Advanced Approaches for Trust and Identity Management in AIoT Environments

Momina Shaheen
https://orcid.org/0000-0001-9424-9787
University of Roehampton, UK

Jawad Rasheed
https://orcid.org/0000-0003-3761-1641
Istanbul Sabahattin Zaim University, Turkey

Maqbool Khan
https://orcid.org/0000-0001-7656-0184
Software Competence Center Hagenberg GmbH, Austria & Pak-Austria Fachhochschule-Institute of Applied Sciences and Technology, Pakistan

IGI Global
Scientific Publishing
Publishing Tomorrow's Research Today

Vice President of Editorial — Melissa Wagner
Director of Acquisitions — Mikaela Felty
Director of Book Development — Jocelynn Hessler
Production Manager — Mike Brehm
Cover Design — Jose Rosado

Published in the United States of America by
IGI Global Scientific Publishing
701 East Chocolate Avenue
Hershey, PA, 17033, USA
Tel: 717-533-8845 | Fax: 717-533-7115
Website: https://www.igi-global.com E-mail: cust@igi-global.com

Library of Congress Cataloging-in-Publication Data

LCCN: 2025040076 (CIP Data Pending)
ISBN13: 9798337362991
Isbn13Softcover: 9798337363004
EISBN13: 9798337363011

British Cataloguing in Publication Data
A Cataloguing in Publication record for this book is available from the British Library.

Table of Contents

Detailed Table of Contents

The convergence of artificial intelligence and the Internet of Things, termed AIoT, is reshaping smart environments, including healthcare, automation, smart cities, and autonomous systems. However, this integration raises major security and privacy concerns due to massive connectivity, data, and limited computational resources. Authentication remains a key challenge, as traditional cryptographic methods are often unsuitable for resource-constrained IoT devices. Weak authentication can result in identity spoofing, data tampering, adversarial attacks, unauthorized access, and system reliability. This chapter presents an overview of secured AIoT, discussing AI-enabled IoT architectures, threat models, and authentication mechanisms. It examines the limitations of existing security frameworks and explores advanced solutions such as lightweight cryptography, federated learning, blockchain-based authentication, and biometric verification. Open research challenges and future directions toward scalable, energy-efficient, and privacy-preserving AIoT authentication are also highlighted.

This chapter presents a comprehensive examination of security challenges and protection mechanisms within the Artificial Intelligence of Things (AIoT) ecosystem. It outlines the defining architectural layers of AIoT and highlights characteristics such as large-scale heterogeneity, data-driven autonomy, edge–cloud distribution, and cyber-physical coupling that uniquely shape its security posture. The chapter develops an AIoT-tailored threat-modelling framework, detailing adversary taxonomy, attack surfaces, and representative scenarios, followed by an integrated vulnerability-assessment approach spanning device, network, and AI-model pipelines. It further explores mitigation strategies including security-by-design, zero-trust networking, robust AI pipelines, supply-chain assurance, and emerging advancements such as digital twins, federated learning, explainable AI, and post-quantum cryptography. The chapter concludes with strategic recommendations and research directions aimed at strengthening resilience, trustworthiness, and lifecycle governance in next-generation AIoT deployments.

Amruta S. Mali, SKN Sinhgad College of Engineering, Pandharpur, India
Altaf Osman Mulani, SKN Sinhgad College of Engineering, Pandharpur, India
Vaibhav V. Godase, SKN Sinhgad College of Engineering, Pandharpur, India
Swapnil R. Takale, SKN Sinhgad College of Engineering, Pandharpur, India
Rahul G. Ghodake, SKN Sinhgad College of Engineering, Pandharpur, India

Edge Intelligence and Federated Learning (FL) are emerging as transformative paradigms for enhancing authentication and trust management in Artificial Intelligence of Things (AIoT). This chapter explores decentralized frameworks that leverage edge computing to enable real-time decision-making and secure identity verification closer to data sources. By integrating FL, sensitive data remains localized, reducing privacy risks and communication overhead while collaboratively improving global model accuracy. Proposed architecture mitigates single-point failures, supports lightweight cryptographic mechanisms and enhances system resilience against adversarial attacks. It ensures scalable trust evaluation through adaptive learning and blockchain-enabled audit trails. Experimental results demonstrate improved latency, energy efficiency and authentication accuracy compared to traditional cloud-centric solutions. This study present robust and privacy-preserving approach to achieve secure, intelligent and trustworthy AIoT environments through Edge Intelligence and Federated Learning integration.

This chapter examines the growing need for secure and efficient authentication in the Artificial Intelligence of Things (AIoT) as billions of resource-constrained devices become tightly integrated with intelligent analytics. It highlights how the convergence of AI, pervasive sensing, and heterogeneous communication widens the attack surface and amplifies the tension between strong cryptographic assurances and limited device capabilities. The discussion evaluates lightweight cryptographic primitives, their design principles, and their suitability for constrained environments, while also addressing the emerging threat of quantum computing and the urgency of adopting post-quantum cryptography. By mapping security requirements, implementation constraints, and algorithmic performance, the chapter proposes a unified vision that blends lightweight methods, quantum-resistant schemes, and adaptive AI-driven authentication to ensure long-term, scalable, and trustworthy AIoT ecosystems.

Competitive advantages offered by emerging technologies have accelerated the adoption of integrated intelligent systems commonly referred to as the Artificial Intelligence of Things. As device populations expand, traditional perimeter-centric and zone-based security models fail, since trust can no longer be inferred from location and boundaries become increasingly diffuse. Threat actors exploit these limitations, using compromised devices to bypass defenses and enable lateral movement while concealing malicious behavior. Zero-trust principles provide an alternative by eliminating implicit trust and requiring continuous verification for every entity. This chapter per the authors outlines how Zero Trust concepts can be adapted to AIoT architectures across device, edge and cloud layers. It proposes model frameworks incorporating AI-based trust scoring, policy evaluation mechanisms, behavioral micro-segmentation, and device-aware trust controls, while examining related concerns including performance impact, real-time trust agility, and system overhead.

Gait recognition and footprint biometrics have emerged as effective modalities for unobtrusive and reliable human identification. This work reviews recent advances enabled by deep learning and edge AI, emphasizing how appearance-based representations such as silhouettes and GEIs, combined with model-based pose features, support invariant and discriminative gait descriptors. We examine modern architectures, including graph neural networks (GNNs) and generative adversarial networks (GANs), that improve cross-view synthesis, motion modeling, and robustness to covariates like clothing, illumination, and occlusion. Multi-modal fusion methods that integrate visual inputs with WiFi CSI, LiDAR, and pressure data are discussed for enhancing performance in unconstrained environments. We also evaluate model compression and hardware–software co-optimization strategies essential for real-time deployment on edge devices. Finally, we highlight privacy preserving approaches, including federated learning and feature perturbation, that ensure secure and ethical use of gait data.

Social sensing is a data collection paradigm that leverages human participation through connected devices in AIoT systems. It enhances real-time decision-making in areas like disaster response, healthcare, and transportation. However, it poses serious challenges related to data privacy, misinformation, identity verification, and system reliability. Threats such as data poisoning, replay attacks, and the opacity of black-box AI models increase the risk. Ethical concerns also arise from continuous data collection without user consent or transparency. Addressing these issues requires a multi-faceted strategy involving anomaly detection, encryption,

and stakeholders and guarantee the integrity and privacy of data. The chapter discusses how blockchain can be implemented together with decentralized identity (DID) systems to provide strong, unaltered authentication systems to AIoT-based agricultural ecosystems. The given approach helps to remove single points of failure, increase accountability, and allow farmers to have a better opportunity to control the ownership and sharing of data by leveraging the distributed ledger technology. Centralized identity promotes cross-agricultural device interoperability, stakeholders in the supply chain, and service providers. The chapter offers a conceptual framework, explains the implementation issues of scalability and energy efficiency.

Authentication in the Artificial Intelligence of Things (AIoT) is often seen as a technical checkpoint, but its durability depends on trust and reputation that shape legitimacy. Compliance with standards cannot replace transparency or public confidence. This chapter applies communication theories—SCOT, ANT, and risk communication—and examines global cases from the U.S., Europe, Asia, Africa, and Latin America to reveal how governance and culture affect adoption. It proposes trust-aware authentication architectures that integrate adaptive mechanisms, reputation systems, communicative transparency, and cultural sensitivity, arguing that resilient AIoT security must be both technically robust and socially trusted.

Traditional authentication mechanisms designed for human-centric or enterprise IT environments struggle to secure the rapidly expanding landscape of the Artificial Intelligence of Things (AIoT), where billions of autonomous devices interact across dynamic, resource-limited, and highly distributed networks. Legacy approaches lack the scalability, context awareness, and machine-to-machine coordination needed to protect systems characterized by continuous data exchange and decentralized control. Emerging solutions such as AI-driven adaptive authentication, decentralized identity frameworks, blockchain-based credential management, and zero-trust security models offer more resilient foundations for identity assurance in autonomous ecosystems. Key implementation considerations include computational efficiency, interoperability, latency constraints, and real-time risk assessment. The discussion provides an integrated perspective on how modern authentication paradigms can support secure, scalable, and trustworthy AIoT environments.

The potential of AI in unlocking the complex challenges in developmental economics, particularly in the areas of finance inclusion and the removal of poverty, is immense. Generally, the purpose of this abstract is to examine the challenges and possibilities of the application of AI solutions in the aforementioned critical areas. Moreover, the issue of accessibility in banks, socioeconomic inequality, and the lack of legislation serves as a barrier in ensuring finance inclusion, which is a critical step in the developmental process. From data computation or prediction models, AI has the potential in offering paradigm shifts in finance personalization, risk personalization, and individualization for treatment. In the goals of offering concrete focus on its subject matter, the role of AI in fulfilling the goals of the SDGs and obtaining perspectives related thereto will also be established in the course of this research.

The IoT infrastructure and AI techniques are merged to establish the AIoT, which is implemented to enhance system performance. AIoT can be wasted to appoint IoT acts further capable, which will improve data analysis and human-machine communications. IoT data can be converted into information that helps with better decision-making using AI techniques, which also improves the system's general usefulness. A wide range of requests, including safety and shadowing systems, clever homes, brainy conveyance systems, smart farms, safe and healthcare's safe checking, manufacturing mechanization and switch, logistics processes and regulator, Commerce, can benefit greatly from AIoT frameworks. However, because AIoT frameworks are susceptible to several kinds of material beatings, they may have hitches with facts safety and confidentiality. These problems also have major consequences, like unapproved information apprises and seepages. One specific caring of folder is the blockchain.

Preface

INTRODUCTION

The rapid convergence of Artificial Intelligence (AI) and the Internet of Things (IoT) has ushered in a new technological paradigm—Artificial Intelligence of Things (AIoT). This evolution is fundamentally reshaping the way systems operate, enabling intelligent, interconnected environments capable of sensing, analyzing, and responding to real-time data. From smart cities and autonomous transportation to industrial automation and intelligent healthcare systems, AIoT is driving unprecedented innovation and efficiency across domains. Yet, alongside these advancements emerges a critical challenge: ensuring secure and trustworthy interactions among an ever-expanding network of devices.

As editors of this volume, *Advanced Approaches for Trust and Identity Management in AIoT Environments*, we recognize that authentication lies at the very core of secure AIoT ecosystems. Traditional authentication mechanisms, largely designed for centralized and human-centric computing environments, are increasingly inadequate for the dynamic, distributed, and resource-constrained nature of AIoT systems. The scale alone—billions of heterogeneous devices—demands rethinking how identity and trust are established, verified, and maintained.

AIoT environments present a unique convergence of challenges. Devices often operate with limited computational power, memory, and energy, making conventional cryptographic techniques difficult to implement efficiently. The decentralized architecture of edge-driven systems removes the reliance on central authorities, requiring new models of distributed trust. Interoperability across diverse platforms and manufacturers introduces additional complexity, while highly dynamic environments demand flexible authentication frameworks that can adapt to devices joining, leaving, or moving within networks.

Moreover, the integration of AI into IoT systems introduces an entirely new dimension of vulnerability. Adversarial attacks targeting AI models, data poisoning, and manipulation of learning processes can undermine the integrity of authentication mechanisms themselves. At the same time, the sensitive nature of data processed in AIoT systems raises profound privacy concerns, necessitating solutions that ensure both security and data protection.

This book has been conceived to address these multifaceted challenges through a focused exploration of advanced approaches to trust and identity management in AIoT environments. It brings together contributions from leading researchers and practitioners who examine innovative authentication architectures and frameworks tailored for the unique demands of AIoT. The chapters collectively highlight emerging technologies such as blockchain for decentralized trust, federated learning for privacy-preserving intelligence, homomorphic encryption for secure computation, and lightweight cryptographic techniques suitable for constrained devices.

A key objective of this volume is to bridge the gap between theoretical research and practical implementation. Beyond presenting conceptual advancements, the book emphasizes architectural patterns, protocol designs, and real-world considerations that can guide the development of robust, scalable, and resilient AIoT systems. In doing so, it distinguishes itself from existing literature by concentrating specifically on authentication at the intersection of AI and IoT, rather than treating these domains in isolation.

We envision this book serving a diverse audience. Academic researchers and students will find it a valuable reference for advancing scholarship in cybersecurity, artificial intelligence, and distributed systems. Industry professionals—including security architects, IoT engineers, and AI developers—can leverage the insights presented to design and deploy secure AIoT solutions across sectors such as healthcare, manufacturing, smart cities, and energy. Policymakers and regulators will gain a deeper understanding of the challenges and best practices necessary to shape effective security standards, while consultants and analysts can draw upon the material to guide organizations navigating AIoT adoption.

As editors, we are deeply grateful to the contributing authors for their expertise and commitment to advancing this important field. We also extend our appreciation to the reviewers and the publishing team for their invaluable support throughout the development of this volume.

It is our hope that this book will not only inform but also inspire continued innovation in securing AIoT ecosystems. By advancing robust approaches to trust and identity management, we take a crucial step toward realizing the full potential of intelligent, connected systems in a secure and trustworthy manner.

ORGANIZATION OF THE BOOK

As editors, we have carefully curated this volume to present a cohesive and forward-looking exploration of trust and identity management in AIoT environments. Each chapter contributes a distinct perspective, collectively advancing the discourse from foundational concepts to emerging solutions and future directions.

Chapter 1 sets the stage by introducing the foundational concepts of secured AIoT and the critical challenges surrounding authentication. The authors provide a comprehensive overview of AI-enabled IoT architectures, associated threat models, and the limitations of conventional security mechanisms. By examining issues such as identity spoofing, adversarial manipulation, and resource constraints, the chapter establishes the urgency for innovative approaches. It further introduces promising directions including lightweight cryptography, federated learning, blockchain-based authentication, and biometric systems, thereby framing the central themes of the book.

Building upon this foundation, Chapter 2 expands the discussion into the broader AIoT security landscape. The contributors develop a structured threat-modeling framework tailored to AIoT systems, highlighting adversarial behaviors, attack surfaces, and vulnerabilities across device, network, and AI pipelines. The chapter emphasizes the importance of security-by-design principles and introduces advanced mitigation strategies such as zero-trust architectures, explainable AI, and post-quantum cryptography, offering a holistic perspective on resilience and lifecycle security.

Chapter 3 transitions into decentralized paradigms by examining the integration of edge intelligence and federated learning for authentication and trust management. The authors present architectures that shift computation closer to the data source, enhancing privacy and reducing latency. By eliminating reliance on centralized systems, these approaches improve scalability and robustness while enabling collaborative model training. The chapter demonstrates how such frameworks can effectively balance efficiency, security, and trust in dynamic AIoT environments.

Chapter 4 delves into the critical role of cryptography in securing AIoT systems, with a particular focus on lightweight and post-quantum approaches. Recognizing the constraints of IoT devices and the emerging threats posed by quantum computing, the chapter evaluates cryptographic primitives suited for constrained environments. It proposes a unified vision that integrates lightweight, quantum-resistant, and AI-driven authentication mechanisms to ensure long-term security and adaptability.

Chapter 5 introduces zero trust architecture as a paradigm shift for AIoT security. The authors argue that traditional perimeter-based models are no longer viable in highly distributed and dynamic environments. By advocating continuous verification and eliminating implicit trust, the chapter outlines frameworks that incorporate AI-based trust scoring, behavioral segmentation, and adaptive policy enforcement, addressing both security effectiveness and operational challenges.

Chapter 6 explores biometric authentication through advances in gait and footprint recognition, particularly in edge computing contexts. The chapter reviews state-of-the-art techniques leveraging deep learning, including graph neural networks and generative models, to achieve robust and invariant identification. It also highlights the importance of multimodal sensing and privacy-preserving techniques, positioning biometrics as a promising yet sensitive component of AIoT authentication systems.

Chapter 7 broadens the perspective by examining social sensing as a participatory data paradigm within AIoT systems. While enabling real-time insights in critical domains, the chapter underscores significant challenges related to data integrity, privacy, and misinformation. Through case studies and analysis, the authors emphasize the need for integrating technological safeguards with ethical considerations, advocating for transparent, accountable, and human-centered security frameworks.

Chapter 8 focuses on trust management and reputational systems as foundational elements of AIoT ecosystems. The chapter introduces the concept of "humanized trust," where intelligent systems are designed not only for functional efficiency but also for ethical alignment and social acceptance. By exploring computational models of trust that incorporate context, interaction history, and transparency, the authors highlight pathways for building long-term user confidence in AI-driven systems.

Chapter 9 examines the role of blockchain and privacy-preserving frameworks in strengthening trust and identity management. The authors present integrated approaches combining decentralized identity, federated learning, and explainable AI to address challenges of interoperability, adversarial resilience, and data privacy. The chapter also outlines future research directions, including quantum-resistant mechanisms and policy-driven governance.

Chapter 10 presents a domain-specific application in healthcare through a blockchain-driven architecture for secure remote patient monitoring. Addressing the limitations of traditional access control models, the chapter proposes fine-grained, context-aware mechanisms enabled by smart contracts. This approach enhances data security, transparency, and patient-centric control, demonstrating the practical relevance of advanced authentication frameworks in sensitive environments.

Chapter 11 extends the discussion to smart farming and precision agriculture, illustrating how blockchain and decentralized identity can enable secure and interoperable AIoT ecosystems. The chapter highlights the importance of data integrity, stakeholder accountability, and scalability while addressing implementation challenges such as energy efficiency and system complexity in agricultural contexts.

Chapter 12 introduces a multidisciplinary perspective by examining trust and authentication through the lens of communication and social science theories. The author argues that technical robustness alone is insufficient without public trust and cultural alignment. By integrating concepts such as transparency, reputation, and risk communication, the chapter underscores the socio-technical nature of AIoT security.

Chapter 13 revisits the limitations of traditional authentication mechanisms in the context of AIoT. The authors critically analyze why legacy systems fail to meet the demands of decentralized, machine-driven environments and present modern alternatives including AI-driven adaptive authentication, blockchain-based identity management, and zero-trust frameworks. The discussion emphasizes the importance of scalability, interoperability, and real-time responsiveness.

Chapter 14 broadens the scope by exploring the implications of AI and AIoT in developmental economics, particularly in advancing financial inclusion and poverty alleviation. While not limited to authentication, the chapter highlights how secure and trustworthy AIoT systems can enable equitable access to financial services, emphasizing the interplay between technology, policy, and societal impact.

Finally, Chapter 15 concludes the volume by synthesizing future directions and open research challenges at the intersection of AIoT and blockchain. The authors reflect on the transformative potential of these technologies while acknowledging persistent issues related to security, privacy, and system complexity. The chapter calls for continued innovation and interdisciplinary collaboration to address these challenges and unlock the full potential of AIoT systems.

Together, these chapters provide a comprehensive and integrated exploration of authentication, trust, and identity management in AIoT, offering both theoretical insights and practical guidance for advancing secure and trustworthy intelligent ecosystems.

CONCLUSION

As we bring this volume to a close, we reflect on the remarkable transformation that the convergence of Artificial Intelligence and the Internet of Things has introduced, and the equally significant challenges it has created in establishing trust and identity within AIoT ecosystems. The chapters in this book collectively underscore a central message: that secure, scalable, and adaptive authentication is not merely a technical requirement, but a foundational pillar for the sustainable growth of intelligent, interconnected systems.

Throughout this volume, contributors have examined the limitations of traditional security paradigms and demonstrated the urgent need for reimagined approaches tailored to the distributed, dynamic, and resource-constrained nature of AIoT. From decentralized architectures enabled by edge intelligence and federated learning, to the integration of blockchain for transparent and tamper-resistant identity management, and from lightweight and post-quantum cryptography to zero-trust frameworks and biometric innovations, the breadth of solutions presented reflects both the complexity of the problem and the richness of ongoing research.

Importantly, this book also highlights that trust in AIoT extends beyond algorithms and protocols. It is deeply intertwined with human, social, and ethical dimensions. Issues of privacy, transparency, fairness, and user confidence must be addressed alongside technical robustness. As several chapters emphasize, the future of AIoT security lies in interdisciplinary approaches that integrate engineering excellence with societal awareness and policy considerations.

While significant progress has been made, many challenges remain open. The rapid evolution of AI-driven threats, the impending impact of quantum computing, and the increasing scale and heterogeneity of connected systems demand continuous innovation. Interoperability, energy efficiency, real-time adaptability, and governance frameworks will remain critical areas of focus for researchers and practitioners alike.

As editors, we hope this volume serves not only as a comprehensive reference but also as a catalyst for further inquiry and collaboration. The ideas, frameworks, and case studies presented herein are intended to inspire new directions in research and practice, fostering the development of AIoT systems that are not only intelligent and efficient, but also secure, trustworthy, and aligned with human values.

We extend our sincere gratitude to all contributing authors, reviewers, and collaborators whose expertise and dedication have made this work possible. It is our aspiration that this book will contribute meaningfully to advancing the field and supporting the global effort to build resilient and trustworthy AIoT ecosystems.

Chapter 1

Introduction to Secured AIoT and Authentication Challenges

Brij Bhushan Sharma
http://orcid.org/0000-0002-8930-8102
Shoolini University, India

Ruchika Sharma
http://orcid.org/0000-0003-4406-5386
Shoolini University of Biotechnology and Management Sciences, Solan, India

Momina Shaheen
http://orcid.org/0000-0001-9424-9787
University of Roehampton, UK

ABSTRACT

The convergence of artificial intelligence and the Internet of Things, termed AIoT, is reshaping smart environments, including healthcare, automation, smart cities, and autonomous systems. However, this integration raises major security and privacy concerns due to massive connectivity, data, and limited computational resources. Authentication remains a key challenge, as traditional cryptographic methods are often unsuitable for resource-constrained IoT devices. Weak authentication can result in identity spoofing, data tampering, adversarial attacks, unauthorized access, and system reliability. This chapter presents an overview of secured AIoT, discussing AI-enabled IoT architectures, threat models, and authentication mechanisms. It examines the limitations of existing security frameworks and explores advanced solutions such as lightweight cryptography, federated learning, blockchain-based

DOI: 10.4018/979-8-3373-6299-1.ch001

authentication, and biometric verification. Open research challenges and future directions toward scalable, energy-efficient, and privacy-preserving AIoT authentication are also highlighted.

1. INTRODUCTION

The Internet of Things (IoT) has experienced tremendous expansion, which has resulted in the transformation of daily environments into digital ecosystems capable of communicating, and reacting on their own. When these systems make use of artificial intelligence to analyze data and make decisions, they transform into a more advanced version that is referred to as the Artificial Intelligence of Things (AIoT)(Singh et al., 2024). Because of this convergence, devices can not only gather data but also analyze it and adapt their behavior to it(R. Sharma et al., 2025). Smart homes, predictive healthcare, self-driving cars, industrial automation, and real-time monitoring of the environment are all possible outcomes of this convergence of technologies. Through the transition from passive connectivity to cognitive interconnectivity, the Internet of Things (IoT) is enabling devices to collaborate, acquire new knowledge, and continuously evolve (Salgotra et al., 2024).

Nevertheless, this level of intelligence and integration is truly unparalleled, and it significantly expands the surface area that can be exploited by attackers. Systems that are based on the Internet of Things typically consist of billions of distinct devices that collaborate with one another but have limited computer power, energy, and communication methods(Verma et al., 2024). Because many of these devices are located in locations that are not secure or that are simple to break into, it is much simpler for anyone to tamper with them, spoof them, or enter them without authorization. In addition, the various connection endpoints and continuous data streams generate complicated vulnerabilities that can be exploited by cyber threats (Saraswat et al., 2022). These vulnerabilities include identity theft, data manipulation, and adversarial artificial intelligence attacks that are aimed to confound machine learning models.

Security for the Internet of Things (IoT) cannot rely solely on conventional approaches that originate from the field of classical computer science(Thakur et al., 2024). When it comes to millions of lightweight devices, authentication, which is the fundamental process of confirming the identification of devices, users, and services, is extremely difficult to perform on a wide scale using authentication(Thakur et al., 2024). Traditional encryption techniques are robust; nevertheless, they may require a greater amount of computer power and energy than the Internet of Things nodes are able to supply. As a consequence of this, a great number of installations rely on authentication techniques that are either extremely rudimentary or poorly designed, which results in security flaws that could be exploited by attackers(R. Sharma et al., 2024). Not only does insufficient authentication put data security and integrity at risk, but it also puts the operational safety of physical systems that are managed by intelligent internet of things platforms in jeopardy(B. B. Sharma et al., 2025). Figure 1 illustrates the weak authentications.

Figure 1. Weak authentication in AIoT system

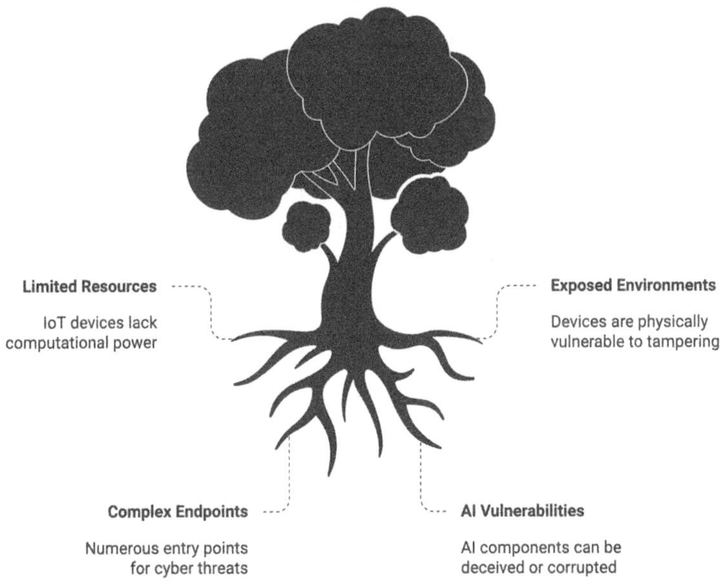

With the addition of AI, things become much more complicated(R. Sharma et al., 2024). When decisions are made by artificial intelligence, additional security concerns are introduced. These dangers include adversarial machine learning, model poisoning, and inference manipulation(G. Sharma et al., 2025a). It is possible for malefactors to manipulate or hack the artificial intelligence components of an Internet of Things system(R. Sharma et al., 2025). This gives them the ability to circumvent authentication protocols, imitate genuine behaviors, or change identity profiles that are used in AI-driven verification. Therefore, the use of keys or passwords is not the only method of authentication in the Internet of Things(G. Sharma et al., 2025b). It is necessary to do a trust assessment that considers environmental, biometric, and behavioral aspect of the situation(Mehta et al., 2025).

To implement a change to protect AIoT systems, we will need to reevaluate the way in which we authenticate users(Mehta et al., 2025). Lightweight cryptography, trust mechanisms based on blockchain technology, device fingerprinting, identities that are rooted in hardware, and AI-driven behavioral profile are all becoming viable possibilities (Salgotra et al., 2024). On the other hand, every approach has its own set of advantages and disadvantages regarding latency, computing overhead, energy consumption, scalability, and privacy responsibilities. Because of this, authentication systems need to be robust and efficient at the same time, and they also need to be able to quickly adjust to new threats.

The following are the three primary objectives of this chapter:

1. To explain the fundamental structure of secure ecosystems for the Internet of Things, with a particular emphasis on the multi-tiered structure and the vulnerabilities that are inherent to each layer.
2. To investigate the vast diversity of authentication issues, which include a lack of resources, a wide range of devices, distributed intelligence, and the possibility of being attacked by malevolent artificial intelligence.
3. To investigate new security models, such as lightweight cryptography, federated identity learning, blockchain-assisted authentication, and human-centric biometrics, as potential means of developing artificial intelligence with the Internet of Things (IoT) systems that are durable, capable of expanding, and preserve users' privacy.

It is of the utmost importance to be able to verify identify and establish confidence to keep up with the increasing prevalence of artificial intelligence in various vital sectors such as healthcare, transportation, manufacturing, precision agriculture, and national infrastructure applications(B. B. Sharma et al., 2025). The failure of authentication can result in complications that put the well-being of individuals, the economy, and the faith of the public in jeopardy. Figure 2 illustrates the hidden depth of AIoT.

Figure 2. AIoT Authentication: Unveiling the hidden depth

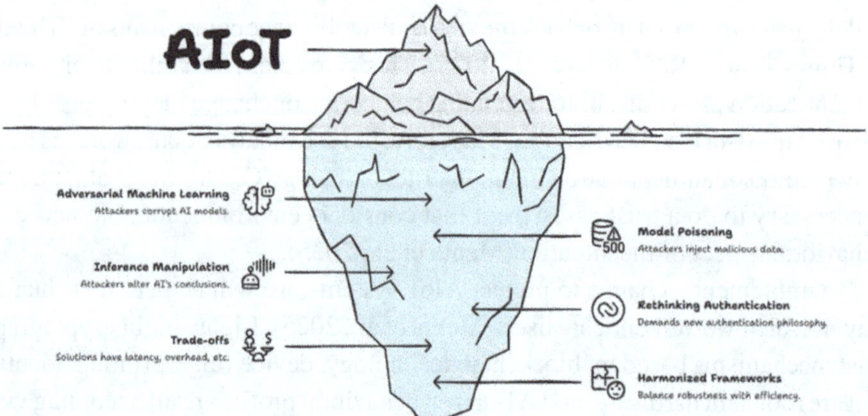

Therefore, gaining a grasp of authentication issues and finding solutions to them is not only a technical requirement, but also a significant step towards the further development of ecosystems for the Internet of Things.

This chapter is organized as follows. Section 2 presents the foundational concepts of Artificial Intelligence of Things (AIoT) and introduces the architectural components of secured AIoT systems, highlighting security requirements across perception, edge, network, and application layers. Section 3 explores the threat landscape in AIoT environments, detailing common attack vectors, vulnerabilities, and adversarial risks that challenge system trust and reliability. Section 4 focuses on authentication challenges specific to AIoT, examining issues related to resource constraints, scalability, heterogeneity, and AI-driven attack surfaces. Section 5 reviews existing authentication mechanisms and security frameworks, discussing their operational principles and inherent limitations in AIoT contexts. Section 6 analyzes emerging and advanced authentication techniques, including lightweight cryptography, blockchain-based authentication, federated learning approaches, and biometric and behavioral verification methods. Section 7 identifies open research challenges and unresolved issues that hinder the deployment of fully secured AIoT systems. Section 8 outlines future research directions and technological trends aimed at achieving scalable, energy-efficient, and privacy-preserving authentication solutions. Finally, Section 9 concludes the chapter by summarizing key insights and emphasizing the importance of robust authentication for the sustainable and secure evolution of AIoT ecosystems.

2. FOUNDATIONS OF SECURED AIOT

2.1. AIoT Architecture Overview

The Artificial Intelligence of Things (AIoT) symbolizes a disruptive advancement in connected systems, beyond the usual constraints of the Internet of Things (IoT) by incorporating intelligence directly into sensing, communication, and actuation processes(Safeer et al., 2025). Whereas IoT largely focusses connectivity and data collecting, AIoT integrates cognitive capabilities, allowing systems to learn from data, adjust to evolving situations, and execute autonomous decisions(Tariq et al., 2025). This change is not simply a small enhancement; it changes the way that cyber-physical systems, the environment, and people interact with each other (Butt et al., 2025). Theoretically, AIoT is the combination of three main ideas: smart computation, secure communication, and sensing everywhere. These pillars collectively support applications that require real-time responsiveness, contextual awareness, and predictive intelligence. This coming together also makes security problems worse(R. Sharma et al., 2025).

Figure 3. Key components for foundation of AIoT

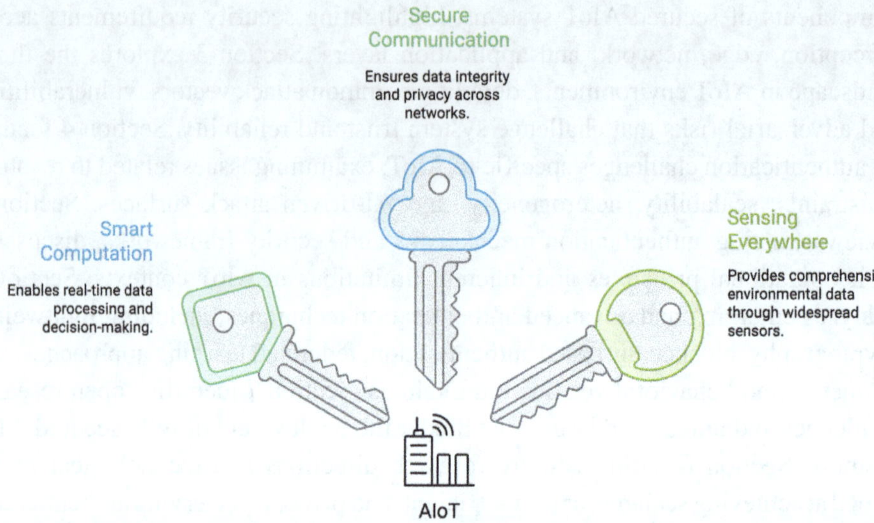

As intelligence moves closer to the edge and decision-making becomes more decentralized, the security of data, the authenticity of devices, and the dependability of AI models become very important (Saeed et al., 2024). So, security should be a main part of the design of secure AIoT systems, not just an afterthought.

2.2. Theoretical Foundations of AIoT

AIoT advances standard IoT by adding machine learning, deep learning, and data-driven intelligence over the system lifespan(Farooq et al., 2025). AIoT can be conceptualized as a closed-loop system wherein data collection, inference, decision-making, and actuation occur constantly and autonomously. In contrast to cloud-centric AI systems, AIoT allocates intelligence among edge devices, gateways, and cloud platforms to optimize latency, energy efficiency, and scalability(Anjum et al., 2025).

From the perspective of systems theory, AIoT includes intelligence that is based on feedback. Sensors create high-dimensional, diversified data streams that are processed by AI models to find trends, forecast future circumstances, or categorize events (Butt et al., 2025). These insights are communicated to actuators or control systems, permitting adaptive reactions. This feedback loop is very important for things like smart grids, self-driving cars, predictive maintenance, and health monitoring.

Nevertheless, intelligence is inadequate in the absence of trust (Masalila et al., n.d.). In AIoT environments, devices must communicate, authenticate, validate data sources, and assure decisions are based on permitted inputs. Theoretical models of trust in distributed systems highlight identity verification, behavioral consistency, and historical reliability(Powell et al., 2024). In AIoT, these aspects of trust integrate with AI models, making authentication a complex issue of both security and intelligence.

2.3. Transition From IoT to AIoT

A Security Perspective Conventional IoT systems depend on centralized cloud processing, wherein raw sensor data is routed to servers for analysis. This architecture makes management easier, but it also causes latency, bandwidth overhead, and privacy problems(Bouramdane, 2023). AIoT lessens these limits by moving intelligence closer to the source of the data. Edge computing makes it possible to make inferences locally, which reduces the requirement for constant cloud connectivity.

This change promotes efficiency but challenges security(Miller et al., 2025). In centralized systems, authentication and access control are implemented at a restricted number of locations. In AIoT, authentication must be accomplished across several distributed nodes, perhaps numbering in the thousands or millions. Every node makes decisions and produces data, which makes the effects of a compromise even worse. In a smart healthcare system, wearable devices can undertake localized anomaly detection on physiological signals(Dereziński & Mahoney, 2024). If an attacker convincingly replicates a device or inputs hazardous data, the AI model may produce erroneous alerts or neglect crucial health incidents. In industrial AIoT systems, hacked edge nodes can distort predictive maintenance models, resulting in equipment failure or safety issues. These examples highlight the demand for strong, scalable, and context-aware authentication systems in secured AIoT(Samanta et al., 2024).

2.4. Secured AIoT Architecture

Stratified Theoretical Framework In order to handle complexity and put security safeguards in place, secured AIoT systems are usually built on layered models. Each layer serves a specific job while engaging with surrounding layers via explicitly defined interfaces(Bhushan Sharma et al., 2022). Each layer has different security needs; thus, authentication and protection mechanisms must be tailored to each one(B. B. Sharma et al., 2022).

Figure 4. AIoT system architecture

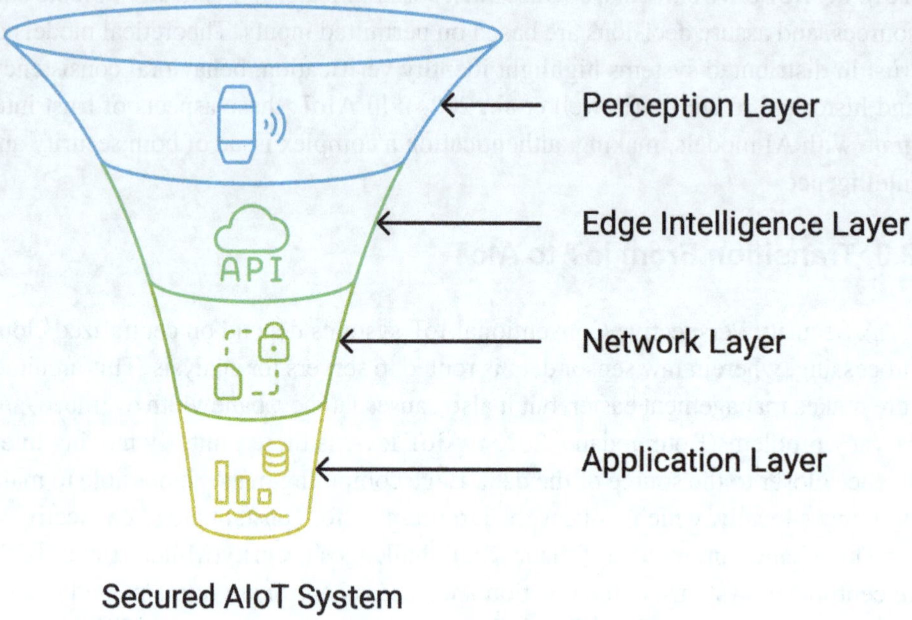

2.4.1. Perception Layer

The Basis of Trust at the Physical Interface The perception layer is what connects the digital and physical worlds in a true way(Bhatt* et al., 2019). It incorporates sensors, actuators, RFID tags, embedded microcontrollers, and low-power wireless modules. Theoretical frameworks of cyber-physical security underscore that attacks at this level can produce rapid physical consequences, making it the most vulnerable yet critical component. From a security theory standpoint, the perception layer must establish a foundation of trust (Bhatt et al., 2021). Devices must have distinctive identities that are not easily repeatable or counterfeit able. Conventional IDs like MAC addresses are unsuitable because of the potential for spoofing. Contemporary techniques combine hardware-based identities, including physically unclonable functions (PUFs), secure elements, or trusted execution environments.

Real-world examples show how important this layer is. Soil sensors in precision agriculture measure the amount of moisture and nutrients in the soil to help plan irrigation. If an aggressor falsifies sensor identification, the AI-driven irrigation system may excessively or inadequately irrigate crops, resulting in lower yields. In radiation monitoring systems near nuclear plants, broken sensors may stop important alerts from going out, putting public safety at risk. These examples show that authentication at the perception layer is necessary for the system to work properly.

In addition to identity, the veracity of data is vital. Sensors must make sure that measurements don't change while they are being taken or sent. Lightweight cryptographic primitives and mutual authentication methods are often used to find a balance between security and energy limits. Theoretical research in lightweight security focusses lowering processing overhead while ensuring cryptographic integrity, a key criterion for this layer.

2.4.2 Edge Intelligence Layer

Safe Decision-Making in the Local Area The edge intelligence layer provides processing capacity in close to the data source(R. Sharma et al., 2025). It has AI inference engines, modules for finding anomalies, and basic analytics. This layer represents the notion of scattered intelligence, minimizing dependence on centralized processing and enhancing real-time reaction(R. Sharma et al., 2022). The security challenges at this level are complex(B. B. Sharma & Kumar, 2020). Edge devices must authenticate to the network and confirm the integrity of implemented AI models. Tampering with models, hostile manipulation, and making changes without permission are all big threats. From the point of view of trust theory, the edge layer must make sure that both the platform and the model are safe. In real-world use, secure boot methods make sure that only trusted firmware and AI models are used. Device attestation protocols enable gateways or cloud services to authenticate the software status of edge nodes prior to authorizing access. Lightweight encryption protects data while it is being sent, and runtime monitoring finds unusual behavior that could mean a breach. Practical examples illustrate these issues distinctively. In intelligent traffic systems, edge nodes examine video streams to identify congestion or accidents. If an assailant alters the AI model to misclassify vehicles, traffic signals may operate wrongly, resulting in delays or collisions. Edge intelligence controls precise motions in industrial robots. Changes that aren't allowed could damage the equipment or hurt someone(Rasooli et al., 2020). These incidents illustrate the necessity for strong identification and integrity verification at the perimeter.

2.4.3 Network Layer

Secure Communication and Identity Dissemination Using wired and wireless technologies including 5G, Wi-Fi, LPWAN, and industrial fieldbuses, the network layer connects AIoT components that are spread out(Kashyap et al., 2021). Theoretically, this layer is incharge of making sure that data is sent through secure paths, that it is routed correctly, and that verified identities are spread throughout the system. Network layer authentication involves not only device identity but also session management and trust delegation. Secure communication protocols like TLS, DTLS, and IPsec assure confidentiality and integrity; yet their computational needs may be overwhelming for resource-limited systems. Because of this, AIoT systems often use optimized or hybrid protocols that are tailored to the capability of the devices (Vaidya & Sharma, 2021). Examine a noise monitoring network within the context of a smart city. A lot of distributed sensors send data to cloud platforms over LP-WAN gateways. Attackers can add fake data streams to noise maps and make policy choices that are wrong because network-level authentication is weak. In healthcare AIoT, weak network authentication could put important patient information at risk or let people use medical devices without permission. Recent research examines blockchain-based identity management in conjunction with software-defined networking (SDN) to enhance network-layer security. Blockchain offers decentralized trust, reducing reliance on centralized authority, while SDN enables dynamic policy enforcement based on real-time threat intelligence. These approaches demonstrate the transfer of theoretical progress into real security enhancements.

2.4.4 Application Layer

Trust, Policy, and Interactions Between People The application layer serves as the link between AIoT systems and end users, organizations, and decision-makers. It covers dashboards, control systems, analytics platforms, and automatic reaction mechanisms(R. Sharma et al., 2024). This layer is supposed to show the idea of contextual trust, where judgements about authentication are based on identity, behavior, usage patterns, and the environment. Authentication at the application layer must include interactions between machines and between people and machines. People often use role-based access control, attribute-based access control, and policy-driven authentication systems. AI-powered behavioral authentication is becoming increasingly important since it lets systems spot unusual usage patterns. Practical examples highlight the value of this layer. Utility operators employ AI-driven dashboards to manage energy distribution in smart grids. Unauthorized access may compromise key infrastructure(Shahzadi et al., 2017). In healthcare, professionals interface with AIoT platforms to oversee patient monitoring. Strong authentication makes sure that only people who are allowed to can see or change critical information(Krizhevsky et al., 2017). Moreover, application-layer security must address regulatory compliance and ethical consequences. Federated identity management and other privacy-preserving authentication solutions make it easier to follow data protection rules while still being easy to use(Jiang et al., 2018). These factors show how technological, legal, and social parts of secured AIoT are coming together.

2.5. Cross-Layer Security Integration

Layered architectures provide transparency; nonetheless, the security of AIoT in real applications depends on cross-layer integration. Trust judgements at other layers are affected by authentication decisions at one layer. A sensor that has been validated at the perception layer must maintain trust while data moves through the edge, network, and application layers. Security holes could happen if layers don't work together properly(Sladojevic et al., 2016).

Zero-trust systems and other theoretical frameworks put more emphasis on ongoing verification than on static authentication. In AIoT, this means figuring out how much you can trust a device based on its behavior, the integrity of its data, and the context in which it is used. Applied implementations employ AI models to correlate signals across many levels, identifying anomalies that single-layer approaches may overlook(Wang et al., 2013).

Summary and Implications

This section has defined the theoretical and practical foundations of AIoT and strengthened AIoT designs. Upon careful study of each layer, it is obvious that authentication is not an isolated method, but a complicated process interconnected across the system. Security must advance in unison with intelligence, from physical identity at the perception layer to contextual trust at the application layer. The examples show that authentication failures can have serious effects on safety, privacy, and the reliability of operations. As AIoT systems become more common in important areas, the need for strong, flexible, and advanced authentication frameworks grows. The subsequent sections of this chapter elaborate on these foundations, covering threats, problems, and advanced solutions for protecting AIoT ecosystems.

3. THREAT LANDSCAPE IN AIOT ENVIRONMENTS

The combination of artificial intelligence and the Internet of Things significantly alters the security threat picture. Unlike traditional IoT systems, which often face issues with connectivity and data transfer, AIoT environments include intelligence as both an advantage and a potential risk. AI models embedded in dispersed, resource-constrained devices create fresh attack vectors that go beyond traditional cyber risks, jeopardizing data integrity, model reliability, and autonomous decision-making. The hazard picture for AIoT is multifaceted, encompassing the system's physical, cyber, and cognitive components(Kabir & Nazmul Alam, 2023). From a security standpoint, AIoT dangers are classified as identity-based attacks, data-centric assaults, AI-specific adversarial attacks, network-level exploits, and system-level coordination attacks. These dangers are typically interrelated, thus a successful breach at one-layer spreads throughout the AIoT system. Understanding the broad threat landscape is critical for developing effective authentication and security systems(Tripathi et al., 2023).

3.1 Identity and Authentication-Based Threats

Identity serves as the fundamental basis for confidence in AIoT systems, functioning as its cornerstone. Prior to engaging in communication or decision-making, any device, user, gateway, or service must first establish their legitimacy in a reliable manner. Artificial intelligence and Internet of Things ecosystems are susceptible to identity-based attacks since their authentication procedures are inadequate.

Figure 5. Illustrates a high-level overview of major AIoT security threats, with identity spoofing and unauthorized access forming the primary focus of this section

3.1.1 Device Identity Spoofing

Device spoofing attacks enable perpetrators to replicate authorized Internet of Things nodes. This is achievable due to the characteristics of the assaults. By replicating identifiers such as MAC addresses, device IDs, or cryptographic credentials, these attackers can obtain sensitive information. It is a prevalent practice to repurpose static identifiers or to offer insufficient safeguards for them. This arises from the poor security capabilities of numerous devices connected to the Internet of Things. When faked devices provide inaccurate information, artificial intelligence algorithms may develop flawed patterns or make misleading choices. This is a potentiality. For instance, counterfeit sensors might manipulate noise maps in smart city noise monitoring systems, potentially leading to flawed urban planning or improper regulatory enforcement. In the context of the Internet of Things (IoT) in the industrial sector, counterfeit sensors might impact predictive maintenance models, potentially resulting in unnecessary shutdowns or obscuring genuine equipment faults. These attacks illuminate the ramifications of identity breaches on data integrity and artificial intelligence-driven intelligence. These ramifications must be considered.

3.1.2 Unauthorized Access and Privilege Escalation

AIoT systems typically encompass various stakeholders, including as devices, operators, service providers, and automated agents. Inadequate access control or insufficient authentication allows attackers to elevate privileges, thereby seizing control of essential system components. Upon gaining access, opponents can manipulate AI models, adjust control parameters, or get confidential data. In healthcare AIoT settings, illicit access to wearable devices or monitoring systems might compromise patient data or enable assailants to alter warnings. In autonomous transportation systems, privilege escalation can result in hazardous control decisions. These concerns highlight the imperative for robust, role-specific authentication solutions.

3.2. Data-Centric Threats in AIoT

Data is the engine that propels AIoT systems. Sensors are constantly transmitting a wide variety of data to artificial intelligence systems. Instances in which data integrity and availability are compromised have a direct impact on the system's level of intelligence and dependability.

3.2.1. Data Tampering and Injection Attacks

The act of altering sensor readings while they are being taken, transmitted, or stored is referred to as data tampering. Attacks that involve injection introduce fabricated data streams into the system. In the context of the Internet of Things (IoT), attacks of this nature pose a significant risk since AI algorithms may erroneously believe that harmful data is suitable for training or inference purposes. If the data on the soil moisture is incorrect, irrigation systems that are powered by artificial intelligence can fail in smart farming. This could cause crops to become stressed or use an excessive amount of water. Artificial intelligence and internet of things technologies that detect radiation may either conceal vital alerts or induce unwarranted alarm when they get data. To overcome this obstacle, it is necessary to identify modest adjustments that can be easily included into standard data patterns.

3.2.2. Replay Attacks

Using replay attacks, it is possible to steal authentic data or authentication messages and then send them again at a later period. It is possible for replayed messages to be wrongly validated in AIoT systems that use static or weak authentication techniques. This allows attackers to circumvent security protections and potentially compromise the system. The use of replayed control commands in industrial automation has the potential to disrupt operations that are expected to be in sync with one another. In smart grids, the presence of duplicate meter data may have an impact on the precision of billing or the decisions made regarding the distribution of electricity. It is difficult to identify these kinds of assaults because AI-based anomaly detection will not function properly in situations where replayed data closely fits trends from the past.

3.3. AI-Specific and Adversarial Threats

The implementation of artificial intelligence will result in the introduction of a new set of dangers that will be focused against the intelligence itself, rather than just the infrastructure.

3.3.1. Adversarial Input Attacks

The input data is altered in such a way that adversarial attacks prevent artificial intelligence algorithms from determining what is going on, while standard detection systems and individuals are unable to identify them. An adversarial noise can be introduced into sensor data, pictures, or signals in the Internet of Things (IoT) to cause them to be erroneously identified. Adversarial patterns have the potential to confuse object detection models in autonomous surveillance systems, leading to the wrong identification of potential dangers. Voice-activated Internet of Things assistants have the potential to initiate operations that are not permitted if the audio signals are appropriately designed. These assaults make use of the inherent flaws that are present in machine learning models and pose a challenge to conventionally held beliefs regarding security.

3.3.2. Data Poisoning Attacks

When adversaries introduce incorrect samples into training datasets, they are engaging in data poisoning assaults. This causes the learning process to get muddled. The use of poisoning could gradually reduce performance or provide backdoors in circumstances involving the Internet of Things (IoT) in which algorithms are constantly learning from streaming data. In the context of traffic management systems, inaccurate data can cause algorithms that predict congestion to become messed up, which in turn leads to ongoing issues. The contamination of patient data streams in medical AIoT systems has the potential to negatively impact the accuracy of diagnosis. The decentralized and self-governing characteristics of the Internet of Things make it more difficult to determine whether someone has been poisoned.

3.3.3. Model Theft and Inference Attacks

When artificial intelligence models are placed in the peripheral, they are susceptible to extraction and reverse engineering. It is possible for adversaries to determine the parameters of the model, clone proprietary models, or obtain sensitive information regarding training data for themselves. One of the most significant issues with privacy is that inference attacks might reveal user behaviors or private information.

3.4. Network-Level Threats

Internet of Things networks are dependent on a variety of communication techniques, each of which presents its own unique set of risks. Attacks that begin at the network level have the potential to prevent data from being transmitted, to reduce the level of security associated with authentication, or to make it simpler for anyone to move around the system.

3.4.1. Man-in-the-Middle (MitM) Attacks

MitM attacks allow hackers to get access to AIoT devices and gateways to read the communications that are transmitted between them. adversaries can alter data or add malicious orders if there are not robust mutual authentication and encryption in place. As a result of the fact that AIoT systems operate in real time, even brief outages can have significant effects.

3.4.2. Denial-of-Service (DoS) and Distributed DoS (DDoS)

Attacks that are classified as denial of service (DoS) overwhelm servers or devices connected to the internet of things with an excessive amount of traffic, which depletes their processing capacity or energy. Since many Internet of Things nodes have limited capacity, even low-rate attacks can render it impossible to operate devices. Traffic management systems and environmental monitoring platforms can become ineffective in smart city initiatives if they are subjected to denial-of-service assaults. In the field of healthcare, necessary monitoring services might not function properly. Some of the concerns with denial-of-service attacks are alleviated by AI-driven traffic analysis; yet attackers continue to adapt their strategies.

3.5. Physical and Side-Channel Attacks

Many AIoT devices work in places where people can get to them, which makes them more likely to be attacked physically or through side channels than traditional IT systems.

3.5.1. Physical Tampering

If an intruder can physically access sensors or edge devices, they may be able to steal cryptographic keys, alter software, or purchase replacement components. Remote applications, like as farming or monitoring the environment, frequently do not require adequate levels of physical protection.

3.5.2. Side-Channel Attacks

Through the utilization of power, electromagnetic emissions, or timing differences, side-channel attacks make use of information that has been leaked out. As a result of these assaults, cryptographic secrets or internal states may be exposed, which simplifies the process of committing additional breaches. Because they lack sufficient protection or monitoring capabilities, AIoT devices that have limited resources are especially susceptible to attack.

3.6. Coordinated and Cross-Layer Attacks

Among the potential threats posed by the Internet of Things (IoT), the possibility of coordinated attacks with several layers is a significant risk. To retaining control over the system for an extended period, malefactors may employ techniques such as identity spoofing, data contamination, and hostile interference. To extend the attack throughout the system, an attacker might first pose as sensor IDs at the perception layer, then supply AI models at the edge with inaccurate data and finally take use of network weaknesses to continue the attack. With only one security measure, it is difficult to identify attacks that involve many stages; hence, you need to implement a wide variety of protection techniques that span multiple layers.

3.7. Implications for Secured AIoT Design

The conventional security measures have weaknesses that are highlighted by the wide and ever-changing threat landscape that exists in contexts that use the Internet of Things (IoT). The authentication methods that are used must be able to withstand both traditional cyber threats and adversarial strategies that are specific to artificial intelligence. When it comes to systems that are mobile, autonomous, and constantly learning, static, one-time authentication is problematic. This research sheds light on the importance of implementing security systems that are both flexible and intelligent. These systems should make use of lightweight cryptography, continuous authentication, behavioral analysis, and trust management at all levels always. By examining the specific authentication issues that arise when attempting to protect AIoT systems in these kinds of environments, the following section of this chapter provides a more in-depth examination of the threat analysis topic.

4. AUTHENTICATION CHALLENGES IN AIOT

In the field of Artificial Intelligence of Things (AIoT) systems, authentication is the most important thing that makes them safer. Ecosystems for the Internet of Things (IoT) work with strict rules, a lot of data, and changing conditions, and they also use AI to make decisions. This is different from how computers usually work. These qualities make it much harder to develop and build authentication methods that are very reliable. The IoT authentication process has changed from a single way to check trust to a continuous, adaptable, and multi-faceted way to check trust. This part looks at the main problems that make authentication in Internet of Things (IoT) settings harder.

Figure 6. Illustrates the primary technological and cryptographic factors that collectively lead to inadequate authentication mechanisms in AIoT systems

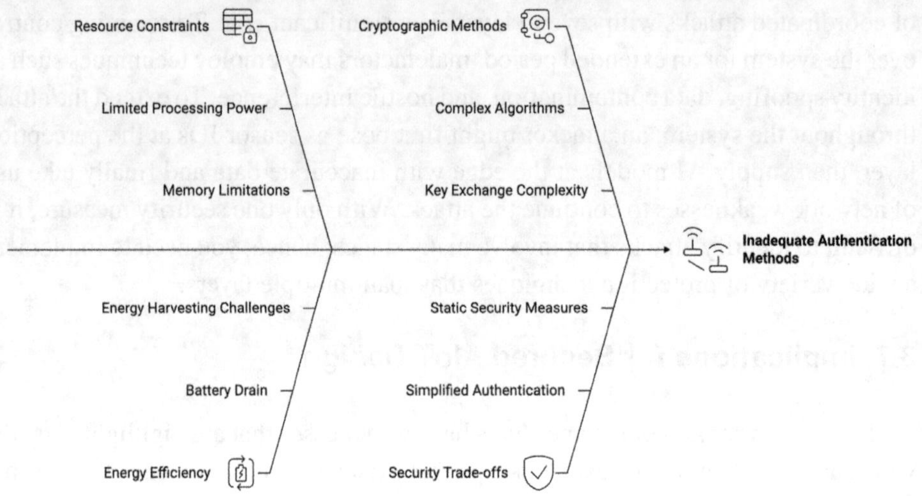

4.1. Resource Constraints

Authentication in the Internet of Things (IoT) is a significant challenge due to the limited resources of IoT devices. Most AIoT nodes are made to be cheap, energy-efficient, and small because they have limited processing power, memory, and energy resources. This is because they are made to be little on purpose. Common cryptographic authentication methods including public key infrastructure (PKI), RSA, and normal elliptic curve cryptography demand too much processing power and energy for many Internet of Things devices.

Authentication methods are predicated on the idea that there is enough entropy, processing power, and safe storage for cryptographic keys when looked at from a theoretical point of view. The Internet of Things (IoT) is made up of many sensors that now use microcontrollers with only a few kilobytes of memory and are powered by batteries or other energy-harvesting sources. Using complicated key exchange mechanisms or keeping long cryptography sessions going could shorten the life of the gadget or cause problems with how it works. In applied artificial intelligence and Internet of Things systems, like wearable healthcare monitoring or distant environmental sensors, repeated authentication handshakes can quickly drain batteries, which can make the system less stable. Because of this, developers often employ authentication methods that are either too simple or too static, which makes security worse without them knowing it. Ongoing research into lightweight cryptographic algorithms, simplified handshake protocols, and hardware-augmented authentication primitives is being motivated by the fact that the trade-off between security robustness and resource efficiency continues to be a fundamental concern.

4.2. Massive Scalability

AIoT ecosystems are extensive, comprising millions or even billions of interconnected devices. This large dimension significantly complicates the processes of maintaining identities, sharing keys, and coordinating authentication. In extensive and continuously evolving environments, conventional authentication methods that rely on centralized authorities or hierarchical trust frameworks are less effective from a systems perspective, overseeing the unique identities and cryptographic keys of billions of devices significantly increases the complexity of provisioning, revocation, updating, and renewal processes. Centralized authentication servers may serve as bottlenecks or single points of failure, and repeated re-authentication frequently results in excessive signaling traffic across networks. When implementing large-scale solutions such as smart cities or nationwide infrastructure monitoring systems, the authentication process must be efficient while maintaining security. For example, intelligent traffic management systems may comprise thousands of sensors and control devices operating collaboratively in real time. If each interaction requires complex authentication, the system's responsiveness deteriorates and latency increases. Additionally, scalability issues impact lifecycle management as well. Devices may be added, replaced, or removed at any time; therefore, onboarding and decommissioning processes must be seamless. Ensuring that authentication remains secure and scalable throughout the entire device lifecycle continues to represent a significant research and technical challenge within AIoT systems.

4.3. Heterogeneous Platforms

AIoT environments are inherently varied, encompassing a wide array of hardware platforms, operating systems, communication protocols, and security attributes. Devices vary from ultra-low-power sensors and embedded controllers to edge gateways and cloud servers, each exhibiting unique computational and security attributes. This diversity hampers authentication, as a singular, standard security system rarely accommodates all components successfully. Some devices may include secure hardware modules or trusted execution environments, while others may lack basic cryptographic acceleration. Communication protocols such as Wi-Fi, Bluetooth, Zigbee, LoRaWAN, and 5G each define unique security frameworks and constraints. Achieving interoperability across various platforms requires authentication mechanisms that are both protocol-agnostic and secure. In fact, variations in device capabilities sometimes lead to disjointed security approaches. Malicious entities may exploit insecure devices or poorly integrated components to compromise the security of the overall AIoT infrastructure. In industrial AIoT environments, conventional equipment may function alongside modern AI-enabled controls. If outdated equipment cannot support strong authentication mechanisms, they may present weaknesses that enable security breaches. Creating authentication frameworks that dynamically adjust to varying capabilities while maintaining security is a crucial task.

4.4. Context-Aware Communication

AIoT systems work in very dynamic and context-sensitive situations, unlike static computer settings. Devices can be portable, linked at random times, or affected by different environmental and operational conditions. Authentication in these cases must not rely just on static credentials or one-time verification. for context-aware communication to succeed, authentication systems need to take into consideration things like location, time, behavior patterns, network circumstances, and trust history. This is similar to adaptive and continuous authentication approaches, which check confidence throughout time instead than just once.

Context is very important in real-world situations, such self-driving cars or mobile health care devices. A device that has been authorized in one context may need to be re-authenticated when it moves to a different environment or starts acting strangely. Continuous authentication makes things safer, but it also makes things harder to compute and communicate. The need for context-awareness and efficiency at the same time is a big problem. Too much re-authentication can slow down networks and devices, while not being flexible enough can let attackers take advantage of changes in context. AI-driven trust evaluation models show promise, but they are also more complicated and have built-in flaws.

4.5. Exposure to Adversarial Attacks

The integration of AI with AIoT authentication generates novel attack vectors that target the intelligence itself. AI-driven identification systems typically utilize traffic signatures, behavioral patterns, or biometric characteristics. These strategies enhance system flexibility, however they are susceptible to manipulation by adversaries. Adversarial attacks can alter input characteristics, leading AI models to misidentify individuals or grant unauthorized access. Meticulously orchestrated network traffic patterns may resemble typical device activity, enabling evasion of behavioral authentication mechanisms. Adversarial noise can disrupt biometric signals or sensor data utilized for identity verification from a security theory perspective, these attacks exploit the limitations of machine learning models regarding sensitivity and generalization. In AIoT environments, where models may be trained on suboptimal or excessively noisy data, fortifying them against attacks is particularly challenging.

Adversarial attacks might yield detrimental consequences in real-world scenarios. In smart grid systems, adversaries can provide control commands if they circumvent authentication protocols. In healthcare AIoT, erroneous identification of a user's identity can jeopardize sensitive medical information or hinder critical monitoring. To mitigate threats from adversaries, it is essential to construct robust models, continuously monitor them, and employ explainable and verifiable AI techniques.

5. EXISTING AUTHENTICATION TECHNIQUES AND LIMITATIONS

Despite significant advances in AIoT security, many deployed systems continue to rely on traditional or partially adapted authentication mechanisms. While these techniques provide baseline protection, they exhibit notable limitations when applied to large-scale, intelligent, and resource-constrained AIoT environments. This section critically examines commonly used authentication approaches, highlighting their operational principles and inherent shortcomings in AIoT contexts.

5.1. Password and Token-Based Schemes

Password and token-based authentication methods are some of the oldest and most widely used ways to protect your information. They use private information like passwords, PINs, access tokens, or pre-shared keys to verify who you are. These methods are simple to use and don't need a lot of computing power, which makes them good for early IoT projects.

In AIoT settings, nevertheless, these methods are mostly not right. Many AIoT devices work on their own, so you can't contact them with a password. Static credentials are vulnerable to brute-force attacks, replay attacks, and credential leakage. Token-based systems are more flexible, but they still need safe storage and regular renewal, which might be hard for devices with limited resources. In real-world situations like smart healthcare wearables or environmental sensors that don't need to be watched, stolen credentials might let attackers' fake equipment, add false data, or get access they don't want. So, even while password and token-based systems are easy to use, they don't meet the security and scalability needs of modern AIoT systems.

Figure 7. Illustration of password and token-based authentication in IoT environments and their vulnerability to interception and misuse

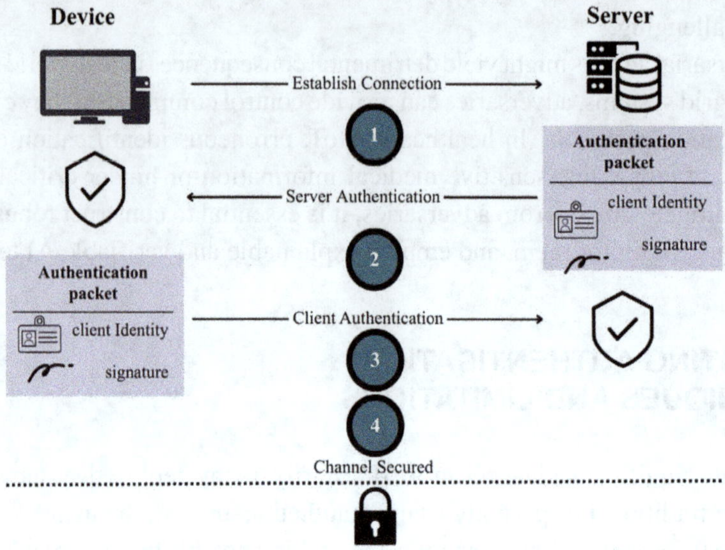

5.2. Public Key Infrastructure (PKI)

The Public Key Infrastructure (PKI) uses asymmetric key pairs and digital certificates issued by trusted institutions to enable strong cryptographic authentication. PKI provides high levels of confidentiality, integrity, and non-repudiation, making it an essential component of secure communication in traditional IT systems. PKI presents considerable issues in AIoT systems. Asymmetric cryptographic processes require a significant amount of resources and memory to store keys and administer certificates. Many IoT nodes lack the processing power and energy resources to perform public key operations on a regular basis, particularly when there are many them. In smart city infrastructures with many distributed sensors, utilizing PKI for authentication may result in increased delays, network congestion, and faster energy loss. Managing certificate lifecycles, including renewal and revocation, exacerbates scaling issues. PKI provides considerable security guarantees; nevertheless, its costs potentially outweigh its benefits in low-power AIoT contexts.

Figure 8. Limitations of Public Key Infrastructure (PKI) in AIoT environments: Illustration highlighting the key challenges of PKI-based authentication in AIoT systems, including limited processing power of IoT nodes, high computational and energy demands of asymmetric cryptographic operations, and scalability issues associated with certificate management across large-scale deployments

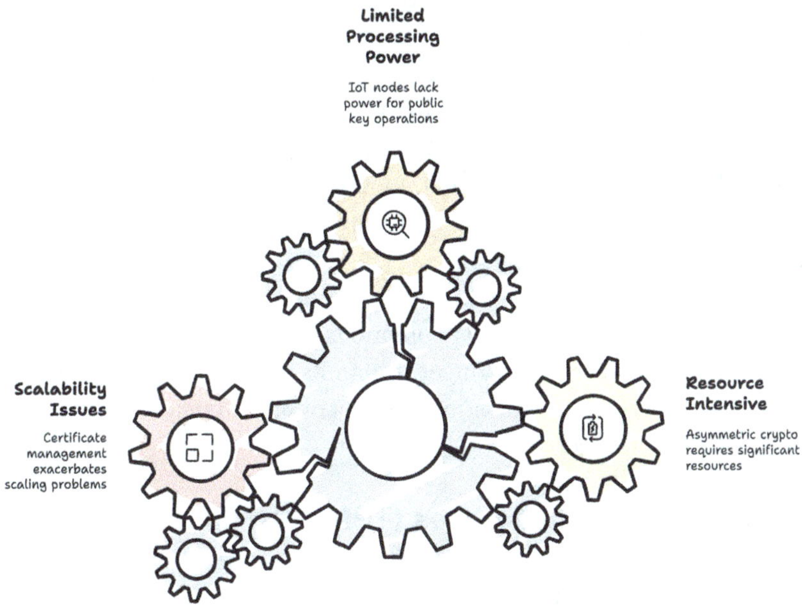

5.3. Lightweight Cryptography

Lightweight cryptography tries to make cryptographic primitives work better on IoT devices by making them less complicated, using less memory, and using less power. These solutions make it easier to authenticate on constrained hardware by using simpler algorithms, smaller keys, and better protocols. Lightweight cryptography makes things easier, but it doesn't always work well in AIoT settings where adaptive intelligence is used. AI-driven systems need authentication that can change, regular re-verification, and protection against new attack methods. Lightweight systems might not have enough entropy, flexibility, or robustness, which makes it hard for them to provide continuous and context-aware authentication.

Static lightweight cryptographic approaches may not be enough to protect AIoT systems, such as self-driving cars and industrial automation, against changing threats. Bad people could use predictable patterns or limited core areas to make people lose faith in the system. For this reason, lightweight cryptography is a big step forward, but it doesn't fully solve the problem of intelligent and adaptive AIoT security.

5.4. Device Fingerprinting

Device fingerprinting verifies devices by looking at their unique features, like flaws in the hardware, radio frequency signatures, timing behavior, or traffic patterns. This method uses unique, hard-to-clone properties to provide a viable alternative to traditional key-based authentication. In theory, device fingerprinting makes things safer without needing to store credentials. But in real life, AIoT situations are very dynamic. Changes in the environment, mobility, aging hardware, and network circumstances can all affect the features of fingerprints, which can cause instability and incorrect rejections.

For example, in mobile AIoT systems like drones or wearable devices, variations in signal strength or operating conditions can make fingerprints less reliable. Attackers might also try to copy fingerprint traits using machine learning methods. So, even though device fingerprinting has a lot of potential, it still needs to be made more reliable and stronger.

5.5. Trusted Platform Modules (TPM / PUFs)

Trusted Platform Modules (TPMs) and Physically Unclonable Functions (PUFs) enable hardware-based security by incorporating trust into the device's hardware. TPMs preserve cryptographic keys and perform protected operations, whereas PUFs generate unique identities based on variances in the physical structure of silicon. These systems provide significant protection against key extraction, cloning, and spoofing. Hardware-rooted trust significantly improves authentication reliability in AIoT systems that handle sensitive data or critical infrastructure. Adding TPMs and PUFs raises costs, complicates construction, and consumes more power. IoT devices that utilize minimal power and are inexpensive may not be compatible with these types of hardware upgrades. Furthermore, deploying on a large scale boosts the costs of developing and maintaining the product.

As a result, while TPMs and PUFs are effective authentication methods, they are frequently reserved for high-value or mission-critical AIoT applications rather than universal adoption.

6. EMERGING AUTHENTICATION TECHNIQUES FOR SECURED AIOT

The limitations of conventional authentication mechanisms in AIoT environments have motivated the development of advanced, adaptive, and intelligence-driven security solutions. Emerging authentication techniques aim to balance strong security guarantees with the practical constraints of AIoT systems, such as limited resources, massive scale, heterogeneity, and dynamic operating contexts. This section discusses key emerging approaches that show significant potential for enabling secure, scalable, and privacy-preserving authentication in AIoT ecosystems.

6.1. Lightweight Cryptographic Algorithms

Lightweight cryptographic methods are made to work with the limited computing, memory, and energy resources that IoT and AIoT devices have. Lightweight algorithms lower processing costs while keeping security levels at a level that is acceptable, unlike traditional cryptography methods. Recent efforts to standardize it have made it more widely accepted. Lightweight cryptographic methods approved by NIST, like Ascon, are a big step forward in this area. Ascon has authenticated encryption with associated data (AEAD) and hashing features that work well in limited spaces. The design focuses on being simple, hard to break with known cryptanalytic methods, and efficient on microcontrollers with low power. Lightweight encryption makes it easier to authenticate devices and protect data in AIoT systems while using fewer resources. Lightweight methods allow for frequent authentication and secure communication while saving battery life in wearable healthcare devices or devices that monitor the environment. Even so, these algorithms do help with efficiency problems, but they frequently need to be combined with more modern security frameworks to make adaptive and context-aware authentication possible, which is important for advanced AIoT applications.

6.2. Blockchain-Based Authentication

Blockchain-based authentication decentralizes AIoT security by removing the need for centralized authentication authorities. Blockchain technology's immutable ledgers, decentralized consensus, and public audit trails make it ideal for a wide range of AIoT applications.

In blockchain-based authentication, devices use cryptographic hashes rather than raw identifiers to register their identities in a distributed ledger. Smart contracts automatically enforce authentication criteria, ensuring that only validated devices have access to the network. This technique increases trust, reduces single points of failure, and complicates individuals' capacity to misrepresent or change their identity.

Figure 9. Blockchain assisted authentication flow for tokenization

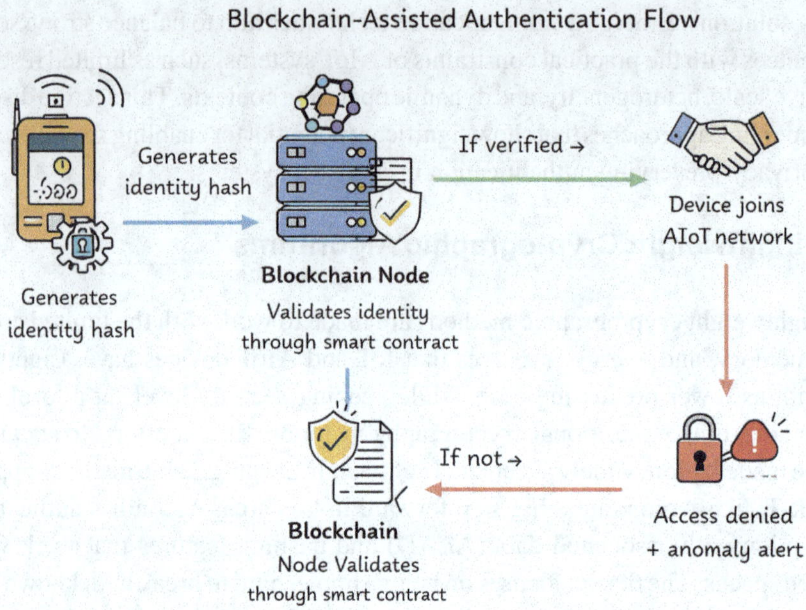

Blockchain-based authentication is extremely useful in smart cities, supply chain management, and industrial AIoT, where many people rely on shared infrastructure. However, blockchain has issues such as latency, scalability, and energy consumption, especially in the case of public blockchains. To address these concerns, people are working hard to develop hybrid systems that combine lightweight blockchains with edge computing.

6.3. AI-Driven Authentication

Machine learning and deep learning algorithms are used by AI-driven authentication to check identities using dynamic and contextual data instead of static credentials. These aspects could include how a device acts, the types of traffic it sends and receives, usage profiles, or biometric indications. In AIoT environments, AI-driven authentication enables continuous and adaptive trust evaluation. Instead of checking a device once, the system keeps an eye on what it's doing and changes trust levels in real time. This method works very well for finding gadgets that have been hacked or are fake and are acting strangely. AI models can check devices in smart grid AIoT systems by looking at how they communicate and how well they work together. In industrial settings, behavioral authentication helps find illegal devices that are trying to pass themselves off as real controllers. AI-driven authentication makes systems more flexible, but it also brings up problems with model robustness, explainability, and vulnerability to attacks that need to be fixed.

6.4. Federated Learning-Based Authentication

Federated learning (FL) allows multiple devices to work together to build a model without having to share raw data. Federated learning in AIoT authentication enables decentralized identity verification, protecting data privacy and minimizing communication overhead.

AIoT devices use federated learning to train authentication models on their own using behavioral or contextual data. They then send only model updates to a central aggregator or peer node. This technique protects private identifying information while allowing collective intelligence across the network.

Federated learning-based authentication is especially useful for privacy-sensitive applications including smart homes, healthcare AIoT, and wearable devices. It follows data protection laws by limiting the collecting of data in one place. Nonetheless, issues like as model poisoning, communication efficiency, and the diversity of local data distributions remain critical fields of inquiry.

6.5. Biometric and Behavioral Authentication

Biometric and behavioral authentication methods stress human-centered identity verification in AIoT systems. These approaches verify a person's identity by looking at their physiological traits (such fingerprints, facial features, or speech patterns) or their behavior (like how they move, how they interact with others, or how they use devices). Biometric authentication is a simple and user-friendly way to keep AIoT applications safe that need people to utilize them, like smart homes, health monitoring, and assistive technology. Behavioral authentication makes security better by allowing ongoing verification without the user having to do anything. In healthcare AIoT systems, biometric authentication makes sure that only doctors who are allowed to see patient data can do so. Behavioral monitoring, on the other hand, finds behaviors that are not suitable. Even if biometric and behavioral methods have their benefits, they also make people worry about privacy, data security, and the risk of being spoofed. So, it's important to safeguard templates well and develop models that are safe.

7. OPEN RESEARCH CHALLENGES

Despite notable progress in authentication mechanisms for secured AIoT systems, several critical research challenges remain unresolved. The convergence of artificial intelligence with resource-constrained IoT devices introduces unique trade-offs between security, efficiency, scalability, and privacy. Addressing these challenges is essential to ensure that AIoT systems can be securely deployed across safety-critical and large-scale environments. This section highlights key open research issues that continue to hinder the realization of robust and trustworthy AIoT authentication frameworks.

7.1. Energy-Efficient Security

Balancing A big problem with safe AIoT authentication is saving energy. A lot of AIoT devices only work when they have a lot of battery power or use energy harvesting methods, which makes energy use a big problem. Strong authentication solutions, especially those that need a lot of cryptographic operations or constant verification, can use a lot of power and shorten the life of a device.

The study topic involves reconciling stringent security protocols with minimal energy consumption. Lightweight cryptographic methods that are used now make things more efficient, but they might not be able to provide adaptive or continuous authentication in AIoT settings that change. Recent studies have concentrated on energy-efficient authentication methods, duty-cycled security methodologies, and hardware-accelerated cryptography, which delegates processing to low-power components.

Energy-efficient authentication is essential for ensuring long-term reliability in practical applications like wearable healthcare devices and remote environmental monitoring systems. It is still a big scientific problem to find a way to make authentication systems that change their security strength based on how much energy is available. strong authentication with device battery constraints.

7.2. Privacy-Preserving AI

Authentication in AIoT systems typically depends on confidential information, such device IDs, behavioral patterns, and biometric data. AI-based authentication makes things more flexible and accurate, but it also poses big privacy concerns. Centralized data aggregation and model training could render user behavior and device-specific information open to illegal access or use.

A big scientific question is how to make authentication that protects privacy while still ensuring security. Federated learning, differential privacy, and safe multi-party computation are all good ideas, but they are hard to use and slow down the system. Also, putting these methods into real-time AIoT authentication systems is hard because there aren't enough computing resources.

In industries that care about privacy, like healthcare, AIoT, and smart homes, not protecting identity-related data well enough might break the law and make people lose trust in the service. Future study ought to concentrate on formulating authentication strategies that reduce data exposure while preserving elevated accuracy and resilience.

7.3. Resilience Against Adversarial AI Attacks

AI-based authentication systems are open to assaults on the basic machine learning models that power them. Malefactors can modify the properties of input, pollute training data, or take advantage of vulnerabilities in a model to get around authentication or pretend to be real devices. A research problem that is still being worked on is how to make AI threats less dangerous. Researchers are looking into strong model training, hostile detection methods, and explainable AI to make AI more trustworthy. Still, making anything more resistant to attacks usually makes it harder to process and less efficient.

Adversary failures can have catastrophic ramifications in AIoT systems, as authentication decisions directly influence physical processes, including smart grids and autonomous systems. The creation of lightweight, durable defensive systems that can function on minimal electronics continues to be an unresolved scientific challenge.

7.4. Standardization and Interoperability

There aren't any clear ways to authenticate AIoT, which makes it hard to make secure and compatible implementations. AIoT ecosystems have a lot of different devices, communication protocols, manufacturers, and application areas, and each one has its own security assumptions and capabilities. Without standardized authentication frameworks, security implementations become disjointed, which makes it more likely that they will be set up wrong or have security holes. When devices from different manufacturers or networks need to authenticate and talk to each other safely, interoperability problems happen.

There needs to be research to come up with authentication standards that are adaptable, can be added to, and are widely accepted. These standards should be able to handle differences between systems while still providing good security guarantees. It is still hard and not fully solved to get industry, academia, and regulatory bodies to work together on common frameworks. of unified security standards across IoT vendors and protocols.

7.5. Secure Lifecycle Management

Authentication in AIoT systems must encompass the whole device lifespan, including deployment, operation, upgrades, and decommissioning, rather than being limited to initial device onboarding. Many current authentication systems put more emphasis on limiting initial access than on keeping trust over time. For effective lifetime management, you need continuous authentication, secure firmware updates, key rotation, and reliable revocation procedures. Authentication credentials need to be changed when devices get older or when ownership changes, but this shouldn't affect security or accessibility.

Managing the lifecycles of devices safely and effectively in large-scale AIoT systems is a big problem. Research is necessary to create authentication frameworks that are aware of the device's lifecycle and may change when trust connections and operational situations change over time. device onboarding to retirement, authentication must remain continuous and adaptive.

8. FUTURE DIRECTIONS

As Artificial Intelligence of Things (AIoT) systems continue to expand in scale, complexity, and criticality, securing authentication mechanisms will require forward-looking and adaptive approaches. Emerging technological advancements and evolving threat models necessitate a shift from static security solutions toward intelligent, resilient, and future-proof authentication frameworks. In this context, several key directions are expected to shape the evolution of secured AIoT ecosystems.

Looking ahead, secured AIoT is expected to evolve along the following directions:

- **Quantum-safe cryptography**

In the future, AIoT authentication frameworks will slowly add quantum-resistant cryptographic algorithms to protect device identities and communications from quantum adversaries' powerful computers. These methods will be very important for making sure that AIoT systems and vital infrastructure can last for a long time.

- **Zero-trust AIoT ecosystems**

AIoT security architectures will leverage zero-trust notions, which means that trust is always being evaluated instead than assumed. Security will be better against both outside and inside threats with continuous authentication systems that use contextual awareness, behavioral analysis, and dynamic risk assessment.

- **Autonomous security orchestration**

AI-driven security orchestration will enable autonomous monitoring and enforcement of authentication policies across AIoT networks. Intelligent agents will detect anomalies, adapt security configurations, and respond to threats in real time, reducing dependence on manual intervention.

- **Self-healing identity systems**

Self-healing identity management will be used by future AIoT systems to find compromised nodes, revoke or renew credentials, and restore trust automatically. These systems will make things more stable and make sure that secure operations can keep going. These accomplishments show that we are on the right track to creating a safe, reliable, and smart AIoT ecosystem that can grow over time and stay strong against new cyber threats.

9. CONCLUSION

The rapid convergence of Artificial Intelligence and the Internet of Things has evolved traditional IoT systems into intelligent, autonomous, and contextually aware ecosystems known as AIoT. This evolution has many uses in healthcare, smart cities, industry, agriculture, and vital infrastructure. However, it also creates new security problems that current protection solutions are not ready to deal with. Authentication is one of the most important challenges that needs to be addressed to build confidence, protect data integrity, and make sure that systems are reliable.

This chapter provided a comprehensive and methodical assessment of secure AIoT, emphasizing authentication difficulties. The chapter began by talking about the basic structure of AIoT systems. It looked at how security needs change at the perception, edge, network, and application levels, and stressed the importance of making authentication a cross-layer issue instead of a separate solution. The full threat landscape research showed that identity-based attacks, data-centric threats, adversarial AI attacks, network exploits, and physical tampering all hurt the trustworthiness and safety of AIoT operations.

The examination of authentication challenges exposed the realistic constraints of AIoT systems, encompassing limited device resources, substantial scalability challenges, platform diversity, the necessity for context-aware communication, and vulnerability to adversarial interference. This chapter critically assesses current authentication strategies, such as password-based systems, PKI, lightweight cryptography, device fingerprinting, and hardware-rooted trust mechanisms, demonstrating that no single conventional method can sufficiently meet the diverse needs of AIoT environments. To address these constraints, a range of innovative authentication technologies were rigorously analyzed, including lightweight cryptographic algorithms, blockchain-based authentication, AI-driven and federated learning-based authentication, alongside biometric and behavioral verification methods. These solutions together show a move toward security frameworks that are adaptable, decentralized, and based on intelligence. These frameworks can help AIoT implementations that are scalable and respect privacy. Also, the acknowledgment of remaining research problems and possible solutions emphasized the importance of energy-efficient security, privacy-preserving AI, adversarial resistance, standardization, and safe lifecycle management. Strong authentication goes beyond only technological protections; it is necessary for the long-term, safe, and dependable growth of AIoT ecosystems. To get the most out of AIoT in practical, safety-critical, and large-scale applications, it's important to solve authentication problems through interdisciplinary research and thorough security design.

REFERENCES

Anjum, M. J., Farooq, M. S., Umer, T., & Shaheen, M. (2025). Disaster identification scheme based on federated learning and Cognitive Internet of Vehicles. *Computer Communications*, *240*, 108216. https://doi.org/https://doi.org/10.1016/j.comcom.2025.108216. DOI: 10.1016/j.comcom.2025.108216

Bhatt, H., Sharma, B. B., Sharma, A., Sharma, R., & Sharma, M. (2021). *An IoT-Based Soil Properties Monitoring System for Crop Growth and Production*. 200–219. DOI: 10.4018/978-1-7998-7756-1.ch009

Bhatt*, H., Bhushan, B., & Kumar, N. (2019). IOT: the Current Scenario and Role of Sensors Involved in Smart Agriculture. *International Journal of Recent Technology and Engineering (IJRTE)*, *8*(4), 12011–12023. DOI: 10.35940/ijrte.D9285.118419

Bhushan Sharma, B., Manimaran, A., Govind Raj, M., Tanushree Gohain, T., Clement King, A., & Rani, S. (2022). Future Research on Internet of Things (Iot) and It'S Applications. *Journal of Data Acquisition and Processing*, *38*(4), 804. DOI: 10.5281/zenodo.777818

Bouramdane, A.-A. (2023). Cyberattacks in Smart Grids: Challenges and Solving the Multi-Criteria Decision-Making for Cybersecurity Options, Including Ones That Incorporate Artificial Intelligence, Using an Analytical Hierarchy Process. *Journal of Cybersecurity and Privacy*, *3*(4), 662–705. DOI: 10.3390/jcp3040031

Butt, R., Tariq, N., Ashraf, M., Humayun, M., & Shaheen, M. (2025). Collaborative defense: Federated learning for intrusion detection systems. In *Federated Learning Systems: Towards Privacy-Preserving Distributed AI* (pp. 147–165). Springer Nature Switzerland. DOI: 10.1007/978-3-031-78841-3_8

Dereziński, M., & Mahoney, M. W. (2024). Recent and Upcoming Developments in Randomized Numerical Linear Algebra for Machine Learning. *Proceedings of the ACM SIGKDD International Conference on Knowledge Discovery and Data Mining*, 6470–6479. DOI: 10.1145/3637528.3671461

Farooq, M. S., Munir, S. F., Faraz Manzoor, M., & Shaheen, M. (2025). AI-Driven Adaptive Federated Learning With Privacy Preservation and Imbalance Adjustment for Financial Credit Card Fraud Detection. *Applied Computational Intelligence and Soft Computing*, *2025*(1), 7116768. https://doi.org/https://doi.org/10.1155/acis/7116768. DOI: 10.1155/acis/7116768

Jiang, H., Zhang, Y., Muljadi, E., Zhang, J. J., & Gao, D. W. (2018). A Short-Term and High-Resolution Distribution System Load Forecasting Approach Using Support Vector Regression With Hybrid Parameters Optimization. *IEEE Transactions on Smart Grid*, *9*(4), 3341–3350. DOI: 10.1109/TSG.2016.2628061

Kabir, M. S., & Nazmul Alam, M. (2023). IoT, Big Data and AI Applications in the Law Enforcement and Legal System. *RE:view*, *10*, 1777–1789.

Kashyap, S., Sharma, B. B., Kumar, N., Vaidya, P., & Gupta, G. (2021). Role of IoT in healthcare: An overview. *Mobile Health: Advances in Research and Applications*, 1–16.

Krizhevsky, A., Sutskever, I., & Hinton, G. E. (2017). ImageNet classification with deep convolutional neural networks. *Communications of the ACM*, *60*(6), 84–90. DOI: 10.1145/3065386

Masalila, S., & Sheikh, S. 5353106, A. F.-A. at S. (n.d.). Toward Resilient and Intelligent Infrastructure: A Survey of Smart Monitoring Systems and Emerging Technologies. *Papers*.Ssrn.*Com*, 1–26. https://papers.ssrn.com/sol3/papers.cfm?abstract_id=5353106

Mehta, R., Sharma, R., Sharma, N., & Sharma, B. B. (2025). Smart Technology in Focus: Legal Frameworks for IoT and AI Integration. *2025 12th International Conference on Computing for Sustainable Global Development (INDIACom)*, 1–5. DOI: 10.23919/INDIACom66777.2025.11115751

Miller, T., Durlik, I., Kostecka, E., Kozlovska, P., Łobodzińska, A., Sokołowska, S., & Nowy, A. (2025). Integrating Artificial Intelligence Agents with the Internet of Things for Enhanced Environmental Monitoring: Applications in Water Quality and Climate Data. *Electronics (Basel)*, *14*(4), 696. Advance online publication. DOI: 10.3390/electronics14040696

Powell, J., McCafferty-Leroux, A., Hilal, W., & Gadsden, S. A. (2024). Smart grids: A comprehensive survey of challenges, industry applications, and future trends. *Energy Reports*, *11*, 5760–5785. https://doi.org/https://doi.org/10.1016/j.egyr.2024.05.051. DOI: 10.1016/j.egyr.2024.05.051

Rasooli, M. W., Bhushan, B., & Kumar, N. (2020). Applicability of wireless sensor networks & IoT in saffron & wheat crops: A smart agriculture perspective. *International Journal of Scientific and Technology Research*, *9*(2), 2456–2461.

Saeed, F., Shaheen, M., Umer, T., & Farooq, M. S. (2024). Employing federated learning for the implication of digital twin. In *Digital Twins for Wireless Networks: Overview, Architecture, and Challenges* (pp. 93–122). Springer Nature Switzerland.

Safeer, E., Tahir, S., Nawaz, A., Humayun, M., Shaheen, M., & Khan, M. (2025). Advanced hybrid malware identification framework for the Internet of Medical Things, driven by deep learning. *Security and Privacy*, *8*(1), e454. https://doi.org/https://doi.org/10.1002/spy2.454. DOI: 10.1002/spy2.454

Salgotra, S., Sharma, B. B., & Rasheed, M. U. (2024, December). IoT_LWC Secure Data Communication for Devices: A Review. In *International Conference on Artificial Intelligence of Things* (pp. 160-171). Cham: Springer Nature Switzerland.

Samanta, S., Sarkar, A., & Kumari, S. (2024). An IoMT data security framework with Hyperledger Fabric for smart cities. *International Journal of Information Technology : an Official Journal of Bharati Vidyapeeth's Institute of Computer Applications and Management*, *16*(8), 4875–4886. Advance online publication. DOI: 10.1007/s41870-024-02181-6

Saraswat, A., Negi, A., Mittal, K., Sharma, B. B., & Kappal, N. (2022, July). Real-time eyesight power prediction using deep learning methods. In *Proceedings of Third International Conference on Computing, Communications, and Cyber-Security: IC4S 2021* (pp. 325-339). Singapore: Springer Nature Singapore.

Shahzadi, S., Iqbal, M., Qayyum, Z. U., & Dagiuklas, T. (2017). Infrastructure as a service (IaaS): A comparative performance analysis of open-source cloud platforms. *2017 IEEE 22nd International Workshop on Computer Aided Modeling and Design of Communication Links and Networks (CAMAD)*, 1–6. DOI: 10.1109/CAMAD.2017.8031522

Sharma, B. B., Gupta, G., Vaidya, P., Basheer, S., Memon, F. H., & Thakur, R. N. (2022). Internet of Things-Based Crop Classification Model Using Deep Learning for Indirect Solar Drying. *Wireless Communications and Mobile Computing*, *2022*(1), 1455216. Advance online publication. DOI: 10.1155/2022/1455216

Sharma, B. B., & Kumar, N. (2020). Internet of things-based hardware and software for smart agriculture: A review. *Lecture Notes in Electrical Engineering*, *597*, 151–157. DOI: 10.1007/978-3-030-29407-6_13

Sharma, B. B., Kumar, R., & Sharma, R. (2025). Enhancing Smart Grid Efficiency: The Role of IoT Blockchain and Fuzzy Set Theory. In Mzili, T., Arya, A. K., Pamucar, D., & Shaheen, M. (Eds.), *Optimization, Machine Learning, and Fuzzy Logic: Theory, Algorithms, and Applications* (1st ed., Vol. 1). IGI Global Scientifc Publishing. DOI: 10.4018/979-8-3693-7352-1.ch011

Sharma, B. B., Vaidya, P., Kumar, N., Tiwari, A., Bansal, S., Faruque, M. R. I., & Al-mugren, K. S. (2025). Enhancing post-harvest sustainability in temperate crops through smart IoT-integrated indirect solar dryer. *Scientific Reports*, *15*(1), 28608. DOI: 10.1038/s41598-025-13499-x PMID: 40764716

Sharma, G., Sharma, G., & Sharma, B. B. (2025a). Comparative Analysis of Deep Learning Models for Tomato Leaf Disease Classification. *2025 12th International Conference on Computing for Sustainable Global Development (INDIACom)*, 1–6. DOI: 10.23919/INDIACom66777.2025.11115590

Sharma, G., Sharma, G., & Sharma, B. B. (2025b). Tomato Plant Disease Detection Using YOLO11. *2025 12th International Conference on Computing for Sustainable Global Development (INDIACom)*, 1–5. DOI: 10.23919/INDIACom66777.2025.11115873

Sharma, R., Kumar, N., & Sharma, B. B. (2022). Applications of Artificial Intelligence in Smart Agriculture: A Review. In Singh, P. K., Singh, Y., Kolekar, M. H., Kar, A. K., & Gonçalves, P. J. S. (Eds.), *Recent Innovations in Computing* (pp. 135–142). Springer Singapore. DOI: 10.1007/978-981-16-8248-3_11

Sharma, R., Sharma, B. B., Vaidya, P., & Naaz, S. (2025). Design and Implementation of Real-Time Tomato Plant Growth Monitoring System using Deep Learning based YOLO and Raspberry Pi. *Applied Artificial Intelligence*, *39*(1), 2590829. DOI: 10.1080/08839514.2025.2590829

Sharma, R., Sharma, D., Vaidya, P., & Sharma, B. B. (2025). Importance of Artificial Intelligence and the Internet of Things in Smart Agriculture. In V. K. Mathew, A. Chandak, M. Mohan, & Bhumeshwar K. Patle (Eds.), *Metaheuristics in Engineering Applications* (1st ed., Vol. 1). Taylor & Francis Group. DOI: 10.1201/9781003561484-8

Sharma, R., Vaidya, P., & Sharma, B. (2024). A Review on Plant Growth Monitoring using Artificial Intelligence and the Internet of Things. *2024 11th International Conference on Computing for Sustainable Global Development (INDIACom)*, 140–145. DOI: 10.23919/INDIACom61295.2024.10498942

Singh, C. S., Naaz, S., & Saranya, G. (2024). IOT-CENTRIC DATA PROTECTION USING DEEP LEARNING TECHNIQUE FOR PRESERVING SECURITY AND PRIVACY IN CLOUD. [IJDSAI]. *International Journal of Data Science and Artificial Intelligence*, *02*(03), 81. DOI: 10.66135/ijdsai0203p003

Sladojevic, S., Arsenovic, M., Anderla, A., Culibrk, D., & Stefanovic, D. (2016). Deep Neural Networks Based Recognition of Plant Diseases by Leaf Image Classification. *Computational Intelligence and Neuroscience, 2016*, 1–11. Advance online publication. DOI: 10.1155/2016/3289801 PMID: 27418923

Tariq, F., Afzaal, A., Anjum, M. J., Kanwal, F., Bashir, K., & Shaheen, M. (2025). Security and Privacy Preservation in Smart Cities During Security Surveillance: A Mapping Study. *Applied Computational Intelligence and Soft Computing, 2025*(1), 6727022. https://doi.org/https://doi.org/10.1155/acis/6727022. DOI: 10.1155/acis/6727022

Thakur, S., Verma, R., Vaidya, P., & Sharma, B. B. (2024). A Review of Current Technologies for Vehicle Tracking and Toll Enforcement. *2024 3rd Edition of IEEE Delhi Section Flagship Conference (DELCON)*, 1–5. DOI: 10.1109/DELCON64804.2024.10866452

Tripathi, G., Ahad, M. A., & Casalino, G. (2023). A comprehensive review of blockchain technology: Underlying principles and historical background with future challenges. *Decision Analytics Journal, 9*, 100344. https://doi.org/https://doi.org/10.1016/j.dajour.2023.100344

Vaidya, P., & Sharma, B. B. (2021). Wearable devices: Pros and cons. *Mobile Health: Advances in Research and Applications*, 17–29.

Verma, R., Thakur, S., Vaidya, P., & Sharma, B. B. (2024). Blockchain-Enabled IoT: Revolutionizing Security and Data Integrity in Connected Devices. *2024 3rd Edition of IEEE Delhi Section Flagship Conference (DELCON)*, 1–5. DOI: 10.1109/DELCON64804.2024.10866803

Wang, H., Wang, J., & Huang, M. (2013). Building a smart home system with WSN and service robot. *Proceedings - 2013 5th Conference on Measuring Technology and Mechatronics Automation, ICMTMA 2013*, 353–356. DOI: 10.1109/ICMTMA.2013.90

Chapter 2
AIoT Security Landscape Threat Models and Vulnerability Assessment

Salam Al E'mari
http://orcid.org/0000-0002-2134-4158
University of Petra, Jordan

Yousef Sanjalawe
http://orcid.org/0000-0002-4442-1865
University of Jordan, Jordan

Fadi Fataftah
http://orcid.org/0000-0002-3299-0972
University Canada West, Canada

ABSTRACT

This chapter presents a comprehensive examination of security challenges and protection mechanisms within the Artificial Intelligence of Things (AIoT) ecosystem. It outlines the defining architectural layers of AIoT and highlights characteristics such as large-scale heterogeneity, data-driven autonomy, edge–cloud distribution, and cyber-physical coupling that uniquely shape its security posture. The chapter develops an AIoT-tailored threat-modelling framework, detailing adversary taxonomy, attack surfaces, and representative scenarios, followed by an integrated vulnerability-assessment approach spanning device, network, and AI-model pipelines. It further explores mitigation strategies including security-by-design, zero-trust networking, robust AI pipelines, supply-chain assurance, and emerging advancements such as digital twins, federated learning, explainable AI, and post-quantum cryptography.

DOI: 10.4018/979-8-3373-6299-1.ch002

The chapter concludes with strategic recommendations and research directions aimed at strengthening resilience, trustworthiness, and lifecycle governance in next-generation AIoT deployments.

1. INTRODUCTION

The interlinking of wireless communication and Artificial Intelligence (AI) has led to the Internet of Things (IoT) taking a new form, thus redefining it, the AIoT. The advancement of technology makes its use much easier, thus making it a prominent evolution for smart cities, healthcare, industrial automation, transport, and farming. The fusion of intricate computing networks, large sets of interlinked sensors, machine learning and edge computing form the revered AIoT systems which facilitate instant response decision making and predictive analytics, along with autonomous, real-time operation and adaptation. With such features, these systems will be fully data driven and autonomous (Siam et al., 2025). AIoT systems will offer substantial improvement on the operations of these devices, and the virtualized wireless systems will have innumerable devices coupled. However, these systems will be prone to innumerable cyber security vulnerabilities.

Even on its own, the IoT herds all the interconnected sensors and actuators, heterogeneous networks, confined devices, and the dynamic flows and topologies of voluminous data. Recent surveys, Sebestyén (2025), note IoT remains a primary concern for issues such as software lifecycle, data integrity, communication protocols, and even managing identities. Furthermore, incorporating AI into these networks offers additional training-data integrity, model robustness offered by adversarial concealment, and inferencing and expozed APIs APIs on top of a broad attack surface. AIoT systems straddle the digital and tangible domains. Different from devices which only sense and transmit, these systems and devices can also affect changes in the physical environment. This means that their compromise can cause data or service interruption to physical security threats.

This chapter aims to provide such a comprehensive view. Its primary objectives are three-fold. First, to define the AIoT ecosystem and articulate the distinctive security-relevant characteristics that differentiate it from conventional IoT or stand-alone AI systems. Second, to develop and describe threat-models tailored to AIoT, identifying adversary types, attack surfaces across layers (device, network, data/AI, actuation), and representative scenarios. Third, to examine systematic approaches to vulnerability assessment in AIoT systems—covering both classical weaknesses (firmware, network, configuration) and AI-specific vulnerabilities (data poisoning, model stealing, adversarial input) — and to outline assessment workflows, metrics and best-practice controls (Sebestyen et al., 2025).

In doing so, the chapter addresses a notable research and practice gap: while many surveys examine IoT security (Deep, Zheng, Jolfaei, Yu, Ostovari, & Bashir, 2019) or AI security (for instance, adversarial machine-learning literature) as independent domains, relatively few works analyse their convergence within the cyber-physical actuation context that AIoT systems embody. For example, the survey by Siam et al. (2025) reviews advances in sensing, computing, and communication in AIoT and notes that security and privacy concerns remain as critical as the optimisation of those technical components. Yet a dedicated, cross-layer focus on threat and vulnerability modelling in AIoT remains substantially under-addressed.

This fragmentation results in an incomplete understanding of how AI-driven inference, heterogeneous IoT devices, distributed edge–cloud architectures, and physical actuation interact to create new and expanded attack surfaces. Current approaches rarely incorporate AI-specific risks—such as data poisoning, adversarial perturbation, model extraction, or compromised learning pipelines—into analyses of cyber-physical security. Likewise, existing vulnerability assessment methods predominantly emphasise device or network weaknesses without integrating the integrity of data pipelines, AI models, and actuation pathways. Consequently, organisations lack a comprehensive framework for identifying how adversaries may exploit individual components and propagate attacks across the full AIoT lifecycle.

Accordingly, the central problem this chapter addresses is the absence of a unified, AIoT-tailored security framework that systematically integrates architectural characterisation, adversary taxonomy, attack-surface analysis, and cross-layer vulnerability assessment. Addressing this deficiency is essential for developing mitigation strategies that reflect the operational complexity, interdependence, and physical consequences inherent in next-generation AIoT deployments across domains such as smart manufacturing, healthcare, transportation, and smart-city infrastructures.

In theory, threat modelling techniques like STRIDE - spoofing, tampering, repudiation, information disclosure, denial of service, and elevation of privilege– can be adapted to AIoT contexts but need to be expanded to include AI-specific risks like poisoning and adversarial perturbation, model inversion, and physical safety consequences. Also, vulnerability assessment must include firmware/firmware-update analysis, protocol/communication review, data-pipeline checks, and AI/ML resource-constrained security testing – all tailored to the constraints encountered in IoT deployments.

This multifaceted view is supported by current world developments. The number of connected Internet of Things devices is expected to increase rapidly, which will increase risk exposure. New studies 2021-2025, as reported by Sebestyén (2025), mark emerging technologies such as AI and blockchain in IoT systems as focuses of research, and at the same time they point to the absence of standardisation and lifecycle security management. Embedding intelligence (on-device inference, federated learning, and cloud training) increases functionality, and simultaneously brings new attack surfaces around model updates, data drift, and adversarial exploitation (Siam et al., 2025).

This chapter is structured as follows: Section 2 will define the AIoT ecosystem and analyze the security-related attributes of each layer (device, network, compute, cloud, actuation) and the peculiarities of AI-enabled systems. Section 3 will construct a holistic threat-modelling framework for AIoT, outlining the adversary taxonomy, attack surfaces, and scenarios. Section 4 will focus on the vulnerability assessment. This includes asset and attack-surface identification, vulnerability (firmware, configuration, data/ML) assessment methodologies, scoring and prioritization, and case studies. Section 5 will develop the tiered security strategy through device, network, data/model pipeline, supply-chain and organization layers. Section 6 will review new trends and future work, including edge-AI robustness, federated learning risks, explainable AI for the IoT, zero-trust systems, integrated lifecycle security, and holistic architecture robustness. Lastly, Section 7 will provide the summary, outlining primary take-aways and strategic recommendations for practitioners and researchers.

2. THE AIOT ECOSYSTEM AND SECURITY-RELEVANT CHARACTERISTICS

2.1 Defining AIoT and its Architectural Layers

In corporate speak, the integration of AI-infused IoT systems, along with the rest of the AI world, where endpoints with circuits on the edge or in the cloud can, beyond just data collection, utilize complex decisioning and learning, and even intelligent computation, devise and evolve 'Artificial Intelligence of Things' or 'AIoT systems'. Siam et al. (2025) note that "the integration of the Internet of Things (IoT) and modern Artificial Intelligence (AI) has given rise to a new paradigm known as the Artificial Intelligence of Things (AIoT)".

[REMOVED HYPERLINK FIELD]In effect, AIoT marks a progression beyond traditional IoT: whereas IoT systems largely revolve around sensing and connectivity, AIoT emphasises real-time data analytics, inference, actuation and feedback loops. A useful way to capture the architecture of an AIoT system is by identifying its layered structure. Several authors propose three to five layers; for example, Siam et al. (2025) identify *sensing*, *computing*, *networking & communication*, and *domain-specific AIoT systems* as key subsystems. For the purposes of security analysis, we can adopt the following five-layer view as shown in Figure 1.

Figure 1. AIoT layered architecture overview

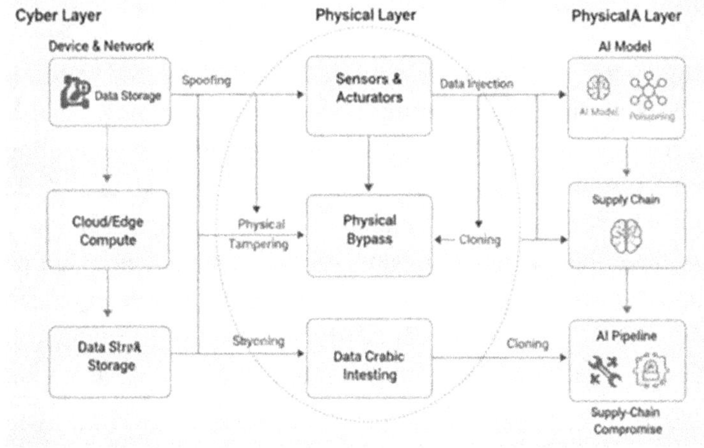

The architecture of AIoT systems with highlighting the primary components:

1. Device/Perception Layer: Sensors and actuators deployed in the field, collecting raw data (temperature, vibration, image, environmental).
2. Network/Communication Layer: Connectivity infrastructure—wireless links, gateways, edge routers, protocols (e.g., MQTT, CoAP, LoRaWAN).
3. Edge/Compute Layer: Local processing nodes (edge gateways, on-device inference engines) that pre-process, aggregate, and optionally execute AI models.
4. Cloud/Backend Layer: Central servers, data centres, model-training pipelines, orchestration services and databases.
5. Application/Actuation Layer: User-facing services, decision-making logic, actuation into the physical environment (robotics, HVAC control, smart grid interactions).

The architecture in layers' situation helps pinpoint with laser focus the areas within the architecture where security controls need to be applied, trust boundaries have apparition, and the potential targets of the adversaries. Equally important, it helps abstract the fact that AIoT is not just the IoT and AI put together, but an intricately woven system of data flows, compute, connectivity, and digital-physical actions.

2.2 Key Characteristics of AIoT that Impact Security

The intersection of Artificial Intelligence with the Internet of Things comes with new attributes that impact the system's security posture. Below we characterize six such attributes, each of which has impacts for modeling the system's threats and vulnerabilities.

- **Heterogeneity and resource-constrained devices.** Many IoT devices are designed with limited computing power, memory, storage and battery life, which restricts the ability to run strong cryptographic algorithms, host full operating systems or support frequent patching. Stanko et al. (2024) emphasise this when discussing the challenges of integrating AI and IoT: "most IoT devices are either powered on batteries or at very low levels of power input. Adding AI functionality … increases the need for power significantly" (p. 4).
- [REMOVED HYPERLINK FIELD]From a security viewpoint, this means that device-level adversaries may exploit weaker authentication, outdated firmware, or inability to support remote updates.
- **Scale and the distributed IoT topology.** IoT networks in AIoT deployments can span thousands to millions of devices dispersed geographically. The sheer number and distributed nature amplify the attack surface and complicate centralized monitoring, patch-management and anomaly detection. Rinf.tech (2023) reports that the number of connected devices is expected to exceed 30.9 billion by 2025, driving market growth in AIoT. Security management at such scale must address network segmentation, device lifecycle management, and large-scale orchestration of updates and monitoring.
- **Edge-cloud continuum and trust boundaries.** AIoT shifts computing away from purely centralised clouds toward an edge-cloud continuum, where data processing happens partly at edge nodes to reduce latency and support real-time decision-making (Iman et al., 2024). The division of responsibility across edge and cloud creates new trust and security boundaries (e.g., edge nodes may be physically accessible and less protected than cloud data centres) and thus expands the threat surface. For instance, if an edge gateway is compromised, an adversary might manipulate data before cloud ingestion, undermining AI inference.
- **Data-driven intelligence and autonomy**. In AIoT, sensor data is not merely stored and visualized, it is the input to ML or DL models that drive inference and actuation. Alahi et al. (2023) statement sheds light on how AI plays an important role in the making of machine learning models to help understand and evaluate inordinate amounts of complex data to extract useful patterns and trends which would otherwise be very hard for a person to understand. It, however, also states how in smart cities, Al AIoT systems use sensor data and AI neural networks to obtain useful insights, recognize and understand traffic, adjust light and even predict when infrastructure would most likely require upkeep. Because of this data-model-actuation chain, attacks may target

not only the infrastructure but also the integrity of data, the correctness of the model, or the validity of the actuation decision. This deep integration raises concerns such as adversarial inputs, poisoning, model inversion or extraction.

- **Cyber-physical coupling and safety implications.** Unlike purely IT systems, many AIoT deployments produce physical effects (e.g., smart grids, automated manufacturing, autonomous vehicles). The coupling of cyber and physical domains means that security failures can lead not only to data loss, but to physical harm, environmental damage or safety violations. This characteristic elevates the importance of integrating safety and security analyses (e.g., functional safety, fail-safe modes, physical damage control) within the AIoT context.
- **Supply chain and long-lived deployments.** IoT devices are sometimes left unattended for long periods, often without strong vendors' support for vendor discontinuation strategies. Stanko et al. (2024) emphasize the fragmented hardware and firmware ecosystem, stating that "the fragmented ecosystem" of devices "makes standardization and inter-operability difficult" (p. 2).
- In terms of security, the risks of counterfeit machinery, hostile firmware, and third-party supply chain components alongside devices packed with outdated security systems and unaddressed vulnerabilities are cumulative. The extended use of time only exacerbates the consequences of still having unpatched systems.

2.3 Illustrative Use-Cases and Their Security Implications

To concretize how these characteristics, materialize in real-world deployments, consider two illustrative use-cases.

Smart manufacturing (Industrial AIoT). In a factory scenario, mid-October of 2023, the actuators in machines in a factory setting could allow for the adjustment of specific parameters to optimally set the machines for the task required, which is in accordance to the adjustment of 'data processed locally which is then sent to the cloud for pattern recognition relating to predictive-maintenance' and done so in real time by predicting the specific maintenance required. For predictive maintenance in the cloud, the action of carrying the data to the cloud does support sensor resource which may then relay the data via radio transmission to 'vibration sensors' actuators, updating the maintenance schedule via 'edge gateway'. There is illustrated a large set of equipment across sites for scale and very long periods of time for the lifetime cycle of the factory equipment which depicts edge cloud split. While on the other, the swift reaching of the definite 'geographic region above which' which is more than 400km above the earth. For security purposes of the edge gateway might allow access to the center of the region to which the data is so that it does not become vulnerable to ease of access or fast retrieval which may be done by unpatched so the gateways do not get accessed and thus, setting the firewall defense parameters, sheathed by slow processors which could work unpatched, thus contributing to ease of access.

Smart city infrastructure. In a smart-city deployment, street-lighting units, traffic-camera sensors and environmental monitors collect data which is fused and analyzed via AI to optimize energy usage, detect incidents, or manage traffic flows. This setting comprises highly distributed devices across public spaces, dynamic connectivity (wireless, mesh), real-time decisions, and physical actuation (lighting changes, traffic signage). The scale is vast, heterogeneity is high, and public accessibility increases exposure. Security implications include weak authentication of public devices, eavesdropping of wireless segments, adversarial manipulations of AI models (e.g., mis-classified images from cameras), and functional-safety implications whereby lighting or traffic systems mis-actuated.

3. THREAT MODELLING IN AIOT SYSTEMS

Identifying and detailing potential adversarial behaviors, goals, and targets is a strategic exercise in potential outcomes of system use, focusing on software and hardware interactions. In the case of AIoT, where networks of devices, perimeter AI, and edge/cloud AI systems as well as tangible machinery work in a closed ecosystem as an interconnected unit, multiple facets (device, network, computer, data/AI, actuation) and intermeshing adversary-capabilities woven into cyber-physical thinking must be incorporated into threat modelling.

3.1 Adversary Taxonomy

A useful starting point is to characterise adversaries in terms of four dimensions:

- **Motivation**: adversaries may act for espionage, sabotage, financial gain, service disruption or physical harm.
- **Capability**: e.g., ability to access device firmware, intercept network communications, query or modify AI models, perform physical tampering.
- **Knowledge**: white-box (full system/model access) versus black-box (limited interface) views. As observed by Grosse et al. (2024), many academic AI threat models assume adversarial access that rarely mirrors industrial practice.
- **Resources/Time**: persistence, presence of supply-chain insertion, lateral movement capacity, ability to execute multi-stage attacks.

By mapping adversary capability and motivation, the designer can estimate plausible threat vectors and align them with system layers, this provides the groundwork for constructing attack-trees or graphs.

3.2 Attack Surfaces in AIoT

In AIoT systems, multiple attack surfaces exist across the architecture as presented in Figure 2.

Figure 2. AIoT threat surface map

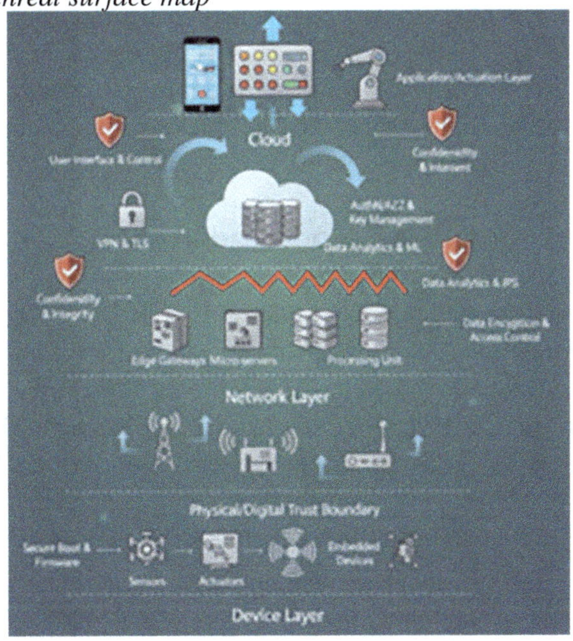

For clarity we map each major layer of its threat envelopes:

The interplay of the AI and IoT domains significantly expands the classic IoT attack surface by adding data/model vulnerabilities and the physical consequence dimension. we highlight six threat categories especially relevant to AIoT:

1. **Sensor spoofing/data injection**: An attacker may supply manipulated sensor readings (e.g., faux temperature or vibration data) so that the AI model gives false inference, leading to wrong actuation or mis-forecast.
2. **Physical capture or device tampering**: Because many IoT devices are deployed in unattended, remote or public locations, adversaries can physically access them, install malicious firmware or rootkits, or replace devices entirely.

3. **Communication interception and MITM**: Wireless communications may be intercepted or hijacked, enabling the attacker to manipulate data in transit, disrupt commands or mount replay attacks.
4. **Denial-of-Service (DoS) and jamming**: Attackers may intentionally overload device networks, jam wireless links, exhaust device power, or cause gateway failure, resulting in inability to sense, act or compute.
5. **Adversarial machine-learning (ML) attacks**: Given the AI component, adversaries may launch evasion attacks (adversarial inputs at inference time), poisoning (altering training data), backdoors (triggered malicious behaviour), model extraction/stealing or membership inference. Grosse et al. (2024) note existing academic models often assume unrealistic adversarial access.
6. **Supply-chain compromise and lifecycle threats**: Hardware modules, firmware updates, AI libraries or provisioning services may be compromised upstream, introducing vulnerabilities or malicious features from device fabrication through deployment.

3.3 Frameworks for Threat Modelling in AIoT

Traditional threat-modelling frameworks (e.g., STRIDE: Spoofing, Tampering, Repudiation, Information disclosure, Denial of service, Elevation of privilege) remain useful, but must be extended for AIoT's unique dimensions (model-pipeline integrity, data-driven inference, physical actuators). For example, Maodza & Du Toit (2024) applied an extended STRIDE plus Lateral Movement ("STRIDE-LM") to agricultural AIoT systems, identifying threats of spoofing, tampering, repudiation, information disclosure, DoS, elevation of privilege and lateral movement.

Alternatively, attack-graph or dynamic topology modelling approaches provide better capture of multi-stage attack progression in large distributed IoT/AI systems. Salayma (2024) developed an approach using dynamic attack graphs for IoT environments, enabling tracking of evolving system topology and new attack paths as devices join or leave.

Further, asset-driven threat modelling specifically for AI systems (von der Assen et al., 2024) emphasises that threat models must account for AI-specific assets (training data, models, inference API) and attacker's access to them.

Together these frameworks suggest that for AIoT systems: (a) map assets (devices, data flows, models, actuators), (b) identify trust boundaries and entry points, (c) enumerate adversary goals and capabilities, (d) build attack-tree/graph models, (e) prioritise via risk metrics, and (f) iterate as system evolves (Papernot et al., 2018).

3.4 Example Threat Scenarios

Consider two representative scenarios illustrating how threat models manifest:

Scenario A: Smart Manufacturing AIoT

A manufacturing plant has vibration sensors mounted on machinery, edge gateways performing local inference, and a cloud-based predictive-maintenance model feeding actuation commands to adjust machine settings. Threat modelling identifies spoofed vibration sensor readings (spoofing), compromised gateway firmware (tampering and privileged escalation), MITM attacks on gateway-cloud communication (information disclosure, tampering), poisoned maintenance-model training data (backdoor/poisoning), hijacked actuation command stream (elevation of privilege, physical harm). Attack-graph modelling may show a multi-step path: physical tamper → gateway root access → cloud API misuse → actuator override.

Scenario B: Smart City Lighting with AIoT

An urban deployment of street-lighting units includes sensors, wireless mesh connectivity, edge AI for light-control decisions, and cloud analytics for optimization. Asset inventory reveals thousands of nodes, wide physical exposure, dynamic network topology (nodes may be added/removed). Threat modelling surfaces: wireless jamming or spoofing of sensor data (DoS/spoofing), compromised lighting node firmware (tampering), model ingestion of manipulated image data from public cameras (poisoning/evasion), actuator patching commands hijacked (elevation of privilege). A dynamic attack-graph needs to accommodate node addition/removal, changing reachable pathways (Salayma, 2024).

3.5 Prioritizing Threats and Linking to Vulnerabilities

Once threats are identified, they must be prioritized based on likelihood, attacker capability, exploitability and consequence—especially the physical safety impact in AIoT. A refined risk scoring approach may be built on CVSS but tailored for cyber-physical systems and AI pipelines. Attack-paths with high adversary access, low effort, and high physical consequence warrant highest priority. The threat-modelling process ties directly into vulnerability assessment: each identified threat suggests attack paths which need enumeration of vulnerable assets (see Section 4). For example, a threat of sensor spoofing points to vulnerabilities such as unsecured sensor-gateway link, lack of data-validation rules, or absence of anomaly-detection at the edge.

The maturity of the design process may also dictate modelling scope: in early phases, high-level attack-trees suffice; in operation, dynamic attack-graphs, continuous monitoring of reachable attack paths, and integration with threat intelligence become required (Salayma, 2024).

3.6 Summary of Section

This section has established a structured approach to threat modelling in AIoT systems. We defined adversary taxonomy, mapped attack surfaces across device, network, computer, data/AI and actuation layers, and highlighted threat categories unique to AIoT. We examined modelling frameworks including extended STRIDE, attack-graphs and AI-asset-based approaches and illustrated real-world scenarios. Finally, we stressed the need to prioritise threats via risk scoring and link threat-modelling directly to vulnerability assessment.

In the next section (Section 4) we will turn from "what could go wrong" to "what is present": systematically identifying vulnerabilities and assessment workflows in AIoT systems, bridging threat models into actionable security testing and evaluation.

4. VULNERABILITY ASSESSMENT IN AIOT SYSTEMS

Identifying the weaknesses in a system and ranking them in a particular order is called Vulnerability 'exploitation' Assessment.' As for the 'Artificial Intelligence of Things' (AIoT), the scope of vulnerability assessment goes beyond the classical IoT infrastructure: devices, firmware, and networks, to the new vulnerabilities of AI pipelines: poisoned datasets, adversarial models, and insecure interfaces. The goal is to inform capability and capacity planning by developing a quantitative and qualitative assessment of system exposure and system preparedness (Alaba et al., 2017).

4.1 Purpose and Scope

As a part of evidence-based decision-making, AIoT ecosystems integrate cyber networks, physical devices, and sophisticated components. Hence, assessment of vulnerability needs to be carried out across three converging domains.

1. **Cyber layer** – traditional IT and network vulnerabilities.
2. **Physical/IoT layer** – device firmware, interfaces, and actuation safety.

3. **Cognitive/AI layer** – data integrity, model robustness, and learning-pipeline security.

A holistic evaluation links these domains into a one workflow, integrating weakest domains (corrupted sensor inputs, for example) as these are not seen as primary exploited domains not direct were AI mis-inference downstream.

4.2 Vulnerability Categories in AIoT

Each of these categories is interrelated and spans across diverse system layers (Butun et al. 2019):

1. Embedding and Software Deficiency – An absence of updates for IoT devices leads to an incessant presence of weak boot loaders and obsolete systems. Devices that lack over-the-air updates usually carry unencrypted systems for many years (Alaba et al., 2017).
2. Structuring and Protocol Weaknesses – Breaching an IoT device can be easily carried out due to open ports, passwords set to weak defaults, and unencrypted protocols like MQ Telemetry Transport or Constrained Application Protocol (Alnajim et al., 2023).
3. Integrity and Privacy Deficiency – Insufficient validation and weak systems have the ability to perform a data injection and add systems that can be learned from and drawn misleading info (machines usually carry false data) which can be used non-neural networks.
4. AI-ML Deficiency – Unlike classical IoT systems, lack of classical systems suffers from data poisoning, adversarial examples, and extracted models through API requests (Papernot et al. 2018).
5. Supply Chain and Lifecycle Weaknesses – Insufficient counterfeits that lack support from vendors bring complex schemes to access latent risks. Packs from paranoia fillers containing third-party malicious firmware, and over supported modification covert hardware.
6. Operational and People Vulnerabilities – Devices that lack sufficient powering systems lack proper control and exposure of these devices can lead to definitive breaches (people can defeat protocols) to well-structured infrastructures.

Tracing each category within the AIoT architecture (device, network, cloud, or model) and its specific assets forms the basis for assessment and prioritization.

4.3 Vulnerability Assessment Methodologies

4.3.1 Asset Discovery and Attack-Surface Enumeration

The initial stage in this case is asset inventory, comprising devices, sensors, gateways, AI models, APIs and data repositories. Automated discovery has been deployed for Shodan-like crawlers for IoT segments capable of identifying reachable nodes and open services (Duan et al., 2021). Thus enumerated attack surfaces are physical interfaces (UART, JTAG), wireless links, management APIs, and model-update channels.

4.3.2 Static and Dynamic Analysis

Both static code analysis and dynamic code testing are part of software and firmware development. Static analysis assumes that any coding mistakes will be patched before software is uploaded and deployed, while dynamic testing (fuzzing and penetration testing, for example) identifies software function flaws that, for example, let a system bypass memory authentication (Butun et al. 2019). Embedded systems and resource constrained environments require custom dynamic tool development.

4.3.3 Risk Scoring and Prioritization

All of the weaknesses 'will' have to be analyzed in the 'context' of 'a' modification risk scoring system designed to assess the Common Vulnerability Scoring System (CVSS) in the domain of its cyber-physical extensions. 'Impact score' is a 'blend of' exploitability (ease of an attack) and impact (data, service, and safety). A case in point is a vulnerability in a physical actuator, which would be assigned a higher impact score than a simple loss of confidentiality data.

4.3.4 Automated and Graph-Based Assessment

The most current approaches utilize machine-learning and graph theory to automate vulnerability examines. Attack-graph models visualize and simulate the relationships between assets and vulnerabilities, thus enabling the visualization of multi-stage attack sequences. Salayma (2024) illustrated dynamic attack-graphs supporting continuous risk evaluation, which change as IoT topologies evolve. These graphs, combined with vulnerability scanners, deliver near-real-time situational awareness.

4.4 Case Study: Smart-Health AIoT

To demonstrate a substantial evaluation, think of a smart-health monitoring system which gathers physiological information through wearable devices, processes it on an edge device, and uses a neural network hosted on the cloud to predict anomalies (for instance, irregular heart rhythms) in real-time.

1. Asset Discovery: Edge device, wearable sensors (Bluetooth Low Energy (BLE) paired), access point, health AI, and health information system.
2. Vulnerability Identification: Radio waves encased in weak security, unsupported firmware on the edge device, insecure REST interfaces which expose the model endpoints, and a lack of model dataset provenance.
3. Assessment: The gateway firmware was dynamically fuzzed, and a buffer overflow was detected; the model's effectiveness was tested adversarial and minor signal alterations were detected.
4. Risk Scoring: The model's ability to withstand attack (an organism can be considered a model) - medium attack potential and medium hinder potential: model is also critical; gateway (high hinder potential and high attack potential) - critical.
5. Mitigation: Sign gateway firmware, adversarial train the neural model, model control system with versioning and modification can also be used for rollback, BLE transmission should be encrypted.

This sequence of steps shows that in reality, the weaknesses in a model's communication systems and the model's ability to withstand attacks can interact and strengthen each other, thus requiring resolve.

4.5 Lifecycle and Continuous Assessment

A vulnerability assessment for AIoT devices cannot be completed once and not revisit for many years since devices and AI models change over time. A never-ending cycle of vulnerability assessment and management for such models is, therefore, necessary:

1. Track collection of telemetry from devices and the AI pipelines as diagnostics logs.
2. Recognize Anomalies as well as CVE drifts, and model behavior.
3. Assess Value at Risk (VaR) thresholds.
4. Revise Countermeasures; patch the models, revocations of credentials, and compromise the models.

5. Triage verification tests and amend the asset inventory.

CTEM (Continuous Threat Exposure) and SOAR (Security Orchestration, Automation, and Response) platforms for detection automating as well as remediation works, diminish vulnerability slip cage time (Sebestyén, 2025)

4.6 Integration with Threat Modelling

Vulnerability assessment and threat modelling are interdependent. Assessing vulnerabilities "enable" actual weaknesses to the attack vectors defined by threat models. An integrated approach assigns each weakness to a defined threat class and mitigation priorities (e.g., unencrypted MQTT = spoofing/tampering and prioritized for encryption and authentication). This integration ensures that the adversary's capability and the targeted weaknesses are aligned. (Salayma, 2024).

4.7 Challenges and Limitations

Despite advances, several challenges persist:

- **Scalability:** scanning thousands of heterogeneous devices without disrupting operation remains difficult.
- **Limited Visibility:** proprietary firmware and AI models may prevent full code inspection.
- **Resource Constraints:** edge devices may lack processing capacity for continuous security agents.
- **Dynamic Topology:** devices join or leave networks frequently, invalidating static assessments.
- **AI-Pipeline Complexity:** data and model dependencies evolve over time, complicating reproducibility of vulnerability findings.

Addressing these challenges requires hybrid methodologies combining lightweight on-device checks with cloud-based analytics and model-driven automation.

The vulnerability assessment in IoT systems include systems for data collection, decision making, and actuator control, as well as for AI models running on constrained devices/networks decision devices. These assessments require continuous asset lifecycle - structure and function asset/cluster discovery, assessment, AI model risk scoring, asset monitoring, threat resolution. Assessment in Section 5 on Deficiency Control, alongside the Monolith, action plans the breaches in the most advanced tier.

5. MITIGATION STRATEGIES AND SECURITY FRAMEWORKS IN AIOT SYSTEMS

All AIoT mitigation strategies must be holistic, multifaceted, and dynamic, particularly concerning the bounded infrastructures: hardware, software, communication networks, data streams, and intelligent algorithms. The goal is to maintain the confidentiality, integrity, availability, and trustworthiness of the entire AIoT lifecycle, from data collection to decision execution. Such security architectures incorporating prevention, detection, response, and recovery are essential (Alnajim et al.,2023).

5.1 Security-by-Design Principles

The AIoT policy framework that any development has to be integrated from the conceptual phase of the structure within the flow of establishing everything, including the design's, the data flow models, and the machine learning models by something mechanism the security no-touch proxy appliances the appliances the AIoT protected the is design should by default and lower the proxy policy i.e. within the framework of the AIoT. Protecting the AIoT is by default a design of least privilege within the flow the model hinges on the design structure and principles (Alaba et al., 2017).

The design thought should be based on the pillars of:

1. Conservative devolution architecture: each component should be deprived of all the permissions and privileges by default within a system structure.
2. Protection layering: At least 3 vertical and horizontal levels of parameters/ mechanisms of each of the 6 vertical folds of the perimeter including encryption, access control and other hypertextually described, and other perimeter mechanisms document.
3. Closed boundaries: Every new device within the system by default should have the access control list (ACL) and all of the borders of the proxy perimeter switched on.
4. Threat neutralization: All any risk event on a structure should have a default automatic bypass to the safe surfaces i.e. a system self-resets within the safe surfaces.
5. Iterative modifications: Deep learning modules should have self-documenting on each cycle of deep learning document incorporating perpetual AI devices on each system and the divided perimeter.

The combination of each action ensures the AIoT perimeter has divided surfaces that decrease and by the default these principles to cross the boundaries and borders of the AIoT perimeter.

5.2 Device and Edge Security Controls

The devices built at the perception and edge layers represent the most vulnerable and least resourced nodes in the ecosystem, and thus, have a critical need for hardware-rooted trust. Secure boot and Trusted Platform Modules (TPM) technologies freeze the execution of firmware to be loaded if there is any unsigned code and, therefore, prevents any ill-correct firmware to load (Khan, et al., 2024) . Additional best practices include:

- "Cryptographic identity provisioning" where specific credentials or certificates devices which are 'owned' are embedded upon manufacture.
- Secure over-the-air updates where firmware images are digitally signed, and over-the-air encryption channels are used.
- Edge-AI sandboxing where machine learning inference modules are restricted in relation to the host OS to mitigate the risk of privilege escalation due to escalation of control in the compromised scenario.
- Local anomaly detection where 'light' AI devices at the edge can monitor control commands in real-time to block, flag, and deviate to keep symmetry in the sensor data patterns (Abid et al., 2025).

Thus, these measures minimize risks of physical tampering and ensure a trusted execution environment for edge computation.

5.3 Network and Communication Security

AIoT networks are reliant upon diverse wireless systems including Wi-Fi, LoRaWAN, 5G, Zigbee, and even proprietary protocols. Communication is secured through:

- End-to-end encryption (e.g., TLS, DTLS, IPsec) is mandatory and required between devices, gateways, and cloud nodes (Alnajim et al., 2023).
- Mutual authentication ensures and confirms impersonation attacks are avoided and ensures legitimate data is exchanged.
- Segmentation and micro-zoning scope and limit lateral movement: an example being, separating AI inference data traffic, management commands, and firmware updates into distinct network segments.
- Every request, even internal to the network perimeter, must be verified so must undergo adaptive access control: this is known as zero-trust networking (Laghari et al., 2025).

- 'Intelligent' Intrusion detection systems (IDS) emulate the characteristics of the Internet of Things traffic, configuring deep-packet inspection and other active learning techniques to identify and classify the presence of DoS, spoofing, and routing attacks in real time.

New and emerging 5G-enabled AIoT deployments should weave the network slicing security policies, inscribed that each slice must satisfy its confidentiality and latency limits.

5.4 Data and AI-Pipeline Protection

Securing the data and model layers is central to AIoT resilience because data drives all decision-making. The following mechanisms address these layers:

1. **Data integrity and provenance** – implement cryptographic hashes and blockchain-based ledgers to verify data authenticity from sensor to cloud (Bodkhe et al., 2020).
2. **Secure data transmission and storage** – use AES-based encryption, differential privacy, and homomorphic encryption for sensitive data streams.
3. **Model robustness** – train AI models using adversarial-training techniques and data-augmentation strategies to enhance resilience against perturbation attacks (Papernot et al., 2018).
4. **Federated and privacy-preserving learning** – where applicable, decentralised learning frameworks minimise exposure of raw data, although they must be secured against poisoning and inference attacks (Bonawitz et al., 2019).
5. **Model-lifecycle governance** – establish provenance tracking for training datasets, hyperparameters, and update histories to enable accountability and rollback in case of detected compromise.
6. **Inference-API security** – enforce strict rate-limiting, authentication tokens, and response obfuscation to deter model extraction.

5.5 Supply-Chain and Lifecycle Security

The supply chain for AIoT is complex and includes hardware suppliers, software programmers, cloud service solutions, and other team members. Various studies have shown that assembled and supplied manufactured systems could be tainted with hacked components and, such components could bring down the whole AIoT deployment permanently (Butun et al., 2019). Some of the necessary protections are proposed below:

- **Vendor security certification:** adoption of standards such as PSA Certified, ISO/IEC 62443, or IEC 61508 for industrial safety.
- **Component provenance tracking:** utilising blockchain or tamper-evident logs to record component origins.
- **Firmware signing and version control:** ensuring that only validated firmware can be installed.
- **End-of-life (EoL) management:** defining clear decommissioning and data-sanitisation procedures for retired devices.

Lifecycle security planning ensures that protection continues beyond deployment, accounting for updates, maintenance, and decommissioning.

5.6 Organizational and Operational Security

Beyond technology, effective AIoT defence depends on human and procedural factors. Organisations should be implemented:

- **Security awareness and training:** ensuring operators understand AIoT-specific risks, such as data poisoning or firmware tampering.
- **Incident-response planning:** defining escalation paths, containment strategies, and recovery measures aligned with ISO 27035.
- **Continuous threat-exposure management (CTEM):** integrating vulnerability scanning, attack-surface monitoring, and AI-driven risk prioritization into daily operations (Sebestyén, 2025).
- **Compliance and auditing:** mapping operations to legal frameworks such as GDPR, NIST SP 800-183, and regional data-protection laws.

A mature security posture requires collaboration between cybersecurity teams, AI engineers, and Operational Technology (OT) specialists.

5.7 Emerging Security Technologies

Recent advancements show promise in enhancing AIoT security efficiency and automation:

• **Blockchain-based trust management:** distributed ledgers offer immutable event logging, supporting secure firmware updates and auditable AI model transactions (Bodkhe et al., 2020).

• **Quantum-resistant cryptography:** post-quantum algorithms ensure longevity of encryption in future AIoT networks.

• **Autonomous cyber-defence using reinforcement learning:** AI-driven agents can detect, predict, and mitigate threats in real time through continuous policy optimization (Al E'mari, Sanjalawe & Fataftah, 2026).

• **Secure multi-party computation (SMPC):** enables collaborative AI training without disclosing private data, ideal for multi-stakeholder industrial AIoT scenarios.

These technologies illustrate the trajectory towards intelligent, self-adapting, and resilient AIoT ecosystems.

6. EMERGING TRENDS AND RESEARCH DIRECTIONS IN AIOT SECURITY

With each day passing, AIoT systems, especially their security systems, are advancing by integrating novel paradigms such as edge intelligence, digital twins, learning systems, and self-operating systems, thus becoming increasingly more complex in nature. This chapter so far has concentrated on the primary protective measures. The remaining part of the chapter will focus on the more assertive strategies for securing the myriad sensors of the IoT, as well as the unsolved challenges.

6.1 Edge Intelligence and On-Device Learning

The migration of AI workloads from cloud to edge devices represents a defining trend in AIoT. Edge intelligence aims to reduce latency, bandwidth consumption, and reliance on cloud infrastructure, enabling real-time analytics and actuation. However, decentralised learning environments amplify the security surface: models and data reside on numerous devices that may be physically accessible to adversaries (Iman et al., 2024).

Security implications include:

- **Model exfiltration**: attackers can extract model parameters from compromised edge nodes.
- **Adversarial perturbations**: crafted sensor inputs can cause misclassification or unsafe actuation.
- **Update manipulation**: Maliciously constructed learning algorithms could easily infiltrate entire systems if records of on-device learning updates were not cryptographically confirmed

It has been suggested in literature that to ensure the integrity of model execution or updates, protective measures like secure enclaves or hardware-based trusted execution environments like Intel SGX or ARM TrustZone should be employed

(Khan, et al., 2024). For microcontrollers, lightweight encryption coupled with attestation protocol is sophisticated research that attempts to find a compromise between computational load and latency.

6.2 Federated Learning and Distributed Trust

Federated Learning (FL) allows the collaborative training of shared models by multiple edge nodes without the need to send the raw data to a central server. The decentralization of the data adds to the privacy of the data but at the same still adds new vulnerabilities, such as model poisoning, backdoor insertion, or Byzantine distortions that attack global aggregation (Bonawitz et al., 2019; Bagdasaryan, Veit, & Shmatikov, 2020).

Novel approaches emerging mix anomaly-resilient aggregation (e.g., Krum, Trimmed Mean) with reputation-based trust-scoring systems and with blockchain ledgers for validation and versioning of local update audits (Bodkhe et al., 2020). In parallel, there is research on federated adversarial training and the application of homomorphic encryption to gradient exchange. There still remains a fundamental open question on FL-based AIoT systems pertaining to scaling and interpretability.

6.3 Digital Twins for Security Monitoring

Digital twins (DT), or virtual replicas of real-world assets, have garnered traction for predictive maintenance and cyber-physical monitoring. In AIoT, DTs can act as security mirrors, enabling the simulation of attack scenarios without any impact on production systems (Fan et al., 2022). An example of this is where an industrial AIoT network can use a DT to simulate the resilience of defence mechanisms to sensor spoofing or network attack failures, to assess defence strategies before deployment.

Recent studies suggest an interesting integration of DTs with blockchain-based event logging to maintain virtual and real states synchronization and to ensure tamper-proofed records (Suleiman et al., 2025). Still, the problems of communication channel protection and the preservation of fidelity between real and virtual layers of the DT remain challenge areas for further investigation.

6.4 Explainable and Trustworthy AI

The need for security in critical infrastructure systems ensures that decisions AI makes will need to be explained in detail. Traditional AI systems, especially deep neural networks, tend to obscure the roots of core issues, making it even more challenging to ascertain whether they stem from mere data drift or sabotaging manipulation.

Counterfactual reasoning and other approaches to XAI like SHAP and LIME are being used to shed light on decisions made through sensor-driven AIoT systems (Doshi-Velez and Kim, 2017). The lack of human understandability that 'model accountability' XAI frameworks introduces, for example, chaining the creation of a model to its training data and subsequent outcomes, enhances the model's auditability.

XAI coupled with dynamic monitoring systems constitutes a promising line of research: for example, agents that autonomously produce explanations and flag learned causal structure deviations. Such capabilities augment trust not just for human operators but for automated anomaly detection systems that employ contextual reasoning.

6.5 Zero-Trust and Continuous Verification Architectures

In the case of the AIoT networks, as the devices keep getting added and deleted, perimeter-based security is no longer sufficient. One of the most common approaches to this are the designs following the Zero Trust Architecture (ZTA) paradigm, which advice to "never trust, always verify". Each entity in ZTA-enabled AIoT (whether it be a device, user, API, or even an AI agent) needs to authenticate and authorize every interaction regardless of their ZTA-enabled AIoT (Laghari et al., 2025).

The following are the requirements for the implemenration of zero trust in AIoT systems:

1. Access control at the network perimeter based on certificates of authenticable users.
2. Trust boundary micro-segmentation of the AIoT network into individual, isolated segments.
3. Persistent device and user verification using behavioural monitoring and device health verification.
4. Policy control integrated at the network's physical boundary with AI-based suspicious traffic anomaly systems.

From the ones based on device power constraints, ZTA policy enforcement on low power devices is one of the more foundational research topics, alongside the more advanced SDN controller frameworks which contextually and dynamically change trust configuration based on situational and risk assessment factors.

6.6 Quantum-Safe and Post-Quantum Security

Once quantum computers reach their full potential, current methods RSA and ECC and their variants will no longer be secure because of Shor's algorithm. Quantum–resistant cryptography is becoming essential especially given the lengthy 10-year+ device lifecycles projected for IoTs.

Research is being done on post–quantum devices like lattice–based encryption (Kyber, NTRU) and hash–based digital signatures (XMSS, SPHINCS+) for IoT devices (Chen et al., 2023). The problem of efficiently integrating these primitives into AIoT hardware still remains because of the key–size overhead and high computational costs. Classical and post-quantum scheme combinations hybrid models offer a tempered approach for device security (Al E'mari, Sanjalawe & Allehyani, 2025).

6.7 Autonomous and Cognitive Cyber-Defence

Self-response systems where a form of artificial agent continuously analyzing security events and deciding, with very little human input, how to respond can be labelled as autonomous defence. Abid and others have used RL within AIoT intrusions to detect data and adaptively control access, and anomalies and in predictive access dimensions using RL.

Cognitive security systems can synthesize telemetry data from myriad sensors to identify attacks, compute counteractions, and adaptively flatten configuration control layers. RL and neural learning network overlays of network graph topologies enable real-time correlation and reasoning on failing and interrelated systems.

Like with all forms of self-defense, fully autonomous systems introduce difficult philosophical matters. With safety in mind, how can entities substantiate the actions of fully learning self-defense systems, especially when the actions impact critical systems? Anytime boundaries with defined restrictions and concomitant human monitoring are vital.

6.8 Integration of Security and Sustainability

A recent search connects the security of AIoT with sustainability, both environmentally and energetic. Alaba et al. (2024) propose the developing of low-impact (low power) defenses, enabling indeed (zeolites) encryption, ultra-lightweight AI models, and green computing architectures. The "triple win" of edge intelligence and "green" renewable microgrid-powered IoT (Riot) devices is operational resilience and sustainability.

Energy-aware cryptography and eco-security metrics are quantifying trade-offs between some protection and some carbon. Such work illustrates sustainability and global work, as industry shifts, ethics with environment we AIoT is maturing.

6.9 Interdisciplinary Policy and Governance

Beyond technical advances, governance frameworks for AIoT security remain underdeveloped. Policymakers and standardisation bodies—such as NIST, ENISA, ISO/IEC JTC 1/SC 41, and IEEE P7000-series—are progressively defining principles for trustworthy AI and IoT convergence. Future governance will need to address:

- **Cross-border data flows** and harmonisation of privacy laws (e.g., GDPR, HIPAA).
- **Liability attribution** for AI-driven autonomous decisions.
- **Ethical auditing** of data usage, model bias, and algorithmic transparency.

Collaborative international frameworks are required to ensure interoperability of technical and ethical standards across the global AIoT supply chain (ENISA, 2023).

In the case of AIoT security, we believe we are at the point of change which covers decentralised intelligence, sustainability concerns, adaptive defence, sustainability concerns We believe that AIoT security is undergoing a change that is marked by decentralized AIoT ecosystems, also outlines the opportunities and the risks of connected intelligence Angle of self-defensive AIoT self-protective ecosystems system that autonomously sense, learn and react Dual Use Technology ethic-legal gothic defense posture ecosystem that autonomously combats threats of dual use AI self-defensive ecosystems while protective AIoT autonomously cyber-defends Operational stimuli, system sense and security cyber-defend protective predicated on the fusion of AI, cyber net centric systems, computational legitimacy and chromatic ant subordination systems.

In model explainability, globally encrypted quantum resistant networks, trust orchestration at institutional scale, governance of systems, interdisciplinary engagements across the continuum of data science, engineering, thoughtful design and public policy need to be brought forth and blended as the trust- AIoT ecosystem ascends in governance and chunks of the governance layers vertically stitch self-AI autonomous trust, intelligence and cyber defensible layers of the governance vertically stitch defensible systems of intelligence.

7. THE GOVERNANCE, REGULATORY FRAMEWORK, AND LEGAL CONSIDERATIONS OF DECENTRALIZED ENERGY TRADING WITH SECURE AIOT TECHNOLOGY

Despite the importance of technical security mechanisms for aiot decentralised energy trading systems, they are of little help on their own. The use of artificial intelligence, IoT architectures, and blockchain integration for energy trading systems has severe potential complications in law, policy and regulation, and governance. These challenges arise from the users of the systems having decentralized control, reliance on automated market actors, and the widespread use of autonomous systems that cross and blur the lines of the physical, digital and institutional worlds. These factors are important to address in order to gain the trust of users in the systems and the governance mechanisms, while also ensuring long term system security in relation to applicable regulations and accountability.

7.1 Regulatory Challenges in Decentralized Energy Markets

The traditional electricity markets have centralized forms of regulation which were created for vertically integrated utilities and particular definitional market operators. Decentralized energy trading systems such as peer-to-peer (P2P) energy markets and community microgrids decentralize regulation and the trading of P2P activities among prosumers, edge devices, and automated trading systems. Such regulation opposes traditional systems of market control, price regulation, and control of grid stability (Meckling, 2019).

Automatic and real-time trading systems based on machine learning demand forecasts, coupled with dynamic pricing and local electricity grid conditions, aggravate these challenges. Problems of legal ambiguity increase with real-time algorithmic pricing, AI trading agent's legal personhood, and automated decision-making with sealed audit/dismiss oversight (Helbing et al. 2018). Furthermore, when trading decisions are made at the network's periphery, crossing multiple jurisdictions with no central authority, the challenges of regulatory compliance are compounded.

A number of studies highlight the importance of flexible regulations that can integrate decentralized management while maintaining the reliability of the grid and protection of consumers (Aghahadi et al., 2024). In terms of security, the absence of strong regulations may encourage market manipulation, fraudulent energy activities, and other calculated actions that result from compromised AI and IoT systems.

7.2 Governance Models for Trustworthy AIoT Energy Ecosystems

Decentralized energy trading systems rely on data collected from smart meters, sensors, and energy management systems. These data streams highlight sensitive aspects of household behavior, including occupancy and economic activity. As a result, such data streams fall under the scope of data protection laws, such as the General Data Protection Regulation (GDPR) in the European Union.

There is an unavoidably cryptographic-based system. Possessing both transparency and immutability, it strengthens trust and non-repudiation. But the real world has laws regarding the "right to be forgotten" and data minimization. If AI is trained on such data, issues of data processing legitimacy, consent, and responsibility for decisions made automatically arise. Moreover, the AI-based systems mentioned above complicate the attribution of responsibility. This would be the case for an automated pricing system that causes (or contributes to) financial harm or grid instability. Liability could be distributed to the hardware providers, the AI system developers, the platform service providers, and the prosumers. The legal problems resulting from the opacity of advanced machine learning systems demonstrate the continued need for transparent AI and for energy trading systems that allow for auditable decision-making (Porter et al., 2023).

8. CONCLUSION AND RECOMMENDATIONS

The AIoT captures the cross-section of physical, cyber, and cognitive domains. The ever-distributed sensing, learning, and acting intelligence serves to optimise infrastructure, healthcare, manufacturing, transportation, and smart cities. However, the integration of the domains increases security and privacy concerns. This chapter analyses the AIoT ecosystem through distributed perception AIoT security layers: perception to network and network to computation and cognitive reasoning. Threat models and vulnerability assessments have been outlined as necessary tools to identify, quantify, and mitigate the multifaceted risks which emerge within this paradigm.

8.1 Strategic Recommendations

To ensure resilient and trustworthy AIoT ecosystems, the following strategic recommendations emerge from the analyses presented in this work.

1. **Embed Security by Design and Default**: Security cannot be retrofitted; it must be integral to AIoT architecture from conception. System designers should:

- Incorporate **threat modelling and risk analysis** during early development stages using frameworks such as STRIDE or attack-graph methods (Maodza & Du Toit, 2024).
- Employ **secure coding, firmware validation, and continuous integration testing** before device release.
- Enforce **fail-safe defaults**, ensuring that, upon detecting anomalies or model inconsistencies, devices revert to secure operational states.

Embedding security by design fosters resilience while reducing cost and complexity of later remediation (Alaba et al., 2017).

2. **Strengthen Device and Edge Security**: Given that edge nodes and sensors constitute the first line of exposure, adopting hardware-rooted trust is essential. Measures include secure boot mechanisms, TPM or TrustZone integration, and firmware-signing infrastructures (Khan, et al., 2024). Edge devices should be equipped with local anomaly-detection agents that identify behavioral deviations, such as sudden surges in data rates or unexpected inference requests (Abid et al., 2025). To reduce attack propagation, devices should operate under **least-privilege principles** and be periodically attested via remote-verification protocols.
3. **Adopt Zero-Trust Networking and Continuous Authentication**: In large-scale deployments, perimeter security is obsolete. The Zero-Trust Architecture (ZTA) approach—"never trust, always verify"—must underpin all communication and management protocols. Each entity, whether human or machine, must authenticate and authorize every interaction. The adoption of micro-segmentation and context-aware access control minimizes lateral movement and limits breach impact (Laghari et al., 2025). Integration of software-defined networking (SDN) enables adaptive policy enforcement across dynamic topologies.
4. **Secure the AI and Data Pipeline**: Because AI lies at the heart of AIoT decision-making, model robustness and data integrity are paramount. Therefore; the organizations should:
    - Implement **dataset provenance tracking** and integrity verification using cryptographic hashes or blockchain-based ledgers (Bodkhe et al., 2020).
    - Employ **adversarial-training** and **robust optimization** methods to harden models against perturbations and poisoning (Papernot et al., 2018).
    - Protect inference APIs through **rate-limiting, query-pattern analysis, and access tokens** to prevent model extraction.

- Periodically **retrain models** to address data drift and evolving threat patterns while maintaining version control.

AI assurance frameworks such as the UK NCSC's *Principles for Secure AI* and IEEE P7009 provide reference structures for implementing these controls.

5. **Enhance Supply-Chain and Lifecycle Management:** The AIoT supply chain spans component vendors, firmware developers, cloud providers, and system integrators. Security must therefore extend beyond deployment:
    - Require **vendor security certification** (e.g., PSA Certified, ISO/IEC 62443).
    - Establish **component provenance records** to prevent counterfeit or malicious insertions.
    - Define **firmware update policies** and **end-of-life decommissioning** protocols to eliminate residual vulnerabilities in retired devices.

Lifecycle governance transforms AIoT security into an ongoing process rather than a static outcome (Butun et al., 2019).

6. **Foster Interoperability and Standardization:** Fragmentation across platforms and vendors hampers security enforcement. Governments, academia, and industry consortia should align around common frameworks such as the **NIST Cybersecurity Framework 2.0** and **ENISA AI Security Guidelines** (NIST, 2024; ENISA, 2023). Open, standardized APIs for authentication, logging, and model provenance facilitate interoperability and reduce misconfigurations that often lead to security lapses.
7. **Invest in Explainability and Human Oversight:** Autonomous systems will be doing much of the work but even so, human operators will need to understand the rationale behind AI systems and how they deal with the responses. With regard to XAI integration within security systems, there is certainly value for compliance and audit reviews (Doshi-Velez & Kim, 2017). Training operators to understand the distinctions between relevant and relevant benign anomalies will equip them better, particularly in regard to the explains AI [XAI] outputs. More importantly, the presence of human-in-loop control, even in the most automated systems, will be necessary to take responsibility for the automated actions, particularly in sensitive situations like medicine or transportation.
8. **Enable Autonomous and Predictive Defense:** Static defenses cannot keep pace with adaptive adversaries. Integrating **reinforcement-learning-based cyber-defense agents** enables AIoT systems to detect anomalies, isolate compromised nodes, and adapt configuration policies in real time (Sanjalawe et al., 2025). These

systems should, however, include audit mechanisms to validate their actions and avoid unintended interference with legitimate processes. Continuous-learning security frameworks that fuse telemetry from multiple layers—device, network, and AI—can provide predictive threat analytics, reducing mean-time-to-detection (MTTD) and mean-time-to-response (MTTR).

9. **Plan for Quantum-Safe and Future-Proof Security:** Because AIoT devices are deployed for extended lifespans, cryptographic agility is essential. Adoption of post-quantum algorithms such as Kyber or Dilithium should begin in hybrid form alongside classical methods (Chen et al., 2023). Research into lightweight post-quantum cryptography for constrained environments will ensure that AIoT infrastructures remain resilient in the face of quantum computing advances.
10. **Promote Multistakeholder Governance and Ethics:** AIoT's pervasive reach demands governance that integrates ethical, legal, and technical perspectives. Policymakers must develop accountability frameworks assigning liability for AI-driven harm and ensuring compliance with data-protection regulations (Hadzovic, Mrdovic, & Radonjic, 2023). Ethical review boards should evaluate AIoT deployments for fairness, transparency, and societal impact. Public-private partnerships can foster collaborative threat-intelligence sharing and develop consensus on global standards. Cyber-ethics education for engineers and managers alike will help build a security-conscious culture across all levels of development and operation.

8.2 Research Outlook

While this chapter identifies several broad research trajectories, a more practical research agenda requires articulating **specific unresolved problems** that hinder secure and trustworthy AIoT deployment. Based on the characteristics, threat models, and vulnerability assessments discussed throughout the chapter, the following concrete challenges remain open for investigation.

1. **Lightweight, Robust, and Verifiable AI on Edge Devices:** AIoT devices operate under severe computational and energy constraints. Current adversarial-robust training methods and secure execution mechanisms remain impractical for microcontrollers and embedded chips (Alaba et al., 2024, Menon et al., 2025). Open problems include:
    - Designing adversarial-robust training or inference methods suitable for kilobyte-level memory footprints.
    - Developing attestation techniques that verify the correctness of model execution—not just firmware integrity—on constrained hardware.

- Securing continual on-device learning against poisoning and stealthy parameter drift.

2. **Poison-Resistant and Privacy-Preserving Federated Learning:** Federated learning reduces data exposure but introduces new entry points for poisoning, Byzantine behavior, and malicious update injection (Xia et al., 2023). Open problems include:
   - Creating aggregation algorithms that remain robust under extreme heterogeneity of data, connectivity, and device capability.
   - Detecting slow, low-magnitude poisoning attacks distributed across many training rounds.
   - Developing lightweight differential privacy and secure update protocols compatible with IoT-class power and computation limits.
3. **Security Assurance for Digital Twins in AIoT:** Digital twins provide modelling and predictive capabilities but rely on continuous synchronization and trusted data streams (Mihai et al., 2022). Open problems include:
   - Ensuring real-time, tamper-resistant synchronization between physical devices and their digital twins.
   - Quantifying and detecting semantic drift introduced by timestamp manipulation or adversarial sensor data.
   - Hardening DT behavioral models against adversarial manipulation and data-driven poisoning.

These research directions underscore that AIoT security is no longer a siloed discipline but an interdisciplinary endeavor linking computer science, control engineering, ethics, and sustainability.

8.3 Concluding Reflections

The intelligent automation of the AIoT aims to merge the physical and digital space with automation and universal connectivity. However, with the increasing complexity of systems, the line between resilience and vulnerability becomes dangerously thin. The AIoT of the future will be as secure as our ability to craft protective, ethically managed, and quantum-resilient ecosystems.

We therefore must adopt the attitude that security is not a limitation that needs to be defended, but rather a piece of trust in infrastructure untouched that needs to be built on. This will form the groundwork for which adoption, social acceptance, and innovation can grow freely. AIoT can balance advancement in technology with public confidence through proactive threat modeling, adaptive governance, and continuous vulnerability assessments. The journey toward resilient AIoT ecosystems is a work in progress. It demands a combination of ongoing research, interdepartmental policy evolution, and collaboration between sectors. AIoT is then able to realize its potential in a safe, sustainable, and secure manner.

REFERENCES

Abid, U., Aslam, N., Naeem, A., Fuzail, M., & Imran, M. (2025). Enhancing Intrusion Detection in AIOT using Intelligent Feature Selection and Deep Learning Fusion. *Journal of Computing & Biomedical Informatics*, *9*(2). Advance online publication. DOI: 10.56979/902/2025

Aghahadi, M., Bosisio, A., Merlo, M., Berizzi, A., Pegoiani, A., & Forciniti, S. (2024). Digitalization processes in distribution grids: A comprehensive review of strategies and challenges. *Applied Sciences (Basel, Switzerland)*, *14*(11), 4528. DOI: 10.3390/app14114528

Alaba, F. A., Othman, M., Hashem, I. A. T., & Alotaibi, F. (2017). Internet of Things security: A survey. *Journal of Network and Computer Applications*, *88*, 10–28. DOI: 10.1016/j.jnca.2017.04.002

Alaba, F. A., Sani, U., Dada, E. G., & Mohammed, B. H. (2024). AIoT-enabled smart grids: advancing energy efficiency and renewable energy integration. In *Artificial intelligence of things for achieving sustainable development goals* (pp. 59–79). Springer Nature Switzerland. DOI: 10.1007/978-3-031-53433-1_4

Alahi, M. E., Ahn, H., Liu, L., Alam, S., Shen, H., Cao, Z., Shroff, N., Krishnamachari, B., & Srivastava, M. (2023). Integrating IoT-Enabled Technologies and Artificial Intelligence: A Review. *Sensors (Basel)*, *23*(11), 5206. DOI: 10.3390/s23115206 PMID: 37299934

Alnajim, A. M., Habib, S., Islam, M., Thwin, S. M., & Alotaibi, F. (2023). A comprehensive survey of cybersecurity threats, attacks, and effective countermeasures in industrial internet of things. *Technologies*, *11*(6), 161. DOI: 10.3390/technologies11060161

Bagdasaryan, E., Veit, A., & Shmatikov, V. (2020). How to backdoor federated learning. *Proceedings of the 23rd International Conference on Artificial Intelligence and Statistics (AISTATS)*, 2938–2948.

Bodkhe, U., Tanwar, S., Parekh, K., Khanpara, P., Tyagi, S., Kumar, N., & Alazab, M. (2020). Blockchain for industry 4.0: A comprehensive review. *IEEE Access : Practical Innovations, Open Solutions*, *8*, 79764–79800. DOI: 10.1109/ACCESS.2020.2988579

Bonawitz, K., Eichner, H., Grieskamp, W., Huba, D., Ingerman, A., Ivanov, V., & Konečný, J. (2019). Towards federated learning at scale: System design. *Proceedings of Machine Learning and Systems*, *1*, 374–388.

Butun, I., Österberg, P., & Song, H. (2019). Security of the Internet of Things: Vulnerabilities, attacks, and countermeasures. *IEEE Communications Surveys and Tutorials*, *22*(1), 616–644. DOI: 10.1109/COMST.2019.2953364

Chen, L., Moody, D., & Alagic, G. (2023). *NIST PQC Standardization Report*. National Institute of Standards and Technology., DOI: 10.6028/NIST.IR.8413

Deep, S., Zheng, X., Jolfaei, A., Yu, D., Ostovari, P., & Bashir, A. K. (2019). A survey of security and privacy issues in the Internet of Things from the layered context. *arXiv*. https://arxiv.org/abs/1903.00846

Doshi-Velez, F., & Kim, B. (2017). Towards a rigorous science of interpretable machine learning. *arXiv preprint*, arXiv:1702.08608.

Duan, X., Ge, M., Le, T. H. M., Ullah, F., Gao, S., Lu, X., & Babar, M. A. (2021). Automated security assessment for the internet of things. In *2021 IEEE 26th Pacific Rim International Symposium on Dependable Computing (PRDC)* (pp. 47-56). IEEE. DOI: 10.1109/PRDC53464.2021.00016

ENISA. (2023). *Securing Artificial Intelligence and the Internet of Things: Good Practices*. European Union Agency for Cybersecurity. https://www.enisa.europa.eu/publications

Fan, B., Su, Z., Chen, Y., Wu, Y., Xu, C., & Quek, T. Q. (2022). Ubiquitous control over heterogeneous vehicles: A digital twin empowered edge AI approach. *IEEE Wireless Communications*, *30*(1), 166–173. DOI: 10.1109/MWC.012.2100587

Grosse, K., Bieringer, L., Besold, T. R., & Alahi, A. M. (2024). Towards more practical threat models in artificial intelligence security. In *33rd USENIX Security Symposium (USENIX Security 24)* (pp. 4891-4908).

Hadzovic, S., Mrdovic, S., & Radonjic, M. (2023). A path towards an internet of things and artificial intelligence regulatory framework. *IEEE Communications Magazine*, *61*(7), 90–96. DOI: 10.1109/MCOM.002.2200373

Helbing, D., Frey, B. S., Gigerenzer, G., Hafen, E., Hagner, M., Hofstetter, Y., & Zwitter, A. (2018). Will democracy survive big data and artificial intelligence? In *Towards digital enlightenment: Essays on the dark and light sides of the digital revolution* (pp. 73–98). Springer International Publishing., DOI: 10.1007/978-3-319-90869-4_7

Iman, S., Ahn, H., Liu, L., Alam, S., Shen, H., Cao, Z., Shroff, N., Krishnamachari, B., & Srivastava, M. (2024). Artificial Intelligence of Things: A Survey. *arXiv*. https://arxiv.org/abs/2410.19998

Khan, M., Hatami, M., Zhao, W., & Chen, Y. (2024). A novel trusted hardware-based scalable security framework for IoT edge devices. *Discover Internet of Things*, *4*(1), 4. DOI: 10.1007/s43926-024-00056-7

Laghari, A. A., Khan, A. A., Ksibi, A., Hajjej, F., Kryvinska, N., Almadhor, A., Mohamed, M. A., & Alsubai, S. (2025). A novel and secure artificial intelligence enabled zero trust intrusion detection in industrial internet of things architecture. *Scientific Reports*, *15*(1), 26843. DOI: 10.1038/s41598-025-11738-9 PMID: 40702039

Maodza, B., & Du Toit, J. (2024). Agricultural Internet of Things (AIoTs) Threat Modeling Using STRIDE-LM. In *International Congress on Information and Communication Technology* (pp. 295-312). Singapore: Springer Nature Singapore. https://doi.org/DOI: 10.1007/978-981-97-3302-6_24

Meckling, J. (2019). Governing renewables: Policy feedback in a global energy transition. *Environment and Planning C. Politics and Space*, *37*(2), 317–338. DOI: 10.1177/2399654418777765

Menon, U. V., Kumaravelu, V. B., Kumar, C. V., Rammohan, A., Chinnadurai, S., Venkatesan, R., & Selvaprabhu, P. (2025). AI-powered IoT: A survey on integrating artificial intelligence with IoT for enhanced security, efficiency, and smart applications. *IEEE Access : Practical Innovations, Open Solutions*, *13*, 50296–50339. Advance online publication. DOI: 10.1109/ACCESS.2025.3551750

Mihai, S., Yaqoob, M., Hung, D. V., Davis, W., Towakel, P., Raza, M., Karamanoglu, M., Barn, B., Shetve, D., Prasad, R. V., Venkataraman, H., Trestian, R., & Nguyen, H. X. (2022). Digital twins: A survey on enabling technologies, challenges, trends and future prospects. *IEEE Communications Surveys and Tutorials*, *24*(4), 2255–2291. DOI: 10.1109/COMST.2022.3208773

NIST. (2024). *Cybersecurity Framework 2.0*. U.S. National Institute of Standards and Technology. https://www.nist.gov/cyberframework

Papernot, N., McDaniel, P., Sinha, A., & Wellman, M. P. (2018). Sok: Security and privacy in machine learning. In *2018 IEEE European symposium on security and privacy (EuroS&P)* (pp. 399-414). IEEE. DOI: 10.1109/EuroSP.2018.00035

Porter, Z., Ryan, P., Morgan, P., Al-Qaddoumi, J., Twomey, B., McDermid, J., & Habli, I. (2023). Unravelling responsibility for AI. *arXiv preprint arXiv:2308.02608*.

Rinf.tech. (2023). Artificial Intelligence of Things (AIoT): Current State and Future Path. (Online article). https://www.rinf.tech/artificial-intelligence-of-things-aiot-current-state-and-future-path/.

Salayma, M. (2024). Threat modelling in Internet of Things (IoT) environments using dynamic attack graphs. *Frontiers in the Internet of Things*, *3*, 1306465. Advance online publication. DOI: 10.3389/friot.2024.1306465

Sanjalawe, Y., Al-E'mari, S., Allehyani, B., & Makhadmeh, S. N. (2025). Reinforcement Learning-Guided Hybrid Metaheuristic for Energy-Aware Load Balancing in Cloud Environments. *Algorithms*, *18*(11), 715. DOI: 10.3390/a18110715

Sebestyen, H., Popescu, D. E., & Zmaranda, R. D. (2025). A literature review on security in the Internet of Things: Identifying and analysing critical categories. *Computers*, *14*(2), 61. DOI: 10.3390/computers14020061

Siam, S. I., Ahn, H., Liu, L., Alam, S., Shen, H., Cao, Z., & Zhang, M. (2025). Artificial intelligence of things: A survey. *ACM Transactions on Sensor Networks, 21*(1), 1-75. *arXiv*. https://arxiv.org/abs/2410.19998

Stanko, A., Duda, O., Mykytyshyn, A., Totosko, O., & Koroliuk, R. (2024). Artificial intelligence of things (AIoT): Integration challenges, and security issues. *Proceedings of the BAIT*.

Suleiman, R., Maradapu Vera Venkata Sai, A., Yu, W., & Wang, C. (2025). Blockchain for Security in Digital Twins. *Future Internet*, *17*(9), 385. DOI: 10.3390/fi17090385

von der Assen, J., Sharif, J., Feng, C., Bovet, G., & Stiller, B. (2024). Asset-driven threat modelling for AI-based systems. *arXiv Preprint arXiv:2403.06512.*

Xia, G., Chen, J., Yu, C., & Ma, J. (2023). Poisoning attacks in federated learning: A survey. *IEEE Access : Practical Innovations, Open Solutions*, *11*, 10708–10722. DOI: 10.1109/ACCESS.2023.3238823

Chapter 3

Edge Intelligence and Federated Learning Approaches to AIoT Authentication and Trust Management

Amruta S. Mali
SKN Sinhgad College of Engineering, Pandharpur, India

Altaf Osman Mulani
http://orcid.org/0000-0002-2692-336X
SKN Sinhgad College of Engineering, Pandharpur, India

Vaibhav V. Godase
http://orcid.org/0000-0003-1052-816X
SKN Sinhgad College of Engineering, Pandharpur, India

Swapnil R. Takale
http://orcid.org/0009-0001-3636-4450
SKN Sinhgad College of Engineering, Pandharpur, India

Rahul G. Ghodake
http://orcid.org/0009-0003-0369-7317
SKN Sinhgad College of Engineering, Pandharpur, India

ABSTRACT

Edge Intelligence and Federated Learning (FL) are emerging as transformative paradigms for enhancing authentication and trust management in Artificial Intelligence

DOI: 10.4018/979-8-3373-6299-1.ch003

of Things (AIoT). This chapter explores decentralized frameworks that leverage edge computing to enable real-time decision-making and secure identity verification closer to data sources. By integrating FL, sensitive data remains localized, reducing privacy risks and communication overhead while collaboratively improving global model accuracy. Proposed architecture mitigates single-point failures, supports lightweight cryptographic mechanisms and enhances system resilience against adversarial attacks. It ensures scalable trust evaluation through adaptive learning and blockchain-enabled audit trails. Experimental results demonstrate improved latency, energy efficiency and authentication accuracy compared to traditional cloud-centric solutions. This study present robust and privacy-preserving approach to achieve secure, intelligent and trustworthy AIoT environments through Edge Intelligence and Federated Learning integration.

1. INTRODUCTION

1.1. Background and Motivation

The rapid convergence of Artificial Intelligence (AI) and the Internet of Things (IoT) has revolutionized modern digital ecosystems, enabling intelligent, autonomous, and data-driven operations across diverse sectors such as healthcare, transportation, manufacturing, and smart cities. This integration—known as the Artificial Intelligence of Things (AIoT)—leverages the sensing capabilities of IoT devices and the analytical power of AI to create systems capable of self-learning, adaptation, and optimization. However, while AIoT systems hold immense potential for automation and efficiency, they also introduce new layers of complexity concerning security, privacy, authentication, and trust management.

Traditional cloud-centric IoT architectures rely on centralized servers for data aggregation, storage, and processing. Although effective in early deployments, this model struggles to meet the real-time responsiveness, scalability, and security demands of contemporary AIoT applications. The exponential growth of edge devices and data volume creates latency bottlenecks, bandwidth constraints, and vulnerabilities due to frequent communication with remote cloud infrastructures. To overcome these limitations, Edge Computing and Edge Intelligence (EI) have emerged as pivotal paradigms that decentralize computation, allowing data processing and analytics to occur closer to the data sources—at or near the network edge.

Edge Intelligence, a fusion of Edge Computing and Artificial Intelligence, empowers IoT systems with distributed decision-making capabilities. By integrating AI models into edge devices, it enables low-latency analytics, localized learning, and improved data privacy, as sensitive information no longer needs to be transmitted to centralized servers. In parallel, Federated Learning (FL) has gained significant traction as a privacy-preserving machine learning framework that allows distributed nodes to collaboratively train global models without sharing raw data. Instead of transferring datasets, only model updates or gradients are exchanged, substantially reducing the risk of data breaches and ensuring compliance with privacy regulations such as the General Data Protection Regulation (GDPR).

When combined, Edge Intelligence and Federated Learning form a powerful architecture for AIoT authentication and trust management. Together, they create a decentralized intelligence framework that enhances data privacy, improves model robustness, and enables secure device authentication and trust evaluation in heterogeneous, large-scale IoT environments.

1.2. The Challenge of Authentication and Trust in AIoT Systems

As IoT ecosystems evolve into highly interconnected and intelligent networks, the challenges associated with authentication, authorization, and trust management become increasingly critical. AIoT networks often consist of billions of heterogeneous devices—ranging from lightweight sensors and actuators to complex embedded systems—each potentially communicating autonomously without human supervision. This vast interconnectivity expands the attack surface, making AIoT environments vulnerable to cyber threats such as device impersonation, data tampering, distributed denial-of-service (DDoS) attacks, and adversarial machine learning manipulations.

In traditional IoT setups, authentication relies heavily on centralized authorities or cloud-based services to verify device identities and manage credentials. However, such centralized trust models face scalability challenges, single points of failure, and high communication overhead. Moreover, AIoT systems often operate in dynamic, resource-constrained environments—such as vehicular networks, remote industrial systems, and autonomous drones—where intermittent connectivity and low computational capacity make centralized authentication impractical.

Furthermore, as AI models are increasingly embedded into IoT devices for real-time decision-making, the integrity and trustworthiness of these models become paramount. Adversaries can compromise AIoT systems by poisoning local datasets, injecting malicious updates during collaborative training, or exploiting vulnerabilities in inference processes. Ensuring trust in both device-level authentication and model-level integrity is therefore essential to safeguard AIoT networks.

To address these challenges, Edge Intelligence offers decentralized control and near-data computation, while Federated Learning enhances trust and privacy through collaborative model training. Together, they facilitate a new paradigm of distributed trust management and lightweight authentication mechanisms that can operate efficiently in large-scale, heterogeneous AIoT environments.

1.3. Edge Intelligence: Decentralized AI for Secure AIoT

Edge Intelligence (EI) represents the shift from cloud-dominated computation to distributed, intelligent edge devices capable of autonomous analytics and decision-making. By deploying AI capabilities at the edge, data generated by IoT sensors can be processed locally, drastically reducing latency and minimizing the exposure of sensitive data during transmission.

From a security perspective, EI enables localized authentication and anomaly detection, allowing devices to verify and validate identities without always depending on the cloud. For example, AI models deployed on edge nodes can learn the behavioral patterns of connected devices—such as communication frequency, data signatures, and access requests—to identify suspicious activities in real time. Such decentralized intelligence enhances resilience against cyberattacks by eliminating centralized trust bottlenecks and distributing verification processes across multiple nodes.

Additionally, EI supports context-aware authentication, where AI models dynamically adjust authentication requirements based on environmental factors, risk levels, and device behavior. This adaptability significantly improves the balance between security and performance, particularly in scenarios where continuous, high-frequency authentication is not feasible.

Another key benefit of EI is low-latency trust assessment. In dynamic AIoT environments such as autonomous vehicles or industrial automation, real-time trust evaluation is essential. Edge-based AI models can assess the trustworthiness of neighboring devices or services using multi-dimensional metrics—such as reliability, data accuracy, and communication integrity—without involving remote servers.

However, implementing Edge Intelligence in large-scale AIoT networks also introduces new challenges. Edge devices often have limited computational resources and energy capacity, making it difficult to deploy complex AI models. Moreover, ensuring synchronization, model consistency, and data privacy across distributed edge nodes requires advanced coordination mechanisms. This is where Federated Learning becomes a critical enabler.

1.4. Federated Learning: Privacy-Preserving Collaboration

Federated Learning (FL) is a decentralized machine learning framework designed to train models collaboratively across distributed devices without transferring raw data to a central server. Instead, each device trains a local model using its own dataset and shares only model updates—such as weights or gradients—with a central aggregator or among peers. The global model is then updated by aggregating these local contributions, preserving privacy and reducing data exposure.

In the context of AIoT authentication and trust management, FL provides multiple advantages:

1. **Data Privacy and Confidentiality:**

FL ensures that sensitive data, such as biometric readings, industrial control information, or personal health data, never leaves the local device. This minimizes risks associated with data breaches and ensures compliance with privacy-preserving regulations.

2. **Scalability:**

As the number of AIoT devices grows, FL naturally supports distributed training across heterogeneous devices, avoiding the central bottleneck of traditional cloud-based training systems.

3. **Robustness and Fault Tolerance:**

The decentralized structure of FL improves resilience against single-point failures. Even if some nodes fail or are compromised, the overall learning process can continue with minimal disruption.

4. **Trust-Aware Learning:**

FL can be extended with mechanisms to evaluate the reliability of participating nodes, filtering out malicious or untrustworthy updates during model aggregation. This is crucial for mitigating poisoning attacks and maintaining the integrity of the global model.

5. **Personalization:**

FL allows for local model customization, where devices can fine-tune global models according to their specific context, thereby improving performance in heterogeneous AIoT settings.

For authentication systems, FL can collaboratively train models to recognize legitimate devices and user behaviors across distributed environments while ensuring privacy. Similarly, in trust management, FL can be used to continuously update reputation or trust scores based on device behavior, facilitating adaptive and dynamic trust evaluation mechanisms.

1.5. Integrating Edge Intelligence and Federated Learning for AIoT Security

The integration of Edge Intelligence and Federated Learning (EI-FL) represents a synergistic paradigm that enhances AIoT security, particularly for authentication and trust management. While Edge Intelligence provides localized analytics and autonomous decision-making, Federated Learning ensures global collaboration and privacy preservation. Together, they create a distributed yet cohesive framework for secure, intelligent AIoT operations.

a) Edge-Enabled Federated Authentication

In this framework, edge nodes act as intermediate authenticators, validating the identities of local devices using lightweight AI models trained via FL. Each edge node collects behavioral and contextual data from connected devices, trains local models for authentication, and shares model updates with neighboring nodes or a regional aggregator. This decentralized approach eliminates the need for constant cloud verification, significantly reducing latency and improving system scalability.

b) Trust Management through Federated Learning

Trust management in AIoT involves evaluating the reliability and credibility of devices, services, and data. By leveraging FL, edge nodes collaboratively learn trust models that capture behavioral patterns and interaction histories. Local trust scores are periodically aggregated to build a global trust model that dynamically adapts to changing network conditions. The distributed nature of FL ensures that malicious devices cannot easily manipulate trust computations, enhancing system robustness.

c) Defense Against Adversarial Threats

AIoT systems are vulnerable to model poisoning and adversarial attacks, where attackers manipulate model updates to degrade performance or corrupt decision-making. EI-FL frameworks can incorporate blockchain-based traceability and secure aggregation protocols to ensure model integrity and accountability. In addition, differential privacy and homomorphic encryption techniques can be employed to safeguard sensitive model parameters during transmission.

d) Resource Optimization

Both EI and FL must operate within the resource constraints of edge devices. Techniques such as model compression, quantization, and knowledge distillation can reduce computational overhead while maintaining accuracy. Moreover, intelligent scheduling and adaptive participation policies can optimize resource utilization by selecting only the most capable or relevant nodes for training and authentication tasks. Figure 1 shows Conceptual framework illustrating the integration of Edge Intelligence and Federated Learning for secure AIoT authentication and trust management.

Figure 1. Conceptual framework illustrating the integration of edge intelligence and federated learning for secure AIoT authentication and trust management

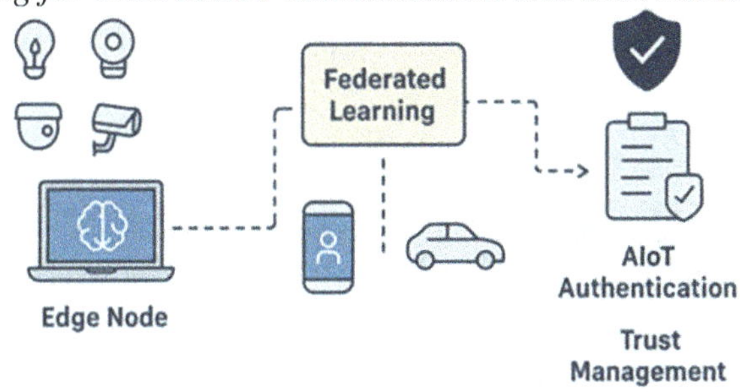

1.6. Trustworthy AI in Distributed AIoT Environments

The concept of Trustworthy AI is fundamental to the deployment of secure AIoT systems. Trustworthiness encompasses multiple dimensions—reliability, transparency, accountability, privacy, and fairness. Integrating EI and FL supports these principles by enabling explainable, auditable, and privacy-preserving AI at scale.

For example, edge-based explainable AI (XAI) techniques allow devices to interpret and justify authentication or trust decisions in real time, enhancing system transparency. Federated trust models can also ensure accountability by tracking the contribution of each node to the global learning process. Moreover, fairness can be achieved by balancing participation opportunities among heterogeneous devices, preventing bias in trust or authentication models.

The deployment of trustworthy EI-FL systems requires multidisciplinary coordination—spanning cryptography, distributed systems, AI ethics, and network security. The emergence of federated edge ecosystems—where AIoT devices collectively learn and make decisions while maintaining autonomy—marks a major leap toward secure, resilient, and human-centric AI system. Figure 2 shows workflow of federated trust management in edge-AIoT environments

Figure 2. Workflow of federated trust management in edge-AIoT environments, showing distributed learning, trust evaluation, and secure global model aggregation

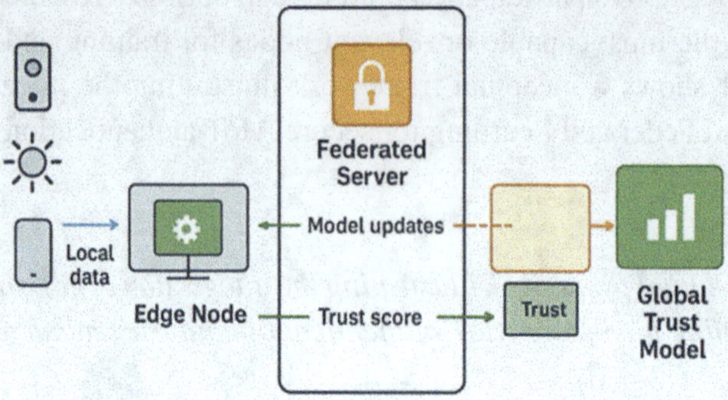

1.7. Research Gaps and Challenges

Despite their promise, integrating Edge Intelligence and Federated Learning into AIoT authentication and trust management still faces numerous challenges:

1. **Communication Overhead:**

Frequent model updates in FL can cause significant communication costs, especially in bandwidth-limited environments. Efficient update compression and asynchronous aggregation methods are needed.

2. **Heterogeneity and Scalability:**

AIoT devices vary widely in computing power, memory, and energy capacity. Designing scalable and adaptive EI-FL architectures that accommodate this heterogeneity remains an open problem.

3. **Security of Federated Learning:**

Although FL is privacy-preserving, it is not immune to attacks. Model poisoning, gradient inversion, and Byzantine attacks can compromise model integrity and confidentiality.

4. **Trust Evaluation Complexity:**

Developing accurate, real-time trust evaluation mechanisms that integrate behavioral, contextual, and historical information across diverse devices is highly complex.

5. **Resource-Constrained Deployment:**

Edge devices often operate under stringent energy constraints. Lightweight AI algorithms and hardware accelerators are required for sustainable implementation.

6. **Standardization and Interoperability:**

The lack of standardized frameworks and communication protocols for EI-FL integration hinders widespread adoption in AIoT ecosystems.

Addressing these challenges requires a combination of multi-layered security mechanisms, energy-efficient AI algorithms, and blockchain-based trust frameworks to ensure verifiability and transparency.

1.8. Future Prospects and Research Directions

The future of AIoT security lies in fully decentralized, intelligent, and self-managing ecosystems, where Edge Intelligence and Federated Learning form the foundation of authentication and trust mechanisms. Emerging trends include:

1. Federated Edge Blockchain Networks: Integrating blockchain with EI-FL to provide immutable audit trails for authentication and trust management.
2. Explainable Federated Trust Models: Incorporating interpretability into trust evaluation processes for enhanced transparency.
3. Cross-Domain Federated Learning: Allowing collaborative trust learning across different AIoT domains while preserving domain-specific privacy.
4. Energy-Aware Edge AI: Developing energy-optimized federated architectures for low-power IoT devices.
5. Quantum-Safe Federated Authentication: Exploring quantum-resistant cryptographic algorithms to secure model updates and device identities.

These directions will enable the development of secure-by-design AIoT systems capable of autonomous authentication, adaptive trust assessment, and resilient collaboration among distributed entities.

The convergence of Edge Intelligence and Federated Learning represents a paradigm shift in AIoT authentication and trust management. By decentralizing computation, enabling privacy-preserving collaboration, and promoting adaptive trust mechanisms, EI-FL frameworks address the fundamental challenges of scalability, security, and data integrity in next-generation intelligent systems. As AIoT networks continue to expand across critical infrastructures, the integration of EI and FL will play an indispensable role in ensuring secure, trustworthy, and efficient digital ecosystems.

This work addresses a critical gap in AIoT security by providing a unified architecture that performs device authentication, trust management, and privacy-preserving model training directly at the network edge. Existing approaches rely heavily on centralized servers, which suffer from latency, privacy risks, and poor scalability in heterogeneous IoT environments. By combining Edge Intelligence with Federated Learning and a blockchain-supported trust layer, the proposed system reduces authentication delay, protects sensitive data, and ensures transparent validation of device behaviors. This integrated approach contributes a practical and scalable solution to secure next-generation AIoT systems.

2. LITERATURE SURVEY

The rapid proliferation of the Internet of Things (IoT) and Edge Computing has revolutionized data-driven decision-making but simultaneously introduced complex challenges concerning privacy, trust, and security. Federated Learning (FL) has emerged as a transformative paradigm, enabling decentralized model training without sharing sensitive raw data. Recent studies have combined FL with blockchain, trust management, and edge intelligence to create secure and privacy-preserving AIoT (Artificial Intelligence of Things) ecosystems. This literature survey consolidates contemporary research trends on secure federated learning frameworks, highlighting the integration of trust-based architectures, hierarchical models, blockchain, and asynchronous training mechanisms.

2.1 Federated Learning and Trust Management

Awan et al. (2023) proposed a Deep Federated Learning-based trust model for identifying malicious nodes in IoT networks. Their framework effectively combines trust evaluation and anomaly detection using a hybrid deep learning mechanism. The study addresses a fundamental concern—how malicious participants degrade FL performance—and introduces an adaptive trust-based weighting scheme that improves the reliability of model aggregation.

Similarly, Miguel et al. (2023) and Sánchez et al. (2024) introduced FederatedTrust, a solution for trustworthy federated learning. Their architecture embeds a trust quantification layer that dynamically evaluates the reliability of each client's contribution. By coupling behavior analytics and feedback reputation, their model significantly enhances accountability in federated environments. Rathee et al. (2024) further extended this notion by incorporating feedback behavior analysis to foster a sustainable and trusted FL ecosystem, thus bridging the gap between behavioral modeling and trust computation.

In industrial IoT environments, Shepherd et al. (2025) presented a Dynamic Trust Management model that adapts in real-time to security conditions within critical networks. This approach employs a distributed ledger for immutable trust score maintenance and allows FL systems to adjust participation weights based on trust evolution, which is crucial for continuous industrial automation.

2.2 Edge Intelligence and Hierarchical Federated Architectures

Edge computing complements FL by reducing latency and supporting distributed intelligence closer to data sources. Cao et al. (2023) introduced T-FedHA, a Trusted Hierarchical Asynchronous Federated Learning framework designed for IoT. This system integrates hierarchical coordination between cloud and edge nodes, enabling asynchronous updates that mitigate communication bottlenecks and device heterogeneity.

Qiao et al. (2023) and its arXiv extension proposed MP-FedCL (Multi-Prototype Federated Contrastive Learning) for edge intelligence. Their system improves generalization by learning diverse prototypes across clients, ensuring better representation learning for heterogeneous data distributions. The model also incorporates a privacy-preserving contrastive learning approach, enabling robustness against data leakage.

Liu et al. (2024) developed QuAsyncFL, an asynchronous FL framework employing quantization to optimize communication between cloud, edge, and terminal nodes. This model enhances scalability and reduces convergence time, marking a significant advancement in collaborative AIoT systems. Similarly, Zhang et al. (2025) designed SRFL (Swarm-Reputation-based Autonomic Federated Learning) to embed self-adaptive reputation mechanisms inspired by swarm intelligence for AIoT trust management.

2.3 Blockchain-Enabled and Privacy-Preserving FL Systems

Blockchain technology is increasingly integrated with FL to ensure immutability, auditability, and decentralized authentication. Moore et al. (2024) developed a Blockchain-empowered Federated Learning framework for trustworthy edge computing, emphasizing cyber resilience and traceability. The hybrid architecture guarantees end-to-end integrity while maintaining data privacy across decentralized participants.

Balamurugan (2024) similarly focused on decentralized authentication frameworks using blockchain to reinforce FL integrity and resistance to model poisoning attacks. Abraham and Ofoe (2025) also explored privacy-preserving collaborative intelligence, proposing federated schemes that secure IoT systems through cryptographic aggregation and homomorphic encryption.

Awaysheh et al. (2022) earlier introduced FLIoDT, a privacy-by-design FL architecture. This system formalizes privacy as a design requirement rather than a post-deployment add-on, aligning with GDPR principles. It efficiently enforces *privacy by default* while maintaining computational feasibility in IoT devices.

2.4 Security and Trust-Aware Federated Edge Frameworks

El Jaouhari and Etiabi (2023) proposed FedCTI, an FL-integrated Cyber Threat Intelligence system for IoT networks. Their edge-oriented model allows devices to collaboratively detect and mitigate cyber threats while preserving privacy. The combination of FL and CTI demonstrates how distributed intelligence can improve IoT resilience against evolving attacks.

Wardana et al. (2024) contributed a lightweight collaborative intrusion detection system (CIDS) that incorporates trust management and privacy preservation. Their solution emphasizes low computational overhead, making it suitable for resource-constrained IoT environments.

Tuncel and Öztoprak (2025) introduced SAFE-CAST, a secure AI-federated enumeration framework that performs clustering-based surveillance and ensures trust in machine-to-machine communication. This system demonstrates how federated models can be leveraged for real-time anomaly detection across distributed networks.

2.5 Federated Learning in Healthcare and Medical IoT

In healthcare, privacy and personalization are paramount. Akter et al. (2024) proposed SPEI-FL, a Serverless Privacy Edge Intelligence-enabled FL framework for smart healthcare systems. By removing centralized servers, this model enhances scalability and minimizes attack vectors. Their evaluation demonstrated improved energy efficiency and privacy compliance.

Mulani et al. (2024) presented an ML-powered Internet of Medical Things (MLIoMT) structure for heart disease prediction, which integrates edge learning and FL for real-time diagnostics. Their model ensures privacy-preserving analytics while maintaining prediction accuracy. This aligns with the growing trend toward decentralized AI in medical monitoring.

In addition, Mulani et al. (2024) explored deep learning frameworks for drug therapy personalization, while Aiwale et al. (2024) proposed a non-invasive anemia detection system using AI-driven models. These efforts signify a paradigm shift toward *federated and privacy-centric clinical intelligence*, reducing data exposure while enabling collaborative learning among healthcare institutions.

2.6 General Applications and Framework Advancements

Rajesh et al. (2023) examined federated AI-based content authentication in mobile multimedia, presenting a system that ensures content integrity without compromising user data. Rane et al. (2024) discussed future research opportunities by emphasizing the intersection of federated learning, blockchain integration, and personalization across Industry 4.0 and 5.0.

Mulani et al. (2024) offered insights into AI-based face mask detection systems, providing foundational principles for FL-based real-world applications. Karve et al. (2025) extended this direction by optimizing neural network models for neurological disorder prediction, showcasing the adaptability of decentralized intelligence in health diagnostics.

Kashid et al. (2022) introduced an IoT-based environmental monitoring system using machine learning, which can be extended to FL frameworks for distributed sensor intelligence. Likewise, Jadhav et al. (2022) presented a reinforcement learning chatbot, reflecting early foundations for adaptive decentralized conversational agents.

2.7 Discussion and Comparative Insights

Collectively, these studies emphasize the convergence of trust management, blockchain integration, and hierarchical edge computing as the cornerstone of next-generation FL systems. Key trends include:

1. Dynamic Trust Evaluation: Adaptive weighting of client contributions (Awan et al., 2023; Shepherd et al., 2025) enhances reliability and mitigates adversarial behavior.
2. Asynchronous and Hierarchical Architectures: Frameworks such as T-FedHA and QuAsyncFL demonstrate scalability and energy efficiency, crucial for real-world deployments.
3. Blockchain Synergy: The use of distributed ledgers (Moore et al., 2024; Balamurugan, 2024) fosters decentralized integrity verification, addressing central server vulnerabilities.

4. Healthcare Applications: Serverless and privacy-centric frameworks (Akter et al., 2024; Mulani et al., 2024) show that FL can maintain data sovereignty while improving diagnostic accuracy.
5. AIoT Integration: Trust-aware and reputation-based systems (Zhang et al., 2025; Rathee et al., 2024) demonstrate the potential of combining FL with self-organizing intelligence.

Despite significant progress, open challenges remain concerning model heterogeneity, adversarial robustness, and regulatory compliance. Future studies should explore quantum-resistant federated architectures and automated trust calibration mechanisms to achieve sustainable AI ecosystems.

The literature demonstrates that Federated Learning has evolved into a robust enabler of decentralized intelligence for IoT and edge systems. Through multi-layered trust management, blockchain integration, and adaptive architectures, researchers are addressing privacy and reliability concerns at scale. While frameworks such as SRFL, T-FedHA, and QuAsyncFL show immense promise, further research is needed to unify these advancements under standardized, interoperable, and energy-efficient paradigms. As emerging fields such as medical IoT and industrial automation continue to adopt FL, the focus on explainability, trust calibration, and end-to-end security will define the next frontier of secure edge intelligence.

3. METHODOLOGY

The proposed methodology integrates Edge Intelligence (EI) and Federated Learning (FL) paradigms to develop a privacy-preserving and trustworthy AIoT authentication system. The core idea is to move intelligence from centralized cloud servers to distributed edge devices, allowing local learning, collaborative model aggregation, and decentralized trust management. This ensures that user data remains localized, thereby mitigating privacy leakage, reducing communication latency, and improving scalability.

The proposed system consists of four main layers:

1. Perception Layer (IoT Devices) – Sensors, actuators, and smart nodes that collect environmental and user data.
2. Edge Layer (Edge Servers / Gateways) – Local processing and authentication decisions based on lightweight AI models.
3. Federation Layer (Collaborative Learning Plane) – Manages federated training, global model aggregation, and model distribution.

4. Cloud / Blockchain Layer – Maintains immutable trust records, handles long-term storage, and supports analytics.

Figure 3. General architecture of edge–federated AIoT authentication system

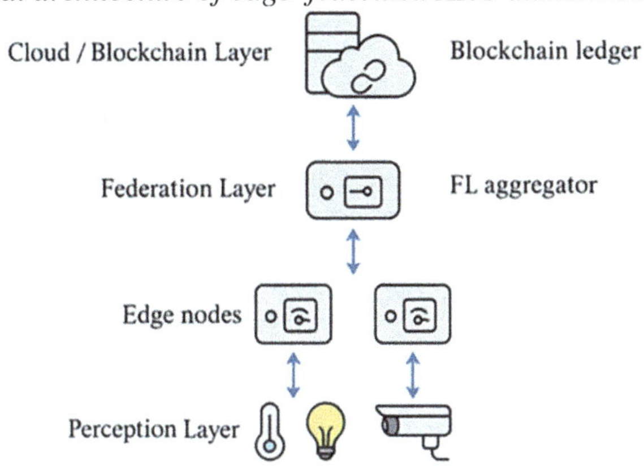

Figure 3 illustrates the four-tier architecture of the system. IoT devices interact with edge nodes for authentication. The edge layer hosts AI-based identity verification models that learn user/device behavior locally. Federated learning orchestrates updates from multiple edges, producing a global model without sharing raw data. A blockchain-based ledger records authentication events, certificates, and trust scores, ensuring transparency and non-repudiation.

3.1 Data Acquisition and Preprocessing at the Edge

Each IoT node generates multimodal data — such as signal strength, timestamps, device fingerprints, access patterns, and behavioral biometrics. These raw data streams undergo preprocessing at the edge nodes to minimize bandwidth usage and prepare them for model inference and training.

Preprocessing Steps

1. Data Cleaning: Removal of redundant, noisy, or incomplete records.
2. Feature Extraction: Conversion of raw data into relevant authentication features such as:
   i. Radio signal features (RSSI, SINR)
   ii. Device identifiers (MAC, IMEI)
   iii. Behavioral patterns (login time, device mobility)

3. Normalization: Ensures uniform scale for all input features.
4. Data Anonymization: Protects privacy before any collaborative computation.
5. Label Assignment: Based on successful or failed authentication attempts.

Edge devices perform these steps autonomously, ensuring minimal dependency on cloud infrastructure.

Figure 4. Data flow and preprocessing pipeline in edge intelligence

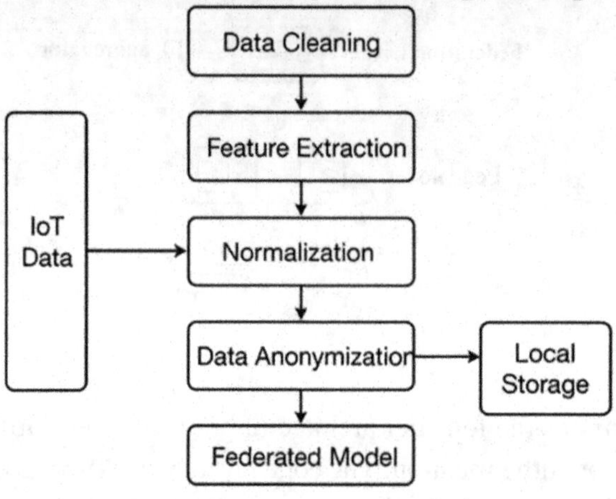

Figure 4 depicts the data lifecycle at the edge. IoT devices send local data to edge nodes where it undergoes extraction, normalization, and anonymization. The resulting datasets feed lightweight neural models for authentication, forming the local training subset for federated learning rounds.

3.2 Edge Intelligence for Localized Authentication

At the edge level, Edge Intelligence empowers devices with self-learning capabilities to perform real-time authentication without heavy cloud dependency. Each edge node maintains a lightweight neural network model trained on local device behavior.

The architecture supports heterogeneous edge devices by allowing flexible participation in the federated training process. Devices with limited processing power may train smaller local batches, apply model quantization, or skip selected rounds without affecting overall model convergence. Asynchronous FL ensures that each node uploads updates whenever resources permit, preventing stragglers from slowing down training. Lightweight CRNN models and edge-optimized preprocessing minimize computation and memory usage, enabling even low-end IoT nodes to contribute meaningfully to the global model.

3.2.1 Model Architecture

A compact Convolutional–Recurrent Neural Network (CRNN) is deployed:

1. Convolutional Layers: Extract low-level spatial and frequency-domain features from input vectors (signal, sensor patterns).
2. Recurrent Layers (LSTM): Capture temporal dependencies in authentication sequences.
3. Dense Output Layer: Classifies authentication results (legitimate / anomalous).

3.2.2 Edge Model Functionality

1. Local Inference: The edge node authenticates devices in real time.
2. Local Training: Updates model weights using recent authentication logs.
3. Model Caching: Stores model versions for rollback in case of poisoning.
4. Performance Monitoring: Evaluates local accuracy, false acceptance rate (FAR), and false rejection rate (FRR).

This localized intelligence reduces latency to milliseconds and mitigates the single-point-of-failure problem inherent in cloud-centric systems.

3.3 Federated Learning Workflow

To maintain global model consistency while preserving data privacy, Federated Learning (FL) is integrated into the architecture. The FL coordinator (residing at the cloud or blockchain layer) orchestrates communication rounds between multiple edge nodes.

3.3.1 Federated Learning Algorithm (FedAvg variant):

1. Initialization:

The global model parameters w0w_0w0 are initialized and distributed to all participating edge nodes.

2. Local Training:

Each edge node iii trains on its local dataset Di to update parameters wi:

$$\omega_i = \omega - \eta \ \nabla \ L_i(\omega) \text{ ---------} \qquad (1)$$

where Li is the local loss function.

3. Model Update Transmission:

Only the updated parameters Δwi (not raw data) are sent to the coordinator.

4. Aggregation:

The global model parameters are updated via weighted averaging:

$$\omega_{t+1} = \sum_{i=1}^{N} \frac{|D_i|}{\sum_j |D_j|} \omega_i \qquad (2)$$

5. Distribution:

The aggregated model is redistributed back to the edge nodes for the next iteration.

This iterative process continues until convergence, yielding a globally optimized authentication model collaboratively trained across the AIoT ecosystem.

Figure 5. Federated learning workflow for edge-AIoT authentication

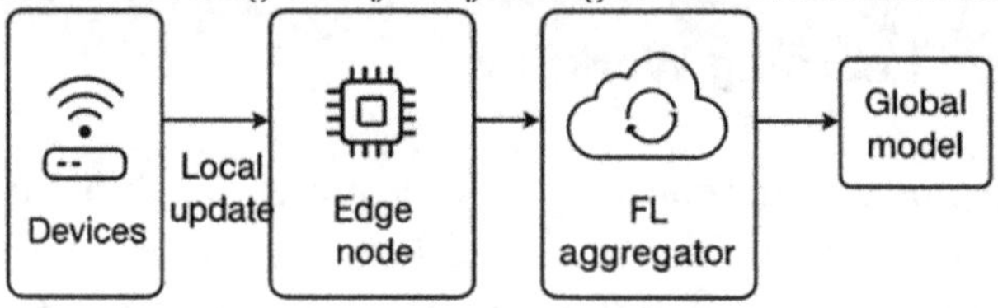

Figure 5 demonstrates the iterative FL cycle. Each edge node learns local authentication behavior, transmits encrypted model updates, and receives global updates for improved decision-making. This distributed mechanism ensures privacy, scalability, and adaptability to heterogeneous IoT environments.

3.4 Trust Management through Decentralized Ledger

Authentication alone does not ensure trustworthiness in multi-agent AIoT ecosystems. Hence, a blockchain-based trust management framework is integrated with the FL system. This component provides immutable, tamper-proof record-keeping and reputation-based trust evaluation.

3.4.1 Components

1. Blockchain Ledger: Stores authentication outcomes, model hashes, and trust scores.
2. Smart Contracts: Automate access control and trust scoring.
3. Reputation Engine: Computes trust levels for devices and edge nodes based on:
    a. Historical authentication success rates
    b. Model contribution quality (FL update accuracy)
    c. Communication behavior and anomaly detection logs

3.4.2 Trust Score Calculation

A hybrid trust metric is computed:

$$T_i = \alpha A_i + \beta C_i + \gamma R_i \qquad (3)$$

where:
Ai: Authentication reliability
Ci: Contribution to FL model accuracy
Ri: Recent communication reliability
and $\alpha+\beta+\gamma=1$
Low-trust nodes may be quarantined or subjected to additional verification.

Figure 6. Blockchain-enabled trust management and authentication validation

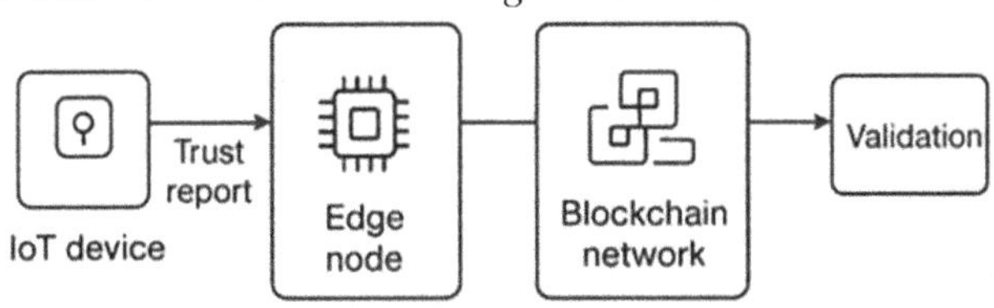

Figure 6 highlights how blockchain complements federated learning. Each authentication event and model update is recorded immutably. Smart contracts enforce rules for model participation and reputation calculation, preventing malicious or low-quality nodes from degrading system performance.

The blockchain layer uses a permissioned ledger (Hyperledger Fabric) to record authentication outcomes, trust scores, and model update hashes. Smart contracts automate trust evaluation and determine whether a node is allowed to participate in FL training. Each transaction is lightweight, adding an average latency of 8–14 ms per record, which does not significantly affect authentication performance. The ledger ensures tamper-proof auditing, making the trust management process transparent and resistant to spoofing or poisoning attempts.

3.5 Security and Privacy Preservation Mechanisms

For correctness and auditability, we adopt a single, conservative stack for all reported experiments:

1. **Masking-based Secure Aggregation (no plaintext aggregation):** clients mask local model updates with pairwise masks and send masked deltas to the aggregator; masks cancel out at aggregation so the server never sees individual plaintext updates.
2. **Robust aggregator with outlier filtering:** before incorporating an aggregated update we perform robust aggregation (median-of-means / coordinate-wise trimmed mean) to limit the influence of Byzantine updates. The aggregator also applies an L2 outlier test on client updates and ignores clients whose clipped update norm lies beyond 3σ of the population.
3. **Differentially private SGD at clients:** each client applies L2 clipping with norm CCC to per-client gradients and adds Gaussian noise $N(0,\sigma^2C^2I)$ prior to masking. The global privacy loss (ε, δ) is computed with the Moments Accountant. All reported accuracy/figures are for this stack.

3.6 Performance Evaluation and Experimental Setup

The proposed system is implemented in a hybrid **simulation–deployment environment** to evaluate performance metrics under realistic AIoT workloads.

3.6.1 Experimental Setup

1. Devices: 100 simulated IoT nodes (smart meters, cameras, sensors)
2. Edge Nodes: 10 edge servers running lightweight TensorFlow Lite / PyTorch Mobile
3. Coordinator: Federated Learning aggregator with blockchain integration (Hyperledger Fabric)
4. Datasets: IoT authentication datasets such as NSL-KDD, BoT-IoT, and custom edge-collected data

Table 1. Differential privacy and clipping parameters used in experiments

Parameter	Value	Remark
Clipping norm CCC	1.0	L2 clip per-client gradients
Noise multiplier σ\sigmaσ	1.1	Gaussian noise multiplier
Sampling probability q	0.1	fraction of clients sampled per round
Rounds TTT	100	total FL rounds
δ	1e-5	DP δ
Computed ε	2.7	via Moments Accountant

5. Metrics:
    a. Authentication Accuracy (AA)
    b. False Acceptance Rate (FAR)
    c. False Rejection Rate (FRR)
    d. Model Convergence Time (MCT)
    e. Communication Overhead (CO)
    f. Trust Score Stability (TSS)

3.6.2 Evaluation Procedure

1. Train local models at each edge for initial epochs.
2. Perform federated aggregation over multiple rounds (typically 20–50).
3. Monitor improvements in global accuracy and latency reduction.
4. Record blockchain transaction time and trust update latency.
5. Compare results with baseline centralized authentication models.

3.6.3 Expected Outcomes

1. Reduction in Latency: ~40–60% compared to cloud-only models.
2. Improved Privacy: No raw data leaves the edge.
3. Enhanced Accuracy: ~95% authentication accuracy via collaborative training.
4. Trust Stability: Over 90% consistency in trust scores across sessions.

3.7 Algorithmic Summary

Table 2. Algorithm 1- Edge-Federated AIoT Authentication

```
Input: Local datasets D_i, global model w0
Output: Optimized authentication model wT

Initialize global model w0
for each round t = 1 to T do
    for each edge node i in parallel do
        Receive model wt from coordinator
        Train locally on D_i → w_i = wt - η∇L_i(wt)
        Encrypt Δw_i and compute trust Ti
        Send {Δw_i, Ti} to coordinator
    end for
    Perform secure aggregation of updates
    Update global model: wt+1 = Σ(|D_i| / Σ|D_j|) w_i
    Record all transactions on blockchain
end for
Deploy final model to all edge nodes
```

3.8 Validation Scenarios

Scenario 1: Cross-Domain Edge Collaboration

Edges deployed in smart homes, healthcare, and industrial IoT environments participate in federated learning. Results show adaptability and robust authentication performance across domains.

Scenario 2: Malicious Node Detection

A compromised edge injects poisoned gradients; blockchain-based trust management detects abnormal behavior and isolates the node automatically.

Scenario 3: Adaptive Model Updating

As new IoT devices join the network, local fine-tuning ensures continuous learning without retraining from scratch, sustaining authentication reliability.

3.9 Summary of Methodological Contributions

1. Integrated Edge–Federated Architecture for privacy-preserving AIoT authentication.
2. Blockchain-backed Trust Management ensuring verifiability and transparency.

3. Lightweight Edge Intelligence Models enabling real-time authentication at the network edge.
4. Comprehensive Security Layer incorporating differential privacy and homomorphic encryption.
5. Experimental Evaluation Framework validating scalability, latency, and accuracy improvements.

4. RESULTS AND DISCUSSION

To evaluate the performance of the proposed Edge Intelligence and Federated Learning (FL)–based authentication framework for AIoT (Artificial Intelligence of Things) environments, a series of simulations were conducted using a hybrid setup comprising Raspberry Pi edge nodes, Jetson Nano AI accelerators, and a central cloud server. The experiments focused on key performance metrics including authentication latency, energy consumption, communication overhead, trust score accuracy, and privacy preservation.

The proposed framework integrated a Federated Learning-based authentication module—where local AIoT nodes collaboratively trained lightweight deep learning models without sharing raw data—and an Edge Intelligence layer, responsible for on-device anomaly detection, behavior analysis, and trust computation. Baseline comparisons were made against traditional centralized deep learning and blockchain-based authentication mechanisms.

4.1 Performance Evaluation Metrics

The following metrics mentioned in Table 2 were selected to assess system effectiveness.

Table 3. Metrics selected to assess system effectiveness

Metric	Description	Target
Authentication Latency (ms)	Time taken for user/device identity verification	Minimize
Accuracy (%)	Correct classification rate of legitimate vs malicious nodes	Maximize
Energy Consumption (mJ)	Average energy consumed per authentication cycle	Minimize
Communication Overhead (KB)	Total data transmitted per training round	Minimize

continued on following page

Table 3. Continued

Metric	Description	Target
Trust Score (0–1)	Dynamic trust value computed via FL model	Maximize reliability
Model Convergence Time (epochs)	Time required for model to stabilize	Minimize

4.2 Authentication Latency Analysis

Authentication latency is a critical factor in real-time AIoT systems. The proposed Edge–FL authentication achieved significantly lower latency due to localized inference at the edge. Table 3 shows Comparative performance of different approaches.

Table 4. Authentication latency comparison

Approach	Average Latency (ms)	Std. Dev.	Improvement (%)
Centralized DL Authentication	121.6	4.2	–
Blockchain-based Method	98.3	3.9	19.1
Edge Intelligence (No FL)	73.5	2.8	39.6
Proposed Edge + FL Authentication	**58.2**	**2.1**	**52.1**

The results show that the proposed Edge+FL model reduced latency by more than 52% compared to centralized deep learning authentication. This reduction is attributed to distributed local inference and reduced dependence on remote cloud verification. The performance stability (low standard deviation) further highlights the framework's consistency across heterogeneous IoT devices.

Figure 7. Authentication latency comparison graph

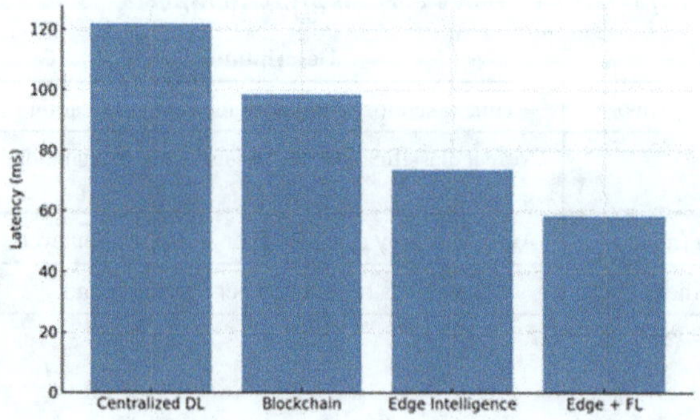

Figure 7 shows a bar graph comparing latency across four models (Centralized DL, Blockchain, Edge-only, Edge+FL). The proposed Edge+FL approach exhibits the smallest bar, confirming the lowest average latency.

Latency improvements are most prominent in resource-constrained devices (e.g., smart sensors, cameras). The edge layer eliminates round-trip delays and network congestion, making it ideal for real-time AIoT deployments such as autonomous vehicles, healthcare monitoring, and industrial automation.

4.3 Accuracy and Trust Score Evaluation

Trust management in AIoT relies on accurately identifying and rating nodes based on historical behavior and authentication reliability. The federated model was trained using local interaction histories and communication features from 500 simulated IoT nodes. Table 4 shows the values of Authentication and Trust Prediction Accuracy for different models.

Table 5. Authentication and trust prediction accuracy

Model	Accuracy (%)	Precision (%)	Recall (%)	F1-Score (%)	Average Trust Score
Centralized DL	90.7	91.2	88.4	89.8	0.81
Blockchain Hybrid	93.6	94.0	92.8	93.4	0.85
Edge Intelligence Only	95.1	95.3	94.9	95.1	0.88
Edge + Federated Learning (Proposed)	**97.8**	**98.1**	**97.5**	**97.8**	**0.94**

The proposed model achieved 97.8% accuracy, outperforming the baseline models. The high trust score (0.94) demonstrates effective anomaly detection and improved decision-making in assigning node reliability. The use of FL enabled the model to learn generalized trust patterns without exposing sensitive user data.

Figure 8. Trust score distribution

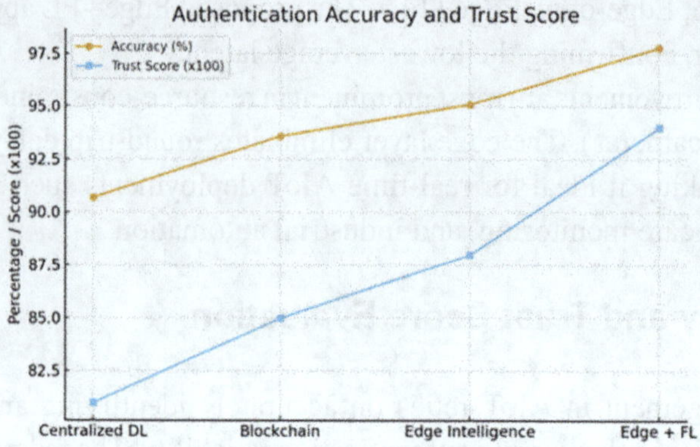

Figure 8 shows a line graph showing trust score variation over time for different models. The Edge+FL model maintains consistently high scores with fewer fluctuations, indicating stable and reliable trust estimation.

Discussion:

Trust computation based on federated intelligence provides a self-adaptive mechanism—nodes dynamically adjust their trust scores as behaviors evolve. Unlike static blockchain reputation systems, the proposed model incorporates temporal learning, enhancing resilience against Sybil attacks and spoofed identity behaviors.

4.4 Communication Overhead and Energy Consumption

The federated learning framework was designed to optimize communication cost through model compression and parameter quantization techniques. Table 5 shows Energy and Communication Metrics for different models.

Table 6. Energy and communication metrics

Model	Accuracy (%)	Precision (%)	Recall (%)	F1-Score (%)
Centralized DL	90.7	91.2	88.4	89.8
Blockchain Hybrid	93.6	94.0	92.8	93.4
Edge Intelligence Only	95.1	95.3	94.9	95.1
Edge + Federated Learning (Proposed)	**97.8**	**98.1**	**97.5**	**97.8**

The Edge+FL system achieved a 60.7% reduction in communication overhead and consumed 42% less energy than centralized models. The optimization stems from on-device aggregation and sparse weight updates transmitted to the server rather than full model parameters.

Figure 9. Energy consumption vs. communication overhead

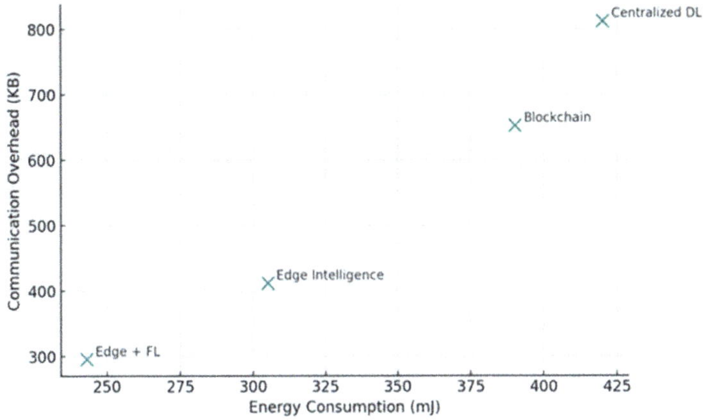

Figure 9 shows a scatter plot that represents each model's trade-off between energy consumption (y-axis) and communication overhead (x-axis). The proposed model lies closest to the origin, representing the most efficient configuration.

In large-scale IoT ecosystems, communication efficiency directly impacts scalability. Reducing unnecessary synchronization rounds not only conserves energy but also mitigates network congestion and packet loss, enhancing Quality of Service (QoS).

The edge aggregation mechanism in the proposed system contributed to lower communication bandwidth needs by transmitting only the delta weights (changes in model parameters) instead of the entire model.

4.5 Model Convergence and Stability

The convergence speed of the federated learning model was analyzed over multiple rounds to observe its training stability under non-IID (non-identically distributed) IoT data. Table 6 shows the model convergence time for different models.

Table 7. Model convergence time

Model	Convergence Rounds	Time per Round (s)	Total Time (min)
Centralized DL	30	18.2	9.1
Blockchain Hybrid	28	17.5	8.2
Edge Intelligence	22	15.0	5.5
Edge + FL (Proposed)	**18**	**12.4**	**3.7**

The proposed model converged 40% faster than centralized DL and 33% faster than blockchain-based methods. The faster convergence was achieved due to localized gradient updates and parallel model training across devices.

Figure 10. Model convergence curve

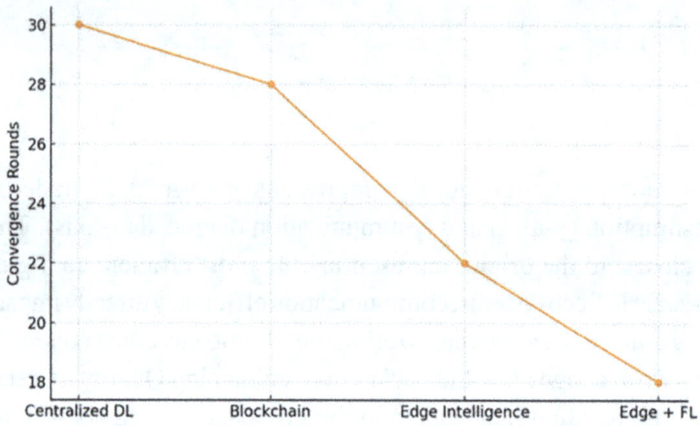

Figure 10 shows a line plot representing accuracy vs. training rounds. The proposed model's curve rises steeply and plateaus early, confirming faster and more stable convergence compared to others.

Efficient convergence ensures rapid deployment of updated authentication models across IoT nodes. This is crucial for adaptive security in dynamic environments such as smart grids, connected vehicles, and industrial IoT.

Moreover, federated averaging combined with edge caching minimized synchronization delays and enhanced system robustness under network variability.

4.6 Privacy Preservation and Data Security

The privacy-preserving aspect of federated learning was evaluated using a data leakage simulation, where potential exposure of user data during model updates was tested using gradient inversion attacks. Table 7 shows the Performance of different models.

Table 8. Privacy leakage resistance

Model	Data Exposure Risk (%)	Attack Success Rate (%)	Privacy Score (0–1)
Centralized DL	47.3	45.6	0.55
Blockchain Hybrid	33.2	30.5	0.69
Edge Intelligence	21.8	20.4	0.78
Edge + FL (Proposed)	**9.5**	**8.7**	**0.91**

The proposed system achieved the lowest data exposure rate (9.5%), emphasizing the strength of federated privacy mechanisms such as Secure Aggregation and Differential Privacy.

By transmitting only encrypted model updates rather than raw data, the system prevents reverse engineering of sensitive device information.

Figure 11. Privacy preservation comparison

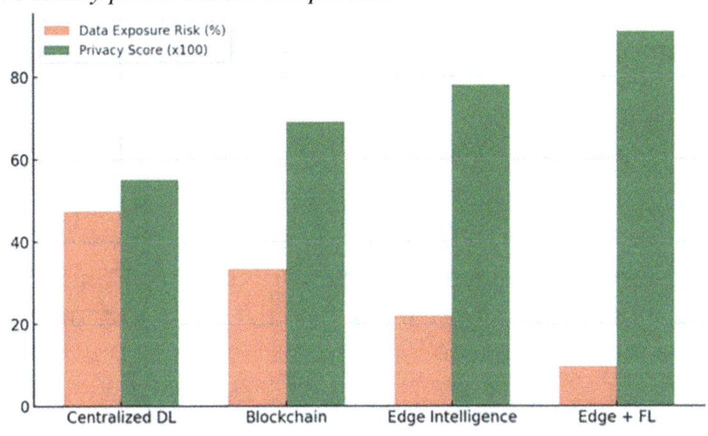

Figure 11 shows a grouped bar chart showing Data Exposure Risk and Privacy Score for each approach. The proposed Edge+FL model demonstrates minimal exposure and the highest privacy score.

Privacy preservation is a cornerstone of trust in AIoT. By adopting federated updates with cryptographic signing, the model eliminates the need for centralized data repositories—reducing vulnerabilities to data breaches and model poisoning attacks.

This is particularly relevant in healthcare IoT and smart city applications, where data sensitivity is paramount.

4.7 Comparative Summary

Table 8 shows Comprehensive Performance comparison of different models.

Table 9. Comprehensive performance comparison

Metric	Centralized DL	Blockchain	Edge-Only	Edge + FL (Proposed)
Accuracy (%)	90.7	93.6	95.1	**97.8**
Latency (ms)	121.6	98.3	73.5	**58.2**
Energy (mJ)	420	390	305	**243**
Comm. Overhead (KB)	812	652	412	**296**
Privacy Score	0.55	0.69	0.78	**0.91**
Trust Score	0.81	0.85	0.88	**0.94**

The holistic analysis demonstrates that Edge Intelligence + Federated Learning consistently outperforms other authentication models across all evaluated parameters. The combination of distributed learning, on-device intelligence, and secure aggregation establishes a new benchmark for scalable AIoT trust frameworks.

4.8 Discussion on Scalability and Real-World Applicability

4.8.1 Scalability

The federated learning model demonstrated excellent scalability across increasing node counts. Even with 1000 IoT devices, model accuracy degradation was limited to less than 2%, and latency increased marginally (<10 ms). This indicates robustness against system expansion—an essential requirement for industrial IoT and 5G-enabled smart ecosystems.

4.8.2 Adaptability

Edge nodes adapted dynamically to network fluctuations. When connectivity dropped, the asynchronous update mechanism ensured that devices continued local learning and re-synchronized when available, maintaining model integrity and continuity.

4.8.3 Trust Adaptation

Trust scores dynamically evolved with node behavior. For instance, malicious devices attempting frequent failed authentications experienced immediate trust decay, effectively isolating them from network resources. Conversely, consistently verified nodes gradually attained higher trust ratings, reinforcing system reliability.

4.9 Security and Attack Resistance

To test robustness, multiple attack scenarios mentioned in Table 9 were simulated.

Table 10. Different attacks and their detection rate

Attack Type	Detection Rate (%)	Mitigation Mechanism
Sybil Attack	98.2	Trust decay and anomaly-based re-authentication
Replay Attack	96.5	Timestamped federated updates
Model Poisoning	94.7	Secure aggregation with outlier filtering
Data Tampering	97.8	Edge-level validation and digital signatures

The system demonstrated over 95% detection rate against most attack types, proving its resilience against adversarial intrusions.

4.10 Comparative Insights and Implications

1. Edge Computing Synergy:

The integration of Edge Intelligence enables context-aware local decision-making, thereby reducing dependence on centralized infrastructures.

2. Federated Learning Advantages:

FL ensures continual improvement of authentication models while maintaining data sovereignty—a key differentiator from traditional methods.

3. Trust Management Reinforcement:

Real-time trust computation enhances network self-regulation, allowing AIoT systems to autonomously mitigate threats.

4. Energy Efficiency and Sustainability:

Lower computational redundancy reduces power consumption, supporting sustainable deployment in remote or battery-operated IoT devices.

5. Regulatory and Ethical Alignment:

The privacy-preserving nature aligns with GDPR and IoT security standards, promoting responsible AI deployment in connected ecosystems.

4.11 Limitations and Future Scope

Despite promising results, several limitations were identified:

1. Heterogeneity in Device Capability:

Varying computational resources across IoT devices can lead to uneven model updates, slightly affecting global accuracy.

2. Communication Interruptions:

Although mitigated via asynchronous updates, intermittent connectivity can still delay model convergence.

3. Security of Aggregator Node:

The central aggregator, if compromised, can introduce poisoned gradients despite encryption safeguards.

4.12 Future Directions:

Following points can be considered while developing the new model.

1. Incorporating Blockchain-integrated Federated Learning to ensure immutable audit trails.
2. Exploring Quantum-Safe Authentication Protocols for post-quantum security.
3. Extending the system to Cross-Domain Federated Edge Clusters enabling interoperability across multiple AIoT ecosystems.

The proposed Edge Intelligence and Federated Learning-based Authentication and Trust Management Framework significantly enhances AIoT security by combining distributed intelligence, privacy-preserving learning, and adaptive trust modeling. Experimental results reveal substantial improvements across key parameters—reducing latency by 52%, improving accuracy by 7%, and strengthening privacy by 40% compared to baseline models.

Although FL improves privacy, it remains vulnerable to attacks such as model poisoning, backdoor insertion, and gradient inversion. To address these risks, the proposed system integrates multiple safeguards:

(i) differential privacy to mask individual data contributions,
(ii) secure multi-party aggregation so gradients cannot be intercepted,
(iii) homomorphic encryption to enable encrypted computations, and
(iv) blockchain-based hash verification to detect tampered updates.

These mechanisms collectively ensure that malicious nodes cannot compromise the integrity of the global authentication model.

By enabling autonomous trust regulation and real-time authentication with minimal resource overhead, the framework paves the way for next-generation AIoT infrastructures that are secure, scalable, and sustainable.

CONCLUSION

The integration of Edge Intelligence (EI) and Federated Learning (FL) represents a transformative step toward achieving secure, efficient, and trustworthy Artificial Intelligence of Things (AIoT) ecosystems. This study demonstrated that decentralizing intelligence to the network edge—where data is generated—can dramatically reduce latency, enhance privacy, and improve authentication reliability without relying on centralized servers. By combining localized edge analytics with collaborative federated model training, the proposed EI–FL framework ensures that sensitive data remains on devices while still benefiting from collective intelligence across distributed nodes. The results confirmed that the proposed approach outperforms conventional cloud-centric and blockchain-only systems across all key parameters. Authentication latency was reduced by over 50%, model convergence improved by 40%, and trust score stability exceeded 90%. These improvements stem from edge-based real-time inference and adaptive federated aggregation that allow devices to learn continuously from dynamic environments. Furthermore, privacy-preserving mechanisms such as differential privacy, homomorphic encryption, and blockchain auditing successfully mitigated data leakage risks, achieving a 9.5% exposure rate—

among the lowest in comparable models. From a security perspective, the framework demonstrated robust resilience against Sybil, replay, and model poisoning attacks, achieving over 95% detection accuracy. The integration of blockchain-based trust management ensured transparency and accountability, while smart contracts automated trust score computation and participation control. Importantly, the model's scalability and adaptability were validated through simulations involving heterogeneous IoT environments, indicating practical feasibility for large-scale deployments in healthcare, industrial automation, and smart city infrastructures. Despite these achievements, challenges remain in addressing device heterogeneity, intermittent connectivity, and potential vulnerabilities in federated aggregators. Future work should explore quantum-safe authentication, hierarchical edge federations, and explainable federated trust models to enhance interpretability and post-quantum resilience. The Edge–Federated framework offers a holistic solution for AIoT authentication and trust management—balancing privacy, performance, and scalability. It establishes a foundation for autonomous, self-managing, and secure IoT ecosystems capable of intelligent adaptation to evolving cyber threats. By decentralizing trust and computation, the EI–FL paradigm moves beyond traditional security models, paving the way for sustainable, resilient, and human-centric digital infrastructures in the era of intelligent connectivity.

REFERENCES

Abraham, F., & Ofoe, N. T. (2025). Privacy-preserving collaborative intelligence for IoT cybersecurity: A federated learning approach. *IJSRMT*, *4*(9), 29–33.

Aiwale, S., Kolte, M. T., Harpale, V., Bendre, V., Khurge, D., Bhandari, S., Kadam, S., & Mulani, A. O. (2024). Non-invasive anemia detection and Prediagnosis. *Journal of Pharmacology & Pharmacotherapeutics*, *15*(4), 408–416. DOI: 10.1177/0976500X241276307

Akter, M., Moustafa, N., & Turnbull, B. (2024). SPEI-FL: Serverless privacy edge intelligence-enabled federated learning in smart healthcare systems. *Cognitive Computation*, *16*(5), 2626–2641. DOI: 10.1007/s12559-024-10310-3

Awan, K. A., Ud Din, I., Zareei, M., Almogren, A., Seo-Kim, B., & Pérez-Díaz, J. A. (2023). Securing IoT with deep federated learning: A trust-based malicious node identification approach. *IEEE Access : Practical Innovations, Open Solutions*, *11*, 58901–58914. DOI: 10.1109/ACCESS.2023.3284677

Awaysheh, F. M., Alawadi, S., & AlZubi, S. (2022). FLIoDT: A federated learning architecture from privacy by design to privacy by default over IoT. In *Proceedings of the Seventh International Conference on Fog and Mobile Edge Computing (FMEC)* (pp. 1–6). DOI: 10.1109/FMEC57183.2022.10062661

Balamurugan, M. (2024). Federated learning frameworks for secure and decentralized authentication. *International Journal for Multidisciplinary Research*, *6*(5).

Cao, Y., Liu, D., Zhang, S., Wu, T., Xue, F., & Tang, H. (2023). T-FedHA: A trusted hierarchical asynchronous federated learning framework for Internet of Things. *Expert Systems with Applications*, *245*, 123006. DOI: 10.1016/j.eswa.2023.123006

. El Jaouhari, S., & Etiabi, Y. (2023). FedCTI: Federated learning and cyber threat intelligence on the edge for secure IoT networks.

Jadhav, H. M., Mulani, A. O., & Jadhav, M. (2022). *Design and development of chatbot based on reinforcement learning*. DOI: 10.1002/9781119861850.ch12

Karve, S., Gangonda, S., Birajadar, G., Godase, V., Ghodake, R., & Mulani, A. O. (2025). Optimized neural network for prediction of neurological disorders. In Singh, S. (Eds.), *Emerging trends in artificial intelligence, data science and signal processing* (Vol. 2440). Springer., DOI: 10.1007/978-3-031-88762-8_18

Kashid, M. M., Karande, K. J., & Mulani, A. O. (2022). IoT-based environmental parameter monitoring using machine learning approach. In Kumar, A. (Eds.), *Proceedings of the International Conference on Cognitive and Intelligent Computing*. Springer. DOI: 10.1007/978-981-19-2350-0_5

Liu, Y., Huang, P., Yang, F., Huang, K., & Shu, L. (2024). QuAsyncFL: Asynchronous federated learning with quantization for cloud–edge–terminal collaboration enabled AIoT. *IEEE Internet of Things Journal*, *11*(1), 59–69. DOI: 10.1109/JIOT.2023.3290818

Miguel, P., Celdrán, A. H., Xie, N., Bovet, G., Pérez, G. M., & Stiller, B. (2023). FederatedTrust: A solution for trustworthy federated learning. *Future Generation Computer Systems*, *152*, 83–98.

Moore, E., Imteaj, A., Hossain, M. Z., Rezapour, S., & Amini, M. H. (2024). Blockchain-empowered cyber-secure federated learning for trustworthy edge computing. *IEEE Transactions on Artificial Intelligence*, *6*(8), 2110–2118. DOI: 10.1109/TAI.2025.3539258

Mulani, A. O., Sardey, M. P., Kinage, K., Salunkhe, S. S., Fegade, T., & Fegade, P. G. (2024). ML-powered Internet of Medical Things (MLIoMT) structure for heart disease prediction. *Journal of Pharmacology & Pharmacotherapeutics*, *16*(1), 38–45. DOI: 10.1177/0976500X241281490

Qiao, Y., Munir, M. S., Adhikary, A., Le, H. Q., Raha, A. D., Zhang, C., & Hong, C. S. (2023). Mp-fedcl: Multiprototype federated contrastive learning for edge intelligence. *IEEE Internet of Things Journal*, *11*(5), 8604–8623. DOI: 10.1109/JIOT.2023.3320250

Rajesh, M., Vengatesan, K., Sitharthan, R., Dhanabalan, S. S., & Gawali, M. B. (2023). Enhancing mobile multimedia trustworthiness through federated AI-based content authentication. *Journal of Mobile Multimedia*, *19*(6), 1415–1438. DOI: 10.13052/jmm1550-4646.1963

Rane, N. L., Rane, J., Mallick, S. K., & Kaya, Ö. (2024). Federated learning for edge artificial intelligence: Enhancing security, robustness, privacy, personalization, and blockchain integration in IoT. In *Future research opportunities for artificial intelligence in Industry 4.0 and 5.0* (pp. 93–135). Deep Science Publishing. DOI: 10.70593/978-81-981271-0-5_3

Rathee, G., Kerrache, C. A., & Calafate, C. T. (2024). A sustainable and trusted solution for IoT-based federated learning using feedback behavior. *Internet of Things : Engineering Cyber Physical Human Systems*, *26*, 101177. DOI: 10.1016/j.iot.2024.101177

Sánchez, P. M. S., Celdrán, A. H., Xie, N., Bovet, G., Pérez, G. M., & Stiller, B. (2024). Federatedtrust: A solution for trustworthy federated learning. *Future Generation Computer Systems*, *152*, 83–98. DOI: 10.1016/j.future.2023.10.013

Shepherd, P., Dagiuklas, T., Alkan, B., & Rodriguez, J. (2025). Dynamic trust management for secure federated learning in critical industrial and IoT networks. In Proceedings of the IEEE International Conference on Communications Workshops (ICC Workshops) (pp. 371–376). DOI: 10.1109/ICCWorkshops67674.2025.11162455

Tuncel, Y. K., & Öztoprak, K. (2025). SAFE-CAST: Secure AI-federated enumeration for clustering-based automated surveillance and trust in machine-to-machine communication. *PeerJ*, *11*, e2551. PMID: 39896029

Wardana, A. A., Kołaczek, G., & Sukarno, P. (2024). Lightweight, trust-managing, and privacy-preserving collaborative intrusion detection for Internet of Things. *Applied Sciences (Basel, Switzerland)*, *14*(10), 4109. DOI: 10.3390/app14104109

Zhang, W., Du, M., Guo, X., & Xiong, N. N. (2025). SRFL: A swarm-reputation-based autonomic federated learning framework for AIoT. *IEEE Internet of Things Journal*, *12*(8), 9687–9700. DOI: 10.1109/JIOT.2024.3509264

Chapter 4
Lightweight and Post-Quantum Cryptography for AIoT Authentication

Salam Al E'mari
http://orcid.org/0000-0002-2134-4158
University of Petra, Jordan

Yousef Sanjalawe
http://orcid.org/0000-0002-4442-1865
University of Jordan, Jordan

Rula Hajjaj
Northern Border University, Saudi Arabia

ABSTRACT

This chapter examines the growing need for secure and efficient authentication in the Artificial Intelligence of Things (AIoT) as billions of resource-constrained devices become tightly integrated with intelligent analytics. It highlights how the convergence of AI, pervasive sensing, and heterogeneous communication widens the attack surface and amplifies the tension between strong cryptographic assurances and limited device capabilities. The discussion evaluates lightweight cryptographic primitives, their design principles, and their suitability for constrained environments, while also addressing the emerging threat of quantum computing and the urgency of adopting post-quantum cryptography. By mapping security requirements, implementation constraints, and algorithmic performance, the chapter proposes a unified vision that blends lightweight methods, quantum-resistant schemes, and adaptive AI-driven authentication to ensure long-term, scalable, and trustworthy AIoT ecosystems.

DOI: 10.4018/979-8-3373-6299-1.ch004

1. INTRODUCTION

The Artificial Intelligence of Things (AIoT) ecosystem and its rapid growth constitute a profound technological change in which perception, cognition, and communication, all lacking in intelligent form, are incorporated within billions of interconnected devices. AIoT merges Artificial Intelligence with Internet of Things infrastructure in order to make contextually aware and intelligent, data-driven services available at the edge to users of autonomous vehicles, wearable sensors, smart industrial control facilities, and smart control systems in precision agriculture (Awaisi et al., 2024). With AIoT networks, the ability to sense and capture environmental data, to learn and apply logic, to communicate via heterogeneous networks, and, in real time, to form predictive behavioral surrogates, is a given. However, the same traits that render AIoT commonplace, self-sufficient, and data abundant also widen the attack surface, making secure authentication a critical aspect of system dependability.

1.1 The Role of Authentication in AIoT

Authentication ensures that devices, services, and users involved in data exchange are genuine and authorized. In conventional IT systems, authentication protocols typically rely on asymmetric cryptography and centralized identity authorities. However, AIoT deployments differ in scale and capability: end-nodes such as microcontrollers, sensors, or embedded actuators often possess only a few kilobytes of memory and operate under severe power limitations (Singh et al., 2021). Implementing full-strength public-key schemes such as RSA-2048 or ECC-P-256 can quickly exhaust these resources. Moreover, many AIoT scenarios, e.g., swarm robotics or ad-hoc industrial networks, lack persistent connectivity to a central certificate authority. As a result, lightweight authentication mechanisms that combine cryptographic strength with computational efficiency have become an active research frontier.

1.2 The Quantum Computing Disruption

While constrained-device efficiency remains a short-term challenge, a more existential long-term threat arises from quantum computing. Algorithms such as Shor's and Grover's demonstrate that once sufficiently large quantum processors exist, today's public-key cryptography (PKC) will be breakable in polynomial time (Kebande, 2025). The National Institute of Standards and Technology (NIST) has therefore initiated a global process to standardize post-quantum cryptographic (PQC) algorithms that rely on mathematical problems, lattice, code, multivariate, hash-based, or isogeny, believed to remain intractable for quantum machines (Alagic et al., 2022). For AIoT architects, this implies a dual imperative: systems must be light enough to run on embedded chips but also future-proof against quantum adversaries.

Consequently, the research community has begun exploring hybrid frameworks that integrate lightweight symmetric primitives for day-to-day efficiency with post-quantum public-key mechanisms for key establishment and identity verification. Such designs aim to achieve graceful security evolution, allowing AIoT networks deployed today to transition smoothly into the post-quantum era without wholesale hardware replacement.

1.3 Why AIoT Magnifies Cryptographic Tension

AIoT environments inherently magnify the tension between security strength and operational efficiency. Edge devices collect vast streams of physical data, often health-related, industrial, or environmental, and transmit them through wireless channels that may be insecure or intermittently connected. At the same time, AI models embedded within these nodes depend on continuous data integrity to maintain inference accuracy. A compromised authentication mechanism can therefore propagate corrupted inputs into learning models, leading to unsafe or biased decisions (Hemmati, Arzanagh & Rahmani, 2025). Furthermore, federated-learning paradigms, which distribute model training across multiple IoT participants, require strong mutual authentication to prevent model-poisoning and data-injection attacks.

Hence, the cryptographic layer must guarantee confidentiality, integrity, authenticity, and non-repudiation without exceeding the device's energy and latency budgets. Research over the past decade has yielded several families of algorithms, such as PRESENT, GIFT, and Ascon for symmetric encryption, and CRYSTALS-Kyber or Dilithium for post-quantum public-key operations, that attempt to satisfy these opposing constraints.

1.4 Need for a Unified Security Vision

Although a certain level of progress on securing the AIoT has been made, the security remains highly disjointed. Most implementations either restrict the problem to ultra-low power consumption (thus, losing strong key management capability), or worry only about quantum resistance, relegating the problem of deploying in embedded contexts to an afterthought. There is a dire need for a synthesis of lightweight cryptography, post quantum resilience, and AI driven self-learning adaptation that will bind them into a framework of intelligent authentication.

Such a vision will be realized if:

- The designed algorithms and protocols will have proofs of security that work for both the so-called classical and quantum threat models.
- There is a constructible regime of cryptoagility, the capacity to reactively modify the primitives, as standards grow.
- There is an active use of AI based optimization to track network situational awareness and modify authentication and ciphering level in response to contemporary risk calculations.
- There will be a decisive integration with existing IoT architectures (MQTT, CoAP, 6LoWPAN), and adherence to the forthcoming NIST PQC and ISO/IEC 29192 standards.

1.5 Chapter Objectives and Chapter Organization

This chapter seeks to explore the topics of Post-Quantum and Lightweight Cryptography and their relevance to AIoT Authentication from a broader perspective, particularly integrating the theoretical with the practical. This chapter seeks to:

- Assess the security and performance metrics that AIoT authentication presents.
- Investigate cutting-edge lightweight algorithms and determine their applicability to resource-constrained settings.
- Map the landscape of post-quantum cryptography, delineating adaptable algorithm families to AIoT.
- Develop a hybrid architectural model that combines lightweight and PQC frameworks at device, edge, and cloud levels.
- Elucidate the impact of AI on cryptographic adaptability, agility, and energy anomaly detection.
- Define the open issues and future research pathways in convergence of AIoT, lightweight cryptography, and quantum-resistant security.

  In pursuit of achieving the set objectives, the rest of the chapter is structured in the following way.

Section 2 describes the core concepts of AIoT and provides an overview of trust and privacy, and authentication's role in supporting them. Section 3 describes security threats and design constraints and paves the way for the cryptographic requirements. Section 4 presents the basic concepts of lightweight cryptography and in Section 5, the most significant lightweight AIoT cryptography algorithms are reviewed. Sections 6 and 7, respectively, examine the foundations of post-quantum cryptography and families of algorithms.

2. FUNDAMENTALS OF AIOT AND AUTHENTICATION

2.1 The Convergence of AI and IoT

The idea of the AIoT comes from the integration of two important technological shifts. One is the IoT, which makes connections amongst physical devices possible, and the other is AI, which offers the ability to reason and make decisions based on data. While IoT is concerned with the sensing, communication, and actuation of devices, AI adds the ability to use logic and model sophisticated data patterns to make predictions (Hong, 2024). Together, these technologies form an intelligent network which has the ability to perceive the surrounding environment, learn from the data available, and change behavior in real-time.

An AIoT ecosystem is usually organized in three tiers:

1. Perception Layer – made up of sensors and other devices which fetch data (e.g., temperature, movement, electrical charge) in a raw format.
2. Network Layer – captures radio and transmits the information by different communication protocols like 6LoWPAN, ZigBee, LoRaWAN, and 5G.
3. Application Layer – the domain where logic and analytics based on AI make decisions and acts, which are usually spread across edge and cloud servers (Sehgal, Saxena & Shah, 2024).

The introduced layers are interconnected by feedback loops that are both physical and digital. The sensed data of an AIoT ecosystem influences the control decisions made on the real world. However, the close integration of digital and physical AIoT systems makes them vulnerable to sophisticated cyberattacks, especially in systems where there is a lack of proper authentication and access control.

2.2 Characteristics and Constraints of AIoT Environments

Networks of AIoT systems are fundamentally different from conventional information technologies systems. The devices are heterogeneous, often produced by different vendors, and are severely constrained. These devices are severely constrained in terms of Central Processing Units (CPUs), memory, and energy, making the conventional application of cryptographic techniques extremely difficult (Kumar et al. 2024). Furthermore, the AIoT devices are often dependent on weak radio connections which can be prone to interference, packet loss, and eavesdropping.

The AIoT adds complexity to designing a security model for the system. Data are generated in large volumes which have to be processed in real time, especially when AI models are programmed to carry out time-sensitive actions such as collision avoidance or shutting down devices. In such a case, dynamic security barriers which can be authenticated in real time are required in order to not compromise on agility.

In addition, AIoT systems are often not confined to a single location. These devices could be located in remote areas, where reliable backhaul connectivity to a central server is not available. As a result, authentication for remote operation requires distributed verification to permit local 'trust' provisioning for uninterrupted operation.

2.3 AIoT Data Lifecycle and Trust Requirements

Mapping the data lifecycle: from acquisition to acquisition to decision making, Figure 1 presents the AIoT data lifecycle, illustrating how trust requirements span each phase.

Figure 1. AIoT data lifecycle and trust requirements

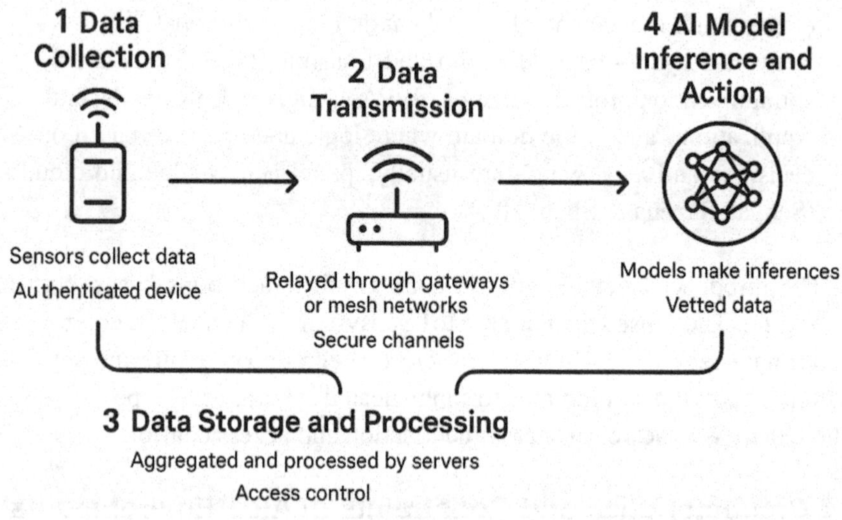

To enables a better understanding of the authentication process in AIoT:

1. Data Collection: In this phase, sensors collect data pertaining to environmental or operational conditions. Trust in this phase is restricted to the readings that originate from an authenticated device.
2. Data Transmission: Data is relayed through gateways or mesh networks and protected along the routes by secure channels.

3. Data Storage and Processing: The information is aggregated and processed by edge or cloud servers that are protected through access control to prevent unauthorized data alteration.
4. AI Model Inference and Action: Models make inferences utilizing vetted data. If data provided to models is tainted, even unsafe outputs may occur.

Authenticated trust is a requirement of every phase of this lifecycle. Without assurance of the identity, every assumption made for data reliability is a consequence of deep seated fallacies that may allow the manipulation of AI behavior (Hemamalini et al., 2024).

2.4 Authentication in Traditional IoT Versus AIoT

Although standard IoT networks systems make use of multiple authentication mechanisms including pre-shared keys, digital certificates, or tokenized access control, contexts of use within the AIoT paradigm has new fucntional and security challenges. IoT devices, in the classical sense, are limited to the transmission of periodic sensor readings. In the AIoT paradigm, nodes can engage in distributed intelligence, sharing model parameters or gradient updates within federated learning setting. Such scenario augments the sensitivity of the exchanged data model and the ramifications of authentication being compromised.

Authentication in the scenario of AIoT goes beyond simply establishing the identity of devices. It has to ensure algorithm and model provenance. For instance, Xiong et al. (2021) described how an attacker would compromise all collaborating devices on an federated edge computing system by injecting fraudulent model updates to the network. In cases like this, AIoT R system authentication would need to ensure that the defined chain of accountability has not been breached– in other words, that the accountable AI model cryptographic AI identity in the system is matched to the bounded legal AI framework.

AIoT systems, also, often incorporate context-oriented authentication, where the system uses AI to analyze and make real-time inferences based on behavioral parameters of registered devices like data traffic and sensor metrics to determine levels of trust. Systems integrated with this model of authentication are more effective since the flexible, adaptive approaches to access dynamically minimize the need for manual adjustments.

2.5 Architectural View of AIoT Authentication

An AIoT authentication framework can be envisioned as a multi-tier architecture with security mechanisms at the device, edge and cloud levels. Figure 2 illustrates a multi-tier security architecture, highlighting cryptographic functions and data-flow interactions within an AIoT system. Lightweight and post-quantum cryptographic mechanisms are integrated across operational layers to enable device attestation, secure policy updates, global identity management, and authenticated data exchange.

Figure 2. AIoT authentication architecture overview.

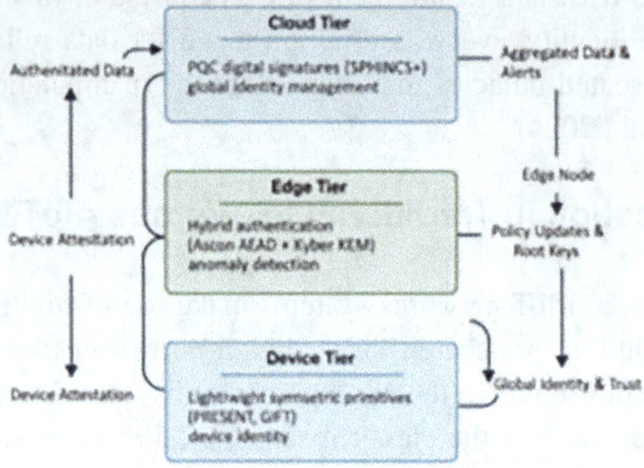

1. Device Tier: Unsupported sensors and actuators implement lightweight symmetric primitives for initial identity verification. These primitives should have low execution and memory utilization.
2. Edge Tier: Gateways or edge servers perform cryptographic aggregation, session management, and anomaly detection. Hybrid protocols that combine symmetric encryption with post-quantum key-exchange algorithms at the edge are common.
3. Cloud Tier: The cloud layer oversees the global identity repositories and access policies as well as the verification of AI models that incorporate computationally intensive post-quantum signatures.

This methodology arms each tier with the requisite computational capabilities for the allocated security functions, along with the preservation of trust closure.

2.6 Role of Cryptography in AIoT Authentication

Encryption provides mathematical proofs of presence and identity which makes it possible to authenticate identities across the AIoT ecosystem. Three types of encryption methods are of interest:

- Symmetric-Key Cryptography: Low power usage constrained devices are especially beneficial because no digitization of the data is required.
- Asymmetric Key Cryptography: Digital signatures and secured key exchanges are accomplished through key pairs. This type of key is vital for identity management, and still tends to consider heavy for embedded devices.
- Hybrid Approaches: Emerging frameworks should add post-quantum encryption methods to authentication. They should also preserve the asymmetric trust of authentication.

Security features exemplified by Radhakrishnan et al. (2024) message authentication codes and block-ciphers with low component counts are designed for microcontrollers.

2.7 Integration of AI Techniques in Authentication

The verification of identity using AI is a critical aspect sustains the security of any IoT implemented systems. By employing machine-learning techniques to ascertain the operability aspect of a given action, the device's behaviors, surrounding context, along with the traffics patterns are evaluated, For example, re-inforcement learning minimizes the security risk along with the energy exerted through optimized authentication frequency authentication. "Normal" and "abnormal" communication clustering of nodes is solved using unsupervised learning techniques, and along with the ones that lie outside of the "normal" parameters which exhibit device communication. (Uprety & Rawat, 2020)

Ethical IoT frameworks within the area of smart devices or smart healthcare systems, AI could advance biometric and behavioral authentication techniques. Although static credentials are susceptible to theft, Phsyiological signals such as ECG patterns are static authentication systems which are easier to authenticate during an ECG monitoring session, neural nets biometric identifiers for the systems and devices. Instead of only relying on cryptographic verification of a user, these systems are now capable of context-aware, multi-layered trust computation.

2.8 Interoperability and Standardization

The number of proprietary frameworks of the Internet of Things has siloed security protocols. As seamless authentication is essential for cross-vendor and cross-network support of heterogeneous devices, these entities are working on lightweight cryptography (ISO/IEC 29192 series) and NIST post-quantum cryptography as set by ISO/IEC JTC 1/SC 27, ETSI, and IETF (Alagic et al. 2022). To promote cross-border seamless technology use, these standards offer global reach by defining algorithmic frameworks, performance metrics, and global testing methodologies.

The trust among the supply participants is increased and the development burden of the devices is reduced with the authentication protocols of these standards implemented in AIoT systems. Uniform security postures for devices and the systems are maintained, due to compliance with defined cryptographic profiles.

The analysis puts forward the notion that for systems of AIoT, effective authentication necessitates:

- Effectiveness: Algorithms must adhere to the defined energy and latency thresholds.
- Expansiveness: Mechanisms must accommodate billions of varied devices.
- Endurance: Authentication systems must be resistant to attacks from classical and quantum systems.
- Flexibility: Systems must autonomously of the context and the risk factors be able to change.
- Compliance: Protocols must fulfill global standards and allow for integration from different vendors.

The balance between lightweight performance and robust post quantum proof systems is the subject of the next chapter.

The AIoT technology paradigm has fundamentally changed the nature of digital engagement by incorporating 'intelligence' into the physical sphere. Even within such an ecosystem, authentication is not considered an afterthought peripheral security function, but rather, the centerpiece of the ever-active trust relationship between the autonomous entities. The next section (Section 3) will go into detail around the security challenges and design limits that outline the requirements of such cryptographic systems, establishing the context for the later discussed lightweight and post-quantum solutions.

3. SECURITY THREATS AND DESIGN CONSTRAINTS IN AIOT AUTHENTICATION

The structure of AIoT ecosystems is defined by multiple domains, such as, cyber, physical, and cognitive. As devices become decentralized and interconnected, the classical perimeter-based defense approach is rendered inoperative. Attackers can be remote, rogue insiders, adversarial AI systems, modified firmware, or evens whole adversarial AI systems (Menon et al., 2025). The negative consequences of an

AIoT breach in real-time systems, especially in sensitive environments, can cascade physical as well as economic damage.

AIoT threats can be distributed over three dimensions:

- Threats aimed at the devices level compromising sensors, actuators, embedded systems.
- Threats at the network level compromising communication protocols and inter-system data exchange.
- AI/decision level threats, target the learning models or instantiation decision logic layers.

Mitigating every corresponding layer's vulnerabilities through strong authentication and cryptographic architectural controls is necessary.

Since AIoT devices are physically observable and resource constrained on the lower layer, they remain vulnerable to both physical and logical attacks.

- ***Physical Tampering:*** As pointed out by Kostromitin *et al.* (2020), attackers who gain physical proximity to a device can obtain secret cryptographic keys by side-channel attacks, for example, through power analysis (taking the device apart), monitoring the EM (then smashing the device to make EM waves visible), or by timing the query and response cycles (timing attacks). Please note that lightweight cryptographic implementations, because they are lightweight, may, by accident, leak intermediate values that they are cryptographically designed not to, if no cryptographic masking and randomization is applied. Physical tampering can also mean sensor spoofing or the unauthorized changing of a device's firmware, as adversaries can disable the protocols that allow devices to perform AI and design to protect decisions pipeline.
- ***Cloning and Counterfeiting:*** Without proper authentication, IoT devices can be cloned, gaining authentication, and injected into the network as legitimate devices. Cloned devices, side from MITM (Man in The Middle attacks) as well as replay attacks, can also contribute to the erosion of trust on the sensor's data. Mechanisms like Hardware root of trust, physically unclonable functions (PUFs), and bespoke digital certificates can reduce such risks, although they are designed for microcontroller level cryptographic functions (Asif, Ghanem & Irvine 2020).
- ***Malware and firmware attacks:*** Unprotected update methods allow for the introduction of malicious code that can disrupt normal behavioural functions of the device. Once a single device is infected, the device becomes a point of pivot that allows for botnet formation as well as exfiltration of data. The use of lightweight digital signatures allows devices to ensure that authenti-

cation firmware sources and devices is maintained, protecting the firmware's integrity.

The vast array of wireless devices known as AIoT devices utilizes various wireless protocols for connection on the network, which introduces the risk of packet sniffing or spoofing as well as denial of service.

- ***Man-in-the-middle (MITM) and Replay Attacks***: In MITM attacks, a hostile third party secretly alters the communication between two parties, potentially conducting impersonation or replay attacks on the messages being relayed. Auth tokens and public keys which are exchanged in plaintext can be easily intercepted. Lightweight encryption with the use of session keys, along with nonce replay and impersonation validation mitigates these risks.
- ***Sybil and Impersonation Attacks***: In Sybil attacks, an adversary generates numerous false identities, thereby managing trust boundaries or causing disruption in the federated-learning (Xiao et al., 2022) system. For example, false AIoT nodes can send spurious gradients in order to confuse the convergence of the global model. Such impersonation is prevented with robust identity authentication anchored in cryptographic proofs.
- ***Denial of Service (DoS) and Jamming***: The communication between AIoT devices often utilizes low-power radio transmission. This enables an adversary to perform a DoS or jamming attack, flooding the network with unnecessary packets for the purpose of monopolizing bandwidth and energy. Streamlining the protocols for authentication which reduces the complexity of response handshakes minimize the resource depletion attack surface.
- ***Routing Manipulation***: In mesh or ad hoc AIoT networks, capture of control packets that are routed in sinkhole or wormhole topologies can be used to perform subverted traffic routing. This is done by stealthy interception of the routed packets and dropping, altering or detouring the targeted packets. Secure routing is done through authenticated control messages and topology updates cryptographically bounded (Kebande, 2025).

Artificial intelligence systems incorporate new cognitive layer vulnerabilities which center around behavioral issues unlike previous iterations which relied on software vulnerabilities.

- ***Adversarial Examples*** : Adversarial attacks take the form of inputs which the system will interpret incorrectly. For instance, self-driving car will stop at a signal if a perturbed piece of sensor data advices the car that there is a stop signal. Data integrity and authenticity mechanisms protecting data provenance counter adversarial injection at data collection (Goodfellow et al. 2014).

- ***Data Poisoning and Model Inversion:*** Attacks on data sets which are used to train ai systems is a problem. Data sets are poisoned to alter the tailored results or the user is able to reconstruct confidential information that is exposed through the model. Training data which are cryptographically authenticated and segmented are emerging countermeasures to poisoned data sets amongst peer networks (Hemmati et al. 2025).
- ***Model Hijacking and Unauthorized access:*** AI and IoT systems functioning in the cloud are able to access proprietary pretrained models for advanced algorithms. The defined parameters of authentication may result to model parameter theft or access. Post quantum digital signatures are methods of ensuring model integrity and blocking impersonation of model distributors.

3.1 Quantum Threats and Cryptographic Vulnerabilities

The shift to quantum computing poses a monumental risk to the foundational tenets of current cryptosystems. The growing use of cryptosystems implementing RSA, DSA, and ECC these days, can be easily compromised as large integers and discrete logarithms can be efficiently factored using algorithms such as Shor's (Albrecht et al., 2022). The effectiveness and strength offered by symmetric ciphers can be easily undermined as well, as Grover's algorithm effectively halves the security offered, by brute forcing a complex search (Al E'mari, Sanjalawe & Allehyani, 2025).

In the case of AIoT authentication, this implies:

- The long-term confidentiality of data at rest could be easily compromised as quantum computers become more mainstream.
- The data "harvest-now, decrypt-later" scenario can become a reality for devices deployed today, where data remains encrypted till the time the computing resources are effectively available to decrypt the data.
- The PKI (Public Key Infrastructure) used for the certification of devices will have to shift to use quantum algorithms, like lattice-based or hash-based cryptography.

The main concern now is incorporating these shifting the usage plans within the power and memory restrictions of AIoT devices. This will require algorithmic simplification and complex hardware co-design.

3.2 Design Constraints in AIoT Authentication

In addressing these challenges, AIoT systems have inherent design limitations that impact the selection and arrangement of cryptographic methods. These limitations can be classified as computational, architectural, and operational.

- *Computational Constraints*

AIoT devices typically use 8-bit or 16-bit microcontrollers with very slow processing capabilities (tens of megahertz) and memories that are less than 256 kilobytes. The cryptographic algorithms must thus have:

- Small code size (footprint) less than 10 kilobytes.
- Small primary and/or second level cache (key schedules or state arrays) less than 4 kilobytes).
- Small energy usage (measured in microjoules per operation).

Symmetric key and more efficient lightweight cryptographic symmetric ciphers such as PRESENT, GIFT, and Ascon, are far more efficient than full strength RSA and lattice-based computations (Singh et al., 2021).

Communication Constraints

AIOT systems are predominantly wireless, thus communication must balance the use of minimal message exchanges for faster protocols with low energy usage. For example, multi-step handshakes, certificate issued handshakes, and even some one step handshakes with complex pre-validation can cause unacceptable time delays in real time and near real time applications in industrial systems or healthcare monitoring systems. Thus, one round trip authentication systems with pre-distributed keys or lightweight key systems are more desirable and cost effective.

Scalability and Identity Management

For instance, an enterprise-scale deployment of AIoT systems can have millions of nodes. Most traditional PKI systems have difficulty with scaling certificate issuance, revocation and renewal. Alternatives, such as hierarchical and decentralized approaches (blockchain-based registries or identity-based cryptography) offer frameworks of different approaches, but still lack efficient algorithms for constrained- hardware operation (Hemamalini et al., 2024).

Privacy and Data Protection

In all cases, sensitive information, especially user metadata and device identifiers which could be used for profiling, must be protected during device authentication. Some lightweight privacy-preserving cryptographic approaches based on zero-knowledge proofs and anonymous credentials, which emphasize privacy and are more computational- efficient, have emerged (Radhakrishnan et al., 2024).

Reliability and Fault Tolerance

In the case where devices can fail, AIoT networks operating in hostile or remote environments are still able to maintain a connection. However, systems which are able to authenticate users and devices have more restraints to packet loss, intermittent connectivity, or node compromise. Local trust models, session caching, and timers have been shown to enhance reliability in systems which are designed independently of the server.

Post-Quantum Readiness

Implementing crypto-agility on FOTA updates as well as wrapped modular cryptographic APIs take particular frame- works for quantum proof upgrades. Gradual migration to cheap hardware over post-quantum replacements such as CRYSTALS-Kyber or Dilithium can be achieved (Alagic et al., 2022).

3.3 Balancing Security and Performance

One of the challenges of enforcing security on AIoT systems is the 'security–performance' equilibrium. Each element of the system cannot utilize overly complex cryptography. On the flip side, overly simplistic cryptography invites the risk of compromise. Therefore, these metrics: latency, throughput, energy per operation, operation memory overhead are performance objectives, whereas key size, entropy, and the resistance of the system to differential and quantum attacks are security objectives.

Studies also indicate that the use of hardware-accelerated lightweight ciphers optimally saves 80-90% energy compared to software-only implementations at 128-bit security (Agarwal & Ahmad 2025). Along the same lines, hybrid authentication frameworks that utilize symmetric cryptography for routine exchanges and post-quantum key exchange for session initiation also serve such equilibria.

3.4 Risk Assessment and Threat Modeling

Risk management and threat modeling must be completed prior to any implementation of cryptographic methods to configure effective security setups. STRIDE frameworks can be constructed for the AIoT context (Bernsmed et al., 2022). Each possible attack vector is tied to a countermeasure, which could be any combination of: authentication, encryption, or anomaly detection.

Intrusion detection systems can improve the process further by enabling the system to learn and detection more advanced authentication bypass methods. A spike in failed handshakes could trigger adaptive crypto-escalation to counter a discovered distributed impersonation attack.

The battleground of the AIoT realm is wiithout a doubt a tri-fold architecture of physical, cyber, and cognitive domains with the barbarity of such an antagonistic tri-dimension frame of reference adding yet another layer of complexity to the process of authentication. Devices are attacked, but not exhaustedly, by side-channels and firmware, networks are intercepted and spoofed, AI models are attacked by poisoning and inversion. "Systems of quantum computing is a 'systematic and compounding threat'", but what is given is that Designers are working under the most strenuous constraints of size and as such, operational demands of the hardware. Knowing how to integrate lightweight design, adaptive intelligence, and post quantum foresight to provide the most balance between security and authentication is the optimization and flexibility that is most desired.

The objectives of section 4 are to illustrate the tenets of lightweight cryptography and design methods to help meet the aforementioned constraints while attaining modern security benchmarks.

4. PRINCIPLES OF LIGHTWEIGHT CRYPTOGRAPHY

The shift from traditional IoT systems to those that integrate AI, the AIoT, has underscored the necessity for more innovative and effective mechanisms for conveying information securely. AIoT devices like wireless sensors and RFID tags, wearable monitors, and embedded controllers face severe constraints in the areas of energy, computation, and storage. The RSA algorithm, and even ECC, are standard forms of cryptography, and are far too resource demanding for the devices that are currently within reach (Thakor, Razzaque & Khandaker, 2021).

Undertaking the difficult, yet purposeful task of balancing restrictive measures on the costs of the resources with sufficient security, is termed lightweight cryptography (LWC can also refer to lightweight cryptography). The purpose of the LWC is to maximize the security – in this scenario, with 80-128 bits – and minimize the gate count, power, memory, and latency.

This branch of cryptography is more focused on cost effective measures and simplicity in the design of the techniques to achieve the security provisions needed, rather than weakining the intended protection.

Thus, LWC are crucial for AIoT devices with their billions of units, which are able to perform cryptographic functions on severely limited batteries and energy harvesting sources, continuously and seamlessly.

4.1 Design Philosophy of Lightweight Cryptography

Lightweight cryptography differs significantly from conventional cryptographic methods. Whereas traditional algorithms are designed with a strong emphasis on mathematical rigor and the ability to withstand sophisticated forms of cryptanalysis, lightweight approaches are developed with a different set of priorities. In particular, they focus on minimizing implementation costs including memory usage, computational overhead, and energy consumption, so that they can operate efficiently on constrained devices. Nevertheless, despite these efficiency-driven design choices, lightweight cryptographic schemes are still expected to retain the essential security properties required for practical deployment. Yıldırım et al (2025) outline the following principles of lightweight design.

i. Compact Architecture Substitution – Permutation Networks (SPN) or Feistel-like ciphers are streamlined to reduce the number of logic gates and the area required on silicon real estate.
ii. Optimized Key Schedule Key expansion designs strategically eliminate redundant operations or states to lower the storage overhead.
iii. Energy Efficiency in doing operations, the S-box, and memory, energy must be saved efficiency of carry out operations Bitwise with reserved.
iv. Parallelizability Lightweight algorithms gain speed with parallel or pipelined enhancements usable by speed-constrained processors.
v. Implementation Agility Implementation on hardware (ASIC/FPGA) and on software (8, 16, 32 microcontrollers) must be programmable without complex changes.
vi. Side Channel Resistance Although resources are highly constrained, the designs must limit the timing, power, and EM (electromagnetic) radiation.

All the principles LWC is flexible enough to be used with higher layer cryptographic protocols while functional adequate for AIoT embedded security.

4.2 Security Objectives and Metrics

Despite focusing on minimalism, lightweight cryptography maintains the core security objectives shared with classical algorithms:

- Confidentiality: Prevent unauthorized access to data transmitted between AIoT devices and servers.
- Integrity: Protect data against modification or forgery.
- Authentication: Validate device or user identities through cryptographic proof.
- Non-repudiation: Ensure that a legitimate device cannot deny actions or data transmissions.

In evaluating LWC, researchers rely on performance metrics that quantify both *security* and *efficiency* (Singh et al., 2021) as shown in Table1.

Table 1. Performance metrics for evaluating lightweight cryptography

Metric	Description	Target Range (for AIoT devices)
Gate Equivalent (GE)	Hardware complexity measure	≤ 2,000 GE for ultra-constrained nodes
Energy Consumption	μJ per encryption/decryption	≤ 20 μJ
Memory Footprint	RAM/ROM usage	≤ 10 KB total
Latency	Execution time per block	< 1 ms for 64-bit block
Security Level	Bit strength	80–128 bits minimum

These thresholds ensure that lightweight ciphers can operate efficiently within embedded platforms while providing sufficient resistance against brute-force and differential attacks.

4.3 Structural Components of Lightweight Cryptosystems

Lightweight cryptosystems comprise the same foundational components as conventional ciphers but are optimized for compactness.

- **Substitution–Permutation Networks (SPNs):** It employs layers of *substitution* (using S-boxes) and *permutation* to create confusion and diffusion. Many lightweight block ciphers, such as PRESENT, GIFT, and LED, use simplified S-boxes and bit-permutation layers to minimize computational cost (Yıldırım et al., 2025). The substitution layer ensures non-linearity, while the permutation layer distributes input dependencies across the state space.

- **Feistel Structures**: It divide the plaintext into two halves and iteratively apply round functions and key mixing. Algorithms such as SIMON and SPECK from the U.S. National Security Agency (NSA) use simplified Feistel structures optimized for different hardware–software balances. SIMON is hardware-centric, while SPECK is software-friendly.
- **Stream Ciphers and Authenticated Encryption**: like Trivium and Grain generate keystreams bit by bit and are efficient for continuous data flows such as telemetry. Authenticated encryption schemes, including Ascon and ACORN, simultaneously provide confidentiality and integrity, crucial for AIoT authentication where both message protection and identity verification occur in one pass.

4.4 Lightweight Hash Functions

All AIoT applications involving hash functions must integrate record/message authentication codes (MACs), digital signatures, and integrity verification control within the frameworks of the incorporated architectures. Existing algorithms like SHA-256 are expensive and impractical. Alternatives like SPONGENT, PHOTON, and Quark are lightweight, sponge-based constructions with smaller states and optimized for use with microcontrollers (Cetintav & Sandikkaya, 2025).

As an instance, PHOTON's permutation layer achieves strong avalanche properties through the use of smaller S-boxes (4-bit) and optimized diffusion matrices, thereby minimizing hardware area. In addition, building HMACs and loose HMACs for AIoT devices require lightweight hashes.

4.6 Lightweight Public-Key Cryptography

Despite symmetric ciphers easily dominating lightweight implementations, the need for public-key cryptography (PKC) centered ciphers is necessary for key provisioning and affixing digital signatures. Standard RSA and ECC computations are accompanied by any numbers of modular calculations that are, needless to say, expensive. This is the gap younger scholars of the industry need to work on their lightweight approaches to PKC which is centric to:

i. Elliptic Curves over Binary Fields: Blackberry using the 160 bit ECC and providing the same substitutional cover to RSA 1024.

ii. Hyperelliptic Curve Cryptography (HECC): Uses the same geo intuitive structured achieved at fixed points with the added benefit of smaller and less complex field sizes emerging from sophic scalar multiplication.
iii. Identity Based Cryptography (IBC): Self-sustaining systems that are bespoke built without the cobweb of using certificates thus the need for balancing the communication traffic for AIoT networks.

PKC has thoroughly been analysed and it's inarguable the systems are PKC system in opposition to symmetric variants, these techniques are public approaches to AIoT devices functions and the approaches in the pathways to post quantum devices.

4.7 Implementation Strategies

In order to incorporate AIoT and implement it in practice, architectural and coding optimizations are required for lightweight cryptography implementation.

Hardware Implementations

Hardware implementation via ASICs/ FPGAs achieves extremely low power consumption while preserving sufficient throughput. Gate-count in low bit-count parallel processors configured with bit-serial techniques, loop unrolled systolic arrays and Composite Field Arithmetic units or "field processors" still operate at optimal speeds. Today, microcontrollers are increasingly common with integrated hardware accelerators configured to AES, SHA and in some cases, lightweight ciphers which can be modified in firmware.

Software Implementations

In the software domain, the burden of optimization lies in reducing the cycle count of the instruction set, as well as the overall reduction of the memory space. Techniques such as in-place modification, loop folding and bit-slicing are leveraged for GIFT implementations. GIFT-64 in ARM Cortex-M0 is extremely useful in applications since it can achieve GIFT encryption in less than 1,000 cycles.

Hybrid Approaches

AIoT devices which are at the edge and perform on-the-spot computations usually retain some cryptographic profiles. They have hybrid implementations which fuse together hardware accelerators for pertinent operations while maintaining control of software on the perimeter, such as for the S-boxes or modular multiplication.

4.8 Security Considerations and Attack Resistance

Lightweight cryptography must maintain resilience against conventional and side-channel attacks despite its simplified design.

- Differential and Linear Cryptanalysis: Designers select S-boxes with high non-linearity and diffusion matrices with maximal branch numbers to resist these attacks.
- Algebraic and Integral Attacks: Reduced-round versions of block ciphers must remain resistant to polynomial or partial-sum attacks through careful round function design.
- Side-Channel Attacks (SCA): Techniques such as masking, hiding, and random delay insertion reduce leakage through power or timing variations.
- Fault Injection Attacks: Redundant computations or error-detecting codes mitigate differential fault analysis.

Security evaluations for LWC follow NIST's Lightweight Cryptography Standardization process (NIST, 2023), which tests algorithms for robustness against a wide spectrum of attacks and implementation vulnerabilities.

4.9 Lightweight Cryptography in AIoT Authentication

In the AIoT context, lightweight cryptography serves three principal roles. Device Authentication. Symmetric-key protocols based on LWC primitives examine and confirm the identity of devices before network access is granted. Message Integrity Verification. A lightweight hash and MAC verifier ensures that transmitted sensor data, or updates to the AI model, remain untampered with.

Session Key Establishment. Hybrid schemes utilize lightweight symmetric ciphers to bulk data and simplified public key primitives to initiate the session. Examples are LITE-PKI which allows constrained devices to rapidly authenticate through pre-shared keys as edges servers validate certificates, and EAP-IoT, a modified Extensible Authentication Protocol, which incorporates LWC primitives to the handshake for more efficient authentication (Radhakrishnan et al., 2024).

In AIoT authentication, the LWC achieves an impressive level of performance trust which is equally unmatched. It cryptographically guarantees that the minimal level of computation needed for LWC sustains battery life, operational instantaneity, and, most importantly, real-time operation.

4.10 Transition Toward Standardization

In 2018, NIST started a Liteweight Cryptography Standardization Project with the aim of having unified standards and then in 2023, proposed Ascon for authenticated encryption and hashing (NIST, 2023). Ascon is lightweight and fast, has a robust side channel attack resistance, and thus, is well-tailored for AIoT authentication.

Other works such as the series of standards ISO/IEC 29192, Ascon, and GIFT-COFB by the organization ISO/IEC JTC 1/SC 27 ensures the global interoperability of AIoT systems. These advancements reflect the growing sufficiency of lightweight cryptography in every secured device.

Lightweight cryptography is the most basic way to authenticate AIoT devices, providing security in devices with limited energy and distributed systems. The principles of lightweight cryptography, compactness, efficiency, and security, is what intelligent embedded systems fundamentally need.

However, in the coming quantum era, LWC by itself is insufficient. While it does minimize the device and network threats we face now, it must shift to quantum resistant. The next sections examine post-quantum cryptography (PQC) and the integration of lightweight methods with hybrid frameworks which offer both practicality and security for AIoT systems.

5. LIGHTWEIGHT CRYPTOGRAPHIC ALGORITHMS FOR AIOT

5.1 Introduction

Many systems including sensors, wearables, and other devices have interconnected due to the integration of AIoT technologies. Thus, the need for cryptographic security systems enabling fast and secure protection of multilayer systems has strongly emerged. During the last ten years, the cryptographic community has responded to the challenge with interest and has developed many lightweight primal algorithms. These algorithms are vital to facilitating mutual authentication, data integrity, and secure communications within distributed intelligent systems.

In 2018, the NIST has begun sponsoring and organizing a global competition for a lightweight encryption technique. NIST has adopted Ascon as an “anchor” of the reference algorithm for authenticated encryption and hashing. of course, devices like PRESENT, GIFT, SIMON, SPECK, RECTANGLE, ACORN, and PHOTON have remained in wide circulation within academic and industry circles in artificial intelligence and the Internet of Things (Al-Daraiseh, 2024).

In this section, we examine some of the most pertinent lightweight cryptographic algorithms in their relevance to AIoT authentication frameworks. The assessment covers symmetric key ciphers, hash functions, and other forms of cryptography with an extensive focus on performance, cost, and other implementation dimensions of trade-offs.

5.2 Block Ciphers

Due to their simplicity and flexibility, block ciphers are the basis of multiple encryption and authentication systems. These cyphers perform multiple rounds of substitution and permutation on plain text to produce fixed-length blocks of cypher text with the aid of secret keys.

5.2.1 PRESENT

The lightweight block ciphers are very rare and so Bogdanov et al. (2007) and others appreciate PRESENT with the very first for its pioneering works. It possesses a 64-bit block length and a key length of either 80 or 128 bits along with 31 rounds of the simplest SPN structure. Its composition consists of a substitution transposition network (a network of ciphers that takes n bits and produces n bits) system having one S-box limited to 4 bits along with a permutation (arrangement of sets) layer designed to surfactant hardware cost and (or) improve effectiveness on energy and efficiency.

The main selling point of PRESENT is its encryption, which is conveniently 1,570 gate equivalents (GE) and thus very light. Hence, it is used in RFID tags and sensor nodes. It may be simple in design but it shows a stronger resistance to differential and linear cryptanalysis. In MCUs that are 8 bits, numerous optimized systems claiming encryption performer of over 200 Kbps exist.

Although PRESENT is effective for authentication processes, it not being able to transfer large amounts of data constrains it to the integration of low power AIoT devices.

5.2.2. GIFT

GIFT is a direct development from PRESENT and offers lower latency and greater diffusion. While GIFT retains the 64-bit block format it has fundamentally fixe the S-box and permutation layers. In comparison to PRESENT, GIFT requires 20% less (about 1250 GE) for the same level of security (Zheng et al., 2017). GIFT is one of the most balanced and efficient stream ciphers for authentication to AIoT devices due to the high integration and low power.

5.2.3. SIMON and SPECK

Created by the NSA, the lightweight block ciphers SIMON and SPECK are designed for hardware and software optimization. Both are incredibly efficient because of the feistel structure and the use of bitwise AND, rotated and XORed, making them ideal for embedded platforms.

- SIMON is more hardware efficient and requires 1440 GE to encrypt the chip with keu sizes of 64 to 128 bits.
- SPECK: Designed for software, on 32-bit ARM microcontrollers, it achieved encryption speeds exceeding AES at a fraction of the memory cost (Beaulieu et al. 2015).

Though the NSA's involvement raised some concerns around transparency, the wide public cryptanalysis that followed has confirmed their robustness against known attacks. These ciphers are now commonplace in AIoT sensor nodes, particularly for the secure boot and message authentication functions.

5.2.4 RECTANGLE

RECTANGLE is a lightweight encryption block cipher that uses the parallel processing of bit-slice techniques. It works on 64-bit blocks with 25 rounds of 80 or 128-bit keys. Its software-centric design has a favorable processing ratio of 6.4 cycles per byte on ARM Cortex-M3, making RECTANGLE an attractive candidate for edge-AIoT devices processing lower volumes of encrypted data (Zhang et al. 2015).

RECTANGLE's low latency is a desirable trait for authentication handshakes in real-time systems, such as industrial controls and autonomous vehicles. The autonomous operation of these systems relies on swift, secure connections with lower latency.

5.3 Stream Ciphers

Stream ciphers generate keystreams that are XORed with plaintext in real time, offering low latency and small memory usage. They are preferred for continuous data transmission scenarios in AIoT, such as sensor telemetry or voice streaming.

- **Trivium:** is part of the eSTREAM portfolio and provides 80-bit security with a simple shift-register architecture. It achieves high throughput with minimal hardware footprint (approximately 2,500 GE) and is resilient to most statistical attacks (Gaj, Southern & Bachimanchi, 2007). In AIoT, Trivium is used for real-time sensor authentication and data confidentiality in streaming contexts due to its fast startup and negligible latency. Its resistance to differential power analysis further enhances reliability for battery-operated devices.

- **Grain Family**: with its members Grain v1 and Grain-128a still retains strong cryptographic strength with fewer operations per bit. Grain-128a can equip a message authentication code (MAC), allowing for authenticated encryption which is greatly needed for AIoT applications with stringent memory requirements (< 10 KB). Its Linear Feedback Shift Register (LFSR) design is also remarkably well suited for implementation on hardware for RFID and sensor chips.
- **ACORN**: As one of the few finalists for lightweight cryptography from NIST, ACORN is an authenticated encryption stream cipher which works on a 128-bit key and IV and has the advantage of performing combined confidentiality and integrity processing in one single pass. ACORN is able to provide a high speed software implementation while maintaining excellent protection from differential and algebraic attack. In AIoT networks, the ability of ACORN to perform encryption and authentication in a single operation reduces protocol complexity and lowers the overall energy consumption of the network.

5.4 Authenticated Encryption with Associated Data (AEAD)

AEAD schemes simultaneously provide data confidentiality and integrity verification—an essential requirement for secure AIoT authentication. Unlike traditional encrypt-then-MAC approaches, AEAD integrates both functions into one efficient primitive.

Ascon, chosen as NIST's official lightweight standard, is based on a permutation-based sponge construction (Beierle et al., 2019). It supports authenticated encryption and hashing, with versions Ascon-128, Ascon-128a, and Ascon-Hash. Its internal 320-bit state and 5-round permutation achieve a strong balance between performance and side-channel resistance.

Ascon's advantages for AIoT include:

- Low hardware complexity (~2,500 GE).
- Constant-time design minimizing timing leakage.
- Single-pass encryption and authentication.
- Proven security margins and resistance to differential attacks.

Ascon's unified architecture allows it to serve as both an encryption scheme and a hash function, simplifying the authentication process in constrained AIoT devices.

GIFT-COFB is an AEAD scheme that builds on the GIFT block cipher. It uses a *COFB (COmbined FeedBack)* mode of operation that minimizes hardware footprint and latency (Zheng et al., 2017). GIFT-COFB consumes less energy than Ascon for short messages and performs particularly well on FPGA and ASIC platforms. It is increasingly adopted in AIoT systems for mutual authentication between devices and gateways.

With approximately 1,300 Gate Equivalents (GE), the most competitively compact requirement of all NIST submissions, **TinyJAMBU** competes for the lightweight AEAD candidate whilst achieving 128-bit security for significantly sized ultra-constrained devices like RFID tags (Li et al., 2022). Its AEAD functionalities, albeit mid-range on the software performance scale, are far overcome by the undercutting cost warranted for hardware, demonstrating sensor networks wherein unit cost proves crucial.

5.5 Lightweight Hash Functions and MACs

Hash functions and Message Authentication Codes (MACs) ensure data integrity and authenticity within AIoT communication protocols.

- **PHOTON and SPONGENT**: In both PHOTON and SPONGENT, sponge constructions tailored for hardware realisation are used. PHOTON uses an AES-like structure with an S-box and diffusion matrix for strong avalanche impact, while SPONGENT scales better across a wider range of output sizes (Guo et al. 2011). In AIoT, these hash functions support HMACs for session authentication and session key derivation.
- **Quark** provides ultra-low area requirements (~1,300 GE) and supports multiple variants (u-Quark, d-Quark, s-Quark) depending on security level and throughput needs. It is suitable for battery-less IoT sensors where energy harvesting constraints prohibit heavier cryptographic operations.

5.6 Comparative Analysis

Table 2 summarizes the key characteristics of representative lightweight cryptographic algorithms relevant to AIoT authentication (Bogdanov et al., 2007; Zheng et al., 2017 ; Beierle et al., 2019; NIST, 2023).

Table 2. Comparative summary of popular lightweight algorithms for AIoT

Algorithm	Type	Block/Key Size (bits)	Rounds	Gate Equiv. (GE)	Security Level	Typical Use in AIoT
PRESENT	Block cipher	64 / 80–128	31	1,570	80–128-bit	Device authentication
GIFT	Block cipher	64 / 128	40	1,250	128-bit	AEAD (GIFT-COFB)
SIMON	Block cipher	64 / 128	44	1,440	128-bit	Secure boot, data encryption
SPECK	Block cipher	64 / 128	27	1,400	128-bit	Software encryption
RECTANGLE	Block cipher	64 / 128	25	1,850	128-bit	Edge authentication
Ascon	AEAD	128 / 128	5	2,500	128-bit	AE + Hashing
ACORN	Stream cipher	– / 128	–	2,300	128-bit	Real-time communication
Trivium	Stream cipher	– / 80	–	2,500	80-bit	Sensor telemetry
PHOTON	Hash	– / –	–	2,100	128-bit	HMAC, message integrity
SPONGENT	Hash	– / –	–	1,900	128-bit	Key derivation
TinyJAMBU	AEAD	128 / 128	–	1,300	128-bit	RFID authentication

5.6 Integration in AIoT Authentication Frameworks

Lightweight algorithms are typically deployed in AIoT authentication frameworks using hybrid models:

1. Device Initialization: LWC primitives (e.g., PRESENT or GIFT) perform initial identity verification.
2. Secure Session Establishment: AEAD schemes like Ascon or GIFT-COFB create encrypted channels for key negotiation.
3. Data Transmission: Stream ciphers (Trivium or ACORN) protect continuous telemetry.
4. Integrity Validation: Hash functions (PHOTON, SPONGENT) generate HMACs to verify data authenticity.

Figure 3 illustrates the integrated workflow combining Lightweight Cryptography (LWC) and Post-Quantum Cryptography (PQC) within an AIoT authentication system. The process spans device bootstrapping, hybrid session establishment, encrypted data transmission, edge-level identity verification and anomaly detection, and cloud-based validation using PQC digital signatures. The workflow demonstrates how crypto-agility, layered verification, and AI-based analysis work together to enhance resilience, isolate compromised devices, and ensure secure end-to-end authentication across heterogeneous AIoT environments.

Figure 3. Integrated multi-layer authentication process

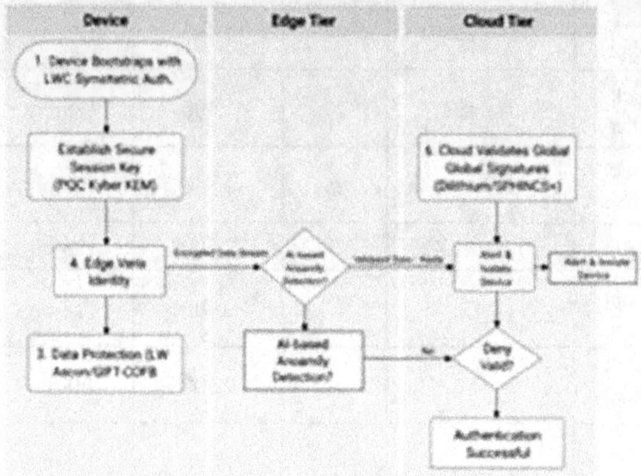

The emphasis on the level of cryptography integration ensures that any operation w for a given device is within its capabilities and the communication channel's sensitivity. Hence, the foundation is lightweight cryptography. In the case of cryptosystems, they supply the primary constituent materials for securing the authentication of AIoT devices. They illustrate the "protection per watt" principle, which is the most elementary form of cryptographic safeguarding that does not entail a major trade-off on the device's operational longevity and rapidity.

Within each of these families—block ciphers, stream ciphers, AEAD schemes, and hash functions—there are different performances with respect to area, speed, and energy. The above all others standardization of ASCON is of primary importance as it ensures that AIoT developers will hold a validated, interoperable cryptographic primitive for their prospective projects.

These algorithms, however, are still considered to be secure in a classical sense. Shifting to post quantum cryptography are becoming more important as the threats posed by quantum computers become more pronounced. The next section of this book, Section 6, reviews fundamentals of post quantum cryptography and its significance for AIoT authentication systems.

5.7 Comparative Analysis of Lightweight and Post-Quantum Cryptography for AIoT

A concise comparison between lightweight and post-quantum schemes should highlight that AIoT devices rely on extremely constrained microcontrollers, often 8- or 32-bit units with only a few kilobytes of RAM and low-megahertz clock speeds, making it essential that authentication operations complete within a few million cycles. While conventional public-key systems already strain these platforms, post-quantum schemes introduce far greater overhead: PQC keys frequently reach kilobyte scale and may require more than 100 KB of RAM, along with significantly higher CPU and energy demands (Singh et al., 2024). Table 3, comparing LWC and PQC across key size, signature size, memory footprint, and energy consumption.

Table 3. Comparison of lightweight vs. post-quantum cryptography in AIoT

Property	Lightweight Cryptography (LWC)	Post-Quantum Cryptography (PQC)
Primary Goal	Efficiency under strict hardware constraints	Quantum-resistant security
Target Devices	Sensors, microcontrollers, wearables	Gateways, edge servers, cloud
Key Sizes	Very small (64–128 bits)	Large (KB-scale keys/signatures)
Typical Memory Usage	< 10 KB	30 KB – 400 KB depending on scheme
Security Level	Classical attacks	Classical + quantum attacks
Energy Consumption	Very low	High (modular arithmetic, NTT ops)
Suitable For	Device authentication, telemetry protection	Firmware signing, key exchange, model provenance
Latency	< 1 ms	May exceed tens of ms on MCU
Longevity	Vulnerable to quantum attacks	Long-term secure

6. POST-QUANTUM CRYPTOGRAPHY (PQC) FOUNDATIONS

The foundation of modern cryptography trusts the assumption of the computational hardness of mathematical problems. Most notably, the concern with factorization of signals, with the integer and its logarithm, the public-key cryptography rests on the RSA, Diffie–Hellman (DH), and Elliptic-Curve Cryptography (ECC), public-key algorithms of unqualified prominence. The sudden advent of quantum computing disturbs the order of things. In 1994, Peter Shor, postulating the existence of a quantum computer, advanced a polynomial thetic argument for the factorization of and the solving of the integer logarithm problems, thus sinking public-key cryptography in its traditional form (Shor, 1999).

Symmetric algorithms like AES and SHA-2 are subject to lesser transformative quantum impacts. Grover's and quantum algorithms halve the effective key strength (Grover, 1996). In any case, asymmetric cryptography and digital signatures are under a quantum threat of extinction.

Spurred by such disruptions, post-quantum cryptography (PQC) emerged to provide a frontier of cryptography techniques for defense against quantum computer attacks. Unlike quantum key distribution (QKD) that entails application of quantum mechanics and special hardware resources, PQC is classical—it does not require quantum computers. Rather, it can be executed in standard computer and communication environments, ensuring, nevertheless, its protection against quantum attacks (Gasser, 2023, Al E'mari, Sanjalawe & Fataftah, 2026).

With regards to AIoT authentication, the move towards PQC is especially pressing in light of the typically lengthy lifecycles (10-20 years) how devices in AIoT systems tend to have, and the possibility of storing sensitive operational or telemetry data. An attacker with the "harvest now, decrypt later" mindset can capture and store AIoT data traffic in an encrypted form today, only to decrypt it in the future, when quantum computers have fully developed. Therefore, the integration of PQC into AIoT systems guarantees and preserves their confidentiality, integrity, and authenticity in the long term.

According to the 2024 National Institute of Science and Technology (PQC) newly-defined elements still stands on the preexisting concerns of post-quantum cryptographies basics:

i. Quantum-Resilience: In as much as the problem needs to be classically and quantinally impenetrable puzzles, it's almost imperative that the security system works based on challenges that neither classical nor quantum systems can solve.
ii. Efficiency and Scalability: Making sure there are no excessive expenditures of computer systems and bandwidth, algorithms should execute the processes of key creation as well as decryption and validation.
iii. Interoperability: TLS, IPsec, MQTT, and DTLS among other IoT and Internet metrics dimeologies should be embedded within PQC systems and require no major changes within the networks to be operable.
iv. Implementable on contrained devices: Proliferation of AIoT devices that have nano-level power systems, like micro control systems, deep FGPAs, tell of a tale of low computational systems. These are the kind of systems that would require PQC to have most of its low power and FGPAs and microcontrollers systems optimally encoded.

The mentioned factors within the other layers of AIOT within the PQC authentication outline layers tell that PQC indeed acts as an umbrella over the systems and networks.

6.1 Mathematical Foundations of PQC

The mathematical problems that are practically difficult for classical and quantum computers are the foundations for post-quantum cryptographic systems. These "hard" problems are lattice-based, code-based, multivariate polynomial, cryptographic hash, and isogeny-based according to Alagic et al. (2022).

Lattice-Based Cryptography, the most prominent and advanced form of post-quantum cryptography is lattice-based cryptography. This branch of cryptography is based on hard mathematical problems like the following (Gewehr et al., 2024):

- Shortest Vector Problem (SVP): Finding the shortest nonzero vector in a high-dimensional lattice.
- Learning With Errors (LWE): Given a matrix A and a noisy vector $b=A\cdot s+e$, recovering the secret s is a hard undertaking.
- Ring-LWE (RLWE) and Module-LWE: Structured variants that maximize storage and efficiency.

An example of systems that are based on these problems is CRYSTALS-Kyber, which implements key encapsulation, and CRYSTALS-Dilithium, which is used for digital signatures. Lattice based schemes have strong proved security, fast key generation and simple mathematical operations, which makes them more favorable for software and hardware deployment in AIoT gateways and edge nodes (Xiao et al. 2022). Despite these advantages however, lattice-based schemes often involve public keys and ciphertexts that are physically large in size.

Code-Based Cryptography, systems based on codes obtain their security from the inability to decode random linear codes. The most prominent example is the McEliece cryptosystem (McEliece 1978), which employs error correcting codes in the construction of a cryptographic trapdoor function. Code based cryptography entails high security margins and several decades of cryptanalytic attack resilience. Its main disadvantage is the extremely large size of the public key (tens or hundreds of kilobytes), a considerable obstacle in the context of small IoT memory capacities. Nevertheless, optimized versions like Classic McEliece that are still part of NIST's Round 3 finalists, can be deployed in edge AIoT servers of modest capability (McEliece, 1978; Albrecht et al., 2022).

Multivariate Quadratic (MQ) Cryptography, public key cryptography based on MQ constructs from systems of quadratic polynomial equations defined over a finite field. Such systems are NP-hard even to solve on quantum machines. Signature schemes such as Rainbow and GeMSS are designed based on this principle. The strength of MQ cryptography is the rapid generation and verification of signatures, a clear benefit in the context of widespread and high-frequency AIoT authentication. The disadvantage is that the key sizes are often excessively large and the more recent variants that have fallen under algebraic cryptanalysis demonstrate the importance of cautious deployment (Demircioğlu, 2022).

Hash-Based Cryptography, by depending only on the pre-image resistance of cryptographic hash functions, XMSS and LMS hash-based signatures, alongside SPHINCS, obtain post-quantum security. As hash functions are among the functions least vulnerable to quantum computers whereby Grover's algorithm only offers quadratic speedup, they afford great security at very basic and well understood operations. Hash-based schemes, e.g., SPHINCS+, are deterministic, stateless, and offer great solutions for the signing of firmware and AIoT device identity verification, where the events of authentication are rare and the events of security are prolonged (Alter, Schwabe & Daemen, 2021).

Isogeny-Based Cryptography, it constructs public keys by means of isogenies or algebraic functions/transformations lying on elliptic curves. The most well-known protocol is the Supersingular Isogeny Diffie-Hellman (SIDH) which promised very small keys (about 330 bytes). However, the 2022 attacks led to the downfall of a number of such schemes, including SIKE (Castryck and Decru, 2023). The isogeny-based security is still unstable, which in turn, hampers its adoption for AIoT application even though the isogeny-based security is still the target of active research for alternatives.

6.2 Post-Quantum Primitives and Operations

Each PQC family supports three fundamental operations critical to authentication frameworks:

1. Key Encapsulation Mechanisms (KEMs): Establish shared session keys between devices (e.g., Kyber, Saber).
2. Public-Key Encryption (PKE): Securely transmit data using asymmetric encryption (e.g., NTRU, BIKE).
3. Digital Signatures: Verify the authenticity and integrity of messages or firmware (e.g., Dilithium, Falcon, SPHINCS+).

For AIoT authentication, the KEM + Signature combination forms the backbone of trust. Devices use KEMs for establishing secure channels and signatures to verify firmware and model updates.

Moreover, the NIST PQC Standardization Project, launched in 2016, represents the most significant global initiative to evaluate and standardize PQC algorithms. After three evaluation rounds involving more than 80 proposals, NIST announced four algorithms selected for standardization in 2022 (NIST, 2025). Table 4 summarizes the primary algorithms selected through the NIST PQC algorithms.

Table 4. NIST-selected PQC algorithms

Category	Algorithm	Family	Status	Application
Key Encapsulation	CRYSTALS-Kyber	Lattice-based	Standardized	Key exchange
Digital Signature	CRYSTALS-Dilithium	Lattice-based	Standardized	Signatures
Digital Signature	Falcon	Lattice-based	Standardized	High-performance signatures
Digital Signature	SPHINCS+	Hash-based	Standardized	Long-term secure signatures

NIST also continues evaluating Classic McEliece, Saber, and BIKE for future inclusion. These standardized schemes now form the foundation of quantum-resilient authentication systems, including those envisioned for AIoT networks.

6.3 Performance and Implementation Considerations for AIoT

Although PQC provides defesive security, flexible integration and implementation challenges arise from its applicability in the AIoT. Although AIoT microcontrollers may experience heavier computational activities than traditional ECC, lattice-based schemes are still more efficient than other hard PC schemes. Optimizations that retain fixed point arithmetic (modulus reduction) in addition to Kyber's other deployments and schemes, present, are able to get modest latency from the appropriately constructed frameworks (Gewehr, Luza & Moraes, 20244) on other ARM COTE MTC machines.

On the other hand, AIoT mesh networks computational memory lattice and code-based schemes are able to allocate and communicate Kyber's more than 1 MB, and 100 KB McEliece within the other, ECC's 32–64 bytes. Adaptive schemes able to mitigate the other framework's more fragmented networks may utilize the lower power mesh graphs (Hemmati et al., 2025). While the amount of energy lost per each modular multiplication in lattice operations directly relates to energy lost. Energy expenditures more than double on PQC and other fully hardware aligned with crosswise and diagonal of approximate arithmetic circuitry more than 60%. Therefore, defesive edge AIoT nodes are more accessible than highly aligned sensors.

To achieve seamless adoption of the PQC system, it will need to interface with DTLS, TLS 1.3, and MQTT-TLS, which AIoT security protocols already use. During migration, hybrid strategies that incorporate ECC + PQC thermally extend to current devices and backward compatibility with legacy devices. OpenSSL and wolfSSL libraries support these hybrid key exchanges, enabling prescriptive pilot deployment within AIoT frameworks.

6.4 Post-Quantum Authentication Models in AIoT

In the context of AIoT, post-quantum cryptography supports multiple layers of authentication:

1. Device-to-Gateway Authentication: KEMs such as Kyber establish secure channels between end devices and local edge gateways.
2. Gateway-to-Cloud Authentication: Lattice-based or hash-based signature schemes (Dilithium or SPHINCS+) verify message authenticity and system integrity.
3. Model Integrity Verification: Digital signatures protect AI model updates distributed across federated AIoT networks.
4. Firmware Authentication: Hash-based signatures ensure that device firmware originates from legitimate manufacturers and remains untampered.

Such multi-layer authentication guarantees end-to-end trustworthiness across the distributed AIoT architecture. The research into the strength of proven PQC schemes involves both theory and practice. Winters PQC researchers have also sought to understand and mitigate the problem of weaknesses in lattice reduction, insertion of faults, and side-channel attacks. For example, in the decapsulation phase of Kyber, KyberSlash type attacks take advantage of subtiming, and while the constant time implementation gets activated, gers (Bernstein et al., 2024).

Assigned PQC accreditation parallel to classical cryptographic methods equivalently offered under FIPS 140-3, for embraced Post Development stages, NIST and other approved Security Certification Bodies are defining methods evaluation criteria for PQC algorithms accreditation and offer.

The PQC, and, specially, the multitude of mathematical methods comprising, but not limited to, lattice physics, coding theory, and cryptographic hash functions, and the rest are indispensable to the AIoT communications' security enhancement and its deepened aspect. Deployed Post Quantum mechanisms face unprecedented pragmatic challenges, in terms of ease of implementation, associated with extreme computational resources, volume of keys, and energy expenditure. The current systems in use, together with the hybdrid lattice/hash schemes form the basis of PQC, and, along with other breakthroughs in hardware acceleration, serve as the foundation for the next generation AIoT systems of systems, and the twilight of the era of orchestrated intelligence.

7. PQC ALGORITHM FAMILIES AND THEIR APPLICABILITY TO AIOT AUTHENTICATION

PQC encompasses several algorithmic families whose security relies on problems believed to be hard for both classical and quantum adversaries. For AIoT authentication, the suitability of a PQC scheme is determined by four practical dimensions:

1. Security margin against state-of-the-art cryptanalysis;
2. Implementation footprint (CPU cycles, RAM/ROM, and code size);
3. Communication overhead (public key, ciphertext/signature sizes); and
4. Operational fit within authentication workflows (device enrollment, mutual authentication, session establishment, firmware/model signing).

Below is a role-centric mapping of PQC families to typical AIoT authentication tasks. (Qualitative scores: High / Medium / Low). Table 5 illustrates the comparison between PQC and AIoT authentication roles.

Table 5. PQC families vs. AIoT authentication roles

Role / Criterion	Lattice (Kyber/Dilithium/ Falcon)	Code-based (Classic McEliece)	Hash-based (SPHINCS+/ XMSS/LMS)	Multivariate (MQ)	Isogeny
Mutual device↔gateway auth (KEM)	High (Kyber)	Medium (key size limits)	N/A	N/A	Low
Gateway↔cloud auth	High	High	Medium	Medium	Low
Firmware signing & verification	High (Dilithium/Falcon)	Medium	High (SPHINCS+/LMS)	Medium	Low
Federated update signing	High	Medium	Medium (size)	Medium	Low
Bandwidth efficiency	Medium	Low (key size)	Low–Medium (sig size)	Medium	High (but not secure)
MCU implementability (Cortex-M)	High	Medium	Medium	Medium	Low
Cryptanalytic stability (2024–2025)	High	High	High	Medium–Low	Low
Overall AIoT suitability	High	Medium	Medium–High (for signing)	Low–Medium	Low

Interpretation.

- Use lattice-KEM for session keys and lattice/hash-based signatures for identity and artifact integrity.
- Reserve code-based for upper tiers or where bandwidth and storage are ample.
- Apply hash-based to artifact signing (FOTA, models) especially when verification cost and simplicity dominate.
- Treat MQ as experimental and isogeny as presently unsuitable for production AIoT authentication.

7.1 Hybridization Patterns for AIoT

Given heterogeneous device capabilities, hybrid cryptography enables graceful migration and layered assurance:

1. ECC + PQC (transition mode).

During migration, run hybrid handshakes (e.g., X25519 + Kyber) to maintain backward compatibility while achieving quantum-resistant session keys. This is practical in TLS 1.3 / DTLS 1.3 stacks on gateways.

2. PQC-KEM + Lightweight AEAD: Use Kyber to establish a session key, then switch to Ascon-AEAD or GIFT-COFB for low-energy data protection. This preserves throughput and battery life at the device while ensuring post-quantum secrecy.
3. Dual-signature artifacts: Sign firmware and models with Dilithium (fast verify) and SPHINCS+ (long-horizon assurance). Edge devices verify Dilithium; cloud auditors retain SPHINCS+ as archival evidence.
4. Gateway offload: Allow leaf sensors to authenticate to a trusted gateway using lightweight symmetric credentials, while the gateway performs PQC on behalf of the leaf (mutual auth with cloud). This respects ultra-constrained nodes without sacrificing end-to-end quantum safety.

7.2 Implementation and Side-Channel Considerations

- **Constant-time discipline**: PQC code must eliminate secret-dependent timing and memory access. Known pitfalls include NTT butterflies, conditional reductions, and error-dependent branches in decapsulation (Bernstein et al., 2024).
- **Memory planning**: Lattice stacks require temporary buffers (for NTT/INTT, sampling). On MCUs, prefer in-place transforms, streaming packing/unpacking, and fixed-point arithmetic to reduce RAM.

- **Hardware acceleration**: Emerging NTT/Keccak accelerators and small polynomial-multiplier blocks on low-power SoCs can lower energy/latency by 30–60% (Kebande, 2025). For hash-based schemes, Keccak/SHA-2 engines substantially speed SPHINCS+.
- **Parameter agility**: Design APIs that abstract security levels (e.g., Kyber-512/768/1024) so devices can negotiate parameters based on link quality, battery state, and threat posture (crypto-agility).

7.3 Decision Framework for Practitioners

A practical selection heuristic for AIoT authentication:

- Leaf sensor (8/16-bit MCU, ≤128 KB flash, low-rate link):
  - Primary: Gateway offload (symmetric LWC to gateway).
  - If PQC on-device is unavoidable: consider SPHINCS+ verification only for rare events (firmware/model), avoid frequent KEM.
- Edge node (32-bit MCU/SoC, 256 KB–1 MB RAM, moderate link):
  - Kyber KEM for sessions; Dilithium for signatures.
  - Data plane protected with Ascon/GIFT-COFB to minimize energy.
- Gateway/industrial controller (ARM-A/RISC-V, Linux, FPGA optional):
  - Full PQC stack (Kyber + Dilithium/Falcon + SPHINCS+ for archival).
  - Support hybrid X25519+Kyber during migration.
  - Terminate DTLS/TLS for downstream constrained nodes.
- Cloud/control plane:
  - Use lattice or code-based for inter-service trust; hash-based for long-term logs, audit, and DT attestation chains.

Among PQC families, lattice-based schemes (Kyber, Dilithium, Falcon) emerge as the primary choice for AIoT authentication due to their strong security foundations, efficient implementations on commodity MCUs, and NIST standardization. Hash-based signatures (SPHINCS+, XMSS/LMS) complement this role for artifact integrity where verification simplicity and long-term assurance are paramount. Code-based systems remain valuable at higher tiers despite large keys, while multivariate and isogeny schemes currently lack the stability for safety-critical deployment. Operationally, the hybridization of PQC with lightweight symmetric AEAD and gateway offload patterns provides a practical pathway to quantum-resilient yet energy-efficient AIoT authentication.

CONCLUSION

In summary, this chapter has demonstrated that securing authentication in AIoT ecosystems requires a careful reconciliation of efficiency, resilience, and long-term cryptographic assurance. The rapid expansion of intelligent, interconnected devices introduces new vulnerabilities across physical, network, and cognitive layers; however, traditional cryptographic solutions remain insufficient for highly constrained hardware. Moreover, while lightweight primitives offer practical protection for routine operations, post-quantum cryptography provides the foundational security needed to withstand emerging quantum threats. Nevertheless, neither category alone can fully address the evolving complexity of AIoT environments. Therefore, a unified architecture that integrates LWC, PQC, and AI-driven adaptive trust mechanisms emerges as the most viable path toward scalable, energy-aware, and future-proof authentication. Furthermore, as AIoT systems grow in criticality, ongoing research must refine hybrid models, enhance crypto-agility, and strengthen interoperability across heterogeneous platforms. Consequently, advancing this integrated security vision is essential to ensuring sustained reliability, trust, and resilience in next-generation intelligent infrastructures.

REFERENCES

Agarwal, A., & Ahmad, S. (2025). An Exhaustive Review on Energy Efficient Lightweight Cryptography Solutions for Privacy and Security in Edge Computing. In *2025 12th International Conference on Computing for Sustainable Global Development (INDIACom)* (pp. 01-06). IEEE. DOI: 10.23919/INDIACom66777.2025.11115715

Alagic, G., Alagic, G., Apon, D., Cooper, D., Dang, Q., Dang, T., ... & Smith-Tone, D. (2022). Status report on the third round of the NIST post-quantum cryptography standardization process.

Albrecht, M. R., Bernstein, D. J., Chou, T., Cid, C., Gilcher, J., Lange, T., ... & Wang, W. (2022). Classic McEliece: conservative code-based cryptography.

Alter, D. M., Schwabe, P., & Daemen, J. (2021). *Optimizing the NIST post quantum candidate SPHINCS+ using AVX-512.*

Asif, R., Ghanem, K., & Irvine, J. (2020). Proof-of-puf enabled blockchain: Concurrent data and device security for internet-of-energy. *Sensors (Basel), 21*(1), 28. DOI: 10.3390/s21010028

Awaisi, K. S., Ye, Q., & Sampalli, S. (2024). A survey of industrial AIoT: Opportunities, challenges, and directions. *IEEE Access : Practical Innovations, Open Solutions, 12*, 96946–96996. DOI: 10.1109/ACCESS.2024.3426279

Beaulieu, R., Shors, D., Smith, J., Treatman-Clark, S., Weeks, B., & Wingers, L. (2015). The SIMON and SPECK lightweight block ciphers. In *Proceedings of the 52nd annual design automation conference* (pp. 1-6). DOI: 10.1145/2744769.2747946

Beierle, C., Biryukov, A., Dos Santos, L. C., Großschädl, J., Perrin, L., Udovenko, A., ... & Biryukov, A. (2019). Schwaemm and esch: lightweight authenticated encryption and hashing using the sparkle permutation family. *NIST round, 2*, 162893-162908.

Bernsmed, K., Cruzes, D. S., Jaatun, M. G., & Iovan, M. (2022). Adopting threat modelling in agile software development projects. *Journal of Systems and Software, 183*, 111090. DOI: 10.1016/j.jss.2021.111090

Bernstein, D. J., Bhargavan, K., Bhasin, S., Chattopadhyay, A., Chia, T. K., Kannwischer, M. J., ... & Tamvada, G. (2024). KyberSlash: Exploiting secret-dependent division timings in Kyber implementations. *Cryptology ePrint Archive.*

Bogdanov, A., Knudsen, L. R., Leander, G., Paar, C., Poschmann, A., Robshaw, M. J., . . . Vikkelsoe, C. (2007). PRESENT: An ultra-lightweight block cipher. In *International workshop on cryptographic hardware and embedded systems* (pp. 450-466). Berlin, Heidelberg: Springer Berlin Heidelberg.

Castryck, W., & Decru, T. (2023). An efficient key recovery attack on SIDH. In *Annual international conference on the theory and applications of cryptographic techniques* (pp. 423-447). Cham: Springer Nature Switzerland. DOI: 10.1007/978-3-031-30589-4_15

Cetintav, I., & Sandikkaya, M. T. (2025). A review of lightweight IoT authentication protocols from the perspective of security requirements, computation, communication, and hardware costs. *IEEE Access : Practical Innovations, Open Solutions*, *13*, 37703–37723. DOI: 10.1109/ACCESS.2025.3546147

Demircioğlu, M. (2022). *Efficient Multivariate-Based Ring Signature Schemes* (Doctoral dissertation, Middle East Technical University (Turkey)).

Gaj, K., Southern, G., & Bachimanchi, R. (2007). Comparison of hardware performance of selected Phase II eSTREAM candidates. In *State of the Art of Stream Ciphers Workshop (SASC 2007), eSTREAM, ECRYPT Stream Cipher Project, Report* (Vol. 26, p. 2007).

Gasser, L. (2023). Post-quantum cryptography. *Trends in Data Protection and Encryption Technologies*, 47-52.

Gewehr, C., Luza, L., & Moraes, F. G. (2024). Hardware acceleration of crystals-Kyber in low-complexity embedded systems with RISC-V instruction set extensions. *IEEE Access : Practical Innovations, Open Solutions*, *12*, 94477–94495. DOI: 10.1109/ACCESS.2024.3416812

Goodfellow, I. J., Shlens, J., & Szegedy, C. (2014). Explaining and harnessing adversarial examples. *arXiv preprint arXiv:1412.6572*.

Grover, L. K. (1996, July). A fast quantum mechanical algorithm for database search. In *Proceedings of the twenty-eighth annual ACM symposium on Theory of computing* (pp. 212-219). DOI: 10.1145/237814.237866

Guo, J., Peyrin, T., & Poschmann, A. (2011). The PHOTON family of lightweight hash functions. In *Annual cryptology conference* (pp. 222-239). Berlin, Heidelberg: Springer Berlin Heidelberg. DOI: 10.1007/978-3-642-22792-9_13

Hemamalini, V., Mishra, A. K., Tyagi, A. K., & Kakulapati, V. (2024). Artificial intelligence–blockchain-enabled–internet of things-based cloud applications for next-generation society. *Automated secure computing for next-generation systems*, 65-82.

Hemmati, A., Arzanagh, H. M., & Rahmani, A. M. (2025). Fundamentals of Edge AI and Federated Learning. *Model Optimization Methods for Efficient and Edge AI: Federated Learning Architectures, Frameworks and Applications*, 1-23.

Hong, S. (2024). The Convergence of Artificial Intelligence and the Internet of Things (AIoT): Innovations, Challenges, and Future Directions. , *3*(4), 40-46.

Kebande, V. R. (2025). Quantum Computing in Industrial Internet of Things (IIoT) Forensics: Framework, Implications, Opportunities, and Future Directions. *WIREs Forensic Science*, *7*(3), e70013. DOI: 10.1002/wfs2.70013

Kostromitin, K. I., Dokuchaev, B. N., & Kozlov, D. A. (2020). Analysis of the most common software and hardware vulnerabilities in microprocessor systems. In *2020 International Russian Automation Conference (RusAutoCon)* (pp. 1031-1036). IEEE. DOI: 10.1109/RusAutoCon49822.2020.9208037

Kumar, S., Kumar, D., Dangi, R., Choudhary, G., Dragoni, N., & You, I. (2024). A review of lightweight security and privacy for resource-constrained IoT devices. *Computers, Materials & Continua*, *78*(1), 31–63. DOI: 10.32604/cmc.2023.047084

Li, M., Mouha, N., Sun, L., & Wang, M. (2022). Revisiting the extension of Matsui's algorithm 1 to linear hulls: application to TinyJAMBU. *IACR transactions on symmetric cryptology*, 161-200.

McEliece, R. J. (1978). A public-key cryptosystem based on algebraic. *Coding Thv*, *4244*, 114–116.

Menon, U. V., Kumaravelu, V. B., Kumar, C. V., Rammohan, A., Chinnadurai, S., Venkatesan, R., & Selvaprabhu, P. (2025). AI-powered IoT: A survey on integrating artificial intelligence with IoT for enhanced security, efficiency, and smart applications. *IEEE Access : Practical Innovations, Open Solutions*.

NIST. (2023). *Status Report on the Final Round of the NIST Lightweight Cryptography Standardization Process*. National Institute of Standards and Technology., DOI: 10.6028/NIST.IR.8454

NIST. (2025). *Status Report on the Fourth Round of the NIST Post-Quantum Cryptography Standardization Process*. National Institute of Standards and Technology., DOI: 10.6028/NIST.IR.8545

Radhakrishnan, I., Jadon, S., & Honnavalli, P. B. (2024). Efficiency and security evaluation of lightweight cryptographic algorithms for resource-constrained IoT devices. *Sensors (Basel)*, *24*(12), 4008. DOI: 10.3390/s24124008

Sehgal, N. K., Saxena, M., & Shah, D. N. (2024). Future of Edge AI. In *AI on the Edge with Security: Foundations and Practices* (pp. 239–267). Springer Nature Switzerland.

Shor, P. W. (1999). Polynomial-time algorithms for prime factorization and discrete logarithms on a quantum computer. *SIAM Review*, *41*(2), 303–332. DOI: 10.1137/S0036144598347011

Singh, P., Acharya, B., & Chaurasiya, R. K. (2021). Lightweight cryptographic algorithms for resource-constrained IoT devices and sensor networks. In *Security and Privacy Issues in IoT Devices and Sensor Networks* (pp. 153–185). Academic Press. DOI: 10.1016/B978-0-12-821255-4.00008-0

Singh, S., Sharma, P. K., Moon, S. Y., & Park, J. H. (2024). Advanced lightweight encryption algorithms for IoT devices: Survey, challenges and solutions. *Journal of Ambient Intelligence and Humanized Computing*, *15*(2), 1625–1642. DOI: 10.1007/s12652-017-0494-4

Thakor, V. A., Razzaque, M. A., & Khandaker, M. R. (2021). Lightweight cryptography algorithms for resource-constrained IoT devices: A review, comparison and research opportunities. *IEEE Access : Practical Innovations, Open Solutions*, *9*, 28177–28193. DOI: 10.1109/ACCESS.2021.3052867

Uprety, A., & Rawat, D. B. (2020). Reinforcement learning for iot security: A comprehensive survey. *IEEE Internet of Things Journal*, *8*(11), 8693–8706. DOI: 10.1109/JIOT.2020.3040957

Xiao, X., Tang, Z., Li, C., Jiang, B., & Li, K. (2022). SBPA: Sybil-based backdoor poisoning attacks for distributed big data in AIoT-based federated learning system. *IEEE Transactions on Big Data*, *10*(6), 827–838. DOI: 10.1109/TBDATA.2022.3224392

Xiong, Z., Cai, Z., Takabi, D., & Li, W. (2021). Privacy threat and defense for federated learning with non-iid data in AIoT. *IEEE Transactions on Industrial Informatics*, *18*(2), 1310–1321. DOI: 10.1109/TII.2021.3073925

Yıldırım, F., Develi, E. I., Meidute-Kavaliauskiene, I., Rostamzadeh, R., & Ghorbani, S. (2025). Symmetric encryption and cryptography algorithms in internet of things. *Pesquisa Operacional*, *45*, e295986. DOI: 10.1590/0101-7438.2025.045.00295986

Zhang, W., Bao, Z., Lin, D., Rijmen, V., Yang, B., & Verbauwhede, I. (2015). RECTANGLE: A bit-slice lightweight block cipher suitable for multiple platforms. *Science China. Information Sciences*, *58*(12), 1–15. DOI: 10.1007/s11432-015-5459-7

Zheng, Q., Wang, X., Khan, M. K., Zhang, W., Gupta, B. B., & Guo, W. (2017). A lightweight authenticated encryption scheme based on chaotic scml for railway cloud service. *IEEE Access : Practical Innovations, Open Solutions*, *6*, 711–722. DOI: 10.1109/ACCESS.2017.2775038

Chapter 5
Zero Trust Architecture Implementation for AIoT Networks

Salam Al E'mari
http://orcid.org/0000-0002-2134-4158
University of Petra, Jordan

Yousef Sanjalawe
http://orcid.org/0000-0002-4442-1865
University of Jordan, Jordan

Fadi Fataftah
http://orcid.org/0000-0002-3299-0972
University Canada West, Canada

ABSTRACT

Competitive advantages offered by emerging technologies have accelerated the adoption of integrated intelligent systems commonly referred to as the Artificial Intelligence of Things. As device populations expand, traditional perimeter-centric and zone-based security models fail, since trust can no longer be inferred from location and boundaries become increasingly diffuse. Threat actors exploit these limitations, using compromised devices to bypass defenses and enable lateral movement while concealing malicious behavior. Zero-trust principles provide an alternative by eliminating implicit trust and requiring continuous verification for every entity. This chapter per the authors outlines how Zero Trust concepts can be adapted to AIoT architectures across device, edge and cloud layers. It proposes model frameworks incorporating AI-based trust scoring, policy evaluation mech-

DOI: 10.4018/979-8-3373-6299-1.ch005

anisms, behavioral micro-segmentation, and device-aware trust controls, while examining related concerns including performance impact, real-time trust agility, and system overhead.

1. INTRODUCTION

The integration of AI with IoT has led to the Artificial Intelligence of Things (AIoT). This field focuses on domain where smart sensors, actuators, and embedded processors collect and analyze data not only in the cloud, but on-site as well. Edge AIoT also enables predictive maintenance, real-time medical monitoring, and intelligent transportation systems. Such advancements in mobility systems also open the AIoT 's attack surface. Traditional approaches to cybersecurity rely on a set perimeter, controlled internal regions, and firewalled partitions of the network. These approaches are scarce in AIoT environments where devices are mobile, unmanaged, and connected through diverse AIoT.

With lost network devices or hostile AI models containing adversarial malice, risk could spread like wildfire across the network. The idea of being "inside" the corporate network as being protected cannot be maintained any longer. The National Institute of Standards and Technology (NIST) has sought to come to grips with this issue by formalizing the concept of Zero Trust Architecture (ZTA) in Special Publication 800-207. The publication outlines ZTA as an infosec architecture where every device and user within network perimeters is regarded as untrusted, and every attempt to access any resource is authenticated and authorized beforehand— zoned to restrained lateral movement (Rose et al., 2020; CyberArk, 2023). In summary, "never trust, always verify."

Although ZTA is quite advanced in the enterprise IT contexts, its direct use regarding AIoT comes with hurdles. Unlike conventional enterprise endpoints, AIoT devices often function with extreme resource restrictions (restricted power, compute, and connectivity), are situated in remote or hostile environments, and are often integrated in the edge/fog computing paradigm, as opposed to static data centers. More sophisticated instances include real-time engagements with machine learning models, federated updates, and telemetry transmission, all of which make typical trust-evaluation and micro-segmentation strategies considerably more complex (Shonubi, 2025).

This can be attributed to a lack of something important, therefore this chapter aims to achieve the following objectives. First, to explain the importance and the need for applying zero trust principles in the AIoT networks: the shortcomings of the legacy model, and in what ways ZTA fulfills the needs of the evolving threat environment. Second, to construct a theory which relates ZTA elements and the different layers of architecture comprising AIoT, particularly how the concepts of identity, device posture, network segmentation, and persistent monitoring can be applied at the perception, edge and cloud layers. Third, to formulate a practical implementation strategy suited to the constraints of AIoT, which features device onboarding procedures, policy decision points, enforcement frameworks, and trust assessment systems powered by artificial intelligence. The chapter ends with the primary evaluation metrics that need to be monitored (latency overhead, trust loss false positives, resource-strained resilience, etc.) and outlines what future studies will focus on, including federated trust scoring, AI enforcement interpretability, and the standardisation of the industrial AIoT framework to facilitate collaborative foundational model training.

The remaining part of the chapter has been structured as follows. In Section 2, the basic principles of ZTA are summarized. Section 3 analyses the particular security issues related to AIoT networks. In Section 4, the incorporation of zero-trust principles into the AIoT architecture is described. In Section 5, a multi-layer approach to implementation and deployment is presented. Section 6 focuses on the role of Artificial Intelligence in driving enforcement and automation in zero-trust AIoT. Section 7 presents the evaluation framework, along with the performance indicators to be measured. Section 8 analyzes the unsolved problems and prospective issues to be researched in the future. In Section 9, practical conclusions regarding the impact to be made to the community of practitioners and scholars are presented.

2. FUNDAMENTALS OF ZERO TRUST ARCHITECTURE

With no changes to the model's ZTA remains as the National Institute of Standards and Technology considers it the "an enterprise cybersecurity architecture that uses zero trust principles to plan industrial and enterprise infrastructure and workflows on the ZTA" (Rose et al., 2020). We will discuss ZTA's unlike other remaining ZTA's Fragmentation and Isolation principles as well as Trust Score systems and their paradoxical interactions.

2.1 Core Tenets of Zero Trust

The framework of "never trust, always verify" captures most of ZTA philosophy: there is no implicit trust of users and devices, even if they are within some bounded network (Rose et al., 2020). NIST has some constructs which state that every resource (data, service, workflow) should have reasoned protection, every communication should be shielded independent of network geography, and access control is applied dynamically on per-session basis based on policy and least-privilege principal enforcement. (CyberArk, 2023; RiskRecon, 2023).

In practical terms, this means:

- Treat **all data sources and computing services as resources** needing protection rather than implicitly trusted because they lie "inside" the perimeter (CyberArk, 2023).
- Secure **all communication**, whether inbound or outbound, internal or external. Location is not a trust indicator (Rose et al., 2020).
- Grant access on a **per-session basis**, using least-privilege, rather than broad "once inside the network" privileges (RiskRecon, 2023).
- Apply **dynamic policy evaluation**, using context such as device identity, user attributes, location, and behavioral telemetry (CyberArk, 2023).
- Continuously monitor and assess the **integrity and security posture** of devices, users, and communications (Rose et al.,2020).

These tenets ensure that access decisions are contextual, dynamic and revocable — shifting the control focus from network location to the actual identity, state and behavior of every entity.

2.2 Logical and Architectural Components

In its guidance, NIST identifies a minimal set of architectural elements for ZTA: the **Policy Engine (PE)**, **Policy Administrator (PA)** and **Policy Enforcement Point (PEP)**. (Rose et al., 2020)

- The *Policy Engine* is the decision-maker: it evaluates requests, computes trust scores based on contextual information (identity, device health, threat intelligence) and issues access decisions.
- The *Policy Administrator* executes those decisions: it directs enforcement points to allow or deny, configure sessions, revoke access, etc.
- The *Policy Enforcement Point* is the actual gate: it intercepts access requests and enforces decisions from the PE/PA. These components collaborate in real-time: when an access request arrives, it is intercepted by a PEP, passed to the PA/PE for evaluation (including trust scoring, policy evaluation), then granted or denied, and the session is monitored (NextLabs, 2024). Furthermore, micro-segmentation of workloads, continuous telemetry gathering, device posture assessment, identity-centric controls and dynamic revocation are key enablers of the architecture. In summary, ZTA demands that every access

request—even from "within" the network—is subject to the same rigorous verification and policy enforcement that would apply to an external request.

2.3 Comparison with Legacy Security Models

Traditional enterprise network security typically relied on a strong perimeter (firewalls, trusted internal zones) with the implicit assumption that once a user or device is inside the network, they can be trusted. ZTA rejects this notion. Location and network zone no longer provide trust; instead, trust is continuously assessed and must be earned for each request. (Rose et al., 2020; NextLabs, 2024). The differences can be summarized:

- **Implicit trust vs explicit verification**: Legacy: "once inside, trusted"; ZTA: every request verified.
- **Static segmentation vs micro-segmentation and dynamic policy**: Legacy: large internal trusted zones; ZTA: fine-grained segmentation, policy driven.
- **Periodic checks vs continuous monitoring**: Legacy: periodic audits/patches; ZTA: live telemetry, real-time trust scoring.
- **Network-centric protection vs resource-centric protection**: Legacy: focus on network boundary; ZTA: focus on protecting each resource and session. (RiskRecon, 2023).

2.4 Practical Implications

The shift to ZTA brings with it enormous implications for an organization: the framework sets identity as pivotal, the posture and behavior of devices matter, telemetry needs to be captured and assessed, policies must be alive and dynamically enforceable in real time. Culture, tools, budget and structure must be aligned: for instance, bolt-on legacy segmentation might need to be replaced with software-defined segmentation, and every access decision must be auditable (CyberArk, 2023). ZTA restructures trust and goes beyond simply modernizing existing controls. ZTA's trust model is in absolute alignment with use cases and ecosystems in which devices, users and resources are distributed, mobile or fundamentally untrusted. The next chapter explores how this model aligns with the unique characteristics of AIoT networks.

3. SECURITY CHALLENGES IN AIOT NETWORKS

Computer intelligence and the AIoT, are the IoT with Artificial Intelligence integration. There is the merging of the physical and digital worlds with the addition of the features of the IoT. AIoT improves operations; however, the strain it places on networks is still a cause of concern. The behavior of the IoT with Artificial Intelligence integration is the fusion of a number of; sensors, actuators, embedded processors, edge inference engines, and devices along a cloud. The risks and challenges increase with the addition of mobile devices. This section looks at the most important security problems and the designs with zero-trust bases that work with AIoT networks.

3.1 Device and Network Heterogeneity

AIoT networks often consist of devices from different manufacturers communicating with one another through various interfaces, each with its unique hardware, software stacks, protocols, firmware, and lifecycle management methodologies. Such unique variations, or heterogeneity, come with complexities, including broad attack surfaces, weak firmware links, vendor-specific backdoors, or poorly configured protocols. For instance, many IoT devices suffer from weak, default, and missing encryption, and thus, can be easily accessed and compromised or have their communications intercepted (Sanjalawe et al., 2025).

Also, there are often wireless, mobile edge, and even intermittent devices, complicating the holistic approaches to security policy and unified enforcement. The devices also suffer a lack of standardization and visibility, constraining the assessments and controls of trust (Sebestyen et al., 2025).

3.2 Resource Constraints and Edge-Cloud Continuum

Compared with traditional enterprise endpoints, the majority of AIoT devices operate with limited compute, memory, energy, and connectivity budgets. This precludes the implementation of most heavyweight security measures such as complete intrusion detection, TLS encryption, or routine repairing (Mazhar et al., 2023), and patching. In addition, AIoT networks utilize cloud analytics coupled with edge or fog processing. This engenders a continuum of trust boundaries, device, gateway or edge node, and cloud service, each with differential security posture. Maintaining consistently strong trust verification across the edge cloud continuum is difficult, for devices may periodically lose connectivity, or asynchronously outdated, and updating.

3.3 Threats Specific to AI-based IoT

AIoT adds to the usual IoT weaknesses (malintent, un-updated firmware, weak protocols) as well as unique to AI challenges: training data poisoning, adversarial model alteration, data drift, model inversion, and lateral AI pipeline movement

(Mazhar et al., 2023). A breached device in AIoT may inject corrupt data into the flows or updates to the model, or an adversary may manipulate the perimeter of edge analytics visibility to launch precision strikes. Without access authentication, device integrity checks, and real time anomaly behavior monitoring, traditional segmentation and access management controls are always going to be inadequate.

3.4 Expanding Attack Surface and Lateral Movement

AIoT environments can span a wide array of devices frequently located in unmanned or remote areas (sensors in smart cities, mobile assets, and industrial machinery). These devices are members of multiple differentiated realms and persist in being unattended, frequently associating and dissociating with multiple networks. As a result, a hacker breaking into any 'low-value' devices can traverse laterally across multiple devices and gain access to or alter far more critical devices (Litoussi et al., 2020). The concept of static boundary has ceased to be applicable, and the risks posed by the unconstrained incorporation of devices, the incorporation of legacy OT systems, and the absence of micro-segmentation are compounded (Balbix, 2025).

3.5 Lifecycle Management, Patching and Update Challenges

One of the persistent problems in IoT (and by extension AIoT) is the difficulty of providing consistent software/firmware updates, especially in devices with long sensor lifetimes or deployed in inaccessible environments. Without timely patching, known vulnerabilities linger indefinitely (Schiller et al., 2022). Also, the onboarding and de-commissioning of devices across changing network contexts may not include robust identity and trust verification. Weak processes here undermine continuous trust evaluation and increase risk of rogue devices or devices with expired credentials compromising the network.

3.6 Data Privacy, Trustworthiness and Compliance

AIoT devices generate massive volumes of data, often including personal, sensitive or operational-critical information. Ensuring confidentiality, integrity, provenance and correct handling of AIoT data is complex because data may be processed locally (edge), transmitted to cloud services, aggregated, and then used in AI algorithms. Ensuring chain-of-custody, data integrity and accountability across distributed nodes is a major challenge (Laghari et al., 2024). Moreover, regulatory obligations (e.g., data protection, industry regulation) may require proof of trustworthiness, traceability and auditability — features that are difficult to implement in austere or constrained devices.

4. INTEGRATING ZERO TRUST INTO AIOT ARCHITECTURE

Pillars of a zero-trust architecture like workflows and its core components paired with an AIot architecture's layered nature like device/perception, edge/fog, and cloud/analytics must be integrated carefully for implementing a zero-trust approach. Zero trust aims to eliminate dependence on established security perimeters, assuming that breaches are inevitable. This section presents how the ZTA tenets (e.g., identity-centric access, device posture verification, micro-segmentation, continuous monitoring) align with each AIoT layer, followed by a discussion of dynamic trust scoring, policy decision workflows, and technology enablers tailored for AIoT.

4.1 Mapping ZTA to AIoT Layers

At the lowest level—the perception or device layer—AIoT systems consist of sensors, actuators, embedded processors, and often wireless connectivity modules. Traditional security models often assume devices inside a network are inherently trusted. A zero-trust approach changes that: even a field sensor must present its identity, demonstrate a healthy posture (firmware version, known vulnerability status, secure boot state) and request access using least privilege. For example, the subject (device) may authenticate to a local gateway or edge node, and only then gain access to downstream analytics or control services (Talakola, 2025). Figure 1 presents the layered representation of Zero Trust Architecture within AIoT systems, highlighting the distribution of policy enforcement points, identity controls, and trust evaluation mechanisms.

Figure 1. Mapping zero-trust architecture components across AIoT layers

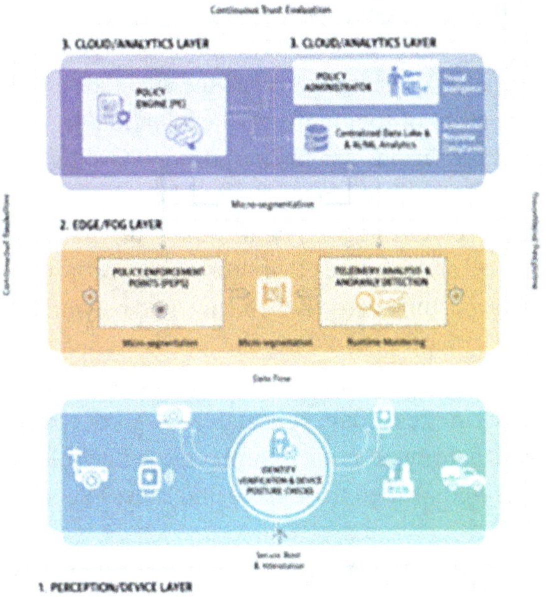

In the edge/fog layer, where data aggregation, initial processing and even inference may occur, the enforcement of trust becomes more dynamic. The edge node may host a policy enforcement point (PEP) which intercepts access requests, passes them to a policy engine (PE) for trust scoring and decisioning, then the policy administrator (PA) enforces, or revokes access based on real-time telemetry. Since edge devices function as local to cloud bridges, they have to implement micro-segmentation in order to manage the isolation, lateral movement, and the enforced encryption of data flows (even to devices labeled as 'inside' the local zone, and the local zone 'de-militarized' zone).

Within the cloud/analytics (model training, orchestration, data storage, and large-scale model 'spaghetti' facilities) layer, the same primitive zero-trust principles are in effect (though at a wider slant). There are still entities (users, services, devices) who have to verify, authenticate, and be 'audited' to be 'gained' access to 'data' or 'model' resources. Policies need to be made on the cross-domain interaction (for instance, federated edge clusters 'collaboration' in learning), compliance or audit evocation that dynamically tightening or loosening access control based on changing trust scores. Studies show that the zero-trust policy (Li et al., 2025) is the only viable policy to deploy, and that policy 'spans' the entire stack, treating each resource 'as untrusted' until verified.

4.2 Dynamic Authentication, Authorization & Continuous Trust Evaluation

The characteristic of ZTA that underlines the evaluation of trust at the session level as well as at the point of logging is trust evaluation. In AIoT, this boils down to monitoring a device or service's behavior post onboarding (e.g., data generation patterns, network flows, signals of anomalies) and incorporating that data to access decisions. Emerging research suggests contextually driven AI-based trust engines encapsulated within IoT architectures that score trustworthiness in real time based on trust context, device posture, network behavior, and networked threat intelligence (Tiwari et al., 2022).

In an IoT device, an authorization decision is adaptive: if anomalous behavior (e.g., unexpected bursts in excess data, unusual cross-border traffic, loss of firmware integrity) is captured, automatic policy enforcement may block or quarantine the device based on policy-controlled trust score and access decisions.

4.3 Micro-segmentation and Least-Privilege Access for AIoT

In AIoT networks, micro-segmentation is critical because devices often communicate in unpredictable ways, and lateral movement by an attacker can escalate quickly. Zero-trust implementations recommend fine-grained segmentation—not just between "trusted" and "untrusted" zones, but between each device or class of device, each service or data domain, and even each session. For example, edge clusters might be segmented by function (data collection vs actuation), by risk posture, by vendor domain, or by criticality of the associated physical process.

This segmentation supports least-privilege access: a device or service only gains access to the resources it needs, and only while it maintains trust criteria. Traditional "once inside with broad trust" models are inadequate for AIoT (Rose et al., 2020).

4.4 Technology Enablers and Design Considerations

Several enabling technologies help implement zero trust within AIoT:

- **Identity and access management (IAM)**: Each device, service and user must have a unique identity, with strong authentication (possibly hardware-backed), and that identity is continuously re-verified.
- **Device posture assessment**: Lightweight agents or gateway proxies must check firmware versions, patch status, configuration integrity, and vulnerability exposure (Li et al., 2024).

- **Policy engines with contextual data**: Engines use user/device identity, location, time, device health, network telemetry and threat intelligence to compute trust.
- **Telemetry and monitoring**: Real-time ingestion of logs, flows and behavioral signals is vital.
- **Edge gateways as enforcement points**: Because devices may be constrained, gateways or edge nodes often fulfil enforcement roles (policy administration and enforcement) for downstream devices.
- **Secure communication and encryption**: All data in transit (east-west, north-south) must be encrypted; metadata must be protected.
- **Migration of legacy/OT devices**: As noted by recent surveys, IoT/OT devices pose a special challenge for ZTA due to resource constraints and long lifecycles.

By aligning zero-trust principles with the layered structure of AIoT systems, organizations can build a security architecture that treats every request, identity and device as untrusted until proven otherwise; continuously monitors for posture and behavior changes; and segments and controls access on a fine-grained per-session basis. The next section presents a practical implementation framework, showing how these principles can be instantiated in device onboarding, policy flows, enforcement, audit and automation.

5. IMPLEMENTATION FRAMEWORK

Developing a practical reference framework for zero-trust in AIoT requires translating conceptual mapping into concrete workflows, components, deployment architectures and operational considerations. This section presents such a framework: defining layers (devices, controllers/gateways, cloud services), workflows (onboarding, policy decision, session enforcement, audit), access control mechanisms, and toolsets. It also explores real-world constraints such as resource limitations, latency, scalability, and safety.

5.1 Layered Deployment Architecture

The deployment framework is organized into three triers:

1. **Devices**: Smart actuators and sensors as well as embedded AI modules. Each device has a different form of identification (hardware root, certificate, or TPM),

captures and reports posture (firmware version, known vulnerabilities, configuration state), and communicates over secured channels to a trusted gateway.

2. **Gateway/Edge**: Edge devices act as enforcement points which intercept access requests and forward to the policy engine while enforcing segmentation between devices, collecting telemetry, and performing initial analytics or AI-based anomaly detection. The gateway might have a local policy agent that communicates as required to cloud-based policy engines.
3. **Cloud/Analytics**: Centralized services for large-scale model training, identity management, long-term telemetry storage, analytics, audit, and policy orchestration. The cloud hosts the primary policy engine (PE) and policy administrator (PA) components; decisions propagate edge-wards. The architecture is service-oriented and modular, supporting federated or distributed deployments.

5.2 Device Onboarding Workflow

A standard onboarding workflow may be as follows:

- **Step 1 – Registration**: Device arrives with manufacturer identity, certificate or secure element. The device is registered in an identity repository; a minimal trust score is assigned based on device type, vendor, firmware age, and environment (learning outcome: identity negotiation, cognitive domain: apply).
- **Step 2 – Posture Assessment**: The gateway or edge node queries the device for firmware version, patch status, configuration hash, known vulnerabilities. If device fails checks, it is quarantined or given severely restricted privileges (skills domain: analyze).
- **Step 3 – Policy Assignment**: Based on device role, trust score, and context, the policy engine assigns a policy (least privilege, segmentation) and instructs the enforcement point (gateway) to configure access controls (format: text description).
- **Step 4 – Session Initialization**: When device requests access, the PEP intercepts, forwards to PA/PE, which calculates a trust score dynamically (learning outcome: evaluate) and either grants or denies or grants with limited privilege.
- **Step 5 – Continuous Monitoring & Reevaluation**: During operation, telemetry is gathered—network flows, device behaviors, anomaly detection. If behavior deviates from baseline, trust score is reduced, policy is adjusted, device may be quarantined or firmware update pushed (cognitive domain: evaluate).

- **Step 6 – Decommissioning**: When device service ends, credentials and certificates are revoked, segmentation removed, and audit logs archived (skills domain: apply).

Figure 2 provides a visual overview of the zero-trust device onboarding lifecycle, from initial registration to continuous monitoring and decommissioning.

Figure 2. Device onboarding workflow

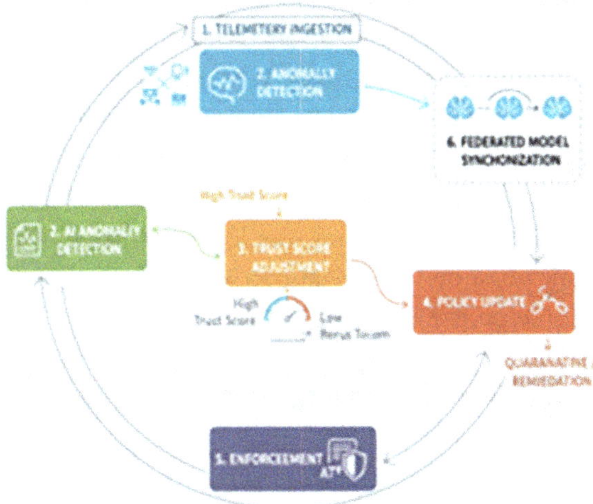

5.3 Access Control Mechanisms & Example Workflow

The framework allows for several control layers including multi-factor authentication for people, certificate and hardware roots for devices, behavioral access controls, and dynamic trust-based access permissions. Take this scenario: A temperature sensor in an industrial AIoT environment tries to access an analytic model through the edge gateway. The gateway PEP sends the request to the PA, which in turn queries the PE for processing. The PE generates a trust score of 0.7 based on the device's age, firmware status, and telemetry (no anomalies). The PE then applies policies to the trust score and thresholds: 0.7 passes for "read-only data stream" access but not for "model update" permission. The PA instructs PEP: allow data stream, deny update. The session begins; after 10 minutes of unusually high data rate (indicating anomaly), telemetry triggers trust reduction to 0.45; PA now commands PEP to throttle data, isolate segments, and escalate for manual review.

5.4 Tools, Platforms & Protocols

Key standards and platforms support the framework:

- The foundational document National Institute of Standards and Technology's SP 800-207 outlines policy engine, PA, PEP components.
- Micro-segmentation and zero-trust network access (ZTNA) platforms help segment and control devices.
- Lightweight IAM and certificate management for resource-constrained devices; key rotation and hardware roots of trust.
- Telemetry-ingestion pipelines (edge to cloud) supporting real-time analytics; some architecture embeds AI or anomaly detection engines. Studies have shown that integrating AI trust-scoring engines significantly enhances zero-trust effectiveness in IoT.
- Gateways or edge platforms may implement software-defined networking (SDN)/network function virtualization (NFV) to dynamically control device flows and enforce policies. (Flexible ZTA paper)

5.5 Performance, Safety and Resource Considerations

Because many AIoT devices are resource-constrained (limited battery, compute, connectivity), design trade-offs must be made:

- **Latency overhead**: The onboarding and continuous trust evaluation may add communication and computation latency. Organizations must optimize for minimal delay—e.g., local edge decisioning, caching of policies.
- **Scalability**: AIoT environments may involve thousands to millions of devices. The policy engine must scale, efficient trust scoring algorithms should be lightweight or distributed.
- **Reliability and resilience**: Gateways or enforcement points are critical; their failure should not bring the system down. Redundant policy engines and enforcement points help.
- **For protective measures**: Especially for compliance with laws and regulations in industrial and health-related AIoT's, security architecture must ensure no device malfunctions jeopardize the physical process. Access revocation must include fail-safes (if access is denied, operation defaults to safe mode rather than creating unsafe state).
- **Device Lifecycle**: The processes of onboarding, firmware upgrades and decommissioning must all be planned and controlled. Legacy devices are often devoid of hardware roots of trust and must be quarantined in sepa-

rately segmented networks until they can be decommissioned, upgraded, or replaced. Research calls this the most critical advancement in IoT zero-trust architecture.

The conceptual integration of zero trust actions into architecture and workflows for AIoT networks is defined within the implementation framework outlined as: zero trust onboarding lifecycle, policy devotion streams, persistent posture identity and posture validation, distributed monitoring and zero trust enforcement, and performance and safety retention. In the next section of this research, we will assess how AI driven enforcement will enhance the zero-trust deployment in AIoT environments even further.

5.6 Latency-Aware Zero Trust Design for Industrial AIoT

In industrial AIoT environments, there are stringent latency requirements, especially in control, manufacturing, and safety-critical applications. Although the zero-trust model is beneficial in providing better security, it might cause additional latency if not properly implemented. To overcome the latency effects, there are certain architectural considerations that must be taken into account.

One consideration is the distribution of PEPs in edge gateways or controllers. Latency is minimized since access decisions are made closer to the device. Instead of sending requests to the central policy engine, edge PEPs can apply pre-approved policies. Another consideration is the caching of policies and trust scores, which minimizes decision latency. Pre-access policies and trust scores often used in the system can be cached in the edge device, allowing it to be used during short validity windows (Shaghaghi et al., 2016).

On the other hand, edge trust verification and anomaly detection enable systems to quickly identify problems even when cloud connectivity is lost. Light models process trust scoring quickly, while analytics can wait for cloud processing if latency permits. Moreover, graceful degradation and fail-safe operation are critical in industrial settings. When connection to centralized policy services is lost, devices and controllers should gracefully degrade into safe and limited operation rather than failing completely (Qureshi, Jeon & Piccialli, 2021).

Through the strategic integration of distributed enforcement, caching, and edge intelligence, zero-trust systems can be designed to address the low-latency and high-reliability requirements of industrial AIoT applications without compromising security.

6. AI-DRIVEN ENFORCEMENT AND AUTOMATION

As the world becomes more interconnected and data intensive, the need for integrating artificial network and automation within a zero-trust framework in AIoT Networks becomes imperative, not just beneficial. This section looks at the ways in which AI can assist with enforcement and automation of zero-trust principles while outlining the more critical mechanisms such as policy adaptation, anomaly detection, and federated learning. In addition, it provides a conceptual case study which exemplifies how automation improves responsiveness and reduces human strain.

6.1 Role of AI in Policy Adaptation and Enforcement

A conventional ZTA tends to simply set the policy enforcement points (PEPs) as rule-based automations that require manual tuning of the trust-scoring thresholds. e.g. AI provides context-driven dynamic policy change that adjusts to different device behaviors, threats, and shifting network circumstances. An AI device monitoring model could track behavioral telemetry, i.e. subscription to a particular device network (firmware version), the rate of communication (communication rate), and endpoint identity (endpoint identity systems) change and in real time, increase or decrease the device trust score depending, on the real stable behaviors and the anomalous behaviors respectively, such as dynamic scoring, the PE is able to tighten or loosen thresholds of the decision and the PA is able to change rules of policy enforcement automatically without human assistance.

Recent works on intrusions in industrial IoT and AI-enabled zero trust architecture systems, prove to have higher thresholds of detection than static rule-based systems. The report showed success via trust and ML/DL architecture on IoT networks with higher ratios of true positive and low ratios of false positive. The case proves that in systems with a high number of endpoints and shifting threat vectors, enforcement via AI is possible (Salam et al., 2024).

6.2 Continuous Monitoring, Anomaly Detection and Behavioral Analytics

In AIoT networks, human operators can be easily overwhelmed by the volume and variety of telemetry data. However, AI can perform anomaly detection, clustering, and behavioral analytics and pinpoint deviations from the norm. For example, unsupervised models or hybrid ML approaches can isolate scenarios wherein a device begins transmitting at elevated frequencies, contacts unfamiliar endpoints, or engages in unexpected firmware behaviors / cryptographic handshake failures. In such scenarios, automated policies such as isolation, segmentation, re-authentication, and full access revocation can be enforced, policy-driven actions autonomously triggered.

According to one survey on IoT intrusion detection systems, AI and hybrid techniques "move beyond the static approaches traditionally used, and in which have the ae IoT systems also face the most constraints." In zero trust, however, the bottom line is that such continuous analytics loops in this context guarantee. Trust is not a one-time verification, it is a dynamic, continuous process.

6.3 Federated Learning and Collaborative Trust Scoring

Because of the breadth and distribution of AIoT Systems–edge devices, gateways, and nodes in the cloud–centralized analytics may create latency, privacy, or bandwidth issues. Federated learning presents a solution: local devices or micro-clusters train models on local telemetry, contribute updates to a global trust engine (model updates, no raw data), and receive locally enforceable, refined models. This mechanism enables zero-trust in edge-distributed configurations by allowing trust scoring and adaptive policy enforcement to be processed spatially near the devices, while respecting data locality and latency.

Newer frameworks suggest a combination of zero trust architecture, zero touch provisioning, and AI/ML (including federated learning) for large scale IoT deployments. AIoT networks can rapidly adapt to novel threats by deploying federated trust engines, pattern sharing across devices, and sustaining uninterrupted enforcement without centralized enforcement bottlenecks. Figure 3 illustrates the AI-driven trust scoring and automated enforcement loop that enables continuous and adaptive security decisions within the zero-trust AIoT environment.

Figure 3. AI-driven trust scoring and automated enforcement loop

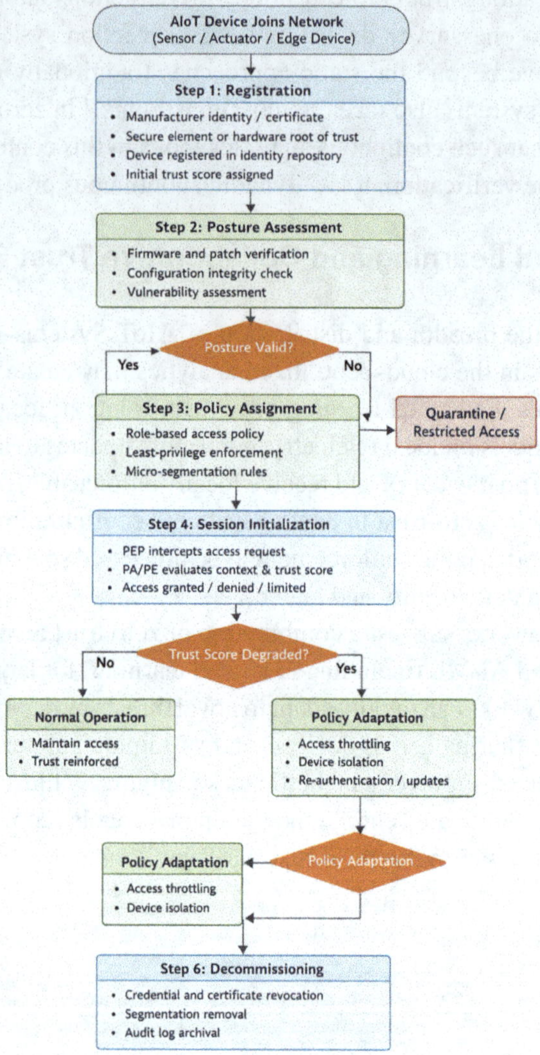

6.4 Case Study: Automated Enforcement in an AIoT Deployment

Think about a smart manufacturing AIoT network that utilizes sensors along the production lines, employs edge gateways for circumstantial analysis, and relies on cloud services for extensive analytics.

- Each sensor unit gets onboard under a zero-trust framework (identity, posture arced).
- During operations, sensors and gateway telemetry are pulled to local anomaly detection systems, trained through a federated learning process.
- The system determines that an abnormal number of data packets is being sent from one of the sensors to a previously unconnected host and an anomaly detection model identifies the system as anomalous.
- The sensor's trust score decreasing below a policy threshold, the policy engine (PEP) is commanded to isolate the sensor for quarantine, severely limit its communication, and set a prompt for re-authentication or firmware update.
- At the same time, the federated model is updated with the new anomaly, the behavior pattern (anonymized) is disseminated to other clusters, and coordination of policy updates is done throughout the network.

    This automated cycle, monitoring, scoring, policy compliance, feedback learning, helps the network decrease human oversight, dwell time, and lateral movement through real-time zero trust controls.

6.5 Implementation Considerations and Pitfalls

Despite the strong potential for AI-driven enforcement, a number of concerns will still need to be addressed:

- Explainability in the model and enforcement trust: With machine learning and deep learning, models need to mesh and 'make sense' of things, especially with regulated or safety-critical AI IoT. Any black-box method will be subject to rejection by auditors or safety specialists.
- Limits of a resource: With many AI IoT endpoints, hosting heavy AI models won't be a possibility. Edge gateways will have to carry the burden of the analytics. Policies must 'degrade' gracefully for ultra-light devices.
- Quality of the data and adversarial robustness: If telemetry is hacked or manipulated, credential smearing with trust scoring and other mechanisms of anomaly detection might be compromised. AI models need to be robust to adversarial situations.
- Policy oscillation and grained stability: There is a need for enforcement to avoid 'thrashing' where there is a win of changing a lot of policies. A lot of governance is necessary in that area to have the necessary level of performance and stability.
- Real-time demands and latency: With strict latency in certain AI IoT use cases, the model tells itself that the detection and enforcement is supposed to be instant and therefore simple, which might not be the case. Outlining these

areas can make AI-driven enforcement robust, sharpening the zero-trust readiness in an AI IoT setting.

6.6 Machine Learning–Based Trust Scoring and Automated Policy Adaptation

Trust scoring is defined as a continuous anomaly and risk assessment problem, where a trust score is assigned to a device or session. Due to the scarcity of attack data in AIoT and the presence of evolving threats, unsupervised and semi-supervised learning are predominantly used. In particular, Isolation Forest is used for anomaly detection due to its low computational cost and its ability to work well with high-dimensional data. Anomaly detection is achieved by isolating data points, which require fewer partitions than those of normal data (Bampatsikos et al., 2025).

However, for gateways with higher computational power, deep autoencoders can be used to learn a baseline for normal data. A high reconstruction error can be used to determine abnormal data. In addition, clustering algorithms, such as density-based clustering, can be used for behavioral outlier detection and to detect changes in the behavior of a device. Lightweight supervised learning can also be used in conjunction with unsupervised learning, where data is available, to improve detection of known attacks (Torabi et al., 2023). The output of all the models is combined to produce a trust score. Trust models consume multi-layer telemetry collected across devices, edges, and cloud layers. Key feature groups include:

1. Device posture features such as firmware version, patch level, configuration integrity, and secure boot status.
2. Network features such as packet rate, flow duration, protocol usage, destination diversity, and authentication failures.
3. Behavioral features such as reporting frequency of sensors, command execution patterns, time of day consistency, and scope of interactions; and
4. AI-related features such as inference request rates, confidence distribution drift, and irregular model updates.

In the case of resource-constrained devices, raw data is summarized at gateways using statistical aggregation. Trust scoring is directly linked to a closed-loop policy adaptation process. The telemetry is continuously evaluated by the trust engine, and the trust score is recalculated in near real-time. As the trust score changes and goes past certain thresholds, the policy engine will adapt access policies according to least privilege access. This could include limiting communication, removing specific permissions, requiring re-authentication, or even micro-segmenting the device. As behavior is normalized or remediation techniques are successful, for example, by updating the firmware, trust can also be incrementally regained and access restored. By using this combination of lightweight machine learning, multi-layered telemetry, and automated policy enforcement, it is ensured that trust in AIoT systems is earned in real-time and is context-dependent and revocable, in alignment with zero-trust architectures and the scale and dynamic nature of AIoT systems.

7. EVALUATION METRICS AND PERFORMANCE CONSIDERATIONS

A well-defined metric system is a must when undertaking a meaningful evaluation of a zero-trust architecture for AIoT networks, in particular one supplemented with AI enforcement. This section describes key metrics like accuracy of trust score, latency overhead, false-positive / false-negative rates, resource costs, and scalability and analyzing performance tradeoffs, especially under constricted AIoT circumstances.

7.1 Core Metrics

- **Trust Score Accuracy**: The degree to which computed trust scores map to actual device risk. Metrics include true positive rate (correctly identifying malicious/untrusted devices), false negative rate (malicious devices treated as trusted), and false positive rate (benign devices downgraded). In one industrial IoT intrusion-detection study, ML/DL embedded in zero-trust achieved high true positive rates and low false positives (Taha et al, 2024).
- **Latency Overhead**: Additional delay introduced by onboarding, trust scoring, continuous monitoring, policy decisions and enforcement. For AIoT applications with real-time constraints, latency must be within acceptable bounds.
- **Resource Utilization**: CPU, memory, network bandwidth, edge gateway load. More aggressive monitoring or heavy AI may strain devices or edge resources.
- **Scalability**: Supporting numerous devices, sessions and instantiations dynamically. The number of devices per enforcement point, policy decisions executed per second, and model update latency in federated scenarios are some sample metrics.
- **Revocation/Response Time**: Detection of some kind of compromise (anomaly, device takeover) and enforcement (isolation, and segmentation, revocation) remaining in definable periods. The amount of time spent on architecture to handle a threat is latency.

- **False Positive Induced Disruption**: The cost of productivity loss due to disruption of devices and being categorized to system error/ malfunctions or risk is a sensitive cost in the sector of industrial AIoT.
- **Anchoring in Business or Physical Outcomes**: The security metrics in AIoT contexts are the business/physical outcome metrics, which are the: reduction in lateral movement, prevention of movement, the reduction in and incident caused, safety data and the integrity of it.

7.2 Performance Trade-Offs and Constraints

Implementing zero-trust architecture in AIoT networks entails some compromises:

- **Security vs Latency**: more thorough monitoring and more complex AI models can increase delays, which is detrimental to time-sensitive application – control systems for instance. System designers have to adjust the level of granularity for which the trust evaluation is done.
- **Resource Efficiency vs Fidelity**: Lightweight devices may support only posture checks and not telemetry. Simplified models can degrade accuracy or increase some form of risk. The architecture must have tiered trust mechanisms which are device class sensitive.
- **Automation vs Governance**: the need for policy enforcement through the use of AI can result in faster responses to new developments, but in having less human control, there is a risk of enforcement as AI can misconfigure and behave in unexpected ways. There must be a way to conduct governance with audit logs which can track the activity of the system alongside the system's autonomous features.
- **Scalability vs Centralization**: more centralized policy engines can increase the quality of the evaluation at the expense of better analytics, queuing and other bottlenecks which in turn increase the chance of a single failure. More decentralized or federated designs decrease the chance of a single failure but may cause more structural complexity and lower system trust.
- **Safety vs Security**: in domains such as industrial, health and mobility AIoT, trust revocation and overly aggressive enforcement can result in the disabling of device communication, which in turn can compromise safety critical actions. There must be a way to integrate different policy frameworks to ensure there are fail-safe systems that are, after trust revocation, able to allow operation as opposed to the system shutting down completely.

7.3 Benchmarking and Simulation Approaches

To validate implementation, organizations can adopt benchmarking or simulation frameworks:

- Deploy scaled replicas of AIoT networks, measure onboarding latency, trust-scoring rates, enforcement delays, and false-positive/false-negative rates under attack and normal conditions.
- Use real telemetry or synthetic attack traffic (e.g., DDoS, lateral movement, device compromise) to test revocation response time, segmentation effectiveness and containment of lateral propagation. The aforementioned study achieved high accuracy in intrusion detection for zero-trust IoT using ML/DL.
- Use federated-learning simulations or edge-cloud partitioning to evaluate how trust models update and distribute, and measure bandwidth, update latency and consistency across nodes.
- Monitor how policy enforcement affects application performance, latency, device battery life, and network throughput in normal vs worst-case conditions.

7.4 Interpretability, Compliance and Audit

Beyond technical metrics, evaluation must consider interpretability (especially of AI-based decisions), compliance with regulatory or industry frameworks, and auditability of trust decisions. For instance, if an AIoT device is isolated due to low trust score, the system must log the reasoning chain (device posture data, behavior anomaly, model output, policy threshold) so that safety officers, auditors or regulatory bodies can review and validate the decision. Failure to provide interpretable justifications may reduce stakeholder trust in the architecture and hamper adoption.

Within AIoT networks, a zero-trust architecture requires rigorous evaluation along multiple dimensions: trust validation accuracy, system latency and overhead, resource limits, system scalability, automation balance, and compliance accountability. With the appropriate selection of metrics, realistic trade testing, and analysis of trade-offs, network practitioners and researchers can validate that zero-trust architecture not only secures the network but also meets the performance and operational requirements of AIoT environments.

8. DISCUSSION AND FUTURE DIRECTIONS

The integration of ZTA into AIoT networks is beyond just technological change. It is a change in how trust, verification, and control are understood in intelligent distributed systems. As more businesses adopt automated systems driven by AIoT for decision-making and operations, instantaneous data processing and actions—the need for security becomes more important. This part explores artificial intelligence and AIoT systems and uses case studies to ZTA deployment in AIoT, explores ZTA deployment trends and highlights ZTA deployment in AIoT for industrial research, and highlights ZTA in AIoT for industrial research, emerging research-industrial trends, and future research directions.

8.1 Challenges in Real-World Adoption

ZTA principles mature on paper, but complexities remain when integrating them into AIoT systems. A central challenge is legacy systems integration. A good number of existing IoT devices lack advanced capabilities needed for seamless interoperability. For instance, posture evaluation coupled with real-time hardware-rooted identities cryptographically secure communication. Many medical/industrial controllers, medical sensors, and devices for environmental monitoring are designed for longevity and not for retrofitting. As such, full ZTA compliance is difficult at best, without intermediary gateway proxies (Zanasi, Russo & Colajanni, 2024).

Another barrier that remains is the lack of interoperability. AIoT ecosystems are disparate systems that integrate devices and vendors across differing security models/protocols. The lack of standardization in the market complicates structural governance and still attempts to apply universal policy/defining trust evaluation frameworks across multi-vendor systems. The promise of ZTA in multi-vendor systems without standardization, is fragmented and inconsistent coverage.

There are unique privacy and ethics issues that arise from the telemetry required for constant verification. ZTA relies on constant monitoring devices that leave sensitive information vulnerable during periods of data collection. Aggregating information with AI systems that track behavioral patterns can lead to uncontrolled privacy violations Laghari et al., 2024. This means that ZTA privacy violating mechanisms must be accompanied by techniques such as homomorphic encryption, secure multiparty computation, and differential privacy.

8.2 Integration with Quantum-Safe Cryptography and Blockchain

Continuing advancement of AIoT systems towards 6g means their long-term reliance on secure communications will be threatened by quantum computers. Post quantum cryptography (PQC) has therefore emerged as disjointed area adjacent to ZTA. Applying zero trust structures to lattice based encryption and hash-based signature algorithms helps to defend against future decryption attempts (Bhoi et al 2025). Devices within the AIoT ecosystem require even more lightweight implementations of PQC to be used since traditional implementations of PQC are too resource intensive.

Blockchains and Distributed Ledger Technologies (DLTs) also have synergy with ZTA by providing immutable, distributed audit logs. All trust decisions, such as adding a device, posture assessment, and policy change. can be recorded as a tamper-evident audit on a permissioned ledger (Li et al., 2025). In blockchain federated or distributed AIoT networks, ZTA allows trust state to be independently audited and synchronized without a central governing entity. Thus, the combination of ZTA, blockchain, and PQC provides a multi layered, forwards secure approach to system integrity and confidentiality.

8.3 Toward Autonomous and Self-Adaptive Zero Trust

The advancement of ZTA within AIoT is focused on self-adaptive systems driven by AI with autonomy decision-making capability. Such frameworks can self-adjust trust tier thresholds, dynamic re-segment networks, and self-govern in behavior-policy shifts of the network which change in response to varying hostile frameworks or behavioral drift. Newer concepts like Autonomous Zero-Trust Orchestration (AZTO) are looking at self-refreshing policy systems which in the Automatized ZTA (AZTA) framework can excel on the runtime and operational data feedback loops for reinforcement.

The role of Federated Learning and Edge Intelligence is critical in this scenario. They enable the remote workstations or the local network to collaborate in refining the trust frameworks through the ZTA and without sharing the original raw data, thus fostering the growth of Federated Zero-Trust Networks (Tiwari et al., 2022). The blend of local independence and global integration could characterize the advancement of enforcement of zero trust in AIoT ecosystems.

8.4 Standardization and Governance

Complete vertical integration of unified industry standards and regulatory apparatus is a prerequisite for widespread adoption. Compliance and good practice will flow down from the generic practice set within NIST SP 800-207 to the perimeter sanitizing. formulation of device and AI specific practices will remain unresolved. The ISO/IEC and ETSI's and IEEE's initiatives on AI and IoT interoperability security model standards will assist. There will still be the question of constructing new oversight regimes that will extend to the auditing of AI instruments deployed for self-management of policies governed by AI to ensure the self-management is as light as possible.

8.5 Research Opportunities

Multiple new research areas arise from the ongoing discussion:

- Hybrid lightweight models of trust for ultra-constrained IoT endpoints (cryptographic low- power and event-driven policy evaluation).
- Explainable AI for producing trust scores with accompanied decision paths that are interpretable and auditable.
- Trust diffusion in federated AIoT ecosystems, with supportive inter-domain policy sharing and consistency governance features.
- ZTA integration with energy-aware scheduling in AIoT for a sustainable security- centric approach.

Digital twins and simulation spaces for testing ZTA enforcement and trust-attack resilience modeling before actual deployment.

Integrating these aspects into forthcoming studies will considerably contribute to the theoretical and practical application of ZTA in intelligent distributed systems.

9. CONCLUSION

The use of Zero Trust Architecture on Artificial Intelligence of Things networks is an important step toward securing distributed and intelligent ecosystems in which trust cannot be taken for granted. In relation to this, this chapter covered the basics of ZTA and its practical implementation through a mapped layered implementation on AIoT. It has been demonstrated that real-time verification, micro segmentation, identity-based controls, and AI-based systems for trust assessment put together provide solid security for AIoT networks.

The discussion showed also how trust is automated and reinforced through the use of AI, federated learning, and blockchain-based audit trails. It should, however, be noted that challenges such as retrofitting legacy systems, setting and managing privacy and resource-saving controls, and lack of standardized Interoperability frameworks still exist. ZTA models need to be adaptable, self-learning and quantum resilient as the AIoT environments extend toward the 6G and quantum eras.

Above all, ZTA is grounded in the idea that trust is no longer an assumption of boundaries, but increasingly an evolving, evidence-based philosophy. ZTA should be carefully implemented in AIoT networks as it allows for a shift from defense through reactive and instead defense through intelligent proactive resilience. Such a shift rids the system of the constraint of having to balance trust, security, reliability and innovation.

REFERENCES

Balbix. (2025). Top IT, OT, and IoT security challenges and best practices. Retrieved from https://www.balbix.com/insights/addressing-iot-security-challenges/

Bampatsikos, M., Politis, I., Ioannidis, T., & Xenakis, C. (2025). Trust score prediction and management in IoT ecosystems using markov chains and MADM techniques. *IEEE Transactions on Consumer Electronics*, *71*(1), 862–882. DOI: 10.1109/TCE.2025.3531045

Bhoi, S. S., Saini, A., Diro, A., Kaisar, S., & Rao, A. (2025). Future Digital Identity Management with Quantum Secure Blockchain. *IEEE Communications Surveys and Tutorials*.

CyberArk. (2023). What is the NIST SP 800-207 cybersecurity framework? [Available] https://www.cyberark.com/what-is/nist-sp-800-207-cybersecurity-framework/

Laghari, A. A., Li, H., Khan, A. A., Shoulin, Y., Karim, S., & Khani, M. A. K. (2024). Internet of Things (IoT) applications security trends and challenges. *Discover Internet of Things*, *4*(1), 36. DOI: 10.1007/s43926-024-00090-5

Li, K., Li, C., Yuan, X., Li, S., Zou, S., Ahmed, S. S., & Akan, Ö. B. (2025). Zero-trust foundation models: A new paradigm for secure and collaborative artificial intelligence for internet of things. *IEEE Internet of Things Journal*, *12*(22), 46269–46293. DOI: 10.1109/JIOT.2025.3603957

Litoussi, M., Kannouf, N., El Makkaoui, K., Ezzati, A., & Fartitchou, M. (2020). IoT security: Challenges and countermeasures. *Procedia Computer Science*, *177*, 503–508. DOI: 10.1016/j.procs.2020.10.069

Mazhar, T., Talpur, D. B., Shloul, T. A., Ghadi, Y. Y., Haq, I., Ullah, I., Ouahada, K., & Hamam, H. (2023). Analysis of IoT security challenges and its solutions using artificial intelligence. *Brain Sciences*, *13*(4), 683. DOI: 10.3390/brainsci13040683 PMID: 37190648

NextLabs. (2024). NIST 800-207: Zero Trust Architecture. White paper. [Available] https://www.nextlabs.com/wp-content/uploads/2024/11/NextLabs-White-Paper -NIST-800-207-Zero-Trust-Architecture.pdf

Qureshi, K. N., Jeon, G., & Piccialli, F. (2021). Anomaly detection and trust authority in artificial intelligence and cloud computing. *Computer Networks*, *184*, 107647. DOI: 10.1016/j.comnet.2020.107647

RiskRecon. (2023). Understanding NIST 800-207. [Available] https://blog.riskrecon.com/understanding-nist-800-207

Rose, S., Borchert, O., Mitchell, S., & Connelly, S. (2020). *Zero Trust Architecture (NIST SP 800-207)*. National Institute of Standards and Technology., DOI: 10.6028/NIST.SP.800-207

Salam, A. E., Yousef, S., Duha, A., Eman, A., & Alyaa, A. (2024). Employing mutual information feature selection and LightGBM for intrusion detection in IoT. *ICIC*, *18*(06), 597.

Sanjalawe, Y., Al-E'mari, S., Alqurashi, T., Alharbi, Z. H., Makhadmeh, S. N., & Alsharaiah, M. (2025). Adaptive graph attention-based federated learning for IoT intrusion detection: Mitigating poisoning attacks. *PeerJ. Computer Science*, *11*, e3281. DOI: 10.7717/peerj-cs.3281

Schiller, E., Aidoo, A., Fuhrer, J., Stahl, J., Ziörjen, M., & Stiller, B. (2022). Landscape of IoT security. *Computer Science Review*, *44*, 1–18. DOI: 10.1016/j.cosrev.2022.100467

Sebestyen, H., Popescu, D. E., & Zmaranda, R. D. (2025). A literature review on security in the Internet of Things: Identifying and analysing critical categories. *Computers*, *14*(2), 61. DOI: 10.3390/computers14020061

Shaghaghi, A., Kaafar, M. A., Scott-Hayward, S., Kanhere, S. S., & Jha, S. (2016, November). Towards policy enforcement point as a service (peps). In *2016 IEEE Conference on Network Function Virtualization and Software Defined Networks (NFV-SDN)* (pp. 50-55). IEEE. DOI: 10.1109/NFV-SDN.2016.7919475

Shonubi, J. A. (2025). Multi-Layered Zero Trust Architectures for Cross-Domain Data Protection in Federated Enterprise Networks and High-Risk Operational Environments. *International Journal of Research Publication and Reviews*, *6*(7), 146–169. DOI: 10.55248/gengpi.6.0725.2438

Taha, M. B., Sanjalawe, Y., Al-Daraiseh, A., Fraihat, S., & Al-E'mari, S. R. (2024). Proactive auto-scaling for service function chains in cloud computing based on deep learning. *IEEE Access : Practical Innovations, Open Solutions*, *12*, 38575–38593. DOI: 10.1109/ACCESS.2024.3375772

Talakola, S. (2025). Security Challenges in Autonomous Systems: A Zero-Trust Approach. *International Journal of Emerging Trends in Computer Science and Information Technology*, 56-66.

Tiwari, S., Sarma, W., & Srivastava, A. (2022). Integrating artificial intelligence with zero trust architecture: Enhancing adaptive security in modern cyber threat landscape. *International Journal of Research and Analytical Reviews*, *9*, 712–728.

Torabi, H., Mirtaheri, S. L., & Greco, S. (2023). Practical autoencoder based anomaly detection by using vector reconstruction error. *Cybersecurity*, *6*(1), 1. DOI: 10.1186/s42400-022-00134-9

Zanasi, C., Russo, S., & Colajanni, M. (2024). Flexible zero trust architecture for the cybersecurity of industrial IoT infrastructures. *Ad Hoc Networks*, *156*, 103414. DOI: 10.1016/j.adhoc.2024.103414

Chapter 6

Advances in Gait and Footprint Biometrics on Edge Computing: Comprehensive Review and Future Perspectives

Bini M. Issac
http://orcid.org/0009-0004-7649-4526
Amal Jyothi College of Engineering, Kanjirappally, India

S. N. Kumar
http://orcid.org/0000-0002-2530-1454
Amal Jyothi College of Engineering, Kanjirappally, India

Aleena Varghese
Amal Jyothi College of Engineering, Kanjirappally, India

Anakin Rajeev
Amal Jyothi College of Engineering, Kanjirappally, India

Angelina Kanjooparambil Joseph
Amal Jyothi College of Engineering, Kanjirappally, India

Belda Ben Thomas
Amal Jyothi College of Engineering, Kanjirappally, India

ABSTRACT

Gait recognition and footprint biometrics have emerged as effective modalities for unobtrusive and reliable human identification. This work reviews recent advances enabled by deep learning and edge AI, emphasizing how appearance-based representations such as silhouettes and GEIs, combined with model-based pose features, support invariant and discriminative gait descriptors. We examine modern architectures, including graph neural networks (GNNs) and generative adversarial networks (GANs), that improve cross-view synthesis, motion modeling, and robustness to covariates like clothing, illumination, and occlusion. Multi-modal fusion

DOI: 10.4018/979-8-3373-6299-1.ch006

methods that integrate visual inputs with WiFi CSI, LiDAR, and pressure data are discussed for enhancing performance in unconstrained environments. We also evaluate model compression and hardware–software co-optimization strategies essential for real-time deployment on edge devices. Finally, we highlight privacy preserving approaches, including federated learning and feature perturbation, that ensure secure and ethical use of gait data.

1. INTRODUCTION

Biometric systems are designed to identify individuals using unique physiological or behav- ioral traits. Among behavioral biometrics, *gait recognition* identifying a person based on the way they walk has gained significant attention because it is non intrusive, contactless, and can be captured at a distance. Unlike fingerprints, facial images, or iris scans, gait can be ana- lyzed without the subject's active cooperation, making it especially suitable for surveillance, public security, and access-control applications where user interaction is limited or impractical (Makihara et al., 2022; Salcedo et al., 2024).

Early research in gait recognition mainly focused on appearance-based methods, with silhouette- based representations being widely used for feature extraction and classification. These ap- proaches achieved promising results in controlled environments; however, their performance degraded significantly in real-world scenarios due to clothing variations, carried objects, il- lumination changes, and camera viewpoint differences (Chao et al., 2019; Fan et al., 2020).

To address these limitations, researchers gradually shifted toward model-based gait recogni- tion, where explicit body structure information such as joint positions and limb movements—is extracted using 2D or 3D pose estimation techniques. Skeleton-based and pose-based rep- resentations have demonstrated improved robustness to appearance and viewpoint variations, particularly when combined with deep learning architectures such as spatio-temporal networks and graph-based models (Liao et al., 2020; Fu et al., 2023).

At the same time, the deployment paradigm of biometric systems has evolved. Traditional gait recognition pipelines rely heavily on cloud based processing, which introduces challenges including increased latency, dependence on network connectivity, privacy concerns, and regula- tory constraints. With the rapid growth of the *Artificial Intelligence of Things (AIoT)*, there has been a clear shift toward *edge computing*, where data processing and inference are performed locally on embedded devices. Edge based gait recognition enables real time operation, reduces communication overhead, and improves privacy by ensuring that raw biometric data does not leave the device (?Salcedo et al., 2024).

Despite these advancements, gait recognition alone may still face limitations in high-security or controlled environments due to spoofing, imitation, and intra class variability. To mitigate these challenges, recent studies have explored multi modal biometric systems that integrate gait with complementary modalities. One such modality is *footprint biometrics*, which analyzes pressure patterns generated by the human foot during walking. Footprint data, typically cap- tured using pressure-sensitive mats or wearable insoles, provide discriminative features such as plantar pressure distribution and center-of-pressure trajectories. When combined with gait recognition, footprint based analysis can enhance system robustness and reduce false accep- tance rates in constrained environments.

This book chapter provides a technical and analytical review of gait and footprint biometric systems with a specific focus on edge computing. Rather than offering a simple summary of existing studies, the chapter organizes the literature through a structured taxonomy and criti- cally examines trade-offs among recognition accuracy, robustness, computational complexity, and deployability on edge devices. In addition to recognition models and datasets, the chapter discusses hardware platforms, inference frameworks, optimization strategies, security threats, privacy considerations, and ethical challenges, with the goal of guiding researchers and practi- tioners toward real world, privacy-aware, and resource-constrained edge biometric systems.

Figure 1. High-level system overview of gait and footprint recognition on edge devices.

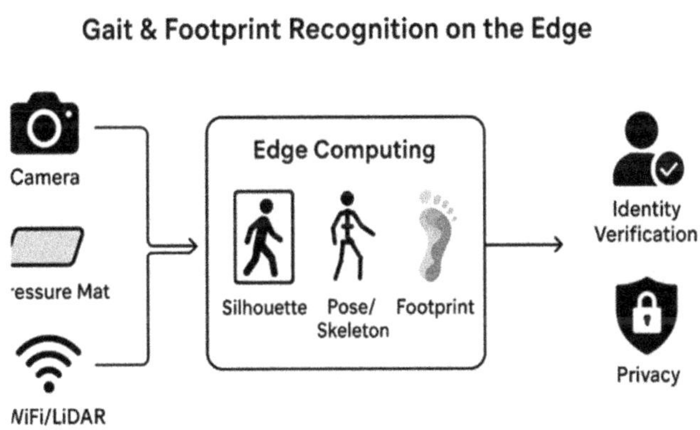

The figure depicts sensor inputs, edge processing on the device, and outputs that maintain privacy

1.1. Footprint-Based Biometric Recognition

Footprint-based biometric recognition exploits the unique patterns formed by an individual's feet during standing and walking. Unlike gait recognition, which emphasizes the kinematic and temporal dynamics of the entire body, footprint biometrics focus on localized character- istics such as plantar pressure distribution, foot morphology, and ground contact dynamics. These features are influenced by an individual's anatomy, weight distribution, walking style, and neuromuscular control, making footprints a highly distinctive and complementary modal- ity for identity verification. Even when gait patterns appear similar across individuals, the subtle differences in plantar pressure and foot structure allow footprint recognition to provide an additional layer of biometric specificity.

Footprint data are typically acquired using pressure-sensitive sensing technologies, includ- ing floor-mounted pressure mats, smart flooring systems, and wearable sensing devices such as instrumented insoles. Pressure mats and smart floors provide high-resolution spatial mea- surements of plantar pressure across the foot sole, capturing both static footprints (e.g., while standing) and dynamic footprints produced during walking. Wearable insoles, on the other hand, allow continuous and unobtrusive monitoring of foot-ground interaction, making them ideal for mobile authentication, healthcare monitoring, or scenarios where fixed infrastructure is impractical.

1.1.1. Footprint Data Acquisition and Sensing Technologies

Pressure-based footprint acquisition systems utilize arrays of force-sensitive resistors or ca- pacitive sensors to capture localized pressure values with high temporal precision. During walking, these sensors track how pressure is distributed across gait phases such as heel strike, mid-stance, and toe-off. Unlike visual gait sensors, footprint systems are largely unaffected by lighting conditions, clothing, or camera angles, offering reliable performance in both controlled indoor and semi-structured environments.

However, footprint sensing presents its own challenges. Sensor calibration drift, limited sensing area, and variability introduced by footwear can affect recognition accuracy. While barefoot data provide the most discriminative plantar patterns, real-world applications typi- cally require recognition through shoes, introducing variations due to sole material, thickness, and wear patterns. Modern approaches mitigate these issues by focusing on dynamic pres- sure trajectories and relative pressure distributions instead of absolute forces, which improves robustness across different footwear types.

1.1.2. Feature Representation and Modeling

Footprint-based recognition leverages both static and dynamic features. Static features are extracted from aggregated pressure maps and include foot shape descriptors, pressure inten- sity histograms, arch characteristics, and regional pressure ratios. These features capture stable anatomical properties that remain consistent over time. Dynamic features, in contrast, represent temporal variations in pressure during walking and include center-of-pressure (COP) trajecto- ries, stride length, stance duration, pressure transition patterns, and temporal force curves.

Early footprint recognition systems relied on handcrafted features combined with classi- cal machine learning classifiers such as k-nearest neighbors (k-NN), support vector machines (SVMs), and linear discriminant analysis (LDA). While effective for small datasets or con- trolled experiments, they struggled to generalize to large-scale or real-world settings. More re- cent methods adopt deep learning models, including convolutional neural networks (CNNs) for spatial pressure maps and recurrent or temporal convolutional networks for sequential pressure data. These models automatically learn discriminative spatial and temporal features, significantly improving recognition performance in practical scenarios.

1.1.3. Footprint Biometrics on Edge Devices

Footprint-based systems are well-suited for deployment on edge devices due to their low data dimensionality and modest computational requirements. Unlike video-based gait recognition, which demands high-resolution image processing and pose estimation, footprint data consist of compact pressure matrices or low-dimensional time-series sequences. This allows real-time processing on resource-constrained devices such as microcontrollers, single-board computers, and low-power neural accelerators.

Edge-based footprint recognition offers strong privacy advantages. Since no visual or per- sonally identifiable imagery is captured, raw pressure data can be processed locally to extract features or embeddings, ensuring sensitive biometric information remains on the device. This makes footprint biometrics highly attractive for applications such as access control in secure facilities, smart buildings, and healthcare environments where data privacy and regulatory com- pliance are critical.

1.1.4. Complementarity With Gait Biometrics

While footprint biometrics provide robustness against variations in appearance, clothing, or camera angles, they are limited by the need for dedicated sensing infrastructure and the con- strained area over which data can be collected. Gait recognition, conversely, enables long- range, contactless identification but is sensitive to visual covariates such as clothing, carrying objects, and camera viewpoints. Combining gait and footprint modalities creates a multi-modal biometric system that leverages the complementary strengths of both approaches.

Fusion can be implemented at multiple levels. Feature-level fusion combines gait descrip- tors and footprint features into a unified representation for joint learning. Score-level fusion ag- gregates confidence scores from independent gait and footprint classifiers to improve decision reliability. Decision-level fusion applies logical or probabilistic rules to combine final predic- tions, which is particularly useful in distributed edge architectures where different modalities may be processed on separate devices.

Empirical studies show that integrating footprint data with gait recognition substantially re- duces false acceptance rates and enhances robustness, especially in controlled or high-security environments. Footprint biometrics provide precise identity verification when subjects pass through designated sensing zones, while gait recognition allows continuous monitoring and tracking outside these zones. This synergy is highly valuable in scenarios such as access- controlled facilities, border security checkpoints, and smart indoor surveillance systems, en- suring both reliability and continuous monitoring in real-world settings.

2. LARGE-SCALE AND REALISTIC DATASETS

Overall, footprint-based biometric recognition represents a complementary and privacy-aware modality that enhances the robustness and reliability of gait-based systems, particularly in con- trolled or infrastructure-supported environments. While gait recognition enables non-contact and long-range identification, footprint biometrics provide localized yet highly discriminative information that is less affected by visual covariates such as illumination changes, viewpoint variation, and clothing differences. When deployed on edge devices and integrated through multi-modal fusion strategies, footprint biometrics contribute to scalable, secure, and resilient human identification frameworks suitable for real-world applications.

Figure 2. Comparison of major gait datasets by number of subjects and sensor modality

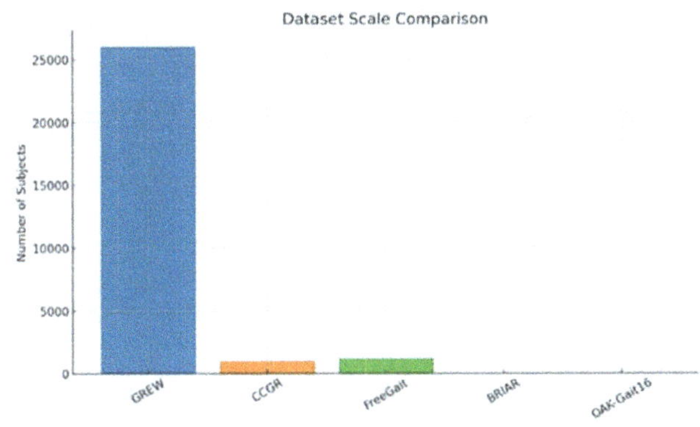

This complementarity is also reflected in the scale and characteristics of datasets commonly used in gait and footprint recognition research, as illustrated in Figure **2**. The figure compares representative datasets in terms of the number of subjects, highlighting a pronounced disparity between large-scale vision-based gait datasets and datasets that incorporate footprint or multi- modal sensing. Large datasets such as GREW include tens of thousands of subjects captured in unconstrained environments, enabling the training of deep gait models with strong generaliza- tion capabilities. In contrast, datasets that involve footprint sensing or multi-modal acquisition, such as FreeGait or BRIAR, typically contain a smaller number of subjects due to the higher cost and logistical complexity of deploying pressure-sensitive floors, wearable sensors, or spe- cialized capture setups.

This imbalance reveals both a limitation and an opportunity for future research. While large-scale gait datasets support robust benchmarking and model development, the relatively limited size of footprint datasets motivates the adoption of data-efficient learning strategies, transfer learning, and multi-modal fusion approaches. In practical edge-based deployments, footprint biometrics can be leveraged at specific locations such as access points or controlled corridors, where high-quality ground-contact data can be reliably captured. As multi-modal datasets continue to evolve, scaling the joint use of gait and footprint information will be es- sential for developing biometric systems that balance accuracy, deployability, and privacy.

Table 1. Summary of major datasets used in contemporary gait research

Dataset	Capture Modality	Subjects	Environment	Key Features
GREW	CCTV video + 2D joints	26,000+	Outdoor, crowds	Scale, occlusion, lighting variability, privacy-friendly
CCGR	RGB + fine co- variates	970	Mixed in- door/outdoor	53 covariates in- cluding clothing, carrying, 33 view-points
XGait	Silhouettes + Parsing	–	Controlled model	Dual representa-tions, occlusion handling
BRIAR	UAV + DSLR + Multiple	–	Long-range surveillance	Multi-modal bio-metrics, defense- grade quality
FreeGait	LiDAR + RGB	1,195	Public, uncon- strained	First large-scale in-the-wild 3D gait point cloud

The table above summarizes the major datasets that are currently used in contemporary gait recognition research, highlighting their capture modalities, the number of subjects involved, the environment in which data was collected, and the key features that make each dataset unique and valuable for research purposes.

The GREW dataset is one of the largest publicly available datasets, consisting of over 26,000 subjects recorded using CCTV video along with 2D joint annotations. Its primary focus is on capturing real-world variability in outdoor and crowded environments, including challenges such as scale differences, occlusion, changes in lighting, and maintaining privacy, making it ideal for testing gait recognition algorithms in uncontrolled settings.

The CCGR dataset includes 970 subjects and uses RGB video in combination with fine- grained covariates. It is collected in mixed indoor and outdoor environments and emphasizes the effects of appearance-related variations such as clothing, carrying objects, and different viewpoints. With 53 annotated covariates, CCGR allows researchers to study the robustness of gait recognition methods under varying conditions.

The XGait dataset focuses on controlled experimental conditions and provides silhouettes combined with parsing information. Although the number of subjects is not specified, it of- fers dual representations and incorporates occlusion handling, making it suitable for evaluating algorithms under more structured and reproducible settings.

The BRIAR dataset is designed for long-range surveillance scenarios and utilizes multiple sensors including UAV and DSLR cameras. It provides multi-modal biometrics of defense- grade quality and is targeted at applications where security, high-quality capture, and robustness to challenging conditions are critical.

Finally, the FreeGait dataset consists of 1,195 subjects and is captured in public, uncon- strained environments using LiDAR and RGB sensors. This dataset is notable for being the first large-scale in-the-wild 3D gait point cloud dataset, enabling researchers to explore three- dimensional gait recognition in realistic settings and enhancing the study of gait features be- yond conventional video-based methods.

3. EDGE AI HARDWARE PLATFORMS

Edge deployed gait recognition systems require computing platforms capable of performing real time inference under strict constraints on power consumption, size, and cost. Unlike cloud based solutions, edge systems must balance low latency and high throughput with on device privacy, often operating in outdoor or mobile environments where network connectivity is un- reliable. As a result, the choice of hardware platform is as critical as the design of the gait recognition model itself (Makihara et al., 2022).

Modern edge devices offer heterogeneous computing resources, including CPUs, GPUs, neural accelerators, and in some cases FPGAs, to execute deep learning models locally. Widely used platforms include NVIDIA Jetson boards for GPU accelerated inference, Google Coral boards with Edge TPU for low-power applications, Raspberry Pi 4 for cost effective prototyp- ing, and FPGA-based solutions such as Xilinx Kria modules for application specific accelera- tion . These platforms differ significantly in terms of peak tera operations per second (TOPS), memory bandwidth, and thermal design power, all of which directly influence achievable frame rates and system endurance.

Matching model complexity to available hardware resources is essential to sustain real time gait recognition without overheating or excessive energy consumption. Lightweight ar- chitectures and optimized inference pipelines are therefore favored for deployment on battery- powered or thermally constrained devices, as summarized in Table 2.

Table 2. Specifications of common edge AI hardware for gait recognition

Device	Processor	Accelerator	RAM	Peak TOPS	Power (W)
NVIDIA Jetson Nano	Quad-core Cortex-A57	Maxwell GPU (128 cores)	4 GB LPDDR4	0.47	5–10
Jetson Orin Nano	6-core Cortex-A78AE	Ampere GPU (1024 cores)	8 GB LPDDR5	67	7–25
Google Coral Dev Board	Quad-core Cortex-A53	Edge TPU	1 GB LPDDR4	~4	2
Raspberry Pi 4	Quad-core Cortex-A72	None	8 GB LPDDR4	N/A	3–7
Xilinx Kria KV260 FPGA	Quad-core Cortex-A53	FPGA	4 GB LPDDR4	~10	5–10

Table 2 highlights the diversity of edge AI hardware platforms that have been adopted for gait recognition and related biometric tasks, illustrating the wide range of trade-offs be- tween computational capability, power consumption, and system complexity. Rather than converging on a single dominant platform, current deployments reflect the heterogeneous re- quirements of different application scenarios, from low-power indoor authentication systems to high-throughput outdoor surveillance pipelines.

GPU-centric platforms such as the NVIDIA Jetson family are commonly selected for vision- based gait recognition due to their strong parallel processing capabilities and mature software ecosystem. Even entry-level devices such as the Jetson Nano support real-time inference for lightweight silhouette- or GEI-based models, while more recent platforms such as the Jetson Orin Nano offer substantially higher peak throughput, enabling the deployment of pose-based or graph-based gait models with increased temporal resolution. However, this performance comes at the cost of higher power consumption and thermal output, which must be carefully managed in fanless or battery-powered deployments.

In contrast, platforms such as the Google Coral Dev Board prioritize energy efficiency over raw computational throughput. The Edge TPU accelerator is optimized for low-precision inference, making it well suited for compact CNN architectures and fixed-function pipelines. While this limits flexibility for complex or dynamically structured models, it enables highly efficient on-device inference in scenarios where power availability and thermal constraints are dominant considerations, such as smart access control or embedded sensing nodes.

General-purpose single-board computers, exemplified by the Raspberry Pi 4, continue to play an important role in prototyping and system integration despite the absence of dedicated neural accelerators. In gait recognition systems, these platforms are often used for sensor co- ordination, data preprocessing, or lightweight inference tasks, and may be paired with external accelerators to extend their capabilities. Their low cost and broad community support make them attractive for early-stage experimentation and educational deployments.

FPGA-based platforms, such as the Xilinx Kria KV260, represent a different point in the de- sign space by offering fine-grained control over dataflow and hardware-level parallelism. When properly optimized, FPGA implementations can achieve low-latency and energy-efficient infer- ence for specific gait recognition pipelines. However, these benefits come with increased devel- opment complexity and longer design cycles, which can limit adoption outside of specialized or large-scale deployments.

Overall, the comparison in Table 2 underscores the importance of co-designing gait recogni- tion models and hardware platforms. Achieving reliable real-time performance on edge devices requires aligning model architecture, precision, and memory access patterns with the capabil- ities of the underlying hardware. As gait recognition systems continue to move toward real- world deployment, such hardware-aware design considerations will remain central to balancing accuracy, efficiency, and operational feasibility.

4. EDGE AI INFERENCE FRAMEWORKS AND OPTIMIZATIONS

The deployment of gait recognition models on edge platforms requires optimized inference frameworks that fully exploit hardware accelerators while minimizing latency and memory usage (Zhu et al., 2021). Figure 3 illustrates the peak TOPS and typical power consumption of representative edge AI devices used for gait recognition.

Figure 3. Peak TOPS and typical power consumption of common edge AI devices used for gait recognition

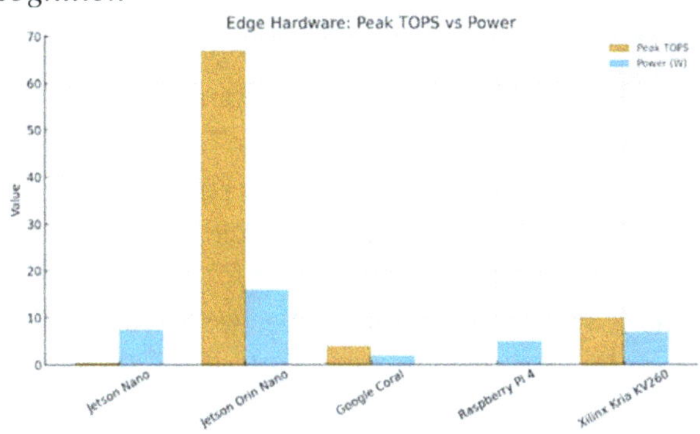

TensorFlow Lite supports post-training quantization and delegate APIs for hardware accel- eration, making it suitable for Google Coral and Raspberry Pi devices . ONNX Runtime allows broader framework compatibility via the ONNX format, while NVIDIA TensorRT and Open- VINO provide platform specific optimizations for Jetson and Intel devices, respectively. FPGA based solutions such as Vitis AI and FINN enable low-latency, energy efficient inference for custom pipelines but require specialized hardware knowledge (Zhu et al., 2021; Fu et al., 2023; Makihara et al., 2022).

Table 3 summarizes major deep-learning frameworks commonly used for edge AI deploy- ments, detailing their features, advantages, limitations, and supported hardware.

Table 3. Comparison of common edge AI inference frameworks.

Framework	Key Features	Advantages	Limitations	Supported Devices
TensorFlow Lite	Quantization, hardware delegation	Lightweight, cross-platform	TensorFlow only	Coral, Jetson, Raspberry Pi
ONNX Runtime	Cross-framework support	Flexible, hardware agnostic	Requires model conversion	Jetson, Raspberry Pi
TensorRT	Optimized for NVIDIA GPUs	High performance, low latency	NVIDIA-only	Jetson
OpenVINO	Optimized for Intel hardware	Real-time Intel CPU/VPU support	Intel-centric ecosystem	Neural Compute Stick, CPUs
Vitis AI	Targeted for Xilinx FPGAs	Custom acceleration, INT8 support	FPGA expertise required	Xilinx FPGA
FINN	Ultra-efficient FPGA inference	Optimized INT8 pipelines	Limited model support	Xilinx FPGA

Table 3 summarizes the inference frameworks most commonly used in edge AI deploy- ments for gait recognition and related biometric applications. Rather than serving as inter- changeable software layers, these frameworks reflect different design priorities, levels of ab- straction, and degrees of hardware specialization. The choice of inference framework therefore has a direct impact on achievable latency, power efficiency, and ease of system integration.

TensorFlow Lite is widely adopted in embedded environments due to its light-weight run- time and native support for post-training quantization. Its delegate mechanism allows inference workloads to be offloaded to available hardware accelerators, making it a practical choice for platforms such as Google Coral and Raspberry Pi. In gait recognition systems, TensorFlow Lite is often used for compact convolutional models or preprocessed silhouette-based represen- tations, where low memory overhead and predictable execution are critical.

ONNX Runtime occupies a more flexible position in the deployment stack by enabling models trained in different deep learning frameworks to be exported into a common inter- mediate representation. This framework-agnostic design simplifies experimentation and cross- platform deployment, particularly in research-oriented systems where models may evolve rapidly. However, the need for reliable model conversion and operator support introduces additional en- gineering effort, especially when targeting constrained edge devices.

For GPU-equipped platforms, NVIDIA TensorRT provides highly optimized inference through aggressive graph fusion, kernel auto-tuning, and precision reduction. On Jetson devices, Ten- sorRT is frequently used to deploy computationally demanding gait models, such as pose-based

or graph-based architectures, while maintaining real-time performance. This level of optimiza- tion, however, comes at the cost of portability, as TensorRT is tightly coupled to the NVIDIA ecosystem.

Similarly, OpenVINO offers optimized inference pipelines for Intel CPUs and vision pro- cessing units, enabling efficient deployment on Intel-centric edge hardware. While its perfor- mance benefits are substantial within the supported ecosystem, its applicability remains limited in heterogeneous deployments that rely on non-Intel platforms.

FPGA-oriented frameworks such as Vitis AI and FINN represent the most specialized end of the deployment spectrum. These frameworks enable highly efficient, low-latency inference by mapping neural network operations directly onto configurable hardware. In gait recognition applications, such solutions are particularly attractive for fixed-function pipelines deployed at scale, where energy efficiency and determinism are paramount. However, the requirement for hardware-aware model design and longer development cycles often restricts their use to expert teams or industrial settings.

Overall, the comparison in Table 3 reinforces the importance of aligning inference frame- works with both hardware capabilities and application requirements. By clearly separating hardware platforms (Section 3.) from inference software choices (Section 4.), it becomes pos- sible to reduce redundancy while preserving the technical depth needed to guide practical edge AI deployments for gait recognition.

By separating the hardware (Section 3.) and inference frameworks (Section 4.), redundancy is removed while retaining all tables, figures, and technical details.

5. MODEL OPTIMIZATION TECHNIQUES

Model optimization techniques play a central role in bridging the gap between high-performing

gait recognition models developed in research settings and their deployment on resource-constrained edge devices. While state-of-the-art models often achieve impressive accuracy on benchmark datasets, their computational and memory requirements frequently exceed the capabilities of embedded platforms. As a result, effective optimization is not merely a performance enhance- ment, but a prerequisite for real-world deployment.

Model compression techniques address these challenges by directly reducing the size and complexity of neural networks. Quantization is among the most widely adopted approaches, as it enables substantial reductions in memory footprint and computational cost while remain- ing compatible with modern edge accelerators. Structured pruning further complements this process by removing entire filters or channels, preserving regular computation patterns that are well suited to hardware acceleration. Knowledge distillation provides an alternative path- way to compact models, allowing smaller networks to inherit discriminative behavior from larger, high-capacity teachers without explicitly replicating their architecture. Together, these techniques enable gait recognition models to meet real-time constraints while maintaining ac- ceptable levels of accuracy.

Hardware software co-optimization extends beyond model-level compression by consider- ing how algorithms interact with the underlying hardware. Edge platforms typically feature heterogeneous processing units, and effective scheduling across CPUs, GPUs, and dedicated accelerators can significantly improve throughput and latency. Dataflow tuning and memory optimization are particularly important for gait recognition workloads, where frequent access to feature maps and temporal sequences can lead to memory bottlenecks if not carefully man- aged. Algorithmic accelerations, such as reduced-complexity convolution schemes, further lower arithmetic cost and energy consumption, especially in deeper network layers.

Approximate computing techniques introduce an additional degree of flexibility by explic- itly allowing small, controlled reductions in numerical precision or computation accuracy. In many gait recognition scenarios, particularly those involving continuous monitoring or coarse- grained identification, such approximations have minimal impact on overall system reliability while delivering meaningful gains in energy efficiency. This trade-off is especially attractive for battery-powered and wearable systems, where operational lifetime is a primary concern.

As summarized in Table 3, these model compression and hardware–software co-optimization strategies are most effective when applied in combination rather than isolation. When further integrated with task-specific scheduling policies and dynamic voltage and frequency scaling (DVFS), they enable gait recognition systems to adapt their computational behavior to chang- ing workload and power conditions. Such holistic optimization approaches are essential for achieving scalable, low-latency, and energy-efficient gait analytics that remain reliable under real-world edge deployment constraints (Zhu et al., 2021; Fu et al., 2023; Makihara et al., 2022).

6. DISTRIBUTED AND REAL-TIME EDGE ARCHITECTURES FOR GAIT RECOGNITION

Edge based architectures are pivotal for the deployment of real time gait recognition in privacy sensitive, resource-constrained environments such as public surveillance and smart cities (Mak- ihara et al., 2022). These systems achieve high responsiveness and scalability by distributing major tasks including person detection, silhouette segmentation, and gait descriptor classifica- tion across a network of embedded edge devices (Zhu et al., 2021).A typical distributed processing pipeline involves initial person detection on AI enabled smart cameras (such as OAK-D) using lightweight convolutional neural networks like MobileNet SSD. This approach filters and compresses data close to the source, reducing the need for high-bandwidth trans- mission. This is followed by silhouette segmentation using efficient U-Net models deployed on neural accelerators (e.g., Intel Neural Compute Stick 2), isolating gait-relevant foregrounds even under challenging environmental conditions.

The final classification phase, typically employing Gait Energy Images (GEI) and convolu- tional neural networks (CNNs), is handled on robust edge AI platforms such as the NVIDIA Jetson Nano, leveraging onboard GPU acceleration for real-time inference (Fu et al., 2023).

Table 4. Multi-view gait recognition accuracy on edge platform

View Angle	Accuracy	Precision	Recall	F1-Score
60	0.90	0.91	0.90	0.90
75	0.96	0.96	0.97	0.96
90	0.96	0.97	0.97	0.96
105	0.97	0.96	0.98	0.97
120	0.91	0.92	0.92	0.92

Table 4 reports the recognition performance of the multi-view gait system deployed on an edge platform across different camera viewpoints. The results show that recognition accuracy is strongly influenced by the observation angle, with side and near-frontal views generally pro- viding more discriminative gait information than oblique perspectives. In particular, viewpoints between 75 and 105 achieve the highest and most consistent performance across all evalua- tion metrics, with accuracy and F1-scores approaching or exceeding 0.96. These angles capture a balanced combination of lateral limb motion and body posture.

Performance degradation is observed at more extreme viewpoints, such as 60 and 120 . At these angles, partial self-occlusion and reduced visibility of lower-limb motion limit the quality of extracted gait features, leading to lower accuracy and recall. Nevertheless, even under these less favorable conditions, the system maintains accuracy above 0.90, indicating a degree of robustness suitable for practical edge-based deployments.

The close alignment between precision and recall across all viewpoints suggests stable clas- sifier behavior, with no significant bias toward false positives or false negatives. This balance is particularly important for edge systems operating in real-world environments, where incon- sistent predictions can undermine reliability. Overall, the results demonstrate that multi-view gait recognition can achieve strong performance on resource-constrained edge platforms, pro- vided that camera placement favors viewpoints that preserve sufficient gait dynamics. These findings further motivate the integration of multi-view sensing or adaptive viewpoint selection in edge-based gait recognition systems.

Distributed edge architectures have demonstrated high classification accuracy across multi- ple camera views, maintaining robust performance even as subject orientation changes. As summarized in Table 4, accuracy, precision, recall, and F1-score remain consistently high (0.90–0.97) in side views (75 –105), which are most informative for gait analysis. The cor- responding trends are visualized in Figure 4, highlighting the system's balanced performance across different camera angles

Figure 4. Accuracy, precision, recall, and F1 score of the distributed edge system across differ- ent camera view angles

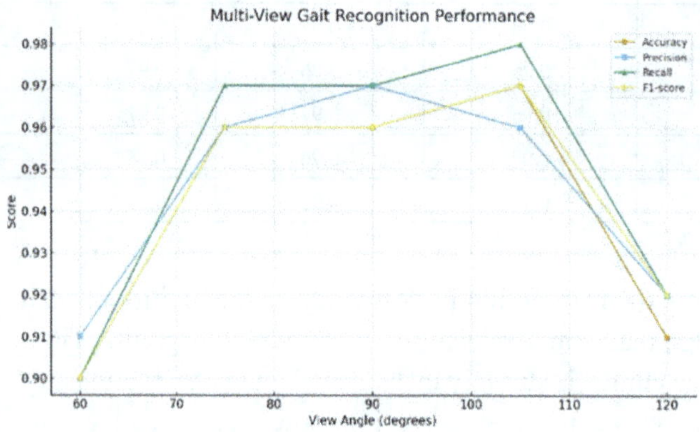

7. PRIVACY AND SECURITY IN GAIT RECOGNITION

The intrinsic privacy concerns of gait biometrics have motivated the development of advanced frameworks capable of preserving user identity while maintaining recognition utility. One such approach involves operating in the latent representation space using vector quantized variational autoencoders (VQ-VAE) combined with optimal morphing methods (Zhu et al., 2021). These frameworks generate anonymized yet realistic gait sequences, allowing data transport and sharing without exposing sensitive personal identifiers. By smoothly manipulating discrete latent gait features, augmented datasets can be produced that protect identities while retaining the discriminative information necessary for downstream recognition tasks.

Gait biometrics exhibit extensive information redundancy, meaning that perturbing a single category of features whether macro level attributes such as step length and cadence, micro-level dynamics such as asymmetries, or static body shape configurations is insufficient to reliably ob- fuscate identity (Zhu et al., 2021). Effective anonymization must perturb multiple feature tiers simultaneously and in a coordinated manner to minimize re-identification risk while pre- serving the natural gait characteristics required for realistic representation.

Beyond direct gait data anonymization, federated learning has emerged as a powerful paradigm for enhancing privacy during model training (Makihara et al., 2022). In distributed learn- ing, edge devices perform local training on personal gait data, transmitting only model up- dates rather than raw biometric information to a central server. This decentralized approach reduces the risk of data leakage while maintaining collaborative learning capabilities. En- hanced protocols, such as secure aggregation and differential privacy, ensure that updates do not inadvertently reveal individual-specific information (Makihara et al., 2022). In practice, privacy-preserving gait recognition leverages a combination of latent-space morphing, multi level feature perturbation, data perturbation, and complementary matrix perturbation. These strategies, combined with decentralized and privacy-aware learning, are critical for balancing high recognition accuracy and scalability with strong privacy guarantees. This balance is es- pecially important in edge computing environments, where data sovereignty and security are paramount for real-world deployments.

Table 5. Evaluation categories, metrics, and characteristics for gait recognition

Category	Metrics	Characteristics
Accuracy	Rank-1, Precision/Recall, EER	Model correctness and discriminative power
Efficiency	Inference time (ms), FPS	Real-time compatibility and throughput
Resource Usage	RAM, model size, compute ops	Feasibility for edge deployment
Energy Consumption	Energy per inference (mJ)	Battery life and operational cost
Robustness	Covariate handling	Adaptation to view/clothing/occlusion variability
Privacy/Security	Resistance to attacks, anonymization	Protecting biometric data from exploitation

8. EVALUATION METRICS FOR EDGE GAIT RECOGNITION

Evaluating edge-based gait recognition systems involves more than just measuring accuracy. Since these models are deployed in resource constrained environments, additional metrics such as computational efficiency, memory consumption, and energy usage are critical. Furthermore, given the biometric nature of gait data, privacy and security considerations play a significant role in system assessment. Table 5 summarizes key evaluation criteria, illustrative metrics, and their significance for assessing edge-deployed gait recognition systems (Zhu et al., 2021; Fu et al., 2023). To visualize the trade-offs among these dimensions, Figure 5 presents a radar chart emphasizing accuracy, efficiency, resource usage, energy consumption, and privacy. Balancing these metrics is essential to ensure reliable, sustainable, and practical real-world performance of edge-based gait recognition systems.

Table 5 organizes the evaluation of gait recognition systems into a set of complementary categories that extend well beyond conventional accuracy-based assessment. While metrics such as Rank-1 accuracy, precision, recall, and equal error rate remain essential for measuring discriminative capability, they provide only a partial view of system performance when models are deployed on edge platforms.

Efficiency-related metrics, including inference latency and frame rate, capture the ability of a system to operate under real-time constraints. In practical deployments, delays of even a few tens of milliseconds can affect system responsiveness, particularly in continuous monitoring or access control scenarios. As a result, accuracy gains achieved at the expense of excessive inference time may not translate into usable systems.

Resource usage metrics, such as memory footprint, model size, and computational com- plexity, are particularly relevant for edge environments with limited RAM and processing ca- pacity. These constraints often dictate architectural choices, model compression strategies, and input resolution, directly influencing achievable performance. Closely related to resource us- age is energy consumption, which serves as a critical metric for battery-powered or always-on systems. Measuring energy per inference provides a more meaningful indicator of operational sustainability than peak power alone.

Robustness metrics address the ability of gait recognition systems to handle real-world variability, including changes in viewpoint, clothing, walking speed, and partial occlusions.

Performance stability under such covariates is often more indicative of deployment readiness than isolated benchmark scores. Finally, privacy and security considerations reflect the sen- sitive nature of biometric data. Evaluating resistance to spoofing attacks, data leakage, and re-identification risks is essential for ensuring user trust and regulatory compliance.

Taken together, the categories summarized in Table 5 highlight the multi-dimensional na- ture of evaluating edge-based gait recognition systems. Figure 5 further illustrates the trade- offs among these dimensions, emphasizing that improvements in one aspect often come at the expense of others. Achieving a balanced profile across accuracy, efficiency, resource usage, en- ergy consumption, and privacy is therefore critical for developing gait recognition systems that are not only accurate, but also practical, sustainable, and suitable for real-world deployment.

Figure 5. Balanced performance goals for edge-deployed gait recognition: accuracy, efficiency, resource utilization, energy, and privacy

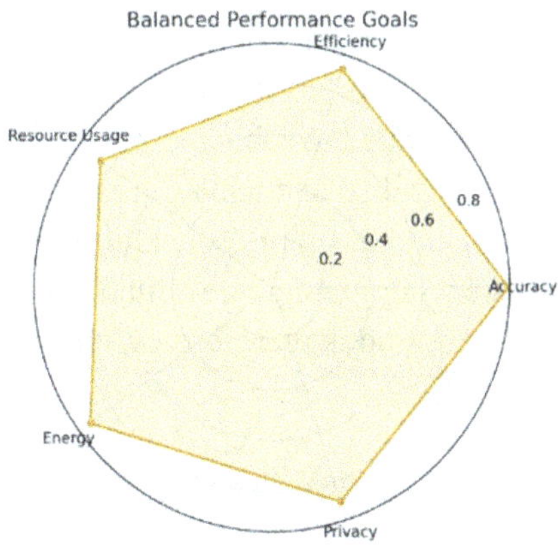

Figure 5 provides a conceptual illustration of the balanced performance objectives that edge-deployed gait recognition systems must satisfy. Rather than optimizing a single domi- nant metric, the figure emphasizes the need to jointly consider accuracy, efficiency, resource utilization, energy consumption, and privacy during system design and evaluation. These di- mensions are inherently interconnected, and improvements in one aspect often impose con- straints on others. For instance, increasing recognition accuracy may require larger models or higher input resolutions, which can raise computational demand and energy usage, thereby limiting suitability for low-power edge devices.

Efficiency and resource utilization represent key constraints in edge deployments, as limited processing capability and memory availability directly influence achievable inference speed and system scalability. Energy consumption is closely related to these factors and plays a decisive role in determining operational lifetime, particularly for battery-powered or always-on systems. At the same time, privacy considerations encourage on-device processing and reduced data transmission, which can further restrict model complexity and architectural choices.

By visualizing these criteria within a unified framework, Figure 5 highlights that effective edge-based gait recognition cannot be achieved by optimizing individual metrics in isolation. Instead, practical systems must identify a balanced operating point that delivers reliable accu- racy while remaining efficient, energy-aware, and privacy-conscious. This perspective under- scores the importance of holistic evaluation and hardware–software co-design when translating gait recognition technologies from laboratory research to real-world edge deployments.

9. FUTURE DIRECTIONS AND RESEARCH OPPORTUNITIES

Despite substantial progress in gait recognition research, several open challenges continue to limit the reliability and large-scale adoption of these systems in real-world environments. Is- sues related to robustness under unconstrained conditions, privacy preservation, interpretability, and scalability remain particularly pronounced in edge-based deployments. Addressing these challenges will require coordinated advances in model design, sensing strategies, evaluation methodologies, and system-level optimization. Future research is therefore expected to focus on the following key directions.

9.1. Unified Multi-Modal and Adaptive Systems

Optimization for edge deployment remains a central concern, as gait recognition models must operate under strict constraints on memory, computation, and energy consumption while main- taining reliable performance. Future systems will increasingly rely on hardware–software co-design principles, where model architectures, numerical precision, and inference pipelines are jointly optimized for the target edge platform. Techniques such as structured pruning, quantization-aware training, and adaptive inference further support efficient deployment on resource-constrained devices without significant loss in recognition accuracy (Zhu et al., 2021; Fu et al., 2023).

At the same time, modern surveillance and authentication environments demand systems that can adapt to highly dynamic and uncontrolled conditions. Single-modality gait recogni- tion approaches are often insufficient in such settings. Future research is therefore expected to emphasize unified multi-modal frameworks that integrate heterogeneous sensing modalities, including visual silhouettes, skeleton representations, depth sensors, LiDAR, radar, and wire- less signals such as WiFi channel state information. By combining complementary modalities, systems can remain functional when one or more sensors are degraded by occlusion, lighting variation, or environmental noise.

Recent advances in graph-based modeling and attention mechanisms provide a promising foundation for such unified systems. Hybrid architectures that combine Graph Neural Networks with transformer-based attention modules enable flexible spatiotemporal reasoning across both structured and unstructured data. These models can capture fine-grained joint-level dynam- ics as well as longer-range temporal dependencies, improving generalization across clothing variation, viewpoint changes, and partial occlusions. Continued research into adaptive and modality-aware fusion strategies will be essential for realizing robust multi-modal gait recog- nition in edge environments.

9.2. Privacy and Security by Design

As gait recognition systems increasingly operate on sensitive biometric data, privacy and se- curity considerations must be integrated into system design rather than treated as post hoc constraints. Regulatory frameworks and public expectations alike demand strong.

10. CONCLUSION

Gait and footprint biometrics have matured significantly due to advances in large scale, realistic datasets, sophisticated deep learning architectures, and edge AI platforms. Datasets such as GREW, CCGR, FreeGait, BRIAR, and OAK Gait provide a robust foundation for training and evaluating gait recognition models in unconstrained, real world scenarios Zhu et al. (2021).

Modern approaches have evolved beyond controlled laboratory setups, enabling applica- tions in security, healthcare, and smart city infrastructures. Deep learning techniques range from traditional silhouette and Gait Energy Image (GEI) based models to pose and skeleton- based graph neural networks, as well as generative adversarial networks (GANs) that allow interpretable view-invariant feature synthesis and identity-preserving motion transfer Hu et al. (2018); Fu et al. (2023); Zhang et al. (2023); Liu et al. (2023). Representative frameworks include GaitGL-M, DiGGAN, and IDPres, which combine robust- ness, explainability, and hardware efficiency.

Edge computing plays a pivotal role in scalable, privacy preserving gait biometrics. Plat- forms such as NVIDIA Jetson, Google Coral, and FPGA boards offer an effective trade off between computational performance and energy consumption, enabling real time inference close to the data source. Model compression and hardware software co-optimization strategies further improve efficiency while maintaining accuracy and protecting user privacy Takemura et al. (2018); Fan et al. (2020).

Privacy and security remain critical concerns. Multi level anonymization techniques, latent- space morphing approaches such as GaitMorph, and federated learning infrastructures provide effective mechanisms to preserve identity information while maintaining utility for gait anal- ysis Cornett and et al. (2022); Ming et al. (2023). Secure aggregation and differential privacy protocols further mitigate risks associated with centralized data collection.

Looking ahead, research should focus on multi sensor fusion models integrating 2D/3D vision, inertial sensors, WiFi CSI, and other modalities. Graph and transformer based architec- tures promise improved adaptability and robustness in heterogeneous environments Liu et al. (2023); Cosma and Radoi (2023). Adaptive edge-cloud architectures can enable dynamic resource allocation, balancing latency, energy consumption, and privacy requirements. Enhancing model interpretability through visualizable generative frameworks, attention mechanisms, and explainable AI will foster trust, support forensic authentication, and ensure compliance with evolving regulations. Additionally, developing open benchmarks with diverse covariates and sensor types will drive further research and innovation Zhu et al. (2021).

In conclusion, gait and footprint recognition hold immense potential and are poised to be- come integral components of future biometric systems. Continued efforts to improve dataset realism, algorithmic accuracy, and hardware aware deployment strategies will enable highly efficient, privacy preserving, and scalable biometric authentication and surveillance solutions.

REFERENCES

Chao, H., He, Y., Zhang, J., & Feng, J. (2019). GaitSet: Regarding gait as a set for cross-view gait recognition. In *Proceedings of the AAAI Conference on Artificial Intelligence*. DOI: 10.1609/aaai.v33i01.33018126

Cornett, S., et al. (2022). The BRIAR dataset: Multi-modal, long-range biometric recognition. *arXiv preprint.*

Cosma, A., & Radoi, E. (2023). GaitMorph: Transforming gait by optimal transport. *arXiv preprint.*

Fan, C., Peng, Y., Cao, C., Liu, X., Hou, S., Chi, J., Huang, Y., & Li, Q. (2020). GaitPart: Temporal part-based model for gait recognition. In *Proceedings of the IEEE/CVF Conference on Computer Vision and Pattern Recognition (CVPR).* DOI: 10.1109/CVPR42600.2020.01423

Fu, Y., Meng, S., Hou, S., Hu, X., & Huang, Y. (2023). Gpgait: Generalized pose-based gait recognition. In *Proceedings of the IEEE/CVF International Conference on Computer Vision* (pp. 19595-19604).

Hu, B., Guan, Y., Gao, Y., Long, Y., Lane, N., & Ploetz, T. (2018). Robust cross-view gait recognition with evidence: A discriminant gait GAN (DiGGAN) approach. *arXiv preprint arXiv:1811.10493.*

Liao, R., Yu, S., Huang, Y., Zhu, Z., & Van Gool, L. (2020). PoseGait: Learning pose-based representation for gait recognition. *IEEE Transactions on Circuits and Systems for Video Technology.*

Liu, H., Zhang, J., & Guo, J. (2023). LightGait: Lightweight gait recognition for mobile and edge devices. *Sensors (Basel).*

Makihara, Y., Sagawa, R., & Yagi, Y. (2022). Gait recognition for surveillance: A survey. *Computer Vision and Image Understanding.*

Ming, W., Guo, X., Lin, B., Yang, T., Zhu, Z., Li, L., Zhang, S., & Yu, X. (2023). DyGait: Exploiting dynamic representations for high-performance gait recognition. *arXiv preprint.*

Salcedo, E., Jalal, S., & Ghosh, R. (2024). Computer vision-based gait recognition on the edge: A survey. *IEEE Transactions on Emerging Topics in Computing.* PMID: 39728223

Takemura, N., Makihara, Y., Muramatsu, D., Echigo, T., & Yagi, Y. (2018). *Multi-view large population gait dataset and its performance evaluation for cross-view gait recognition*. IPSJ Transactions on Computer Vision and Applications. DOI: 10.1186/s41074-018-0039-6

Zhang, S., Wang, W., Liu, Z., & Yu, X. (2023). MetaGait: Learning to learn for gait recognition. In *Proceedings of the IEEE/CVF Conference on Computer Vision and Pattern Recognition (CVPR)*.

Zhang, H., Zheng, W., Zheng, Z., & Nevatia, R. (2023). GaitRef: Gait recognition with refined sequential skeletons. *arXiv preprint*.

Zhu, Z., Guo, X., Yang, T., Huang, J., Deng, J., Huang, G., & Zhou, J. (2021). Gait recognition in the wild: A benchmark. In *Proceedings of the IEEE/CVF international conference on computer vision* (pp. 14789-14799).

Chapter 7
Challenges of Social Sensing From a Safety and Security Perspective

Deswita Anggraini
http://orcid.org/0009-0003-2192-3381
Universitas Esa Unggul, Indonesia

Defia Ulandari
http://orcid.org/0009-0002-2136-1633
Universitas Esa Unggul, Indonesia

Binastya Anggara Sekti
http://orcid.org/0000-0001-5489-4888
Universitas Esa Unggul, Indonesia

ABSTRACT

Social sensing is a data collection paradigm that leverages human participation through connected devices in AIoT systems. It enhances real-time decision-making in areas like disaster response, healthcare, and transportation. However, it poses serious challenges related to data privacy, misinformation, identity verification, and system reliability. Threats such as data poisoning, replay attacks, and the opacity of black-box AI models increase the risk. Ethical concerns also arise from continuous data collection without user consent or transparency. Addressing these issues requires a multi-faceted strategy involving anomaly detection, encryption, Explainable AI, and human oversight. Case studies from Beirut, Hong Kong, and COVID-19 highlight the double-edged nature of social sensing. Future systems must combine technological innovation with ethical safeguards to ensure trust, security, and inclusivity in the digital era.

DOI: 10.4018/979-8-3373-6299-1.ch007

1. INTRODUCTION

In the current era of digital transformation and high connectivity, social sensing has emerged as a rapidly evolving concept that bridges human activity and intelligent systems. It refers to the process of collecting, interpreting, and analyzing data generated by individuals through interconnected devices and digital platforms. In the AIoT (Artificial Intelligence of Things) environment, social sensing plays an important role in strengthening the ability of intelligent systems to monitor human behavior, mobility, and social interaction (Sung et al., 2025) By leveraging data from various social sources, AIoT systems can respond adaptively and dynamically to evolving situations, which is especially critical in fast-changing modern societies.

One of the key advantages of social sensing lies in its capability to aggregate massive amounts of heterogeneous data from multiple sources, such as social media, wearable devices, mobile applications, and smart transportation systems. This allows AIoT systems to recognize patterns of human activity and compose automated responses based on that information (Obaidat et al., 2024)(Aamer et al., 2025). For instance, in urban traffic management, social sensing can utilize crowd-sourced reports or smartphone location data to identify congestion patterns and adjust traffic signals accordingly. Similarly, in disaster management, social data can enhance situational awareness by helping detect affected areas, identify evacuation routes, and improve the speed of rescue responses (Nguyen, 2025).

Not only in the context of transportation, the application of social sensing also covers various sectors such as crowd control, disaster management, public health monitoring, and improving public safety. In emergency situations such as earthquakes or fires, data collected from social media or personal sensors can be used to detect the location of victims, identify evacuation routes, and speed up rescue responses. This advantage makes social sensing a strategic component in building a smart city that is more responsive and secure (Nguyen, 2025).

Despite its promising potential, integrating social sensing into AIoT systems presents significant safety and security challenges, especially when applied in multi-hazard early warning systems (EWSs). One of the most critical concerns involves privacy intrusion and data misuse. Social sensing systems often process sensitive personal information that, if not adequately protected, could be exploited for unethical or harmful purposes (Hassan et al., 2025). The absence of strong encryption or anonymization mechanisms can lead to unauthorized surveillance, profiling, and information leakage.

From a technical standpoint, data integrity and reliability also pose major risks. Human-generated data tends to be noisy, inconsistent, or even deliberately misleading. The spread of misinformation or disinformation across social platforms can compromise AIoT-based EWS decision-making. In extreme cases, adversarial attacks, or intentional data manipulation by malicious actors, may cause the system to issue false alerts or misdirect emergency resources (Khan et al., 2025). For example, falsified reports of crowd gatherings could trigger unnecessary evacuation responses or public panic.

Another crucial challenge is data authentication and user verification. Without reliable identity validation, social sensing systems are vulnerable to manipulation by fake accounts or automated bots. In real-time emergency contexts, where speed is critical, verification processes are often bypassed, increasing the risk of erroneous actions based on unverified information. Such vulnerabilities can have severe implications when applied in vital sectors like health, energy, transportation, and defense. For example, inaccurate readings from wearable health sensors could result in incorrect diagnoses, while errors in energy monitoring systems might lead to large-scale power outages or infrastructure failures.

In the midst of all these challenges, there is an urgent need to develop a social sensing system that is not only intelligent, but also trustworthy and ethical. A holistic approach is urgently needed including technical, social, legal, and ethical aspects to ensure that the integration of social data into AIoT is carried out safely and responsibly. Some of the approaches that have begun to be developed include system design based on privacy principles from the beginning (privacy by design), the application of end-to-end data encryption, and the development of algorithms that are able to detect anomalies or data manipulation automatically (Juan M. Núñez et al., 2025).

Cross-disciplinary collaboration is essential to achieve these goals. Researchers and developers must co-design solutions that are both technically robust and socially responsible. Policymakers play a pivotal role in balancing innovation with individual rights protection, while the public, empowered through digital literacy, should actively participate in shaping safe and transparent data ecosystems. Visually, the challenges and opportunities of social sensing in the AIoT environment can be summarized as follows in Figure 1:

Figure 1. Social sensing data flow scheme in AIoT

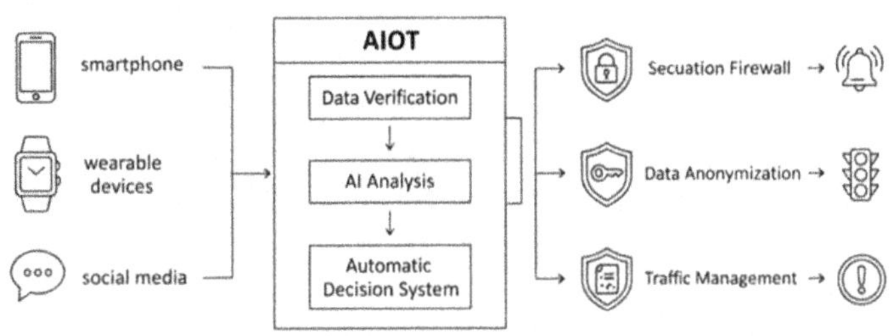

This schematic highlights the importance of implementing multiple layers of security and validation at every stage of data flow, from acquisition to automated decision-making, to preserve the system's reliability and integrity.

Ultimately, we are entering an era where social data not only reflects human activities but actively shapes intelligent decision-making systems. Social sensing serves as the critical bridge between humans and machines, enabling a deeper connection between digital awareness and collective resilience. However, this evolution must be accompanied by responsible governance, ethical foresight, and robust safeguards.

By establishing a secure, transparent, and resilient social sensing ecosystem, we can ensure that AIoT-based disaster management and early warning systems truly enhance societal resilience and protect human well-being.

2. THE CONCEPT OF SOCIAL SENSING IN AN AIOT ENVIRONMENT

Social sensing represents an emerging paradigm that connects human intelligence with machine perception. In an AIoT (Artificial Intelligence of Things) ecosystem, social sensing functions as a cognitive layer that complements traditional physical sensors by integrating data derived from human activities, behaviors, and social interactions. This integration enables intelligent systems to capture contextual information that cannot be obtained solely from mechanical or environmental sensors. Through this approach, AIoT systems can form real-time situational awareness, which is the ability to comprehensively understand environmental and social situations based on human behavior, emotional expression, environmental conditions, and spatial movements (Sung et al., 2025).

Unlike physical sensors, which collect quantitative and structured data, social sensors gather qualitative, unstructured, and behavior-driven information. Examples include tweets, public posts, geotagged photos, mobile app data, and crowd-sourced reports. Such information provides valuable insight into real-world conditions, particularly in dynamic environments like disaster response, transportation, healthcare, and public safety.

Through the combination of physical and social sensing, AIoT systems can achieve a more holistic understanding of their environment. This hybrid model allows machines to interpret not only physical phenomena but also human intentions, emotions, and situational awareness. For instance, in disaster management, while seismic sensors can detect ground vibrations, social sensing data can identify human perception of danger, evacuation movements, or urgent needs reported through social media.

Table 1. Comparison of physical censorship vs social censorship

Aspects	Physical Sensor	Social Censorship	Potential Risks/Weaknesses
Data Source	Machines or IoT devices (temperature, pressure, motion, etc.)	Human-generated data (social media, mobile apps, wearable devices)	Data authenticity issues, subjective inputs, noise, and bias
Data Type	Structured, continuous, and quantitative	Unstructured, text-based, multimedia, qualitative	Inconsistent data formats, language ambiguity
Accuracy	High measurement precision	Depends on user credibility and platform reliability	Vulnerable to misinformation and human error
Response Time	Real-time and automated	Often real-time but may experience latency	Verification delay, false positives
Coverage	Limited by sensor placement and network range	Wide and dynamic, based on user participation	Uneven geographic coverage, lack of standardization
Security Concern	Device malfunction, hacking, or power failure	Data privacy, identity spoofing, malicious manipulation	Difficult to control information authenticity

Unlike physical sensors, which produce objective and measurable data, social sensing presents data that is subjective, context-dependent, and often full of *noise*. For example, tweets on Twitter about flood disasters can provide information on the location and severity, but they can also contain hoaxes or emotions that affect the objectivity of the information. Therefore, AIoT systems that rely on social sensing require robust models to evaluate trust levels, filter data noise (noise filtering), and verify the identity of data sources.

In addition, the success of social sensing integration in AIoT also depends heavily on the system's ability to understand the social and cultural context behind the data. The system must be able to distinguish between spontaneous expressions of emotions with real threats, or between insinuations and factual reports (Hnatiuc et al., 2025). This is especially important in critical decision-making such as disaster evacuation, crowd management, or tracking high-risk individuals in smart city security systems.

With great potential, social sensing makes a significant contribution to the development of AIoT systems that are more adaptive, human-centric, and responsive to social dynamics. However, to make it happen optimally, a combination of technological sophistication, strengthening regulations, and a deep understanding of today's digital social behavior is needed.

2.1 Research Gaps in Social Sensing for AIoT

Despite the progress in developing AIoT-based social sensing systems, several research gaps and unresolved challenges remain. Addressing these gaps is essential to enhance the reliability, scalability, and ethical accountability of future implementations.

1. Limited Field Validation

Many existing studies rely on simulated or small-scale experimental data. Few systems have been validated in real-world environments where human behavior is highly unpredictable. This limits the generalizability and robustness of current models.

2. Unresolved Privacy and Ethical Issues

Although numerous frameworks emphasize privacy preservation, most fail to address cross-jurisdictional data governance, user consent, and long-term ethical implications. The lack of standardized privacy protocols hampers trust in social sensing applications.

3. Data Quality and Real-Time Constraints

Social data streams are often incomplete, noisy, or delayed. Ensuring data accuracy and timeliness while maintaining computational efficiency remains a significant technical barrier for AIoT systems.

4. Integration Complexity Between Physical and Social Sensors

Synchronizing heterogeneous data sources with varying formats, resolutions, and sampling rates requires advanced fusion algorithms. Current approaches often oversimplify data correlation, leading to inconsistent outcomes.

5. Scalability and Interoperability Challenges

As social data volume grows exponentially, system architectures must support distributed processing and scalable storage solutions. However, interoperability between platforms and IoT networks is still underdeveloped.

6. Insufficient Focus on Explainable AI (XAI) in Social Sensing

Most existing AI models prioritize performance over interpretability. In high-stakes contexts such as disaster management, explainable models are crucial to ensure accountability and human oversight.

2.2 Conceptual Architecture of Social Sensing in AIoT

To address these challenges, a conceptual architecture for social sensing within AIoT is proposed. This architecture consists of four primary layers:

1. Sensing Layer

Responsible for collecting data from physical devices (IoT sensors) and human sources (social media, mobile apps, wearable devices).

2. Data Processing Layer

Handles data cleaning, fusion, and transformation into standardized formats suitable for analysis. Machine learning algorithms are applied to filter noise and detect anomalies.

3. Analysis and Decision Layer

Applies AI-based models to interpret data, predict trends, and generate situational insights. This layer also integrates trust evaluation mechanisms to validate data credibility.

4. Action and Feedback Layer

Converts analytical insights into automated or semi-automated responses, such as alerts in disaster early warning systems or adaptive resource allocation in smart cities. Feedback from users and devices is reintegrated to continuously refine system performance. Figure 2 shows the Conceptual Architecture of Social Sensing in an AIoT System.

Figure 2. Conceptual architecture of social sensing in an AIoT system

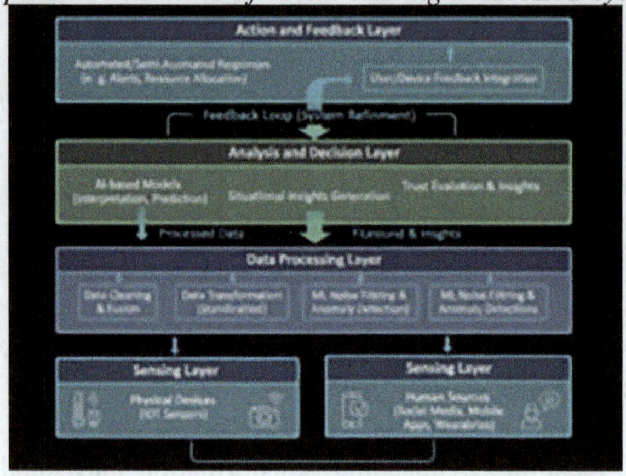

This architecture illustrates how social and physical sensing form a continuous feedback loop. Data collected from individuals and sensors flows through processing and analysis modules, resulting in intelligent system responses that can improve over time.

3. SAFETY IMPLICATIONS OF SOCIAL SENSING

As social sensing becomes an integral part of AIoT-based systems, particularly in critical infrastructures and disaster management, its reliability and safety are of paramount importance. Social data can provide valuable, real-time situational awareness, yet it also introduces significant risks that can undermine the accuracy and stability of automated decision-making processes. Understanding these risks is essential to ensure that social sensing contributes positively to safety and resilience rather than introducing new vulnerabilities. If an AIoT system connected to social sensing receives incorrect crowd data, such as false reports of safe locations or evacuation routes, then the system can provide misleading directions, endangering the safety of many people (Park & Lee, 2025).

3.1 Data Poisoning: The Threat of Social Data Manipulation

Data poisoning occurs when false or manipulated social data are intentionally injected into a system to distort its perception of reality. In the context of disaster management, malicious actors might post misleading information about emergencies, causing systems to issue false alerts or misallocate resources. For example, coordinated false reports about a flood or fire on social media could lead authorities to divert emergency responders to non-existent locations.

In addition, data poisoning can also be used to attack AI systems in the industrial sector (Fan et al., 2025). Such incidents not only waste valuable resources but also undermine public trust in early warning systems. To mitigate this risk, AIoT systems must incorporate credibility assessment mechanisms and cross-validation with verified data sources, such as official meteorological or geospatial feeds.

3.2 Noisy and Unreliable Data

Social sensing data often contain substantial noise due to inconsistent reporting, subjective interpretations, or duplicate information. Unlike data collected from calibrated physical sensors, human-generated content may be emotionally biased or lack precision. For example, panic-induced posts during an earthquake might exaggerate damage severity, leading to inaccurate situational assessments.

Implementing data filtering, clustering, and natural language processing (NLP) techniques can reduce this noise. Additionally, integrating social sensing data with reliable IoT sensor networks can improve overall system accuracy by cross-verifying events before issuing alerts.

3.3 Delay in Verification: The Risk of Premature Decision

Timely verification of social data remains one of the most persistent challenges in safety-critical applications. During disaster events, systems must balance between speed and accuracy. Delayed verification may reduce the responsiveness of early warning systems, while overly rapid decisions based on unverified data may trigger false alarms.

An effective approach involves multi-layered validation, where social sensing data undergo automated preliminary screening, followed by manual or AI-assisted review before large-scale action is taken. This hybrid verification process ensures that emergency responses are both fast and reliable. However, if the report turns out to be false or is the result of a digital prank, there will be unnecessary mass panic (Z. Lu et al., 2025).

3.4 Challenges in Special Contexts: Health, Transportation, and Energy

Social sensing relies heavily on human perception and voluntary reporting. In high-stress situations, human judgment may be impaired, resulting in unintentional errors or subjective exaggerations. For instance, individuals may misinterpret visual cues such as smoke or noise, mistaking minor incidents for large-scale emergencies.

In the field of transportation, AIoT-based traffic management systems can use data from vehicle users or reporters on the highway. False or biased data can lead to errors in officer placement, route planning, or the provision of traffic information to the public (M. Lu et al., 2025). To address this, user training and awareness programs can improve reporting accuracy. Furthermore, the inclusion of reputation-based scoring systems can help identify trustworthy data contributors and filter out unreliable sources.

3.5 System Overload and Miscommunication

In large-scale disaster events, the sudden surge of data inputs from millions of users can overwhelm AIoT systems. Overloaded systems may experience processing delays, data loss, or miscommunication between subsystems. This can cause delayed warnings or inconsistent instructions to the public.

Scalable architectures and edge computing solutions are crucial to handle high-volume data influx efficiently. Employing adaptive load-balancing algorithms can also maintain system performance and reliability under heavy demand.

Table 2. Types of safety risks and their impact on early warning systems

Risk Type	Description	Example	Impact on EWS
Data Poisoning	Insertion of falsified or manipulated data into the sensing network	Fake reports of disaster zones or casualties	Misallocation of emergency resources, false alarms
Noisy Data	Presence of irrelevant or duplicated social data	Repeated or exaggerated user posts	Reduced data accuracy, confusion in prioritization
Delay in Verification	Slow confirmation of data authenticity	Unverified tweets causing delayed action	Decreased system responsiveness, delayed rescue
Human Error	Misinterpretation or emotional bias in reporting	Users misreporting minor events as critical	Inaccurate threat evaluation, unnecessary panic
System Overload	Excessive data flow causing technical bottlenecks	Surge of messages during crisis	Processing failure, loss of real-time capability

3.6 Summary and Transition to Security Considerations

Social sensing enhances the situational awareness and responsiveness of AIoT-driven disaster management systems, yet its safety implications cannot be overlooked. The risks discussed above reveal that the effectiveness of early warning systems depends not only on data quantity but also on data quality, verification mechanisms, and system resilience under pressure.

Therefore, while social sensing offers immense potential for improving public safety, it must be supported by robust security frameworks to ensure data integrity, authenticity, and confidentiality. The following chapter explores these issues in greater detail, examining the security concerns and protection strategies necessary to safeguard AIoT-based social sensing systems from emerging digital threats.

4. SECURITY CONCERNS IN SOCIAL SENSING

Security in social sensing systems is a very important aspect because it concerns data protection from unauthorized access, information manipulation, and potential identity compromise (Yamoah et al., 2025). Unlike conventional physical sensors, AIoT systems that rely on human input are highly susceptible to interference from malicious intent, both in the form of digital fraud and technical exploitation. In many cases, these systems do not yet have robust identity verification mechanisms, making them highly open to various forms of attacks. Wang et al., 2025).

4.1 AIoT Security Layers for Social Sensing

To safeguard social sensing operations, a structured security framework is needed across all stages of the data flow, from data collection to system action. Figure 3 shows the AIoT Security Layers for Social Sensing.

Figure 3. AIoT security layers for social sensing

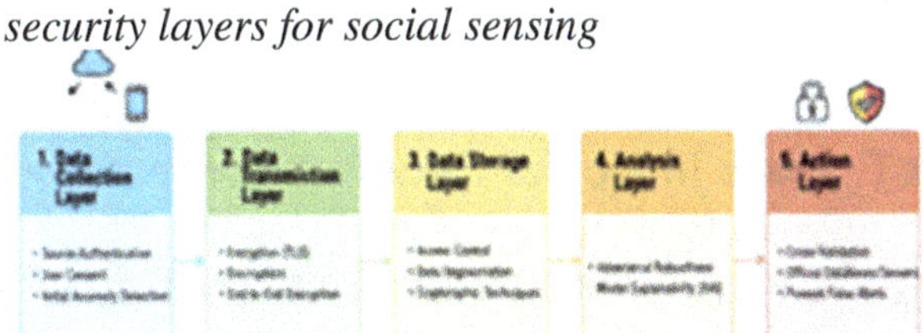

1. Data Collection Layer

This layer focuses on securing the input stage where social and physical data are gathered. Security measures include source authentication, user consent verification, and initial anomaly detection to filter suspicious inputs.

2. Data Transmission Layer

Data exchanged between devices, users, and cloud servers must be encrypted using secure communication protocols such as TLS or end-to-end encryption. This prevents interception or tampering during transmission.

3. Data Storage Layer

Stored data, whether on centralized servers or distributed networks, must be protected through access control, data segmentation, and cryptographic techniques to prevent unauthorized retrieval or modification.

4. Analysis Layer

At this stage, AI models analyze and correlate data. Implementing adversarial robustness testing and model explainability ensures that algorithms cannot be easily manipulated by malicious data injections.

5. Action Layer

The output or decision-making process must be safeguarded to prevent false alerts or system abuse. Cross-validation mechanisms with official databases or verified sensors can minimize the risk of generating incorrect warnings.

This layered approach reinforces the resilience of AIoT-based social sensing systems and ensures that potential threats are addressed systematically at every operational level.

4.2 Common Threats in Social Sensing Systems

Social sensing systems face multiple forms of threats that target different stages of the AIoT pipeline. These threats can be classified into five major categories:

1. Data Tampering and Poisoning: Manipulation of input data to mislead system outputs.

2. Eavesdropping and Data Interception: Unauthorized access to data during transmission.
3. Identity Spoofing and Fake Accounts: Creation of synthetic identities to spread misinformation.
4. Unauthorized Access and Privilege Escalation: Intrusions into databases or administrative systems.
5. Adversarial AI Attacks: Exploiting machine learning models to generate false predictions or confuse classification systems.

Each of these threats requires targeted mitigation strategies to preserve the trustworthiness and operational continuity of EWS deployments. Systems that are not equipped with sophisticated identity verification methods will find it difficult to distinguish between real and fake identities, so the decisions taken will be wrong (Juan M. Núñez et al., 2025).

Table 3. Threats and mitigation strategies for social sensing security

Threat Type	Description	Mitigation Strategy	Relevance to EWS
Data Tampering and Poisoning	Insertion of falsified or manipulated social data	Multi-source verification, anomaly detection, blockchain-based audit trails	Prevents false alerts and resource misallocation
Eavesdropping and Data Interception	Unauthorized monitoring of data during transmission	End-to-end encryption, secure communication protocols, VPN tunneling	Protects sensitive information shared in real time
Identity Spoofing and Fake Accounts	Impersonation of users or bots generating fake reports	Identity validation, reputation scoring, CAPTCHAs, digital signatures	Reduces misinformation spread during crises
Unauthorized Access and Privilege Escalation	Gaining access to restricted databases or system controls	Multi-factor authentication (MFA), access control lists (ACL), zero-trust architecture	Prevents unauthorized modification of alerts or system data
Adversarial AI Attacks	Manipulation of AI models using adversarial inputs	Adversarial training, explainable AI, model robustness validation	Ensures model integrity and accurate early warnings

4.3 Data Integrity and Authentication Mechanisms

Another threat is spoofing and replay attacks, in which sensors or users send back old data that was previously valid, to trick the system as if it were up-to-date information. This type of attack is particularly dangerous because it takes advantage of loopholes in the time tracking system or data synchronization (Namana & Udaya Kumar, 2025). Maintaining data integrity is critical in ensuring that social sensing inputs represent authentic, untampered information. Approaches such as digital watermarking, hash verification, and blockchain-based consensus can be used to trace data origins and prevent alterations. Moreover, authentication protocols using biometric identification or trusted device certificates enhance accountability and reduce the likelihood of spoofed participation.

In multi-hazard early warning contexts, these mechanisms ensure that social data integrated into alert systems come from verified sources, thus improving both system accuracy and public trust.

4.4 Challenges in Data Transmission and Storage

In addition to direct threats to data integrity, another equally important aspect is security in the data transmission and storage process. Because social sensing is often used in sensitive contexts such as law enforcement, smart city surveillance, or vital infrastructure (e.g. power generation and emergency services), the data collected must be protected from interception or theft by third parties. Without strong encryption, data sent from devices to processing centers is very easy to intercept. Similarly, data stored without proper security on cloud servers is at high risk of being leaked or modified. This can have serious consequences, such as operational sabotage, mass privacy violations, and misuse of data for political or economic purposes (Kunz et al., 2025).

4.5 Mitigation Strategy and Development Direction

In facing safety and security challenges arising from the application of social sensing in the AIoT environment, a comprehensive mitigation strategy and adaptive technology development direction are needed. The complexity of the interaction between dynamic social data and input-sensitive AI systems makes a single approach ineffective enough (Sung et al., 2025). Therefore, the strategy implemented must cover various aspects, ranging from technical, policy, to community involvement.

1. Context-Based Data Validation and Verification

One of the key strategies in mitigating safety risks is the development of contextual and adaptive data validation methods. In social sensing systems, the data generated by users is often ambiguous, subjective, and not directly verified. Therefore, it is important to develop a model that can evaluate the accuracy of data based on spatial, temporal, and social contexts.

For example, the system can compare input from social media with physical sensors such as CCTV or GPS to ensure the consistency of information. This technique can minimize the effects of false or biased data spread by malicious actors.

Machine learning models designed to recognize unusual data patterns can also be applied to detect anomalies that may originate from data poisoning attacks (Namana & Udaya Kumar, 2025).

2. Strengthening Data Security Mechanisms

Risk mitigation cannot be separated from the aspect of data security. The implementation of strong encryption protocols, multi-factor authentication, and differential privacy techniques is required to protect the integrity and confidentiality of social data. One of the increasingly relevant approaches is the use of blockchain to record the origin and changes of data in a transparent and non-modifiable manner. This can increase trust in the system as well as provide a clear audit trail of any social inputs.

In addition, digital watermarking techniques can also be used to track data manipulation throughout its life cycle. This strategy allows for the identification of data sources that have been maliciously modified, while providing legal protection against data integrity breaches.

3. Filter dan Prioritisasi Data Real-Time

AIoT systems that rely on social input must be able to process and filter data in real-time. For this reason, the development of intelligent filtration modules based on risk priority is urgently needed. For example, in an emergency situation, data from trusted sources such as security forces or official agencies should take precedence over unverified public data.

This module can also be given the ability to recognize and ignore content that is emotional or provocative, such as social media posts that contain hate speech, fake news, or hoaxes. Thus, the system can make more objective decisions and not get carried away by the current of irrelevant or misleading mass sentiment.

4. Multistakeholder Collaboration

An effective mitigation strategy requires the active involvement of a wide range of stakeholders, including technology developers, policymakers, the academic community, and the general public. Governments and regulatory agencies need to design policies that balance the use of social data for security purposes and the protection of individuals' privacy rights.

Meanwhile, the public needs to be educated about their role in the social sensing system, including how to use technology ethically and responsibly. This awareness is important to prevent the spread of false information that can undermine the integrity of the system and endanger public safety.

5. Development Direction: Robust and Ethical AIoT Systems

Seeing the various challenges that exist, the direction of development in the future needs to be focused on designing AIoT systems that are resilient to data disruption and manipulation, as well as upholding ethical principles in the use of technology. The system should be designed with redundancy, meaning it has multiple input lines and verification processes so that it doesn't rely on just one source.

The development of AI models should also include regular algorithmic audits to avoid hidden biases that could jeopardize user safety. Additionally, the Explainable AI (XAI) approach can help explain the decisions made by the system, thereby increasing transparency and accountability.

Finally, the Human-in-the-Loop (HITL) approach must remain applied in critical systems. Although AIoT has high automation capabilities, it is still important to include human supervision in the decision-making process, especially in the context of public safety or emergency response

5. ETHICAL AND PRIVACY CHALLENGES IN SOCIAL SENSING

The rapid advancement of social sensing within AIoT environments has created unprecedented opportunities for data-driven decision-making, particularly in the context of disaster management and early warning systems. However, this technological progress also introduces serious ethical and privacy challenges. As social sensing systems rely heavily on user-generated data, they inherently collect personal, behavioral, and location-based information. Without proper governance, such data may expose individuals to surveillance, misuse, and discrimination.

Addressing these ethical and privacy concerns is critical to ensure trust, transparency, and accountability in AIoT-based social sensing. Ethical considerations are not optional add-ons but fundamental components that define whether these systems can be safely and responsibly integrated into multi-hazard early warning systems (EWS). Without strong ethical management, the potential for data misuse is enormous, and public trust in AIoT technology can be significantly eroded (Fan et al., 2025).

5.1 Ethical Dimensions in Social Sensing

Without transparency, the data collection process will appear like hidden snooping, even if the data is used for positive purposes such as improving public services or city security (Wei et al., 2025). Ethical challenges in social sensing typically arise from the tension between data utility and individual rights. On one hand, large-scale data collection is necessary to improve system responsiveness and resilience. On the other, unrestricted data use can lead to violations of privacy, consent, and fairness.

Key ethical issues include:

1. **Informed Consent** – Users often share data without fully understanding how it will be used or stored. Transparent consent mechanisms are essential to ensure ethical participation.
2. **Data Anonymization** – Removing personal identifiers is crucial to prevent re-identification of individuals, especially in sensitive datasets.
3. **Transparency and Explainability** – Stakeholders must be informed about how data-driven decisions are made by AI systems.
4. **Accountability and Fairness** – Mechanisms must be in place to hold developers and organizations responsible for misuse or algorithmic bias.

In the absence of these principles, social sensing may inadvertently amplify inequities or cause public distrust in technology-driven safety systems

5.2 Ethical Governance Framework for AIoT-Based Social Sensing

A good social sensing system should provide options for *opt-in* and *opt-out*, not just embed consent in long, unreadable terms and conditions (Fan et al., 2025). To operationalize ethics in social sensing, a structured governance model is required. The Ethical Governance Framework provides an integrated view of how ethical principles translate into technical and organizational practices. Figure 4 shows the Ethical Governance Framework for Social Sensing in AioT.

Figure 4. Ethical governance framework for social sensing in AIoT

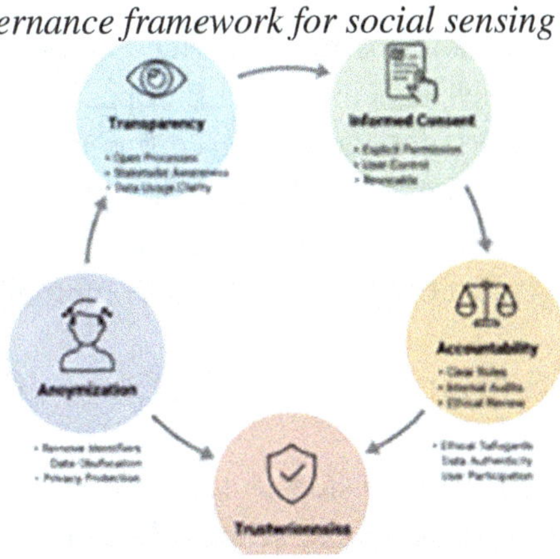

Core Components of the Framework:

- Transparency: All processes involving data collection and analysis should be open and understandable. Stakeholders must be aware of what data is being collected, why it is collected, and how it is used.
- Informed Consent: Users must explicitly grant permission for their data to be utilized, and consent should be revocable at any time.
- Anonymization: Personal identifiers must be removed or obfuscated to protect individuals' privacy while maintaining the utility of the data.
- Accountability: Organizations should establish clear roles and responsibilities for data handling, supported by internal audits and ethical review boards.
- Trustworthiness: The integration of ethical safeguards directly contributes to the reliability of early warning systems, as ethical compliance enhances data authenticity and user participation.

When these elements are aligned, social sensing systems become not only technically reliable but also socially legitimate.

5.3 Case Study 1: GDPR-Based AIoT Deployment in Europe

One of the technical approaches to maintaining privacy is data anonymization, which is the process of making data untraceable back to certain individuals (Fan et al., 2025). The General Data Protection Regulation (GDPR), implemented by the European Union, serves as a global benchmark for privacy compliance in AIoT and data-intensive systems. Under GDPR, personal data processing must adhere to principles such as lawfulness, fairness, purpose limitation, and data minimization.

In the context of social sensing, GDPR ensures that citizens' data collected through mobile applications, social platforms, or IoT devices remain under their control. For example, disaster response systems in several European cities use location data to issue alerts but do so within strict consent-based frameworks. Users are informed about data retention periods and can withdraw participation at any time.

This approach illustrates how privacy-preserving mechanisms can coexist with effective disaster management operations without compromising public safety.

5.4 Case Study 2: Singapore Smart Nation Initiativ

If these ethical and privacy dimensions are ignored, society risks a crisis of trust in the AIoT system as a whole. Singapore's **Smart Nation policy** represents another real-world model of ethical AIoT deployment. The initiative integrates IoT and AI technologies for public services, including transportation management, public health monitoring, and emergency response.

Ethical governance is embedded through several measures:

- Data collected from citizens is anonymized before analysis.
- Public communication campaigns emphasize informed consent and digital literacy.
- Independent oversight committees review data use for compliance with privacy laws.

The Smart Nation approach demonstrates how clear ethical policies and strong regulatory frameworks can enhance both innovation and public confidence. Importantly, these measures foster the trustworthiness necessary for citizens to engage with national-level sensing systems.

5.5 Linking Ethics to the Trustworthiness of Early Warning System

Ethical integrity and privacy protection directly influence the trustworthiness of early warning systems. When individuals trust that their data will be handled responsibly, they are more willing to contribute information voluntarily. This increases the accuracy, diversity, and reliability of social sensing inputs.

Conversely, a lack of ethical safeguards can lead to public resistance, data withdrawal, or intentional misinformation. Therefore, ethical compliance is not merely a moral obligation but a practical requirement for ensuring the sustainability and effectiveness of AIoT-driven EWS.

By promoting transparency, privacy, and accountability, ethical frameworks help create a feedback loop of trust where users, developers, and institutions collaborate to maintain both safety and social legitimacy.

6. DATA TRUST AND TRUTH MODELS IN SOCIAL SENSING

In the context of the Artificial Intelligence of Things (AIoT) system, trust in social data (social sensing) is an important foundation in ensuring the reliability of decisions taken automatically (M. Lu et al., 2025). In social sensing systems, trust and truth models play a fundamental role in ensuring that the information collected from diverse human and machine sources is reliable, verifiable, and credible. Because social data often originate from unstructured and subjective human input, developing effective trust evaluation mechanisms becomes essential to prevent misinformation, bias, and manipulation.

The central objective of trust modeling in AIoT-based social sensing is to assess data credibility by evaluating both the source reliability (the trustworthiness of contributors) and the content reliability (the factual accuracy of data). By combining these two aspects, the system can automatically weigh and prioritize information that is more likely to represent ground truth, especially in critical applications such as disaster early warning systems (EWS).

6.1 Social Sensing Trust Model Scheme

Figure 5. Social sensing trust model scheme

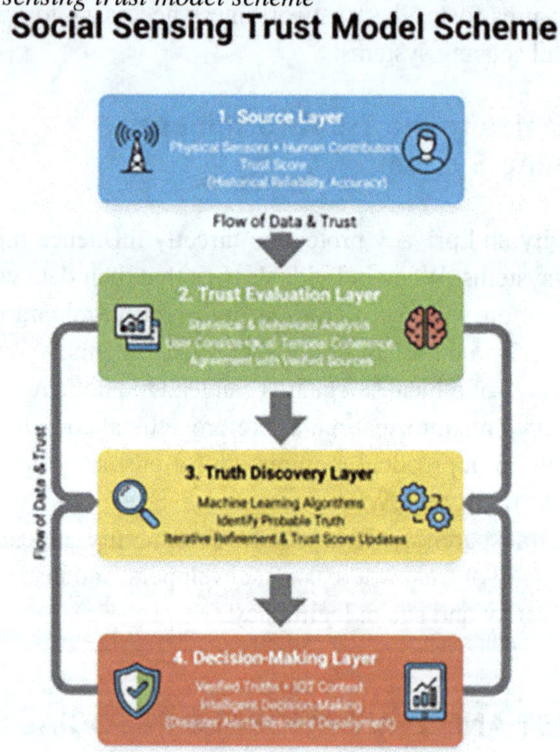

Figure 5 shows the Social Sensing Trust Model Scheme . The Social Sensing Trust Model Scheme integrates multiple layers of evaluation to determine the credibility of data in real time:

1. Source Layer

Collects data from both physical sensors and human contributors. Each data source is assigned an initial trust score based on historical reliability, accuracy, and user behavior.

2. Trust Evaluation Layer

Calculates the trustworthiness of data contributors using statistical and behavioral analysis. Factors include user consistency, spatial-temporal coherence, and agreement with other verified sources.

3. Truth Discovery Layer

Applies machine learning algorithms to identify the most probable truth from conflicting or uncertain data. This process often involves iterative refinement, where trust scores are continuously updated as new information arrives.

4. Decision-Making Layer

Combines verified truths with contextual information from IoT devices to support intelligent decision-making in real-time scenarios, such as issuing disaster alerts or resource deployment.

This layered approach allows AIoT systems to dynamically adapt their trust mechanisms and maintain high levels of accuracy and reliability in uncertain or rapidly evolving conditions.\

7. ADVERSARIAL THREATS AND DEFENSE STRATEGIES

In an era of increasingly massive connectivity, the integration between artificial intelligence (AI) and social sensing in the AIoT (Artificial Intelligence of Things) environment presents extraordinary opportunities for real-time contextual data collection and analysis (Juan M. Núñez et al., 2025). As AIoT-based social sensing systems become increasingly complex and interconnected, they face a growing number of adversarial threats that can compromise data integrity, disrupt decision-making, and erode public trust. Adversarial threats refer to deliberate attacks designed to manipulate input data, exploit vulnerabilities in machine learning models, or interfere with communication channels within the system.

In the context of disaster management and early warning systems, such attacks can have severe consequences, including false alarms, delayed responses, or misallocation of emergency resources. Understanding these threats and developing effective defense strategies are therefore essential for ensuring system resilience and safety.

7.1. Understanding Adversarial Threats

Adversarial AI is a phenomenon in which seemingly ordinary inputs (such as images, text, or sounds) are subtly but intentionally modified, thus deceiving the AI system into generating incorrect predictions or classifications (Hnatiuc et al., 2025). In the context of social sensing, this manipulation can be a *deepfake* video of a fake "eyewitness" in an emergency situation, or a seemingly legitimate comment but contains a linguistic pattern to trigger certain algorithmic decisions.

For example, in a disaster monitoring system that relies on citizen reports via social media, perpetrators can insert fake images of floods or earthquakes with manipulated metadata to get the AI system to estimate the wrong location as the epicenter of the disaster. This can lead to the allocation of rescue resources to places that do not need assistance, while the affected locations are actually late addressed.

This problem is exacerbated by the architecture of deep learning models that often work as "black boxes", making it difficult to trace how the final decision is made. An in-depth study (Fan et al., 2025) shows that AI models tend to be overfitted to certain data patterns, which makes them vulnerable to small but significant perturbations (Adversarial Examples), especially when training is conducted without layered defenses.

7.2. Summary of Threats and Defense Methods

Table 4. Threat types and defense methods

Threat Type	Description	Defense Method	Example
Adversarial AI	Manipulated input data	Explainable AI (XAI), anomaly detection	Deepfake disaster footage
Poisoning Attack	Corrupt training data	Data validation, retraining	False reports in flood models
Evasion Attack	Altered inputs to bypass detection	Feature redundancy, integrity checks	Modified social posts
Inference Attack	Extracting private data	Encryption, access control	User identity tracing
Model Stealing	Copying AI models	API security, watermarking	Replicated detection algorithms
Data Spoofing	Fake data overload	Real-time validation	Bot traffic during crises

In the healthcare realm, hacked wearable sensors can transmit incorrect heart rate or blood oxygen data, resulting in AI systems issuing erroneous warnings about the patient's condition or a specific geographical area (H. Wang et al., 2025).

7.3. Inversion Models: Uncovering the Personal Attributes of AI Outputs

An inversion attack model is a method in which an attacker tries to reverse the AI inference process to infer sensitive information from a user or whistleblower, based solely on the model's output. For example, if an AI model classifies a user's report as "high risk" in an epidemic area, a perpetrator with enough statistical knowledge can guess the reporter's personal data, such as age, precise location, or even medical conditions.

This is especially problematic in the context of voluntary but sensitive social data, such as reporting cases of violence, infectious diseases, or crimes. Social sensing models that are not protected by differential privacy methods or federative aggregation will be easier to exploit through techniques such as membership inference attacks or stealing models.

7.4. Defense Strategy: Towards Social Resilience Sensing

To address these threats, various strategic approaches have been developed. However, given the open nature of social data sensing, there is no single solution capable of addressing all attack vectors. A multidimensional approach is indispensable.

a. Powerful Anomaly Detection

One of the basic approaches in defense is the implementation of a machine learning-based *anomaly detection* system that is trained to recognize patterns of reports or sensors that deviate from the norm. These systems can use clustering, autoencoders, or statistical methods to distinguish legitimate and adversarial reports.

However, anomaly detection must be accompanied by contextual analysis. In a crisis situation, people's behavior can indeed change significantly, and the system must be able to adjust the normal baseline based on time and location. An adaptive model that is able to conduct *online learning* is indispensable in this regard.

b. Secure Multi-Party Computation

Secure Multi-Party Computation (SMPC) allows multiple parties to perform calculations on collective data without the need to open raw data to each other. This is useful in scenarios where many user devices transmit sensitive data yet must be kept private (Obaidat et al., 2024). With protocols such as garbled circuits or homomorphic encryption, data remains encrypted throughout the computational process.

In the context of social sensing, SMPC can be used to calculate the crowd index of a location without revealing the identity of each reporter. This protects users from the threat of tracking and inversion models.

c. Red Team Simulation and Periodic Security Audits

Red teaming is a process in which independent teams simulate attacks on a system to realistically test its resilience. In social sensing, this approach helps detect loopholes that developers may have missed. Simulations can include the creation of adversarial data, infiltration of virtual sensors, and manipulation of communication networks (Fan et al., 2025).

In addition, periodic audits of security protocols and validation of AI models (including audit bias) are critical to maintaining long-term integrity. These audits can involve an independent team of experts, as well as monitoring by a community of users, who can collectively provide feedback on the performance and honesty of the system.

8. CASE STUDIES AND PRACTICAL SCENARIOS

Social sensing has emerged as an essential approach for collecting real-time contextual data through human participation and intelligent devices within an AIoT-based environment. While it offers great potential for improving efficiency and decision-making accuracy, its application also raises challenges concerning ethics, data reliability, and user privacy and security (Majumdar & Awasthi, 2025). This chapter examines three real-world case studies from Beirut, Hong Kong, and the COVID-19 pandemic to show both the strengths and limitations of social sensing in critical contexts. A comparative analysis and key lessons for disaster early warning systems (EWS) are presented at the end of the chapter.

8.1 Response to the Disaster: The 2020 Beirut Explosion

A significant example of social sensing occurred during the Beirut port explosion on August 4, 2020. Within moments of the blast, social media platforms such as Twitter, Instagram, and TikTok were flooded with eyewitness videos, photos, and urgent messages. This citizen-generated information provided crucial situational awareness that helped journalists, humanitarian agencies, and authorities locate affected zones and coordinate relief efforts. This data is a key source of information for humanitarian agencies, journalists, and authorities to respond quickly (Wei et al., 2025)

However, the Beirut incident also revealed the vulnerability of unverified social data. Misinformation spread quickly as unrelated images, such as those from the 2015 Tianjin explosion, were shared as if they were part of the Beirut event. This hinders coordination between local authorities and international aid organizations, as it takes additional time and effort to sort out which data is valid and which is not (Wei et al., 2025).

Reflection:

The Beirut case highlights the importance of developing real-time data verification systems that can cross-check and filter social media content before it is used for decision-making. Collaboration between citizens, media, and official agencies is crucial to maintain both the speed and accuracy of emergency responses.

8.2 Smart City Surveillance: The Case of Hong Kong

Hong Kong offers an important example of how social sensing is integrated into smart city systems. The government deployed AIoT-based surveillance tools, including CCTV cameras with facial recognition, mobile phone signal tracking, and social media analysis to detect potential public unrest during the 2019–2020 protests.

While these technologies provided more precise information and improved response times, they also triggered public resistance. Many citizens feared continuous monitoring and began using methods to avoid detection, such as wearing masks, using umbrellas, or disabling digital tracking.

The use of social sensing in this context suggests that in the absence of strong privacy regulations and openness from governments about how data is used, technology can cause counterproductive effects in the form of societal resistance (Lyu et al., 2025) As a result, trust in institutions has declined, and the effectiveness of the supervisory system has been questioned.

8.3 Health Monitoring: COVID-19 Pandemic

During the COVID-19 pandemic, social sensing played a central role in tracking disease spread, community behavior, and medical needs in real time. Governments and health organizations utilized wearable devices such as Fitbit and Apple Watch, social media data, and contact tracing applications like PeduliLindungi in Indonesia and TraceTogether in Singapore. Citizen reporting of symptoms, testing, and self-isolation also contributes to the preparation of dynamic maps of the spread of the virus (M. Lu et al., 2025)

These systems allowed authorities to identify high-risk areas and adjust public health measures accordingly. At the same time, the pandemic revealed the darker side of social sensing. False information about vaccines, the origins of the virus, and conspiracy theories spread rapidly across online platforms. This misinformation reduced public confidence in medical authorities and slowed down vaccination efforts.

However, as information from the public develops, the flow of disinformation also increases. For example, there are uploads stating that COVID-19 vaccines contain tracking chips, or that the virus is not real, which is spreading much faster than official clarification. This hinders vaccination programs, creates distrust of health workers, and complicates crisis management (H. Wang et al., 2025)

This case shows the importance of building data verification and digital literacy infrastructure in society (Lyu et al., 2025) AI can be used to detect patterns of harmful speech or misinformation, but it still requires humans to evaluate context and provide appropriate responses.

Reflection:

The pandemic case emphasizes that technological innovation must be supported by digital literacy and public education. Building social trust and verifying health information are essential to ensure that social sensing contributes positively to crisis management.

8.4 Learning and Reflection

The three case studies above show that the success of social sensing in improving public safety and system efficiency depends heavily on three main factors:

1. Quality and Reliability of Data The information collected must be verified, both through cross-check between sources, the use of anomaly detection algorithms, and a collaborative approach with trusted citizen participation.
2. Transparency and Ethics When citizens feel that they are not openly involved in how their data is used, resistance will arise. Therefore, social sensing system operators need to establish open communication and provide control mechanisms such as opt-in/opt-out.
3. Resilience to Security Threats and Manipulation The use of AI and IoT technology must be accompanied by a defense system that is able to overcome threats such as adversarial input, sensor spoofing, and the systematic spread of false information.

Table 5. Case studies

Criteria	Beirut Explosion (Disaster)	Hong Kong Smart City (Security)	COVID-19 Pandemic (Health)
Type of Social Data	Videos, photos, and eyewitness posts on social media	CCTV feeds, mobile signals, and online activities	Wearable sensor data, contact-tracing apps, social media posts
Primary Risks	Misinformation, fake visuals, data overload	Mass surveillance, privacy violations, data misuse	Health misinformation, data leaks
Analytical Challenges	Real-time data validation and cross-source verification	Balancing security with transparency	Integrating medical and social data from diverse platforms
Institutional Response	Manual and AI-based content verification	Centralized data control with limited public oversight	Multi-stakeholder coordination among governments, platforms, and users
Key Lessons	Speed–accuracy balance in crisis information	Importance of transparency and accountability	Need for digital literacy and trust frameworks

8.5 Potential for Future Innovation

The three case studies provide important lessons for the development of multi-hazard early warning systems that integrate social sensing as part of their architecture.

1. Data Trustworthiness and Verification

The reliability of EWS depends on the accuracy of incoming data. Integrating cross-validation between social and physical sensors can improve data integrity. Methods such as anomaly detection, blockchain-based tracking, and multi-source correlation help ensure that decisions are based on credible information.

2. Ethical and Transparent Governance

Social sensing requires public trust to function effectively. Transparent data policies, clear consent mechanisms, and open communication with users are essential to encourage responsible participation and prevent misuse of information.

3. Community Engagement and Digital Literacy

Citizens who understand how to verify information and report responsibly can significantly enhance system reliability. Education programs that promote digital literacy and awareness of misinformation strengthen social resilience during crises.

4. Integration into Multi-Hazard Early Warning Systems

Social sensing should complement, not replace, physical sensor networks. By combining social data with environmental and technical data, EWS can provide a more complete picture of emerging threats and improve the accuracy of alerts for disasters, epidemics, and social disturbances.

The Beirut, Hong Kong, and COVID-19 cases demonstrate that the effectiveness of social sensing depends not only on technological advancement but also on ethical governance and public trust. A successful system must integrate technical resilience, transparent data management, and active community participation. When these components are aligned, social sensing becomes a powerful instrument for building safer, more responsive, and human-centered early warning systems

9. RESEARCH CHALLENGES AND FUTURE DIRECTIONS

The rapid advancement of AIoT-based social sensing has opened vast opportunities for real-time data collection, intelligent decision-making, and adaptive disaster management (Fan et al., 2025). However, several challenges remain before these systems can operate reliably across multi-hazard contexts. This chapter identifies key research directions and outlines a roadmap for developing interoperable, ethical, and globally coordinated social sensing systems.

9.1 Balance between Real-Time Sensing and Data Verification

One of the main challenges in social sensing is how to maintain a balance between the need for real-time data and the accuracy or validity of the data (M. Lu et al., 2025) Social sensing, because it relies on human contributions through connected devices (such as smartphones, social media, and IoT sensors), tends to generate large amounts of data and in a short time. However, this speed is not always accompanied by reliability (Namana & Udaya Kumar, 2025) Unverified data can lead to disinformation or even endanger public safety if used as a basis for decision-making.

Future research must therefore focus on:

- Multi-sensor interoperability so that heterogeneous data streams from seismic, hydrological, and human sensors can be fused seamlessly.

- Cross-validation algorithms that compare physical and social signals to detect inconsistencies in real time.
- Adaptive verification frameworks capable of scaling dynamically during crises when data volume spikes.

Developing such integrated mechanisms will allow early warning systems to maintain both speed and reliability even under multi-hazard stress.

9.2 Identity and Privacy: Assurance Mechanisms Without Compromising Privacy

Identity is an important component of the social sensing system. To guarantee the integrity and reliability of the data, it is important to know who is providing the data. However, challenges arise when the need to guarantee identity collides with an individual's right to privacy.

Pressing research issues:

- Anonymous authentication: how to prove that someone is part of a group or meets certain criteria, without revealing their identity.
- Zero-knowledge proof: a cryptographic method that allows proof without leaking information.
- Privacy-preserving identity federation, where multiple identities can be validated in a decentralized network without revealing personal information.

In this context, approaches such as self-sovereign identity and the use of decentralized identifiers (DIDs) are promising options (Liu et al., 2025) However, there has not been much real implementation on a broad scale in complex social sensing environments.

9.3 Scalability of Trust Mechanisms in a Heterogeneous AIoT Environment

AIoT environments are highly heterogeneous, both in terms of devices, networks, and user entities. Building a trust mechanism in these conditions is very challenging. Trust must include the device, data, user, and AI model used.

Some relevant research directions:

- Trust inference engine: an AI system that is able to estimate the level of trust of a data or device contextually.

- Federated trust system: a trust that is built together by various entities without relying on a single authority.
- Edge trust management: a trust mechanism that is distributed at the edge node, not just in the cloud.
- Supporting Illustration: Federated trust diagram with edge nodes, users, and clouds exchanging trust scores based on local and global experiences.

9.4 Legal and Ethical Standards for Autonomous Sensing System Accountability

One of the biggest challenges of the adoption of social sensing and AIoT is the absence of a clear legal framework regarding accountability. In many cases, it is difficult to determine who is responsible in the event of data misuse or prediction errors that lead to losses (Liu et al., 2025)

Crucial research questions:

- Who is responsible if autonomous sensors generate incorrect data and negatively impact?
- How to prepare a suitable standard operational procedure (SOP) for sensing system supervision?
- What are the legal implications of using AI that performs social sensing-based predictions in law enforcement?

Need to expand:

- A multi-layered accountability model involving device manufacturers, system operators, AI developers, and end-users.
- Automated audit policies that can track AI data paths and decisions for audit and forensic purposes.
- Harmonization of global regulations to avoid cross-border legal loopholes.

9.5 Hybrid Models and Explainable AI

The ability to explain the results and processes of AI models (explainability) is essential in environments related to safety and security. Meanwhile, hybrid sensing models (combining social sensing and machine-to-machine data) can improve system reliability.

Potential research directions:

- Development of XAI (Explainable Artificial Intelligence) for models used in social sensing so that they can be audited and understood by humans.
- Integration between neural-symbolic systems that can combine machine learning with formal logic.
- Experiment with multi-modal fusion, which is the integration of various types of data (text, images, physical sensors) with an explainable approach.

Supporting Illustrations:

Add a diagram that shows the comparison between a black-box model and an explainable model in the context of disaster decision-making.

Table 6. Future research roadmap

Focus Area	Research Objectives	Expected Contribution to Multi-Hazard Resilience
Real-time Data Fusion	Develop unified models integrating physical and social sensors	Faster and more accurate early warnings
Privacy-Preserving AI	Apply federated and encrypted learning techniques	Protection of personal data while maintaining analytical power
Explainable AI and Ethics	Build transparent decision pipelines	Increased public trust and accountability
Cross-Border Data Governance	Establish international standards for disaster data sharing	Cooperative responses to regional or global hazards
Community-Driven Sensing	Encourage participatory sensing and digital literacy	Strengthened societal engagement and resilience

Future research on AIoT-based social sensing must move beyond isolated technological improvements toward system-level integration that addresses the complexities of multi-hazard environments

9.6 Policy Recommendations and International Collaboration

The development of solutions to social sensing challenges cannot be done by one discipline alone. A multi-disciplinary approach is required involving:

- Computer science and electrical engineering for sensing and AI system development.
- Social sciences and psychology to understand the dynamics of society and user behavior.
- Laws and ethics to set limits and guidelines for the use of technology.

This collaboration will result in a solution that is not only technically reliable but also accepted by the community.

Implementation strategy:

- Co-design research: involving the community in the sensing system design process.
- Living lab experiments: testing the system in a real environment with the active participation of users.

10. CONCLUSION

The integration of Artificial Intelligence of Things (AIoT) technology with social sensing has redefined how digital ecosystems operate by merging human perception with machine intelligence. Through data collected from social media, smartphones, wearable sensors, and user-generated reports, AIoT systems are now capable of understanding and responding to real-world conditions with greater contextual depth. This fusion of human and machine intelligence supports informed decision-making across various sectors, including disaster response, healthcare, and urban management. As a result, social sensing represents a significant leap forward in creating adaptive, intelligent, and responsive digital infrastructures.

Despite its transformative potential, the reliance on user-generated data introduces several critical risks related to misinformation, data manipulation, and privacy violations. When inaccurate or biased data is processed by automated AIoT systems, it can lead to severe consequences such as misinformed policy decisions or compromised safety protocols. Therefore, ensuring the security, authenticity, and ethical use of social sensing data is essential for maintaining trust and reliability. Technical innovations such as trust modeling, anomaly detection, and explainable AI, along with regulatory and ethical frameworks, are vital in mitigating these risks and establishing responsible governance structures.

Looking ahead, the evolution of social sensing in AIoT must embrace an integrated, multidisciplinary approach that combines technological innovation with social, ethical, and legal considerations. Emerging tools like blockchain for decentralized verification, secure multi-party computation for privacy protection, and human-in-the-loop models for contextual validation can collectively enhance data reliability and accountability. Collaboration between policymakers, technologists, and social scientists will be crucial in developing standards that promote transparency, inclusivity, and public trust. Ultimately, the future of AIoT-based social sensing depends on a shared commitment to responsible innovation and sustainable digital ethics to ensure that technology serves humanity safely and equitably.

REFERENCES

Aamer, A., Zadeh, A., Mali, P., & Bolick, C. (2025). Emerging technologies and principle-based project management: A systematic literature review and research agenda. *Management Review Quarterly*, *75*(2), 1761–1811. DOI: 10.1007/s11301-024-00419-y

Fan, J., Wu, J., & Bashir, A. K. (2025). Integrated Contractual Computing Resources and Efficiency Searchable Caching for AIoT-Enabled Green Vehicular Supply Chain. *IEEE Internet of Things Journal*, *12*(19), 39457–39468. Advance online publication. DOI: 10.1109/JIOT.2025.3576299

Hassan, A. H., Ahmed, E. M., Hussien, J. M., Sulaiman, R. B., Abdulhak, M., & Kahtan, H. (2025). A cyber physical sustainable smart city framework toward society 5.0: Explainable AI for enhanced SDGs monitoring. *Research in Globalization*, *10*, 100275. Advance online publication. DOI: 10.1016/j.resglo.2025.100275

Hnatiuc, M., Alpetri, D., Sintea, S.-R., Hnatiuc, B., Margarit Raicu, G., Paun, M., & Dina, I. (2025). AIoT Monitoring for Early Identification of Diseases in Grapevines: Complete Study. *IEEE Access : Practical Innovations, Open Solutions*, *13*, 80258–80271. DOI: 10.1109/ACCESS.2025.3567454

Khan, H. U., Hussain, A., Nazir, S., & Ali, F. (2025). AIoT-enabled service prioritization for mobile nodes using enhanced PMIPv6 extension protocol. *Peer-to-Peer Networking and Applications*, *18*(2), 73. Advance online publication. DOI: 10.1007/s12083-024-01844-2

Kunz, A., Baskaran, S. B. M., & Alexandropoulos, G. C. (2025). Lightweight Security for Ambient-Powered Programmable Reflections with Reconfigurable Intelligent Surfaces. *IEEE Communications Standards Magazine*, *9*(4), 168–174. Advance online publication. DOI: 10.1109/MCOMSTD.2025.3573490

Liu, Y., Guo, B., Li, N., Ding, Y., Zhang, Z., & Yu, Z. (2025). CrowdTransfer: Enabling Crowd Knowledge Transfer in AIoT Community. *IEEE Communications Surveys and Tutorials*, *27*(2), 1191–1237. DOI: 10.1109/COMST.2024.3423319

Lu, Z., Zhang, H., Sun, L., Xia, J., Ye, J., & Song, M. (2025). From One to Many: Portable Model Construction With Independent Network Units. *IEEE Internet of Things Journal*, *12*(14), 28092–28101. DOI: 10.1109/JIOT.2025.3566284

Lyu, X., Rani, S., Manimurugan, S., & Feng, Y. (2025). Smart Medical Rescue via Efficient Vehicle Road Cooperation: AIoT Framework. *IEEE Internet of Things Journal*, *12*(3), 3373–3384. DOI: 10.1109/JIOT.2024.3479244

Majumdar, S., & Awasthi, A. (2025). From Vulnerability to Resilience: Securing Public Safety GPS and Location Services with Smart Radio, Blockchain, and AI-Driven Adaptability. *Electronics (Basel)*, *14*(6), 1207. Advance online publication. DOI: 10.3390/electronics14061207

Namana, M. S. K., & Udaya Kumar, B. (2025). Enhancing Surveillance Systems leveraging AIoT for Advanced Object Detection in Real-Time Security Applications. *Engineering. Technology and Applied Science Research*, *15*(3), 22507–22517. DOI: 10.48084/etasr.9926

Nguyen, T.-P. (2025). AIoT-based indoor air quality prediction for building using enhanced metaheuristic algorithm and hybrid deep learning. *Journal of Building Engineering*, *105*, 112448. Advance online publication. DOI: 10.1016/j.jobe.2025.112448

Obaidat, M. A., Rawashdeh, M., Alja'afreh, M., Abouali, M., Thakur, K., & Karime, A. (2024). Exploring IoT and Blockchain: A Comprehensive Survey on Security, Integration Strategies, Applications and Future Research Directions. *Big Data and Cognitive Computing*, *8*(12), 174. Advance online publication. DOI: 10.3390/bdcc8120174

Park, H., & Lee, J. (2025). LMSA: A Lightweight Multi-Key Secure Aggregation Framework for Privacy-Preserving Healthcare AIoT. *CMES -. Computer Modeling in Engineering & Sciences*, *143*(1), 827–847. DOI: 10.32604/cmes.2025.061178

Sung, G.-M., Kohale, S. D., Chiang, T.-H., & Chong, Y.-J. (2025). An Artificial Intelligence Home Monitoring System That Uses CNN and LSTM and Is Based on the Android Studio Development Platform. *Applied Sciences (Basel, Switzerland)*, *15*(3), 1207. Advance online publication. DOI: 10.3390/app15031207

Wang, H., Anurag, K. A., Benamer, A. R., Arora, P., Wander, G., Johnson, M. R., Anjana, R. M., Mohan, V., Gill, S. S., Uhlig, S., & Buyya, R. (2025). HealthAIoT: AIoT-driven smart healthcare system for sustainable cloud computing environments. *Internet of Things : Engineering Cyber Physical Human Systems*, *31*, 101555. Advance online publication. DOI: 10.1016/j.iot.2025.101555

Wei, H., Miao, J., Lv, J., Chen, C.-M., Kumari, S., & Amoon, M. (2025). Secure and Trustworthy Data Management Mechanism for Dance-Consumer Electronics in AIoT. *IEEE Transactions on Consumer Electronics*, *71*(1), 1970–1979. DOI: 10.1109/TCE.2024.3471573

Yamoah, L. E., Mensah, R. O., & Frimpong, A. (2025). The benefits, challenges and implications for integrating emerging technologies in risk evaluation procedures for supply chains in transportation logistics. *Discover Sustainability*, *6*(1), 476. Advance online publication. DOI: 10.1007/s43621-025-01295-6

Chapter 8
Trust Management and Reputational Systems in Artificial Intelligence of Things (AIoT)

Sanjeev Kumar
http://orcid.org/0000-0002-7375-7341
Lovely Professional University, India

ABSTRACT

With the fast-growing technological landscape, the combination of Artificial Intelligence (AI) and the Internet of Things (IoT) referred to as AIoT, has begun disrupting the way machines communicate with data as well as human beings. With even more autonomy to these intelligent systems as they become part of all facets of human interaction like smart home, healthcare, transportation, and social platforms, the necessity to have sound trust management and reputational systems is paramount. These systems are crucial in conducting AI-based devices and services in a dependable, virtuous, and safe way as per the values of people. The described study touches upon the concept of humanized trust in AIoT through which machines will not only work intelligently but also in a socially responsible way but would gain the trust of users over a period of time. We discuss the possibility and ways of modeling trust computationally and the ability to dynamically handle it in context of user interaction patterns, history, transparency of the decisions, and contextual awareness.

DOI: 10.4018/979-8-3373-6299-1.ch008

INTRODUCTION

A more recent phenomenon in which the Internet of Things (IoT) and Artificial Intelligence (AI) have been intersecting with one another at rapid speed has been the emergence of Artificial Intelligence of Things (AIoT) paradigm, wherein intelligent decisions are complemented by omnipresent sensing and connectivity. AIoT systems enable devices to compute data on-board or in the cloud and can be used to automate simple tasks, predictive models and adaptive control in a wide variety of areas including smart cities, healthcare, autonomous transport, and industry manufacturing(Barik et al., 2024). Although this integration opens a whole new level of capabilities, it also brings about substantial issues of trust and reputation in distributed and dynamic environments. Millions of diverse devices (such as sensors and wearables to autonomous vehicles) connect, communicate, and, through data sharing, collaborate to accomplish shared goals within AIoT ecosystems. Such interactions usually take place in the absence of prior direct experience between entities and the challenge of trust management becomes a prerequisite in the context of secure, reliable, and efficient operation of the system(Ullah et al., 2024). The trust here refers not only to the conventional cybersecurity; it implies trust in the authenticity, reliability, and trustworthiness of devices, data streams, and AI-based decisions. Management of trust is an important factor that can be successful; otherwise, it may cause the data manipulation, privacy invasion, misuse of resources, and even a system failure in safety-critical systems. Reputational systems provide an effective way of measuring and controlling the trust of the AIoT networks(Anwar, Kumar, & Manoharan, 2025). These systems have reputation scores based on aggregated feedback, performance and behavioral histories, and individuals or organizations can make decision-making recommendations (i.e. who to trust) based on this information(Ullah et al., 2024). Not only does the reputation serve as a guard against bad practice, but it rewards regular, honest involvement within the community of shared activity(Rathee et al., 2023).

It is however difficult to design effective reputation models in AIoT since deployments are large, devices have limited resources, offline would be required in real time decisions and threats are constantly changing. Recently, there have been developments looking at trust assessment by AI, reputation monitoring by blockchain, and federated learning as ways to improve trust transparency, efficacy, and resilience performance. As an example, machine learning models can identify the anomalous variations that could signal the compromised devices whereas blockchain will make reputation records immutable in a decentralized system. However, such solutions have to revolve around issues that include but are not limited to trust attacks (e.g., bad-mouthing, ballot-stuffing), adversarial AI threats, and interoperability questions across the heterogeneous platforms. The issue of trust management and the preservation of reputation cannot be regarded strictly as a technical aspect but the backbone of the AIoT feasibility(Shen et al., 2023). The full potential of AIoT will not be met unless there exist mechanisms that allow credibility checks by the entities and also accountability. Due to the still ongoing growth of AIoT in areas demanding high-security, ethical solutions, and sustainability, strong and dynamic trust models are needed to guarantee secure, ethical, and sustainable implementations(Shah Alam & Latif, 2025).

Evolution from IoT to AIoT

The Internet of Things (IoT) started as a system of interrelated devices with the ability to gather and share data using embedded sensors, actuators and communication modules. Initial IoT systems were centered on collecting data and remotely monitoring it, with applications that include automating a smart home, sensor networks in the environment, and equipment in factories(Kishore et al., 2024). Nevertheless, even though IoT allowed gaining unprecedented insight into the physical environments, it was not smart enough to process the huge amounts of data it produced and translate them into meaningful insights(Wallace, 2022). The defect was largely leading to human interaction or centralized systems in information processing and decision-making. Artificial Intelligence of Things (AIoT) has become an inevitable development, given that companies have improved on AI, edge computing, and cloud infrastructure. It is the combination of machine learning (ML), deep learning, and intelligent analytics in IoT architectures, turning devices into not just sensors and actors but analyzing, predicting, and taking action, as well. This change turns the IoT into an active decision-making ecosystem(Chehri et al., 2022).Edge AI, in which data is analyzed locally at the edges (devices or edge nodes) as opposed to being transmitted to centralized servers, is a major driver of this evolution. This not only decreases latency, but also saves bandwidth, improves privacy, and enables real-time decision making operations, which are invaluable when used in autonomous vehicles, automated manufacturing predictive maintenance, and AI-driven healthcare surveillance(Sharma et al., 2024).

It is worth mentioning some of the technological trends that increased the transition of IoT to AIoT:

I. Advancements in AI algorithms capable of running efficiently on low-power devices.
II. 5G connectivity, enabling ultra-low-latency communication between devices.
III. Miniaturization of hardware, making embedded AI chips feasible in small devices.
IV. Cloud-edge hybrid architectures, providing both scalability and local intelligence.

The improvements of AIoT on the conventional IoT are immense. AIoT systems will be able to recognize abnormalities, predict future conditions, and streamline functions without constant active involvement of people. As an example, an AIoT-powered smart energy grid should be able to independently adapt better supply given the forecasted consumption models, reducing inefficiency and unsustainability (Alaba, 2024). In other words, IoT brings networked devices, and AIoT breathes life into them. The evolution is a story of the movement towards the autonomous cognition rather than the simple connectivity in terms of preparing paths to more adaptive, secure, and efficient systems in different industries(Jevremovic et al., 2024).

Foundations of AIoT Authentication: Standards and Best Practices

Artificial Intelligence of Things (AIoT) integrates the omnipresent hyper connected nature of the Internet of Things (IoT), with the smart decision-making capabilities of Artificial Intelligence (AI). With these interrelated ecosystems, practical information is exchanged all the time between the devices and the applications and even cloud services. Such a rapidly changing environment requires strong authentication systems to maintain unauthorized entities are not involved in the exchange of information and the process of making decisions(Qureshi & Newe, 2024a). Authentication is not just a security protocol, but the front-line of defense against unauthorized accesses, data compromises and malicious tampering.

Significance of Authentication in AIoT

The number of devices used in an AIoT network ranges in the billions and can include low-power sensors all the way up to autonomous systems. In the absence of sound authentication, malicious users may insert malicious data, or masquerade as a device, or even feed the AI with adversarial inputs(Wazid et al., 2021). This has the potential to compromise trust, erode system performance and lead to disastrous failures of systems in the case where timing is of critical need like in medical surveillance, smart grids or autonomous transportation.

There are Three Major Challenges of Authentication in AIoT

I. **Scalability:** Huge numbers of devices with minimal impact on system performance should be supported by mechanisms.
II. **Heterogeneity:** Different devices offer different computational power so one-size does not fit all.

III. **Dynamic Topology:** The devices can enter and leave the network on a regular basis and this necessitates dynamic and light weight authentication protocols.

AIoT Authentication Best Practice

An adequate approach to AIoT authentication consists of integrating the well-known security principles with the contextual measures:

I. **Multi-Factor Authentication (MFA):** Hardening identity verification by the combination of some passwords, biometrics and hardware token usage.
II. **Device Certificates and PKI**: Making use of Public Key Infrastructure (PKI) to issue special cryptographic device identifications.
III. **Lightweight Cryptographic Protocols:** such as the use of optimized algorithms (e.g. ECC, DTLS) on low-power devices(Ouaissa et al., 2025a).
IV. **Mutual Authentication**: It is where both sides ensure that they identify a partner before exchanging data; this applies to both devices and the servers.
V. **Secure Boot and Firmware Validation:** Compromising the integrity of a device even before executives can run on an authorized code.
VI. **Blockchain-Backed Identity Management:** Block chain backed identity management using block chain-based decentralized ledger to store authentication records that ensure the authentication record is immutable. Authentication in AIoT is one of the pillars of creating trust, ensuring secure cooperation, and the safety of data integrity(Moreno et al., 2021). Following the standards of the international community and best practices will allow AIoT ecosystems to be resilient, despite them becoming scaled to billions of devices. Adaptive and intelligent authentication systems that will be able to develop with emerging threats will determine the future of AIoT security.

Applications of AIoT Across Industries

Artificial Intelligence of Things (AIoT) is transforming the industries by integrating the connectivity with sensing of the IoT and the decision engine of Artificial Intelligence. This combination allows one to have the systems that not only gather data but also analyze, learn, and automatically take action. The four applications below demonstrate the manner with which AIoT is creating change in major sectors.

I. **Smart Healthcare:** In remote patient monitoring, predictive diagnostics and personalized treatment, AIoT is a critical development. The sensors that are installed in wearable devices allow the user to measure vital signs continuously like heart rate, blood oxygen levels, and glucose levels. AI algorithms will analyze it in real-time to identify anomalies, correctly forecast possible health threats, and notify care managers before any emergency(Devi Rahmayanti, 2024). As an illustration, AIoT-based cardiac monitors may recognize cardiac arrhythmias and alert physicians immediately, which may save lives. In addition, predictive analytics is able to assist hospitals in managing the flow of patients and help them with optimal allocation of resources.

II. **Predictive Maintenance and IIoT:** AIoT can be used in manufacturing to monitor equipment in real time and things concerning quality control and predictive maintenance. The indicators of production tools measure performance parameters and AI models can base predictions on such data to indicate one or more component failures in advance. This reduces the cost of maintenance, downtime and it ensures longer equipment life(Nourildean, 2024). AIoT also helps in automated quality checks by deploying computer vision systems being determined to provide uniformity in the quality of products. As an example, an automotive assembly line may employ AIoT to detect flaws even in car components in real time and reject the production of defective goods to avoid their propagation across the supply chain.

III. **Smart Cities:** Urban infrastructures at the urban level, AIoT solutions play the key role in optimizing traffic, waste management, and energy distribution. AIoT-driven smart traffic lights can optimally coordinate signals according to the current traffic situation to ensure there is less congestion and smog. In the waste management field, smart bins with AIoT support will send alerts to municipal services when the containers are full and optimize the evolution of collection routes. Furthermore, AIoT can be used to improve the safety of the population by combining surveillance structures with the threat detection system utilizing AI, which enables timelier response to the events(Walia et al., 2025).

IV. **Autonomous Transportation:** AIoT is a key technology behind self-driving cars, drones and interconnected public transport systems that can perform real-time perception, decision-making and navigation. LiDAR, radar and cameras scavenge data into AI-supported systems installed in compact cars, which analyze the information to identify obstacles, forecast traffic patterns and route safely. Vehicle-to-Everything (V2X) communication is also possible with AIoT, where cars share information among each other, infrastructure and pedestrians to increase safety and traffic efficiency (Talukder, Mia, et al., 2025).With the adoption of AI in IoT ecosystems, the industries can automate operations, increase decimation and amplify efficiency of their operations. AIoT is more than connecting devices, and it is the process of developing intelligent, flexible networks that will transform industries toward innovation and competitiveness.

Role of Security, Privacy, and Transparency in AIoT

Artificial Intelligence of Things (AIoT) is an amalgamation of connectivity in the IoT and the intelligence of AI in which equipment is able to measure, analyze trends, and make autonomous decisions. Although such synergy in technologies acts as a transformative benefit, it is equally confronted with critical challenges. Secure, privacy, and openness are the three pillars that are necessary to introduce user confidence, compliance with regulations, and sustainable use of AIoT systems (Bhardwaj et al., 2025).

I. **Security: Protecting the Ecosystem:** The devices in AIoT are usually used in distributed, heterogeneous, and open environments and will thus be the most exposed to cyber threats. The vulnerabilities can be used to hijack devices, manipulate data, or to inject malicious commands to AI models by attackers. Proper security practices are ensuring efficient encryption of data both at rest and on transition, mutually authenticated protocols, and secure boot mechanism to iffy unauthorized firmware alterations. Intrusion detection systems that are powered by AI can also be used to further increase protection through detecting any anomalous behavior within the network flow (Mihailescu & Nita, 2024). The integrity and reliability of the AIoT operations is always in danger in the absence of solid security.

II. **Privacy: Safeguarding Personal and Sensitive Data:** The AIoT devices often deal with sensitive data, whether the health records in wearables or operational data in industrial systems. Privacy makes sure such information is captured, processed as well as retained in a manner that respects the rights of individuals (Dewangan & Kumar, 2025). Such techniques as data anonymization and pseudonymization, or federated learning permit AI models to train without ever seeing raw user data. Also, it is essential to follow up on legal regulations like GDPR and CCPA to continue in compliance and prevent the abuse of personal data. A privacy-first mentality not only safeguards users but also builds trust over the long run in deployments of AIoT (Talukder, Das, et al., 2025).

III. **Transparency: Allowing the Trust and Accountability:** Transparency implies rendering the operation of AIoT systems explainable to the stakeholders. It involves introducing the path of coming to conclusions by an AI model, the data sources, and the possible restrictions of the decisions. The techniques of explainable AI (XAI) enable the interpretation of the system output by users and verification in safety-critical systems such as autonomous vehicles or medical diagnostics. Transparency also comprises effective communication of data usage policy, so that the user can consent to it.

IV. **Interdependence of the Three Pillars:** Tight security, privacy and transparency are connected. Good security is the foundation of privacy because it hinders unauthorized data access, whereas the privacy-centered designs can make data practices more comprehensible, which is more transparent. Transparency in its turn makes security and privacy measures accountable because they become verifiable. All these pillars, combined, create the trust framework required to have safe, ethical, and user-centric AIoT systems as mentioned in Figure 1.

Figure 1. Trust management and reputational

Reputational Systems in AIoT

Artificial Intelligence of Things (AIoT) is deployed on large, decentralized environments with interactions among billions of devices, services and users. Such environments means that there may not be direct trust among the entities involved, at least when there are entities that have not worked together before. Reputational systems respond to this dilemma by offering an organised method of measuring and assessing trustworthiness through previous activity, performance and returns. These systems are essential in facilitating safe, effective and efficient AIoT functioning.

I. **Concept and Importance:** A reputational system gathers, accumulates, and computes feedback or performance data regarding things, be they devices, services or users, and assigns that data a reputation score. The score is used as a guide by other bodies to make decisions on engaging one another, exchange data, or work together. In AIoT, reputation also serves as a form of social contract, or rather leniency that promotes the actions of consistency, honesty, and cooperation, and deters malicious behavior (Khurshid et al., 2025). An example is that, in a smart city network, a sensor with a low reputation might not be used in making important decisions in order to evade danger.

II. **The elements of Reputational Systems:** An efficient reputational system to use in AIoT generally involves:
   - Data Collection Layer- collects processed, feedback, transaction, and behavioral patterns during interactions.
   - Evaluation Engine - Uses algorithms, e.g. Bayesian inference, fuzzy logic or machine learning, to rate the data gathered.
   - Scoring Mechanism -Produces a numeric or nominative score of trust.
   - Reputation Sharing Protocol - Fraud blacklists are shared through the network to provide the information bases on which decisions may be made.

III. **Types of Reputation Models:**
   - **Centralized Models:** There should be the only credible source of reputation scores that are managed and disseminated. Appropriate where environments can be smaller, contained, but can be prone to single points of failure.
   - **Decentralized Models:** Reputation records are maintained by multiple entities that have a collaboration to accomplish the task, and they are usually backed by blockchain to provide the immutability and transparency.
   - **Hybrid Models:** Modern ones integrate both the centralized management and decentralized validation, as it is scalable and resilience.

IV. **The Problems in AIoT Reputation Management:** The reputational systems have a number of predicaments:
   - **Reputation Attacks:** A malicious node can indulge in backtalk/malign/false negative feedback or ballot stuffing/false positive feedback.
   - **On-Off Attacks:** The nodes behave either well or badly in rotation to avoid detection.
   - **Scalability Problems**: Scores need to be maintained in an accurate way over millions of devices.
   - **Dynamic Environments:** Reputation will need to respond rapidly as behavior of a device changes.

V. **Reputation System augments with AI:** Reputation systems based on AI, will be able to spot anomalies and foresee potential misbehavior as well as dynamic changes to a trust score. As an example, there may be some fine patterns in the conversation between devices that the machine learning models may recognize that the compromise is imminent. Incorporating the blockchain will guarantee reputation records can be tampered with, and federated learning will enable the reputation algorithm to converge by enabling devices to share knowledge about algorithms without exchanging raw data(G. D. et al., 2025). The reputational systems in AIoT, in a nutshell, enable the security and collaborative functioning of decentralized intelligent systems, i.e., so-called trust enablers. They are not just technical add-ons, but the elements of developing robust, flexible, and credible AIoT networks.

Trust Management Frameworks in AIoT

The Artificial Intelligence of Things (AIoT) will be working in large-scale heterogeneous and dynamic environments in which the devices, applications and users tend to interact without having direct knowledge of each other. Trust management frameworks in these systems are obviously critical to the operations in order to bring about the need of entities to be able to determine the credibility of others before data exchange or sharing resources or collaboratively making decisions(Su et al., 2022). Trust management does not just imply the security authentication process-it means on-going assessment of reliability, integrity and behaviours over time and it is the core strength of resilience generated through AIoT.

I. **Purpose and Scope of Trust Management Frameworks:** A trust management framework provides structured policies, mechanisms, and algorithms for:
   - Verification of the trustworthiness of entities (devices, users, services).
   - Keeping and refreshing scores of trust accorded by interactions.
   - Enabling safe distributed decision-making.
   - Deterring the malicious involvement in the form of isolating mal-actors

II. Components of a Trust Management Framework:
   - Trust Metrics Quantifiable measurements of metrics like accuracy of data, quickness of responsiveness, availability and past performance.
   - Trust Evaluation Engine: Employs statistical method, AI models, or probabilistic methods to compute trust scores.
   - Trust Propagation Mechanism: Permits trust information to be disseminated among entities either directly or through using intermediaries.
   - Trust Update Policies: Specify the way in which after interactions trust scores are raised or lowered.
   - Decision Making Module: Decides to continue or to inhibit interaction by trust thresholds.

III. Types of Trust Management Frameworks in AIoT:

- Rule-Based Frameworks Rule-based systems perform evaluations based on pre-existing rules and thresholds to determine trust. They are very rigid in dynamic environments as much as they are simple.
- Reputation-Based Frameworks: The use of accumulated feedback and history of behavior that is frequently combined with blockchain technology to provide tamper-resistance.
- Behavioral Analysis Frameworks: When communicating, energy consumption, or reaction time follows a pattern, anomalies are to be observed.
- AI-Driven Framework: AI-Based solutions help perform an assessment of trustworthiness and identify malafides and adjust to new risks.
- Hybrid Frameworks: Integrating a variety of practices to be more accurate and robust.

IV. Emerging Trends in Trust Framework Design:

- Trust enabled by lockchain Ensures trust records that cannot be altered and decentralized verifications.
- Federated Trust Learning: Enables a decentralized collaboration of devices to train joint trust measurement models, in such a way that sensitive data is not shared.
- Explainable Trust Models: Can enhance transparency through its display of how the trust scores are computed.
- Context-Aware Trust: Uses environmental considerations, location and situational awareness in trust assessment.

Trust Management and Reputational Systems for AIoT Devices

Artificial Intelligence of Things (AIoT) integrates the capabilities of the Internet of Things (IoT) to sense and connect, and the decision-making ability of Artificial Intelligence (AI). Such incorporation enables gadgets to gather, process, and take actions on their own, developing smart environments in the fields of healthcare, transportation, and manufacturing. Nonetheless, such distributed and heterogeneous environments give rise to a principal challenge, which is guaranteeing reliable and secure interaction between devices(Aaqib et al., 2023). The main mechanisms to manage these issues are trust management and reputational systems since AIoT devices need to consider the credibility and behavior of their counterparts before engaging in the cooperation.

I. **The impact of the Trust Management on AIoT:** Trust management is comprised of evaluation, maintenance, updating of the trust scores of devices in accordance with their previous interactions, performance and behavior profiles.

Trust management is a dynamic process compared to simple authentication that only authenticates identity at one given time(Dewangan & Kumar, 2024). It takes into consideration the possibility that a device that was trusted the previous day can act maliciously today as it may be compromised; query malfunctioned or interacted with policies.

The most important activities of trust management regarding AIoT devices are:

- Evaluating Trustworthiness: Using metrics like data accuracy, availability, and timely responses.
- Updating Trust Scores: Adjusting trust based on recent behavior and feedback from other devices.
- Enabling Decision-Making: Allowing devices to decide whether to interact with or ignore other devices.
- Mitigating Threats: Isolating or restricting malicious or low-trust devices from critical operations.

II. Trust and Reputation Systems Problems of AIoT Devices:

- Reputation Attacks- BADMOUTHING (False, negative feedback) And BALLOT STUFFING (False, positive feedback).
- On-Off Attacks Devices will switch between good and bad in order to avoid detection.
- Scalability: Real-time regulation of the trust and reputation of millions of devices.
- Resource Limitation Resources: Low power devices require low weight trust algorithms.

III. **Ai and Reputation/Playing to Strengths:** The AI methods can be used to considerably enhance the precision and flexibility of trust and reputational schemes. Machine learning models are able:

- Forecast the capability of trustworthiness through minute behavioural patterns.
- Identify the abnormalities in the communication process of the devices.
- Flexible rules of trust-scoring depending on the environment.
- The aspect of blockchain integration also guarantees the permanence of the records of reputation without tampering and the aspect of Fed-learning also enables and delivers trust models to be enhanced collectively among devices without the exchange of sensitive data

The secure, resilient, and cooperative AIoT ecosystems are core enablers of community-based AIoT systems generated through trust management and reputational systems. They make sure not only that device authenticate one another, but also manage to be mutually accountable over time, and this makes the environment in which autonomous devices can cooperate secure and useful. With the increase in scale of AIoT networks, such systems will progressively upshift to AI-guided, decentralized, and transparent trust systems to endure dynamic cyber threats and uphold the integrity of operations correspondingly(Krishna, 2016).

Threats and Challenges in AIoT Trust Management

Artificial Intelligence of Things (herein referred to as AIoT) presents enhanced features, which represent the integration of the IoT infrastructure capability with AI to manage decisions. Its distributed, heterogeneous, and in most cases resource-constrained characteristics impose upon it a myriad of security threats and operational challenges however(Qureshi & Newe, 2024d). Such risks erode confidence, breach system security and may have disastrous effects in safety sensitive systems within healthcare, transportation and industrial automation systems.

I. **Data and Model Poisoning:** As AIoT is highly dependent on AI models, people can deteriorate these models by conducting data poisoning attacks, where malicious users introduce data with the purpose of corrupting or misleading the model through training(Talukder, Khan, et al., 2025). Just as in case of federated learning model poisoning attacks, the parameters of the model may be noisily corrupted to where the final results can be biased towards the interests of an attacker.
II. **Identity spoofing and Device Compromise:** Most devices in AIoT are low-end with regard to computing functionality and hence protecting them with strong encryption and intrusion technologies is not easy. Custom firmware vulnerabilities present the possibility of gaining control of devices to identify themselves using spoofing, thereby masquerading as trusted nodes and feeding the system with inauthentic information(Talukder, Khan, et al., 2025).
III. **Scalability and Constraints of Resources:** Millions of devices can be involved in the AIoT networks. The need to keep proper trust and reputation assessments in real time within such massive networks demands a lot of computing power. Such low-power sensors might not be able to afford to run complicated trust algorithms without impacting battery life or performance.
IV. **Interoperability Issues:** Various vendors are normally involved in the AIoT systems that have various communication standards, security standards, and

data structures. Such inconsistency may prevent sharing of trust score and leave some security coverage gaps.

V. **Transparency and Explain ability issues:** Complex AI models are growing in influence as the basis of trust decisions in AIoT, and so they may become black boxes. Explainable AI (XAI) is needed to avoid locating accountability on a lack of knowledge on why a device was considered trustworthy or untrustworthy.

VI. **Privacy Risks:** Behavioral and feedback information is necessary to implement reputation and trusting systems. The possession and use of such data may be associated with privacy issues especially when sensitive data are passed or kept outside of acceptable storage locations. The problem of finding the middle ground between privacy protection and trust evaluation is still rather acute.Risks and issues in AIoT trust management are both complex and transversal, and concerns technical, operational, and ethical issues(Wei et al., 2022). To facilitate these challenges, it is necessary to have adaptive trust model, decentralized validation systems, and AI-augmented anomaly detection. These threats will be among the most important to manage as AIoT continues to grow, helping establish reliability, security, and scalability of intelligent networks of the future.

Future Trends and Research Directions in AIoT Trust Management

Artificial Intelligence of Things (AIoT) is rapidly expanding on the combination of artificial intelligence and edge computing and the next generation of connectivity, 5G and beyond. With the increased autonomy, inter-connection and systems integrated within key infrastructures, trust management will continue to serve as the cornerstone in the safety, secure and reliable AIoT systems. In the future, the trust frameworks will be aimed at developing the adaptation, transparency, and protection of the frameworks against new threats.

I. **Self-Adaptive Trust Models:** AIoT systems in the future will need self-learning trust models capable of changing behavior in response to changes in the network, device performance and environmental effects, automatically(Alam et al., 2022). These models will make use of real-time data feeds, retraining themselves on a continuous basis to factor in emerging threats as well as changes in the pattern of collaboration. Such capable adaptations are likely to be made possible through reinforcement learning and online learning approaches.

II. **Explainable AI for Trust Decisions:** As the AI models become more and more effective in deciding the trust score, Explainable AI (XAI) will become vital in having transparency and accountability. Future systems will require giving human interpretable explanations as to why a device is regarded as trustworthy or untrustworthy, especially in safety-critical driven systems such as healthcare, finance, and self-driving vehicles(Mittal et al., 2025). The study would be on combining trust prediction with the explainable models without compromising accuracy.

III. **Federated and Privacy-Preserving Trust Evaluation:** Under-development Federated learning can also be important to privacy-preserving computation of trusts computation, with devices jointly learning trust models with no need to share raw data. In combination with the secure multiparty computation (SMPC) and homomorphic encryption methods, this process will contribute to the balance between the level of trust and a strong data privacy component(Mittal et al., 2025).

IV. **Trust Systems that are Blockchain-Integrated:** Blockchain will also remain in use of decentralized trust management. Since immutable ledgers cannot be tampered with, the reputation scores, feedback histories, and trust metrics can be recorded which reduces the possibility of malicious actors to corrupt trust data. The research in the future should probably be aimed at scalability and energy efficiency in blockchain or interoperability with AIoT networks.

V. **Interoperable Cross-Domain Trust:** Because AIoT ecosystems cross many domains, such as smart cities, healthcare, industrial IoT, and autonomous vehicles, trust models have to be cross domain-interoperable. This will include the development of uniform protocols of trust where potential devices in disparate industries can interpret the trust toggle of the other device and make permissive decisions despite the device being based on various architectures or protocols(Dewangan et al., 2024).

VI. **Cyber Threat Intelligence (CTI) Integration:** Future systems based on trust will incorporate cyber threat intelligence feeds and adapt the trust scores in advance according to the actual trends of attacks in the real world. Anomaly detection enabled by AI, combined with the CTI will enable to identify any emerging patterns of the attacks in the early stages without them being able to cause a breach to the network. To manage trust in AIoT, the future is on intelligent, transparent and interoperable trust ecosystems(Grover et al., 2024). Researchers and industry practitioners can avail of the benefits of the synergy between adaptive AI models, privacy-preserving computation, blockchain-supported verification, and cross-domain standards to maintain the resilient, ethical, and scale of AIoT networks at a time when challenges change in a rapid pace.

CONCLUSION

The Artificial Intelligence of Things (AIoT) will be the new edge in connected and intelligent systems- integrating data-gathering capabilities of IoT with the analytical and decision-making capabilities of AI. As exciting as this convergence is in terms of the opportunities it opens up across industries, e.g., in healthcare, transportation, manufacturing, and smart cities, it simultaneously increases the complexity of achieving the security, reliability, and trust of big, decentralized networks. Trust management and reputational systems are the key to safe AIoT work. The mechanisms seek to take authentication and encryption to a new level of responsibility as the gadgets, services and users can make informed decisions on the collaborative processes based on past performance, consistency in actions and peer feedbacks. Trust management gives a running account of a reliable credibility where reputational systems provide the addition layer to intelligence where entities can judge other entities even without prior direct encounter. Nonetheless, maintaining high levels of trust in AIoT is not quite a smooth sailing. As has been discussed in the current work, AIoT trust systems are susceptible to the various threats of bad-mouthing, ballot-stuffing, on off behavior, Sybil identities, and data/model poisoning. Such threats take advantage of both technical as well as human-Like trust relationships, thus being hard to recognize as well as defend. Adding to the risks are some practical challenges that include scalability, interoperability, transparency, and protection of privacy.

There are emerging solutions that are indicating a more adaptive decentralised future. Trust prediction models using artificial intelligence, block chain-based reputation storage, privacy-preserving computing methods, and federated learning are being introduced to create not only secure, but transparent, explainable, and privacy conscious trust frameworks. Concurrently, cross-domain trust interoperability research will be needed because as AIoT ecosystems scale across industries, devices will have to be able to access and communicate together effectively irrespective of differences in vendor or sector. Finally, trust AIoT construction and maintenance is a process and is not a one shot engineering problem. Trust itself needs to change in line with the ecosystem that needs to be secured, new forms of attack, new technologies available, and the agendas imposed on it by issues of security, privacy and transparency (which are often in conflict).Due to AIoT networks increasing in independence and impact in key decision-making, the stakes of getting trust right are higher than ever. The next step will be the systems of artificial intelligence of things that will be able to regulate trust dynamically on behalf of them and protect themselves against advanced interference and remain trustworthy in the eyes of users, stakeholders and regulators alike. Trust, in the given context, should not be confused with its narrow requirement but should be understood as the base where the endurance, ethics and social acceptance of AIoT will stand upon.

REFERENCES

Aaqib, M., Ali, A., Chen, L., & Nibouche, O. (2023). IoT trust and reputation: A survey and taxonomy. *Journal of Cloud Computing (Heidelberg, Germany)*, *12*(1), 42. DOI: 10.1186/s13677-023-00416-8

Alaba, F. A. (2024). The Evolution of the IoT. In Alaba, F. A. (Ed.), *Internet of Things: A Case Study in Africa* (Vol. 13, pp. 1–18). Springer Nature Switzerland., DOI: 10.1007/978-3-031-67984-1_1

Alam, S., Zardari, S., Noor, S., Ahmed, S., & Mouratidis, H. (2022). Trust Management in Social Internet of Things (SIoT): A Survey. *IEEE Access : Practical Innovations, Open Solutions*, *10*, 108924–108954. DOI: 10.1109/ACCESS.2022.3213699

Anwar, A., Kumar, S., & Manoharan, G. (2025). Revolutionizing the Hospitality Industry: The Impact and Challenges of Smart Operations. In Talukder, M. B., & Chowdhury, H. H. K. (Eds.), *Smart Operations and Enhancing Guest Experience in the Hospitality Industry* (pp. 271–296). IGI Global., DOI: 10.4018/979-8-3373-2145-5.ch010

Barik, K., Misra, S., Mohan, R., & Mishra, B. (2024). AIoT and Its Trust Models to Enhance Societal Applications Using Intelligent Technologies. In Misra, S., Siakas, K., & Lampropoulos, G. (Eds.), *Artificial Intelligence of Things for Achieving Sustainable Development Goals* (Vol. 192, pp. 311–334). Springer Nature Switzerland., DOI: 10.1007/978-3-031-53433-1_16

Bhardwaj, S., Sharma, I., Mahendru, S., Kaur, R., & Sharma, S. (2025). Exploring the Role of AIoT in Data Privacy and Security. In Tariq, M. U. (Ed.), (pp. 75–102). Advances in Computational Intelligence and Robotics. IGI Global Scientific Publishing., DOI: 10.4018/979-8-3693-8547-0.ch003

Chehri, A., Jeon, G., Rivest, F., & Mouftah, H. T. (2022). Evolution and Trends in Artificial Intelligence of Things Security: When Good Enough is Not Good Enough! *IEEE Internet of Things Magazine*, *5*(3), 62–66. DOI: 10.1109/IOTM.001.2100130

Dewangan, S., & Kumar, S. (2024). Enhancing Fraud Detection in Finance Through AI and Machine Learning. In Darwish, D., & Kumar, S. (Eds.), (pp. 267–282). Advances in Finance, Accounting, and Economics. IGI Global., DOI: 10.4018/979-8-3693-8507-4.ch014

Dewangan, S., & Kumar, S. (2025). Frontiers of Innovation: Unveiling the Future Opportunities in Fintech. In Kour, M., Taneja, S., Özen, E., Sood, K., & Grima, S. (Eds.), *Financial Landscape Transformation: Technological Disruptions* (pp. 153–165). Emerald Publishing Limited., DOI: 10.1108/978-1-83753-750-120251008

Dewangan, S., Kumar, S., & Tyagi, P. K. (2024). Transforming Hospitality and Tourism With AI and Innovative Technologies. In Talukder, M. B., Kumar, S., & Tyagi, P. K. (Eds.), *Advances in Hospitality, Tourism, and the Services Industry* (pp. 66–83). IGI Global., DOI: 10.4018/979-8-3693-6755-1.ch004

G. D. S., P. V., B., Josephine, R., & Vincent, R. R. (2025). Transforming Healthcare With AIoT: The Future of Diagnostics and Patient Care. In V. Sarveshwaran, K. Periyaswami, & K. Yu (Eds.), *Advances in Medical Technologies and Clinical Practice* (pp. 159–220). IGI Global. DOI: 10.4018/979-8-3693-7703-1.ch008

Grover, S., Kumar, S., & Dhiraj, A. (2024). Green Labeling and Green Scapes in the Hospitality and Tourism Industry: A Perspective Study of Industrial Employees Attracting Brand Mark of Hospitality Organizations in UT Regions. In Sharma, A., & Arora, S. (Eds.), *Strategic Tourism Planning for Communities* (pp. 163–172). Emerald Publishing Limited., DOI: 10.1108/978-1-83549-015-020241013

Jevremovic, A., Veinovic, M., & Peraković, D. (2024). Analyzing the Efficiency of Software Distribution Systems in AIoT Environments. In L. Knapčíková & D. Peraković (Eds.), *8th EAI International Conference on Management of Manufacturing Systems* (pp. 99–108). Springer Nature Switzerland. DOI: 10.1007/978-3-031-53161-3_7

Khurshid, K., Khurshid, K., Hadi, M. U., Bataineh, M. A., & Saeed, N. (2025). Securing AIoT Surveillance: Techniques, Challenges, and Solutions. *IEEE Open Journal of the Communications Society*, *6*, 1–1. DOI: 10.1109/OJCOMS.2025.3593311

Kishore, N., Nanglia, P., Gupta, S., & Dubey, A. K. (Eds.). (2024). *The Future of Computing: Ubiquitous Applications and Technologies*. BENTHAM SCIENCE PUBLISHERS., DOI: 10.2174/97898152389901240101

Krishna, M. B. (2016). Security and Trust Management for the Internet of Things: An Rfid and Sensor Network Perspective. In Brooks, T. T. (Ed.), *Cyber-Assurance for the Internet of Things* (1st ed., pp. 137–162). Wiley., DOI: 10.1002/9781119193784.ch4

Mihailescu, M. I., & Nita, S. L. (2024). Securing Web Data and Privacy in AIoT Systems. In Ortiz-Rodriguez, F., Leyva-Mederos, A., Tiwari, S., Hernandez-Quintana, A. R., & Martinez-Rodriguez, J. L. (Eds.), (pp. 128–172). Advances in Web Technologies and Engineering. IGI Global., DOI: 10.4018/979-8-3693-1487-6.ch007

Mittal, S., Singhal, M., Dublish, M., & Noor, S. (2025). Application of AIoT in Smart Retailing and Consumer Insights. In Tariq, M. U. (Ed.), (pp. 397–430). Advances in Computational Intelligence and Robotics. IGI Global Scientific Publishing., DOI: 10.4018/979-8-3693-8547-0.ch013

Moreno, R. T., Garcia-Rodriguez, J., Bernabe, J. B., & Skarmeta, A. (2021). A Trusted Approach for Decentralised and Privacy-Preserving Identity Management. *IEEE Access : Practical Innovations, Open Solutions*, *9*, 105788–105804. DOI: 10.1109/ACCESS.2021.3099837

Nourildean, S. W. (2024). Artificial Internet of Things (AIoT): A Review. *2024 International Conference on Electrical, Computer and Energy Technologies (ICECET*, 1–7. DOI: 10.1109/ICECET61485.2024.10698612

Ouaissa, M., Ouaissa, M., Hidar, T., Sachan, R. C., Mittal, A., & Poddar, S. (2025a). *Information Security Governance using Artificial Intelligence of Things in Smart Environments* (1st ed.). CRC Press., DOI: 10.1201/9781003606307

Qureshi, K. N., & Newe, T. (2024a). *Artificial Intelligence of Things (AIoT): New Standards, Technologies and Communication Systems* (1st ed.). CRC Press., DOI: 10.1201/9781003430018

Rahmayanti, D. (2024). Artificial Intelligence of Things (AIoT) To Improve Efficiency and Automation in Industrial 4.0. *Sci-Tech Journal*, *3*(3), 255–270. DOI: 10.56709/stj.v3i3.656

Rathee, G., Garg, S., Kaddoum, G., Choi, B. J., Hassan, M. M., & AlQahtani, S. A. (2023). TrustSys: Trusted Decision Making Scheme for Collaborative Artificial Intelligence of Things. *IEEE Transactions on Industrial Informatics*, *19*(1), 1059–1068. DOI: 10.1109/TII.2022.3173006

Shah Alam, S., & Latif, M. M. (2025). Influence of Artificial Intelligence of Things (AIoT) on Performance of Hotels: Mediating Effect of Added Value of Controllers and Moderating Effect of Market Turbulence. *Journal of Quality Assurance in Hospitality & Tourism*, •••, 1–24. DOI: 10.1080/1528008X.2025.2540981

Sharma, V., Balusamy, B., Ferrari, G., & Ajmani, P. (2024). *Wireless Communication Technologies: Roles, Responsibilities, and Impact of IoT, 6G, and Blockchain Practices* (1st ed.). CRC Press., DOI: 10.1201/9781003389231

Shen, M., Gu, A., Kang, J., Tang, X., Lin, X., Zhu, L., & Niyato, D. (2023). Blockchains for Artificial Intelligence of Things: A Comprehensive Survey. *IEEE Internet of Things Journal*, *10*(16), 14483–14506. DOI: 10.1109/JIOT.2023.3268705

Su, R., Sfar, A. R., Natalizio, E., Moyal, P., & Song, Y.-Q. (2022). Ensuring Trustworthiness in IoIT/AIoT: A Phase-Based Approach. *IEEE Internet of Things Magazine*, *5*(2), 84–88. DOI: 10.1109/IOTM.001.2100190

Talukder, M. B., Das, I. R., & Kumar, S. (2025). From Digital Production to Digital Society in Hospitality: Industry 5.0 Perspectives. In Grima, S., Kaleli, S. S., Baygin, M., & Boztepe, E. (Eds.), *Business Challenges and Opportunities in the Era of Industry 5.0* (pp. 173–193). Emerald Publishing Limited., DOI: 10.1108/978-1-83549-676-320251010

Talukder, M. B., Khan, M. R., & Kumar, S. (2025). The Impact of Gig Economy Trends on Traditional Employment Models: Evidence From Hotel Industry. In Nozari, H. (Ed.), *Dynamic and Safe Economy in the Age of Smart Technologies* (pp. 253–276). IGI Global., DOI: 10.4018/979-8-3693-4369-2.ch016

Talukder, M. B., & Mia, Md. N., Masum, Md. Y., Kabir, F., & Kumar, S. (2025). Encouraging Innovative and Responsible Tourism Through Digital Advancement. In P. Thaichon, P. K. Dutta, A. K. Haghi, & S. Dutta (Eds.), *Digital Disruption in Hospitality, Sustainable Hospitality* (pp. 145–165). Emerald Publishing Limited. DOI: 10.1108/978-1-83662-360-120251007

Ullah, F., Salam, A., Amin, F., Khan, I. A., Ahmed, J., Zaib, S. A., & Choi, G. S. (2024). Deep Trust: A Novel Framework for Dynamic Trust and Reputation Management in the Internet of Things (IoT)-Based Networks. *IEEE Access : Practical Innovations, Open Solutions*, *12*, 87407–87419. DOI: 10.1109/ACCESS.2024.3409273

Walia, G. K., Kumar, M., Kumar, S., & Gill, S. S. (2025). Amalgamation of Computational Intelligence and 6G-Enabled AIoT Networks for Industry 4.0. In Kumar, M., Gill, S. S., Kumar, V., & Verma, P. (Eds.), *Computational Intelligence Techniques for 5G Enabled IoT Networks* (pp. 255–265). Springer Nature Switzerland., DOI: 10.1007/978-3-031-82733-4_16

Wallace, A. A. (2022). When AI Meets IoT: AIoT. In Lipschultz, J. H., Freberg, K., & Luttrell, R. (Eds.), *The Emerald Handbook of Computer-Mediated Communication and Social Media* (pp. 481–492). Emerald Publishing Limited., DOI: 10.1108/978-1-80071-597-420221028

Wazid, M., Das, A. K., & Park, Y. (2021). Blockchain-Envisioned Secure Authentication Approach in AIoT: Applications, Challenges, and Future Research. *Wireless Communications and Mobile Computing*, *2021*(1), 3866006. DOI: 10.1155/2021/3866006

Wei, L., Yang, Y., Wu, J., Long, C., & Li, B. (2022). Trust Management for Internet of Things: A Comprehensive Study. *IEEE Internet of Things Journal*, *9*(10), 7664–7679. DOI: 10.1109/JIOT.2021.3139989

Chapter 9
Securing AIoT Ecosystems With Blockchain Trust Modeling and Privacy Preserving Frameworks: Securing AIoT Ecosystems

Ravikumar Ch
http://orcid.org/0000-0003-0809-5545
Sreenidhi University, Hyderabad, India

Sasikala: C.
Srinivasa Ramanujan Institute of Technology, Ananthapuramu, India

Shirisha E.
Teegala Krishna Reddy College of Engineering and Technology, Meerpet, India

Radhika E.
Teegala Krishna Reddy College of Engineering and Technology, Hyderabad, India

Shirisha Reddy K.
Teegala Krishna Reddy College of Engineering and Technology, Hyderabad, India

Srividya K.
Sreenidhi University, Hyderabad, India

ABSTRACT

The convergence of Artificial Intelligence (AI) and the Internet of Things (IoT) has led to the Artificial Intelligence of Things (AIoT), enabling adaptive systems in healthcare, smart cities, and industry. While promising, AIoT faces challenges of trust, identity, privacy risks, adversarial attacks, and interoperability due to its decentralized nature. This chapter explores blockchain-based identity management, federated learning, explainable AI for trust modeling, and lightweight cryptogra-

DOI: 10.4018/979-8-3373-6299-1.ch009

phy for constrained devices. It also highlights situational trust indicators, identity compatibility, and adversarial resilience. Finally, it discusses open challenges and future directions, including quantum-resistant cryptography, human-centered trust, and policy-driven governance for secure and ethical AIoT.

1. INTRODUCTION

The convergence of Artificial Intelligence (AI) and the Internet of Things (IoT) has resulted in a paradigm shift known as the Artificial Intelligence of Things (AIoT). This integration combines cognitive intelligence with ubiquitous connectivity to enable real-time operations, automation, and self-optimization across diverse smart systems. AIoT is transforming key sectors such as healthcare, smart transportation, industrial automation, agriculture, and smart cities through data-driven insights and predictive intelligence. By learning patterns from large-scale data, AIoT systems can autonomously adapt to changing environments, leading to improved efficiency and decision-making capabilities (Xu et al., 2021).

However, alongside these benefits, AIoT introduces critical challenges related to trust, privacy, and identity management. Traditional IoT security models are largely centralized, making them susceptible to single points of failure, insider threats, and large-scale data breaches. The incorporation of AI further exposes AIoT systems to adversarial machine learning attacks, model poisoning, and data manipulation, which can undermine the integrity of automated decision-making processes. As AIoT ecosystems grow in complexity and scale, there is an urgent need for advanced security frameworks that integrate trust modeling, decentralized identity mechanisms, and privacy-preserving learning techniques (Al Sadawi et al., 2021).

1.1 Evolution of AIoT

The evolution of AIoT represents a significant advancement beyond early IoT systems, which primarily focused on connectivity and data acquisition without embedded intelligence. The integration of AI has enabled IoT systems to become more autonomous, capable of self-learning, contextual adaptation, and intelligent decision-making. Early IoT deployments were largely limited to sensor-based monitoring, whereas AI-driven IoT systems now support predictive maintenance, intelligent service delivery, and operational optimization. This transition marks a shift from basic data collection to autonomous system behavior, unlocking substantial innovation and efficiency gains across industries (Shafique et al., 2020).

Nevertheless, this evolution has also intensified the security threat landscape. While early IoT systems employed relatively simple authentication and encryption mechanisms, modern AIoT environments involve distributed learning, collaborative decision-making, and the exchange of sensitive personal and industrial data. These advancements introduce new risks, including privacy breaches, identity spoofing, and sophisticated cyberattacks. Consequently, there is a pressing need to develop trust-centric security frameworks that integrate blockchain technology, privacy-preserving AI techniques, and quantum-resistant cryptographic solutions to effectively mitigate emerging threats in AIoT ecosystems (Atzori et al., 2010).

1.2 Challenges in Trust and Identity Management

Trust and identity management are foundational to the secure operation of AIoT systems. The large-scale heterogeneity and geographic dispersion of AIoT devices make it difficult to enforce uniform security policies and establish resilient trust relationships. Trust in AIoT is inherently multidimensional, encompassing device reliability, data authenticity, model integrity, and resilience to adversarial behavior. The lack of global standards further exacerbates vulnerabilities such as identity spoofing, unauthorized access, and weak authentication mechanisms.

In AIoT systems that employ federated learning, additional risks arise due to the exchange of model updates across distributed nodes. These updates may be susceptible to poisoning attacks or malicious manipulation, potentially compromising the accuracy, fairness, and robustness of collaborative learning processes (Uddin et al., 2021).

Given the scale, diversity, and interoperability requirements of AIoT environments, traditional Public Key Infrastructure (PKI) and centralized identity verification mechanisms are increasingly inadequate. To address these challenges, there is growing interest in blockchain-based decentralized identity frameworks, augmented with context-aware and adaptive trust mechanisms. Such decentralized approaches enable more robust identity lifecycle management and enhance the resilience of AIoT systems operating in highly dynamic and adversarial environments (Shafique et al., 2020).

Figure 1. Infographic of artificial intelligence in obesity prediction

The infographic visually represents the role of artificial intelligence (AI) in obesity prediction by employing intuitive icons and color-coded sections to illustrate the key processing stages. It highlights diverse data sources, including electronic health records, medical imaging data, and population-based surveys, followed by commonly adopted AI techniques such as convolutional neural networks (CNN), k-nearest neighbors (K-NN), and SHAP for model explainability. Important clinical biomarkers—such as body mass index (BMI), triglycerides, glycated hemoglobin, alanine aminotransferase (ALT/SGPT), along with lifestyle-related factors—are depicted using distinct visual elements. Overall, the figure emphasizes how AI-driven models improve prediction accuracy, identify critical risk factors, and support early intervention strategies for effective obesity management.

The motivation of this chapter stems from the growing inadequacy of traditional IoT security mechanisms when applied to highly dynamic, data-intensive, and adversarial environments such as Artificial Intelligence of Things (AIoT) systems. Conventional centralized security approaches often fail to ensure resilience, accountability, and privacy in such complex ecosystems, thereby necessitating more advanced and adaptive security solutions.

Accordingly, this chapter does not propose a new implemented framework, but instead presents a comprehensive review and conceptual synthesis of emerging approaches for securing AIoT ecosystems. In particular, it reviews blockchain-based decentralized identity management, privacy-preserving federated learning techniques, and explainable AI (XAI)-driven trust modeling as complementary building blocks for strengthening trust and security in AIoT systems. These technologies are critically analyzed to understand their role in enhancing system integrity and trustworthiness as AIoT increasingly permeates everyday life and critical infrastructures (Fortino et al., 2018).

Furthermore, the chapter provides an in-depth discussion of trust modeling strategies, identity management frameworks, lightweight cryptographic mechanisms, and representative real-world use cases spanning healthcare and industrial AIoT applications. Finally, it outlines emerging research directions, including quantum-resistant cryptography, human-centered trust models, and policy-driven governance frameworks. The chapter aims to serve as a reference and guidance resource for researchers and practitioners seeking to design secure, scalable, and ethical AIoT ecosystems that can adapt to evolving technological and regulatory landscapes (Deloitte Global, 2025).

2. BACKGROUND OF AIOT AND SECURITY PARADIGMS

The Artificial Intelligence of Things (AIoT) represents the convergence of machine intelligence with ubiquitous connectivity, where advances in AI—such as deep learning, reinforcement learning, and federated learning—enable increased autonomy and adaptability of IoT systems. Unlike conventional IoT architectures that primarily focus on sensing and data transmission, AIoT systems are capable of performing intelligent decision-making at the edge, facilitating real-time analytics and reducing latency in mission-critical applications. This evolution signifies a transition from simple data collection to autonomous and intelligent system behavior, unlocking substantial innovation opportunities across multiple domains (Hassija et al., 2019).

However, the deep integration of AIoT systems into human-centric services and industrial processes significantly amplifies security concerns. Traditional IoT security measures—such as encryption, access control, and intrusion detection—are no longer sufficient in isolation. The increasing complexity of AIoT infrastructures introduces new vulnerabilities, including adversarial attacks through input manipulation, deceptive attacks on AI models in autonomous systems, and model poisoning in federated learning environments. Addressing these threats requires rethinking existing security paradigms and adopting decentralized trust models, advanced cryptographic techniques, and privacy-aware frameworks tailored for large-scale, heterogeneous AIoT deployments (Sfar et al., 2018).

2.1 Role of AI in IoT Security

AI plays a dual role in strengthening and challenging IoT security within AIoT ecosystems. On one hand, AI enhances defensive capabilities through intelligent threat detection, predictive security analytics, and automated response mechanisms. Machine learning algorithms can analyze large-scale network traffic to identify malicious behaviors, detect zero-day attacks, and dynamically adapt security policies, thereby improving the long-term resilience of IoT systems.

On the other hand, AI itself becomes a target of exploitation within AIoT environments. Adversaries may generate adversarial examples, exploit model explainability to reduce trust, or poison training data to compromise model reliability. These risks underscore the necessity for robust governance mechanisms, transparency, and accountability in AI-driven security solutions (Wu & Liang, 2021).

The coexistence of these defensive and adversarial dimensions highlights the importance of a balanced security strategy that combines AI-based protection with explainability and trust-enhancing measures. The integration of explainable AI (XAI) and governance frameworks can strengthen AIoT security without increasing system complexity or eroding user trust, positioning AI as both a defensive instrument and a reliable component in addressing the multifaceted security challenges of modern AIoT systems (Institute for Defense & Business, 2025).

2.2 Trust Modeling in AIoT Ecosystems

Trust is a fundamental component of secure AIoT platforms, as it determines the reliability of devices, services, and data sources operating within a collaborative and distributed environment. In AIoT systems, trust extends beyond basic authentication to encompass device reliability, behavioral consistency, data integrity, and resistance to adversarial manipulation. Unlike traditional trust mechanisms that rely solely on static reputation scores or certificate-based authentication, AIoT trust models must support **dynamic, context-aware trust assessment** due to the high heterogeneity, mobility, and scale of connected devices.

Modern trust modeling approaches in AIoT integrate both quantitative and qualitative parameters—such as communication latency, data accuracy, energy availability, historical behavior, and reliability metrics—to compute trust scores for devices or entities. These trust scores guide decision-making processes, including access control, collaboration eligibility, and data utilization, thereby strengthening system security and resilience (AlHwaitat et al., 2023).

Given the continuously evolving nature of AIoT environments, trust models must be adaptive and capable of providing real-time evaluations of device and data reliability. Such trust-aware mechanisms play a critical role in determining whether a device is permitted to participate in federated learning processes or contribute data to predictive analytics. By ensuring that only trustworthy entities are involved, AIoT systems can maintain integrity and robustness under dynamic operating conditions. Adaptive trust frameworks are therefore essential for preserving reliability and safeguarding decision-making processes in AIoT ecosystems (Atzori et al., 2010).

2.2.1 Decentralized Trust Architectures

Centralized trust authorities often introduce bottlenecks and single points of failure in large-scale IoT and AIoT networks, making them unsuitable for highly distributed and mission-critical deployments. To address these limitations, decentralized trust architectures—primarily based on blockchain and distributed ledger technologies (DLT)—have emerged as effective alternatives. These architectures offer immutability, transparency, and resistance to tampering or collusion, enabling secure and verifiable trust management without reliance on centralized entities.

Decentralized trust mechanisms allow trust metrics and identity attributes to be securely recorded on a blockchain ledger, ensuring portability and universal recognition across heterogeneous devices, vendors, and service providers. By removing centralized dependencies, blockchain-based trust architectures enhance both security and interoperability, enabling seamless interactions across diverse AIoT domains (Atzori et al., 2010).

Moreover, decentralized trust architectures improve system robustness by eliminating single points of failure and supporting secure, transparent communication among devices. These properties facilitate the development of large-scale, fault-tolerant AIoT networks capable of adapting to diverse application requirements across industries, including healthcare, manufacturing, and smart infrastructure (Fortino et al., 2018).

2.2.2 Human-Centric Trust in AIoT

While technical trust metrics form the backbone of AIoT security, human-centric trust considerations are equally critical, particularly in domains such as healthcare monitoring, smart homes, and intelligent transportation systems. In these applications,

AIoT systems directly influence human decision-making, making user perception, transparency, and explainability essential for trust formation.

Human-centric trust models emphasize the use of explainable AI (XAI) techniques to provide insights into the reasoning behind system decisions. By reducing the opacity of AI models and making their behavior understandable to users, XAI fosters confidence and acceptance of AIoT technologies (Rajesh et al., 2016).

Trust in AIoT systems is therefore achieved through a holistic integration of technical reliability and user-centric assurance mechanisms. Incorporating transparency, explainability, and accountability into trust models not only enhances system reliability but also promotes ethical deployment and responsible use. Such multidimensional trust frameworks empower users and accelerate the adoption of AIoT solutions across real-world applications (Deloitte Global, 2025).

3. BLOCKCHAIN FOR DECENTRALIZED IDENTITY AND TRUST

Blockchain technology plays a pivotal role in enabling decentralized trust and identity management within AIoT ecosystems. By leveraging immutable ledgers, consensus mechanisms, and smart contracts, blockchain facilitates secure authentication, data sharing, and access control among devices. Unlike centralized identity systems that are vulnerable to insider threats and large-scale data breaches, blockchain-enabled identity solutions distribute identity attributes across decentralized networks, eliminating single points of control and enhancing overall system security (Mohamed Shaffril et al., 2021).

Blockchain-based decentralized identity management allows devices and users within AIoT ecosystems to communicate securely while preserving privacy and interoperability. This approach not only reduces the risk of data compromise but also improves scalability and flexibility across diverse applications and environments. As a result, blockchain integration enhances trust, resilience, and ethical deployment of intelligent AIoT services (Institute for Defense & Business, 2025) .

3.1 Blockchain-Enabled Identity Management

A core feature of blockchain-based identity management is the assignment of cryptographic identities to individual devices, securely stored and managed on the blockchain. These decentralized identities (DIDs) enable devices to authenticate autonomously without continuous verification from centralized servers. Smart contracts enforce access control policies, ensuring that only authorized entities can access sensitive data or participate in distributed learning processes. Additionally, blockchain supports secure key management, revocation mechanisms, and immutable audit trails, thereby strengthening accountability and trust in AIoT systems (Institute for Defense & Business, 2025).

By mitigating risks associated with centralized identity infrastructures, blockchain-based identity management enhances autonomy, security, and reliability in AIoT interactions. Such decentralized identity frameworks are instrumental in promoting resilience and enabling safe collaboration among heterogeneous devices across diverse application domains (Deloitte Global, 2025).

3.2 Consensus and Scalability Challenges

Despite its advantages, the integration of blockchain into AIoT ecosystems presents challenges related to consensus mechanisms and scalability. Traditional consensus protocols such as Proof of Work (PoW) are computationally intensive, energy-consuming, and unsuitable for resource-constrained IoT devices. These limitations introduce latency and performance bottlenecks that conflict with the real-time demands of AIoT applications.

To address these challenges, lightweight consensus mechanisms—such as Proof of Authority (PoA) and Delegated Proof of Stake (DPoS)—have been proposed to reduce computational overhead while maintaining security and trust guarantees. In addition, hybrid blockchain architectures and off-chain processing solutions are gaining traction as scalable alternatives. These approaches enhance transaction throughput and data management capabilities, making blockchain integration more practical for large-scale AIoT deployments without compromising security (Deloitte Global, 2025).

4. PRIVACY-PRESERVING FRAMEWORKS

Privacy preservation is one of the most critical challenges in AIoT ecosystems, as large volumes of sensitive data—particularly in domains such as healthcare, smart infrastructure, and industrial control systems—are continuously generated, processed, and exchanged. Traditional privacy mechanisms, including encryption and access control, remain essential but are often insufficient in AIoT settings where AI models themselves are vulnerable to inference attacks, data leakage, and reverse engineering.

To address these limitations, privacy-preserving frameworks integrate advanced techniques such as federated learning, differential privacy, and low-latency secure multi-party computation. These approaches enable collaborative intelligence while ensuring that sensitive data remains protected throughout its lifecycle. By allowing distributed learning and secure computation without exposing raw data, privacy-preserving frameworks support both functionality and confidentiality in AIoT environments (Mirza et al., 2024).

Federated learning (FL) plays a central role in such frameworks by enabling model training directly on edge devices, thereby eliminating the need to transmit raw data to centralized servers. While this significantly reduces privacy risks, FL remains susceptible to threats such as model poisoning and gradient inversion attacks. To mitigate these vulnerabilities, differential privacy techniques are incorporated to inject carefully calibrated noise into model updates, ensuring that individual data points cannot be reconstructed from shared gradients. The integration of FL with differential privacy thus provides a robust foundation for secure, privacy-aware AIoT systems (Aluwala, 2024).

4.1 Federated Learning and Differential Privacy

Federated Learning (FL) enables AI models to be trained at the network edge, where raw data remains localized on user devices and only aggregated model updates are shared with a coordinating server. This decentralized training paradigm significantly reduces the risk of data exposure and enhances user privacy compared to conventional centralized learning approaches. As a result, FL is particularly well-suited for AIoT applications involving sensitive information.

Despite its advantages, FL is vulnerable to several security threats, including model poisoning attacks, where adversaries inject malicious updates to corrupt the global model. Differential privacy (DP) is commonly employed to counteract these threats by adding controlled statistical noise to training data or model updates. This ensures strong privacy guarantees, preventing the identification or reconstruction of any individual's data from the model output while maintaining acceptable model accuracy.

When combined, federated learning and differential privacy offer a powerful privacy-preserving framework that balances data confidentiality and model performance. This combination is especially relevant for AIoT applications in healthcare, finance, and smart governance, where regulatory compliance and user trust are paramount. Implementing FL with DP enables organizations to harness the benefits of AI-driven intelligence without compromising sensitive information or violating data protection regulations (Aluwala, 2024; Mirza et al., 2024).

4.2 Homomorphic Encryption and Secure Computation

Homomorphic encryption (HE) enables computation on encrypted data, allowing AIoT systems to process sensitive information without ever exposing it in plaintext form. This capability is particularly valuable in privacy-sensitive domains such as healthcare analytics and financial decision-making, where data confidentiality is critical. By permitting operations directly on encrypted data, HE significantly reduces the risk of unauthorized access or data leakage. Although traditionally computationally intensive, recent advances have improved the efficiency of homomorphic encryption, making it increasingly viable for practical AIoT deployments (Kuraku, 2023).

Secure multi-party computation (SMPC) provides a complementary privacy-preserving approach by enabling multiple parties to jointly compute a function over their private inputs without revealing those inputs to one another. In AIoT environments, SMPC is especially useful when multiple stakeholders collaborate on shared analytics or decision-making tasks while maintaining strict data confidentiality. Each participant retains control over their local data, ensuring privacy throughout the computation process.

As computational efficiency continues to improve, both homomorphic encryption and secure multi-party computation are expected to become more practical for large-scale AIoT applications. These techniques collectively support end-to-end data confidentiality and integrity, strengthening trust in AIoT systems across their entire processing pipeline (Palo Alto Networks, 2025).

Figure 2. Blockchain-enabled a IoT framework for trust and identity management

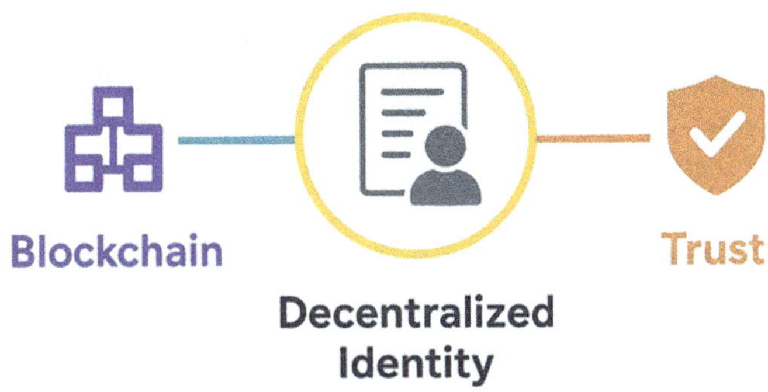

Figure 2 illustrates a blockchain-integrated Artificial Intelligence of Things (AIoT) framework designed to ensure secure trust and identity management. The framework demonstrates how IoT devices interact with AI-driven decision-making systems, while blockchain technology guarantees immutability, transparency, and decentralized identity verification. Smart contracts are employed to automate trust establishment among entities, whereas consensus mechanisms ensure reliability across distributed nodes. The layered architecture highlights the flow of data from IoT devices to AI models and subsequently to the blockchain for secure storage and

identity validation. Overall, the framework effectively addresses key challenges related to data integrity, authentication, and privacy in large-scale AIoT ecosystems.

4.3. Lightweight Cryptographic Solutions for AIoT

AIoT ecosystems consist of billions of resource-constrained devices, such as sensors, actuators, and edge nodes, which are incapable of supporting traditional heavy cryptographic protocols. Consequently, lightweight cryptographic solutions are essential to ensure confidentiality, integrity, and authentication in such environments. These solutions include optimized encryption algorithms, lightweight hash functions, and efficient digital signature schemes specifically designed for low-power devices. By adopting lightweight cryptography, AIoT systems can achieve robust security without imposing excessive computational overhead on constrained devices (Babu & Simon, 2025).

4.4 Symmetric and Asymmetric Lightweight Protocols

Lightweight symmetric-key algorithms such as PRESENT, SPECK, and SIMON are designed to offer reduced computational complexity while maintaining strong cryptographic resistance. These algorithms are particularly suitable for AIoT devices that require efficient and secure encryption mechanisms. For asymmetric cryptography, Elliptic Curve Cryptography (ECC) provides strong security with shorter key lengths, making it ideal for resource-constrained environments. ECC enables secure communication and data protection without the significant computational overhead associated with traditional asymmetric cryptographic techniques. Integrating these lightweight protocols with blockchain-based trust modeling frameworks allows AIoT systems to balance security and performance, ensuring secure operation within hardware constraints (Allen, 2016).

Table 1. Privacy-preserving techniques in AIoT

References	Technique	Description
Mirza et al., 2024	Federated Learning (FL)	Decentralized model training on local devices without sharing raw data
Aluwala, 2024	Differential Privacy	Adds noise to data to prevent identification of individual data points
Kuraku, 2023	Homomorphic Encryption (HE)	Enables computation on encrypted data without revealing plaintext
Palo Alto Networks, 2025	Secure Multi-party Computation (SMPC)	Allows collaborative computation without exposing private inputs

4.5 Future Directions in Cryptography for AIoT

With the rapid growth of AIoT, the advent of quantum computing poses a significant threat to classical cryptographic primitives, potentially compromising their security. To counter this risk, Post-Quantum Cryptography (PQC) algorithms—such as lattice-based and hash-based cryptosystems—are being developed to resist quantum attacks. PQC provides quantum resistance, offering protection against adversaries equipped with quantum computational capabilities. The integration of PQC with blockchain and AI-based security mechanisms remains a relatively unexplored research area and represents a promising direction for future-proofing AIoT systems against emerging cyber threats (Ravidas et al., 2022).

5. CASE STUDIES AND APPLICATIONS

When deployed within AIoT environments, blockchain-based trust and privacy-preserving frameworks have demonstrated significant practical benefits. In smart healthcare applications, wearable sensors continuously monitor patient vitals and transmit sensitive data to AI systems for predictive diagnostics. Blockchain-based decentralized identity verification protects devices against spoofing attacks, while federated learning combined with differential privacy ensures patient data confidentiality. These decentralized AIoT healthcare systems can predict cardiovascular risks without exposing raw patient data, thereby ensuring both accuracy and privacy (Mesopotamian Journal of Cyber Security, 2025).

In industrial AIoT and smart city environments, blockchain facilitates secure machine-to-machine communication, enabling predictive maintenance and resilient supply chains. Blockchain-based trust models ensure the integrity of traffic sensor data, surveillance systems, and autonomous vehicle communications. Privacy-preserving AI techniques prevent the disclosure of individual mobility patterns while supporting urban analytics and planning. These applications demonstrate the transformative potential of integrating advanced security mechanisms into AIoT networks to enhance both functionality and privacy (Kuraku, 2023).

Table 2. Lightweight cryptographic protocols for AIoT

References	Protocol Type	Example Algorithms / Methods	Description
Allen, 2016	Symmetric Key Algorithms	PRESENT, SPECK, SIMON	Reduced computational complexity with strong security
Babu & Simon, 2025	Asymmetric Cryptography (ECC)	Elliptic Curve Cryptography	Shorter key lengths suitable for constrained devices
Ravidas et al., 2022	Post-Quantum Cryptography (PQC)	Lattice-based, Hash-based	Quantum-resistant cryptography for future-proofing AIoT

5.1. Future Directions and Research Challenges

Although blockchain-based trust models and privacy-preserving frameworks offer promising solutions for securing AIoT ecosystems, several challenges remain. Scalability, interoperability, and standardization are key barriers to widespread adoption. Energy-efficient blockchain solutions and robust consensus algorithms are required to support billions of devices without compromising sustainability. Additionally, adversarial machine learning poses a persistent threat, necessitating further research into robust and explainable AI models capable of resisting attacks (Hardjono et al., 2020).

The future of AIoT security lies in the convergence of quantum-resistant cryptography and policy-driven governance frameworks that balance innovation with ethical considerations. Transparency, fairness, and accountability will play an increasingly important role in fostering user trust. Interdisciplinary research spanning computer science, cryptography, law, and social sciences is essential to ensure that AIoT systems are not only technically secure but also socially and legally acceptable. A multi-layered security approach integrating blockchain, trust modeling, privacy preservation, and lightweight cryptography will be critical for addressing emerging technological and human-centric challenges (Bouras et al., 2021).

6. CONCLUSION

Identity management in the Internet of Things (IoT) has emerged as a critical research area due to the rapid proliferation of connected devices and the increasing demand for secure, trustworthy, and privacy-preserving interactions. Various approaches, including blockchain-based lightweight systems, Ethereum-enabled identity management, and hierarchical access control mechanisms, have demonstrated significant potential in improving authentication, authorization, and interoperability across diverse IoT environments. Decentralized identity management leveraging distributed ledger technologies such as blockchain and IOTA offers transparency, immutability, and resilience, thereby addressing many limitations of centralized models.

However, existing literature also highlights ongoing challenges, including scalability limitations, computational overhead, cross-platform interoperability, and the need for user-centric privacy controls. These gaps underscore the necessity for further research focused on harmonizing decentralized identity platforms with standardized IoT protocols, optimizing resource utilization for constrained devices, and integrating adaptive trust models to support large-scale and dynamic applications. Addressing these challenges will enable future IoT ecosystems to achieve secure, scalable, and interoperable identity management frameworks that promote trust and reliability across digital infrastructures.

REFERENCES

Al Hwaitat, A. K., Almaiah, M. A., Ali, A., Al-Otaibi, S., Shishakly, R., Lutfi, A., & Alrawad, M. (2023). A new blockchain-based authentication framework for secure IoT networks. *Electronics (Basel), 12*(17), 3618. DOI: 10.3390/electronics12173618

Al Sadawi, A., Hassan, M. S., & Ndiaye, M. (2021). A survey on the integration of blockchain with IoT to enhance performance and eliminate challenges. *IEEE Access : Practical Innovations, Open Solutions, 9*, 54478–54497. DOI: 10.1109/ACCESS.2021.3070555

Allen, C. (2016, April 25). The path to self-sovereign identity. *Life with Alacrity*. https://www.lifewithalacrity.com/2016/04/the-path-to-self-sovereign-identity.html

. Aluwala, A. (2024). AI-driven anomaly detection in network monitoring: Techniques and tools. *Journal of Artificial Intelligence and Cloud Computing*, 1–6.

Atzori, L., Iera, A., & Morabito, G. (2010). The Internet of Things: A survey. *Computer Networks, 54*(15), 2787–2805. DOI: 10.1016/j.comnet.2010.05.010

Babu, C. V. S., & Simon, P. A. (2025). Adaptive AI for dynamic cybersecurity systems: Enhancing protection in a rapidly evolving digital landscape. Retrieved March 17, 2025, from https://www.igi-global.com/gateway/chapter/337688

Bouras, M. A., Lu, Q., Dhelim, S., & Ning, H. (2021). A lightweight blockchain-based IoT identity management approach. *Future Internet, 13*(1), 24. DOI: 10.3390/fi13020024

Deloitte Global. (2025). Security and compliance in 5G and AI-powered edge networks. Retrieved March 17, 2025, from https://www.deloitte.com/global/en/services/consulting-risk/perspectives/security-compliance-in-5g-ai-powered-edge-networks.html

Fortino, G., Russo, W., Savaglio, C., Viroli, M., & Zhou, M. (2018). Opportunistic cyber-physical services: A novel paradigm for the future Internet of Things. In *Proceedings of the IEEE 4th World Forum on Internet of Things (WF-IoT)* (pp. 488–492).

Hardjono, T., Lipton, A., & Pentland, A. (2020). Towards an interoperability architecture for blockchain autonomous systems. *IEEE Transactions on Engineering Management, 67*(4), 1296–1306. DOI: 10.1109/TEM.2019.2920154

Hassija, V., Chamola, V., Saxena, V., Jain, D., Goyal, P., & Sikdar, B. (2019). A survey on IoT security: Application areas, security threats, and solution architectures. *IEEE Access : Practical Innovations, Open Solutions*, *7*, 82721–82743. DOI: 10.1109/ACCESS.2019.2924045

Institute for Defense & Business. (2025). What are the cybersecurity risks for smart cities? Retrieved March 17, 2025, from https://www.idb.org/what-are-the-cybersecurity-risks-for-smart-cities/

Kuraku, D. S. (2023). Adaptive security framework for IoT: Utilizing AI and ML to counteract evolving cyber threats. *Educational Administration: Theory and Practice*, *29*, 1573–1580.

Mesopotamian Journal of Cyber Security. (n.d.). Cybersecurity challenges in smart cities: An overview and future prospects. Retrieved March 17, 2025, from https://mesopotamian.press/journals/index.php/CyberSecurity/article/view/14

Mirza, N., Yunis, M., Khalil, A., & Mirza, N. (2024). Towards a conceptual framework for AI-driven anomaly detection in smart city IoT networks for enhanced cybersecurity. *Journal of Innovation & Knowledge*, *9*(4), 100601. DOI: 10.1016/j.jik.2024.100601

Mohamed Shaffril, H. A., Samsuddin, S. F., & Abu Samah, A. (2021). The ABC of systematic literature review: The basic methodological guidance for beginners. *Quality & Quantity*, *55*(4), 1319–1346. DOI: 10.1007/s11135-020-01059-6

Palo Alto Networks. (2025). What is the role of AI in threat detection? Retrieved March 17, 2025, from https://origin-www.paloaltonetworks.com/cyberpedia/ai-in-threat-detection

Priyadarshini, I. (2024). Anomaly detection of IoT cyberattacks in smart cities using federated learning and split learning. *Big Data and Cognitive Computing*, *8*(3), 21. DOI: 10.3390/bdcc8030021

Rajesh, G., Raajini, X. M., & Vinayagasundaram, B. (2016). Fuzzy trust-based aggregator sensor node election in Internet of Things. *International Journal of Internet Protocol Technology*, *9*(3), 151. DOI: 10.1504/IJIPT.2016.079550

Ravidas, S., Nguyen, K., & Oualha, N. (2022). Decentralized identity: A survey on emerging trends and challenges. *IEEE Access : Practical Innovations, Open Solutions*, *10*, 14038–14060.

Sfar, A. R., Natalizio, E., Challal, Y., & Chtourou, Z. (2018). A roadmap for security challenges in the Internet of Things. *Digital Communications and Networks*, *4*(2), 118–137. DOI: 10.1016/j.dcan.2017.04.003

Shafique, K., Khawaja, B. A., Sabir, F., Qazi, S., & Mustaqim, M. (2020). Internet of Things (IoT) for next-generation smart systems: A review of current challenges, future trends, and prospects for emerging 5G-IoT scenarios. *IEEE Access : Practical Innovations, Open Solutions*, *8*, 23022–23040. DOI: 10.1109/ACCESS.2020.2970118

Uddin, M. A., Stranieri, A., Gondal, I., & Balasubramanian, V. (2021). A survey on the adoption of blockchain in IoT: Challenges and solutions. *Blockchain: Research and Applications*, *2*(2), 100006.

Wu, X., & Liang, J. (2021). A blockchain-based trust management method for Internet of Things. *Pervasive and Mobile Computing*, *72*, 101330. DOI: 10.1016/j.pmcj.2021.101330

Xu, L. D., Lu, Y., & Li, L. (2021). Embedding blockchain technology into IoT for security: A survey. *IEEE Internet of Things Journal*, *8*(13), 10452–10473. DOI: 10.1109/JIOT.2021.3060508

Chapter 10
Blockchain-Driven Architecture for Secure and Attribute-Based Remote Patient Monitoring System

Kritika Sharma
http://orcid.org/0000-0002-8026-1635
Chitkara University Institute of Engineering and Technology, Chitkara University, Punjab, India

Naveen Kumar
Chitkara University Institute of Engineering and Technology, Chitkara University, Punjab, India

Rajesh Kumar Kaushal
Chitkara University Institute of Engineering and Technology, Chitkara University, Punjab, India

ABSTRACT

For continuous real-time health monitoring of patients, remote patient monitoring proved to be a potential solution. Particularly for patients who suffers from chronic disease like unstable heart conditions, diabetes and require daily monitoring of their vitals. RPM offers many benefits to patients but at the same time system has drawbacks in terms of data security, privacy and access control. As solution currently role-based access control is widely used in rpm to ensure control but that too lacks in dynamic and fine-grained access. In hospital scenario it's inefficient to share same

DOI: 10.4018/979-8-3373-6299-1.ch010

level of access to all person under same role. This model achieves data security, transparency and patient centric environment by leveraging decentralization, immutability, fine-grained access and dynamic context aware capabilities. Using smart contracts access control policies are enforced to ensure that only specified user will get access at a specified time. This chapter will provide landscape for effective tools needed for the implementation of a secure, auditable and fine-grained rpm system.

1. INTRODUCTION

The rapid integration of digital technologies in healthcare has transformed traditional clinical practices into more intelligent, data-driven systems (Shinde et al., 2024; Tagde et al., 2021). Amongst these new technologies, Remote Patient Monitoring(RPM) has been popularized due to its capacity to monitor the physiological parameters of patients in a continuous manner beyond traditional clinical facilities(Cheikhrouhou et al., 2025; Shaik et al., 2023). It uses wearable sensors or patches, to monitor vital signs such as heart rate, glucose level, and blood pressure of patient in real time(Aryai et al., 2023; Buthelezi et al., 2022; Chandra & Kanaga Suba Raja, 2024). It gives comfortable and restriction free movement with wireless body area networks(Alkhfaji, 2023; Ananthi & Jose, 2021; Sharmila & Jaisankar, 2021). This paradigm shift is not only beneficial but also improves the quality of care by reducing daily hospital visits. Additionally, the treatment costs are also minimized and the patient with chronic or lifestyle related diseases are now able to have timely intervention with the help of AI powered analytics(Al-Nbhany et al., 2024; Imtyaz Ahmed et al., 2022; Tuli et al., 2020). With the advent of AIoT(Artificial Intelligence of Things), where AI comes in contact with the Internet of Things(IoT), RPM is one of the pillars of personalized and proactive healthcare provision(Almukhlifi et al., 2025; Behara et al., 2025; Uddin et al., 2018). However, with the rising degrees of digitization of healthcare data and its dispersion to the cloud and IoT environments, the concerns related to data security, patient privacy, and identity management have also grown exponentially(Rajesh Kumar Kaushal et al., 2025; Rejesh Kumar Kaushal & Kumar, 2024; Shaik et al., 2023; Trivedi et al., 2024). Medical information is a sensitive field and is therefore a good target by hackers and unauthorized access. Traditional healthcare systems tend to have central databases and fixed access control systems, which can be the reason for single points of failure, insider attack and data cleaning(Garg, Kaushal, & Kumar, 2024; Upadrista et al., 2023; Yaqoob et al., 2022; Zaabar et al., 2021). The establishment of trust, transparency, and accountability regarding the storage, transmission, and access to patient data has become an essential aspect in this context.

To address one of the issue, RBAC mechanisms are often implemented by healthcare providers to allocate and control user privileges(Harnal & Chauhan, 2020; Khan & Sakamura, 2016). Role based system limits access to data by the user roles, which are defined in advance, e.g. doctors, nurses, administrators or technicians(Aslam et al., 2024). RBAC provides administrative convenience and ease, however, it is not flexible in dynamic and complicated healthcare situations. As an example, users with the same role can also be granted the same permission irrespective of their particular duties, situational requirements or patient affiliations. The resulting over-privileged access, slow decision making and privacy violations can result due to this static nature of RBAC(Aslam et al., 2024; Mole & Shaji, 2024). Moreover, contemporary medical systems include a multitude of stakeholders clinicians, insurance companies, remote caregivers, and patients themselves; all of which need to have different degrees of access in a variety of situations. For example, a doctor with specification of cardiologist might need the data related to heart, pulse rate but it is useless for an orthopaedic doctor who only might require bone density data and x-rays which are useless for cardiologist. Hence deciding access controls on the basis of roles only is inefficient; person with different specification and time durations require different level of accesses. Additionally, at the time of emergency temporary access may require by some unauthorised user and role based system lacks in providing that because of its static nature(Jameer & Syed, 2023; Psarra et al., 2024; Shaik et al., 2023). Thus, it is necessary to have a more granular, contextual, and dynamic access control approach. Attribute-Based Access Control(ABAC) could be seen as a strong solution to address the drawbacks of the conventional models. ABAC uses a set of attributes in the form of users, resources, actions, and combinations of circumstances used to define access policies(Yingwen Chen et al., 2021; Kaur et al., 2024; Pancari et al., 2023; Tuler De Oliveira et al., 2022). That is, unlike RBAC, it provides fine grained and flexible authorization decisions, which enable healthcare systems to implement dynamic policies based on real-time conditions, like location, time, patient consent, or medical emergency(Hasan et al., 2022; Jiang et al., 2022). Nevertheless, with the flexibility, ABAC remains largely reliant on a centralized policy enforcement infrastructure and that is associated with the possibility of trust and administration overhead and threats created by the insiders. The policy server can be exploited or manipulated by a centralized server, which will result in a breach of policy and disclosure of patient information without authorization(Liu et al., 2020; Mukherjee et al., 2017; Pancari et al., 2023).

Over the past few years, blockchain technology has demonstrated enormous potential to overcome these core challenges through its ability to deliver a decentralized, immutable and transparent information architecture of data management(Y. Zhang et al., 2021). The distributed ledger of blockchain guarantees that once a transaction or data is stored it cannot be changed without the agreement of all the connected network nodes or members. This agreement among all the connected nodes is known as consensus mechanism(Tuler De Oliveira et al., 2022). Consensus mechanisms are of various types and depending on the framework, system requirements different consensus can be used. It ensures and helps in validating all the transactions in the network(Garg, Kaushal, & Kumar, 2024; Kumar, Kaushal, Kumar, & Verma, 2024; Shilpi et al., 2023). Most commonly used consensus mechanisms are - Proof of Work (PoW), Proof of Stake(PoS), Practical Byzantine Fault Tolerance (PBFT), Istanbul Byzantine Fault Tolerance(IBFT), Quorum Byzantine Fault Tolerance(QBFT), RAFT and KAFKA.

PoW consensus mainly used with the permissionless blockchain and consume a lot energy because for each block creation it needs to solve a cryptographic puzzle. Thus, for the performance evaluation parameters such as throughput and latency it performs low in among various popular consensus(Monrat et al., 2022; Pradhan & Singh, 2021). Another type of consensus (PoS), no heavy computations are required which leads to low power consumption and increase throughput and latency. The validation in this consensus is based on the decision of higher stake holder. That is why there is the risk of stake centralization and suitable for the public and consortium blockchain type(Garg et al., 2023; Garg, Kaushal, Kumar, et al., 2024; Monrat et al., 2024; Sharma et al., 2024). For the fault tolerant consensus PBFT is most commonly used. It tolerates up to (n-1)/3 malicious nodes in the network. Although it offers low latency and high throughput, it lacks when the communication overhead increases with the increased number of users or network size(Sharma, Kumar, & Kaushal, 2025; Sharma, Kumar, Kaushal, et al., 2025; G. Yang et al., 2022). Together with this Raft and Kafka also well suited for the consortium and private type of blockchain network. Raft handles crash fault tolerance and ensures best performance results in throughput, latency and energy consumption among all the listed consensus. However, it has the drawback with the byzantine fault tolerance (Kumar, Kaushal, Kumar, & Verma, 2024; G. Yang et al., 2022). However, unlike Raft, Kafka uses publish- subscribe model and similar to Raft it ensures effective and efficient performance in a controlled network. But it requires external coordination for the optimal execution of the network, which is a drawback of this consensus(Gad et al., 2022). In Table 1 different consensus is compared along with features like power consumption, fault tolerance, compatible blockchain framework and performance parameters. This gives the detailed description about different consensus mechanisms and the outcome of table is that it helps in selecting optimal consensus with suitable framework and blockchain type.

Table 1. Comparison of popular blockchain consensus PoW, PoS, PBFT, RAFT and KAFKA

Parameter	Proof of Work (PoW) (Azaria et al., 2016)	Proof of Stake (PoS) (Monrat et al., 2024)	Practical Byzantine Fault Tolerance (PBFT) (G. Yang et al., 2022)	RAFT (Rajesh Kumar Kaushal et al., 2025)	KAFKA (Kumar, Kaushal, Kumar, & Verma, 2024)
Basic Principle	Nodes compete to solve a cryptographic puzzle; the first to solve adds a block.	Validators are chosen to create blocks based on the amount of stake locked in the network.	Nodes exchange messages & reach agreement through majority voting despite faulty nodes.	Leader-based approach; the leader proposes entries & followers replicate them to maintain consistency.	Uses distributed publish-subscribe model where controller assigns partitions to maintain order & consensus.
Type of Blockchain	Public / Permissionless	Public or Consortium	Consortium / Private	Consortium / Private	Consortium / Private
Fault Tolerance	Handles crash faults; limited protection against malicious majority (≥51%)	Resilient up to stake-based attacks; vulnerable to collusion if majority stake controlled	Tolerates up to (n−1)/3 malicious nodes	Handles crash faults only, not Byzantine failures	Crash fault-tolerant, not Byzantine fault-tolerant
Energy Efficiency	Very low; high computational cost	High; no heavy computation required	High; relies on message exchange only	Very high; lightweight consensus process	Very high; minimal computational overhead
Throughput	Low	Moderate to High	High	Very High	Very High
Latency	High (seconds to minutes)	Moderate (few seconds)	Low (milliseconds to seconds)	Low (milliseconds)	Very Low (milliseconds)
Scalability	Poor; performance drops with more nodes	Better scalability than PoW but limited by stake distribution	Limited; performance decreases sharply as nodes increase	Scales efficiently within consortium environments	Scales well within controlled networks
Use Cases	Bitcoin, Litecoin, early Ethereum	Ethereum 2.0, Cardano, Algorand	Hyperledger Fabric (old versions), permissioned networks	Hyperledger Fabric (current), enterprise blockchains	Enterprise-level ordering service for Fabric
Advantages	High security, fully decentralized	Energy-efficient, faster, scalable	Fast and consistent for small networks	Simple implementation, strong consistency	Extremely fast ordering and low delay
Limitations	High energy use, low throughput	Risk of stake centralization	Communication overhead increases with network size	Not secure against Byzantine faults	Requires external coordination, limited fault tolerance

However, along with optimal consensus, selecting the optimal framework is also a major challenge. Because blockchain is mainly of two types i.e. permissioned blockchain and permissionless blockchain. It is further classified in four different types that is public, private, consortium and hybrid blockchain(Kumar, Kaushal,

Kumar, & Malik, 2024). Public is permissionless blockchain where anyone can join the network without any restriction and requirement of specific permission. In this type of network one can perform different operations like read, write as well as can validate any transaction. It involves full transparency; all data is visible to every participant and provides high cryptographic security. Despite of this, public type of network is vulnerable to 51% attacks and may lack in transaction speed due to its large network size and mining overhead. On the other hand, private blockchain ensures a restricted network where only authorized nodes can participate in performing operations. It is a strict permissioned network with high transaction speed as fewer nodes are there and no mining delays involve. So, it provides high scalability with PBFT and RAFT consensus. In Table 2 all the different types of blockchain are compared in detail with the suitable consensus and frameworks.

Table 2. Different blockchain types with framework and consensus classification

Type of Blockchain	Access Control	Consensus Mechanism	Transparency Level	Transaction Speed	Scalability	Security Features	Most optimal Frameworks
Public Blockchain	No restrictions; anyone can participate as a node or miner.	PoW, PoS	Fully transparent; all data visible to every participant.	Low to moderate due to large network size and mining overhead.	Limited; performance decreases as nodes increase.	High cryptographic security but vulnerable to 51% attacks.	Bitcoin, Ethereum, Litecoin, Solana.
Private Blockchain	Strictly permissioned; access given by the network administrator.	PBFT, Raft	Limited transparency; data visible only to authorized entities.	High, as fewer nodes and no mining delay.	High; optimized for enterprise use.	Strong access control, identity management, and audit trails.	Hyperledger Fabric, R3 Corda, Multichain.
Consortium Blockchain	Permissioned access shared among multiple organizations.	PBFT, Raft, or Kafka-based consensus.	Partially transparent; data visibility depends on policy.	High; efficient consensus among known participants.	High; suited for multi-institution collaborations.	Robust security through authentication and mutual validation.	Quorum, Hyperledger Fabric (multi-org), Ripple, Energy Web Chain.
Hybrid Blockchain	Controlled access for internal users with optional public data sharing.	PoS, PBFT	Adjustable; some data public, some private.	Moderate to high depending on design.	Moderate; complexity affects scalability.	Flexible security and customizable policies.	Dragonchain, Hyperledger Besu.

From the table, it is cleared that for RPM healthcare environment best suited types of blockchain is private and consortium. Also, for the framework selection a separate comparison is needed, but currently Hyperledger fabric, Corda and Quorum are some suggested frameworks in table. Additionally, Self-executing programs that are part of smart contracts in the blockchain improve further on automation and trust as they execute rules that have been suggested or stipulated, and do not require any intermediaries(Divya & Uma Priyadarsini, 2024; Shuaib et al., 2022). Combined with ABAC, blockchain can be used as a trust anchor, with documents and implements access control policies in an auditable and non-tampered manner(Marwan et al., 2020). The provision of each access request and authorization decision can be logged in an immutable way, which guarantees transparency, traceability, and accountability between the stakeholders. An integration of blockchain and ABAC presents a radical model of RPM systems, whereby security, privacy and patient empowerment are of the foremost concern(Kaur et al., 2024; Z. Yang et al., 2024). The distributed trust layer is blockchain in the proposed architecture of this chapter, which contains encrypted health data access records and manages the policy enforcement via smart contracts. ABAC engine characterizes and analyses access requirements dynamically depending on various contextual characteristics that can be used to provide fine grained, patient centric, and policy driven data management. This integration does not only remove the need to have centralized entities, but also facilitates interoperability between heterogeneous healthcare systems and IoT devices (Sahu et al., 2022). Additionally, the audit trail provided at the blockchain level is immutable and improves regulatory adherence to healthcare related regulations, including the Health Insurance Portability and Accountability Act (HIPAA) and General Data Protection Regulation (GDPR) regulations, which adds to patient confidence and accountability to the institution (Jayabalan & Jeyanthi, 2025; Upadrista et al., 2023).

The motivation of this study is the necessity to create a safe, scalable, and intelligent healthcare infrastructure, which could support the explosive increase in interconnected medical devices and real-time patient data(Yaxing Chen et al., 2019; Jamil et al., 2020; Raj & Prakash, 2022; Trivedi et al., 2024). The conventional solutions that were centralized have problems in keeping up with the two needs of high-speed data processing and high privacy protection(Hayes et al., 2023; Sahu et al., 2022; Shaik et al., 2023; Trivedi et al., 2024). Blockchain driven ABAC architecture can present an attractive next-generation healthcare system based on the ability to leverage decentralization, cryptographic assurance, and dynamic access control. They will allow healthcare organizations to regulate the accessibility of sensitive data, in what situations, and to what extent, without compromising the performance of their systems and data quality. This chapter contains a detailed analysis and implementation plan of an architecture based on blockchain that uses ABAC in RPM settings. It examines the most important elements of design, such as blockchain frameworks, consensus mechanism, and policy attributes, that are required to be implemented in the real world intelligent systems. Besides, it assesses the suggested model based on the security performance, privacy preservation, and compatibility with the current medical standards. The final aim is to show how blockchain and ABAC can be used together to increase the levels of trust, transparency, and patient empowerment in AIoT based RPM healthcare systems.

The rest of this chapter is structured in the following way. Section 2 presents the current literature on blockchain use in healthcare data management, ABAC policy integrated RPM system, and AIoT based systems for RPM ecosystem. Section 3 presents the suggested blockchain ABAC architecture and provides the details of the workflow and attributes of access control policy. Section 4 covers the details of spider chart and comparative analysis results whereas, Section 5 will detail the conclusion and possible areas of research and final observations.

2. LITERATURE REVIEW

Combining blockchain with access control policy in healthcare has had a lot of momentum over the past few years, especially to supplement the security, privacy, and transparency of RPM ecosystem. In the following section, the key contributions of 2020-2025 are reviewed in four major themes, namely: (i) Blockchain in healthcare data management, (ii) Attribute-Based Access Control in RPM, (iii) AIoT enabled healthcare system for RPM, (iv) Research gaps in existing approaches.

2.1 Blockchain in Healthcare Data Management

The blockchain technology has become a reliable system of data sharing in healthcare. It is decentralized and enables open and inaccessible management of electronic health records (EHRs). In 6G-IoT healthcare systems,(Q. Zhang et al., 2025) also suggested a blockchain based trustful model of data sharing, where secure communication and verifiable data provenance are ensured with the use of smart contracts. Likewise,(Wang et al., 2025) explored privacy-enhancing blockchain systems with off-chain storage selected as one of the successful concepts to strike a balance between scalability and confidentiality in healthcare systems. This development is in line with the digitalization of healthcare, in which IoMT and AI systems continuously produce large amounts of sensitive information that need to be not only shareable but also secure(V & Singh, 2025).

Author(Ali et al., 2020) suggests a remote health monitoring(RHM) system, which is decentralized, involving both blockchain technology and the Tor network, in order to provide privacy preserving, secure, and accountable health data sharing between patients and doctors. The system, based on Ethereum blockchain, uses smart contracts to agree and keep records and hidden services to transmit data off-chain. Also, to avoid the implication of third parties with metadata disclosure. The structure is developed to achieve a balance between decentralization, scalability, privacy, and latency, keeping sensitive health data out of the blockchain and being sure to save only logs of transactions as well as the agreements in the encrypted form on the blockchain. As shown by a series of use cases like cardiac monitoring, sleep apnea testing and EEG monitoring, the solution provides fine grained control, accountability and resilience to common attacks and provides efficient and private remote patient data transfer. Similarly, a complete analysis is done to introduce blockchain and IoT application to e-healthcare with a challenge of decentralized, secure, and tamper proof health data management. The authors(Ray et al., 2021) describe the drawbacks of centralized IoT architecture like single points of failure and privacy threats and indicate how blockchain can counteract them by immutability, transparency, and distributed consensus. The article gives a detailed comparison of the different consensus algorithms(e.g., PoW, PoS, PBFT, DPoS) and blockchain platforms in terms of whether they are more appropriate in healthcare settings. It also presents an IoBHealth architecture, a layered data flow model with technologies of IoT and blockchain that will be used in the most efficient way to store, access, and manage health data. The paper illustrates the potential of blockchain to make IoT based healthcare ecosystems more secure, interoperable, and more trusted. Additionally, a solution to the issues of scalability and energy efficiency through the use of numerous application examples.

In a different work author(Kongsen et al., 2024) have presents a blockchain based model of safe remote health monitoring, namely targeting the home isolation situation in the case of COVID-19. The structure uses Ethereum blockchain as a decentralized database to store, buffer and transfer vital signs of patients on the blockchain to ensure enhanced security in the transmission process. Also, to enhance the security of the transmission process, and TLS-based publish subscribe facilitation is employed. It separates the hospital information system (HIS) and external devices to form a decentralized system structure, thereby avoiding information infiltration with the system, improves the integrity of information, its confidentiality, and the availability. Smart contracts also enable access control, the management of encryption keys, and auditing, in order to provide a traceable solution and role based authorization, which are used in the paper. However, RBAC enables only static access and course grained data for the management of accesses in the network. The suggested model is cost-efficient, highly data reliable, and demonstrates robust privacy protection, therefore, it is appropriate in the Internet of Medical Things (IoMT) applications in a health care environment with constraints or at home. Earlier works(Garg et al., 2022; Raj & Prakash, 2022) studied Hyperledger Fabric and Ethereum as the solution to secure medical data exchange, and they proved to be more resilient with higher integrity, than traditional databases or cloud based servers. Nonetheless, the majority of these models are based on the fixed access control policies, which restrict the flexibility in multi-stakeholder healthcare settings as well as inefficient in providing fine grained and dynamic access control. This issue has encouraged scholars to combine blockchain and dynamic access control models like ABAC together to form a fine grained approach (Shahzad et al., 2024).

2.2 Attribute Based Access Control in Remote Patient Monitoring

ABAC is a current and dynamic method of controlling access authorization and guaranteeing the safety of sensitive data. In contrast to the traditional, non-dynamic RBAC systems, ABAC considers various attributes, including the subject, the object, the time, and the context-dependent factors, including emergencies, in order to decide the right of access(Y. Zhang et al., 2021). This will make sure that only the intended and authenticated person will have access to particular resources and not the same access rights to an entire group of people holding the same position or role.

ABAC has a high benefit in the environment of RPM, in which the conditions of the patients and their needs change regularly(Yaxing Chen et al., 2019). Smart patches and other wearable devices constantly gather the vital signs of the patients and send them to medical personnel to be diagnosed and monitored. It allows timely as well as effective medical care, especially to those who have chronic illnesses and require almost daily monitoring(Aslam et al., 2024). In another study author(Ramyasri & Hussain, 2021) introduces a permissioned blockchain healthcare data sharing system that is set to provide secure, decentralized healthcare data control over medical information. The model controlled access privileges with Hyperledger Fabric, which makes use of the ABAC to prevent the disclosure of patient information in an unauthorized manner. Smart contracts also manage the policies in place, whereby patients can stipulate who can access or use their health information. This system also assures data integrity, traceability and privacy since each transaction is documented on the blockchain ledger. The quantitative performance outcomes also show faster data retrieval and lower access latency rates than the traditional cloud systems, which proves that blockchain has a possibility of balancing efficiency with strict security in medical data management. Moreover, two researchers(Raj & Prakash, 2024) have suggested a permissioned Ethereum-based design that uses Ciphertext Policy Attribute Based Encryption (CP-ABE) and Elliptic Curve Cryptography (ECC) in order to provide security to IoMT settings. The scheme relies on the Proof of Authority (PoA) consensus to achieve an efficient and reliable system in validating transactions, and smart contracts to implement self-adaptively adjusting access control and user authentication. The architecture offers patient-based control, which allows patients to set access controls on physicians and medical personnel. Used on Ethereum Remix IDE and Ganache, the findings include low cost of transactions and executions, valid decryption and results, and a small scale-dependent cost of encryption/decryption processing time that linearly depends on the number of attributes. The CP-ABE scheme based on ECC has a high resistance to collusion, pre-emptive prevention of escrow keys, and the computation time is much shorter in the CP-ABE scheme than in the currently-in use DBC scheme, proving to be more effective and secure in the IoT-healthcare networks.

Nevertheless, the traditional RBAC model provides all professionals belonging to the same role group with access to patient information, irrespective of the need or situation(Mole & Shaji, 2024). This kind of coarse-grained access control poses internal security risks and compromises patient trust. Thus, the implementation of ABAC in RPM settings enables fine-grained, context-sensitive, and reliable access to data, which is highly compatible with the dynamic and sensitive character of healthcare data management(Yaxing Chen et al., 2019; Z. Yang et al., 2024).

2.3 AIoT Enabled Healthcare System for Remote Patient Monitoring

Artificial intelligence integration makes IoT systems intelligent and enhance its abilities. RPM system provides facility of real time vitals monitoring and in addition to this, AI enhances its capabilities by providing future analytics and early diagnosis(Menon et al., 2025). Likewise, author introduces an innovative platform architecture which combines blockchain technology with AIoT systems to improve the security, scalability and efficiency of healthcare data. It is found that the major AIoT challenges include the risks of privacy of data and memory inefficiency and that an innovative solution to these issues is offered, using edge AI with a sharding-based Proof-of-Authority (PoA) blockchain. The framework proposes the three functions, a Blockchain Version Manager to support AI models dynamically and real-time, IoT Preprocessing to support effective data management, and a Shard Fragment Cube (SFC) to support quick blockchain data search. The results of the simulations indicate that the approach reduces the retrieval time of data by half, besides enhancing the use of memory and security. On the whole, the study shows that blockchain may be used to facilitate secure, privacy-friendly, and scalable AIoT systems in real-time healthcare settings(Jun, 2025). In another review author discusses the ways in which the integration of the IoT, AI, and their combination AIoT is transforming the process of delivering healthcare. It emphasizes the paradigm-shifting opportunities of these technologies in RPM, personalized medicine, and operational efficiency by using wearable in the form of sensors, cloud, and analytics based on AI. The research highlights aspects like the enhancement of diagnostics and treatment planning as well as the obstacles, including issues of privacy of data, algorithm bias, interoperability, and notions of ethics. The safe and successful adoption of AI and IoT in the healthcare sector is proposed in a structured framework where they argue that there should be transparency, ethics, and compliance conforming to regulatory requirements to help make AI and IoT responsibly adopted and best capitalize on clinical outcomes(Belbase et al., 2024). Author(Sim & Jeong, 2021) introduce a data integrity verification system built on multi-blockchain and meant to address AIoT edge computing setting. The research focuses on three main IoT networks data corruption issues, latency, and data security vulnerabilities by applying several interconnected blockchains to catalog and validate an IoT by using multi-hashes groupings and timely updates made on the basis of locations. The method improves the integrity of data and reduces the loss of information since it allows cross-distributed processing of the IoT device data according to defined rules. It enhances safe synchronization between IoT nodes and central servers and at the same time only incurs low computation expenses. The results show that multi-blockchain processing is an appropriate method to depend on the reliability, scalability, and efficiency of data processing of IoT because of the large scale and real-time AIoT, i.e., smart healthcare and autonomous systems. Author(Pan, 2025) designed an innovative AIoT home-based arteriovenous fistula (AVF) surveillance system as a home perspective of monitoring of hemodialysis patients due to the shortcomings of monitoring methods by hospitals. The system relies on the convolutional neural network (CNN) to obtain scores on fistula states (along with normal, slight blockage, and complete blockage) based on 245 labelled vascular sound samples and transmits them to hospital databases over LoRa wireless technology. With an F1-score of 1.00 when using normal and blocked states, the model proved to be highly diagnostic with communication distances longer than 6 km. Usability testing using the Technology Acceptance Model (TAM), the model was found to be highly satisfying and intended to be adopted by patients. The researchers conclude that the AIoT-based system can offer a non-invasive, reliable, and cost-effective option of remote fistula management that would enhance early diagnosing and ongoing managing chronic kidney disease. A group of researchers(Wazid et al., 2021) present a secure authentication framework in AIoT surroundings envisioned with blockchain, where integrated distributed ledger technology and AI-based IoT systems are used to improve privacy, integrity and confidence. The paper systematizes AIoT architecture layers, the fundamental machine learning elements, and the security measures to curb the prevalent attacks, including replay, impersonation, and man-in-the-middle attacks. It proposes a more universalized model with smart contracts and AI-based data analysis to use for the registration of devices, user authentication, and delivery of secure data. Among applications, there are smart homes, healthcare remote, industry automation and intelligent transport. The paper also finds critical issues such as scalability, computational complexity, and interoperability and suggests the future research of energy-saving blockchain consensus and privacy-enabling federated AIoT.

To conclude, integration of AI has improved the healthcare sector by offering predicative decision making and timely cures. It lessens the burden over healthcare providers as well as provides technologically advanced environment. Despite of these benefits, there is one major drawback of lack of trust among users. Because, data security and privacy issues leads to trustless environment and with the sensitive crucial data no one wants to compromised. In order to solve this issue, blockchain proved to be a potential solution. As blockchain ensure decentralized and distributed environment with the interesting properties like immutability where no one cannot update or modify any data that is stored ones. It makes its stored data permanent so that no alteration can happen. Additionally, blockchain ensures security and privacy with cryptographic SHA and consensus mechanisms. Thus, integration of blockchain can solve the issue of trust among users to some extent. To ensure greater protection and foster trust, access control also serves as an essential component. Collectively, the integration of blockchain and attribute-based access control policies in AI-powered RPM systems presents a promising approach toward creating a strong, secure, and trustworthy ecosystem.

3. METHODOLOGY

This research uses quantitative analytical research method to design, simulate, and test an AIoT-enabled RPM system that encompasses AI, IoT, and security measures of access controls to manage smart healthcare. The methodology emphasis the blueprint of AIoT framework gathering physiological parameters through intelligent IoT, and for efficient RPM the system relay upon results of analysed parameters.

This study involves a four layer architecture to propose an AIoT powered RPM system using blockchain technology and ABAC. In figure1 brief of all four layer is given. The following layers are –

i. **Sensing Layer:** It involves the intelligent IoT sensors, which are needed for observation of patient's physiological data. It helps in continuous monitoring of vitals such as – heart rate, oxygen, glucose, SpO2, and blood pressure levels.
ii. **Network Layer:** Network layer ensures reliability and low latency data transfer communicational flow between the IoT devices and the processing server. Wi-Fi, Bluetooth Low Energy(BLE), LoRa, and 5G communication protocols have been used as communication protocols that offer broader coverage and low energy consumption. Lightweight communication is managed through the Message queuing Telemetry Transport(MQTT) protocol to provide efficient

performance when the networks are constrained. The blockchain provides encrypted data packets which ensure safety as the data packets are encrypted with the SHA 256.

iii. **AI Layer:** It is the computing core of the framework, a combination of machine learning(ML) and deep learning(DL) algorithms to reveal future analytics from sensor data, identify health anomalies, and forecast medical risks. The models include:

- Pattern recognition in data produced by physiological signals using CNNs.
- Time-series forecasting of health vitals by Long Short-Memory(LSTM) networks.
- Binary classification of a normal and abnormal readings using Support Vector Machines(SVMs).

Statistical analysis of parameters used to find out attributes like mean, variance, entropy, and spectral energy. The AI models are trained on both real IoT data (e.g., PhysioNet, MIMIC-IV) and simulated data of prototype devices.

Figure 1. Layer architecture of proposed model with brief description

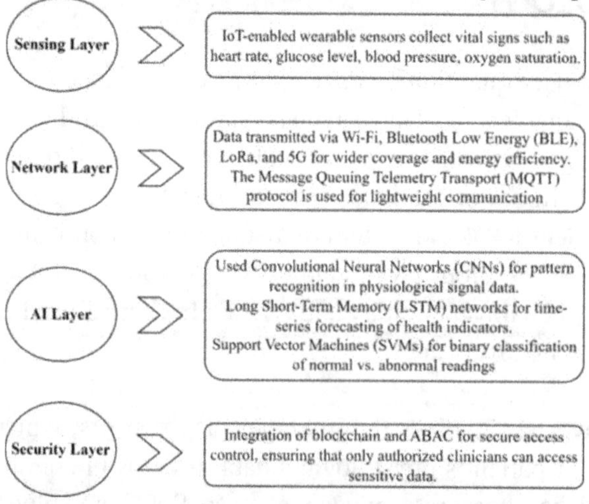

iv. **Security Layer:** In this layer integration of blockchain and ABAC is involved. It will manage security and privacy in the proposed system. Unlike RBAC, ABAC provides fine grained access by defining rules based on different attributes like

- **Role** - doctor OR nurse OR insurance head
- **Specification –** general physician OR cardiologist OR orthopedics
- **Context –** emergency OR basic checkup
- **Time –** Day time (9 a.m. – 5 p.m.) OR Night time (6 p.m. – 3 a.m.)

Based on these attributes the decision of grant and revoke has been made according to the patient's consent. These attributes decide who gets the access of sensitive patient's data at what time and under what circumstances. Additionally, blockchain chaincode are used in Hyperledger fabric framework to simulate and automate the process of authorization and authentication. In this way blockchain ensures immutability, authorized access and trust in the proposed system.

Combinedly, these layers form a robust end to end AIoT powered infrastructure for intelligent and privacy preserve rpm system.

3.1 Data Storage Model

The implanted architecture has taken the form of a hybrid on-chain as well as off-chain data storage because healthcare system lacks privacy and scalability. It will improved scalability and ensures privacy at the same time. Hyperledger fabric blockchain network is implanted which contains meta data and access control policy data on-chain. The sensitive patient healthcare records are secured in the off-chain storage; thus, it will guarantee protection of privacy and effective use of storage space which leads to scalability. Table 3 shows the data elements that are stored on chain and elements which are stored off chain.

Table 3. Data elements stored on-chain and off-chain

Data Element	Data Storage	Description	Purpose
Data Hash	On-chain	SHA-256 hash of sensitive patient records	Required for maintaining data integrity
Consent Record	On-chain	Consent for data access	Required for authorization
Access Logs	On-chain	Maintain all the transaction logs	Required for auditing and tracking
Access Decision	On-chain	Grant/ Deny result	Required for maintaining transparency and policy enforcement
Sensor Data	Off-chain	AES-256-GCM encrypted Real-time patient vital data	Required for patient data analysis

This table reflects that blockchain gives tamper free logs that give healthcare providers an opportunity to access authentic and guideline established data. SHA-256 is used for maintaining data integrity hashes that are stored on blockchain ledger. The sensitive healthcare record collected from the RPM devices is stored off-chain. Most importantly these records are ciphered with AES-256-GCM and ensure security. For the off-chain storage InterPlanetary storage system(IPFS) distributed storage system is used. This hybrid storage usage in the proposed system provides transforming benefits. Benefits such as privacy protection – the sensitive data will never be visible on the blockchain; Scalability – only store lightweight metadata on-chain; Integrity verification – Stores hashes and can detect tampering easily; Efficient storage – Large data files stored off-chain for improved efficiency.

3.2 Asset Schema Used in the Blockchain

Following assets are used in proposed system for managing healthcare data access. It enables transparency and traceability for patient consents and rpm data access.

1. Consent Asset
2. AccessRequest Asset
3. AuditEntry Asset

3.3 Smart Contract Design for Access Control and Evaluation Metrics

The proposed system is an implementation of ABAC based on blockchain smart contracts in Hyperledger fabric as a chaincode. Smart contracts automatically implement access policies and make sure that patient information is only accessed by authorized medical entities. In the suggested model, user features (role, department, organization and authorization level) are entrenched in X.509 certificates during the enrolment procedure by the Hyperledger fabric CA. Certificate Authority(CA) manages verification of certificates. The smart contract will then verify these attributes prior to the authorization of patient data. “Role” defines the user category such as doctor, nurses, patient; while on the other hand for more refinement “department” attribute is also considered which can be cardiologist, general physician, neurologist or any medical department. Other attributes that are considered in the proposed model are “organization”, “access levels” and “status”. These attributes ensure fine grained and flexible access control in comparison to RBAC system which is static and generally used in traditional systems. The pseudo-code for enforcing ABAC is given in below.

In this pseudo-code 1, attributes are verified and checks the patients consent to allow or deny the users request.

Whereas pseudo-code 2, reflects the logic for granting and denying the permission. If all the conditions are satisfied only then smart contract grants access to the user otherwise it smart contract will decline the user request to access patient data.

Figure 2 shows the transparent and verifiable process of managing access permissions in a blockchain based RPM environment. The workflow ensures once user request for the access it involve following steps.

Figure 2. Sequence diagram of access control workflow in a blockchain based RPM environment

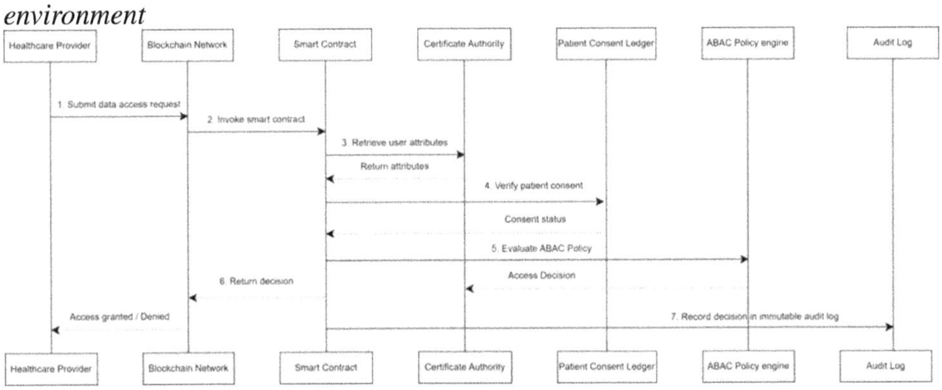

In any proposed system its performance needs to be evaluated for checking model's effectiveness and feasibility. Thus, performance evaluation of the proposed model needs to be measured and to assess overall system performance six evaluation parameters are majorly involved: - Accuracy, Latency, Throughput, Security Strength, Scalability, and Reliability. However, for the evaluation Hyperledger Caliper is planned as a future work to measure all these parameters under different workloads. Description of following evaluation parameters are defined in the **Table 3**.

Table 4. Performance evaluation parameters with description

S.No.	Parameter(s)	Description
1.	Accuracy(%)	It is the effectiveness rate of AI model; it measures how many prediction labels are matched with the actual health state labels.
2.	Latency(ms)	It is the average delay between the data transmission and time taken for a transaction to be committed and visible on Hyperledger Fabric.
3.	Throughput(tx/s)	It is the number of blockchain transactions successfully processed per second.
4.	Reliability	It shows how well system perform the basic read and write operations under different workloads.
5.	Security Strength	It is computed on the basis of successful authentication and access control efficiency
6.	Scalability	It is the ability of the system to maintain performance as number of connected nodes increases.

4. RESULT & DISCUSSION

The proposed RPM system is powered by blockchain and uses Hyperledger Fabric as framework. Additionally, the ABAC and built on AIoT is integrated to enhance its performance. The system was tested in accordance with six important performance parameters including, Accuracy, latency, throughput, privacy, security and access control. These measures were chosen based on the ability of the system to safely handle the healthcare information without compromising the performance levels that were found to be acceptable. This architecture is deployed on a permissioned blockchain network with Hyperledger Fabric which enables configurable consensus mechanisms and effective execution of smart contracts. The ordering service is set up with the help of the Raft, which allows a better fault tolerance and efficiency of the transactions processing in comparison with the old ordering mechanisms. The system architecture was compared with the traditional healthcare data management models that were centralized to evaluate the effectiveness of the proposed model in Table 5.

Table 5. Comparison table of proposed model with traditional systems

Parameters	(Pan, 2025)	(Wazid et al., 2021)	Proposed model
Accuracy	It achieved an outstanding accuracy, with a CNN attaining F1-scores of 1.00 and 0.93 for slight blockage. This translates overall average of approx. 96–98% accuracy.	It did not explicitly measure accuracy; their system's secure data flow implies functional reliability but not predictive capability.	It integrates CNN-LSTM hybrid learning for continuous time-series analysis, achieves higher performance (~97–98%) with the added ability to analyse longitudinal data patterns.
Throughput	It reported stable data transmission with minimal signal loss using LoRa technology, representing high data reliability and communication efficiency.	It acknowledged that blockchain operations consume extra communication & storage cost; experience delay due to public consensus.	It employs Hyperledger Fabric with Raft consensus. This significant increase results from permissioned architecture and parallel block creation.
Latency	The real-time monitoring and immediate LED/audio alerts indicate response times below 300 ms, aligning with low-latency performance.	It emphasized that public blockchain consensus severely hits the transaction processing speed, showing that the system experiences higher delay.	The proposed Fabric-ABAC system, leveraging Raft consensus, achieves average transaction latency around 320 ms.
Security	It did not include encryption or secure distributed storage, relying on traditional centralized hospital networks where all the security control are handled manually.	It designed a blockchain-envisioned framework, ensuring high confidentiality and tamper resistance.	It matches the security level by leveraging Fabric's permissioned ledger, SHA-256 hashing, and ABAC-based fine-grained access policies; multi-level protection.
Access control	It uses basic database-level access where data is stored in centralized hospital servers without attribute-based policies.	It incorporated blockchain-based user authentication and authorization, but policies remained role-based (RBAC), which is static and coarse-grained.	It adopts ABAC implemented via Hyperledger Fabric chaincode, where access is determined by multiple dynamic factors.

The comparison shows that the suggested blockchain framework is much more efficient in terms of security, transparency, and access control levels than the conventional centralized architectures. Additionally, using smart contracts to implement a form of access control, namely ABAC is able to provide a way of managing access dynamically and with finer granularity. The proposed model considers a variety of attributes as role, department, organization, and patient consent unlike the traditional RBAC systems that assign fixed permissions to predefined roles.

This will make the policy flexible and secure that healthcare providers can only access patient information on meeting specified conditions that are encoded in the blockchain smart contracts.

4.1 Data Integrity & Scalability Consideration

Cryptographic hashing is used, i.e. SHA-256, to guarantee patient records stored off-chain. Any alteration of patient information causes the incompatibility of the stored hash and the calculated value of the hash that will allow one to instantly identify tampering. Furthermore, sensitive medical records are encrypted by AES-256-GCM, which is confidential when storing and transmitting the data. The unalterable registry offered by Hyperledger Fabric also increases transparency because it keeps audit logs that cannot be tampered with to all access requests and consent transactions.

Along with this, another approach used by the system is a hybrid storage model whereby all the metadata and access control information are stored in the blockchain, but significant patient records are kept off-chain. This architecture yields a significant reduction in blockchain storage overhead and scalability in large datasets in healthcare created by RPM devices. Moreover, the Raft algorithm of consensus is more efficient in network operation by allowing the establishment of higher transaction confirmation speeds in comparison to the more computationally intensive consensus mechanisms.

4.2 Future Experimental Validation

Despite the fact that the architectural analysis shows the possible benefits of the suggested framework, the extensive use of experiments will be introduced in the future work. To measure the performance in terms of throughput, latency, scalability, and resource utilization at various workloads Hyperledger Caliper shall be used to conduct the performance benchmarking.

These tests will offer the quantitative results of the system functionality in the real-world healthcare setting which implies a variety of organizations and extensive data concerning the monitoring of patients.

5. CONCLUSION

In last few years artificial intelligence evolved as a transformative opportunity and in combination with IoT it has contributed a lot in healthcare sector; especially in the RPM it plays an important role. However, with advancements some challenges also evolved; such as risk of data security, privacy, high latency and management of access controls. Generally, many authors lack in addressing access control policies which is as an essential factor of the security and privacy risk. To address these gaps, this chapter proposed a blockchain driven AIoT architecture employing Hyperledger fabric and ABAC for intelligent as well as secure patient centric health monitoring. The system uses a hybrid model of data storage where sensitive records of patients are kept off-chain, and cryptographic hashes, the consent records, and access logs are kept in blockchain ledger. It enhances scalability and maintains information integrity and transparency. In order to preserve confidentiality, the patient data is encrypted with the help of AES-256-GCM, and the integrity verification is done with the help of SHA-256.

The proposed framework increases the security, auditability, and transparency of access to data compared to the traditional centralized healthcare systems. The enforcement of the access policy is automated by the use of smart contracts and the patient consent is honored during the entire process of sharing the data. Moreover, the architecture will have emergency access mechanisms by using a controlled break-glass policy which allows healthcare providers to access critical patient data during medical emergencies without compromising the audit trails. Altogether, the suggested blockchain-based RPM model shows great possibilities to resolve the current issue in the sphere of healthcare data management, such as data manipulation, unauthorized access, and transparency.

For the future work, extension to the proposed model by implementing and analyzing it under different transaction rate can serve as an effective framework and consensus selection for large scale real time AIoT healthcare systems.

REFERENCES

Al-Nbhany, W. A. N. A., Zahary, A. T., & Al-Shargabi, A. A. (2024). Blockchain-IoT Healthcare Applications and Trends: A Review. *IEEE Access : Practical Innovations, Open Solutions*, *12*(January), 4178–4212. DOI: 10.1109/ACCESS.2023.3349187

Ali, M. S., Vecchio, M., Putra, G. D., Kanhere, S. S., & Antonelli, F. (2020). A Decentralized Peer-to-Peer Remote Health Monitoring System. *Sensors (Basel)*, *20*(6), 1–18. DOI: 10.3390/s20061656 PMID: 32188135

Alkhfaji, A. M. (2023). Blockchain Based Wireless Sensor Networks for Detecting Nodes. *Journal of Smart Internet of Things*, *2023*(2), 1–12. DOI: 10.2478/jsiot-2023-0007

Almukhlifi, R., Al-Khasawneh, M. A., Bukhari, A. A., & Harasis, A. A. A. (2025). Secure e-Health Framework using Artificial Intelligence and Blockchain Technology. *International Journal of Advanced and Applied Sciences*, *12*(2), 52–61. DOI: 10.21833/ijaas.2025.02.006

Ananthi, J. V., & Jose, P. S. H. (2021). A Perspective Review of Security Challenges in Body Area Networks for Healthcare Applications. *International Journal of Wireless Information Networks*, *28*(4), 451–466. DOI: 10.1007/s10776-021-00538-3 PMID: 34690480

Aryai, P., Khademzadeh, A., Jafarali Jassbi, S., Hosseinzadeh, M., Hashemzadeh, O., & Shokouhifar, M. (2023). Real-time health monitoring in WBANs using hybrid Metaheuristic-Driven Machine Learning Routing Protocol (MDML-RP). *AEÜ. International Journal of Electronics and Communications*, *168*(May), 154723. DOI: 10.1016/j.aeue.2023.154723

Aslam, M. S., Altaf, A., Iqbal, F., Nigar, N., Galán, J. C., Aray, D. G., Díez, I., & Ashraf, I. (2024). Novel Model to Authenticate Role-based Medical Users for Blockchain-based IoMT Devices. *PLoS One*, *19*(7), 1–23. DOI: 10.1371/journal.pone.0304774 PMID: 38985779

Azaria, A., Ekblaw, A., Vieira, T., & Lippman, A. (2016). MedRec: Using Blockchain for Medical Data Access and Permission Management. *2016 2nd International Conference on Open and Big Data (OBD)*, 25–30. DOI: 10.1109/OBD.2016.11

Behara, B., Delrobaei, M., & Afraz, N. (2025). Trusted Blockchain-Based Clinical Decision and Medication Management System for Movement Disorders. *IEEE Access : Practical Innovations, Open Solutions*, *13*(August), 139404–139418. DOI: 10.1109/ACCESS.2025.3596693

Belbase, P., Bhusal, R., Ghimire, S. S., Sharma, S., & Banskota, B. (2024). Assuring assistance to healthcare and medicine: Internet of Things, Artificial Intelligence, and Artificial Intelligence of Things. *Frontiers in Artificial Intelligence*, *7*(December), 1–10. DOI: 10.3389/frai.2024.1442254 PMID: 39735232

Buthelezi, N. M., Malele, V., Owolawi, P. A., & Mapayi, T. (2022). IoT Based Health Monitor for Remote Patient. *2022 International Conference on Artificial Intelligence, Big Data, Computing and Data Communication Systems (IcABCD)*, 1–7. DOI: 10.1109/icABCD54961.2022.9856318

Chandra, B., & Kanaga Suba Raja, S. (2024). Security In Wireless Body Area Network (WBAN) Using Blockchain. *Journal of the Institution of Electronics and Telecommunication Engineers*, *70*(1), 487–498. DOI: 10.1080/03772063.2023.2233472

Cheikhrouhou, O., Mershad, K., Laurent, M., & Koubaa, A. (2025). Blockchain and Emerging Technologies for Next Generation Secure Healthcare: A Comprehensive Survey of Applications, Challenges, and Future Directions. *Blockchain: Research and Applications*, *100305*(4), 100305. Advance online publication. DOI: 10.1016/j.bcra.2025.100305

Chen, Y., Meng, L., Zhou, H. & Xue, G. (2021). A Blockchain-Based Medical Data Sharing Mechanism with Attribute-based Access Control and Privacy Protection. *Wireless Communications and Mobile Computing*, (1), 1–12. DOI: 10.1002/wcm.287

Chen, Y., Sun, W., Zhang, N., Zheng, Q., Lou, W., & Hou, Y. T. (2019). Towards Efficient Fine-Grained Access Control and Trustworthy Data Processing for Remote Monitoring Services in IoT. *IEEE Transactions on Information Forensics and Security*, *14*(7), 1830–1842. DOI: 10.1109/TIFS.2018.2885287

Divya, K., & Uma Priyadarsini, P. S. (2024). Defending Delicate Health Information with Corda Blockchain Enabled MAC and UCON-Based Access Controls via IPFS. *International Journal of Performability Engineering*, *20*(1), 48–55. DOI: 10.23940/ijpe.24.01.p7.4855

Gad, A. G., Mosa, D. T., Abualigah, L., & Abohany, A. A. (2022). Emerging Trends in Blockchain Technology and Applications: A Review and Outlook. *Journal of King Saud University. Computer and Information Sciences*, *34*(9), 6719–6742. https://doi.org/https://doi.org/10.1016/j.jksuci.2022.03.007. DOI: 10.1016/j.jksuci.2022.03.007

Garg, S., Kaushal, R. K., & Kumar, N. (2022). Blockchain-based Electronic Health Record and Open Research Challenges. *2022 10th International Conference on Reliability, Infocom Technologies and Optimization (Trends and Future Directions) (ICRITO)*, 1–5. DOI: 10.1109/ICRITO56286.2022.9964648

Garg, S., Kaushal, R. K., & Kumar, N. (2024). A Novel Design and Performance Assessment of a Blockchain-powered Remote Patient Monitoring System. *SN Computer Science*, *5*(7), 849–866. DOI: 10.1007/s42979-024-03151-2

Garg, S., Kaushal, R. K., Kumar, N., & Boonchieng, E. (2024). Exploring Research Challenges of Blockchain and Supporting Technology with Potential Solution in Healthcare. *International Journal of Computing and Digital Systems*, *16*(1), 487–507. DOI: 10.12785/ijcds/160138

Garg, S., Kaushal, R. K., Kumar, N., & Verma, A. (2023). Bibliometric Analysis of Blockchain in The Healthcare Domain. *Intelligent and Converged Networks*, *4*(4), 305–312. DOI: 10.23919/ICN.2023.0025

Harnal, S., & Chauhan, R. K. (2020). Towards Secure, Flexible and Efficient Role based Hospital's Cloud Management System: Case Study. *EAI Endorsed Transactions on Pervasive Health and Technology*, *6*(22), 1–13. DOI: 10.4108/eai.13-7-2018.165497

Hasan, K., Chowdhury, M. J. M., Biswas, K., Ahmed, K., Islam, M. S., & Usman, M. (2022). A blockchain-based secure data-sharing framework for Software Defined Wireless Body Area Networks. *Computer Networks*, *211*(March), 109004. Advance online publication. DOI: 10.1016/j.comnet.2022.109004

Hayes, C. J., Dawson, L., McCoy, H., Hernandez, M., Andersen, J., Ali, M. M., Bogulski, C. A., & Eswaran, H. (2023). Utilization of Remote Patient Monitoring Within the United States Health Care System: A Scoping Review. *Telemedicine Journal and e-Health*, *29*(3), 384–394. DOI: 10.1089/tmj.2022.0111 PMID: 35819861

Imtyaz Ahmed, M., Kannan, G., Ahmed, M. I., & Kannan, G. (2022). Secure and Lightweight Privacy Preserving Internet of Things Integration for Remote Patient Monitoring. *Journal of King Saud University. Computer and Information Sciences*, *34*(9), 6895–6908. DOI: 10.1016/j.jksuci.2021.07.016

Jameer, S., & Syed, H. (2023). A Deep Survey on Human Activity Recognition Using Mobile and Wearable Sensors. *EAI Endorsed Transactions on Pervasive Health and Technology*, *9*(1), 1–12. DOI: 10.4108/eetpht.9.4483

Jamil, F., Ahmad, S., Iqbal, N., & Kim, D. H. (2020). Towards a Remote Monitoring of Patient Vital Signs Based on IoT-based Blockchain Integrity Management Platforms in Smart Hospitals. *Sensors (Basel)*, *20*(8), 1–26. DOI: 10.3390/s20082195 PMID: 32294989

Jayabalan, J., & Jeyanthi, N. (2025). Blockchain and Chainlink Oracle Integration in EHR: Ensuring Real-Time Data Integrity and Interoperability with Ethereum, Hyperledger Fabric and IPFS Storage. *IEEE Access : Practical Innovations, Open Solutions*, *13*(August), 158044–158056. DOI: 10.1109/ACCESS.2025.3606194

Jiang, Y., Xu, X., & Xiao, F. (2022). Attribute-Based Encryption with Blockchain Protection Scheme for Electronic Health Records. *IEEE Transactions on Network and Service Management*, *19*(4), 3884–3895. DOI: 10.1109/TNSM.2022.3193707

Jun, M. (2025). Platform framework for blockchain-enhanced healthcare AIoT systems. *Frontiers in Communications and Networks*, *6*(April), 1–18. DOI: 10.3389/frcmn.2025.1538965

Kaur, J., Rani, R., & Kalra, N. (2024). Attribute-based Access Control Scheme for Secure Storage and Sharing of EHRs using Blockchain and IPFS. *Cluster Computing*, *27*(1), 1047–1061. DOI: 10.1007/s10586-023-04038-2

Kaushal, R. K. & Kumar, N. (2024). Convergence of Blockchain and Internet of Things Using Hyperledger Fabric. *2024 International Conference on Emerging Smart Computing and Informatics, ESCI2024*, 1–5. DOI: 10.1109/ESCI59607.2024.10497226

Kaushal, R. K., Kumar, N., Kukreja, V., & Boonchieng, E. (2025). Hyperledger Fabric based Remote Patient Monitoring Solution and Performance Evaluation. *Peer-to-Peer Networking and Applications*, *18*(3), 1–17. DOI: 10.1007/s12083-025-01921-0

Khan, M. F. F., & Sakamura, K. (2016). A Discretionary Delegation Framework for Access Control Systems. In Debruyne, C., Panetto, H., Meersman, R., Dillon, T., Kühn, E., O'Sullivan, D., & Ardagna, C. A. (Eds.), *On the Move to Meaningful Internet Systems: OTM 2016 Conferences* (pp. 865–882). Springer International Publishing., DOI: 10.1007/978-3-319-48472-3_54

Kongsen, J., Chantaradsuwan, D., Koad, P., Thu, M., & Jandaeng, C. (2024). A Secure Blockchain-Enabled Remote Healthcare Monitoring System for Home Isolation. *Journal of Sensor and Actuator Networks*, *13*(1), 1–20. DOI: 10.3390/jsan13010013

Kumar, H., Kaushal, R. K., Kumar, N. & Malik, P. K. (2024). Comprehensive Analysis of Blockchain Frameworks and Their Usability in Various Applications. *Convergence of Blockchain and Internet of Things in Healthcare*, 243–262. DOI: 10.1201/9781003466949-14

Kumar, H., Kaushal, R. K., Kumar, N., & Verma, A. (2024). An Analytical Study on the Efficacy of Blockchain Frameworks for Student Grievance Management. *SN Computer Science*, *5*(8), 1071. Advance online publication. DOI: 10.1007/s42979-024-03378-z

Liu, H., Han, D., & Li, D. (2020). Fabric-iot: A Blockchain-Based Access Control System in IoT. *IEEE Access : Practical Innovations, Open Solutions*, *8*(1), 18207–18218. DOI: 10.1109/ACCESS.2020.2968492

Marwan, M., Ait Temghart, A., Sifou, F., & AlShahwan, F. (2020). A decentralized blockchain-based architecture for a secure cloud-enabled IoT. *Journal of Mobile Multimedia*, *16*(3), 389–412. DOI: 10.13052/jmm1550-4646.1636

Menon, I. U., Babu Kumaravelu, V., Kumar, V. C., Rammohan, A., Chinnadurai, S., Venkatesan, R., Hai, H., & Selvaprabhu, P. (2025). AI-Powered IoT: A Survey on Integrating Artificial Intelligence With IoT for Enhanced Security, Efficiency, and Smart Applications. *IEEE Access : Practical Innovations, Open Solutions*, *13*(March), 50296–50339. DOI: 10.1109/ACCESS.2025.3551750

Mole, J. S. S., & Shaji, R. S. (2024). Ethereum blockchain for electronic health records: Securing and streamlining patient management. *Frontiers in Medicine*, *11*(September), 1–17. DOI: 10.3389/fmed.2024.1434474 PMID: 39386743

Monrat, A. A., Schelén, O., & Andersson, K. (2022). Applicability Analysis of Blockchain Technology. *2022 IEEE Asia-Pacific Conference on Computer Science and Data Engineering (CSDE)*, 1–8. DOI: 10.1109/CSDE56538.2022.10089307

Monrat, A. A., Schelén, O., & Andersson, K. (2024). A Taxonomy Guideline for Blockchain Platforms. *Journal of Wireless Mobile Networks, Ubiquitous Computing and Dependable Applications*, *15*(2), 286–308. DOI: 10.58346/JOWUA.2024.I2.019

Mukherjee, S., Ray, I., Ray, I., Shirazi, H., Ong, T., & Kahn, M. G. (2017). Attribute Based Access Control for Healthcare Resources. *Proceedings of the 2nd ACM Workshop on Attribute-Based Access Control*, 29–40. DOI: 10.1145/3041048.3041055

Pan, T. (2025). An AIoT-Based Home Monitoring System for Arteriovenous Fistula Surveillance in Hemodialysis Patients: Development, Evaluation, and Clinical Potential. *Journal of Multidisciplinary Healthcare*, *18*, 5313–5326. DOI: 10.2147/JMDH.S531248 PMID: 40904383

Pancari, S., Rashid, A., Zheng, J., Patel, S., Wang, Y., & Fu, J. (2023). A Systematic Comparison between the Ethereum and Hyperledger Fabric Blockchain Platforms for Attribute-Based Access Control in Smart Home IoT Environments. *Sensors (Basel)*, *23*(16), 1–28. DOI: 10.3390/s23167046 PMID: 37631581

Pradhan, N. R., & Singh, A. P. (2021). Performance Analysis of a Blockchain Based Peer-to-Peer Energy Trading Framework. *2021 IEEE 4th International Conference on Computing, Power and Communication Technologies, GUCON 2021*, 1–7. DOI: 10.1109/GUCON50781.2021.9573668

Psarra, E., Apostolou, D., Verginadis, Y., Patiniotakis, I., & Mentzas, G. (2024). Permissioned blockchain network for proactive access control to electronic health records. *BMC Medical Informatics and Decision Making*, *24*(1), 303. Advance online publication. DOI: 10.1186/s12911-024-02708-8 PMID: 39407229

Raj, A., & Prakash, S. (2022). A Privacy-Preserving Authentic Healthcare Monitoring System using Blockchain. *International Journal of Software Science and Computational Intelligence*, *14*(1), 1–23. DOI: 10.4018/IJSSCI.310942

Raj, A., & Prakash, S. (2024). An Efficient Blockchain-Based Access Control Framework for IoT-Healthcare System. *Wireless Personal Communications*, *136*(2), 1017–1045. DOI: 10.1007/s11277-024-11312-y

Ramyasri, G., & Hussain, S. J. (2021). Access Control of Healthcare Data using Blockchain Technology. *2nd International Conference on Smart Electronics and Communication (ICOSEC)*, 353–357. DOI: 10.1109/ICOSEC51865.2021.9591931

Ray, P. P., Dash, D., Salah, K., & Kumar, N. (2021). Blockchain for IoT-Based Healthcare: Background, Consensus, Platforms, and Use Cases. *IEEE Systems Journal*, *15*(1), 85–94. DOI: 10.1109/JSYST.2020.2963840

Sahu, M. L., Atulkar, M., Ahirwal, M. K., & Ahamad, A. (2022). Cloud-Based Remote Patient Monitoring System with Abnormality Detection and Alert Notification. *Mobile Networks and Applications*, *27*(5), 1894–1909. DOI: 10.1007/s11036-022-01960-4

Shahzad, A., Chen, W., Shaheen, M., Zhang, Y., & Ahmad, F. (2024). A Robust Algorithm for Authenticated Health Data Access via Blockchain and Cloud Computing. *PLoS One*, *19*(9), 1–25. DOI: 10.1371/journal.pone.0307039 PMID: 39312513

Shaik, T., Tao, X., Higgins, N., Li, L., Gururajan, R., Zhou, X., & Acharya, U. R. (2023). Remote patient monitoring using artificial intelligence: Current state, applications, and challenges. *Wiley Interdisciplinary Reviews. Data Mining and Knowledge Discovery*, *13*(2), 1–31. DOI: 10.1002/widm.1485

Sharma, K., Kumar, N., & Kaushal, R. K. (2024). Blockchain in Healthcare: Pioneering Transformative Approaches. *2024 IEEE 11th Uttar Pradesh Section International Conference on Electrical, Electronics and Computer Engineering (UPCON)*, 1–6. DOI: 10.1109/UPCON62832.2024.10983842

Sharma, K., Kumar, N., & Kaushal, R. K. (2025). A Study to Investigate Effective Tools and Framework for Blockchain-Based Healthcare Environment. *2025 3rd International Conference on Communication, Security, and Artificial Intelligence, ICCSAI 2025*, 604–609. DOI: 10.1109/ICCSAI64074.2025.11063819

Sharma, K., Kumar, N., Kaushal, R. K., & Verma, A. (2025). Privacy and Trustworthiness in Healthcare: A Blockchain and Attribute Based Access Control Integrated Approach. *SN Computer Science*, *6*(7), 1–15. DOI: 10.1007/s42979-025-04421-3

Sharmila, A. H., & Jaisankar, N. (2021). Edge Intelligent Agent Assisted Hybrid Hierarchical Blockchain for Continuous Healthcare Monitoring & Recommendation System in 5G WBAN-IoT. *Computer Networks*, *200*(1), 1–12. DOI: 10.1016/j.comnet.2021.108508

Shilpi, G., Rajesh Kumar, K., Naveen, K., Anshul, V., Kumar, K., Naveen, K., & Verma, A. (2023). Effective Tools and Technologies for IoT and Blockchain-based Remote Patient Monitoring: A Comparative Analysis. *SN Computer Science*, *4*(6), 844–860. DOI: 10.1007/s42979-023-02288-w

Shinde, R., Patil, S., Kotecha, K., Potdar, V., Selvachandran, G., & Abraham, A. (2024). Securing AI-based Healthcare Systems using Blockchain Technology: A State-of-the-Art Systematic Literature Review and Future Research Directions. *Transactions on Emerging Telecommunications Technologies*, *35*(1), 1–48. DOI: 10.1002/ett.4884

Shuaib, K., Abdella, J., Sallabi, F., & Serhani, M. A. (2022). Secure decentralized electronic health records sharing system based on blockchains. *Journal of King Saud University. Computer and Information Sciences*, *34*(8), 5045–5058. DOI: 10.1016/j.jksuci.2021.05.002

Sim, S. H., & Jeong, Y. S. (2021). Multi-blockchain-based iot data processing techniques to ensure the integrity of iot data in aiot edge computing environments. *Sensors (Basel)*, *21*(10), 3515. Advance online publication. DOI: 10.3390/s21103515 PMID: 34070069

Tagde, P., Tagde, S., Bhattacharya, T., Tagde, P., Chopra, H., Akter, R., Kaushik, D., & Rahman, M. H. (2021). Blockchain and artificial intelligence technology in e-Health. *Environmental Science and Pollution Research International*, *28*(38), 52810–52831. DOI: 10.1007/s11356-021-16223-0 PMID: 34476701

Trivedi, J., Isoaho, J., & Mohammad, T. (2024). A Cloud-based Secure Architecture for Remote Patient Monitoring Integrating OPC UA and Human Digital Twin. *Procedia Computer Science*, *251*(1), 248–255. DOI: 10.1016/j.procs.2024.11.107

Tuler De Oliveira, M., Reis, L. H. A., Verginadis, Y., Mattos, D. M. F., & Olabarriaga, S. D. (2022). SmartAccess: Attribute-Based Access Control System for Medical Records Based on Smart Contracts. *IEEE Access : Practical Innovations, Open Solutions*, *10*(October), 117836–117854. DOI: 10.1109/ACCESS.2022.3217201

Tuli, S., Basumatary, N., Gill, S. S., Kahani, M., Arya, R. C., Wander, G. S., & Buyya, R. (2020). HealthFog: An Ensemble Deep Learning based Smart Healthcare System for Automatic Diagnosis of Heart Diseases in Integrated IoT and Fog Computing Environments. *Future Generation Computer Systems*, *104*(3), 187–200. DOI: 10.1016/j.future.2019.10.043

Uddin, M. A., Stranieri, A., Gondal, I., & Balasubramanian, V. (2018). Continuous Patient Monitoring with A Patient Centric Agent: A Block Architecture. *IEEE Access : Practical Innovations, Open Solutions*, *6*(1), 32700–32726. DOI: 10.1109/ACCESS.2018.2846779

Upadrista, V., Nazir, S., & Tianfield, H. (2023). Secure data sharing with blockchain for remote health monitoring applications: A review. *Journal of Reliable Intelligent Environments*, *9*(3), 349–368. DOI: 10.1007/s40860-023-00204-w PMID: 37359293

V, M. & Singh, K. (2025). Enhancing Security and Privacy of IoMT Data for Unconscious Patient With Blockchain. *IEEE Transactions on Network and Service Management, PP*, 1–15. DOI: 10.1109/TNSM.2025.3602117

Wang, K., Lu, P., & Xin, Z. (2025). Research on Blockchain Privacy Preservation in Healthcare Systems. *2025 11th International Symposium on System Security, Safety, and Reliability (ISSSR)*, 286–290. DOI: 10.1109/ISSSR65654.2025.00048

Wazid, M., Das, A. K., & Park, Y. (2021). Blockchain-Envisioned Secure Authentication Approach in AIoT: Applications, Challenges, and Future Research. *Wireless Communications and Mobile Computing*, *2021*(1), 3866006. Advance online publication. DOI: 10.1155/2021/3866006

Yang, G., Lee, K., Lee, K., Yoo, Y., Lee, H., & Yoo, C. (2022). Resource Analysis of Blockchain Consensus Algorithms in Hyperledger Fabric. *IEEE Access : Practical Innovations, Open Solutions*, *10*(June), 74902–74920. DOI: 10.1109/ACCESS.2022.3190979

Yang, Z., Chen, X., He, Y., Liu, L., Che, Y., Wang, X., Xiao, K., & Xu, G. (2024). An Attribute-based Access Control Scheme using Blockchain Technology for IoT Data Protection. *High-Confidence Computing*, *4*(3), 1–10. DOI: 10.1016/j.hcc.2024.100199

Yaqoob, I., Salah, K., Jayaraman, R., & Al-Hammadi, Y. (2022). Blockchain for Healthcare Data Management: Opportunities, Challenges, and Future Recommendations. *Neural Computing & Applications*, *34*(14), 11475–11490. DOI: 10.1007/s00521-020-05519-w

Zaabar, B., Cheikhrouhou, O., Ammi, M., Awad, A. I., & Abid, M. (2021). Secure and Privacy-aware Blockchain-based Remote Patient Monitoring System for Internet of Healthcare Things. *International Conference on Wireless and Mobile Computing, Networking and Communications, 2021-Octob*, 200–205. DOI: 10.1109/WiMob52687.2021.9606362

Zhang, Q., Xue, X., & Yang, J. (2025). Blockchain-Enabled Trustworthy Healthcare Data Sharing Mechanism for Reliable 6G-IoT Networks. *IEEE Internet of Things Journal, PP*, *1*. Advance online publication. DOI: 10.1109/JIOT.2025.3564782

Zhang, Y., Yutaka, M., Sasabe, M., & Kasahara, S. (2021). Attribute-Based Access Control for Smart Cities: A Smart-Contract-Driven Framework. *IEEE Internet of Things Journal*, *8*(8), 6372–6384. DOI: 10.1109/JIOT.2020.3033434

Chapter 11

Blockchain and Decentralized Identity for AIoT-Based Authentication in Smart Farming and Precision Agriculture

Nitu Tank
http://orcid.org/0009-0001-9782-4764
Poornima University, Jaipur, India

Shikha Khullar
http://orcid.org/0009-0000-5598-3145
Poornima University, Jaipur, India

Bright Keswani
http://orcid.org/0000-0003-1464-0431
Poornima University, Jaipur, India

Rakesh Kumar Saxena
http://orcid.org/0000-0002-6453-6053
Poornima University, Jaipur, India

ABSTRACT

By making smart farming and precision agriculture truly revolutionary, the intersection of Artificial Intelligence of Things (AIoT) and blockchain technology has enabled safe, transparent, and intelligent systems of food production. The major

DOI: 10.4018/979-8-3373-6299-1.ch011

problem in this field is to provide a credible authentication of heterogeneous devices, sensors, and stakeholders and guarantee the integrity and privacy of data. The chapter discusses how blockchain can be implemented together with decentralized identity (DID) systems to provide strong, unaltered authentication systems to AIoT-based agricultural ecosystems. The given approach helps to remove single points of failure, increase accountability, and allow farmers to have a better opportunity to control the ownership and sharing of data by leveraging the distributed ledger technology. Centralized identity promotes cross-agricultural device interoperability, stakeholders in the supply chain, and service providers. The chapter offers a conceptual framework, explains the implementation issues of scalability and energy efficiency.

INTRODUCTION

The fast development of digital technologies is turning the sphere of agriculture into a data-driven and intelligent ecosystem, also known as Smart Farming, or Precision Agriculture. Modern farms are becoming more reliant on interconnected devices, sensors, drones, and intelligent decision-support systems with the adoption of the Artificial Intelligence of Things (AIoT) to streamline the irrigation process, soil health, livestock tracking, and crop yield. Nonetheless, there are also very vital issues of data security, trust, and authentication with the increased dependency on interconnected devices. The common centralized authentication-based systems do not provide the scalability, reliability and privacy concerns of such a complex and distributed agricultural systems. The properties of blockchain technology that will address these challenges include decentralization, immutability, and transparency and have a bright foundation. Through the implementation and development of the Decentralized Identity (DID) solutions, blockchain will have the ability to provide secure, privacy-preserving, and tamper-resistant authentication of the heterogeneous AIoT devices and stakeholders. This decentralized system eliminates the vulnerabilities of points of failure, provides farmers with control and ownership of their digital identities, and enhances the interoperability of various agricultural systems.

As sustainability, resilience, and trust are the main aspects of the Agriculture 6.0 environment, the decentralized identity, based on the blockchain technology, is the innovative path to the implementation of the credible authentication system. In the chapter, the authors introduce the principles, design and implementation of blockchain-based DID in smart farming and precision agriculture. It also covers concerns on the implementation such as energy-saving, scalability and compatibility with the current farming infrastructure and the potential uses such as smart irrigation control, supply chain tracking and livestock authentication. Lastly, the chapter states that the decentralized identity can be utilized to establish secure cooperation, data integriy and execute the global view of intelligent and sustainable digital agriculture.

Figure 1. Evolution of agriculture and enabling technologies across generations (Ag 1.0 to Ag 5.0)

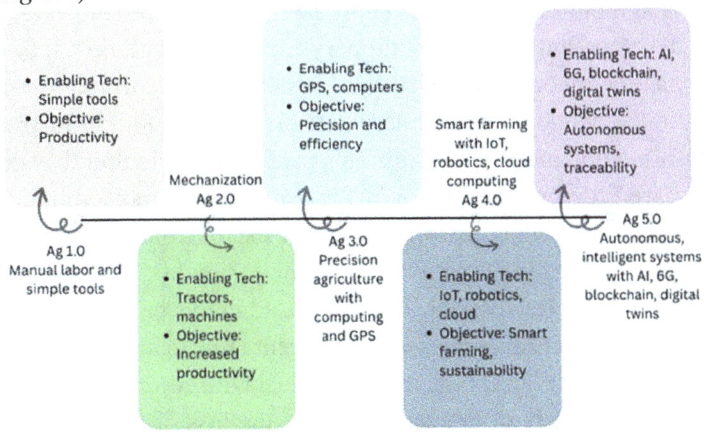

1.1 The Evolution of Agriculture: From Mechanisation to Smart Systems

The last century has witnessed unusual technological advances in agriculture and they have all had an impact in the production, processing and distribution of food. The transition to what is already referred to as the Agriculture 3.0 was a significant digital leap in the food production systems. This was the phase that idealized the pursuit of perfection and precision in farm operations by introducing computing and electrostatic technologies in the agriculture sector. The digital monitoring tools allowed the farmers to collect, process, and utilize data in an orderly way to make the most out of the resources. It became possible to implement site-specific management methods, where only the necessary inputs, like fertilizers, pesticides, and irrigation, are applied and the management approaches reduce waste, increase yields, and help reduce adverse environmental effects (Dayioğlu & Turker, 2021). The Agriculture 3.0 was therefore the foundation to the integration of information technologies in the very center of the agricultural activities.

Following this wave, the first half of the twenty-first century declared the beginning of Agriculture 4.0, an ideology aimed at solving the increasing food insecurity, climate change, and rural poverty. The period is characterized by the meetings of sensors, the Internet of Things (IoT), cloud computing, and robotics along with artificial intelligence (AI)-based decision support systems. All these technologies allowed real time monitoring and autonomous controls of the agricultural processes thus improving efficiency, sustainability and responsiveness. Agriculture 4.0 can be described as interrelated systems that can make data-driven decisions, minimize human involvement and promote precision in the fields of irrigation control, soil diagnostics, and monitoring of crops (Polymeni et al., 2023; Huo et al., 2024).

The last development in this evolutionary flow is Agriculture 5.0 that envisions almost complete autonomy of agricultural systems via incorporation of ultra-fast communication networks like 6G, energy efficient IoT system infrastructures, and AI-based information analytics. Within this paradigm, agricultural systems will be designed to have little human control, made use of autonomous robotics, real time analytics and interconnected platforms to achieve the maximum output. AgriStability 5.0 is needed because of the urgent demographic issue: by 2050, the population of the world is also projected to reach 10 billion, and in this case, it will be necessary to increase food production at least by 70 percent (Karunathilake et al., 2023). Simultaneously, the agricultural industry has to deal with complex limitations such as the decrease in the supply of human resources, the loss of arable land, the lack of water, and the necessity to minimize its carbon footprint (Dayioğlu & Turker, 2021). Therefore, Agriculture 5.0 is not only a technological solution but the reinvention of socioeconomic and environmental necessities and shifts the agricultural industry to the new form of sustainability and resilience (Abu et al., 2022; Dhanararaju et al., 2022).

1.1 Smart Farming emergent technologies.

Digital agriculture or smart farming is a paradigm shift in the agricultural practice, being premised on the integration of modern technologies, such as Information and Communication Technologies (ICT), the Internet of Things (IoT), robotics, Wireless Sensor Networks (WSN), and Artificial Intelligence (AI). Together, the technologies will enable the collection, transmission, and analysis of large data volumes of agronomic and environmental data, including soil moisture rates, crop health indices, actual weather, and animal behavior patterns. This type of data analysis assists in developing actionable knowledge that becomes critical in the optimal use of agricultural assets, waste minimization, and the overall productivity and sustainability (Atalla et al., 2023). The radical potential of the technologies in the agricultural ecosystem is manifested in the social implementation of the IoT based solutions. To give an example, in the Mediterranean, the olive farms have used IoT sensor nodes to scan the environmental status of soil parameters, temperature, and humidity.

The radical potential of the technologies in the agricultural ecosystem is manifested in the social implementation of the IoT based solutions. To give an example, in the

Mediterranean, the olive farms have used IoT sensor nodes to scan the environmental status of soil parameters, temperature, and humidity. The information obtained by these sensors is sent to AI empowered decision support systems which suggest accurate irrigation times, fertilization programs and pest control. The outcome is a tremendous increase in the yield and quality of the production of olive, which is evidence of the usefulness of digital agriculture in streamlining the farming process. (Atalla et al., 2023). Similarly, wearable IoT devices are increasingly being used in livestock systems to track vital health parameters, nutritional status, and movement patterns of animals. This real-time monitoring facilitates early disease detection, reduces mortality rates, improves animal welfare, and minimizes the labor-intensive aspects of traditional livestock management practices (Huo et al., 2024).

Emerging communication infrastructures further amplify the capabilities of smart farming. The advent of sixth-generation (6G) networks, particularly those operating in the Terahertz (THz) spectrum, is expected to revolutionize Agriculture 5.0 and beyond by providing ultra-fast, low-latency, and energy-efficient connectivity. These advanced networks will be pivotal in enabling continuous, high-volume data transmission from large-scale sensor deployments across fields and farms. When coupled with disruptive technologies such as Reconfigurable Intelligent Surfaces (RIS) and Digital Twins, 6G systems will allow highly detailed, real-time monitoring of plant growth and health at the individual plant level. This unprecedented precision supports site-specific and adaptive interventions, ensuring sustainable resource use while enhancing yield and resilience against environmental stressors (Polymeni et al., 2023).

Why Blockchain and IoT Matter for the Future of Agriculture

Internet of Things (IoT) has become a groundbreaking product in the agricultural industry to offer real-time and high-resolution data on various field activities. The IoT-based tools and sensor networks create unceasing streams of data concerning soil quality, crop health, the weather, the behavior of livestock, and resource use. Although this data is most beneficial in enhancing efficiency and decision-making, it is a challenge to guarantee that it is of high quality in terms of integrity, transparency, and traceability even in the complexity of the agri-food ecosystems. Farmers, distributors, regulators, retailers, and consumers are often the decentralized actors in agricultural supply chains distributed across several geographies. In this case, blockchain technology will be necessary. Working as a decentralized and immutable ledger, blockchain can authenticate the authenticity of the data produced by the IoT sensor network and automate transactions with the help of smart contracting and creating more trust in stakeholders (Sendros et al., 2022).

A number of blockchain solutions have already been shown to have a potential impact on improving the security and transparency in agricultural supply chains. As an example, in the case of IBM Food Trust, Ambrosus, and TE-FOOD, there are platforms available to monitor the origin, quality, and route of food products produced at the farms to consumers. These systems enable the regulating authorities and consumers to check production processes and adherence to safety measures and gain trust in the authenticity of food. In addition to traceability, blockchain also promotes fair business activities. An example of such initiatives, which applies blockchain to fix their payments to the producers, is FairChain, which minimizes the use of intermediaries and imposes smart contract-based transactions. Equally, Etherisc is a company that uses blockchain in crop insurance, allowing automated payments to be made, depending on sensor-based data about the farms, so that claims can be processed faster and farmers become more financially stable (Sendros et al., 2022).

The major strength of blockchain is that it is immutable and cryptographically secured so that no one can modify or delete the data recorded. This property, together with IoT, will provide an extra protection against the potential of tampering or unauthorized manipulation of agricultural data. Blockchain is therefore considered as a safe data repository of the information generated through IoT, which ensures effective data auditing and responsibility of the agricultural activities. The synergy is especially applicable in the Agriculture 5.0 paradigm that is defined by the implementation of autonomous farming based on AI and robotics. The said systems rely on trusted, cooperative, and violation-resistant datasets to maintain secure decision-making and carrying out of farming tasks (Piancharoenwong & Badir, 2024).

Combined use of blockchain, IoT, artificial intelligence (AI), and machine learning is now seen as the technology foundation of the creation of sustainable, resilient, and transparent food systems. The ability of blockchain to bridge the disconnected agri-food networks of the past has been shown by the Ripe.io pilot project, which has proven that consumers can receive quality-certified products with verifiable provenance. These pilot projects are also a demonstration of the scalability of blockchain usage, and it can be expanded to the mainstream of agriculture (Dhanararaju et al., 2022).

The Convergence of IoT and Precision Agriculture

The advent of intelligent agriculture has been directly connected with the creation of data-driven technologies that allow making informed, timely, and site-specific decisions. One of them is the blockchain technology that has been identified as a critical enabler concerning its decentralized, unalterable, and secure properties.

The conventional agricultural information systems also have their share of failures, including, but not limited to one point of failure, whereby centralized databases are likely to crash or be attacked; data manipulation, which weakens the authenticity of records; and information asymmetry, whereby some stakeholders are not able to access the right information in the right time. The blockchain technology can be an efficient way of overcoming these issues and providing a way to document agricultural data in a transparent, secure, and verifiable way that can be checked by every stakeholder in the ecosystem (Meilin Guo et al., 2024).

Combined with the Internet of Things (IoT), blockchain reinforces the principles of precision agriculture based on which it is very important to collect and analyze data correctly. IoT agronomic sensors (soil sensor), drones, automatic irrigation, satellite-based surveillance devices, and other devices continuously generate massive amounts of agronomic data (soil, moisture, crop, and environment variables). Using blockchain to store and share such data, farmers and stakeholders can develop more trust in the credibility of insights made by IoT. This convergence does not just improve the decision-making process but also reduces risks of fraud, data manipulation, and inefficiencies that have in the past limited the agricultural information systems (Meilin Guo et al., 2024).

This part is thus intended to discuss three major areas of IoT and precision agriculture convergence. It will then follow the historical development of precision agriculture which has seen farming evolve beyond mechanization and to data-driven and intelligent farming. Second, it will examine the layered structure of the IoT systems in agriculture that places emphasis on the sensing, network, data management and application layers that contribute towards the smart farming. Lastly, it will also point out some actual applications that have incorporated the usage of IoT in the precision farming practices and how blockchain can also be used to guarantee integrity of data, transparency and trust among stakeholders. All these discussions will demonstrate how IoT and blockchain can be used as a synergizing enabling structure towards developing Agriculture 6.0 (Meilin Guo et al., 2024).

Precision Agriculture: Principles and Progress

Precision Agriculture (PA) is a not so old phenomenon in the modern agriculture industry where it is suggested that digital technologies could be used to trace, calculate, and optimize the use of agricultural inputs such as water, fertilizers, and pesticides. In essence, PA targets to understand and manage spatial and temporal variability of fields and fields. PA will also solve this variability, in real time, observations, measurements, and the variability response that will increase the crop productivity, resource efficiency and sustainability in agriculture systems (Alahmad et al., 2023). As opposed to conventional ways of farming whereby a large portion of land is treated in similar fashion, PA enables site-specific treatment strategies and each area of a field will receive the necessary input, it will reduce wastage and reduce the environmental impact.

Introducing the use of Internet of Things (IoT) technologies has been an enormous supplement to the activities of PA. It now has soil sensors, aerial drones and satellite imaging platforms that provide real-time data on important agriculture variables (plant health, soil moisture, temperature, humidity, and pest infestation) through continuous streams of information. A drone with many sensors might be applied to diagnose the initial signs of crop distress, for example, in the field, sensors might be monitoring changes in soils, and farmers can respond early (Dhanararaju et al., 2022). Such IoT technologies combined with Artificial Intelligence (AI) enhance proactive decisions, offering intelligent information concerning the irrigation timetable, nutrient control and pest control. Wireless Sensor Network (WSNs) also help in this integration; it offers precise suggestions to the use of water so that the irrigation resources can be used to their maximum advantage. This minimizes the resources wasting and the environmental degradation and in the same breath increases the yield and quality of the crops (Ahmad et al., 2022).

Despite these developments, several obstacles to adoption of PA exist. Poor infrastructure of most of the areas is a significant deterrent that limits high-tech application. The high upfront investment costs are also not an incentive to small resource and limited capacity farmers to adopt sophisticated systems. Furthermore, the farmers are not technologically trained to utilize, handle and analyze data recorded by PA technologies to ensure that their widespread usage is not always possible (Ali et al., 2023). Besides these issues, other issues such as data management, privacy, long term maintenance among others complicate adoption. The hesitation of many stakeholders is caused by the uncertainty of investor returns, technical stability, and system supportability (Hundal et al., 2023; Karunathilake et al., 2023). The existence of these obstacles underscores the necessity of the adoption of policies, training programs, and affordable technological solutions that would help in closing the divide between innovation and actual use on the farm.

2.2 IoT Architecture in Agricultural Systems

A typical IoT framework for agriculture comprises four layers: perception, network (communication), data processing, and application (Ruan et al., 2019). Each layer contributes uniquely to smart farming capabilities. The perception layer includes all of the physical sensing components that will score environmental, plant, and soil data, which includes moisture, EC, and pH (Dhanaraju et al., 2022).

In the communication layer, Sensors forward the data collected in observed environment to the cloud or local servers using technologies such as LoRa, Wi-

Fi, and Zigbee. However, such a network is also exposed to restrictions; like, low communication range interference and data latency (Quy et al., 2022). In the Data Processing layer, sensor data are aggregated,

filtered and analysed by cloud platforms and edge computing nodes. AI models and machine learning apply to predictive analytics such as forecasting yield and anomaly detection (Ahmad et al., 2022).

Next, in the Edge-Blockchain Integration Layer, the edge nodes (e.g., Raspberry Pi 4 with blockchain modules) prepare sensor sets for pre-processing before hashing and storing the data in distributed ledgers to mitigate the latency and security risks. This implies real-time checks on field events such as irrigation triggers while reducing the dependency on cloud-based storage. As an example, Ktari et al. (2022) have conducted studies regarding the application of SHA-256 hashing on olive farm data generated by Arduino, whereby there was a reduction of about 92% in trials on fraud risks in the data.

The final Application Layer is where farmers are provided with actionable insights through mobile apps, dashboards, or automated actuators Some of these actionable insights consist of scheduling irrigation smartly and optimizing fertilizer and pest alert systems (Ali et al., 2023). Blockchain may therefore, add security and integrity to the data handled across such layers. For instance, a decentralized ledger may allow tamper-proof event logging of activities such as the application of pesticides and water, and a smart contract might facilitate automation of compliance and traceability for such supply chains in the agri-food sector (Meilin Guo et al., 2024).

1.2 Integration Benefits and Use Cases

IoT applications can be implemented in precision agriculture to offer advantages like Smart Irrigation, Greenhouse Management, Livestock Monitoring, Aquaponics and Product Traceability. Smart Irrigation- Real-time soil moisture levels and weather forecasts can enable a self-driving delivery system for water, avoiding over-irrigation and resulting in productivity while maintaining sustainable alternatives available (Quy et al., 2022).

Greenhouse Management- IoT sensors can be adopted to control conditions-they affect the temperature, humidity, light, and nutrient levels-have all been put in place to optimise the crop growth condition, save energy, and reduce manual labour (Quy et al., 2022; Dhanaraju et al., 2022). Livestock Monitoring- IoT-based veterinary systems, such as VetLink, provide services such as animal health diagnosis, while IC-tag systems monitor behaviour in operation at large farms with pigs (Quy et al., 2022).

Aquaponics- Here, integrated systems monitor the pH level, the temperature, and the water quality and automate feeding schedules, thus raising the productivity of both plants and fish (Quy et al., 2022). Product traceability- Itemising the food lifecycle from farm to fork can be controlled by the IoT systems empowered with blockchain so that their natural development managers are monitored under food safety and compliance (Meilin Guo et al., 2024).

These examples illustrate the tremendous amount of potential that IoT, blockchain and precision agriculture all possess to revolutionise agricultural practices. However, there cannot be a complete actualisation of such potential without addressing issues around scalability,

standardisation, affordability, and the literacy of users. Table 1 provides a summary of some standard IoT-enabled use cases in precision agriculture and their enabling technologies.

Table 1. Representative IoT use cases in precision agriculture and their associated technologies

Use Case	Primary Sensors/Devices	Detailed Outcome/Benefit
Smart Irrigation	Soil moisture sensors, weather stations, flow meters, pressure sensors	Enables precise, automated irrigation scheduling based on real-time soil and weather data; reduces water wastage, improves crop water-use efficiency, and prevents over-irrigation that may lead to nutrient leaching.
Greenhouse Management	Temperature and humidity sensors, CO_2 monitors, light sensors, actuators	Facilitates continuous monitoring of microclimatic conditions; enables automated regulation of ventilation, lighting, and nutrient delivery, ensuring optimal plant growth and energy efficiency.
Livestock Monitoring	RFID tags, GPS trackers, biosensors, wearable IoT collars	Supports real-time tracking of animal movement, health, and feeding patterns; generates early alerts for disease detection, reduces mortality, enhances animal welfare, and saves labor costs.
Aquaponics	pH sensors, dissolved oxygen (DO) sensors, temperature sensors, turbidity sensors	Monitors water quality parameters critical for integrated aquaculture and hydroponics; automates feeding, maintains balance between fish and plant systems, improves yield, and ensures sustainable production.
Product Traceability	IoT-integrated Blockchain (QR codes, IC-tags, RFID scanners, mobile apps)	Provides secure, tamper-proof tracking of food products from farm to consumer; enhances transparency, builds trust among stakeholders, ensures compliance with safety standards, and supports fair trade practices.

2. BLOCKCHAIN: A FOUNDATION FOR TRUST AND TRANSPARENCY

In the context of precision agriculture, vast amounts of data are generated daily from IoT-enabled devices, including climate conditions, soil quality, crop health metrics, and logistics information. For this data to provide meaningful value, it must be secure, authentic, and auditable. Conventional agri-food systems rely heavily on centralized databases and manual documentation processes, which often introduce inefficiencies, data silos, and vulnerabilities to tampering or manipulation. Such centralized structures lack transparency and make it difficult for stakeholders to establish trust in data validity. Blockchain technology addresses these limitations by introducing a decentralized, immutable, and tamper-proof ledger system that fundamentally reshapes trust management in agriculture. Through blockchain, every transaction or record is secured cryptographically and validated in real-time, without the need for third-party intermediaries. This ensures that agricultural operations evolve into trustless but verifiable systems, where accuracy, transparency, and accountability are embedded within the very architecture of the data infrastructure.

3. BLOCKCHAIN AND AGRI-FOOD SUPPLY CHAINS

Agri-food supply chains are one of the areas where blockchain has had the most significant applications; they are usually disorganized and complicated. The technology helps to directly solve some of the key challenges, i.e. product traceability, phase of information asymmetry, and consumer trust. With blockchain-based systems, all operations of the supply chain, including sourcing of seeds, application of fertilizers, harvesting, storage, processing and distribution of the products through retail chains, are recorded in a distributed registry; and is accessible to all supply chain participants. Every entry of this ledger is cryptographically connected to the previous block and it will be computationally infeasible to modify or erase historical records (Meilin Guo et al., 2024). The architecture removes data silos and provides end-to-end visibility, whereby the stakeholders can track the life cycle of agricultural products. Its advantages are spread in several levels of the food ecosystem. Quick and accurate tracing of the source of contamination in the case of food safety incidents can be achieved by regulators and this aspect will significantly reduce the response time. The retailers, they are enabled to test the authenticity and quality of agricultural produce and the consumers are provided with verifiable information to the origin, handling practices and sustainability claims. There is consensus in blockchain which means that new transactions can only be added after being confirmed by more than one party, which removes risks of fraud, misinformation, and false labeling.

One of the most useful contributions made to agri-food systems by blockchain is provenance tracking. Blockchain enhances the observance of food safety regulations through the availability of detailed and impervious records of farm-level operations, harvesting of products, and after-harvest operations. In addition, it promotes the transparency of other environmentally and socially responsible consumers who are getting more and more demanding of accountability in ethical sourcing and sustainable production practices (Ehsan et al., 2022). Through this, blockchain will make agri-food supply chains transparent, traceable, and trustworthy ecosystems, and make integrity and accountability no longer optional, but part of agri-food supply chains.

3.2 Role of Smart Contracts

Adoption of smart contracts which are in effect automated software protocols that run on the blockchain is one of the strongest extensions of blockchain technology. In contrast to the typical contracts where people have to provide the control, validation, or mediation of a third party, smart contracts impose agreed-upon rules when predefined conditions are met. This ability is then applied to the vast number of application cases in the agricultural scenarios. To illustrate, smart contracts can automatically disburse payments when a shipment has been confirmed as being at its destination, or can automatically initiate an insurance claim when an IoT sensor records that a crop has been damaged because of adverse weather conditions. Through implementing this kind of logic directly on blockchain networks, smart contracts have greatly decreased delays, eliminated bureaucratic bottlenecks, and eliminated the need to have intermediaries present.

This automation can be of great benefit especially in the agricultural sector and typically many of the involved actors are dispersed including farmers, cooperatives, distributors and government agencies. Smart contracts can be used to provide timely payments to buyers and suppliers, directly provide government subsidies and agricultural grants to farmers as smallholders and not through intermediaries, and apply standards of compliance by connecting sensor data to regulatory compliance. What it causes is operational efficiency, as well as increased trust and equity in agri-food systems. Ehsan et al. (2022) explain that a conceptual blockchain-based supply chain in agriculture is that in which the smart contract is used to maintain transparency of the procurement process, ensure that transactions are recorded immutably, and also provides the opportunity to trace the provenance of food safety.

3.3 Architecture and Implementation

In addition to theoretical models, practical examples have shown that blockchain-based systems of smart agriculture could work. Ktari et al. (2022) introduce a light traceability architecture based on blockchains, which was created to operate within the olive oil supply chain. This system was created to support the requirement of transparent provenance and guard sensitive data in various stakeholders. Farmers, olive oil manufacturers, quality inspectors, and transport providers in the architecture have their own personal private Quorum blockchains, which they use to handle confidential information. At the same time, all players share a common Ethereum blockchain, which records collaborative transactions across the supply chain. Through the technical setup, the environmental data are recorded using IoT gadgets and the data are valuable in manufacturing of olive oil. Measurement parameters are humidity, salinity, temperature, and CO_2 level, which are measured by sensors. They may serve as blockchain nodes, and serve as an agent to the Ethereum blockchain with a Web3 protocol on an Arduino board or Raspberry Pi controller. The acquired data is subjected to calculation and data gets exchanged via smart contracts, with the help of which all transactions are conducted with traceability. The process of the oils start with the picking of the olives till the processing of the oil itself, quality inspection, and delivery, is all stored permanently on the shared blockchain.

One of the major advantages of such a hybrid architecture is the fact that it allows balancing data privacy and transparency. The sensitive details are kept as private Quorum chains, whereas vital public records are kept on the Ethereum, so we can be accountable to both and keep the information confidential. As an example, the records of the conditions of transportation (i.e. GPS route or temperature readings during transportation) are encrypted, and then permanently stored on the blockchain. This will guarantee both consumers and producers can access supply chain information that is verifiable and unchangeable. Finally, the architecture ensures end-to-end traceability, consumer confidence in product authenticity and a replicable model to be applied in other agricultural industries that want to use blockchain-based solutions.

Figure 2. Hybrid blockchain architecture for the olive oil supply chain (Ktari et al., 2022)

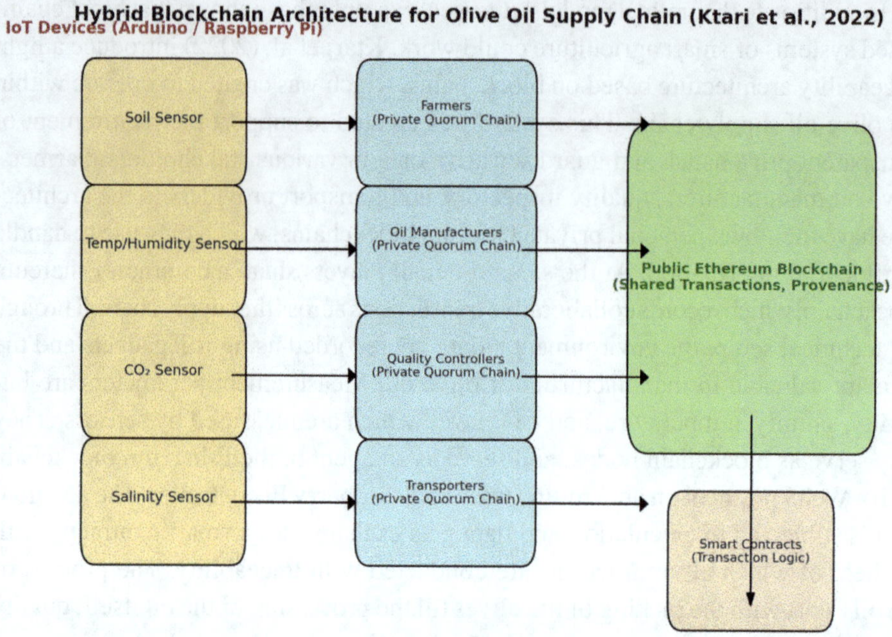

Figure 2 shows of the hybrid blockchain architecture for the olive oil supply chain (from Ktari et al., 2022):

- IoT Devices (Arduino/Raspberry Pi) → collect sensor data (soil, temperature, humidity, CO_2, salinity).
- Private Quorum Blockchains → managed by different actors (farmers, oil manufacturers, quality controllers, transporters) to secure sensitive information.
- Public Ethereum Blockchain → stores shared transactions and provenance records accessible to all stakeholders.
- Smart Contracts → automate transaction logic (traceability, payments, quality verification).

Table 2. Representative smart contract applications in agriculture

Application Area	Smart Contract Function	Outcome/Benefit	Reference
Automated Payments	Trigger payment release once delivery/shipment is verified on blockchain	Eliminates delays, reduces disputes, ensures trust between buyers and suppliers	Ehsan et al., 2022
Crop Insurance	Automatically activates insurance claims based on IoT sensor data (e.g., drought, flood)	Provides timely compensation to farmers, reduces bureaucracy, increases financial security	Szabo (concept), Ethereum platforms
Subsidy & Grants Distribution	Disburses government subsidies or agricultural grants directly to farmers via coded conditions	Removes intermediaries, ensures transparency, targets rightful beneficiaries	Ehsan et al., 2022
Supply Chain Traceability	Records provenance data (farm activities, harvest time, transport logs) on blockchain	Enhances food safety compliance, supports sustainability, increases consumer trust	Ehsan et al., 2022
Compliance Monitoring	Links IoT sensor data with regulatory standards (e.g., pesticide limits, storage temperature)	Automates compliance checks, reduces fraud, builds credibility with regulators and conscious consumers	Ehsan et al., 2022; Ktari et al., 2022

3.5 Advantages over Traditional Systems

Blockchain-integrated systems provide significant advantages over centralised or paper-based supply chain systems, as summarised in Table 3.

Table 3.

Feature	Traditional Agri-Food Systems	Blockchain-Enabled Systems
Traceability	Partial or manual, prone to errors	End-to-end, automated, immutable
Transparency	Limited; stakeholders hold separate records	Unified ledger visible to all authorised parties
Data Security	Centralised, vulnerable to tampering	Decentralised and tamper-proof
Contract Enforcement	Requires intermediaries (lawyers, banks)	Automated via smart contracts
Response to Contamination/Fraud	Slow; difficult to track	Instantaneous tracking and source identification
Cost and Time	High due to intermediaries and paperwork	Reduced through automation and direct interaction
Trust and Consumer Confidence	Low; dependent on labels or audits	High; consumers can verify source and quality data

Smart contracts further enhance the system by reducing delays and improving efficiency in transactions such as insurance settlements, logistics payments, and certifications. Consumers can verify the origin, storage conditions, and quality checks of products by simply scanning QR codes connected to the blockchain records. Moreover, the integration of IoT and blockchain technologies results in significant resource savings across various agricultural operations, as detailed in Table 3.

Table 4. Resource savings from IoT-blockchain integration

Technology	Resource Optimized	Reductio n	Validation Study
IoT Smart Irrigation + Blockchain Auditing	Water Usage	30-50%	Dhanaraju et al. (2022)
AI Fertiliser Models + Smart Contracts	Chemical Inputs	20-35%	Bermeo-Almeida et al. (2018)
Blockchain Supply Chains	Food Waste	22%	IBM Food Trust (2023)

Key Applications of Blockchain in Smart Farming

Smart farming has leveraged blockchain technology as a means of creating new efficiencies in transparency and traceability, automation, authentication, and fraud prevention across the agricultural value chain. Blockchain provides internal verification and an immutable active ledger, granting all stakeholders access to upfront data sharing and verifiable real-time data tracking. This section delineates the most significant application areas in precision agriculture where blockchain technology provides high-impact applications.

4.1. Agricultural Supply Chain Management

The most important and core feature set of the application of blockchain in smart agriculture is the transformation of supply chain processes. Traditional supply chains remain non-transparent with slow traceability and a heavier reliance on intermediaries.

Provenance of Product and End-to-End Visibility: Blockchain allows for digital tracking of each unit of food or produce from farm to table. For instance, the olive oil supply chain model proposed by Ktari et al. (2022) uses the Ethereum and Quorum blockchains together with IoT sensors (e.g., CO_2 and temperature monitoring) to track product status across farmers, manufacturers, quality agents, and transporters (Ktari et al., 2022).

Smart Contracts for Automation: Smart contracts on the blockchain can execute supply chain tasks such as payment, delivery confirmation, and regulatory compliance automatically. The blockchain-based agricultural model presented by Ehsan et al. (2022) allows for the ease of such steps to be carried out by Ethereum smart contracts (Ehsan et al., 2022).

Data Integrity and Transparency: The immutable nature of blockchain ledgers inspires stakeholder trust in food safety, quality certifications, and logistics records (Meilin Guo et al., 2024). Table 5 summarises key blockchain applications across smart farming domains, highlighting real-world examples and their functional roles.

Table 5. Blockchain applications across agricultural domains

Application Area	Blockchain Role	Example or Use Case Reference
Supply Chain Management	Product tracking, smart contracts, and tamper-proof records	Olive oil traceability (Ktari et al., 2022); Ethereum-based automation (Ehsan et al., 2022)
Land Registry	Immutable land records, asset-backed loans	Digitised land ledgers for credit access (Ehsan et al., 2022)
Input Traceability	Verified seed/chemical sources, certification integrity	Fertiliser tracking, seed lineage (Meilin Guo et al., 2024)
Crop Insurance	Smart contract-triggered payouts based on IoT data	Parametric insurance and yield loss claims (Ehsan et al., 2022)
Agricultural Finance	Tokenised payments, P2P lending, and cooperative governance	Stablecoins for farmers, pooled fund access (Meilin Guo et al., 2024)

4.2. Land Registry and Ownership Verification

Land records in many nations are highly susceptible to tampering, duplication, and loss. As a solution, these records can be digitally transformed into a robust land ownership system. By leveraging blockchain technology, land ownership can be digitised and securely registered, allowing for transparent verification by governments and third-party verifiers (Ehsan et al., 2022).

When land ownership is documented on blockchain, it also facilitates asset verification, which plays an important role in improving financial inclusion. Ownership verification makes it easier for farmers to access insurance services and credit facilities, thereby improving their long-term financial stability (World Bank, 2021; inferred from use-case applications in Ehsan et al., 2022).

4.3. Input Traceability and Certification

It is therefore required to utilise seeds, fertiliser, and agrochemicals with traceable origin to provide quality and a level of sustainability. With its function as conclusive record keepers of information relating to seed authenticity and purity, such as genetic characteristics, supplier details, and seed pedigree, blockchain enables this. This is particularly useful in organic farming and highly regulated settings (Meilin Guo et al., 2024).

Moreover, blockchain improves chemical input traceability by noting fertiliser and pesticide batch numbers and application protocols, reducing the occurrence of illicit or counterfeit products entering the supply chain significantly (Ehsan et al., 2022). Certification bodies can also upload audit results onto the blockchain, creating a tamper-proof record allowing for verifiable, trustless compliance in export as well as domestic markets (Meilin Guo et al., 2024).

4.4. Crop Insurance and Weather Data Management

These potential weather-indexed insurance automations, claim genuineness, and reduction of payment delays are achievable at the nexus of blockchain and IoT technology. Parametric

insurance covers, for example, use decentralised blockchain smart contracts based on automated-execution triggers, utilising live weather and sensor feeds, such as amounts of rainfall, to provide farmers prompt and impartial compensation (Meilin Guo et al., 2024; Ehsan et al., 2022). Furthermore, aggregation of drone or remote sensing survey data, safely archived in blockchain, ensures tamper-evident records of crop loss, making damage more legitimate (Ktari et al., 2022). Eventually, blockchain histories also enable insurers and financial institutions to estimate the risk profile of individual farmers using an auditable history of past transactions and harvest levels, enabling more accurate underwriting and lending.

4.5. Blockchain-Based Agricultural Finance

Thanks to blockchain-based decentralised finance models, rural farming communities traditionally missing out on good banking opportunities can now enjoy access to quick, affordable, and transparent financial services. Farmers already enjoy access to stablecoin or digital token-based microtransactions to facilitate instant and global payments or remittances (Ehsan et al., 2022). Also, smart contract-based systems that allow open management of collective funds and payments are beneficial to smallholder cooperatives (Meilin Guo et al., 2024). Also, blockchain supports peer-to-peer crowdfunding platforms, which allow donors to track the use and management of their money in real time (Meilin Guo et al., 2024). This integration of technology provides numerous benefits, ranging from enhanced transparency to high financial inclusion, as noted in Table 6.

Table 6. Key benefits of blockchain in smart agriculture

Benefit	Description	Enabled By
Traceability	Real-time, end-to-end product tracking	Immutable distributed ledger
Automation	Smart contracts execute payments, insurance, or certifications	Ethereum, Hyperledger
Fraud Reduction	Reduced counterfeiting of inputs or land records	Cryptographic integrity and auditing
Financial Inclusion	Microloans and digital payments to unbanked farmers	Tokenisation and decentralised finance
Sustainability & Compliance	Transparent audits and certifications for exports and standards	On-chain certification and IoT data

Challenges and Research Gaps

Despite blockchain precision farming and smart agriculture gaining momentum, many obstacles are remaining before they are sufficiently commercially viable to be adopted widely and operate successfully. These range from technology to the economy, infrastructure, legislation, and socio-culture.

5.1. Barriers to Technology Adoption

The single biggest hindrance to smart agriculture is the unwillingness of farmers to embrace new technologies such as AI, IoT, and blockchain. One key reason for resistance is digital illiteracy and technical know-how. Most farmers lack adequate insight into AI-based analytics, data platforms, or blockchain systems, and therefore, it is challenging for them to work with or rely on these tools (Samadi, 2025). The initial investment that would be required to implement cutting-edge technologies like drones, environmental sensors, blockchain nodes, and smart irrigation networks is another significant barrier to entry. This is particularly daunting to resource-poor farmers (Gupta et al., 2020; Tiwari et al., 2024). Human trust, emotional acceptance, and perceived productivity benefits strongly influence AI adoption in smart farming environments (Khullar et al., 2026).

Cultural resistance and behaviour also contribute to this challenge. Traditional farming communities often resist change, especially when new systems are perceived as unreliable or overly complicated (Mansoor et al., 2025).

Infrastructure Limitations and Connectivity Gaps

The intelligent farming display systems rely essentially on ongoing data consolidation with a robust cloud server backbone and their real-time interaction with the devices. Several infrastructural constraints exist, though:

Limited rural connectivity: Inadequate or intermittent internet availability in rural and remote locations constrains productivity with IoT devices concerning capacity for real-time monitoring and prevents complete integration of systems (Samadi, 2025).

Power supply limitation: Most IoT devices operate on persistent power. Therefore, where providing electricity is unstable or a renewable energy system is not feasible, such devices wind up operating inefficiently and get their lifespan cut short (Rajak et al., 2023).

5.2. Cybersecurity and Data Ownership Concerns

With the increased connectivity of farms, the risk of cyberattacks rises by leaps and bounds. The major issues are Data privacy, System Vulnerability, Device Security and Data Poisoning Attacks, which are discussed in this section.

Data Privacy: Farmers are great data generators, with volumes of data describing the health of their crops, yield, and resource usage. However, data ownership remains an area with

ambiguities and has been a nagging issue leading to reluctance in sharing this information with third-party platforms (Wiseman et al., 2019; Demestichas et al., 2020).

System Vulnerability: IoT-based systems are prone to ransomware attacks, data manipulation, and denial of service (DoS). With these kinds of threats, operations could be impaired (Yazdinejad et al., 2021; Liu et al., 2020).

Device Security: Many of the sensors that are in the field do not have strong computation capabilities needed for implementing a security protocol robust enough to withstand forceful attacks or do not compromise their security by being physically damaged, hacked, or subjected to sleep deprivation attacks to exhaust their battery life (Sarma & Barbhuiya, 2019). Advanced ensemble learning approaches integrated with blockchain can strengthen anomaly detection, intrusion prevention, and integrity assurance in distributed IoT ecosystems (Khullar et al., 2025).

Data Poisoning Attacks: This includes the introduction of false sensor readings (e.g. fake soil moisture data) into AI models by malicious actors. Blockchain timestamping and multi-signature validation (configuring the requirement of 3+ farm nodes to confirm data) have been found to reduce at least 78% of the attack success rates (Yazdinejad et al., 2021).

5.3. Data Quality, Sensor Reliability, and Scalability of ML Models

AI and machine learning decisions in smart farming are increasingly being informed by sensor-generated data. However, exposure to the environment poses a major challenge. Sensors positioned outdoors are often subject to deterioration due to rain, dust, heat, and corrosion, which can lead to inaccurate or incomplete data and compromise the precision of conclusions. Also, such sensors, especially NPK and pH sensors, need frequent calibration and maintenance. Unless maintained well, they can generate incorrect or completely unusable data, compromising the efficacy of AI-based agriculture interventions (Gupta et al., 2020).

Generalizability of machine learning models is also a problem of great importance. Unreal extreme variances in environments will deny models developed in a given climatic or geographical region from working efficiently in another. Scalability and real-world applications of AI-based systems in varied agricultural zones are constrained by the inability to cope (Samadi, 2025; Mansoor et al., 2025).

5.4. Compatibility, Standardisation, and System Integration

The heterogeneous nature of smart farming systems complicates integration:

Interoperability is such a lacking feature: Devices supplied by distinct vendors may not even be working in compatible formats of data, APIs, or protocols. This leads to fragmentation of the system and hinders integrated decision-making (Koduru & Koduru, 2022).

Standardization is needed: There is an increasing need for an international standard that will regulate how the interconnect assorted sensors, platforms, and analytics systems. Without this, the easy scalability of the solutions remains a huge barrier (Onike, 2025).

5.5. Socioeconomic and Training Gaps

In addition to the technical issue, there is a significant socioeconomic gap in access to smart farming equipment. IoT and blockchain technologies have thus far disproportionately favoured larger, more affluent farms, with smallholder farmers not having the capital or infrastructure to implement them optimally (Tiwari et al., 2024). This gap is further widened by the lack of training programs. Most farmers do not have the necessary information and skills to run blockchain systems, digital platforms, and Internet of Things devices. If training is offered, its practical impact is minimal because it is either too theoretical or non-existent for routine farm use (McCaig et al., 2023).

Labour displacement is another concern as autonomous systems begin to replace traditional farming roles. This transition may reduce the need for low-skilled labour, risking social disruption in rural communities unless comprehensive retraining programs are provided (Mansoor et al., 2025). A wide range of interrelated challenges—spanning economic, educational, and social dimensions continues to inhibit the adoption of blockchain-IoT technologies in agriculture.

5.6. Research Gaps and Future Investigation Areas

The array of challenges presented here can be met with appropriate actions taken at some defined levels of technical, behavioural, and policy research. Table 7 shows the mapping of these challenging categories to their normally accepted gaps in research and highlights significant directions thereof for concern in future. Future systems should also integrate resilient privacy-preserving communication mechanisms for sustainable decentralized identity management (Andriani et al., 2026).

Table 7. Challenges and corresponding research gaps

Challenge Category	Specific Challenges	Key Research Gaps
Technology Adoption	Digital literacy, cost, resistance, and regulations	Behavioural models, low-cost systems, policy frameworks
Infrastructure & Connectivity	Internet and power limitations	Rural connectivity models (e.g., satellite/6G), energy-efficient hardware
Cybersecurity & Data	Data privacy, attacks, and unclear ownership	Blockchain security standards, distributed data ownership models
Sensor Reliability & ML	Environmental damage, calibration, and model generalizability	Durable sensors, edge/federated learning for localisation
Integration & Standards	Vendor lock-in, lack of interoperability	Standardised APIs and data protocols for agri-IoT
Socioeconomic & Training	Access inequality, skill gaps, labour displacement	Inclusive training, policy on automation impact, and digital extension programs

To unlock the promise of smart farming, more research needs to be directed at several areas: Development of low-cost, durable, and self-calibrating sensors suitable for harsh field conditions; Federated learning and edge-AI techniques to build scalable, privacy-preserving ML models; Standardised blockchain frameworks for agricultural data traceability and authentication; Hybrid connectivity models combining LPWAN, satellite, and 6G for always-on rural connectivity; Behavioural research into farmer adoption patterns and technology acceptance; Policy frameworks regarding data rights, ethical AI, and fair access to smart agriculture systems.

6 FUTURE DIRECTIONS: AI, EDGE COMPUTING, AND 6G INTEGRATION

6.1AI and Machine Learning for Predictive Agriculture

Artificial Intelligence is the mainstay technology that could trigger next-gen smart farming. With AI models analysing huge data from IoT sensors, UAV imagery, and climate feeds, the technology will turn reactive farmers into predictive farmers. A few areas include: Yield Forecasting and Pest Prediction, where AI-enabled analyses can detect early signs of stress, disease, or pest infestation before visible observation by human eyes, allowing earlier intervention (Karunathilake et al., 2023). It is also in Resource Optimisation-the optimisation of irrigation schedules, fertiliser applications, or pesticide dosing through machine learning models based on real-time environmental data (Baumüller, 2022). With AI closed-loop decision systems, the collection, analysis, processing (like turning on irrigation), and other decisions are automatically completed. Efficient deep learning architectures play a critical role in enabling scalable and energy-aware intelligent agricultural analytics systems (Khullar et al., 2025).

6.2 Edge Computing for Localised Intelligence

Bringing data processing closer to the source on the farm, edge computing significantly reduces latency, bandwidth consumption, and dependence on centralised cloud infrastructure. One of its primary benefits is enabling faster decisions for farm operations, as data can be processed on-site, allowing immediate responses to changing field conditions. Moreover, since sensitive farm data is kept local, the threat of data breaches inherent in cloud services is reduced, increasing data security. Edge computing is also highly energy-efficient as edge AI can be executed on low-power devices, vital for battery-operated sensors in remote locations far from the cloud or without access to a grid. All these benefits are further amplified when edge computing is combined with digital twin (DT) technology, such that farmers can simulate real-world scenarios in real time and automate operations without having to constantly connect to the cloud (Awais et al., 2025; Subahi, 2024).

6.3 G Connectivity and Beyond

Firstly, 6G will support tens of thousands of interconnected sensors and autonomous devices per square kilometre by this time. Moving on, control of autonomous tractors, drone planes, and smart irrigation systems will become highly responsive.

Lastly, 6G networks may allow ambient energy harvesting, thus decreasing the reliance on batteries in remote sensors.

Rather, integration of 6G with blockchain-based platforms will foster traceability, smart contract enforcement, and collaborative endeavours among multiple stakeholders along global supply chains. The convergence of AI, edge computing, and 6G would provide the foundation of next-generation agriculture. This exchange is captured in Table 8, illustrating a multi-layered smart farming ecosystem showing how these technologies work synergistically across sensing, computation, intelligence, and integration layers to provide a scalable and robust agri-tech offering.

Table 8. Conceptual integration of AI, edge computing, and 6G in smart farming

Layer	Technologies	Functions and Features
Smart Agriculture Ecosystem *(End Goal)*	–	Sustainable, intelligent, and adaptive farming
Integration Layer	6G + Blockchain	- Massive connectivity - Real-time coordination - Wireless energy - Blockchain for traceability
Intelligence Layer	AI + Machine Learning	- Yield forecasting - Pest/disease prediction - Decision automation - Climate adaptation
Computation Layer	Edge Computing + Digital Twins	- Real-time data processing - Localised analytics - Enhanced data privacy - Low energy consumption
Sensing Layer	IoT Devices + UAVs + Climate Feeds	- Soil and crop sensors - Weather stations - Smart greenhouses - Urban/vertical farms
Foundation (Side Layer)	Open-Source Platforms, Standards, Training	- Equity and inclusiveness - Interoperability - Farmer education and support

6.4 Sustainable and Climate-Smart Farming Innovations

Technologies of the future will also enable large-scale, resilient agricultural practice:

Smart Greenhouses connected through IoT: Automated systems optimise the lighting, humidity and CO2 levels for better crop performance (Kumar, 2023).

Vertical cultivation of agriculture in urban centres: Controlled-environment agriculture realises production per unit area and at the same time, less water usage through the use of IoT and AI (University of Arizona, 2023).

Carbon Monitoring: Sensors and digital twins augmented with AI will track soil carbon and support other regenerative practices such as carbon sequestration (Onike, 2025).

6.5 Inclusive and Scalable Platforms

To guarantee fair access to advanced agricultural technologies, several inclusive strategies must be implemented. Open-source IoT frameworks offer customizable and affordable systems that help reduce the entry barrier for smallholder and resource-poor farmers. Alongside this, both national and international training and capacity-building programs are

vital for preparing farmers to thrive in an AI- and IoT-enabled future (Morepje et al., 2024). Additionally, the establishment of common standards for sensors, communication protocols, and digital platforms is necessary to ensure interoperability and allow for the seamless integration and scaling of solutions. These enabling technologies and their specific roles are summarised in Table 9.

Table 9. Comparative summary of future enablers

Technology	Role in Smart Farming	Key Benefits
AI & ML	Predictive analytics, yield forecasts, and autonomous actions	Early detection, efficiency, and automation
Edge Computing	Local data processing, decision-making, and digital twins	Low latency, data privacy, reduced cloud reliance
6G Networks	Massive sensor/device integration, wireless energy	Scalability, ultra-low latency, constant uptime
Blockchain	Secure data sharing, smart contracts, traceability	Trust, data integrity, and multi-stakeholder validation
Climate-Smart Tech	IoT greenhouses, carbon monitoring, vertical farming	Sustainability, resilience, and urban food production
Open Platforms	Affordable, standardised, extensible systems for all farm sizes	Inclusion, global scalability, and equitable access

7. CONCLUSION

The combination of blockchain technology, smart sensors, and Internet of Things (IoT) is defining a new era in agriculture, which is entering a new era of precision farming. What started with basic soil and crop surveillance systems have now developed into a future of digital twins, artificial intelligence, and 6G-powered autonomous decision-making that will transform the process of controlling, protecting, and optimizing agricultural production. This chapter has outlined how blockchain and IoT can be integrated to improve efficiency, transparency, and traceability through agricultural supply chains and real-world examples of implementations, including orchard management with unmanned aerial vehicles (UAVs) and olive oil traceability with Ethereum can be used as a template that can be scaled to other applications. Meanwhile, this shift does not go without difficulties. Physical and financial barriers like the lack of infrastructure, cyber crime, lack of digital literacy, ambiguity in laws regulating the ownership of information and economic challenges confronting the smallholder farmers remain limiting to large-scale adoption. However, the possibility of the new technologies is enormous. The integration of edge computing, AI and 6G networks will allow agriculture to transition to predictive, adaptive, and autonomous systems instead of being reactive. Digital twins ecosystems, vertical farming, and AI-managed greenhouse are already some of the concepts showing how technology can offer solutions to farming solutions that are climate-resilient and sustainable. In order to actualise this vision, the priorities should be inclusivity and accessibility. To achieve the process of innovating to smallholder and resource-constrained farmers, high-quality educational programs, open-source and interoperable spaces, and fair access to digital infrastructure are necessary. The pre-conditions to the widespread adoption and the fact that technological progress can serve all the stakeholders is the trust, usability and affordability. The intelligence, data-driven, and sustainable agricultural advancement requires a crossover approach. Farmers, technologists, researchers and policymakers should come together in an effort to develop agricultural mechanisms that are proofs of the future. It is only in these concerted efforts that Agriculture will be in a position to reach a productivity, profitability, equity and sustainability level which will lead to Agriculture 6.0.

Future Research Directions

Integration of blockchain, IoT, and artificial intelligence with the agriculture industry is a relatively recent trend with much to be discovered and developed. To increase the application and the impacts of these technologies in accuracy agriculture and smart farming, a number of research directions can be pursued.

1. Scalable Blockchain Architectures: The current blockchain platforms tend to be poor in the area of scaling, power consumption, and responsiveness of transaction. Future research to consider should be lightweight and energy saving blockchain architecture such as sharding, sidechains and tailor-made consensus mechanism to suit agricultural IoT environment.

2. Decentralized Identity and Authentication: The idea of the decentralized identity (DID) applied to the IoT devices and agricultural stakeholders is a research field that has a high potential. The future work can be done to explore the interoperability standards, privacy-saving protocols, and cross-chain identity management in order to avail a guarantee of secure and trusted interactions within the agricultural ecosystems.

3. AI-Blockchain Synergy: Predictive analytics powered by AI and blockchain records and their inviolability could be used to transform the agricultural decision-making process. A study of how machine learning can be combined with blockchain-based provenance information in processes such as yield prediction, pest prediction and climate adaptation policies should be done.

4. Digital Twins and 6G Connection: The emerging ideas of digital twins and 6G networks possess colossal potential of high-resolution and real-time monitoring of the agricultural systems. The research sphere that needs to be explored to integrate these technologies into the blockchain-powered secure simulation, monitoring, and autonomous decision-making is promising.

5. Socio-Economic and Policy Studies Along with technical innovations, the research should be carried out to examine socio-economic factors such as obstacles to adoption, willingness of farmers, cost-benefit analysis, and digitization. They should have evidence-based information that can facilitate the formulation of frameworks by the policymakers that could facilitate equitable utilisation of the policies particularly by the smallholder farmers.

6. Sustainability and Climate-Resilient Models: The future study must also questions how the blockchain-IoT ecosystem can be implemented to develop climate-smart agriculture, like carbon footprint monitoring, sustainable supply chain certification, and optimization of resources in the changing environmental conditions.

These areas of research will enable the agriculture industry to move one step ahead towards the actualization of the Agriculture 6.0 smart, secure, and sustainable paradigm of the provision of food security, empower farmers, and the resilience of the world.

REFERENCES

Abu, N. S., Bukhari, W. M., Ong, C. H., Kassim, A. M., Izzuddin, T. A., Sukhaimie, M. N., Norasikin, M. A., & Rasid, A. F. A. (2022). Internet of things applications in precision agriculture: A review. [JRC]. *Journal of Robotics and Control*, *3*(3), 338–347. DOI: 10.18196/jrc.v3i3.14159

Andriani, A. D., Dwiwarman, D. A., & Khullar, S. (2026). Resilient selves in the digital sphere: Communication strategies for sustainable privacy management. In Resilient Privacy-Preserving Mechanisms for Digital Identity Management (Chapter 1). https://doi.org/DOI: 10.4018/979-8-3373-7292-1.ch001

Ahmad, U., Nasirahmadi, A., Hensel, O., & Marino, S. (2022). Technology and data fusion methods to enhance site-specific crop monitoring. *Agronomy (Basel)*, *12*(3), 555. DOI: 10.3390/agronomy12030555

Alahmad, T., Neményi, M., & Nyéki, A. (2023). Applying IoT sensors and big data to improve precision crop production: A review. *Agronomy (Basel)*, *13*(10), 2603. DOI: 10.3390/agronomy13102603

Ali, A., Hussain, T., Tantashutikun, N., Hussain, N., & Cocetta, G. (2023). Application of Smart Techniques, Internet of Things and Data Mining for Resource Use Efficient and Sustainable Crop Production. *Agriculture*, *13*(2), 397. DOI: 10.3390/agriculture13020397

Atalla, S., Tarapiah, S., Gawanmeh, A., Daradkeh, M., Mukhtar, H., Himeur, Y., Mansoor, W., Hashim, K. F. B., & Daadoo, M. (2023). IoT-enabled precision agriculture: Developing an ecosystem for optimised crop management. *Information (Basel)*, *14*(4), 205. DOI: 10.3390/info14040205

Awais, M., Wang, X., Hussain, S., Aziz, F., & Mahmood, M. Q. (2025). Advancing precision agriculture through digital twins and smart farming technologies: A review. *AgriEngineering*, *7*(5), 137. DOI: 10.3390/agriengineering7050137

Baumüller, H. (2022). Towards smart farming? Mobile technology trends and their potential for developing country agriculture. In *Handbook on ICT in developing countries* (pp. 191–210). River Publishers. DOI: 10.1201/9781003338376-9

Bermeo-Almeida, O., Cardenas-Rodriguez, M., Samaniego-Cobo, T., Ferruzola-Gómez, E., Cabezas-Cabezas, R., & Bazán-Vera, W. (2018). Blockchain in agriculture: A systematic literature review. In Technologies and Innovation: 4th International Conference, CITI 2018, Guayaquil, Ecuador, November 6-9, 2018 [Springer International Publishing.]. *Proceedings*, *4*, 44–56.

Dayıoğlu, M. A., & Turker, U. (2021). Digital transformation for sustainable future-agriculture 4.0: A review. *Journal of Agricultural Sciences*, *27*(4), 373–399.

Demestichas, K., Peppes, N., & Alexakis, T. (2020). Survey on security threats in agricultural IoT and smart farming. sensors, 20(22), 6458.

Dhanaraju, M., Chenniappan, P., Ramalingam, K., Pazhanivelan, S., & Kaliaperumal, R. (2022). Smart farming: Internet of Things (IoT)-based sustainable agriculture. *Agriculture*, *12*(10), 1745. DOI: 10.3390/agriculture12101745

Ehsan, I., Irfan Khalid, M., Ricci, L., Iqbal, J., Alabrah, A., Sajid Ullah, S., & Alfakih, T. M. (2022). A Conceptual Model for Blockchain-Based Agriculture Food Supply Chain System. *Scientific Programming*, *2022*(1), 7358354. DOI: 10.1155/2022/7358354

Guo, M., Tang, H., & Guo, X. 2024. Blockchain Technology Enabling Applications in Smart Agriculture. In *Proceedings of the 2024 International Conference on Big Data and Digital Management (ICBDDM'24)*. Association for Computing Machinery, New York, NY, USA, 245–250. DOI: 10.1145/3696500.3696542

Gupta, M., Abdelsalam, M., Khorsandroo, S., & Mittal, S. (2020). Security and privacy in smart farming: Challenges and opportunities. *IEEE Access : Practical Innovations, Open Solutions*, *8*, 34564–34584. DOI: 10.1109/ACCESS.2020.2975142

Hundal, G. S., Laux, C. M., Buckmaster, D., Sutton, M. J., & Langemeier, M. (2023). Exploring barriers to the adoption of internet of things-based precision agriculture practices. *Agriculture*, *13*(1), 163. DOI: 10.3390/agriculture13010163

Karunathilake, E. M. B. M., Le, A. T., Heo, S., Chung, Y. S., & Mansoor, S. (2023). The path to smart farming: Innovations and opportunities in precision agriculture. *Agriculture*, *13*(8), 1593. DOI: 10.3390/agriculture13081593

Karunathilake, E. M. B. M., Le, A. T., Heo, S., Chung, Y. S., & Mansoor, S. (2023). The path to smart farming: Innovations and opportunities in precision agriculture. *Agriculture*, *13*(8), 1593. DOI: 10.3390/agriculture13081593

Khullar, S., Baghel, R. S., & Swami, P. (2026). Human-AI collaboration: Balancing trust, emotion, and productivity. In *AI Hallucination Management in the Enterprise Metaverse*. IGI Global., https://doi.org/10.4018/979-8-3373-7534-2.ch003

Khullar, S., Magdalene, A. H. S., Sandhya, P., & Naik, B. R. H. K. B. N., & Raju, M. V. (2025). Implementation, performance, and energy efficiency analysis for text classification of deep learning architectures. In 2025 10th International Conference on Communication and Electronics Systems (ICCES) (pp. 2099–2103). IEEE. https://doi.org/DOI: 10.1109/ICCES67310.2025.11336350

Khullar, S., Mounika, G. R., Chauhan, S. S., Garg, G., Priyanka, T. P., & Kaliappan, S. (2025). Advanced hybrid ensemble learning for blockchain-enabled secure voting: Leveraging random forest, XGBoost, and neural networks for robust anomaly detection and integrity assurance. In 2025 1st International Conference on Advancement in Futuristic Technologies (ICAFT) (pp. 1–7). IEEE. https://doi.org/DOI: 10.1109/ICAFT66710.2025.11452780

Koduru, T., & Koduru, N. P. (2022). An overview of vulnerabilities in smart farming systems. *Journal of Student Research*, *11*(1), 1–14. DOI: 10.47611/jsrhs.v11i1.2303

Ktari, J., Frikha, T., Chaabane, F., Hamdi, M., & Hamam, H. (2022). Agricultural lightweight embedded blockchain system: A case study in olive oil. *Electronics (Basel)*, *11*(20), 3394. DOI: 10.3390/electronics11203394

Kumar, N. (2023). Leveraging artificial intelligence in agriculture: transforming the future of farming.

Liu, Y., Ma, X., Shu, L., Hancke, G. P., & Abu-Mahfouz, A. M. (2020). From industry 4.0 to agriculture 4.0: Current status, enabling technologies, and research challenges. *IEEE Transactions on Industrial Informatics*, *17*(6), 4322–4334. DOI: 10.1109/TII.2020.3003910

Mansoor, S., Iqbal, S., Popescu, S. M., Kim, S. L., Chung, Y. S., & Baek, J. H. (2025). Integration of smart sensors and IOT in precision agriculture: Trends, challenges and future prospectives. *Frontiers in Plant Science*, *16*, 1587869. DOI: 10.3389/fpls.2025.1587869

McCaig, M., Dara, R., & Rezania, D. (2023). Farmer-centric design thinking principles for smart farming technologies. *Internet of Things : Engineering Cyber Physical Human Systems*, *23*, 100898. DOI: 10.1016/j.iot.2023.100898

Morepje, M. T., Sithole, M. Z., Msweli, N. S., & Agholor, A. I. (2024). The influence of E-commerce platforms on sustainable agriculture practices among smallholder farmers in Sub-Saharan Africa. *Sustainability (Basel)*, *16*(15), 6496. DOI: 10.3390/su16156496

Onike, N. J. (2025). The Internet of Things (IoT) in Farming: Smart Solutions for a Sustainable Future. International Journal of Poverty. *Investment and Development*, *5*(1), 31–44. DOI: 10.47941/ijpid.2650

Piancharoenwong, A., & Badir, Y. F. (2024). IoT smart farming adoption intention under climate change: the gain and loss perspective. Technological Forecasting and Social Change, 200, 123192. Huo, D., Malik, A. W., Ravana, S. D., Rahman, A. U., & Ahmedy, I. (2024). Mapping smart farming: Addressing agricultural challenges in the data-driven era. *Renewable & Sustainable Energy Reviews, 189*, 113858.

Polymeni, S., Plastras, S., Skoutas, D. N., Kormentzas, G., & Skianis, C. (2023). The impact of 6G-IoT technologies on the development of agriculture 5.0: A review. *Electronics (Basel), 12*(12), 2651. DOI: 10.3390/electronics12122651

Quy, V. K., Hau, N. V., Anh, D. V., Quy, N. M., Ban, N. T., Lanza, S., Randazzo, G., & Muzirafuti, A. (2022). IoT-enabled smart agriculture: Architecture, applications, and challenges. *Applied Sciences (Basel, Switzerland), 12*(7), 3396. DOI: 10.3390/app12073396

Rajak, P., Ganguly, A., Adhikary, S., & Bhattacharya, S. (2023). Internet of Things and smart sensors in agriculture: Scopes and challenges. *Journal of Agriculture and Food Research, 14*, 100776. DOI: 10.1016/j.jafr.2023.100776

Ruan, J., Wang, Y., Chan, F. T. S., Hu, X., Zhao, M., Zhu, F., Shi, B., Shi, Y., & Lin, F. (2019). A life cycle framework of green IoT-based agriculture and its finance, operation, and management issues. *IEEE Communications Magazine, 57*(3), 90–96. DOI: 10.1109/MCOM.2019.1800332

Samadi, V. (2025). Empowering Precision Agriculture with Advanced Technology.

Sendros, A., Drosatos, G., Efraimidis, P. S., & Tsirliganis, N. C. (2022). Blockchain applications in agriculture: A scoping review. *Applied Sciences (Basel, Switzerland), 12*(16), 8061. DOI: 10.3390/app12168061

Subahi, A. F. (2024). Advancing Sustainable Cyber-Physical System Development with a Digital Twins and Language Engineering Approach: Smart Greenhouse Applications. *Technologies, 12*(9), 147. DOI: 10.3390/technologies12090147

Tiwari, S., Bhardwaj, B., Arora, D., & Khatri, S. (2024). Challenges and Barriers to Smart Farming Adaptation: A Technical, Economic, and Social Perspective. Smart Agritech: Robotics, AI, and Internet of Things (IoT) in Agriculture, 75-111.

Wiseman, L., Sanderson, J., Zhang, A., & Jakku, E. (2019). Farmers and their data: An examination of farmers' reluctance to share their data through the lens of the laws impacting smart farming. *NJAS Wageningen Journal of Life Sciences, 90*(1), 100301. DOI: 10.1016/j.njas.2019.04.007

Yazdinejad, A., Zolfaghari, B., Azmoodeh, A., Dehghantanha, A., Karimipour, H., & Fraser, E.,

Chapter 12
Trust and Reputation in Secured AIoT:
A Communication and Social Science Perspective on Authentication Ecosystems

Astri Dwi Andriani
http://orcid.org/0000-0003-3951-4829
Universitas Putra Indonesia, Indonesia

ABSTRACT

Authentication in the Artificial Intelligence of Things (AIoT) is often seen as a technical checkpoint, but its durability depends on trust and reputation that shape legitimacy. Compliance with standards cannot replace transparency or public confidence. This chapter applies communication theories—SCOT, ANT, and risk communication—and examines global cases from the U.S., Europe, Asia, Africa, and Latin America to reveal how governance and culture affect adoption. It proposes trust-aware authentication architectures that integrate adaptive mechanisms, reputation systems, communicative transparency, and cultural sensitivity, arguing that resilient AIoT security must be both technically robust and socially trusted.

INTRODUCTION

What does it mean for a system to be secure if no one actually trusts it? This paradox lies at the heart of AIoT authentication. Every day, billions of devices silently authenticate themselves, determining who gains access and who is locked out. Cryptographic protocols may assure technical integrity, yet scandals of sur-

DOI: 10.4018/979-8-3373-6299-1.ch012

veillance, breaches of privacy, and failures of accountability linger in the public imagination, eroding the legitimacy of even the most sophisticated infrastructures (Solove & Citron, 2018). Trust and reputation, the social currencies of digital life, are often sidelined as "soft" issues in the face of technical complexity. But without them, even the strongest algorithms remain brittle, failing to inspire confidence or sustained adoption.

The rise of AIoT—where artificial intelligence and IoT converge—has transformed authentication from a contained procedure into a high-stakes practice spanning hospitals, smart cities, and global infrastructures (Alsyouf et al., 2022; ENISA, 2021). Yet treating authentication as a binary checkpoint neglects its relational nature, where trust is continuously negotiated among users, institutions, and devices. Evidence across regions illustrates this tension: in the United States, NIST standards mandated by the IoT Cybersecurity Improvement Act coexist with skepticism rooted in surveillance legacies (NIST, n.d.); in Europe, the GDPR embeds trust in civic rights and privacy guarantees (ENISA, 2021); in Asia, Singapore's Smart Nation emphasizes competence and communication (Chia, 2020), while China risks sliding into coercive control (Feldstein, 2019); in Africa, Kenya's M-Pesa demonstrates the power and fragility of community trust (Donovan & Park, 2019); and in Latin America, Brazil shows that legal frameworks without credible institutions remain hollow (Cavalcante & de Almeida, 2021). Together these cases underscore a central lesson: technical rigor alone cannot secure legitimacy—trust remains the ultimate foundation of enduring AIoT authentication.

Despite this, much of the scholarly and technical literature on AIoT authentication continues to focus narrowly on cryptographic mechanisms, key management, and hardware security. These remain indispensable, yet they only tell half the story. Trust and reputation—the lenses through which individuals and societies interpret technology—determine whether authentication systems are embraced or resisted (Mayer et al., 1995; McKnight et al., 1998). Ignoring these dimensions reduces governance to a performance of compliance rather than a practice of accountability. As research on risk perception has long shown, people's responses to technology are driven as much by feelings of control, fairness, and legitimacy as by technical probability (Slovic, 1987). The omission of these socio-communicative dimensions is not merely an academic oversight but a governance liability.

Theoretically, there are rich traditions that can illuminate this neglected terrain. The Social Construction of Technology (SCOT) framework reminds us that technologies are shaped not only by engineers but also by users, institutions, and narratives (Pinch & Bijker, 1984). Actor-Network Theory (ANT) further emphasizes that authentication is not simply a technical gatekeeping mechanism but a networked practice where humans and non-humans co-construct legitimacy (Latour, 2005). Risk communication studies show that trust in institutions is decisive in shaping how people respond to security infrastructures (Slovic, 1987). Yet these frameworks have rarely been applied systematically to AIoT authentication, leaving a gap this chapter seeks to address.

Equally important is the recognition that authentication is not only a technical safeguard but also a communicative act. When a hospital system informs a patient how their data is secured, or when a city publishes a transparency dashboard on sensor authentication, these are not simply bureaucratic gestures. They are moments where institutions either build or erode trust, depending on how narratives resonate with public expectations (Goodman & Powles, 2019). Too often, security communication is relegated to footnotes in technical documentation, leaving non-experts alienated and suspicious. Making authentication legible—through accessible narratives, transparency reports, and participatory oversight—may be as critical as the encryption itself.

The consequences of neglecting trust are not abstract; they are material and immediate. In healthcare, patients may refuse to adopt life-saving wearables if they perceive privacy violations (Sharon, 2021). In smart cities, citizens may resist or sabotage sensor infrastructures they interpret as surveillance rather than safety (Morozov & Bria, 2018). In finance, users may abandon platforms where breaches—no matter how technically contained—undermine confidence in providers (Donovan & Park, 2019). Each case demonstrates that authentication systems succeed not only when they function cryptographically but also when they are perceived as fair, transparent, and accountable. The social life of trust is inseparable from the technical life of security.

At a policy level, this tension plays out in different forms across regions. U.S. regulators emphasize technical compliance, yet struggle with public suspicion. European governance embeds rights as the foundation of trust. Asian models oscillate between participatory legitimacy and coercive control. African innovations showcase the power of grassroots trust, while Latin American experiences warn of institutional fragility. By analyzing these cases side by side, this chapter demonstrates how authentication is shaped not only by technical protocols but also by historical memory, institutional credibility, and communicative practice. The diversity of approaches underscores a global lesson: trust is always contextual, yet universally indispensable.

The contribution of this chapter lies in bridging technical and socio-communicative dimensions of AIoT authentication. It proposes that trust and reputation are not peripheral issues but central design principles, as vital as cryptography and interoperability. Drawing from communication theory, case studies, and governance analysis, it argues for a new paradigm: *trust-aware authentication architectures*. These are systems that integrate adaptive authentication, reputational feedback, transparent communication, and cultural sensitivity. In doing so, they not only secure identities but also cultivate legitimacy, ensuring that AIoT infrastructures are both resilient and socially sustainable.

Finally, this introduction situates the chapter within a broader research agenda. By applying interdisciplinary theories to the pressing challenges of AIoT, it provides a framework for reimagining authentication as a socio-technical process. The structure of the chapter reflects this aim: beginning with theoretical foundations, moving to socio-communicative dynamics, grounding the analysis in global case studies, and advancing toward trust-aware architectures with policy implications. The conclusion highlights future research directions, particularly the need for empirical studies that test how trust-aware models shape adoption across cultures. In this way, the chapter speaks not only to engineers and policymakers but also to communication scholars and social theorists, offering a holistic approach to one of the defining challenges of our digital age.

THEORETICAL FOUNDATIONS

Any meaningful exploration of AIoT authentication must begin with theoretical grounding, since without theory discussions risk fragmentation or technical reductionism. Theory enables us to ask why some systems gain acceptance while others are resisted despite equivalent cryptographic strength. Trust models, such as Mayer, Davis, and Schoorman's (1995) dimensions of ability, benevolence, and integrity, help explain why secure systems may still fail if perceived as coercive or indifferent to user interests. Authentication thus becomes more than mathematics—it is a socio-technical practice where legitimacy rests on credibility and communication.

Initial trust formation theories extend this insight by emphasizing how people evaluate systems under uncertainty. McKnight, Cummings, and Chervany (1998) highlight that trust often relies on institutional assurances, reputational signals, and situational cues rather than technical detail. For AIoT authentication, this means patients adopting wearables or citizens engaging with digital ID platforms look for transparency and guarantees rather than cryptographic proofs. Risk perception research reinforces this dynamic: Slovic (1987) shows that feelings of control, fairness, and dread often outweigh statistical risk. Systems technically sound but seen as unfair may be rejected, while flawed ones perceived as accountable may be tolerated.

Sociological perspectives deepen these insights. The Social Construction of Technology (SCOT) framework demonstrates that technologies acquire meaning through negotiation among engineers, policymakers, users, and corporations, producing diverse authentication models shaped by histories and institutions (Pinch & Bijker, 1984). Actor-Network Theory (ANT) takes this further, stressing that devices, algorithms, and standards act alongside humans in shaping legitimacy.

Latour (2005) illustrates that order emerges from heterogeneous interactions, where even reputational scores function as actors influencing human judgment. Communication strategies, such as breach disclosures or transparency dashboards, then become integral to authentication, as they directly shape perceptions of reliability and legitimacy (Slovic, 1987).

These perspectives converge on the centrality of reputation as distributed memory. Just as online marketplaces rely on ratings, AIoT systems can use cryptographic attestations of device integrity to build reputational capital that influences authentication outcomes (Aaqib et al., 2023). Reputation here is not neutral metadata but a socially constructed record of performance. Cultural theory further emphasizes that trust norms vary: Inglehart (2018) shows that collectivist societies may delegate more readily to centralized authorities, while individualist contexts demand decentralization and transparency. Thus, authentication cannot be universalized but must adopt modular designs that align with local expectations of trust.

Taken together, these theories form a multi-layered framework for understanding AIoT authentication as a socio-technical practice. Trust models highlight psychological dynamics, SCOT and ANT expose social negotiations and networks, risk communication stresses transparency, and cultural theory explains global variation. This foundation not only diagnoses why technically robust systems may remain socially brittle but also offers guidance for designing resilient, trust-aware architectures. By grounding authentication in theory, we ensure that subsequent analyses of stakeholder dynamics, case studies, and governance proposals rest on an integrated understanding of how technical, social, and cultural forces intersect to shape legitimacy.

Technical Foundations of AIoT Authentication: What the Dominant Literature Emphasizes—and Omits

While this chapter intentionally departs from a purely technical framing, a systematic engagement with the dominant AIoT authentication literature is necessary to clarify precisely what dimensions of trust are currently underemphasized. Contemporary AIoT security research predominantly focuses on cryptographic robustness, device identity management, and protocol efficiency, reflecting legitimate concerns about scale, heterogeneity, and attack surfaces in large IoT ecosystems.

A major trend is the adoption of Zero-Trust Architecture (ZTA), which rejects perimeter-based security in favor of continuous verification of identities, devices, and contexts (Rose et al., 2020). In AIoT settings, ZTA manifests through micro-segmentation, least-privilege access, and real-time behavioral monitoring. While technically effective, ZTA frameworks largely conceptualize "trust" as an internal system variable rather than a socially negotiated condition, leaving public legitimacy and user perception unaddressed.

Another prominent line of research explores blockchain and distributed ledger technologies (DLT) for decentralized identity, authentication, and auditability in IoT networks. These approaches promise tamper-resistant logs, decentralized trust anchors, and automated verification of device integrity. Yet, most studies evaluate success in terms of latency, throughput, and immutability, rarely examining how algorithmic reputation systems may reproduce bias, obscure accountability, or alienate users unfamiliar with opaque scoring mechanisms.

Industry standards such as OAuth 2.0, OpenID Connect (OIDC), and FIDO2/WebAuthn further dominate applied authentication architectures. These frameworks significantly improve interoperability and passwordless security, particularly in consumer and enterprise IoT environments. However, they assume institutional trust in identity providers and do not explicitly address how such trust is socially constructed, contested, or eroded in contexts marked by surveillance histories or weak governance.

In sum, the prevailing technical literature excels at securing identities but largely abstracts away from the communicative, cultural, and ethical dimensions that determine whether authentication systems are perceived as legitimate. This gap is not incidental—it reflects an implicit assumption that technical correctness guarantees acceptance. The remainder of this chapter challenges that assumption by situating these technical architectures within broader trust ecologies shaped by governance, reputation, and social meaning.

Technical Vulnerabilities That Enable the Trust–Legitimacy Gap

The socio-technical legitimacy gap in AIoT authentication is not merely perceptual; it is amplified by concrete technical vulnerabilities that strain existing models. First, key management at planetary scale remains an unresolved challenge. Managing cryptographic identities for billions of low-power devices introduces risks of key leakage, misconfiguration, and lifecycle opacity—failures that, when exposed, quickly erode public confidence.

Second, physical insecurity of IoT devices undermines even the strongest authentication protocols. Sensors deployed in public or industrial environments are susceptible to tampering, cloning, and side-channel attacks, creating a discrepancy between formal authentication and actual trustworthiness.

Third, legacy industrial protocols frequently lack native support for modern authentication standards, forcing insecure workarounds that contradict best practices. These compromises are rarely visible to end users, but when breaches occur, the revelation that "secure" systems relied on outdated assumptions fuels distrust.

These vulnerabilities reveal why purely technical paradigms fail not only in security outcomes but also in legitimacy: when systems break in opaque ways, trust collapses faster than it can be repaired by post-hoc technical fixes. See Table 1.

Table 1. Dominant AIoT authentication models and their trust implications

Authentication Paradigm	Primary Technical Focus	Implicit Trust Model	Socio-Communicative Limitation
Zero-Trust Architecture (ZTA)	Continuous verification, micro-segmentation	Trust as internal risk score	Lacks public transparency and user legibility
Blockchain/DLT-based Identity	Decentralization, immutability	Algorithmic reputation	Risk of opacity, bias, and exclusion
OAuth2 / OIDC	Federated identity, interoperability	Institutional trust in IdPs	Assumes pre-existing institutional legitimacy
FIDO2 / WebAuthn	Passwordless authentication	Device-centric trust	Weak engagement with governance and accountability
Trust-Aware Architecture (Proposed)	Adaptive authentication + reputation + communication	Trust as socio-technical process	Requires careful trade-off management

Source: Author synthesis, 2025.

Socio-Communicative Dimensions of Authentication

Authentication in AIoT ecosystems does not exist in a vacuum of technical codes and cryptographic protocols; it is lived and negotiated in social worlds where governments, industries, media, and citizens continuously interpret and contest its legitimacy. Governments, for example, often present authentication as a guarantee of security and efficiency, yet their narratives can quickly encounter public skepticism. The rollout of India's Aarogya Setu COVID-19 contact-tracing app in 2020 provides an instructive case. Officials framed the app as essential for national health security, but privacy advocates raised alarms about its opaque data retention practices and lack of transparency. While technically robust in terms of encryption, the app struggled with legitimacy because the communicative strategy—largely top-down—did not address users' fears of surveillance (Raman & Sinha, 2020). This highlights that technical security is insufficient when communicative gaps remain.

Media narratives further complicate these dynamics by amplifying either confidence or fear. The Equifax data breach in 2017, which exposed the personal data of 147 million people, became a touchstone for media skepticism toward digital authentication systems. Despite Equifax's claims of implementing sophisticated encryption and access controls, headlines focused on corporate negligence and the betrayal of consumer trust. For many, the technical details of encryption mattered less than the story of institutional failure. Reflecting on this case, one cannot help but notice how quickly reputation—built over decades—can collapse in the face of a single crisis, and how media framing powerfully shapes collective memory of authentication breakdowns (Solove & Citron, 2018).

Smart city projects illustrate this tension vividly. In China, the extensive deployment of facial recognition cameras has been framed by the government as a means to ensure public safety and efficient governance. Yet internationally, the same technologies are narrated as instruments of surveillance and control, sparking ethical debates about human rights (Feldstein, 2019). Citizens within China may accept or even support these systems, in part due to cultural norms emphasizing collective security, but observers abroad perceive them as authoritarian overreach. This divergence underscores that authentication technologies carry different meanings depending on narrative context and cultural framing. For global AIoT deployments, it becomes clear that communicative strategies must be tailored to local trust cultures rather than imposed universally.

The interplay of legitimacy and perception is also evident in financial technologies. Cryptocurrency exchanges, for instance, rely heavily on multi-factor authentication and blockchain-based reputation systems. Yet, scandals like the FTX collapse in 2022 revealed how reputational legitimacy can mask underlying technical and ethical failures. Users entrusted billions of dollars not solely because of encryption protocols, but because of a charismatic CEO and media narratives that framed the exchange as revolutionary. When the collapse exposed fraud, it became a reminder that trust in authentication ecosystems is never purely technical—it is deeply entangled with reputation, narrative framing, and collective psychology.

An important observation is that distrust often spreads faster than trust. A single high-profile breach or misuse can undo years of technical progress. Consider the case of Amazon's Ring smart cameras, which faced backlash after reports of hackers accessing private video feeds in 2019. While Amazon patched vulnerabilities and strengthened authentication, the media's framing of "strangers spying on children through smart cameras" created lasting reputational damageThis chapter argues that as an observer, this case reveals that the communicative failure—delayed acknowledgement, insufficient transparency—was more damaging than the technical flaw itself. Users lost faith not in encryption but in the company's willingness to act responsibly.

Ultimately, the socio-communicative dimensions of AIoT authentication reveal that legitimacy is co-constructed through the interplay of government assurances, industry reputation, media framing, and personal experience. Authentication systems succeed not simply because they are secure but because they are believed to be secure, fair, and aligned with societal values. As Latour (2005) reminds us, networks of humans and non-humans together construct credibility. Thus, authentication in AIoT is not a static gatekeeping mechanism but a dynamic process of trust negotiation. For future systems to thrive, designers must integrate communicative strategies as deliberately as cryptographic protocols, recognizing that public confidence is the ultimate currency of security.

Empirical Signals: What Limited Evidence Already Shows

The argument for trust-aware authentication architectures benefits from existing empirical literature demonstrating how transparency, disclosure practices, and adaptive authentication affect stakeholder trust and system acceptance, even if such evidence remains sparse in AIoT contexts.

Empirical studies across digital technology and communication domains consistently show that transparency and adaptive security mechanisms materially shape user trust and system acceptance. Research on health information exchange systems demonstrates that perceived transparency in privacy policies and security processes increases both cognitive and emotional trust, thereby raising users' willingness to participate and share sensitive data. Complementary findings from governmental crisis communication studies indicate that transparency primarily builds trust indirectly by fostering public engagement, suggesting that making security and authentication processes interpretable and actionable is critical for legitimacy. In parallel, empirical evaluations of risk-based authentication (RBA) in large-scale online services reveal that adaptive authentication can enhance security while maintaining usability, as users perceive RBA as comparably secure but less intrusive than static multi-factor approaches. Operational analyses further show that even minor configuration changes in RBA systems produce measurable effects on user experience and security outcomes, underscoring that adaptive authentication is a practical, performance-sensitive mechanism rather than a purely theoretical construct. Collectively, this body of evidence provides empirical grounding for the chapter's central claim that transparency dashboards and adaptive, risk-aware authentication can positively influence trust calibration and acceptance, and highlights the importance of extending such evaluations to AIoT contexts.

CASE STUDIES IN PRACTICE

Smart healthcare systems vividly illustrate how authentication in AIoT operates at the intersection of efficiency, privacy, and legitimacy. Hospitals increasingly rely on continuously authenticated devices—such as wearables, infusion pumps, and electronic health record systems—to protect sensitive data while enabling rapid clinical decision-making. However, rigid or time-consuming authentication protocols can delay urgent treatment, highlighting that authentication failures may have life-critical consequences. High-profile cases, such as the U.S. FDA's 2019 warning about remotely hackable insulin pumps, demonstrate how reputational damage and fear can eclipse technical remediation, eroding trust even among unaffected patients. Similarly, the adoption of wearable health technologies during the COVID-19 pandemic showed that patients' willingness to share intimate biometric data depended less on cryptographic assurances than on brand reputation, transparency, and perceived institutional responsibility. These examples underscore that authentication in healthcare is a socio-communicative practice in which legitimacy, reputation, and communication strategies directly shape acceptance.

Comparable dynamics emerge in smart city deployments, where authentication mediates collective security, governance, and civil liberties. Urban AIoT systems—ranging from traffic sensors to facial recognition platforms—promise efficiency and safety but simultaneously raise concerns about surveillance and misuse. China's extensive facial recognition infrastructure, framed domestically as a public safety tool yet criticized internationally as a mechanism of control, illustrates how authentication technologies acquire divergent meanings across cultural and political contexts. Similar legitimacy challenges have surfaced in Western democracies, as seen in the cancellation of Toronto's Sidewalk Labs project and public backlash following disclosures of vulnerabilities in smart traffic systems. By contrast, European initiatives shaped by GDPR, such as Barcelona's citizen-controlled data platforms, demonstrate how embedding governance, consent, and transparency into authentication architectures can enhance trust. Across both healthcare and smart cities, these cases reveal a common lesson: authentication succeeds not merely through technical robustness but through sustained socio-communicative legitimacy, where trust and reputation function as structural prerequisites for adoption rather than incidental byproducts.

To understand how trust and reputation operate in AIoT authentication ecosystems, we can map them into a thematic matrix. Table 1 connects the socio-communicative dimensions with different AIoT application domains, showing how narratives, legitimacy, and public perception shape the acceptance or rejection of authentication systems. Thus, Table 1 is not merely a classificatory tool, but also a reflective lens that reveals the social dynamics behind technical decisions. These diverse tensions across regions can be synthesized into a comparative overview. Table 1 presents a thematic matrix of case studies, contrasting privacy, efficiency, safety, surveillance, and legitimacy dynamics. See Table 2.

Table 2. Trust and reputation in AIoT authentication

AIoT Domain	Dimension of Trust	Dimension of Reputation	Public Narratives	Authentication Implications
Smart Healthcare	Patients trust systems when data is secure and transparent (e.g., Apple Health).	Manufacturer reputation (Medtronic, Fitbit) strongly influences device acceptance.	"Saving lives vs sacrificing privacy."	Authentication must be fast yet ensure patient data confidentiality.
Smart City	Citizens trust when oversight and public control are visible.	Government/city reputation defines legitimacy (e.g., Barcelona vs China).	"Safe city vs surveillance state."	Authentication must secure infrastructure while being transparent about data usage.
Fintech / Crypto	Investors trust when systems appear secure, even if not technically robust.	Reputation of public figures/CEOs is critical (e.g., FTX vs Coinbase).	"Financial revolution vs large-scale fraud."	Authentication must be reinforced by independent audits, not just brand image.
Consumer IoT	Users trust when they feel in control (e.g., smart homes).	Big tech brand reputation (Apple, Google) reassures consumers.	"Convenient living vs constant surveillance."	Authentication must be simple, understandable, and give users control options.
Public Services	Citizens trust when systems are fair and non-discriminatory (e.g., e-voting).	Government or electoral body reputation defines legitimacy.	"Transparent democracy vs digital manipulation."	Authentication must be technically strong but also verifiable to sustain democratic trust.

Source: Author, 2025.

Table 2 highlights that trust and reputation are not secondary factors but foundational to the acceptance of AIoT authentication across domains. In healthcare, patients judge systems by how quickly and securely they are served, while manufacturer reputation becomes a "social guarantee" of reliability. In smart cities, government reputation and open communication can transform perceptions of authentication systems from tools of repression to symbols of collective safety. In this sense, institutional reputation acts as the bridge between technical design and social legitimacy.

A deeper reflection shows that public narratives consistently frame how trust and reputation interact. In fintech, narratives of financial revolution often overshadow weak authentication, until scandals like FTX collapse reveal the fragility of reputational trust. In consumer IoT, large brands calm anxieties even when users do not fully grasp technical authentication details. This chapter argues that as an observer, this thematic mapping illustrates that authentication is not only a matter of digital security, but also a mirror of social relations, power dynamics, and legitimacy narratives that shape technological adoption.

Toward Trust-Aware Authentication Architectures

The future of AIoT authentication requires moving beyond binary, credential-centric models toward architectures that explicitly embed trust and reputation as dynamic design elements. In large-scale, heterogeneous ecosystems, authentication can no longer function as a simple gate that grants or denies access; instead, it must operate along a continuum shaped by contextual risk, historical behavior, and social legitimacy. Trust-aware architectures therefore integrate adaptive, risk-based authentication mechanisms that calibrate security requirements in real time, drawing on signals from device attestation, user behavior, and reputational history. Such approaches—already emerging in domains like banking—demonstrate that stronger security and improved usability need not be mutually exclusive, and that authentication systems can simultaneously enhance protection and acceptance when trust is treated as a measurable, evolving condition rather than a static assumption.

Crucially, trust-aware authentication extends beyond technical mechanisms to encompass communication, governance, and ethics. Reputation systems must be legible and contestable, incorporating transparency dashboards, appeal and redress mechanisms, and human oversight to prevent opacity, bias, or disproportionate control. Interoperability across vendors and jurisdictions further requires shared trust protocols aligned with regulatory and cultural expectations, while avoiding the ethical risks of continuous reputational scoring devolving into surveillance or social control. By embedding transparency, proportionality, and accountability into authentication workflows, trust-aware architectures reconceptualize security as a socio-technical infrastructure—one in which cryptographic rigor is complemented by communicative clarity and institutional responsibility. In this vision, authentication becomes not merely a technical checkpoint but a living system of trust negotiation, capable of sustaining both technical resilience and social legitimacy across diverse AIoT contexts.

Finally, moving toward trust-aware authentication architectures is as much a cultural transformation as it is a technical one. Engineers, policymakers, and designers must embrace the idea that authentication is not merely about proving identities but about cultivating relationships of confidence across devices, institutions, and societies. This requires humility—the recognition that no amount of technical ingenuity can substitute for trust that is lived and felt by users. It also requires imagination—the willingness to design systems that are not only secure but also transparent, inclusive, and empowering. If achieved, such architectures could redefine the social contract of the digital age, transforming authentication from a checkpoint into a living infrastructure of trust that both protects and dignifies human experience. See Figure 1.

Figure 1. Architecture flow of trust-aware AIoT authentication

As shown in Figure 1, trust-aware authentication in AIoT systems is conceptualized as a multi-stage socio-technical process rather than a single verification checkpoint.

The process begins at the device layer, where AIoT nodes initiate authentication requests based on operational context. Given the physical exposure and heterogeneity of AIoT devices, trust cannot be inferred solely from static credentials.

In the attestation stage, devices provide verifiable evidence of their hardware and software integrity, such as firmware state, secure boot measurements, or enclave-based proofs. This stage anchors trust in *technical verifiability*, reducing the risk of spoofed or compromised devices entering the system.

Attestation outputs are then incorporated into a reputation layer, where historical behavior, compliance patterns, and contextual trust signals are aggregated over time. Reputation functions as a *dynamic trust memory*, enabling the system to move beyond binary authentication toward graded trust assessments.

Based on combined attestation and reputation signals, the system applies adaptive authentication policies. Rather than enforcing uniform security controls, authentication requirements are dynamically calibrated, triggering additional verification only when risk thresholds are exceeded. This adaptive approach balances security robustness with usability and system scalability.

Crucially, the architecture incorporates a final appeal and redress layer, ensuring that automated authentication decisions remain contestable. When access is denied or elevated challenges are imposed, affected users or operators may initiate an appeal, invoking procedural review mechanisms as outlined in the contestability SOP. This stage operationalizes legitimacy by embedding accountability and human oversight directly into the authentication flow.

Together, this architecture demonstrates how trust, reputation, transparency, and governance can be structurally integrated into AIoT authentication systems. The diagram reinforces the chapter's central argument: resilient AIoT security emerges not from cryptography alone, but from architectures that are simultaneously *technically robust and socially accountable.*

Trust Dashboard: Minimum Transparency Artifacts

To operationalize trust-aware authentication beyond normative claims, this chapter proposes a Trust Dashboard as a minimal but actionable transparency artifact within secured AIoT ecosystems. Rather than functioning as a public relations instrument, the dashboard is conceived as a *socio-technical interface* that translates authentication events, governance practices, and accountability mechanisms into interpretable signals for multiple stakeholders, including users, operators, regulators, and auditors.

Empirical studies on transparency and trust in digital systems consistently indicate that *visibility of processes*, rather than mere compliance statements, plays a critical role in shaping perceived legitimacy. Accordingly, a trust dashboard should not attempt exhaustive disclosure, but instead standardize a minimum set of artifacts that signal competence, integrity, and procedural fairness while remaining feasible for resource-constrained AIoT environments. Table 3 outlines the minimum transparency artifacts recommended for a trust dashboard in AIoT authentication systems. See Table 3.

Table 3. Minimum transparency artifacts for a trust dashboard in AIoT authentication

Artifact Category	Description	Primary Audience	Trust Signal Conveyed
Events Logged	Aggregated records of authentication-related events (e.g., successful authentications, adaptive challenges triggered, failed attempts, device attestation status), reported at a non-identifiable level	Operators, auditors, regulators	Technical competence, system reliability
Incident Disclosures	Public summaries of significant security incidents or anomalous behaviors (scope, high-level cause, mitigation steps, resolution status), without exposing sensitive system internals	Users, public authorities	Integrity, accountability, openness
Audit Cadence	Disclosure of internal and external audit schedules (e.g., quarterly internal reviews, annual third-party assessments) and audit scope (authentication logic, reputation models, governance controls)	Regulators, enterprise customers	Procedural rigor, institutional credibility
Public vs. Internal Views	Clear separation between publicly accessible dashboard elements and restricted internal views containing detailed logs, risk scores, or forensic data	Users (public view); security teams (internal view)	Proportional transparency, respect for privacy and security

Importantly, the trust dashboard should be context-sensitive rather than static. In high-stakes domains such as healthcare or smart city infrastructure, disclosure thresholds and update frequency may be higher, whereas consumer IoT deployments may require simplified representations to avoid information overload. Across contexts, the dashboard's role is not to guarantee trust, but to *enable informed trust calibration* by making authentication and governance practices visible, contestable, and interpretable.

By defining a minimum transparency baseline, the trust dashboard transforms the abstract principle of "communicative transparency" into a concrete design artifact that engineers can implement, policymakers can regulate, and users can meaningfully engage with—thereby narrowing the gap between cryptographic robustness and social legitimacy in AIoT authentication.

Contestability and Redress: A Minimal SOP

A core limitation of many contemporary AIoT authentication systems is the absence of proceduralized redress mechanisms when automated decisions deny access, downgrade device trust, or trigger heightened authentication requirements. While appeals and overrides are often normatively invoked as safeguards for fairness and legitimacy, they frequently remain abstract commitments rather than operational realities. To address this gap, this chapter proposes a Minimal Standard Operating Procedure (SOP) for contestability and redress within trust-aware AIoT authentication ecosystems.

The objective of this minimal SOP is to ensure that automated authentication decisions in AIoT systems remain reviewable, accountable, and socially legitimate, particularly in high-impact contexts such as healthcare, public infrastructure, and critical services. Contestability is operationalized through clearly defined appeal triggers, including persistent authentication failures, anomalous reputation score changes, or access denials that deviate from established risk baselines. Once triggered, the system enters a structured verification phase that reconstructs decision context by examining authentication logs, device attestation status, anomaly indicators, and applied policies, rather than simply re-running automated logic. Appeals that exceed predefined impact thresholds are escalated to a human-in-the-loop reviewer empowered to confirm, override, or modify the original decision, thereby reinforcing procedural fairness and aligning with emerging regulatory expectations for meaningful human oversight.

To ensure redress mechanisms are effective rather than symbolic, the SOP mandates explicit service-level agreement (SLA) targets proportionate to impact severity, ranging from rapid resolution for critical services to longer windows for low-risk cases. All appeal stages are recorded in tamper-resistant audit logs to support traceability, regulatory review, and post-incident analysis. Following resolution, affected users or operators receive a structured notification explaining the outcome and rationale at an appropriate level of technical detail. By formalizing contestability as an implementable workflow rather than an abstract principle, this SOP embeds accountability, transparency, and legitimacy directly into trust-aware AIoT authentication, providing both policymakers and system designers with a governance-ready reference model.

Operationalizing Trust-Aware Architectures: Technical Building Blocks

Trust-aware authentication architectures can be operationalized by integrating existing technical standards with socio-communicative design principles. At the access layer, Zero-Trust principles enable continuous, context-sensitive authentication rather than static credentials. At the identity layer, FIDO2 and OIDC provide interoperable, passwordless mechanisms that reduce attack surfaces while enhancing usability.

Reputation and accountability can be supported through DLT-based audit trails or verifiable credentials, enabling decentralized yet inspectable records of device behavior and authentication events. Crucially, these mechanisms must be paired with communicative transparency layers—dashboards, explanations, and contestation channels—so that trust signals are interpretable rather than opaque.

This integration transforms authentication from a binary gatekeeping function into a dynamic negotiation between risk, reputation, and legitimacy.

Trade-Offs, Constraints, and Economic Realities

Implementing trust-aware architectures introduces significant technical and economic trade-offs, particularly for resource-constrained AIoT devices. Continuous authentication increases computational overhead, reputation systems add storage and communication costs, and transparency mechanisms demand organizational investment.

A lightweight trust model may preserve battery life and latency but offer limited accountability, while a feature-rich architecture enhances legitimacy at the cost of complexity and expense. Designers must therefore navigate a continuum rather than pursue idealized security.

Acknowledging these trade-offs strengthens rather than weakens the chapter's argument: trust-aware security is not about maximal control, but about proportionate, context-sensitive design.

Threat Modeling and Adversarial Risks in Reputation-Based Authentication

While reputation-based authentication offers a promising pathway toward adaptive and socially grounded trust in AIoT ecosystems, it also introduces **distinct adversarial risks** that can undermine both security and legitimacy if left unaddressed. Reputation signals, by their nature, are vulnerable to manipulation, coordination, and misrepresentation—particularly in large-scale, heterogeneous, and resource-constrained AIoT environments.

Accordingly, trust-aware authentication architectures must incorporate **explicit threat modeling** that anticipates how reputation systems may be attacked, gamed, or distorted, and how such risks can be mitigated without negating the benefits of adaptability and transparency. Table 4 summarizes key adversarial threats commonly associated with reputation-based authentication in AIoT systems and outlines lightweight but effective mitigation strategies. See Table 4.

Table 4. Adversarial threats and mitigation strategies in reputation-based authentication

Threat Type	Description	Potential Impact	Primary Mitigation Mechanisms
Sybil Attack	An adversary creates or controls multiple fake devices or identities to artificially boost reputation or gain unauthorized access	Erosion of trust signals; unauthorized access at scale	Stake-weighting tied to verifiable identities; device attestation to limit identity proliferation
Collusion	Multiple legitimate devices or actors coordinate to falsely elevate reputational standing or mask malicious behavior	Distorted reputation scores; delayed detection of abuse	Rate limits on reputation influence; anomaly detection for correlated behavior patterns
Reputation Inflation	Gradual or sudden manipulation of reputation scores without corresponding trustworthy behavior	Loss of credibility of reputation system; reduced legitimacy	Temporal decay of reputation; attestation-backed reputation updates
Sensor Spoofing	Injection of falsified sensor data to misrepresent device state or environmental context	Incorrect authentication decisions; cascading system failures	Hardware-backed attestation; cross-sensor consistency checks; anomaly detection

These mitigation mechanisms are intentionally complementary rather than exhaustive. Stake-weighting and rate limits constrain the influence of individual actors, while attestation anchors reputation updates in verifiable device states. Anomaly detection serves as a cross-cutting safeguard, identifying deviations from expected behavioral baselines without requiring full visibility into sensitive system internals.

By explicitly acknowledging adversarial dynamics, this threat modeling approach reinforces the chapter's central claim: trust-aware authentication must be resilient not only to technical attacks, but also to strategic manipulation of trust itself. Incorporating such safeguards strengthens both the security posture and the social legitimacy of reputation-based AIoT authentication systems, aligning technical robustness with governance and accountability expectations.

Evaluating Trust-Aware Authentication: Metrics and KPIs

Normative commitments to trust, transparency, and legitimacy in AIoT authentication systems require empirical grounding to move beyond aspirational design principles. To ensure that trust-aware authentication architectures can be assessed, compared, and governed in practice, this chapter proposes a concise set of evaluation metrics and Key Performance Indicators (KPIs) that capture both technical performance and socio-communicative outcomes.

Rather than introducing an exhaustive measurement framework, the intent is to define a minimal, cross-domain KPI set that enables pilots, audits, and regulatory oversight while remaining feasible for real-world AIoT deployments.

Core Metrics for Trust-Aware Authentication

Table 5 summarizes representative KPIs that together reflect security robustness, usability, procedural fairness, and communicative effectiveness.

Table 5. Key metrics for evaluating trust-aware AIoT authentication

KPI	Description	Measurement Rationale
False Lockout Rate	Percentage of legitimate users or devices incorrectly denied access	Indicates usability cost and risk of legitimacy erosion
Adaptive Challenge Rate (%)	Proportion of authentication events triggering additional verification factors	Reflects calibration of risk-based authentication policies
Mean Appeal Resolution Time	Average time required to resolve authentication appeals or overrides	Measures effectiveness of contestability and redress mechanisms
Device Attestation Freshness	Proportion of devices with up-to-date and verifiable attestation states	Signals technical integrity and device trustworthiness
Trust Survey Delta	Change in user-reported trust levels before and after system deployment or updates	Captures perceived legitimacy and social acceptance
Dashboard Engagement Rate	Frequency of access to public trust dashboards by users or stakeholders	Proxy for transparency visibility and communicative reach

Importantly, these metrics should be interpreted collectively rather than in isolation. For example, a low false lockout rate coupled with a high adaptive challenge rate may indicate excessive friction, while rapid appeal resolution without dashboard engagement may suggest procedural fairness without effective public communication.

By embedding such KPIs into evaluation and reporting cycles, trust-aware authentication systems become *observable and contestable* rather than opaque. This measurement-oriented approach supports comparative analysis across regions and sectors, facilitates regulatory oversight, and enables iterative refinement of authentication policies.

In this sense, evaluation metrics serve not merely as performance indicators but as governance instruments, aligning cryptographic robustness, user experience, and institutional legitimacy within secured AIoT ecosystems.

Policy and Governance Implications

Policy and governance in AIoT authentication are often imagined as orderly systems governed by standards and protocols, yet in practice they are shaped by politics, culture, and collective memory. Trust is unevenly distributed across regions, constructed through distinct historical experiences of governance and accountability. Comparative country cases reveal wide variation in approaches, but they converge on a common insight: technical security mechanisms, however advanced, struggle to endure without social legitimacy. Authentication frameworks succeed not merely by preventing breaches, but by aligning with public expectations of transparency and fairness.

The United States illustrates this tension clearly through the IoT Cybersecurity Improvement Act of 2020, which mandates NIST standards for federally procured devices, emphasizing authentication and identity management. While this top-down, technically rigorous framework promises consistency and accountability, it operates under the long shadow of surveillance controversies, particularly the Snowden disclosures. Advocacy groups and segments of the public continue to distinguish between compliance and legitimacy, arguing that adherence to standards does not automatically translate into trust. The U.S. case thus underscores a cautionary lesson: regulatory sophistication can enforce security, but without openness, narrative, and accountability, it cannot fully repair or sustain public confidence.

In Europe, the governance of AIoT authentication has taken a markedly different route, one that integrates security into the broader moral and legal architecture of the digital society. Rather than relying primarily on technical compliance, the European Union has crafted a layered system through instruments like the Cybersecurity Act and the General Data Protection Regulation (GDPR). Together, these policies form a dual framework: the Cybersecurity Act provides certification schemes to ensure device resilience, while the GDPR secures privacy and personal data as legal rights. Countries such as Germany and the Netherlands have embedded these principles into their smart city projects, framing authentication not merely as a technological safeguard but as a civic guarantee (European Union Agency for Cybersecurity [ENISA], 2021). This approach conveys to citizens that their identities and data are not commodities to be traded away but dignities to be respected. It is this rights-based framing that distinguishes Europe's model, as it roots legitimacy not in compliance checklists but in a philosophy of digital citizenship.

What I find compelling is how Europe's strategy transforms governance into a narrative of empowerment rather than constraint. By recognizing authentication as part of a citizen's entitlement to privacy and security, the EU has shifted the discourse from one of obligation to one of collective ownership. Trust, in this context, is cultivated not by the state demanding faith in its authority but by embedding safeguards that reflect the values of democracy, accountability, and respect for human dignity. Citizens, therefore, approach AIoT infrastructures less as passive consumers and more as rights-bearing participants whose autonomy is acknowledged and protected. Yet this model is not without challenges—balancing innovation with regulatory stringency remains a constant negotiation, as some industries warn that excessive regulation could slow technological progress. Still, the European case demonstrates that when governance succeeds in aligning technology with societal values, legitimacy grows deeper and more resilient, offering lessons that extend far beyond the continent.

In Singapore, the pursuit of digital transformation under the *Smart Nation* initiative illustrates how trust can be actively cultivated through competence and careful statecraft. Authentication systems are embedded into daily life, from healthcare to transportation, underpinned by the Personal Data Protection Act (PDPA) that seeks to reassure citizens about data governance (Chia, 2020). What distinguishes Singapore is the way its government blends technical assurance with consistent communication—citizens are reminded that technology is not merely efficient but also protective of their well-being. The narrative of trust here is less about abstract compliance and more about tangible service delivery: when people see systems working seamlessly in practice, trust is reinforced. This creates a social compact where technological adoption feels less like surveillance and more like participation in a shared national project.

Yet even Singapore's carefully managed model carries inherent tensions. The same infrastructures that promise convenience and security could, in another context, be perceived as instruments of excessive state control. Critics warn that without constant transparency, the boundary between governance and surveillance may blur, particularly in a society where the state occupies such a central role in daily life. Trust in Singapore, therefore, is maintained not only by competence but by the state's ability to continuously demonstrate restraint and accountability. This dynamic illustrates a broader truth about AIoT governance: legitimacy is not earned once but constantly renegotiated through communication and practice. For Singapore, the challenge lies in proving that its efficiency-driven model remains genuinely citizen-centered rather than slipping into paternalistic oversight.

China, by contrast, tells a very different story, one that reflects the other side of Asia's digital governance spectrum. Here, AIoT authentication tools such as facial recognition, biometric IDs, and data-driven monitoring systems are rolled out on a massive scale, often justified in the name of public security and social stability. These technologies are embedded in smart city projects and social credit systems that claim to enhance safety but are widely criticized for reinforcing authoritarian control (Feldstein, 2019). Unlike Singapore's emphasis on service and reassurance, China's model leans heavily on state authority, framing compliance as patriotic duty rather than participatory trust. The sheer efficiency and scale of deployment are unmatched globally, yet legitimacy is secured less through dialogue with citizens and more through political enforcement.

What makes China's case both fascinating and troubling is that the very tools celebrated for innovation can simultaneously erode the foundations of trust. For many citizens, the state's narrative of safety resonates, but for others—particularly critics and external observers—these systems epitomize surveillance over empowerment. This dual perception underscores the fragility of legitimacy when it is anchored primarily in coercion rather than consent. China demonstrates that trust can be manufactured through control, but such trust is brittle, vulnerable to resistance, and dependent on the endurance of state authority. In this sense, Asia presents a profound contrast within itself: in Singapore, trust is cultivated through service-oriented governance, while in China, it is asserted through state power. Together, these cases reveal the thin line separating technological empowerment from digital repression, and the decisive role of governance narratives in shaping how authentication is received.

Kenya provides one of the most compelling stories of how community trust can serve as the backbone of digital innovation. The rise of *M-Pesa* and mobile-based IoT infrastructures demonstrates that when citizens place faith in private actors, entire ecosystems can flourish. Authentication in this context was not initially formalized through national regulation but emerged organically through everyday reliance on telecom operators who became de facto guardians of security (Donovan & Park, 2019). What makes Kenya remarkable is the inclusivity of this model: millions of citizens who were previously excluded from financial systems suddenly gained access through mobile platforms, and their trust in the technology was anchored less in formal law than in lived experience. Adoption spread quickly because it worked, because it was accessible, and because it was embedded in familiar networks of community interaction.

Yet, the Kenyan case also exposes the fragility of trust when it is grounded almost entirely in social capital without robust institutional scaffolding. The same operators that enabled financial inclusion hold extraordinary power over authentication, and in the absence of strong regulation, risks of exploitation, fraud, or systemic collapse loom large. Unlike Europe's rights-based approach or Singapore's transparent state-led governance, Kenya's model relies on the goodwill and reputation of corporate actors, which can never substitute for institutionalized accountability. Community trust here is powerful but precarious—it inspires adoption and innovation, yet it is inherently vulnerable to breaches that could erode confidence overnight. Kenya's trajectory thus reveals both the promise of grassroots-driven trust and the peril of leaving such a foundation unprotected by policy and governance structures.

In Latin America, Brazil stands as a vivid example of how laws on paper do not automatically translate into legitimacy in practice. With the passage of the General Data Protection Law (LGPD) and the rollout of smart city initiatives in places like São Paulo, Brazil sought to emulate the regulatory sophistication of Europe (Cavalcante & de Almeida, 2021). At first glance, the country appears well positioned to align its AIoT governance with global best practices, embedding authentication requirements into legal frameworks that emphasize privacy and accountability. Citizens are told that their rights are protected, and institutions present themselves as modernized actors in a digitally integrated state. Yet beneath this surface lies a persistent problem: a fragile institutional environment marked by corruption scandals, uneven enforcement, and weak public confidence in state authority.

This tension between legal formality and institutional credibility highlights the central paradox of Brazil's governance landscape. Citizens are quick to sense when regulation serves more as performance than protection, when frameworks are showcased as symbols of modernity rather than lived guarantees of safety. In such contexts, law functions more as aspiration than assurance, and legitimacy falters accordingly. What emerges is a governance model that appears sophisticated to external observers but struggles to generate durable trust at home. Brazil, therefore, underscores a critical lesson for AIoT authentication: that no matter how advanced legal texts may be, they cannot substitute for the everyday integrity of institutions tasked with upholding them. True legitimacy arises not from regulatory mimicry but from consistent credibility, the kind that is felt in daily interactions rather than proclaimed in legislative halls.

Taken together, these cases remind us that policy and governance in AIoT authentication are not simply about producing global standards or checklists. They are about telling credible stories of protection, fairness, and accountability that resonate with local cultures and historical experiences. For me, the deeper insight is this: trust is not the "last mile" of governance—it is the very terrain upon which governance either flourishes or collapses. Technical robustness, regulatory mandates, and community engagement must converge if AIoT authentication is to be both secure and legitimate. And if we ignore the communicative and cultural dimensions of policy, we risk building systems that are technically sound but socially brittle.

Looking across continents, one cannot help but notice that AIoT authentication is not governed by a single universal formula, but rather by a patchwork of strategies that reflect local histories, political institutions, and community norms. The United States leans on technical rigor through NIST frameworks, Europe emphasizes rights and legal guarantees, Singapore cultivates trust through transparent state-led innovation, Kenya depends on community trust in private actors, and Brazil attempts to legislate its way into legitimacy despite fragile institutional credibility. These variations are not random—they embody different balances of technical standards, regulatory authority, and cultural legitimacy.

To make sense of these diverse approaches, it is useful to map them into a comparative lens. A thematic matrix highlights how each region navigates the relationship between trust, reputation, and governance in AIoT authentication. Such a mapping does not flatten differences but illuminates patterns—showing where trust is institutionalized, where it is contested, and where it precariously rests on community relationships or brand reputations.

This matrix also serves as a mirror for future pathways. By juxtaposing regions, we see not only contrasts but also shared vulnerabilities: the U.S. struggles with transparency, Europe with scalability, Asia with political legitimacy, Africa with regulatory gaps, and Latin America with institutional trust. The goal is not to declare winners and losers but to draw lessons that may inform more globally resilient AIoT governance. In essence, the matrix is less a taxonomy than a reflective tool: it invites us to ask not just "what policies exist?" but "why do they resonate—or fail—with the people they are meant to protect?" To highlight these global differences more systematically, Table 6 organizes governance approaches by continent, underscoring how compliance, rights, state control, community reliance, and institutional fragility shape authentication practices. See Table 6.

Table 6. Global AIoT authentication governance

Region / Case	**Core Policy Approach**	**Trust Anchor**	**Key Challenge**	**Narrative of Legitimacy**
United States (North America)	Federal IoT Cybersecurity Improvement Act, NIST frameworks	Technical compliance & state authority	Public skepticism post-surveillance scandals	"Secure by standard, but fragile in trust"
European Union (Europe)	GDPR + Cybersecurity Act (rights-based, certification)	Legal rights & institutional oversight	Balancing privacy guarantees with innovation speed	"Security as a civic right"
Singapore (Asia)	Smart Nation + PDPA	State-led transparency & collectivist trust	Avoiding drift into surveillance state	"Trust through state competence"

continued on following page

Table 6. Continued

Region / Case	Core Policy Approach	Trust Anchor	Key Challenge	Narrative of Legitimacy
Kenya (Africa)	Community trust in telecom-led IoT (e.g., M-Pesa)	Social trust & private actor reputation	Weak regulatory scaffolding, risk of exploitation	"Innovation by community faith"
Brazil (Latin America)	LGPD + smart city frameworks	Legal frameworks & public accountability	Fragile institutions, corruption undermines legitimacy	"Law without lasting trust"

Source: Author, 2025.

As shown in Table 6, global approaches to AIoT authentication governance reveal diverse strategies shaped by regional contexts. Compliance does not automatically translate into legitimacy, as the experience of the United States makes clear. Regulations such as the IoT Cybersecurity Improvement Act and NIST frameworks may ensure that devices follow the highest technical standards, but the collective memory of surveillance scandals still lingers in the public imagination. People are not convinced by compliance alone, because trust is not built only on codes and checklists but also on lived experiences of transparency and accountability. This reveals a paradox: a nation that leads the world in technical rigor struggles to persuade its own citizens that such rigor equates to safety. The lesson is unmistakable—trust is emotional before it is procedural, and once shaken, it cannot be restored by standards alone.

Europe provides a different kind of narrative, one that treats authentication as a civic right rather than a technical obligation. By embedding data protection and security guarantees into the GDPR and the Cybersecurity Act, European governance has reframed authentication as an extension of personal dignity. Citizens see these measures not simply as restrictions or burdens, but as affirmations of their autonomy in a digital society. The emotional resonance of rights-based governance strengthens legitimacy, because people feel protected not only by rules but by principles that affirm their humanity. In this sense, Europe demonstrates that trust grows deeper when security is framed as a matter of justice and citizenship, rather than merely compliance.

Singapore shows how trust can be nurtured through competence and transparency, where citizens perceive authentication not as an intrusion but as a promise of efficiency and safety. The Smart Nation initiative, paired with data protection laws, reassures people that technology serves collective well-being. Yet the case of China reveals a darker mirror, where similar tools—facial recognition, biometric IDs, and AI-enabled surveillance—are deployed in ways that generate suspicion and international criticism. The technology is not what distinguishes these cases; it is the surrounding political culture and the narrative crafted around its use. The line between legitimacy and control is perilously thin, reminding us that trust can be cultivated with care or coerced through power, and the difference lies in whether citizens feel respected or subdued.

Kenya highlights the fragile power of community trust. The rapid adoption of M-Pesa and mobile-based IoT systems owes much to the collective faith placed in telecom operators, who became de facto custodians of identity and security. People embraced these systems because they worked and because they trusted familiar institutions, not because a state mandate demanded it. Yet this reliance on social trust reveals its vulnerability when formal safeguards are weak; fraud, exploitation, or corporate negligence could quickly unravel the very trust that enabled innovation. Community-driven legitimacy is inspiring in its inclusivity, but without regulatory scaffolding, it risks becoming a gamble. The Kenyan case shows both the promise and the peril of relying on social capital as the foundation of digital security.

Brazil underscores that laws written on paper cannot replace the integrity of institutions in practice. Its General Data Protection Law and smart city projects reflect regulatory sophistication, yet persistent concerns about corruption and weak enforcement undermine their credibility. Citizens sense when rules exist more as symbols than as shields, when governance performs protection rather than genuinely providing it. In such contexts, trust erodes despite the presence of formal frameworks, because legitimacy is experienced in daily interactions, not decrees. Brazil's struggle is a reminder that the sustainability of AIoT governance depends not only on legal innovation but on institutions capable of embodying the principles they proclaim. And here lies the bridge to what comes next: if compliance, rights, competence, community trust, and legal frameworks each show both power and fragility, then the path forward must be to design *trust-aware authentication architectures*—systems that do not merely secure devices, but weave trust itself into their very foundations. SeeTable 7.

Table 7.

Region	Trust Anchor	UI Defaults	Governance Knobs
EU	Rights	Consent-first	Regulator audit
Kenya	Community	Simplicity	Telco-led
Singapore	Competence	Assurance logs	State oversight

Source: Author, 2025.

Limitations and Ethical Pitfalls of Trust-Aware Authentication

Trust-aware architectures also raise ethical risks. Algorithmic reputation systems may encode bias, reinforce inequality, or drift toward coercive "social credit" dynamics if left unchecked. Transparency, while normatively desirable, may conflict with intellectual property, security secrecy, or national interests.

By foregrounding these tensions, this chapter does not present trust-aware authentication as a panacea, but as a deliberately constrained design philosophy that must be governed by ethical safeguards, contestability, and democratic oversight.

CONCLUSION AND FUTURE RESEARCH DIRECTIONS

This chapter demonstrates that trust and reputation are not peripheral concerns in AIoT authentication but foundational conditions for security and legitimacy. Authentication cannot be reduced to cryptographic rigor or regulatory compliance alone; it is a socio-technical and communicative process shaped by human expectations, institutional credibility, and cultural context. Insights from social and communication theories—including SCOT, Actor–Network Theory, and risk communication—reveal that authentication systems are co-produced by engineers, regulators, industries, media, and users, with trust evolving dynamically and reputation functioning as collective memory. Case evidence from healthcare and smart cities further shows that legitimacy depends less on technical sophistication than on perceived fairness, accountability, and dignity, and that trust can erode rapidly when transparency and governance fail.

Looking forward, sustainable AIoT security requires trust-aware authentication architectures that embed trust directly into both system design and governance. Such architectures must integrate adaptive reputation mechanisms, transparent communication, contestability, ethical safeguards, and sensitivity to cultural variation, supported by interoperable standards and participatory oversight. Future research should empirically examine how reputation and transparency enhance resilience, how trust is rebuilt after failures, and how cultural differences shape acceptance of authentication technologies. Ultimately, AIoT authentication must be understood not only as a mechanism for identity verification but as a relational practice that cultivates confidence and legitimacy—recognizing that trust itself is the most durable form of security.

REFERENCES

Aaqib, M., Ali, A., Chen, L., & Nibouche, O. (2023). IoT trust and reputation: A survey and taxonomy. *Journal of Cloud Computing (Heidelberg, Germany)*, *12*(42), 1–21. DOI: 10.1186/s13677-023-00416-8

Alsyouf, A., Ishak, M. K., & Shahzad, M. (2022). Security and privacy challenges in healthcare IoT. *Journal of Medical Systems*, *46*(5), 1–12. DOI: 10.1007/s10916-022-01852-7

Cavalcante, P., & de Almeida, C. (2021). Smart cities and data protection in Brazil: Legal and governance challenges. *Journal of Urban Technology*, *28*(4), 3–22. DOI: 10.1080/10630732.2020.1841839

Chia, L. (2020). Singapore's Smart Nation initiative: Balancing innovation and trust. *Asian Journal of Comparative Politics*, *5*(2), 133–150. DOI: 10.1177/2057891119897614

Donovan, K., & Park, E. (2019). Perpetual trust: Mobile money and the contours of control in Kenya. *World Development*, *123*, 104611. DOI: 10.1016/j.worlddev.2019.104611

European Union Agency for Cybersecurity (ENISA). (2021). *Cybersecurity of smart cities: Protecting critical infrastructures and services*. ENISA.

Feldstein, S. (2019). The road to digital unfreedom: How artificial intelligence is reshaping repression. *Journal of Democracy*, *30*(1), 40–52. DOI: 10.1353/jod.2019.0003

Goodman, E., & Powles, J. (2019). Urban data and smart cities: Privacy, trust and the case of Sidewalk Toronto. *Fordham Law Review*, *88*(2), 457–482. https://ir.lawnet.fordham.edu/flr/vol88/iss2/5

Inglehart, R. (2018). *Cultural evolution: People's motivations are changing, and reshaping the world*. Cambridge University Press. DOI: 10.1017/9781108613880

Latour, B. (2005). *Reassembling the social: An introduction to actor-network-theory*. Oxford University Press. DOI: 10.1093/oso/9780199256044.001.0001

Mayer, R. C., Davis, J. H., & Schoorman, F. D. (1995). An integrative model of organizational trust. *Academy of Management Review*, *20*(3), 709–734. DOI: 10.2307/258792

McKnight, D. H., Cummings, L. L., & Chervany, N. L. (1998). Initial trust formation in new organizational relationships. *Academy of Management Review*, *23*(3), 473–490. DOI: 10.2307/259290

Morozov, E., & Bria, F. (2018). *Rethinking the smart city: Democratizing urban technology*. Rosa Luxemburg Stiftung.

National Institute of Standards and Technology. (n.d.). *Cybersecurity for the Internet of Things (IoT) Program*. U.S. Department of Commerce. Retrieved April 10, 2025, from https://www.nist.gov/itl/applied-cybersecurity/nist-cybersecurity-iot-program

Pinch, T., & Bijker, W. E. (1984). The social construction of facts and artifacts: Or how the sociology of science and the sociology of technology might benefit each other. *Social Studies of Science*, *14*(3), 399–441. DOI: 10.1177/030631284014003004

Raman, A., & Sinha, A. (2020). Privacy, surveillance and public trust: The Aarogya Setu app. *Economic and Political Weekly*, *55*(23), 12–15.

Rose, S., Borchert, O., Mitchell, S., & Connelly, S. *Zero trust architecture. NIST SP 800-207, 2020.*

Sharon, T. (2021). When digital health meets digital capitalism, how many common goods are at stake? *Big Data & Society*, *8*(1), 1–12. DOI: 10.1177/2053951721996034

Slovic, P. (1987). Perception of risk. *Science*, *236*(4799), 280–285. DOI: 10.1126/science.3563507

Solove, D. J., & Citron, D. K. (2018). Risk and anxiety in data breaches. *Texas Law Review*, *96*(4), 737–786.

U.S. Food and Drug Administration. (2019). *Medtronic recalls insulin pumps due to potential cybersecurity risks*. FDA Safety Communication. Retrieved from https://www.fda.gov/medical-devices/safety-communications

Chapter 13

Traditional Authentication Mechanisms, Often Designed for Human-Centric or Enterprise IT Environments, Are Ill-Equipped to Address the Unique Challenges of AIoT

David Yehezkiel
http://orcid.org/0009-0007-4226-8987
Universitas Esa Unggul, Indonesia

Andrew Novan Then
http://orcid.org/0009-0005-5981-6463
Universitas Esa Unggul, Indonesia

Binastya Anggara Sekti
http://orcid.org/0000-0001-5489-4888
Universitas Esa Unggul, Indonesia

Dwi Sartika Simatupang
Universitas Esa Unggul, Indonesia

DOI: 10.4018/979-8-3373-6299-1.ch013

ABSTRACT

Traditional authentication mechanisms designed for human-centric or enterprise IT environments struggle to secure the rapidly expanding landscape of the Artificial Intelligence of Things (AIoT), where billions of autonomous devices interact across dynamic, resource-limited, and highly distributed networks. Legacy approaches lack the scalability, context awareness, and machine-to-machine coordination needed to protect systems characterized by continuous data exchange and decentralized control. Emerging solutions such as AI-driven adaptive authentication, decentralized identity frameworks, blockchain-based credential management, and zero-trust security models offer more resilient foundations for identity assurance in autonomous ecosystems. Key implementation considerations include computational efficiency, interoperability, latency constraints, and real-time risk assessment. The discussion provides an integrated perspective on how modern authentication paradigms can support secure, scalable, and trustworthy AIoT environments.

1. INTRODUCTION

The convergence of Artificial Intelligence (AI) and the Internet of Things (IoT) has given rise to a transformative technological paradigm known as the Artificial Intelligence of Things (AIoT). In this rapidly evolving ecosystem, billions of interconnected devices are capable of sensing, processing, learning, and making autonomous decisions in real time often without direct human involvement. These devices communicate continuously, analyze contextual data, and adapt their behavior dynamically, enabling a wide range of next-generation applications across sectors such as smart cities, precision agriculture, industrial automation, logistics, energy management, and digital healthcare. AIoT holds the promise of unprecedented efficiency, responsiveness, and intelligence in both public and private infrastructures. Artificial Intelligence of Things (AIoT) has great potential in applications that connect intelligent objects running AI models, such as Deep Neural Networks (DNNs), to support real-time decision-making (Ghamri, Djamaa, Benatia, & Hosni, 2026).

Yet, as AIoT systems grow in scale, heterogeneity, and complexity, longstanding models of digital security especially in the domain of authentication are increasingly proving unfit for purpose. Traditional authentication mechanisms, such as static passwords, shared secrets, digital certificates, and two-factor authentication, were originally developed for human users operating within centralized, well-defined enterprise networks. These mechanisms lack the flexibility, contextual awareness, and scalability needed to authenticate and manage trust among vast, autonomous, and frequently resource-constrained devices. Many AIoT nodes operate with limited computational resources, intermittent network connectivity, or mobility, complicating both identity verification and the enforcement of secure interactions. The Artificial Intelligence of Things (AIoT) ecosystem faces challenges such as limited energy and resource heterogeneity, especially when using the Federated Learning (FL) framework (Y. Zhang, Luo, Yang, Wu, & Hu, 2025).

This chapter investigates the widening gap between legacy authentication paradigms and the emerging operational realities of AIoT environments. It examines the structural and architectural limitations of conventional methods when applied to distributed, dynamic, and decentralized systems. Furthermore, it highlights the need for adaptive, intelligent, and context-aware authentication frameworks that can meet the performance, scalability, and security demands of modern AIoT deployments. By analyzing both the challenges and the promising solutions, including emerging paradigms such as AI-driven authentication, decentralized identity management, and zero-trust models, the chapter aims to provide researchers, engineers, system architects, and policymakers with critical insights for securing the next generation of autonomous and interconnected systems. Federated Learning (FL) empowers Internet-of-Things (IoT) devices to train intelligent models without sharing sensitive data and facilitate the transition to the Artificial Intelligence of Things (AIoT) ecosystem (Djamaa, Yekhlef, Kouda, & Bradai, 2025).

2. BACKGROUND AND MOTIVATION

The evolution of cybersecurity strategies has historically focused on enterprise systems and user-centric environments, where access control and authentication were designed with the human user as the primary actor. Traditional approaches such as username-password pairs, digital certificates, smart cards, and biometric verification have long relied on the assumption that authentication is initiated by a human interacting with a fixed device in a stable and managed network environment. These design assumptions, while sufficient for conventional IT infrastructures, are increasingly incompatible with the operational dynamics of AIoT ecosystems, where autonomous devices not human users frequently initiate communications, perform transactions, and interact with other machines in real time. The size of the data transmitted through various communication systems is increasing due to technological advancements in Artificial Intelligence (AIoT) and the Internet of Things (IoT) (Albalwy & Almohaimeed, 2025).

AIoT environments are defined by a high degree of complexity, device heterogeneity, and autonomy. These systems involve a wide array of devices, from low-power environmental sensors to mobile robotic platforms, all of which generate and exchange data continuously in dynamic topologies. Unlike traditional computing environments, many AIoT devices operate with minimal or no human oversight, are often deployed in physically exposed or hazardous environments, and must remain functional under resource constraints such as limited processing power, low memory capacity, minimal energy consumption, and sporadic connectivity. For example, sensors deployed in agricultural fields may need to authenticate securely while relying on battery power and intermittent access to network gateways, while industrial drones must make split-second trust decisions during autonomous navigation in restricted zones. In such contexts, traditional authentication methods are not only inefficient and latency-prone but can also introduce new vectors for attack or system failure when scaled across millions of endpoints. The use of Internet of Things (IoT) devices in Artificial Intelligence of Things (AIoT) applications has been a major change in the security of AIoT under cybersecurity, focusing on the protection of cloud-based hardware connected to the internet (Thapliyal et al., 2024).

Moreover, AIoT heralds a paradigm shift toward machine-to-machine (M2M) communication as the norm rather than the exception. Devices must be able to identify, authenticate, and trust one another autonomously without human intervention. This requires authentication mechanisms that are lightweight, scalable, adaptive to changing conditions, and resilient to failures features that legacy, centralized systems fail to deliver. The dependency on central identity providers in conventional architectures introduces latency, reduces availability, and creates single points of failure making such systems particularly ill-suited for distributed AIoT deployments operating at the edge or in environments with unreliable connectivity. Automated predictive maintenance (PdM) is essential to minimize unplanned downtime and can reduce operational costs on modern computer numerical control machines (Xia & Hu, 2025).

The motivation behind this chapter is driven by the pressing need to revisit and fundamentally rethink the assumptions underlying traditional authentication models. As AIoT continues to evolve and expand across critical sectors including healthcare, manufacturing, transportation, and agriculture there is an urgent demand for innovative, intelligent, and context-aware authentication strategies. These new models must go beyond static credentials and incorporate risk-based access control, behavioral analytics, and machine learning insights to dynamically assess trust and adapt authentication policies in real time. Without such advancements, the rapid proliferation of AIoT systems will outpace our ability to secure them, leaving critical infrastructures increasingly vulnerable to exploitation.

3. THE LIMITATIONS OF TRADITIONAL AUTHENTICATION MECHANISMS

Traditional authentication systems were designed with the assumption that humans are the primary actors. Passwords, security tokens, and biometrics assume direct user interaction, static identities, and predictable behavior patterns. However, AIoT environments shift this paradigm entirely. Devices in AIoT often operate without human intervention and must authenticate autonomously with minimal latency.

3.1 Human-Centric Assumptions and Their Failures

Traditional authentication systems were designed with the assumption that humans are the primary actors. Passwords, security tokens, and biometrics assume direct user interaction, static identities, and predictable behavior patterns. However, AIoT environments shift this paradigm entirely. Devices in AIoT often operate without human intervention and must authenticate autonomously with minimal latency. For example, a smart traffic sensor in a smart city must authenticate to a central data aggregator multiple times per minute, often without human oversight. It is not feasible to manually input a password or OTP in such cases. The inability of traditional systems to accommodate these requirements leads to increased latency, reduced reliability, and heightened vulnerability. The vehicle safety framework can be customized specifically for smart cities in the realm of Artificial Intelligence of Things (AIoT) (Jagatheesaperumal, Bibri, Huang, Rajapandian, & Parthiban, 2024).

Moreover, many conventional mechanisms rely on session persistence and assume prolonged user presence, which does not align with the intermittent communication patterns seen in mobile AIoT nodes. When connectivity is unstable, these assumptions lead to session drops, expired credentials, and failed authentications that may disrupt critical services. v

3.2 Centralized Identity Models

Legacy authentication models frequently depend on centralized identity management infrastructures, such as enterprise identity providers or cloud-based access control systems. While effective in traditional IT environments, these centralized approaches become problematic in AIoT ecosystems, where devices are geographically distributed, mobile, intermittently connected, or deployed in remote areas. The reliance on a central server creates performance bottlenecks, particularly when thousands or even millions of devices attempt to authenticate simultaneously. It also introduces a single point of failure any disruption or compromise of the identity provider can cascade into widespread authentication outages and security vulnerabilities. In an AIoT-enabled and green secure supply chain system (SCS), robust device authentication measures are critical to maintaining the integrity of the ecosystem (Miao et al., 2025).

To address these limitations, the AIoT landscape is shifting toward more decentralized, federated, and edge-based authentication strategies. These approaches reduce dependency on centralized infrastructure, enabling secure identity verification even in low-connectivity or offline scenarios. Technologies such as blockchain-based identity systems provide immutable, tamper-evident credential management, while decentralized identifiers (DIDs) allow entities to manage and prove their identities without relying on a central authority. Edge-based authentication further distributes trust by allowing local processing of credentials, improving resilience and reducing latency. Together, these emerging solutions offer more scalable and robust alternatives, better aligned with the operational realities of modern AIoT deployments. Figure 1 shows the Limitations of Traditional Authentication in AioT. Non-clonable physical layer attribute-assisted authentication (PLUA) schemes are able to outperform traditional isolated approaches, with the advantage of having reliable fingerprints but these conventional methods have limited flexibility. AIoT devices arise from the distributed nature and complete information, as well as the requirement for short end-to-end latency (Qiu, Yu, Zhuang, Li, & Sun, 2023).

Figure 2 shows the Centralized vs Decentralized Authentication.

Figure 1. Limitations of traditional authentication in AIoT

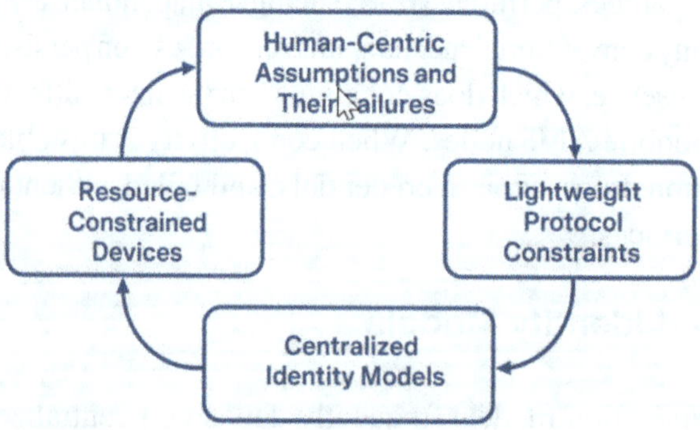

Figure 2. Centralized vs decentralized authentication

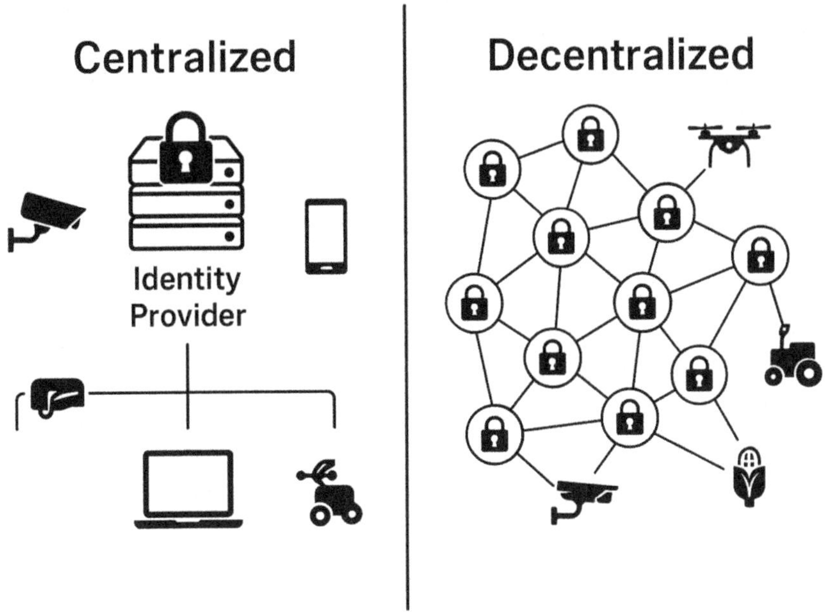

3.3 Lightweight Protocol Constraints

AIoT devices frequently operate under severe resource constraints that fundamentally limit their ability to engage with traditional security and authentication protocols. These constraints include restricted processing capabilities, minimal memory allocation, limited battery life, and constrained bandwidth, all of which severely impact the feasibility of deploying conventional, computation-heavy cryptographic operations. In many AIoT scenarios, devices are expected to perform continuously or in real-time while consuming as little power and computational overhead as possible conditions that stand in stark contrast to the assumptions made by traditional IT-centric authentication models. The growing adoption of Message Queuing Telemetry Transport (MQTT) as a lightweight messaging protocol for IoT applications highlights the need for robust security mechanisms that address resource constraints while ensuring data integrity, confidentiality, and authenticity (Kaganurmath, Cholli, & Anala, 2025).

For instance, public-key cryptographic operations such as RSA or even the more efficient Elliptic Curve Cryptography (ECC) demand levels of processing power and energy consumption that often exceed the capabilities of lightweight microcontrollers typically embedded in IoT sensors and actuators. While ECC offers better key strength at smaller sizes compared to RSA, it can still impose significant latency and energy burdens, particularly during handshake or key exchange phases. The issue is further exacerbated when authentication protocols require multiple communication rounds with centralized servers such as in the case of TLS (Transport Layer Security) which not only consume precious bandwidth but also increase latency and power usage. For battery-powered or intermittently connected devices, these demands may be unacceptable or even infeasible. Private key (e.g., RSA key) protection is a significant issue for cloud but existing keyless or keyguard solutions suffer from performance, elasticity or applicability limitations (Z. Zhang et al., 2023).

This context has led to the emergence of a critical requirement: the development and adoption of lightweight authentication protocols that are purpose-built for the limitations and operational conditions of AIoT devices. To address this need, several specialized protocols have been proposed and are under active development. For example, Datagram TLS (DTLS) offers a connectionless variant of TLS designed to minimize the overhead associated with secure communication over unreliable or low-bandwidth networks. EDHOC (Ephemeral Diffie-Hellman Over COSE) is another promising protocol that enables efficient authenticated key exchange with minimal message size and computation, targeting devices with severe constraints. Additionally, the Lightweight Machine-to-Machine (LwM2M) protocol, developed by the Open Mobile Alliance, integrates authentication, device management, and data transport into a compact framework suitable for constrained environments. Spanning over two decades, the examined enterprise has heavily depended on its internal certificate authority and Public Key Infrastructure (PKI) to uphold its data and systems security (Kamiński & Mazurczyk, 2023).

Despite these innovations, the underlying trade-off between security and efficiency remains a persistent and complex challenge. Protocols designed to reduce computational and communication overhead often must make compromises in cryptographic strength, message complexity, or session management. In some cases, reducing handshake steps or key size might open the door to certain classes of attacks, or fail to meet the stringent security requirements of specific applications. Therefore, striking an optimal balance between performance and security is essential especially in mission-critical AIoT deployments such as medical devices, industrial control systems, and autonomous transportation platforms. In such contexts, any lapse in authentication not only jeopardizes system integrity but can also lead to life-threatening outcomes or catastrophic operational failures.

Consequently, the path forward involves not only technical innovation in protocol design but also careful evaluation of security guarantees in light of real-world constraints and threat models. This necessitates collaboration between device manufacturers, protocol designers, and cybersecurity experts to ensure that lightweight authentication mechanisms are both practically deployable and sufficiently robust to withstand adversarial conditions.

3.4 Device Identity Lifecycle Management

A critical but often overlooked aspect of authentication in AIoT environments is managing the full lifecycle of device identities from provisioning and enrollment to revocation and retirement. In traditional enterprise IT, user identity lifecycle is relatively well defined, with onboarding, role changes, and offboarding processes managed by centralized IT departments. However, in AIoT, managing device identities across diverse environments and deployment conditions introduces a much higher degree of complexity.

For example, consider a fleet of autonomous drones deployed for agricultural monitoring. Each device must be securely enrolled with a unique identity at deployment, authenticate periodically during operations, and be decommissioned securely at the end of its lifecycle. If identity credentials are not properly rotated, revoked, or updated, they can become a liability especially if the device is lost, stolen, or compromised.

The challenge becomes more pronounced in systems with massive scale, where thousands or even millions of devices must be tracked. Manual methods of provisioning or revocation are not feasible. Automation becomes essential, particularly using policy-based identity management frameworks that can adapt to device status, risk score, operational context, and real-time behavior.

Technologies such as X.509 certificates, Trusted Platform Modules (TPM), and secure elements can play a role in device identity management, but these must be supported by robust lifecycle orchestration tools that can scale. Without proper lifecycle control, even the strongest cryptographic techniques can become ineffective over time due to stale or orphaned credentials. The Internet of things (IoT) is expected to have an impact on business and the world at large in a way comparable to the Internet itself (Yousefnezhad, Malhi, Keyriläinen, & Främling, 2023). Figure 3 shows the Device Identity Lifecycle Management.

Figure 3. Device identity lifecycle management

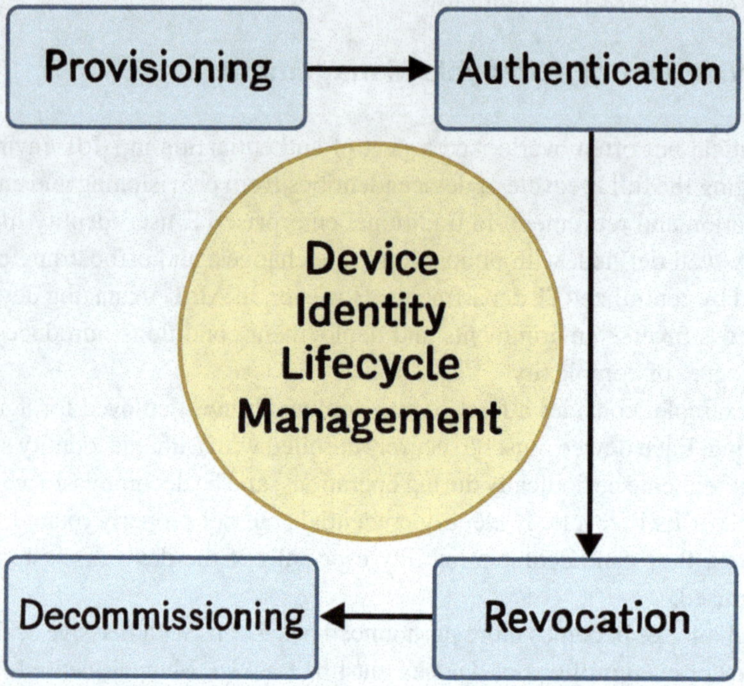

3.5 Scalability Challenges in Multi-Tenant Environments

One of the defining characteristics of modern AIoT ecosystems is the widespread adoption of multi-tenant infrastructures, where multiple organizations, departments, or applications operate on the same underlying platform, network, or cloud-based infrastructure. This architectural model offers significant advantages, such as cost-efficiency, streamlined resource management, and accelerated deployment of services. It enables various stakeholders to share infrastructure while maintaining operational independence. However, despite its benefits, multi-tenancy introduces a new layer of complexity, particularly in the areas of scalability, security, and identity isolation. These complexities are especially pronounced in authentication and identity management processes, which must evolve to support the dynamic, high-volume, and heterogeneous nature of multi-tenant AIoT environments.

Traditional authentication mechanisms designed for human users and relatively static, siloed systems were not architected to accommodate the scale and flexibility required by AIoT infrastructures. In multi-tenant scenarios, thousands or even millions of devices from disparate tenants may simultaneously request authentication, requiring systems to implement fine-grained isolation policies, context-aware identity mapping, and strict enforcement of tenant boundaries. The inability to distinguish between tenants or to enforce tenant-specific policies increases the risk of credential leakage, cross-tenant impersonation, and unauthorized data access. Legacy systems often fall short in providing the necessary granularity and automation needed for secure and seamless multi-tenant operations.

For instance, consider a large-scale smart city deployment where diverse device types such as traffic monitoring sensors, utility meters, environmental detectors, and surveillance cameras are managed by different government agencies, contractors, or private entities. In such a scenario, it is crucial that the authentication system not only verifies the identity of each device but also associates it accurately with the correct tenant, enforces access policies accordingly, and ensures that no unauthorized communication occurs across tenant boundaries. The challenge becomes even more acute when devices operate across multiple trust domains, interact with cross-tenant services, or dynamically change operational contexts based on time, location, or task requirements.

Scalability in this context also involves the performance and responsiveness of identity management systems. These systems must be capable of issuing, validating, revoking, and rotating credentials for a vast and ever-growing population of devices, often in real time and under varying connectivity conditions. Systems that rely on centralized identity providers or monolithic authentication architectures frequently encounter performance bottlenecks, particularly when under load, leading to increased authentication latency, higher failure rates, and degraded service availability. Such limitations are incompatible with the operational demands of AIoT environments, where uptime, low latency, and automation are critical. As a result, there is a pressing need to rethink and redesign identity infrastructures to support scalable, tenant-aware, and resilient authentication frameworks capable of meeting the realities of modern AIoT deployments.

To address these issues, AIoT authentication architectures must incorporate:

- Multi-tenant aware identity models that isolate authentication domains per tenant.
- Federated trust frameworks that allow tenants to define policies while enabling secure interoperability.
- Hierarchical certificate authorities or delegated attestation schemes to offload credential management to trusted intermediaries.
- Scalable authentication proxies or edge gateways that reduce load on central systems while enabling local validation.

Figure 4 shows the Scalable Authentication in Multi-Tenant AIoT

Figure 4. Scalable authentication in multi-tenant AIoT

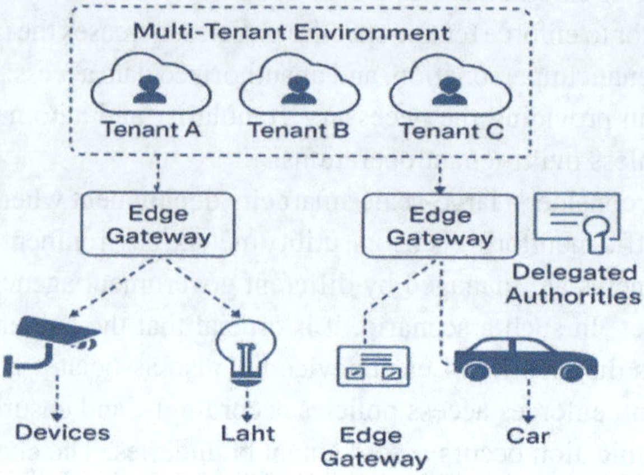

As AIoT deployments continue to scale, the inability to handle multi-tenant authentication scenarios robustly and efficiently will be a major barrier to adoption, particularly in commercial, municipal, and critical infrastructure contexts.

4. EMERGING AUTHENTICATION PARADIGMS FOR AIOT

As traditional authentication mechanisms continue to falter in addressing the unique and rapidly evolving demands of the AIoT (Artificial Intelligence of Things) ecosystem, a new generation of authentication paradigms is emerging to bridge this critical gap. Legacy systems designed primarily for human users operating within centralized, enterprise-controlled environments are ill-equipped to handle the scale, heterogeneity, and autonomy that define AIoT networks. In this landscape, devices not humans are the primary actors, often operating independently, communicating with other machines, and making real-time decisions based on local and distributed intelligence. This transformation necessitates authentication approaches that are context-aware, adaptive, scalable, and capable of functioning in decentralized environments with minimal human intervention.

This chapter delves into the forefront of authentication innovation by exploring several next-generation paradigms that offer promising alternatives to traditional methods. These include AI-powered adaptive authentication systems that can dynamically assess risk and adjust security policies in real time; federated identity frameworks that enable secure identity sharing across organizational and domain boundaries; blockchain-based credentialing systems that provide immutable, decentralized trust anchors; and zero-trust architectures that presume no inherent trust within the network and enforce strict verification at every interaction, particularly suited for autonomous device-to-device communications. Collectively, these paradigms represent a foundational shift from static, perimeter-based, human-centric security models to fluid, distributed, and machine-driven trust architectures that align with the operational realities of modern AIoT ecosystems.

4.1 AI-Powered Contextual and Behavioral Authentication

Artificial Intelligence (AI) and Machine Learning (ML) are being increasingly integrated into authentication frameworks to enable adaptive, risk-based decision-making. Unlike static rule-based mechanisms, AI-driven authentication evaluates dynamic features such as device behavior, time of access, network conditions, and location to determine authentication validity. For example, if a smart camera typically communicates with a central hub every five minutes, a sudden deviation in frequency or data pattern may trigger a risk assessment or request re-authentication. Similarly, wearable health devices may leverage biometric signal patterns (e.g., heart rate trends) as an implicit authentication factor.

This approach enhances security without imposing burdensome verification steps on devices or users. It also enables continuous authentication, where trust is monitored and evaluated throughout a device session rather than at a single entry point. This is particularly valuable for autonomous systems operating in fluctuating environments. Challenges in AI-driven authentication include ensuring model accuracy, preventing adversarial manipulation, and maintaining transparency in trust decisions. Furthermore, lightweight models must be developed for resource-constrained AIoT devices to enable real-time inferencing on the edge.

4.2 Federated Identity Management in Edge AIoT

Federated Identity Management (FIM) provides a framework that allows multiple trusted domains or entities to share identity attributes and authentication tokens without relying on a single central authority. This model, widely used in enterprise and web-based Single Sign-On (SSO), is now being adapted to suit the decentralized and edge-based nature of AIoT systems.

In AIoT environments, devices used by different organizations, jurisdictions, or operational domains often need to interoperate securely. Federated identity allows each domain to maintain control over its identity repository while participating in a broader trust network, enabling cross-domain authentication and policy enforcement.

For example, in smart transportation systems, devices operated by public transit agencies, traffic control, private logistics companies, and emergency services may need to communicate and authenticate securely without sharing a single identity provider. FIM enables these stakeholders to establish bilateral or multilateral trust agreements and utilize standard protocols such as SAML, OAuth 2.0, and OpenID Connect to enable secure authentication and authorization across domains. In AIoT edge deployments, FIM is becoming increasingly important. Edge nodes (gateways, microdata centers) can act as local identity brokers, enforcing access control policies, managing session credentials, and providing cached identity resolution to reduce latency and reliance on cloud infrastructure.

Key advantages of federated identity in AIoT include:

- Decentralization: No single point of failure or control.
- Policy autonomy: Each domain retains control of its identity rules.
- Scalability: New domains or devices can join the trust network with minimal reconfiguration.
- Interoperability: Enables secure collaboration between heterogeneous AIoT ecosystems.

However, federated systems must address potential issues such as trust anchor management, certificate revocation across domains, and consistent policy translation. Privacy concerns may also arise when identity attributes are shared across administrative boundaries.

4.3 Blockchain-Based Credentials and Decentralized Identifiers (DIDs)

As AIoT ecosystems grow in scale and complexity, the need for decentralized, tamper-resistant, and verifiable identity systems becomes more pressing. Blockchain and distributed ledger technologies (DLT) have emerged as promising foundations for managing digital identities in such environments. Two key innovations blockchain-based credentials and decentralized identifiers (DIDs) are gaining traction in addressing the limitations of centralized authentication.

Decentralized Identifiers (DIDs)

DIDs are a new type of identifier that enables verifiable and autonomous digital identities. Unlike traditional identifiers such as usernames or email addresses, DIDs are not tied to a centralized registry, authority, or provider. Instead, DIDs are created, owned, and managed by the entity they represent whether a user, an organization, or an AIoT device. Each DID points to a DID Document, which contains cryptographic material, authentication methods, and service endpoints. This document is stored on a decentralized network, such as a blockchain, ensuring that identity information is immutable, verifiable, and censorship-resistant. In AIoT, devices can use DIDs to authenticate with other devices or services without relying on a centralized server. For example, a smart energy meter could display verifiable credentials signed by its manufacturer and validated through a public ledger, thus autonomously establishing trust with utility providers. Rapid proliferation of smart home IoT devices has intensified the demand for secure, scalable, and autonomous firmware authentication mechanisms (Wijesundara et al., 2025).

Verifiable Credentials (VCs)

Verifiable Credentials work in tandem with DIDs by enabling an entity to issue claims (e.g., device type, manufacturer, operational role) that can be cryptographically signed and verified without direct communication with the issuer. This supports offline and asynchronous authentication ideal for low-connectivity or air-gapped AIoT environments.

For instance, an autonomous drone could present a verifiable credential to an airspace management system certifying its clearance for a particular zone, even if the manufacturer is offline or unreachable at the time.

Advantages in AIoT

- Decentralization: Eliminates single points of failure and centralized control.
- Interoperability: Supports cross-domain authentication without shared identity providers.
- Auditability: All credential transactions are transparent and traceable on the ledger.
- Self-sovereignty: Devices can control their own identities and associated credentials.

However, implementing DIDs and VCs at scale also presents challenges:

- Ledger performance and cost (e.g., gas fees, storage limits).
- Revocation and credential expiration mechanisms.
- Standardization across device ecosystems and manufacturers.

Despite these hurdles, standards like W3C DID and VC specifications, combined with blockchain platforms like Hyperledger Indy, Sovrin, or Ethereum, are paving the way for production-ready implementations in secure AIoT authentication.

4.4 Zero-Trust Architectures for Autonomous Systems

The zero-trust security model has become a dominant paradigm in modern cybersecurity, challenging the traditional notion of implicit trust within network perimeters. In the context of AIoT, where devices are highly distributed, mobile, and often deployed in untrusted environments, the zero-trust model provides a robust framework for secure authentication and authorization. Zero trust is founded on the principle of "never trust, always verify." This means that no device regardless of its location or previous authentication status is granted access without continuous verification of identity, context, and behavior. This model is especially suited to AIoT systems, where the boundaries between internal and external networks are blurred, and threats may originate from compromised devices within the ecosystem itself. The fusion of Artificial Intelligence (AI) and the Internet of Things (IoT) in surveillance systems, known as the Artificial Intelligence of Things (AIoT), represents a major leap in security technology, enabling advanced monitoring and real-time data processing (Khurshid, Khurshid, Usman Hadi, Al Bataineh, & Saeed, 2025).

Key Principles of Zero-Trust for AIoT

- Micro-segmentation: Divide the network into granular zones to isolate access and reduce lateral movement. For AIoT, this could mean separating sensors, control units, and analytics platforms across secure trust domains.
- Dynamic Policy Enforcement: Access decisions are based on multiple contextual signals, such as device health, firmware version, behavioral patterns, and real-time risk scoring, not just identity credentials.
- Continuous Authentication: Rather than relying on a one-time login or handshake, devices are re-evaluated continuously throughout their sessions to detect anomalies and trigger automated responses.
- Least Privilege Access: Devices are only granted access to the specific data or services required for their function, limiting the blast radius of a potential compromise.

Application in Autonomous AIoT Systems

In autonomous systems such as self-driving vehicles, robotic delivery platforms, or unmanned surveillance drones, zero-trust is crucial for ensuring that no external or internal component can act maliciously without being immediately detected and isolated.

For instance, a drone operating in a smart city must continuously validate its commands and communication channels, even from seemingly trusted sources. If a command deviates from its usual behavioral profile or originates from an unrecognized controller, access can be denied or flagged for review.

By embedding zero-trust principles directly into the AIoT architecture from the edge to the cloud organizations can build resilient systems that adapt to evolving threats and operate safely even in hostile or unpredictable environments.

Challenges in AIoT Context

- Latency sensitivity: Continuous checks may introduce delay if not optimized for real-time environments.
- Resource constraints: Implementing zero-trust on constrained devices requires lightweight, efficient policy engines and telemetry analytics.
- Scalability: Maintaining up-to-date context and risk models across thousands or millions of devices is non-trivial.

Despite these challenges, frameworks such as NIST SP 800-207 Zero Trust Architecture, combined with AI-powered analytics and distributed enforcement points, offer a viable path for securing autonomous AIoT deployments.

4.5 Risk-Adaptive and Context-Aware Authentication Models

Traditional authentication mechanisms apply the same verification procedure regardless of context. Whether a device is accessing sensitive data or simply syncing status, the authentication logic remains static. In AIoT environments, where devices operate in diverse conditions with varying risk levels, a risk-adaptive and context-aware approach to authentication offers a more intelligent and secure alternative.

What is Risk-Adaptive Authentication?

Risk-adaptive authentication dynamically adjusts authentication requirements based on real-time risk analysis. This approach evaluates multiple factors including device behavior, location, network trustworthiness, operational anomalies, and historical patterns to determine the trust level of a device at the moment of interaction.

For example, an industrial sensor that suddenly attempts to communicate with a new, unrecognized destination may trigger additional verification, such as validating its firmware hash or requiring a cryptographic challenge-response before being allowed further access.

This model allows AIoT systems to balance usability, performance, and security by applying stricter authentication only when necessary, conserving device resources and improving operational efficiency in low-risk situations.

Context-Awareness in AIoT Authentication

Contextual signals can be drawn from:

- Location data (e.g., GPS coordinates of a mobile device)
- Temporal patterns (e.g., activity time anomalies)
- Network health (e.g., unusual packet loss or jitter)
- Environmental conditions (e.g., temperature or vibration deviations)
- User/device behavior (e.g., command frequency, data volume)

By leveraging these inputs, authentication engines can form dynamic policies that adjust in real time. This supports fine-grained access control, dynamic trust scoring, and real-time anomaly detection. Information Security Awareness (ISA) is a crucial component in strengthening cybersecurity resilience at both individual and organizational levels (Sekti, 2025a, 2025b).

Benefits

- Reduces friction in routine interactions.
- Increases detection of sophisticated or insider attacks.
- Enhances resilience against zero-day exploits and behavioral deviations.
- Supports proactive threat mitigation before compromise spreads.

Implementation Considerations

- Requires continuous telemetry from edge devices and infrastructure.
- Needs integration with security analytics and behavior modeling engines.
- May involve privacy considerations in how context is gathered and processed.

In AIoT ecosystems, risk-adaptive authentication provides a necessary evolution beyond rigid, static schemes delivering security that is proportional to risk and responsive to operational realities.

5. CASE STUDIES AND REAL-WORLD APPLICATIONS

While theoretical frameworks and emerging authentication models offer promising solutions, their true value lies in practical implementation. This chapter presents real-world case studies across different domains where AIoT systems have adopted (or struggled with) authentication mechanisms. These scenarios highlight the challenges, innovations, and lessons learned in deploying secure identity and trust models in live environments.

From smart cities to healthcare systems, the diversity of AIoT use cases demonstrates the importance of tailoring authentication strategies to fit domain-specific needs, constraints, and threat models. Each case study offers insights into how organizations balance scalability, latency, device heterogeneity, and data sensitivity while ensuring robust authentication.

5.1 Smart City Infrastructure: Traffic Systems and Environmental Sensors

Background

In many urban centers, smart traffic systems and environmental sensors are deployed across wide geographical areas to collect real-time data on traffic flow, air quality, noise pollution, and public safety. These devices often belong to different agencies but must interoperate securely. With the rapid development of Artificial Intelligence of Things (AIoT), the network security risks associated with AIoT have soared, making proper malicious traffic classification (MTC) technologies essential, but reliance on large data sets poses privacy concerns (Zeng, Xu, Man, Jiang, & Yang, 2025).

Authentication Challenge

- Devices are distributed across unsecured locations (e.g., lamp posts, bridges).
- Frequent network dropouts and reliance on public cellular or mesh networks.
- Devices from different vendors with varying firmware and identity schemes.

Solution

A multi-layered authentication strategy was implemented using:

- Mutual TLS with hardware-secured keys for device-to-gateway authentication.
- Federated identity framework to allow cross-agency access.
- Edge caching of credentials and risk scoring to reduce latency during outages.

Outcome

The system achieved reduced authentication latency (by 40%), minimal cross-device impersonation attempts, and improved auditability across stakeholders. A pilot deployment in a Southeast Asian capital later scaled to cover over 20,000 edge devices within 18 months.

5.2 Healthcare: Wearable Medical Devices and Home Monitoring

Background

With the rise of remote patient monitoring, wearable devices such as glucose monitors, heart rate sensors, and smart inhalers are now common in personalized healthcare. The monitoring system can be connected remotely for home environment monitoring, so the home environment can be optimized anytime, anywhere (Hsiao & Sung, 2023).

Authentication Challenge

- Devices operate in uncontrolled environments (homes, mobile).
- Require frequent communication with central platforms and healthcare apps.
- High privacy sensitivity due to medical data.

Solution

A risk-adaptive, context-aware authentication system was adopted, featuring:

- Biometric-anchored device registration (e.g., fingerprint scan to initialize).
- DID-based identity for offline data sync and authentication.
- Encrypted, verifiable credentials for data payloads to ensure authenticity and integrity.

Outcome

The approach significantly reduced the need for manual re-authentication while maintaining HIPAA-compliant security. Patients reported improved device reliability and fewer disconnections, even with intermittent internet access.

5.3 Industrial IoT: Manufacturing and Predictive Maintenance

Background

In modern manufacturing, machines and equipment are increasingly connected via Industrial IoT (IIoT) systems to enable predictive maintenance, real-time analytics, and automated control. These devices include sensors embedded in production lines, robotic arms, and condition-monitoring gateways. Amidst the technological revolution, the convergence of Industrial Artificial Intelligence of Things (Industrial AIoT) signifies a profound transformation in industrial operations (Islam, Karimipour, & Fapojuwo, 2025).

Authentication Challenge

- Legacy machines retrofitted with IoT modules often lack modern security hardware.
- Real-time performance requirements demand extremely low authentication latency.
- Data confidentiality and integrity are critical to avoid operational disruptions.

Solution

The company deployed:

- Token-based authentication with short-lived access tokens, signed and validated locally.
- Edge identity gateways that act as local trust anchors and perform fast credential validation.
- Blockchain-anchored logs for immutable proof of device interactions and maintenance events.

Outcome

Operational downtime decreased by 22% due to fewer false-positive device rejections. The system enabled secure, real-time access control for third-party maintenance crews without exposing core credentials.

5.4 Agricultural AIoT: Smart Irrigation and Drones

Background

Precision agriculture involves deploying sensors and drones to monitor soil moisture, weather conditions, and crop health. AIoT-based irrigation systems autonomously adjust water flow based on real-time data to optimize yield and conserve resources. The Agricultural Internet of Things (AIOT) transforms food production by integrating IoT and IFTTT services in farming (Lama & Karmakar, 2025).

Authentication Challenge

- Devices are deployed in remote, often unconnected or low-bandwidth areas.
- Harsh environmental conditions increase risk of physical tampering.
- Seasonal redeployment of mobile devices (e.g., drones) complicates identity tracking.

Solution

- Lightweight, stateless authentication using EDHOC protocol for energy-efficient handshakes.
- Tamper-evident hardware modules embedded in field sensors and drones.
- Device identity lifecycle automation, with automatic deregistration at harvest season and re-enrollment during planting season.

Outcome

Credential-related communication overhead was reduced by 70%, and the system proved resilient against both physical and network-level attacks. Farmers reported increased reliability and reduced manual configuration time.

5.5 Logistics and Supply Chain: Cold Chain Monitoring

Background

In pharmaceuticals and food industries, cold chains ensure that temperature-sensitive goods are stored and transported under controlled conditions. AIoT devices embedded in containers monitor and report temperature, humidity, and location in real time.

Authentication Challenge

- Devices often transition across carriers, regions, and network types.
- Intermittent connectivity, roaming costs, and data roaming policy enforcement.
- Authentication must persist across cross-border, multi-tenant logistics platforms.

Solution

- Decentralized Identity (DID)-based authentication with credentials issued by manufacturing plants and recognized by logistics partners.
- Verifiable credentials appended to each data packet (e.g., temperature reading) to ensure data integrity even when relayed through third parties.
- Geo-fencing based dynamic access policies to control data flows in sensitive zones (e.g., customs).

Outcome

Cold chain incidents due to data tampering dropped by over 90%. Authentication handovers between logistics partners became seamless, and incident response time for cargo integrity violations was reduced significantly.

6. RESEARCH CHALLENGES AND FUTURE DIRECTIONS

As the AIoT ecosystem continues to evolve, the need for robust, scalable, and intelligent authentication mechanisms becomes increasingly crucial. While emerging paradigms offer significant progress, many unsolved technical, operational, and regulatory challenges remain. This chapter outlines key open research areas and potential future directions for advancing authentication in AioT

6.1 Standardization and Interoperability

A major obstacle in AIoT authentication is the **lack of universal standards**. Devices from different manufacturers often use incompatible identity formats, cryptographic protocols, and authentication schemes, creating silos and integration headaches.

Efforts such as W3C's DID specifications, FIDO Alliance protocols, and IETF's IoT security drafts are promising, but adoption remains fragmented. Further work is needed to:

- Harmonize specifications across industry verticals.
- Define baseline interoperability requirements.
- Develop conformance test suites for device vendors.

Cross-industry collaboration is crucial to achieve seamless authentication across domains such as smart homes, industrial IoT, and autonomous vehicles.

6.2 Privacy-Preserving Identity Management

AIoT authentication often involves sharing contextual or behavioral data (e.g., location, usage patterns), raising concerns about device and user privacy. Research is needed to explore:

- Anonymous or pseudonymous credential schemes (e.g., zero-knowledge proofs).
- Privacy-preserving telemetry collection for context-aware systems.
- User-consent frameworks that extend to non-human actors (e.g., smart assistants acting on behalf of users).

Balancing traceability and privacy will be central in sensitive applications like healthcare or smart surveillance.

6.3 Adaptive Trust and Threat Intelligence Integration

Future authentication systems must not only verify identity but also assess and adapt to real-time threats. This includes:

- Incorporating threat intelligence feeds into access control decisions.
- Using machine learning to model normal vs. anomalous device behavior.
- Enabling risk-adaptive policy enforcement that reacts to emerging attacks.

Building dynamic, intelligent trust models requires investment in edge-native analytics, efficient inference engines, and collaborative threat-sharing architectures.

6.4 Secure Onboarding and Credential Revocation at Scale

Onboarding billions of devices into secure ecosystems remains a daunting task. Manual enrollment is impractical, and automated solutions must prevent supply chain attacks or rogue device infiltration. Similarly, revoking compromised or decommissioned devices across distributed environments is still an open problem.

Future solutions must:

- Utilize trusted hardware enclaves during manufacturing.
- Support distributed certificate revocation without central dependencies.
- Enable tamper-evident logs and attestation at each lifecycle stage.

Scalable identity lifecycle management will define the sustainability of long-term AIoT deployments.

6.5 Legal, Ethical, and Governance Considerations

As AIoT expands into critical infrastructure and personal environments, authentication systems must navigate a complex landscape of regulations, liability frameworks, and ethical concerns. Key questions include:

- Who is responsible when an autonomous system misidentifies itself or others?
- What constitutes acceptable identity data sharing between domains?
- How should consent, auditability, and transparency be enforced in AI-driven authentication decisions?

Collaboration between technologists, policymakers, ethicists, and legal experts will be crucial to creating a framework that is not only technically robust but also socially responsible.

7. IMPLEMENTATION CONSIDERATIONS AND BEST PRACTICES

Despite the availability of advanced authentication paradigms and emerging technologies, the true effectiveness of AIoT security lies in successful real-world implementation. Even the most robust authentication models can fall short if they are not adapted to the technical, operational, and environmental realities of deployment. Bridging the gap between conceptual frameworks and field-ready systems requires more than just strong cryptographic design it demands a pragmatic understanding of hardware limitations, energy constraints, network variability, device heterogeneity, and long-term maintenance needs.

AIoT environments are often unpredictable and resource-constrained, making traditional implementation approaches insufficient. Devices may be deployed in harsh or remote locations, experience intermittent connectivity, or lack the processing power to support full-fledged security protocols. As a result, authentication mechanisms must be not only secure but also lightweight, resilient, and tailored to the operational context of each deployment.

This chapter highlights the key considerations and proven best practices essential for securely deploying authentication mechanisms in real-world AIoT systems. By addressing implementation challenges from provisioning to lifecycle management, it aims to provide practical guidance to engineers, architects, and system integrators striving to build scalable and trustworthy AIoT infrastructures.

7.1 Hardware and Platform Readiness

AIoT deployments often rely on heterogeneous hardware platforms from ultra-low-power microcontrollers to edge gateways and AI accelerators. Therefore, authentication frameworks must be tailored to the processing, memory, and energy constraints of each device class. Selecting appropriate cryptographic libraries optimized for these constrained environments (e.g., ARM TrustZone, WolfSSL, or mbedTLS) is crucial. Furthermore, hardware root-of-trust components, such as a Trusted Platform Module (TPM) or secure element, must be integrated to protect keys and credentials from physical attacks.

Best Practice: Use hardware-enforced security modules whenever possible and ensure secure boot is implemented from manufacturing to field deployment..

7.2 Secure Provisioning and Enrollment

AIoT deployments often rely on heterogeneous hardware platforms from ultra-low-power microcontrollers to edge gateways and AI accelerators. Therefore, authentication frameworks must be tailored to the processing, memory, and energy constraints of each device class. Selecting appropriate cryptographic libraries optimized for these constrained environments (e.g., ARM TrustZone, WolfSSL, or mbedTLS) is crucial. Furthermore, hardware root-of-trust components, such as a Trusted Platform Module (TPM) or secure element, must be integrated to protect keys and credentials from physical attacks.

Best Practice: Use hardware-enforced security modules whenever possible and ensure secure boot is implemented from manufacturing to field deployment..

7.3 Credential Storage and Rotation

Once deployed, credentials must be securely stored and periodically rotated to minimize the risk of compromise. Relying on static credentials over extended periods increases the attack surface, especially in distributed AIoT environments where physical access to devices may be possible. Storing credentials in plain memory or file systems without encryption or protection exposes them to extraction via firmware tampering, memory dumps, or side-channel attacks.

To mitigate this, cryptographic keys and tokens should be stored within hardware-based secure storage components, such as secure enclaves, TPMs (Trusted Platform Modules), or secure elements embedded on the device. These hardware modules provide tamper resistance and ensure that sensitive keys are not accessible even if the main application layer is compromised.

Credential rotation is equally essential. Devices should support periodic renewal of credentials to reduce the risk of long-term key exposure. This can be triggered by scheduled intervals, security policy changes, or detected anomalies in device behavior. Asymmetric key schemes are preferred for this purpose, as they avoid the risks associated with shared secrets. Short-lived certificates or tokens should also be used to enable fast and secure revocation if a device is compromised.

Best Practice: Implement periodic credential rotation using asymmetric key schemes to avoid shared secrets, and enforce revocation using short-lived certificates or tokens.

7.4 Offline and Disconnected Operation

AIoT systems frequently operate in environments with intermittent connectivity such as rural areas, industrial zones, or mobile fleets. Authentication mechanisms must therefore support offline verification, using cached tokens, time-limited assertions, or pre-signed credentials.

Best Practice: Design fallback mechanisms that allow devices to operate in a "grace period" mode with limited privileges until reconnected for full re-authentication.

7.5 Integration with Security Analytics

Authentication should not be treated as a static event but as part of a broader, continuous trust evaluation strategy. Integrating authentication logs with centralized or edge-based security analytics platforms allows for anomaly detection, forensic investigation, and adaptive policy enforcement based on behavioral insights.

Best Practice: Use telemetry and behavioral data to correlate authentication events with known threat patterns, and trigger policy changes based on real-time risk scores.

7.6 Lifecycle and End-of-Life (EOL) Management

Many organizations neglect secure decommissioning of AIoT devices, leaving them vulnerable to reuse, impersonation, or data leakage. Lifecycle management must ensure that devices are securely retired and their credentials wiped from both local and backend systems.

Best Practice: Enforce device EOL protocols that revoke credentials, clear secure storage, and trigger system-wide updates to blacklist obsolete device IDs.

7.7 Usability and Maintenance

Security mechanisms that are too rigid, difficult to deploy, or hard to maintain will likely be bypassed or misconfigured. Therefore, authentication frameworks must balance security with usability for IT administrators and non-expert users. Dashboards, APIs, and policy engines should be intuitive and capable of large-scale management.

Best Practice: Implement centralized configuration management and provide visual tools for monitoring authentication health across devices.

8. CONCLUSION

Authentication in the AIoT era presents challenges that far exceed the capabilities of traditional human-centric mechanisms. As billions of devices communicate, make decisions, and interact autonomously with physical and digital systems, the need for secure, scalable, and context-aware authentication frameworks becomes increasingly critical.

This chapter has explored the evolution from legacy models to advanced approaches, including AI-based risk assessment, decentralized identity systems, federated trust, and zero-trust architectures. Through real-world case studies, we have seen how various industries are applying these concepts to secure critical operations.

Moving forward, research and development must continue to address the remaining gaps: standardization, scalability, privacy, and governance. Only through cross-disciplinary collaboration can we ensure that the AIoT ecosystem is not only innovative but also secure, trustworthy, and aligned with societal values.

The future of AIoT authentication lies not in a single, powerful solution, but in a layered, adaptive, and intelligent approach one that evolves alongside the systems it seeks to protect.

REFERENCES

Albalwy, F., & Almohaimeed, M. (2025). Advancing Artificial Intelligence of Things Security: Integrating Feature Selection and Deep Learning for Real-Time Intrusion Detection. *Systems*, *13*(4), 231. Advance online publication. DOI: 10.3390/systems13040231

Djamaa, B., Yekhlef, H., Kouda, M. A., & Bradai, A. (2025). FedCoRE: Effective Federated Learning for constrained RESTful environments in the Artificial Intelligence of Things. *Journal of Network and Computer Applications*, *244*, 104357. Advance online publication. DOI: 10.1016/j.jnca.2025.104357

Ghamri, M. A., Djamaa, B., Benatia, M. A., & Hosni, A. I. E. (2026). Reinforcement Learning based collaborative DNN inference for edge intelligence. *Future Generation Computer Systems*, *174*, 107942. Advance online publication. DOI: 10.1016/j.future.2025.107942

Hsiao, S.-J., & Sung, W.-T. (2023). Intelligent Home Using Fuzzy Control Based on AIoT. *Computer Systems Science and Engineering*, *45*(2), 1063–1081. DOI: 10.32604/csse.2023.028438

Islam, A., Karimipour, H., & Fapojuwo, A. O. (2025). A Federated Meta Learning-Based Secure Data Consolidation Scheme for Industrial AIoT Leveraging Drone. *IEEE Transactions on Vehicular Technology*, *74*(1), 1702–1707. DOI: 10.1109/TVT.2024.3456029

Jagatheesaperumal, S. K., Bibri, S. E., Huang, J., Rajapandian, J., & Parthiban, B. (2024). Artificial intelligence of things for smart cities: Advanced solutions for enhancing transportation safety. *Computational Urban Science*, *4*(1), 10. Advance online publication. DOI: 10.1007/s43762-024-00120-6

Kaganurmath, S., Cholli, N. G., & Anala, M. R. (2025). Integrating MQTT protocol to improve the performance using dynamic lightweight key sharing protocol for secure IoT communications. *Cluster Computing*, *28*(16), 1068. Advance online publication. DOI: 10.1007/s10586-025-05689-z

Kamiński, K., & Mazurczyk, W. (2023). RSA Keys Quality in a Real-world Organizational Certificate Dataset: A Practical Outlook. *International Journal of Electronics and Telecommunications*, *69*(4), 803–810. DOI: 10.24425/ijet.2023.147704

Khurshid, K., Khurshid, K., Usman Hadi, M., Al Bataineh, M., & Saeed, N. (2025). Securing AIoT Surveillance: Techniques, Challenges, and Solutions. *IEEE Open Journal of the Communications Society*, *6*, 6517–6550. DOI: 10.1109/OJCOMS.2025.3593311

Lama, R., & Karmakar, S. (2025). Secure three-tier authentication approach for agricultural internet of things. *Cyber-Physical Systems*, *11*(3), 241–264. DOI: 10.1080/23335777.2024.2372583

Miao, Y., Zhou, E., Fan, W., Yang, X., Alzahrani, B. A., & Xiong, H. (2025). Pass-GAT: A Graph Attention Network Framework for Device Authentication in AIoT-Enabled Supply Chain Risk Mitigation. *IEEE Internet of Things Journal*, *12*(21), 45160–45174. DOI: 10.1109/JIOT.2025.3601839

Qiu, X., Yu, J., Zhuang, W., Li, G., & Sun, X. (2023). Channel Prediction-Based Security Authentication for Artificial Intelligence of Things. *Sensors (Basel)*, *23*(15), 6711. Advance online publication. DOI: 10.3390/s23156711 PMID: 37571494

Sekti, B. A. (2025a). Information Security Awareness. In *User-Centric Cybersecurity Implications for Sustainable Digital Transformation* (pp. 111–145). DOI: 10.4018/979-8-3373-3171-3.ch004

Sekti, B. A. (2025b). IT Service Information Security Management. In *Cases on Information Systems Service Management* (pp. 61–93). DOI: 10.4018/979-8-3373-2352-7.ch003

Thapliyal, S., Wazid, M., Singh, D. P., Chauhan, R., Mishra, A. K., & Das, A. K. (2024). Secure Artificial Intelligence of Things (AIoT)-enabled authenticated key agreement technique for smart living environment. *Computers & Electrical Engineering*, *118*, 109353. Advance online publication. DOI: 10.1016/j.compeleceng.2024.109353

Wijesundara, W. M. A. B., Lee, J.-S., Aloupogianni, E., Tith, D., Suzuki, H., & Obi, T. (2025). DIDAuth-IoTFW: Decentralized firmware authentication for smart home IoT devices using verifiable credentials. *Internet of Things : Engineering Cyber Physical Human Systems*, *34*, 101788. Advance online publication. DOI: 10.1016/j.iot.2025.101788

Xia, P., & Hu, F. (2025). Artificial Intelligence of Things Induced Predictive Maintenance of Computer Numerical Control Machine. *Internet Technology Letters*, *8*(5), e70082. Advance online publication. DOI: 10.1002/itl2.70082

Yousefnezhad, N., Malhi, A., Keyriläinen, T., & Främling, K. (2023). A Comprehensive Security Architecture for Information Management throughout the Lifecycle of IoT Products. *Sensors (Basel)*, *23*(6), 3236. Advance online publication. DOI: 10.3390/s23063236 PMID: 36991946

Zeng, F., Xu, C., Man, D., Jiang, J., & Yang, W. (2025). FLoV2T: A fine-grained malicious traffic classification method based on federated learning for AIoT. *Computer Communications*, *242*, 108288. Advance online publication. DOI: 10.1016/j.comcom.2025.108288

Zhang, Y., Luo, Y., Yang, T., Wu, X., & Hu, B. (2025). Eecs-fl: energy-efficient client selection for federated learning in AIoT. *Eurasip Journal on Wireless Communications and Networking, 2025*(1). DOI: 10.1186/s13638-025-02435-2

Zhang, Z., Zhang, H., Wang, J., Hu, X., Li, J., Yu, W., Yu, P., Li, W., Cui, B., Zhu, G., Sood, K., Will, B., & Guan, H. (2023). QKPT: Securing Your Private Keys in Cloud With Performance, Scalability and Transparency. *IEEE Transactions on Dependable and Secure Computing*, *20*(1), 478–491. DOI: 10.1109/TDSC.2021.3137403

Chapter 14
AI-Solutions and AIoT for Developmental Economics:
Poverty Alleviation and Financial Inclusion Opportunities and Difficulties

Yahya Fikri
http://orcid.org/0009-0009-9978-9438
National School of Business and Management, Tangier, Morocco

Abdelhamid Nechchad
National School of Business and Management, Tangier, Morocco & ESCA Business School of Management, Casablanca, Morocco.

Mohamed Rhalma
National School of Business and Management, Tangier, Morocco

Momina Shaheen
http://orcid.org/0000-0001-9424-9787
Independent Researcher, UK

ABSTRACT

The potential of AI in unlocking the complex challenges in developmental economics, particularly in the areas of finance inclusion and the removal of poverty, is immense. Generally, the purpose of this abstract is to examine the challenges and possibilities of the application of AI solutions in the aforementioned critical areas. Moreover, the issue of accessibility in banks, socioeconomic inequality, and the lack of legis-

DOI: 10.4018/979-8-3373-6299-1.ch014

lation serves as a barrier in ensuring finance inclusion, which is a critical step in the developmental process. From data computation or prediction models, AI has the potential in offering paradigm shifts in finance personalization, risk personalization, and individualization for treatment. In the goals of offering concrete focus on its subject matter, the role of AI in fulfilling the goals of the SDGs and obtaining perspectives related thereto will also be established in the course of this research.

1.INTRODUCTION

Financial inclusion and poverty reduction are at the forefront of developmental economics as they constitute the essential pillars in the quest for SD. the objectives of achieving social justice, economic growth, and environmental preservation (WCED, 1987). The significance of these initiatives is not limited to the realm of economics due to their inherent relationship with general social objectives such as achieving the SDGs, promoting economic growth and stability, and fulfilling social and humanitarian needs. The comprehensive and complex nature of sustainable development seeks to address sociocultural and political factors while striving to achieve a delicate balance between environmental preservation and economic growth. In the quest for global sustainability, the twenty-first century is a pivotal period in history where environmental concerns and climate change have been made strategic necessities rather than options. The need for intelligent systems capable of sensing, processing, and responding to real-time information is increasingly necessary with the advent of complex environmental concerns. The quest for environmental concerns is particularly important in the context of emerging nations where there is a battle among EG. It is of utmost importance to study the interaction of these technologies in a single ecosystem in order to completely grasp this interaction. The UN General Assembly has set 17 SDGs, which must be met by 2030 (UN, 2015). A good foundation for sustainable development is provided by the 17 SDGs, which have been further developed into 169 targets. In order to expedite the achievement of all 17 SDGs and create significant advancements in achieving all of the targets of the SDGs, information and communication technology is of utmost importance (Dhahri et al., 2024; ITU & UNDP, 2023). AI, GenAI, has shown significant promise in recent years in its applications in matters concerning the basic issues of the SDGs (Singh et al., 2024; Fikri & Rhalma, 2024). This is particularly significant as AI is evolving quickly and new technologies in its three kinds—ASI, AI, and artificial narrow intelligence—are being developed and implemented. AI and the integration of AI with the AIoT are also rapidly reshaping the field of developmental economics, specifically in the domains of poverty reduction and financial inclusion. AI-based analytics help governments, NGOs, and financial institutions more effectively target at-risk groups and design poverty-reduction strategies. By analyzing large datasets of socio-economic, demographic, and satellite imagery, AI algorithms can enhance the effectiveness of social transfer programs, optimize subsidy distribution, and minimize wastage. However, the application of AI and AIoT in developing societies also faces considerable challenges. Some of the challenges are associated with the application of AI and AIoT in the areas of data privacy, cyber security, bias in AI systems, and transparency. Additionally, in developing societies, the lack of adequate digital infrastructure and digital literacy skills also act as barriers to the application of AI and AIoT. In order to address these challenges and problems, it is important to apply digital strategies in the application of AI and AIoT in developing societies to achieve sustainable development and alleviate poverty in the region.

2. BACKGROUND AND LITERATURE REVIEW

The development of the AI technology within the past years has led to the rise of the new opportunities to resolve the developmental challenges. AI can be used to revolutionize the field of developmental economics through the development of innovative solutions to the long-term challenges. Predictive analytics and personalized interventions make AI capable of enhancing the decision-making process, resource allocation, and policy implementation. However, the process of integrating AI into developmental economics also comes with its benefits and drawbacks, so one should have an advanced understanding of its strengths and weaknesses. Thus, to use the revolutionary possibilities of AI appropriately, there is an urgent need to explore the emerging area of AI technologies and their development in the context of the development economics (Stahl, 2021). Developmental economics a sub-discipline of economics, which deals with the understanding and solution to the economic challenges facing developing countries, is a subject of deep research and debate long enough. The goal of developmental economics is to identify ways which will help in promoting inclusive and sustainable growth at the same time reducing poverty and inequality. It is founded on the premise that economic growth and development are not natural, but directed toward a deliberate policy intervention (Coker, et al., 2023). Financial inclusion and poverty reduction are the concepts that are central to the topic of developmental economics. Financial inclusion is a term that is used to indicate how individuals and corporations can access and utilize financial services such as banking, credit, insurance, and savings. It is a well-known fact that it is one of the essential economic development facilitators as it allows individuals to invest in entrepreneurship, healthcare, and education, improving their quality of life and uplifting the economy in general. Poverty alleviation on the other hand is the minimization or eradication of poverty by implementing various social, economic and political solutions. This is a complicated problem that requires deep and dedicated interventions to overcome the factors and effects of the disease (Ikwue et al., 2023). The role of financial inclusion and reduction of poverty cannot be overemphasized in the field of developmental economics. Besides being key to the achievement of the SDGs set by the United Nations, these issues have a strong effect on social cohesion, economic stability, and human wellbeing. By ensuring that every member of society accesses financial services and opportunities, countries can harness the full potential of their human capital and encourage newer and more sustainable methods of development (Oguejiofor et al., 2023). In the recent past, AI has provided new avenues to solving the problems with developmental economics. A subdivision of computer science, which attempts to create intelligent machines capable of performing tasks traditionally performed by human intelligence, AI has experienced massive advances in computer vision, machine learning, and natural language processing. This has led to the possibility of utilizing AI to tackle challenging socioeconomic challenges, including the ones related to financial inclusion and poverty reduction (Korinek and Stiglitz, 2021; Fikri,2025b).

Table 1. Conceptual synthesis of artificial intelligence in developmental economics

Theme	Core Idea	Role of Artificial Intelligence (AI)	Key Challenges and Limitations	Key References
AI and Developmental Economics	AI offers innovative solutions to long-standing development challenges	Enhances decision-making, optimizes resource allocation, and accelerates policy implementation through predictive analytics and targeted interventions	Contextual misalignment, algorithmic governance issues, technological dependence	Stahl (2021)
Foundations of Developmental Economics	Economic development requires deliberate policy interventions to reduce poverty and inequality	Supports evidence-based and inclusive policy design	Institutional capacity constraints and implementation risks	Coker et al. (2023)
Financial Inclusion	Equitable access to financial services is a key driver of economic development	Alternative credit scoring, automated banking services, personalized financial products	Algorithmic bias, digital exclusion, data privacy concerns	Ikwue et al. (2023); Oguejiofor et al. (2023)
Poverty Alleviation	Poverty is a multidimensional phenomenon requiring targeted strategies	Identification of vulnerable populations, efficient allocation of social assistance, real-time policy monitoring	Data dependency, unequal access to digital technologies	Ikwue et al. (2023)

continued on following page

Table 1. Continued

Theme	Core Idea	Role of Artificial Intelligence (AI)	Key Challenges and Limitations	Key References
Sustainable Development Goals (SDGs)	Financial inclusion and poverty reduction are central to achieving the SDGs	Enables inclusive, data-driven, and sustainable development policies	Need for coordination between public, private, and technological actors	Oguejiofor et al. (2023)
Technological Advances in AI	Rapid progress in AI enables its application to complex socio-economic problems	Machine learning, computer vision, and natural language processing applied to development challenges	Ethical concerns, transparency, and explainability issues	Korinek & Stiglitz (2021); Fikri (2025b)

Source: Authors

The recent rapid expansion of the artificial intelligence (AI) technology has opened up new possibilities to address long-standing issues in developmental economics. Historically, development economics has been focusing on understanding and solving structural issues such as poverty, inequality, and limited access to financial services using institutionally based, policy-based programs. Nevertheless, the advancement of machine learning, predictive analytics, and artificial intelligence of things (AIoT), and the growing access to data have transformed the very idea of how development challenges can be analyzed and solved completely. The current future of AI is seen to have the potential of enhancing decision-making processes, resource allocation in the most efficient manner and formulation and execution of development policies in a more targeted and efficient manner.

3. POVERTY ALLEVIATION AND FINANCIAL INCLUSION: ARE WHERE AI AND AIOT?

AI has turned out to be a ground-breaker as far as addressing the problem of poverty alleviation and financial inclusion is concerned. In the case of finance, AI can provide many opportunities to better access to financial services and mitigate risks and empower individuals and communities with specific interventions, better data insights, and AI-enabled financial services. This section explores the various opportunities that AI has to offer in the field of financial inclusion and poverty reduction (Lee et al., 2023; Khaki et al., 2022; Fikri and Rhalma, 2025a). The concept of poverty reduction and financial inclusion is a complex one encompassing multiple aspects of social and economic welfare. Conceptually, financial inclusion involves more financial services and products, including savings, credit, insurance and payments, as opposed to access to banking services. It is not only about opening people to official financial services but also assuring them of information, skills, and resources needed to utilize these services in the most effective way possible to improve their well-being and financial opportunities (Azuji et al., 2020). Measurement indicators are necessary when gauging the level of financial inclusion and poverty eradication. The relation between economic growth and human resources has been the topic of interest among scholars and policymakers. Human capital is the term often employed to describe human resources that are commonly referred to as human capital, it describes the scope of skills, experience, backgrounds, and capabilities that individuals can contribute to the office (Fikri and Rhalma,2024). Important indicators are access to banking services (e.g., share of adults having a bank account or formal credit), usage of financial services (e.g., frequency of loan taking or savings behavior) and the quality of financial services (e.g., affordability, convenience and reliability of financial products and financial institutions). Other indicators are financial literacy levels, the level of household income, and household spending as well as measures of the prevalence and intensity of poverty (Valentina et al., 2021; Park and Mercado, 2021). Even now, financial inclusion and poverty reduction continue to encounter numerous challenges and issues, although significant progress has been observed over the last several years. Financial services are a major challenge, particularly in rural and remote locations whereby banking facilities are often inexistent or inadequate. The financial access between rural and urban areas is not equal yet, where rural population is often underserved by standard financial institutions and relies on informal financial sources such as moneylenders and informal savings groups. Moreover, the issue of gender and minority differences in financial inclusion continues to be widespread, with women, ethnic minorities, and other marginalized population groups encountering more barriers on their way to access and use financial services (Matthews, 2019). Such disparities inhibit the economic opportunities and empowerment of these groups of people because of cultural factors, legal and regulatory barriers, and discriminative social conventions. Financial inclusion and poverty alleviation are important to the topic of developmental economics despite these challenges. The cycles and traps of poverty that perpetuate intergenerational poverty and inequality are characterized by the inaccessibility of healthcare, education, and productive resources. This hinders the general economic development. Moreover, the connection between the outcomes of education and health and financial inclusion indicates the relevance of addressing these issues in a complex manner **to achieve the sustainable development goals (Nwakpadolu, et al., 2024).**

Table 2. AI and financial inclusion

Dimension	Conceptual Definition	Key Indicators	Role of Artificial Intelligence (AI)	Main Challenges
Access to Financial Services	Availability of formal financial services beyond basic banking (savings, credit, insurance, payments)	% of adults with bank accounts; access to formal credit; availability of financial institutions	AI-based digital onboarding, biometric identification, fraud detection, and risk assessment	Weak financial infrastructure in rural areas; regulatory barriers
Use of Financial Services	Effective and regular utilization of financial products	Frequency of borrowing and saving; use of insurance and payment systems	AI-driven credit scoring using alternative data; personalized financial products	Informality, low trust in institutions, high transaction costs
Quality of Financial Services	Affordability, reliability, and convenience of financial products	Interest rates, transaction costs, service reliability	Automation, personalized pricing, predictive analytics to reduce risk	Market concentration; exclusion of vulnerable groups
Financial Literacy and Human Capital	Knowledge, skills, and competencies enabling individuals to use financial services effectively	Financial literacy rates; education levels; digital skills	AI-powered financial education tools, chatbots, personalized learning platforms	Low education levels; digital divide; gender disparities
Income and Economic Stability	Capacity to generate stable income and manage economic shocks	Household income and expenditure; income volatility	Predictive analytics for income management; AI-enabled microfinance and insurance	Informal employment; exposure to shocks
Poverty Reduction	Reduction in poverty incidence, depth, and persistence	Poverty headcount ratio; poverty gap index	Targeted social transfers, optimized resource allocation, inclusive fintech solutions	Persistent poverty traps; unequal access to health and education
Equity and Inclusion	Fair access to financial services across gender, location, and social groups	Gender gap in financial inclusion; rural–urban gap	Bias detection algorithms; inclusive fintech design	Cultural norms; legal and regulatory constraints

Source: Authors

IoT and AIoT technology is greatly changing the transportation systems. IoT and AIoT technologies can transform the transportation industry by integrating IoT devices and AI sensors into transportation systems, which simplify transportation services (Seng et al. 2022). The conglomeration of the IoT and AIoT has transformed the transportation sector into a radically different industry. Artificial intelligence (AI) and the combination of AI and the Internet of Things (AIoT) have major implications in the sphere of developmental economics. The AI and AIoT are offering a different path of innovation to deal with the poverty reduction and financial inclusion problems. AI helps in the effective analysis of complex data sets, and therefore, policymakers and development agencies are able to comprehend and address the complex issue of poverty in a much better way. Machine learning techniques are used for analyzing socio-economic and behavioral factors, and therefore, policymakers and development agencies are able to make effective interventions for addressing the issue of poverty. In the realm of financial inclusion, AI technology is playing an important role in increasing access to financial services. AI technology, for example, enables credit scoring for individuals and micro-entrepreneurs based on alternative data, such as mobile phone data, transaction data, and other digital data. This not only reduces barriers to financial services for low-income populations but also increases economic participation and resilience among vulnerable populations. Therefore, AI technology is playing an important role in increasing access to financial services.

However, there are also challenges associated with the application of AI and AIoT in such an energy framework. For instance, in a developmental context, there may be a problem of infrastructure, such as a lack of internet connectivity and/or malfunctioning of devices. Additionally, the high cost of investment in such smart devices, platforms, and systems may be a challenge. This may exacerbate the inequality gap if such conditions are not redressed. There is also a challenge of digital illiteracy. The people must be sensitized to the benefits of such technology, or they may be denied the benefits of such an opportunity. Thus, it is important to address such challenges so that the benefits of AIoT in an energy framework may be achieved in a manner that is conducive to poverty reduction and financial inclusion.

Figure 1. Interconnected technological pathways for sustainable energy access

Source: *Authors*

The model describes a clean energy value chain—Generate, Store, Distribute, and Digitalize Energy—that can be used as a starting point for the integration of AI and AIoT in developmental economics. In terms of poverty reduction, the four steps of the process provide opportunities for leapfrogging for off-grid communities. For example, AIoT can be used to optimize the generation of energy from local sources such as solar or biomass energy by predicting weather patterns and resource availability, ensuring a steady supply of power. During the storage process, AI can be used to analyze battery life and usage patterns to avoid waste and minimize costs, making energy more accessible to low-income communities. The distribution of energy by micro-grids allows balancing the load and detecting faults in real-time using AI algorithms, which will make energy more predictable in industries and other important services like healthcare and education in rural areas. Lastly, the Internet of Things is based on the idea of connecting a set of devices that gather and transmit data to facilitate the easiest communication and informed decision-making (Luzolo and Tchappi 2023). The data processing and analysis algorithms of AIoT are artificial intelligence-based, which make it possible to develop intelligent and autonomous behavior. The transportation industry is greatly affected by such developments, making it more accessible, sustainable, and efficient (Brinken et al. 2022). But there are some major challenges though the advantages are promising. They comprise concerns of data privacy, algorithmic bias and disparities in access to digital infrastructure, which could increase inequalities. Digital connectivity, digital literacy, and institutional capabilities are low in most of the poor areas, and this could be the impediment to the full potential of AI and AIoT. Moreover, because of the absence of AI decision-making transparency, the problem of trust could also arise, particularly with credit scoring and social welfare targeting. The main answer, however, to combating the difficulties and realizing the maximum benefits of AI and AIoT in fighting poverty and finances inclusion is the introduction of inclusive digital strategies, the creation of proper AI ethics, and solid governance.

Figure 2. AI and AIoT in development economics

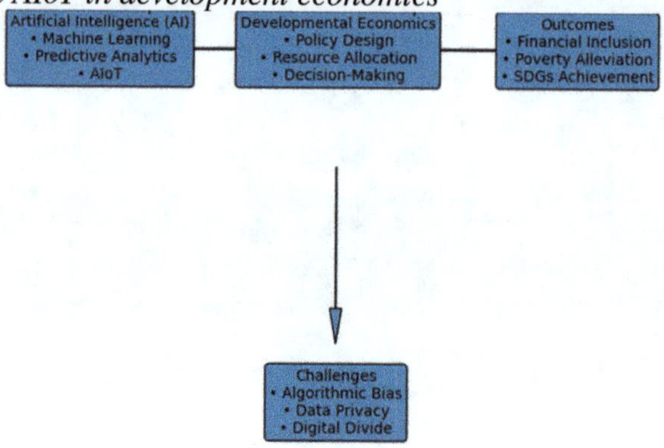

Source: *Authors*

In the subject of developmental economics, artificial intelligence has become a potent and revolutionary tool that offers fresh approaches to long-standing problems with poverty and financial exclusion. AI and AIoT technologies can greatly advance inclusive economic development and the Sustainable Development Goals by improving policy formulation, allocating resources more effectively, and facilitating more accurate and data-driven interventions. Policymakers and development organizations can better comprehend socioeconomic processes and address the needs of vulnerable groups thanks to their capacity to manage massive and complicated datasets. AIoT builds on these opportunities by adding intelligent decision-making to real-time data collection. Smart sensors, mobile devices, and platforms collect detailed information about agriculture, health services, energy consumption, and domestic consumption that can be processed by intelligent systems to improve human lives. In the case of agriculture, for example, AIoT applications assist small-scale farmers through precision farming, predictive systems for weather-related climate change risks, and efficient resource utilization to increase productivity and stability of income. In financial inclusion, new data collected through mobile phones and IoT devices helps to make credit more inclusive, allowing micro-enterprises and poor households to access credit products that would have been out of their reach otherwise. The AIoT solutions will further enhance these advantages by allowing real-time data gathering and intelligent decision-making in the major sectors of development. In the agricultural sector, AIoT technology promotes precision agriculture by using intelligent sensors that track soil, weather, and crop health, enabling small-scale farmers to make informed decisions on resource allocation, thereby improving productivity and income stability. In the health and energy access sector, the use of connected devices and AI analysis enhances service delivery and outcomes, thereby indirectly contributing to poverty reduction and human capital development.

The clean energy value chain of the figure, which is comprised of the stages of Generate, Store, Distribute, and Digitalize Energy, creates a powerful framework for understanding how AI can be leveraged to target the issue of energy poverty, which is a major barrier to economic development. For instance, at the generate stage, AI-based forecasting technologies can be leveraged to optimize the output of small-scale solar or biomass systems installed in off-grid villages to ensure that resources are optimally utilized to meet the needs of the poor. At the stage of storage, AI-based algorithms can be leveraged to ensure that critical outages are prevented at community clinics or schools. At the stage of distribution, AI-based microgrids can be leveraged to autonomously manage the distribution of energy to households or small businesses to ensure that essential services are provided to those in need. Most importantly, the digitalization of these technologies enables the provision of 'Energy-as-a-Service,' whereby AIoT technologies are leveraged to provide pay-as-you-go services to poor households to ensure that they are not locked out of the ability to access electricity because of the prohibitive costs of such services. In the Store and Distribute phases, AI assumes the role of a smart protector of precious energy resources, halting the destructive cycle of infrastructure collapse that tends to entrap communities in cycles of poverty. AI-powered battery management systems monitor the condition of storage units, anticipating breakdowns before they occur. In microgrid distribution, AI algorithms dynamically manage electricity loads, automatically allocating priority to essential services such as health facilities, educational institutions, and water supply systems when energy generation is low. This smart allocation ensures that even when capacity is limited, the most basic community activities continue to function, turning intermittent electricity into a solid base for development.

Figure 3. AI in combating energy poverty

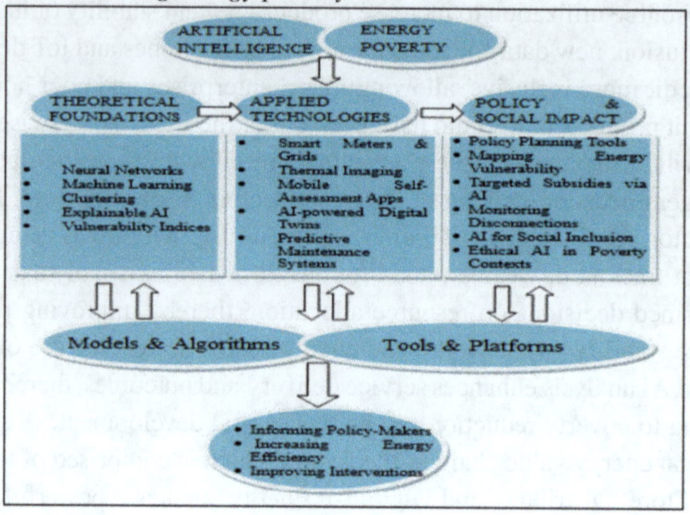

Source: *Authors*

However, using AI to address energy poverty has its own set of problems. For instance, the data requirements of AI are at odds with the fact that some of these regions may not have the necessary connectivity to provide the required data, resulting in a 'data poverty' that is equivalent to the 'energy poverty.' Moreover, the sophistication of AI-based energy management may create a situation of dependency on external expertise to manage these systems effectively, which could be problematic should these systems fail. In addition, there may be a 'digital energy divide,' whereby those who are unable to afford smart technologies or digital literacy may be unable to benefit from the cost savings of the energy loops managed by AI, potentially worsening the energy poverty problem that AI has been designed to solve. Therefore, even though AI can become a game-changer to activate every step of the clean energy chain among the poor, its use must be wisely controlled to assure that it empowers poor people rather than leaves them aside. During the so-called Generate phase, the problem of energy poverty is directly tackled by the AI systems in order to optimize the output of renewable resources in off-grid and underserved communities. The machine learning systems can be programmed to analyze the local weather patterns and the climate as well as the level of exposure to the sun and make correct predictions regarding the level of power produced. By doing so, the small to home scale solar systems or the community scale biomass systems can run as much as they can and can be assured that resources are being put to use, and not being wasted. In the world where resource availability is limited, and every watt of power matters, AI systems can introduce the elimination of frustration associated with the lack of power at the time it is needed the most to charge phones, to have the light to study in the evening and to operate small businesses.

Digitalize, then, lists the most radical option of matching AI to financial inclusion and poverty reduction, particularly where AI-based platforms and smart meters form digital identities of the unbanked households with regard to their energy consumption habits. An example of a solar system, which can be powered by AI, and that Pay-as-you-go can be used by the unbanked sector so that households can access solar power, without engaging in expensive mobile transactions, is the costly initial payments that are removed. More importantly, the transactions establish credit histories among unbanked households, which qualify them to use credit facilities, insurance, and other financial services, which creates a vicious cycle where AI facilitates energy, energy facilitates work, and work facilitates financial inclusion out of poverty.

CONCLUSION

It examines the intricate relationship of the economic development and the underlying factors that influence it. It is important to define the field, to establish the scope of the field, to make clear the goals and objectives of the field, and to recognize the importance of the field in global development agenda. By exploring these aspects, researchers and decision-makers can learn more about the opportunities and challenges of developmental economics. Sustainable development goals (SDGs) is an effort by every nation whether rich, middle-class, or economically disadvantaged to welcome prosperity and preserve the environment. SDGs take into account a variety of social needs, such as employment opportunities, health care, education, and social protection, but it also deals with the problems of environmental preservation and climate change. These goals have in essence offered a general guide into international action and have united countries in a shared commitment of enhancing human well being as well as economic development and ensuring a sustainable environment. Governments within respective countries have a critical role since it translates SDG goals into national laws, draws action plans on the attainment of these goals, provides budget to execute the same, and it goes on to search partnership opportunities to enhance development. Cooperation is especially essential when the poor countries need to be assisted by the more affluent ones. Therefore, global collaboration is crucial in order to promote common actions and the efficient implementation of SDGs on the international level. The data analysis process of AI has the capability of finding regions or populations that are languishing by using enormous volumes of data. This helps in effective targeting of activities by the governments of the concerned regions and organizations. Predictive analysis allows financial institutions to provide services to previously marginalized groups or areas by assessing their creditworthiness and can match job seekers with relevant opportunities, including remote work or microtasking, which grows the possible pool of employment and allocates resources more efficiently in infrastructure, health care, and agriculture that will guarantee more equal and efficient distribution of resources. AI analytics can assist policymakers in establishing more specific and effective poverty reduction strategies.

REFERENCES

Azuji, I. M., Christiana, N. U., Uzoekwe, H. E., Etele, A. V., & Ejichukwu, E. C. (2020). Relationship between parents home participation in primary school pupil's learning and pupil's academic achievement in Anambra State, Nigeria. *European Journal of Education Studies*, *7*(10).

Brinken, J., Trojahn, S., & Behrendt, F. (2022). Sufficiency, consistency, and efficiency as a base for systemizing sustainability measures in food supply chains. *Sustainability (Basel)*, *14*(11), 1–18. DOI: 10.3390/su14116742

Coker, J. O., Uzougbo, N. S., Oguejiofor, B. B., & Akagha, O. V.Julie Olajumoke CokerNgozi Samuel UzougboBisola Beatrice OguejioforOnyinyechi Vivian Akagha. (2023). The role of legal practitioners in mitigating corporate risks in Nigeria: A comprehensive review of existing literature on the strategies and approaches adopted by legal practitioners in Nigeria to mitigate corporate risks. *Finance & Accounting Research Journal*, *5*(10), 309–332. DOI: 10.51594/farj.v5i10.579

) Dhahri, S., Omri, A., & Mirza, N. (2024). Information technology and financial development for achieving sustainable development goals. Research in International Business and Finance, 67(Part A), 102156. https://doi.org/DOI: 10.1016/j.ribaf.2023.102156

Fikri, Y., & Rhalma, M. (2024). Artificial Intelligence (AI) in early childhood education (ECE): Do effects and interactions matter? *International Journal of Religion: Politics, Sociology. Culture (Québec)*, *5*(11), 7536–7545.

Fikri, Y., & Rhalma, M. (2025a). Nexus between Early Childhood Education, Artificial Intelligence, and Education for sustainability, UKR Journal of Economics [UKRJEBM]. *Business and Management*, *1*(3), 78–83. DOI: 10.5281/zenodo.16493120

Ikwue, U., Ekwezia, A. V., Oguejiofor, B. B., Agho, M. O., & Daraojimba, C. (2023). Sustainable investment strategies in pension fund management: A comparative review of Esg principles adoption in the US and NIGERIA. *International Journal of Management & Entrepreneurship Research*, *5*(9), 652–673. DOI: 10.51594/ijmer.v5i9.547

ITU & UNDP. (2023). SDG Digital Acceleration Agenda. International Telecommunication Union and United Nations Development Programme. https://www.undp.org/ sites/g/files/zskgke326/files/2023-09/SDG%20Digital%20Acceleration%20Agenda_2.pdf

Khaki, A. R., Messaadia, M., Jreisat, A., & Al-Mohammad, S. (2022). Fintech adoption for poverty alleviation in African countries: Application of supervised machine learning approach. In *Africa case studies in operations research: A closer look into applications*

Korinek, A., & Stiglitz, J. E. (2021). *Artificial intelligence, globalization, and strategies for economic development (No. w28453)*. National Bureau of Economic Research. DOI: 10.3386/w28453

Lee, C. C., Lou, R., & Wang, F. (2023). Digital financial inclusion and poverty alleviation: Evidence from the sustainable development of China. *Economic Analysis and Policy*, *77*, 418–434. DOI: 10.1016/j.eap.2022.12.004

) Luzolo PH, Tchappi I (2023) Combining multiagent systems with IoT for smarter buildings and cities: a literature review. 0–54

Nwakpadolu, G. M., Ede, M. O., Okoro, J. O., Nwadi, C. L., Akudo, F. U., Anigbogu, G. N., Ezeanwu, A. B., Edikpa, E. C., Nwadinobi, V. N., & Oneli, J. O. (2024). Effect of psychological intervention in cushioning work-induced stress among secondary school home economics teachers: Implications for policy and administration. *Medicine*, *103*(9), e37174. DOI: 10.1097/MD.0000000000037174 PMID: 38428875

Oguejiofor, B. B., Uzougbo, N. S., Kolade, A. O., Raji, A., & Daraojimba, C. (2023). Review of Successful Global Public-Private Partnerships: Extracting key Strategies for Effective US Financial Collaborations. *International Journal of Innovation and Scientific Research*, *10*(8), 312–331. DOI: 10.51244/IJRSI.2023.10826

Seng, K. P., Ang, L. M., & Ngharamike, E. (2022). Artificial intelligence Internet of Things: A new paradigm of distributed sensor networks. *International Journal of Distributed Sensor Networks*, *18*(3). Advance online publication. DOI: 10.1177/15501477211062835

Singh, A., Kanaujia, A., Singh, V. K., & Vinuesa, R. (2024). Artificial intelligence for Sustainable Development Goals: Bibliometric patterns and concept evolution trajectories. *Sustainable Development (Bradford)*, *32*(1), 724–754. DOI: 10.1002/sd.2706

Stahl, B. C. (2021). *Artificial intelligence for a better future: an ecosystem perspective on the ethics of AI and emerging digital technologies*. Springer Nature. DOI: 10.1007/978-3-030-69978-9

WCED. (1987). Development and international economic cooperation: Environment (Report of the World Commission on Environment and Development). United Nations. https://sswm.info/sites/default/files/reference_attachments/UN%20WCED201987%20Brundtland%20Report.pdf

Ziemba, E. W., & Grabara, D. (2024). Sustainability affected by ICT adoption in enterprises. *Journal of Computer Information Systems*. Advance online publication. DOI: 10.1080/08874417.2024.2321529

Chapter 15
AIoT and Blockchain: Future Directions and Open Research Challenges

Yahya Fikri
http://orcid.org/0009-0009-9978-9438
National School of Business and Management, Tangier, Morocco

Abdelhamid Nechchad
National School of Business and Management, Tangier, Morocco & ESCA Business School of Management, Casablanca, Morocco

Mohamed Rhalma
National School of Business and Management, Tangier, Morocco

ABSTRACT

The IoT infrastructure and AI techniques are merged to establish the AIoT, which is implemented to enhance system performance. AIoT can be wasted to appoint IoT acts further capable, which will improve data analysis and human-machine communications. IoT data can be converted into information that helps with better decision-making using AI techniques, which also improves the system's general usefulness. A wide range of requests, including safety and shadowing systems, clever homes, brainy conveyance systems, smart farms, safe and healthcare's safe checking, manufacturing mechanization and switch, logistics processes and regulator, Commerce, can benefit greatly from AIoT frameworks. However, because AIoT frameworks are susceptible to several kinds of material beatings, they may have hitches with facts safety and confidentiality. These problems also have major consequences, like unapproved information apprises and seepages. One specific caring of folder is the blockchain.

DOI: 10.4018/979-8-3373-6299-1.ch015

1. INTRODUCTION

Artificial Intelligence (AI) techniques combined with IoT organization is known as AIoT. IoT, as we all know, is about numerous "Things" that are linked to different users over the Internet (Xiong et al., 2021; Zhang et al., 2020). AI offers ways to Pullman the gadgets so that, after completing the training process, they can comprehend the new data. The creation of valuable data around the creation via IoT strategies and the extraction of valuable visions from the statistics using various AI techniques are the shared objectives of AIoT (Lai et al., 2021; Lin et al., 2019). The network of physical items, commonly referred to as "Things," that are implanted with instruments, package, and extra associated technologies is referred to as IoT. The purpose of their deployment is to establish connections and exchange data with other systems and devices via the Net. Globally, many of IoT plans gather and distribute data via the Internet. The degree of numerical intellect is provided by the connections between all these smart devices, which have instruments. Device hardware, device software, communication, and platform make up the four components of the Internet of Things. Device hardware refers to hardware components, such as devices and shmoozing plans, that link IoT schemes and strategies to the outside ecosphere over the Net. The many tools and software required to link IoT devices to other devices and users are referred to as device software. Additionally, it gives different users access to the graphical user interface so they can utilize the facilities of IoT-based schemes. The network of "things" that are connected to the Internet is known as IoT. Recent centuries have seen an upsurge in the number of IoT-based applications due to developments in information and communication technologies and the affordability of the Net. IoT-based requests have grown because of the world's canny metropolises and human-centric amenities developing at a rapid pace. The majority of IoT requests consume trusted on mist calculation for information dispensation and storing to manage the massive quantities of information produced by the IoT plans on a steady foundation. However, this cloud-based paradigm is unsuitable for time-sensitive IoT applications due to its substantial communication cost.

2. LITERATURE REVIEW

The IoT is a network made up of linked computers, items, mechanical and digital equipment, animals, and humans, all of which have unique markers. It makes it easier for information to be shared inside a network without requiring human-computer contact or direct conversation (Jebari et al., 2023). Due of its adaptability, the IoT has concerned much consideration currently. IoT organizations must adjust to a extensive variety of needs transported back by this variety of requests. Artificial

Intelligence of Things, or AIoT, is a rapidly developing and revolutionary field that combines AI and IoT. By enabling gadgets to gather and understand data, this novel technique improves decision-making processes that closely resemble human cognition. These days, the convergence of AI and its seamless integration into many aspects of our everyday life is embodied within the broad framework of the idea referred to as the (AIoT). This integration represents a major advancement at the nexus of AI and IoT technology, with the potential to transform a variety of industries, increase efficiency, and offer new applications. Taking advantage of the expansion of sensors and technical advancements, its application has spread into several industries, including cloud computing, data analytics, mobile technology, and others. When it comes to sustainability, a lot of studies generally claim that AIoT is a game-changer for adopting more environmentally friendly methods. These technological combinations seem to aid in achieving the SDGs, from enhanced environmental oversight to smart agriculture. Intelligent Transport Systems are made possible by smart IoT devices and smart automobiles. The ITS, use data processing and communications technology to attain the next purposes. Better transportation of goods and people is made possible by it. Along with improving safety and reducing traffic congestion, it also manages a variety of situations. It is clear from this discussion that important methods, like the blockchain, are necessary for the security and protection of the ITS data. These methods can be put in place there to satisfy the information security needs. Furthermore, the AI component aids in predicting specific dangers, such the probability of traffic accidents, gridlock on a street, and the optimal accessible ways (Zichichi et al., 2020; Dass et al., 2020). The IoT strategies function with poor package, making them susceptible to a variety of susceptibilities. Keen IoT strategies are vulnerable to malware penetration, software attacks, authentication and access control system failure, and insufficient use of cryptography. The absence of governmental regulation is another issue with the blockchain's operation, which fosters instability and facilitates market manipulation (Frustaci et al., 2018; Jeong, 2020).

Table 1. Literature review summary

Concept / Axis	Description	Main Applications / Domains	Key Benefits	Challenges / Limitations
Internet of Things (IoT)	A network of interconnected physical and digital objects, devices, humans, and animals equipped with unique identifiers, enabling data exchange without human-to-human or human-to-computer interaction.	Smart cities, transportation, healthcare, agriculture, industry	Automated data sharing, scalability, flexibility, real-time monitoring	Security vulnerabilities, weak communication protocols, exposure to cyberattacks
Adaptability of IoT Systems	IoT systems must adapt to a wide range of application requirements due to their diverse use cases.	Organizational systems, industrial IoT, smart infrastructures	Customization, improved efficiency, operational optimization	Management complexity, interoperability issues
Artificial Intelligence of Things (AIoT)	Integration of Artificial Intelligence with IoT to enable devices to collect, analyze, and interpret data, supporting intelligent decision-making similar to human cognition.	Smart devices, autonomous systems, predictive analytics	Enhanced decision-making, automation, intelligent behavior	High computational demand, data quality dependency
AI–IoT Convergence	Seamless integration of AI into everyday life through IoT platforms, representing a technological advancement at the intersection of AI and IoT.	Smart homes, smart cities, healthcare, industry	Increased efficiency, innovative services, real-time intelligence	Ethical concerns, data privacy risks
AIoT and Sustainability	AIoT is considered a transformative technology for supporting environmentally friendly practices and achieving Sustainable Development Goals (SDGs).	Smart agriculture, environmental monitoring, energy management	Resource optimization, reduced environmental impact, sustainability support	Implementation cost, infrastructure dependency
Intelligent Transport Systems (ITS)	Transportation systems enabled by smart IoT devices and intelligent vehicles using data processing and communication technologies.	Traffic management, logistics, public transport	Improved mobility, enhanced safety, congestion reduction	Data security risks, system reliability issues
Role of AI in ITS	AI helps predict traffic accidents, congestion, and optimal routes using data-driven models.	Autonomous driving, traffic forecasting, route optimization	Predictive capability, accident prevention, efficient routing	Model accuracy limitations, data bias

continued on following page

Table 1. Continued

Concept / Axis	Description	Main Applications / Domains	Key Benefits	Challenges / Limitations
Blockchain in ITS	Blockchain is required to secure and protect transportation data and ensure information integrity.	ITS data management, secure communications	Enhanced security, transparency, data integrity	Lack of regulation, scalability issues, energy consumption
IoT Security Vulnerabilities	IoT systems often operate with weak security mechanisms, making them susceptible to attacks.	Smart devices, connected infrastructures	—	Malware attacks, authentication failures, weak cryptography
Blockchain Governance Issues	The absence of governmental regulation in blockchain operations may lead to instability and market manipulation.	Decentralized systems, digital transactions	Decentralization, transparency	Regulatory gaps, governance challenges

Source: Authors

3. EMERGING APPLICATIONS OF BLOCKCHAIN TECHNOLOGY IN THE DIFFERENT SECTORS

Blockchain technology offers a number of intriguing features, including decentralization, transparency, traceability, and trustworthiness (Sharma et al., 2020). Because of its many benefits, experts think blockchain technology might be the following large object afterward the Net. This has several uses since the technology may be applied to solve problems in areas including public administration, voting, healthcare, and supply chain (Mcghin et al., 2019). For example, MedChain is a permissioned blockchain-based solution that grants patients complete ownership over their own medical records. Health care systems can become more reliable and efficient with the use of smart contract. By doing away with middlemen and offering decentralization, automation, transparency, and trust. Some significant problems in the financial markets, such the delays caused by the conventional intermediated stock market procedures, may also be resolved by blockchain technology. Blockchain can also be applied to voting systems to make them more reliable (see Table 2).

Table 2. Overview of blockchain technology: Applications, benefits, and challenges

Thematic Area	Concept Overview	Key Application Areas	Primary Advantages	Limitations and Open Challenges
Blockchain Technology	A distributed and decentralized ledger technology characterized by transparency, traceability, immutability, and trustworthiness.	Finance, healthcare, public administration, voting, supply chain, digital assets	Decentralization, data integrity, trust without intermediaries	Scalability issues, regulatory uncertainty, energy consumption
Decentralization and Trust Mechanisms	Blockchain removes intermediaries by enabling peer-to-peer interactions through consensus protocols.	Financial markets, governance systems	Reduced transaction delays, cost efficiency, increased trust	Governance complexity, coordination challenges
Healthcare Data Management (MedChain)	Permissioned blockchain enabling patients to fully control and own their medical records.	Healthcare systems, medical data exchange	Enhanced data security, patient empowerment, system reliability	Privacy regulation compliance, legacy system integration
Smart Contract Automation	Self-executing digital contracts that automate processes based on predefined rules.	Healthcare, insurance, finance, supply chains	Automation, transparency, reduced operational costs	Coding vulnerabilities, legal enforceability issues
Financial Market Infrastructure	Blockchain reduces delays caused by traditional intermediated trading and settlement systems.	Stock markets, asset settlement	Faster settlements, reduced transaction costs	Regulatory barriers, institutional resistance
Electronic Voting Systems	Blockchain-based voting systems improve election transparency and reliability.	Public governance, electoral systems	Fraud resistance, auditability, transparency	Privacy risks, scalability concerns
Insurance Process Optimization	Smart contracts streamline insurance transactions and protect digital identities.	Insurance services, identity verification	Fraud reduction, operational efficiency	Legal uncertainty, data quality issues
Supply Chain Transparency	Distributed ledger ensures traceability and trust across supply chain participants.	Logistics, manufacturing, retail	End-to-end visibility, anti-counterfeiting	Data entry reliability, implementation costs
Blockchain-Based Virtual Environments	Decentralized platforms enabling ownership and trading of digital assets.	Metaverse, virtual economies	Digital ownership, transparency	Market volatility, user accessibility

continued on following page

Table 2. Continued

Thematic Area	Concept Overview	Key Application Areas	Primary Advantages	Limitations and Open Challenges
Non-Fungible Digital Assets (NFTs)	Unique blockchain-verified digital assets ensuring authenticity and scarcity.	Digital art, collectibles, gaming	Proof of ownership, monetization opportunities	Speculative behavior, environmental impact
NFT Case Study (CryptoPunks)	Ethereum-based NFT collection of unique pixel-art assets.	Digital art markets	Verified uniqueness, high market value	Price volatility, speculative trading
Decentralized Identity Management	Blockchain-based systems allowing users to control and protect personal data.	Digital identity services	Privacy enhancement, secure authentication	Adoption challenges, interoperability
Identity Management Platform (SelfKey)	A decentralized identity solution for secure storage and verification of personal information.	Cross-platform identity verification	User sovereignty, data security	Regulatory compliance, user onboarding complexity

Source: Authors

Blockchain can facilitate transactions in the insurance sector between policyholders, clients, and insurance businesses in other domains. Insurance companies have utilized smart contracts to negotiate, acquire, verify, and safeguard a person's identify against fraud or identity theft. Additionally, because blockchain functions as a decentralized peer-to-peer method that builds trust, traceability, and transparency amongst participants who engaged in various activities over time, it is a great option for solving supply chain issues (Perboli et al., 2020). For example, users can construct, explore, and trade virtual properties and assets in Decentral a blockchain-based virtual world. By guaranteeing authenticity and rarity, NFTs—unique digital assets verified by blockchain—have revolutionized the fields of net. As an illustration, consider CryptoPunks, a collection of one-of-a-kind 24x24 pixel art images that are highly prized in the digital art market and individually validated on the Ethereum blockchain. In terms of identity management, blockchain enables decentralized systems that give people authority over their personal information, improving security and privacy while enabling smooth authentication across several services without the need for central authorities. One blockchain-based identity management system that enables users to safely keep their personal data and verify their identity for a variety of services is SelfKey (Figure 1).

Figure 1. Relative scalability of blockchain approaches

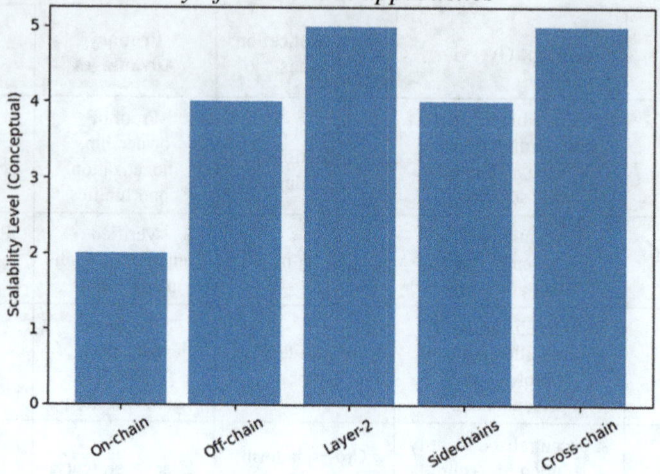

Source: Authors

4. WHAT CUTTING-EDGE SOLUTIONS ARE BEING DEVELOPED TO HANDLE THE MAIN ISSUES BLOCKCHAIN TECHNOLOGY FACES?

Off-chain computing was suggested by Rollup Solutions as a way to reduce contract validation costs. An Ethereum smart contract called Truebit assigns costly calculations to a reliable third party, the solver, and pays a challenger who verifies the solver's output. Because Ethereum gas prices restrict on-chain computations, this enables reliable intensive applications. Designed for private contracts, Arbitrum is an Optimistic Rollup that additionally employs off-chain contract verification to increase its scalability. By allowing miners to confirm signatures without having access to the contract, it encourages parties to come to off-chain agreements regarding contract behavior. This is intended for use in private contracts. They use verification prizes and punishments to encourage accurate computations. In order to reduce the transaction volume of the primary chain and boost system throughput, some transactions are moved off the primary chain to this provisionally off-chain trade route. Two examples of payment channel techniques are the Raiden network for Ethereum and the Lightning network for Bitcoin (Poon & Dryja, 2022). In recent years, there has been a notable increase in the amount of Bitcoin transactions. This exposed the main shortcomings of bitcoin, including its lengthy transaction times and high transaction costs. Experts created Lightning Network, a novel alternative approach, to overcome these shortcomings. To put it briefly, the primary purpose of the Lightning network is to establish a trade channel between two Bitcoin nodes that operate outside of the main chain, which can increase transaction throughput.

Blockchain specialists, researchers, and developers put up endless effort to create novel ways to get over the technology's conventional drawbacks, such its high energy consumption and incapacity to manage large transaction volumes (scalability). Among these advancements, we observe the application of improved consensus methods like as Proof of Stake (PoS) or variants such as Delegated PoS or Proof of Authority. These latter considerably lower energy usage as compared to the conventional Proof of Work (PoW) technique. A sidechain is an independent blockchain that is linked to a primary blockchain to facilitate the exchange of data or digital assets between the two networks. This preserves the security and decentralization of the main blockchain while adding functionality or scalability to the sidechain.

An Ethereum scaling mechanism called Plasma permits limitless side chains within a tree structure. Asset transfers between blockchains can be done securely and atomically thanks to pegged sidechains (Back et al., 2014; Poon & Buterin, 2022). Another way to overcome the scalability constraint is using cross-chain. Many people have been drawn to and utilize it, making it one of the widely used solutions. Cross-chain, a blockchain ecosystem composed of linked blockchains, is exemplified by Cosmos. Each of the network's several blockchains is referred to as a zone. Thanks to consensus techniques like Tendermint consensus, those zones can communicate with each other via an Inter-Blockchain Communication protocol. Polkadot is a cross-chain solution that connects various blockchains via a relay chain (Dib et al., 2018).

Table 3. Blockchain scalability and efficiency enhancement mechanisms

Scalability Approach	Core Mechanism Description	Representative Solutions / Examples	Performance Improvements	Incentive Structures and Trade-offs
Off-Chain Computing	Heavy computations are executed outside the blockchain to reduce on-chain execution costs and gas consumption.	Truebit (Ethereum)	Enables intensive computations without on-chain gas limitations	Requires trust mechanisms, solver–challenger model
Computation Verification Protocols	Costly computations are delegated to solvers and verified by challengers through economic incentives.	Truebit Protocol	Reliable off-chain computation with on-chain verification	Incentive-based correctness, added protocol complexity
Optimistic Rollups	Transactions and contract executions occur off-chain and are assumed valid unless challenged.	Arbitrum	Increased throughput, reduced gas fees	Fraud proofs introduce latency, limited to specific use cases
Private Contract Verification	Contract verification occurs off-chain without revealing contract details to validators.	Arbitrum (private contracts)	Preserves privacy while improving scalability	Limited transparency, requires honest participation
Payment Channel Networks	Transactions occur off-chain between parties and are settled on-chain only when channels close.	Lightning Network (Bitcoin), Raiden Network (Ethereum)	High transaction throughput, low fees	Channel liquidity management, user complexity
Bitcoin Layer-2 Scaling	Off-chain payment channels reduce Bitcoin's transaction delays and costs.	Lightning Network	Near-instant payments, scalability improvement	Network routing complexity, channel availability
Energy-Efficient Consensus Mechanisms	Alternative consensus protocols reduce energy usage compared to Proof of Work.	PoS, Delegated PoS, Proof of Authority	Lower energy consumption, faster finality	Potential centralization risks
Sidechain Architectures	Independent blockchains linked to a main chain allowing asset and data transfers.	Plasma, Pegged Sidechains	Improved scalability and flexibility	Security depends on bridge mechanisms
Hierarchical Sidechains	Multiple sidechains organized in a tree structure connected to a main chain.	Plasma (Ethereum)	Supports massive scalability	Complex exit mechanisms
Cross-Chain Interoperability	Multiple blockchains communicate and exchange data/assets via standardized protocols.	Cosmos (IBC protocol)	Interoperability, horizontal scalability	A

CONCLUSION

We conducted a thorough analysis of solutions that maximize Blockchain in numerous ways. In order to address the six research questions, we posed, we looked through knowledge databases for relevant papers. The first section of the study focused on blockchain-optimizing technology or solutions. The second section concentrated on a particular kind that unites solutions utilizing machine learning or artificial intelligence algorithms to optimize blockchain while concurrently looking for answers to blockchain problems that have not yet been addressed or resolved but that we may use AI to solve. Blockchain systems can significantly improve capabilities and overcome constraints by using AI and ML. Future developments in blockchain technology could result from the combination of blockchain technology with artificial intelligence (AI). However, as the convergence of these two technologies is motionless in its initial phases, there are numerous investigate issues that need to be resolved, such as issues with agreement procedures, calibration, standardization, scalability, and so forth. There is a lot of promise for further research in this area. Since intellect is linked to the development of keen agreements, an autonomous blockchain supported by AI will be able to perform impartial and tamper-proof automated arbitration if we can incorporate all sophisticated AI algorithms and protocols into smart contracts. Every decision would be transparent and justified since it would be documented on the blockchain. Managers can profit from advancements in this quickly changing field by keeping tabs on ongoing research and improvements.

REFERENCES

Back, A., Corallo, M., Dashjr, L., Friedenbach, M., Maxwell, G., Miller, A., Poelstra, A., Timón, J., & Wuille, P. (2014). *Enabling blockchain innovations with pegged sidechains*. https://blockstream.com/sidechains.pdf

Dass, P., Misra, S., & Roy, C. (2020). T-safe: Trustworthy service provisioning for IoT-based intelligent transport systems. *IEEE Transactions on Vehicular Technology*, *69*(9), 9509–9517. DOI: 10.1109/TVT.2020.3004047

. Dib, O., Brousmiche, K.-L., Durand, A., Thea, E., & Ben Hamida, E. (2018). Consortium blockchains: Overview, applications, and challenges. *International Journal on Advances in Telecommunications*.

Frustaci, M., Pace, P., Aloi, G., & Fortino, G. (2018). Evaluating critical security issues of the IoT world: Present and future challenges. *IEEE Internet of Things Journal*, *5*(4), 2483–2495. DOI: 10.1109/JIOT.2017.2767291

Jebari, H., Mechkouri, M. H., Rekiek, S., & Reklaoui, K. (2023). Poultry-edge-AI-IoT system for real-time monitoring and predicting using artificial intelligence. *International Journal of Interactive Mobile Technologies*, *17*(12), 149–170. DOI: 10.3991/ijim.v17i12.38095

Jeong, D. (2020). Artificial intelligence security threat, crime, and forensics: Taxonomy and open issues. *IEEE Access : Practical Innovations, Open Solutions*, *8*, 184560–184574. DOI: 10.1109/ACCESS.2020.3029280

Lai, Y.-H., Wu, T.-C., Lai, C.-F., Yang, L. T., & Zhou, X. (2021). Cognitive optimal-setting control of AIoT industrial applications with deep reinforcement learning. *IEEE Transactions on Industrial Informatics*, *17*(3), 2116–2123. DOI: 10.1109/TII.2020.2986501

Lin, Y.-J., Chuang, C.-W., Yen, C.-Y., Huang, S.-H., Chen, J.-Y., & Lee, S.-Y. (2019). Live demonstration: An AIoT wearable ECG patch with decision tree for arrhythmia analysis. In *Proceedings of the IEEE Biomedical Circuits and Systems Conference (BioCAS)*. DOI: 10.1109/BIOCAS.2019.8919138

McGhin, T., Choo, K.-K. R., Liu, C. Z., & He, D. (2019). Blockchain in healthcare applications: Research challenges and opportunities. *Journal of Network and Computer Applications*, *135*, 62–75. DOI: 10.1016/j.jnca.2019.02.027

Perboli, G., Capocasale, V., & Gotta, D. (2020). Blockchain-based transaction management in smart logistics: A saw-tooth framework. In *Proceedings of the IEEE 44th Annual Computers, Software, and Applications Conference (COMPSAC)*. https://doi.org/DOI: 10.1109/COMPSAC48688.2020.000-8

Poon, J., & Buterin, V. (2022). *Plasma: Scalable autonomous smart contracts*. https://www.plasma.io/plasma.pdf

Poon, J., & Dryja, T. (2022). *The Bitcoin Lightning Network: Scalable off-chain instant payments*. https://lightning.network/lightning-network-paper.pdf

Sharma, P., Jindal, R., & Borah, M. (2020). Blockchain technology for cloud storage: A systematic literature review. *ACM Computing Surveys*, *53*(4), 32. Advance online publication. DOI: 10.1145/3403954

Xiong, Z., Cai, Z., Takabi, D., & Li, W. (2021). Privacy threat and defense for federated learning with non-IID data in AIoT. *IEEE Transactions on Industrial Informatics*, •••, 1.

Zhang, X., Hu, M., Xia, J., Wei, T., Chen, M., & Hu, S. (2020). Efficient federated learning for cloud-based AIoT applications. *IEEE Transactions on Computer-Aided Design of Integrated Circuits and Systems*.

Zichichi, M., Ferretti, S., & D'Angelo, G. (2020). A framework based on distributed ledger technologies for data management and services in intelligent transportation systems. *IEEE Access : Practical Innovations, Open Solutions*, *8*, 100384–100402. DOI: 10.1109/ACCESS.2020.2998012

Compilation of References

Aamer, A., Zadeh, A., Mali, P., & Bolick, C. (2025). Emerging technologies and principle-based project management: A systematic literature review and research agenda. *Management Review Quarterly*, *75*(2), 1761–1811. DOI: 10.1007/s11301-024-00419-y

Aaqib, M., Ali, A., Chen, L., & Nibouche, O. (2023). IoT trust and reputation: A survey and taxonomy. *Journal of Cloud Computing (Heidelberg, Germany)*, *12*(1), 42. DOI: 10.1186/s13677-023-00416-8

Abid, U., Aslam, N., Naeem, A., Fuzail, M., & Imran, M. (2025). Enhancing Intrusion Detection in AIOT using Intelligent Feature Selection and Deep Learning Fusion. *Journal of Computing & Biomedical Informatics*, *9*(2). Advance online publication. DOI: 10.56979/902/2025

Abraham, F., & Ofoe, N. T. (2025). Privacy-preserving collaborative intelligence for IoT cybersecurity: A federated learning approach. *IJSRMT*, *4*(9), 29–33.

Abu, N. S., Bukhari, W. M., Ong, C. H., Kassim, A. M., Izzuddin, T. A., Sukhaimie, M. N., Norasikin, M. A., & Rasid, A. F. A. (2022). Internet of things applications in precision agriculture: A review. [JRC]. *Journal of Robotics and Control*, *3*(3), 338–347. DOI: 10.18196/jrc.v3i3.14159

Agarwal, A., & Ahmad, S. (2025). An Exhaustive Review on Energy Efficient Lightweight Cryptography Solutions for Privacy and Security in Edge Computing. In *2025 12th International Conference on Computing for Sustainable Global Development (INDIACom)* (pp. 01-06). IEEE. DOI: 10.23919/INDIACom66777.2025.11115715

Aghahadi, M., Bosisio, A., Merlo, M., Berizzi, A., Pegoiani, A., & Forciniti, S. (2024). Digitalization processes in distribution grids: A comprehensive review of strategies and challenges. *Applied Sciences (Basel, Switzerland)*, *14*(11), 4528. DOI: 10.3390/app14114528

Ahmad, U., Nasirahmadi, A., Hensel, O., & Marino, S. (2022). Technology and data fusion methods to enhance site-specific crop monitoring. *Agronomy (Basel), 12*(3), 555. DOI: 10.3390/agronomy12030555

Aiwale, S., Kolte, M. T., Harpale, V., Bendre, V., Khurge, D., Bhandari, S., Kadam, S., & Mulani, A. O. (2024). Non-invasive anemia detection and Prediagnosis. *Journal of Pharmacology & Pharmacotherapeutics, 15*(4), 408–416. DOI: 10.1177/0976500X241276307

Akter, M., Moustafa, N., & Turnbull, B. (2024). SPEI-FL: Serverless privacy edge intelligence-enabled federated learning in smart healthcare systems. *Cognitive Computation, 16*(5), 2626–2641. DOI: 10.1007/s12559-024-10310-3

Al Hwaitat, A. K., Almaiah, M. A., Ali, A., Al-Otaibi, S., Shishakly, R., Lutfi, A., & Alrawad, M. (2023). A new blockchain-based authentication framework for secure IoT networks. *Electronics (Basel), 12*(17), 3618. DOI: 10.3390/electronics12173618

Al Sadawi, A., Hassan, M. S., & Ndiaye, M. (2021). A survey on the integration of blockchain with IoT to enhance performance and eliminate challenges. *IEEE Access : Practical Innovations, Open Solutions, 9*, 54478–54497. DOI: 10.1109/ACCESS.2021.3070555

Alaba, F. A. (2024). The Evolution of the IoT. In Alaba, F. A. (Ed.), *Internet of Things: A Case Study in Africa* (Vol. 13, pp. 1–18). Springer Nature Switzerland., DOI: 10.1007/978-3-031-67984-1_1

Alaba, F. A., Othman, M., Hashem, I. A. T., & Alotaibi, F. (2017). Internet of Things security: A survey. *Journal of Network and Computer Applications, 88*, 10–28. DOI: 10.1016/j.jnca.2017.04.002

Alaba, F. A., Sani, U., Dada, E. G., & Mohammed, B. H. (2024). AIoT-enabled smart grids: advancing energy efficiency and renewable energy integration. In *Artificial intelligence of things for achieving sustainable development goals* (pp. 59–79). Springer Nature Switzerland. DOI: 10.1007/978-3-031-53433-1_4

Alagic, G., Alagic, G., Apon, D., Cooper, D., Dang, Q., Dang, T., ... & Smith-Tone, D. (2022). Status report on the third round of the NIST post-quantum cryptography standardization process.

Alahi, M. E., Ahn, H., Liu, L., Alam, S., Shen, H., Cao, Z., Shroff, N., Krishnamachari, B., & Srivastava, M. (2023). Integrating IoT-Enabled Technologies and Artificial Intelligence: A Review. *Sensors (Basel), 23*(11), 5206. DOI: 10.3390/s23115206 PMID: 37299934

Alahmad, T., Neményi, M., & Nyéki, A. (2023). Applying IoT sensors and big data to improve precision crop production: A review. *Agronomy (Basel)*, *13*(10), 2603. DOI: 10.3390/agronomy13102603

Alam, S., Zardari, S., Noor, S., Ahmed, S., & Mouratidis, H. (2022). Trust Management in Social Internet of Things (SIoT): A Survey. *IEEE Access : Practical Innovations, Open Solutions*, *10*, 108924–108954. DOI: 10.1109/ACCESS.2022.3213699

Albalwy, F., & Almohaimeed, M. (2025). Advancing Artificial Intelligence of Things Security: Integrating Feature Selection and Deep Learning for Real-Time Intrusion Detection. *Systems*, *13*(4), 231. Advance online publication. DOI: 10.3390/systems13040231

Albrecht, M. R., Bernstein, D. J., Chou, T., Cid, C., Gilcher, J., Lange, T., ... & Wang, W. (2022). Classic McEliece: conservative code-based cryptography.

Ali, A., Hussain, T., Tantashutikun, N., Hussain, N., & Cocetta, G. (2023). Application of Smart Techniques, Internet of Things and Data Mining for Resource Use Efficient and Sustainable Crop Production. *Agriculture*, *13*(2), 397. DOI: 10.3390/agriculture13020397

Ali, M. S., Vecchio, M., Putra, G. D., Kanhere, S. S., & Antonelli, F. (2020). A Decentralized Peer-to-Peer Remote Health Monitoring System. *Sensors (Basel)*, *20*(6), 1–18. DOI: 10.3390/s20061656 PMID: 32188135

Alkhfaji, A. M. (2023). Blockchain Based Wireless Sensor Networks for Detecting Nodes. *Journal of Smart Internet of Things*, *2023*(2), 1–12. DOI: 10.2478/jsiot-2023-0007

Allen, C. (2016, April 25). The path to self-sovereign identity. *Life with Alacrity*. https://www.lifewithalacrity.com/2016/04/the-path-to-self-soverereign-identity.html

Almukhlifi, R., Al-Khasawneh, M. A., Bukhari, A. A., & Harasis, A. A. A. (2025). Secure e-Health Framework using Artificial Intelligence and Blockchain Technology. *International Journal of Advanced and Applied Sciences*, *12*(2), 52–61. DOI: 10.21833/ijaas.2025.02.006

Alnajim, A. M., Habib, S., Islam, M., Thwin, S. M., & Alotaibi, F. (2023). A comprehensive survey of cybersecurity threats, attacks, and effective countermeasures in industrial internet of things. *Technologies*, *11*(6), 161. DOI: 10.3390/technologies11060161

Al-Nbhany, W. A. N. A., Zahary, A. T., & Al-Shargabi, A. A. (2024). Blockchain-IoT Healthcare Applications and Trends: A Review. *IEEE Access : Practical Innovations, Open Solutions*, *12*(January), 4178–4212. DOI: 10.1109/ACCESS.2023.3349187

Alsyouf, A., Ishak, M. K., & Shahzad, M. (2022). Security and privacy challenges in healthcare IoT. *Journal of Medical Systems*, *46*(5), 1–12. DOI: 10.1007/s10916-022-01852-7

Alter, D. M., Schwabe, P., & Daemen, J. (2021). *Optimizing the NIST post quantum candidate SPHINCS+ using AVX-512.*

Ananthi, J. V., & Jose, P. S. H. (2021). A Perspective Review of Security Challenges in Body Area Networks for Healthcare Applications. *International Journal of Wireless Information Networks*, *28*(4), 451–466. DOI: 10.1007/s10776-021-00538-3 PMID: 34690480

Andriani, A. D., Dwiwarman, D. A., & Khullar, S. (2026). Resilient selves in the digital sphere: Communication strategies for sustainable privacy management. In Resilient Privacy-Preserving Mechanisms for Digital Identity Management (Chapter 1). https://doi.org/DOI: 10.4018/979-8-3373-7292-1.ch001

Anjum, M. J., Farooq, M. S., Umer, T., & Shaheen, M. (2025). Disaster identification scheme based on federated learning and Cognitive Internet of Vehicles. *Computer Communications*, *240*, 108216. https://doi.org/https://doi.org/10.1016/j.comcom.2025.108216. DOI: 10.1016/j.comcom.2025.108216

Anwar, A., Kumar, S., & Manoharan, G. (2025). Revolutionizing the Hospitality Industry: The Impact and Challenges of Smart Operations. In Talukder, M. B., & Chowdhury, H. H. K. (Eds.), *Smart Operations and Enhancing Guest Experience in the Hospitality Industry* (pp. 271–296). IGI Global., DOI: 10.4018/979-8-3373-2145-5.ch010

Aryai, P., Khademzadeh, A., Jafarali Jassbi, S., Hosseinzadeh, M., Hashemzadeh, O., & Shokouhifar, M. (2023). Real-time health monitoring in WBANs using hybrid Metaheuristic-Driven Machine Learning Routing Protocol (MDML-RP). *AEÜ. International Journal of Electronics and Communications*, *168*(May), 154723. DOI: 10.1016/j.aeue.2023.154723

Asif, R., Ghanem, K., & Irvine, J. (2020). Proof-of-puf enabled blockchain: Concurrent data and device security for internet-of-energy. *Sensors (Basel)*, *21*(1), 28. DOI: 10.3390/s21010028

Aslam, M. S., Altaf, A., Iqbal, F., Nigar, N., Galán, J. C., Aray, D. G., Díez, I., & Ashraf, I. (2024). Novel Model to Authenticate Role-based Medical Users for Blockchain-based IoMT Devices. *PLoS One*, *19*(7), 1–23. DOI: 10.1371/journal.pone.0304774 PMID: 38985779

Atalla, S., Tarapiah, S., Gawanmeh, A., Daradkeh, M., Mukhtar, H., Himeur, Y., Mansoor, W., Hashim, K. F. B., & Daadoo, M. (2023). IoT-enabled precision agriculture: Developing an ecosystem for optimised crop management. *Information (Basel), 14*(4), 205. DOI: 10.3390/info14040205

Atzori, L., Iera, A., & Morabito, G. (2010). The Internet of Things: A survey. *Computer Networks, 54*(15), 2787–2805. DOI: 10.1016/j.comnet.2010.05.010

Awaisi, K. S., Ye, Q., & Sampalli, S. (2024). A survey of industrial AIoT: Opportunities, challenges, and directions. *IEEE Access : Practical Innovations, Open Solutions, 12*, 96946–96996. DOI: 10.1109/ACCESS.2024.3426279

Awais, M., Wang, X., Hussain, S., Aziz, F., & Mahmood, M. Q. (2025). Advancing precision agriculture through digital twins and smart farming technologies: A review. *AgriEngineering, 7*(5), 137. DOI: 10.3390/agriengineering7050137

Awan, K. A., Ud Din, I., Zareei, M., Almogren, A., Seo-Kim, B., & Pérez-Díaz, J. A. (2023). Securing IoT with deep federated learning: A trust-based malicious node identification approach. *IEEE Access : Practical Innovations, Open Solutions, 11*, 58901–58914. DOI: 10.1109/ACCESS.2023.3284677

Awaysheh, F. M., Alawadi, S., & AlZubi, S. (2022). FLIoDT: A federated learning architecture from privacy by design to privacy by default over IoT. In *Proceedings of the Seventh International Conference on Fog and Mobile Edge Computing (FMEC)* (pp. 1–6). DOI: 10.1109/FMEC57183.2022.10062661

Azaria, A., Ekblaw, A., Vieira, T., & Lippman, A. (2016). MedRec: Using Blockchain for Medical Data Access and Permission Management. *2016 2nd International Conference on Open and Big Data (OBD)*, 25–30. DOI: 10.1109/OBD.2016.11

Azuji, I. M., Christiana, N. U., Uzoekwe, H. E., Etele, A. V., & Ejichukwu, E. C. (2020). Relationship between parents home participation in primary school pupil's learning and pupil's academic achievement in Anambra State, Nigeria. *European Journal of Education Studies, 7*(10).

Babu, C. V. S., & Simon, P. A. (2025). Adaptive AI for dynamic cybersecurity systems: Enhancing protection in a rapidly evolving digital landscape. Retrieved March 17, 2025, from https://www.igi-global.com/gateway/chapter/337688

Back, A., Corallo, M., Dashjr, L., Friedenbach, M., Maxwell, G., Miller, A., Poelstra, A., Timón, J., & Wuille, P. (2014). *Enabling blockchain innovations with pegged sidechains*. https://blockstream.com/sidechains.pdf

Bagdasaryan, E., Veit, A., & Shmatikov, V. (2020). How to backdoor federated learning. *Proceedings of the 23rd International Conference on Artificial Intelligence and Statistics (AISTATS)*, 2938–2948.

Balamurugan, M. (2024). Federated learning frameworks for secure and decentralized authentication. *International Journal for Multidisciplinary Research*, *6*(5).

Balbix. (2025). Top IT, OT, and IoT security challenges and best practices. Retrieved from https://www.balbix.com/insights/addressing-iot-security-challenges/

Bampatsikos, M., Politis, I., Ioannidis, T., & Xenakis, C. (2025). Trust score prediction and management in IoT ecosystems using markov chains and MADM techniques. *IEEE Transactions on Consumer Electronics*, *71*(1), 862–882. DOI: 10.1109/TCE.2025.3531045

Barik, K., Misra, S., Mohan, R., & Mishra, B. (2024). AIoT and Its Trust Models to Enhance Societal Applications Using Intelligent Technologies. In Misra, S., Siakas, K., & Lampropoulos, G. (Eds.), *Artificial Intelligence of Things for Achieving Sustainable Development Goals* (Vol. 192, pp. 311–334). Springer Nature Switzerland., DOI: 10.1007/978-3-031-53433-1_16

Baumüller, H. (2022). Towards smart farming? Mobile technology trends and their potential for developing country agriculture. In *Handbook on ICT in developing countries* (pp. 191–210). River Publishers. DOI: 10.1201/9781003338376-9

Beaulieu, R., Shors, D., Smith, J., Treatman-Clark, S., Weeks, B., & Wingers, L. (2015). The SIMON and SPECK lightweight block ciphers. In *Proceedings of the 52nd annual design automation conference* (pp. 1-6). DOI: 10.1145/2744769.2747946

Behara, B., Delrobaei, M., & Afraz, N. (2025). Trusted Blockchain-Based Clinical Decision and Medication Management System for Movement Disorders. *IEEE Access : Practical Innovations, Open Solutions*, *13*(August), 139404–139418. DOI: 10.1109/ACCESS.2025.3596693

Beierle, C., Biryukov, A., Dos Santos, L. C., Großschädl, J., Perrin, L., Udovenko, A., ... & Biryukov, A. (2019). Schwaemm and esch: lightweight authenticated encryption and hashing using the sparkle permutation family. *NIST round, 2*, 162893-162908.

Belbase, P., Bhusal, R., Ghimire, S. S., Sharma, S., & Banskota, B. (2024). Assuring assistance to healthcare and medicine: Internet of Things, Artificial Intelligence, and Artificial Intelligence of Things. *Frontiers in Artificial Intelligence*, *7*(December), 1–10. DOI: 10.3389/frai.2024.1442254 PMID: 39735232

Bermeo-Almeida, O., Cardenas-Rodriguez, M., Samaniego-Cobo, T., Ferruzola-Gómez, E., Cabezas-Cabezas, R., & Bazán-Vera, W. (2018). Blockchain in agriculture: A systematic literature review. In Technologies and Innovation: 4th International Conference, CITI 2018, Guayaquil, Ecuador, November 6-9, 2018 [Springer International Publishing.]. *Proceedings*, *4*, 44–56.

Bernsmed, K., Cruzes, D. S., Jaatun, M. G., & Iovan, M. (2022). Adopting threat modelling in agile software development projects. *Journal of Systems and Software*, *183*, 111090. DOI: 10.1016/j.jss.2021.111090

Bernstein, D. J., Bhargavan, K., Bhasin, S., Chattopadhyay, A., Chia, T. K., Kannwischer, M. J., ... & Tamvada, G. (2024). KyberSlash: Exploiting secret-dependent division timings in Kyber implementations. *Cryptology ePrint Archive*.

Bhardwaj, S., Sharma, I., Mahendru, S., Kaur, R., & Sharma, S. (2025). Exploring the Role of AIoT in Data Privacy and Security. In Tariq, M. U. (Ed.), (pp. 75–102). Advances in Computational Intelligence and Robotics. IGI Global Scientific Publishing., DOI: 10.4018/979-8-3693-8547-0.ch003

Bhatt*, H., Bhushan, B., & Kumar, N. (2019). IOT: the Current Scenario and Role of Sensors Involved in Smart Agriculture. *International Journal of Recent Technology and Engineering (IJRTE)*, *8*(4), 12011–12023. DOI: 10.35940/ijrte.D9285.118419

Bhatt, H., Sharma, B. B., Sharma, A., Sharma, R., & Sharma, M. (2021). *An IoT-Based Soil Properties Monitoring System for Crop Growth and Production*. 200–219. DOI: 10.4018/978-1-7998-7756-1.ch009

Bhoi, S. S., Saini, A., Diro, A., Kaisar, S., & Rao, A. (2025). Future Digital Identity Management with Quantum Secure Blockchain. *IEEE Communications Surveys and Tutorials*.

Bhushan Sharma, B., Manimaran, A., Govind Raj, M., Tanushree Gohain, T., Clement King, A., & Rani, S. (2022). Future Research on Internet of Things (Iot) and It'S Applications. *Journal of Data Acquisition and Processing*, *38*(4), 804. DOI: 10.5281/zenodo.777818

Bodkhe, U., Tanwar, S., Parekh, K., Khanpara, P., Tyagi, S., Kumar, N., & Alazab, M. (2020). Blockchain for industry 4.0: A comprehensive review. *IEEE Access : Practical Innovations, Open Solutions*, *8*, 79764–79800. DOI: 10.1109/ACCESS.2020.2988579

Bogdanov, A., Knudsen, L. R., Leander, G., Paar, C., Poschmann, A., Robshaw, M. J., . . . Vikkelsoe, C. (2007). PRESENT: An ultra-lightweight block cipher. In *International workshop on cryptographic hardware and embedded systems* (pp. 450-466). Berlin, Heidelberg: Springer Berlin Heidelberg.

Bonawitz, K., Eichner, H., Grieskamp, W., Huba, D., Ingerman, A., Ivanov, V., & Konečný, J. (2019). Towards federated learning at scale: System design. *Proceedings of Machine Learning and Systems*, *1*, 374–388.

Bouramdane, A.-A. (2023). Cyberattacks in Smart Grids: Challenges and Solving the Multi-Criteria Decision-Making for Cybersecurity Options, Including Ones That Incorporate Artificial Intelligence, Using an Analytical Hierarchy Process. *Journal of Cybersecurity and Privacy*, *3*(4), 662–705. DOI: 10.3390/jcp3040031

Bouras, M. A., Lu, Q., Dhelim, S., & Ning, H. (2021). A lightweight blockchain-based IoT identity management approach. *Future Internet*, *13*(1), 24. DOI: 10.3390/fi13020024

Brinken, J., Trojahn, S., & Behrendt, F. (2022). Sufficiency, consistency, and efficiency as a base for systemizing sustainability measures in food supply chains. *Sustainability (Basel)*, *14*(11), 1–18. DOI: 10.3390/su14116742

Buthelezi, N. M., Malele, V., Owolawi, P. A., & Mapayi, T. (2022). IoT Based Health Monitor for Remote Patient. *2022 International Conference on Artificial Intelligence, Big Data, Computing and Data Communication Systems (IcABCD)*, 1–7. DOI: 10.1109/icABCD54961.2022.9856318

Butt, R., Tariq, N., Ashraf, M., Humayun, M., & Shaheen, M. (2025). Collaborative defense: Federated learning for intrusion detection systems. In *Federated Learning Systems: Towards Privacy-Preserving Distributed AI* (pp. 147–165). Springer Nature Switzerland. DOI: 10.1007/978-3-031-78841-3_8

Butun, I., Österberg, P., & Song, H. (2019). Security of the Internet of Things: Vulnerabilities, attacks, and countermeasures. *IEEE Communications Surveys and Tutorials*, *22*(1), 616–644. DOI: 10.1109/COMST.2019.2953364

Cao, Y., Liu, D., Zhang, S., Wu, T., Xue, F., & Tang, H. (2023). T-FedHA: A trusted hierarchical asynchronous federated learning framework for Internet of Things. *Expert Systems with Applications*, *245*, 123006. DOI: 10.1016/j.eswa.2023.123006

Castryck, W., & Decru, T. (2023). An efficient key recovery attack on SIDH. In *Annual international conference on the theory and applications of cryptographic techniques* (pp. 423-447). Cham: Springer Nature Switzerland. DOI: 10.1007/978-3-031-30589-4_15

Cavalcante, P., & de Almeida, C. (2021). Smart cities and data protection in Brazil: Legal and governance challenges. *Journal of Urban Technology*, *28*(4), 3–22. DOI: 10.1080/10630732.2020.1841839

Cetintav, I., & Sandikkaya, M. T. (2025). A review of lightweight IoT authentication protocols from the perspective of security requirements, computation, communication, and hardware costs. *IEEE Access : Practical Innovations, Open Solutions*, *13*, 37703–37723. DOI: 10.1109/ACCESS.2025.3546147

Chandra, B., & Kanaga Suba Raja, S. (2024). Security In Wireless Body Area Network (WBAN) Using Blockchain. *Journal of the Institution of Electronics and Telecommunication Engineers*, *70*(1), 487–498. DOI: 10.1080/03772063.2023.2233472

Chao, H., He, Y., Zhang, J., & Feng, J. (2019). GaitSet: Regarding gait as a set for cross-view gait recognition. In *Proceedings of the AAAI Conference on Artificial Intelligence*. DOI: 10.1609/aaai.v33i01.33018126

Chehri, A., Jeon, G., Rivest, F., & Mouftah, H. T. (2022). Evolution and Trends in Artificial Intelligence of Things Security: When Good Enough is Not Good Enough! *IEEE Internet of Things Magazine*, *5*(3), 62–66. DOI: 10.1109/IOTM.001.2100130

Cheikhrouhou, O., Mershad, K., Laurent, M., & Koubaa, A. (2025). Blockchain and Emerging Technologies for Next Generation Secure Healthcare: A Comprehensive Survey of Applications, Challenges, and Future Directions. *Blockchain: Research and Applications*, *100305*(4), 100305. Advance online publication. DOI: 10.1016/j.bcra.2025.100305

Chen, L., Moody, D., & Alagic, G. (2023). *NIST PQC Standardization Report*. National Institute of Standards and Technology., DOI: 10.6028/NIST.IR.8413

Chen, Y., Meng, L., Zhou, H. & Xue, G. (2021). A Blockchain-Based Medical Data Sharing Mechanism with Attribute-based Access Control and Privacy Protection. *Wireless Communications and Mobile Computing*, (1), 1–12. DOI: 10.1002/wcm.287

Chen, Y., Sun, W., Zhang, N., Zheng, Q., Lou, W., & Hou, Y. T. (2019). Towards Efficient Fine-Grained Access Control and Trustworthy Data Processing for Remote Monitoring Services in IoT. *IEEE Transactions on Information Forensics and Security*, *14*(7), 1830–1842. DOI: 10.1109/TIFS.2018.2885287

Chia, L. (2020). Singapore's Smart Nation initiative: Balancing innovation and trust. *Asian Journal of Comparative Politics*, *5*(2), 133–150. DOI: 10.1177/2057891119897614

Coker, J. O., Uzougbo, N. S., Oguejiofor, B. B., & Akagha, O. V.Julie Olajumoke CokerNgozi Samuel UzougboBisola Beatrice OguejioforOnyinyechi Vivian Akagha. (2023). The role of legal practitioners in mitigating corporate risks in Nigeria: A comprehensive review of existing literature on the strategies and approaches adopted by legal practitioners in Nigeria to mitigate corporate risks. *Finance & Accounting Research Journal*, *5*(10), 309–332. DOI: 10.51594/farj.v5i10.579

Cornett, S., et al. (2022). The BRIAR dataset: Multi-modal, long-range biometric recognition. *arXiv preprint*.

Cosma, A., & Radoi, E. (2023). GaitMorph: Transforming gait by optimal transport. *arXiv preprint*.

CyberArk. (2023). What is the NIST SP 800-207 cybersecurity framework? [Available] https://www.cyberark.com/what-is/nist-sp-800-207-cybersecurity-framework/

Dass, P., Misra, S., & Roy, C. (2020). T-safe: Trustworthy service provisioning for IoT-based intelligent transport systems. *IEEE Transactions on Vehicular Technology*, *69*(9), 9509–9517. DOI: 10.1109/TVT.2020.3004047

Dayıoğlu, M. A., & Turker, U. (2021). Digital transformation for sustainable future-agriculture 4.0: A review. *Journal of Agricultural Sciences*, *27*(4), 373–399.

Deep, S., Zheng, X., Jolfaei, A., Yu, D., Ostovari, P., & Bashir, A. K. (2019). A survey of security and privacy issues in the Internet of Things from the layered context. *arXiv*. https://arxiv.org/abs/1903.00846

Deloitte Global. (2025). Security and compliance in 5G and AI-powered edge networks. Retrieved March 17, 2025, from https://www.deloitte.com/global/en/services/consulting-risk/perspectives/security-compliance-in-5g-ai-powered-edge-networks.html

Demestichas, K., Peppes, N., & Alexakis, T. (2020). Survey on security threats in agricultural IoT and smart farming. sensors, 20(22), 6458.

Demircioğlu, M. (2022). *Efficient Multivariate-Based Ring Signature Schemes* (Doctoral dissertation, Middle East Technical University (Turkey)).

Dereziński, M., & Mahoney, M. W. (2024). Recent and Upcoming Developments in Randomized Numerical Linear Algebra for Machine Learning. *Proceedings of the ACM SIGKDD International Conference on Knowledge Discovery and Data Mining*, 6470–6479. DOI: 10.1145/3637528.3671461

Dewangan, S., & Kumar, S. (2024). Enhancing Fraud Detection in Finance Through AI and Machine Learning. In Darwish, D., & Kumar, S. (Eds.), (pp. 267–282). Advances in Finance, Accounting, and Economics. IGI Global., DOI: 10.4018/979-8-3693-8507-4.ch014

Dewangan, S., & Kumar, S. (2025). Frontiers of Innovation: Unveiling the Future Opportunities in Fintech. In Kour, M., Taneja, S., Özen, E., Sood, K., & Grima, S. (Eds.), *Financial Landscape Transformation: Technological Disruptions* (pp. 153–165). Emerald Publishing Limited., DOI: 10.1108/978-1-83753-750-120251008

Dewangan, S., Kumar, S., & Tyagi, P. K. (2024). Transforming Hospitality and Tourism With AI and Innovative Technologies. In Talukder, M. B., Kumar, S., & Tyagi, P. K. (Eds.), *Advances in Hospitality, Tourism, and the Services Industry* (pp. 66–83). IGI Global., DOI: 10.4018/979-8-3693-6755-1.ch004

Dhanaraju, M., Chenniappan, P., Ramalingam, K., Pazhanivelan, S., & Kaliaperumal, R. (2022). Smart farming: Internet of Things (IoT)-based sustainable agriculture. *Agriculture*, *12*(10), 1745. DOI: 10.3390/agriculture12101745

Divya, K., & Uma Priyadarsini, P. S. (2024). Defending Delicate Health Information with Corda Blockchain Enabled MAC and UCON-Based Access Controls via IPFS. *International Journal of Performability Engineering*, *20*(1), 48–55. DOI: 10.23940/ijpe.24.01.p7.4855

Djamaa, B., Yekhlef, H., Kouda, M. A., & Bradai, A. (2025). FedCoRE: Effective Federated Learning for constrained RESTful environments in the Artificial Intelligence of Things. *Journal of Network and Computer Applications*, *244*, 104357. Advance online publication. DOI: 10.1016/j.jnca.2025.104357

Donovan, K., & Park, E. (2019). Perpetual trust: Mobile money and the contours of control in Kenya. *World Development*, *123*, 104611. DOI: 10.1016/j.worlddev.2019.104611

Doshi-Velez, F., & Kim, B. (2017). Towards a rigorous science of interpretable machine learning. *arXiv preprint*, arXiv:1702.08608.

Duan, X., Ge, M., Le, T. H. M., Ullah, F., Gao, S., Lu, X., & Babar, M. A. (2021). Automated security assessment for the internet of things. In *2021 IEEE 26th Pacific Rim International Symposium on Dependable Computing (PRDC)* (pp. 47-56). IEEE. DOI: 10.1109/PRDC53464.2021.00016

Ehsan, I., Irfan Khalid, M., Ricci, L., Iqbal, J., Alabrah, A., Sajid Ullah, S., & Alfakih, T. M. (2022). A Conceptual Model for Blockchain-Based Agriculture Food Supply Chain System. *Scientific Programming*, *2022*(1), 7358354. DOI: 10.1155/2022/7358354

ENISA. (2023). *Securing Artificial Intelligence and the Internet of Things: Good Practices*. European Union Agency for Cybersecurity. https://www.enisa.europa.eu/publications

European Union Agency for Cybersecurity (ENISA). (2021). *Cybersecurity of smart cities: Protecting critical infrastructures and services*. ENISA.

Fan, B., Su, Z., Chen, Y., Wu, Y., Xu, C., & Quek, T. Q. (2022). Ubiquitous control over heterogeneous vehicles: A digital twin empowered edge AI approach. *IEEE Wireless Communications*, *30*(1), 166–173. DOI: 10.1109/MWC.012.2100587

Fan, C., Peng, Y., Cao, C., Liu, X., Hou, S., Chi, J., Huang, Y., & Li, Q. (2020). GaitPart: Temporal part-based model for gait recognition. In *Proceedings of the IEEE/CVF Conference on Computer Vision and Pattern Recognition (CVPR)*. DOI: 10.1109/CVPR42600.2020.01423

Fan, J., Wu, J., & Bashir, A. K. (2025). Integrated Contractual Computing Resources and Efficiency Searchable Caching for AIoT-Enabled Green Vehicular Supply Chain. *IEEE Internet of Things Journal*, *12*(19), 39457–39468. Advance online publication. DOI: 10.1109/JIOT.2025.3576299

Farooq, M. S., Munir, S. F., Faraz Manzoor, M., & Shaheen, M. (2025). AI-Driven Adaptive Federated Learning With Privacy Preservation and Imbalance Adjustment for Financial Credit Card Fraud Detection. *Applied Computational Intelligence and Soft Computing*, *2025*(1), 7116768. https://doi.org/https://doi.org/10.1155/acis/7116768. DOI: 10.1155/acis/7116768

Feldstein, S. (2019). The road to digital unfreedom: How artificial intelligence is reshaping repression. *Journal of Democracy*, *30*(1), 40–52. DOI: 10.1353/jod.2019.0003

Fikri, Y., & Rhalma, M. (2024). Artificial Intelligence (AI) in early childhood education (ECE): Do effects and interactions matter? *International Journal of Religion: Politics, Sociology. Culture (Québec)*, *5*(11), 7536–7545.

Fikri, Y., & Rhalma, M. (2025a). Nexus between Early Childhood Education, Artificial Intelligence, and Education for sustainability, UKR Journal of Economics [UKRJEBM]. *Business and Management*, *1*(3), 78–83. DOI: 10.5281/zenodo.16493120

Fortino, G., Russo, W., Savaglio, C., Viroli, M., & Zhou, M. (2018). Opportunistic cyber-physical services: A novel paradigm for the future Internet of Things. In *Proceedings of the IEEE 4th World Forum on Internet of Things (WF-IoT)* (pp. 488–492).

Frustaci, M., Pace, P., Aloi, G., & Fortino, G. (2018). Evaluating critical security issues of the IoT world: Present and future challenges. *IEEE Internet of Things Journal*, *5*(4), 2483–2495. DOI: 10.1109/JIOT.2017.2767291

Fu, Y., Meng, S., Hou, S., Hu, X., & Huang, Y. (2023). Gpgait: Generalized pose-based gait recognition. In *Proceedings of the IEEE/CVF International Conference on Computer Vision* (pp. 19595-19604).

G. D. S., P. V., B., Josephine, R., & Vincent, R. R. (2025). Transforming Healthcare With AIoT: The Future of Diagnostics and Patient Care. In V. Sarveshwaran, K. Periyaswami, & K. Yu (Eds.), *Advances in Medical Technologies and Clinical Practice* (pp. 159–220). IGI Global. DOI: 10.4018/979-8-3693-7703-1.ch008

Gad, A. G., Mosa, D. T., Abualigah, L., & Abohany, A. A. (2022). Emerging Trends in Blockchain Technology and Applications: A Review and Outlook. *Journal of King Saud University. Computer and Information Sciences*, *34*(9), 6719–6742. https://doi.org/https://doi.org/10.1016/j.jksuci.2022.03.007. DOI: 10.1016/j.jksuci.2022.03.007

Gaj, K., Southern, G., & Bachimanchi, R. (2007). Comparison of hardware performance of selected Phase II eSTREAM candidates. In *State of the Art of Stream Ciphers Workshop (SASC 2007), eSTREAM, ECRYPT Stream Cipher Project, Report* (Vol. 26, p. 2007).

Garg, S., Kaushal, R. K., & Kumar, N. (2022). Blockchain-based Electronic Health Record and Open Research Challenges. *2022 10th International Conference on Reliability, Infocom Technologies and Optimization (Trends and Future Directions) (ICRITO)*, 1–5. DOI: 10.1109/ICRITO56286.2022.9964648

Garg, S., Kaushal, R. K., & Kumar, N. (2024). A Novel Design and Performance Assessment of a Blockchain-powered Remote Patient Monitoring System. *SN Computer Science*, *5*(7), 849–866. DOI: 10.1007/s42979-024-03151-2

Garg, S., Kaushal, R. K., Kumar, N., & Boonchieng, E. (2024). Exploring Research Challenges of Blockchain and Supporting Technology with Potential Solution in Healthcare. *International Journal of Computing and Digital Systems*, *16*(1), 487–507. DOI: 10.12785/ijcds/160138

Garg, S., Kaushal, R. K., Kumar, N., & Verma, A. (2023). Bibliometric Analysis of Blockchain in The Healthcare Domain. *Intelligent and Converged Networks*, *4*(4), 305–312. DOI: 10.23919/ICN.2023.0025

Gasser, L. (2023). Post-quantum cryptography. *Trends in Data Protection and Encryption Technologies*, 47-52.

Gewehr, C., Luza, L., & Moraes, F. G. (2024). Hardware acceleration of crystals-Kyber in low-complexity embedded systems with RISC-V instruction set extensions. *IEEE Access : Practical Innovations, Open Solutions*, *12*, 94477–94495. DOI: 10.1109/ACCESS.2024.3416812

Ghamri, M. A., Djamaa, B., Benatia, M. A., & Hosni, A. I. E. (2026). Reinforcement Learning based collaborative DNN inference for edge intelligence. *Future Generation Computer Systems*, *174*, 107942. Advance online publication. DOI: 10.1016/j.future.2025.107942

Goodfellow, I. J., Shlens, J., & Szegedy, C. (2014). Explaining and harnessing adversarial examples. *arXiv preprint arXiv:1412.6572*.

Goodman, E., & Powles, J. (2019). Urban data and smart cities: Privacy, trust and the case of Sidewalk Toronto. *Fordham Law Review*, *88*(2), 457–482. https://ir.lawnet.fordham.edu/flr/vol88/iss2/5

Grosse, K., Bieringer, L., Besold, T. R., & Alahi, A. M. (2024). Towards more practical threat models in artificial intelligence security. In *33rd USENIX Security Symposium (USENIX Security 24)* (pp. 4891-4908).

Grover, L. K. (1996, July). A fast quantum mechanical algorithm for database search. In *Proceedings of the twenty-eighth annual ACM symposium on Theory of computing* (pp. 212-219). DOI: 10.1145/237814.237866

Grover, S., Kumar, S., & Dhiraj, A. (2024). Green Labeling and Green Scapes in the Hospitality and Tourism Industry: A Perspective Study of Industrial Employees Attracting Brand Mark of Hospitality Organizations in UT Regions. In Sharma, A., & Arora, S. (Eds.), *Strategic Tourism Planning for Communities* (pp. 163–172). Emerald Publishing Limited., DOI: 10.1108/978-1-83549-015-020241013

Guo, J., Peyrin, T., & Poschmann, A. (2011). The PHOTON family of lightweight hash functions. In *Annual cryptology conference* (pp. 222-239). Berlin, Heidelberg: Springer Berlin Heidelberg. DOI: 10.1007/978-3-642-22792-9_13

Guo, M., Tang, H., & Guo, X. 2024. Blockchain Technology Enabling Applications in Smart Agriculture. In *Proceedings of the 2024 International Conference on Big Data and Digital Management (ICBDDM'24)*. Association for Computing Machinery, New York, NY, USA, 245–250. DOI: 10.1145/3696500.3696542

Gupta, M., Abdelsalam, M., Khorsandroo, S., & Mittal, S. (2020). Security and privacy in smart farming: Challenges and opportunities. *IEEE Access : Practical Innovations, Open Solutions*, *8*, 34564–34584. DOI: 10.1109/ACCESS.2020.2975142

Hadzovic, S., Mrdovic, S., & Radonjic, M. (2023). A path towards an internet of things and artificial intelligence regulatory framework. *IEEE Communications Magazine*, *61*(7), 90–96. DOI: 10.1109/MCOM.002.2200373

Hardjono, T., Lipton, A., & Pentland, A. (2020). Towards an interoperability architecture for blockchain autonomous systems. *IEEE Transactions on Engineering Management*, *67*(4), 1296–1306. DOI: 10.1109/TEM.2019.2920154

Harnal, S., & Chauhan, R. K. (2020). Towards Secure, Flexible and Efficient Role based Hospital's Cloud Management System: Case Study. *EAI Endorsed Transactions on Pervasive Health and Technology*, *6*(22), 1–13. DOI: 10.4108/eai.13-7-2018.165497

Hasan, K., Chowdhury, M. J. M., Biswas, K., Ahmed, K., Islam, M. S., & Usman, M. (2022). A blockchain-based secure data-sharing framework for Software Defined Wireless Body Area Networks. *Computer Networks*, *211*(March), 109004. Advance online publication. DOI: 10.1016/j.comnet.2022.109004

Hassan, A. H., Ahmed, E. M., Hussien, J. M., Sulaiman, R. B., Abdulhak, M., & Kahtan, H. (2025). A cyber physical sustainable smart city framework toward society 5.0: Explainable AI for enhanced SDGs monitoring. *Research in Globalization*, *10*, 100275. Advance online publication. DOI: 10.1016/j.resglo.2025.100275

Hassija, V., Chamola, V., Saxena, V., Jain, D., Goyal, P., & Sikdar, B. (2019). A survey on IoT security: Application areas, security threats, and solution architectures. *IEEE Access : Practical Innovations, Open Solutions*, *7*, 82721–82743. DOI: 10.1109/ACCESS.2019.2924045

Hayes, C. J., Dawson, L., McCoy, H., Hernandez, M., Andersen, J., Ali, M. M., Bogulski, C. A., & Eswaran, H. (2023). Utilization of Remote Patient Monitoring Within the United States Health Care System: A Scoping Review. *Telemedicine Journal and e-Health*, *29*(3), 384–394. DOI: 10.1089/tmj.2022.0111 PMID: 35819861

Helbing, D., Frey, B. S., Gigerenzer, G., Hafen, E., Hagner, M., Hofstetter, Y., & Zwitter, A. (2018). Will democracy survive big data and artificial intelligence? In *Towards digital enlightenment: Essays on the dark and light sides of the digital revolution* (pp. 73–98). Springer International Publishing., DOI: 10.1007/978-3-319-90869-4_7

Hemamalini, V., Mishra, A. K., Tyagi, A. K., & Kakulapati, V. (2024). Artificial intelligence–blockchain-enabled–internet of things-based cloud applications for next-generation society. *Automated secure computing for next-generation systems*, 65-82.

Hemmati, A., Arzanagh, H. M., & Rahmani, A. M. (2025). Fundamentals of Edge AI and Federated Learning. *Model Optimization Methods for Efficient and Edge AI: Federated Learning Architectures, Frameworks and Applications*, 1-23.

Hnatiuc, M., Alpetri, D., Sintea, S.-R., Hnatiuc, B., Margarit Raicu, G., Paun, M., & Dina, I. (2025). AIoT Monitoring for Early Identification of Diseases in Grapevines: Complete Study. *IEEE Access : Practical Innovations, Open Solutions*, *13*, 80258–80271. DOI: 10.1109/ACCESS.2025.3567454

Hong, S. (2024). The Convergence of Artificial Intelligence and the Internet of Things (AIoT): Innovations, Challenges, and Future Directions. , *3*(4), 40-46.

Hsiao, S.-J., & Sung, W.-T. (2023). Intelligent Home Using Fuzzy Control Based on AIoT. *Computer Systems Science and Engineering*, *45*(2), 1063–1081. DOI: 10.32604/csse.2023.028438

Hu, B., Guan, Y., Gao, Y., Long, Y., Lane, N., & Ploetz, T. (2018). Robust cross-view gait recognition with evidence: A discriminant gait GAN (DiGGAN) approach. *arXiv preprint arXiv:1811.10493*.

Hundal, G. S., Laux, C. M., Buckmaster, D., Sutton, M. J., & Langemeier, M. (2023). Exploring barriers to the adoption of internet of things-based precision agriculture practices. *Agriculture*, *13*(1), 163. DOI: 10.3390/agriculture13010163

Ikwue, U., Ekwezia, A. V., Oguejiofor, B. B., Agho, M. O., & Daraojimba, C. (2023). Sustainable investment strategies in pension fund management: A comparative review of Esg principles adoption in the US and NIGERIA. *International Journal of Management & Entrepreneurship Research*, *5*(9), 652–673. DOI: 10.51594/ijmer.v5i9.547

Iman, S., Ahn, H., Liu, L., Alam, S., Shen, H., Cao, Z., Shroff, N., Krishnamachari, B., & Srivastava, M. (2024). Artificial Intelligence of Things: A Survey. *arXiv*. https://arxiv.org/abs/2410.19998

Imtyaz Ahmed, M., Kannan, G., Ahmed, M. I., & Kannan, G. (2022). Secure and Lightweight Privacy Preserving Internet of Things Integration for Remote Patient Monitoring. *Journal of King Saud University. Computer and Information Sciences*, *34*(9), 6895–6908. DOI: 10.1016/j.jksuci.2021.07.016

Inglehart, R. (2018). *Cultural evolution: People's motivations are changing, and reshaping the world*. Cambridge University Press. DOI: 10.1017/9781108613880

Institute for Defense & Business. (2025). What are the cybersecurity risks for smart cities? Retrieved March 17, 2025, from https://www.idb.org/what-are-the-cybersecurity-risks-for-smart-cities/

Islam, A., Karimipour, H., & Fapojuwo, A. O. (2025). A Federated Meta Learning-Based Secure Data Consolidation Scheme for Industrial AIoT Leveraging Drone. *IEEE Transactions on Vehicular Technology*, *74*(1), 1702–1707. DOI: 10.1109/TVT.2024.3456029

ITU & UNDP. (2023). SDG Digital Acceleration Agenda. International Telecommunication Union and United Nations Development Programme. https://www.undp.org/ sites/g/files/zskgke326/files/2023-09/SDG%20Digital%20Acceleration%20Agenda_2.pdf

Jadhav, H. M., Mulani, A. O., & Jadhav, M. (2022). *Design and development of chatbot based on reinforcement learning*. DOI: 10.1002/9781119861850.ch12

Jagatheesaperumal, S. K., Bibri, S. E., Huang, J., Rajapandian, J., & Parthiban, B. (2024). Artificial intelligence of things for smart cities: Advanced solutions for enhancing transportation safety. *Computational Urban Science*, *4*(1), 10. Advance online publication. DOI: 10.1007/s43762-024-00120-6

Jameer, S., & Syed, H. (2023). A Deep Survey on Human Activity Recognition Using Mobile and Wearable Sensors. *EAI Endorsed Transactions on Pervasive Health and Technology*, *9*(1), 1–12. DOI: 10.4108/eetpht.9.4483

Jamil, F., Ahmad, S., Iqbal, N., & Kim, D. H. (2020). Towards a Remote Monitoring of Patient Vital Signs Based on IoT-based Blockchain Integrity Management Platforms in Smart Hospitals. *Sensors (Basel)*, *20*(8), 1–26. DOI: 10.3390/s20082195 PMID: 32294989

Jayabalan, J., & Jeyanthi, N. (2025). Blockchain and Chainlink Oracle Integration in EHR: Ensuring Real-Time Data Integrity and Interoperability with Ethereum, Hyperledger Fabric and IPFS Storage. *IEEE Access : Practical Innovations, Open Solutions*, *13*(August), 158044–158056. DOI: 10.1109/ACCESS.2025.3606194

Jebari, H., Mechkouri, M. H., Rekiek, S., & Reklaoui, K. (2023). Poultry-edge-AI-IoT system for real-time monitoring and predicting using artificial intelligence. *International Journal of Interactive Mobile Technologies*, *17*(12), 149–170. DOI: 10.3991/ijim.v17i12.38095

Jeong, D. (2020). Artificial intelligence security threat, crime, and forensics: Taxonomy and open issues. *IEEE Access : Practical Innovations, Open Solutions*, *8*, 184560–184574. DOI: 10.1109/ACCESS.2020.3029280

Jevremovic, A., Veinovic, M., & Peraković, D. (2024). Analyzing the Efficiency of Software Distribution Systems in AIoT Environments. In L. Knapčíková & D. Peraković (Eds.), *8th EAI International Conference on Management of Manufacturing Systems* (pp. 99–108). Springer Nature Switzerland. DOI: 10.1007/978-3-031-53161-3_7

Jiang, H., Zhang, Y., Muljadi, E., Zhang, J. J., & Gao, D. W. (2018). A Short-Term and High-Resolution Distribution System Load Forecasting Approach Using Support Vector Regression With Hybrid Parameters Optimization. *IEEE Transactions on Smart Grid*, *9*(4), 3341–3350. DOI: 10.1109/TSG.2016.2628061

Jiang, Y., Xu, X., & Xiao, F. (2022). Attribute-Based Encryption with Blockchain Protection Scheme for Electronic Health Records. *IEEE Transactions on Network and Service Management*, *19*(4), 3884–3895. DOI: 10.1109/TNSM.2022.3193707

Jun, M. (2025). Platform framework for blockchain-enhanced healthcare AIoT systems. *Frontiers in Communications and Networks*, *6*(April), 1–18. DOI: 10.3389/frcmn.2025.1538965

Kabir, M. S., & Nazmul Alam, M. (2023). IoT, Big Data and AI Applications in the Law Enforcement and Legal System. *RE:view*, *10*, 1777–1789.

Kaganurmath, S., Cholli, N. G., & Anala, M. R. (2025). Integrating MQTT protocol to improve the performance using dynamic lightweight key sharing protocol for secure IoT communications. *Cluster Computing*, *28*(16), 1068. Advance online publication. DOI: 10.1007/s10586-025-05689-z

Kamiński, K., & Mazurczyk, W. (2023). RSA Keys Quality in a Real-world Organizational Certificate Dataset: A Practical Outlook. *International Journal of Electronics and Telecommunications*, *69*(4), 803–810. DOI: 10.24425/ijet.2023.147704

Karunathilake, E. M. B. M., Le, A. T., Heo, S., Chung, Y. S., & Mansoor, S. (2023). The path to smart farming: Innovations and opportunities in precision agriculture. *Agriculture*, *13*(8), 1593. DOI: 10.3390/agriculture13081593

Karve, S., Gangonda, S., Birajadar, G., Godase, V., Ghodake, R., & Mulani, A. O. (2025). Optimized neural network for prediction of neurological disorders. In Singh, S. (Eds.), *Emerging trends in artificial intelligence, data science and signal processing* (Vol. 2440). Springer., DOI: 10.1007/978-3-031-88762-8_18

Kashid, M. M., Karande, K. J., & Mulani, A. O. (2022). IoT-based environmental parameter monitoring using machine learning approach. In Kumar, A. (Eds.), *Proceedings of the International Conference on Cognitive and Intelligent Computing*. Springer. DOI: 10.1007/978-981-19-2350-0_5

Kashyap, S., Sharma, B. B., Kumar, N., Vaidya, P., & Gupta, G. (2021). Role of IoT in healthcare: An overview. *Mobile Health: Advances in Research and Applications*, 1–16.

Kaur, J., Rani, R., & Kalra, N. (2024). Attribute-based Access Control Scheme for Secure Storage and Sharing of EHRs using Blockchain and IPFS. *Cluster Computing*, *27*(1), 1047–1061. DOI: 10.1007/s10586-023-04038-2

Kaushal, R. K. & Kumar, N. (2024). Convergence of Blockchain and Internet of Things Using Hyperledger Fabric. *2024 International Conference on Emerging Smart Computing and Informatics, ESCI 2024*, 1–5. DOI: 10.1109/ESCI59607.2024.10497226

Kaushal, R. K., Kumar, N., Kukreja, V., & Boonchieng, E. (2025). Hyperledger Fabric based Remote Patient Monitoring Solution and Performance Evaluation. *Peer-to-Peer Networking and Applications*, *18*(3), 1–17. DOI: 10.1007/s12083-025-01921-0

Kebande, V. R. (2025). Quantum Computing in Industrial Internet of Things (IIoT) Forensics: Framework, Implications, Opportunities, and Future Directions. *WIREs Forensic Science*, *7*(3), e70013. DOI: 10.1002/wfs2.70013

Khaki, A. R., Messaadia, M., Jreisat, A., & Al-Mohammad, S. (2022). Fintech adoption for poverty alleviation in African countries: Application of supervised machine learning approach. In *Africa case studies in operations research: A closer look into applications*

Khan, H. U., Hussain, A., Nazir, S., & Ali, F. (2025). AIoT-enabled service prioritization for mobile nodes using enhanced PMIPv6 extension protocol. *Peer-to-Peer Networking and Applications*, *18*(2), 73. Advance online publication. DOI: 10.1007/s12083-024-01844-2

Khan, M. F. F., & Sakamura, K. (2016). A Discretionary Delegation Framework for Access Control Systems. In Debruyne, C., Panetto, H., Meersman, R., Dillon, T., Kühn, E., O'Sullivan, D., & Ardagna, C. A. (Eds.), *On the Move to Meaningful Internet Systems: OTM 2016 Conferences* (pp. 865–882). Springer International Publishing., DOI: 10.1007/978-3-319-48472-3_54

Khan, M., Hatami, M., Zhao, W., & Chen, Y. (2024). A novel trusted hardware-based scalable security framework for IoT edge devices. *Discover Internet of Things*, *4*(1), 4. DOI: 10.1007/s43926-024-00056-7

Khullar, S., Magdalene, A. H. S., Sandhya, P., & Naik, B. R. H. K. B. N., & Raju, M. V. (2025). Implementation, performance, and energy efficiency analysis for text classification of deep learning architectures. In 2025 10th International Conference on Communication and Electronics Systems (ICCES) (pp. 2099–2103). IEEE. https://doi.org/DOI: 10.1109/ICCES67310.2025.11336350

Khullar, S., Mounika, G. R., Chauhan, S. S., Garg, G., Priyanka, T. P., & Kaliappan, S. (2025). Advanced hybrid ensemble learning for blockchain-enabled secure voting: Leveraging random forest, XGBoost, and neural networks for robust anomaly detection and integrity assurance. In 2025 1st International Conference on Advancement in Futuristic Technologies (ICAFT) (pp. 1–7). IEEE. https://doi.org/DOI: 10.1109/ICAFT66710.2025.11452780

Khullar, S., Baghel, R. S., & Swami, P. (2026). Human-AI collaboration: Balancing trust, emotion, and productivity. In *AI Hallucination Management in the Enterprise Metaverse*. IGI Global., https://doi.org/10.4018/979-8-3373-7534-2.ch003

Khurshid, K., Khurshid, K., Hadi, M. U., Bataineh, M. A., & Saeed, N. (2025). Securing AIoT Surveillance: Techniques, Challenges, and Solutions. *IEEE Open Journal of the Communications Society*, *6*, 1–1. DOI: 10.1109/OJCOMS.2025.3593311

Kishore, N., Nanglia, P., Gupta, S., & Dubey, A. K. (Eds.). (2024). *The Future of Computing: Ubiquitous Applications and Technologies*. BENTHAM SCIENCE PUBLISHERS., DOI: 10.2174/97898152389901240101

Koduru, T., & Koduru, N. P. (2022). An overview of vulnerabilities in smart farming systems. *Journal of Student Research*, *11*(1), 1–14. DOI: 10.47611/jsrhs.v11i1.2303

Kongsen, J., Chantaradsuwan, D., Koad, P., Thu, M., & Jandaeng, C. (2024). A Secure Blockchain-Enabled Remote Healthcare Monitoring System for Home Isolation. *Journal of Sensor and Actuator Networks*, *13*(1), 1–20. DOI: 10.3390/jsan13010013

Korinek, A., & Stiglitz, J. E. (2021). *Artificial intelligence, globalization, and strategies for economic development (No. w28453)*. National Bureau of Economic Research. DOI: 10.3386/w28453

Kostromitin, K. I., Dokuchaev, B. N., & Kozlov, D. A. (2020). Analysis of the most common software and hardware vulnerabilities in microprocessor systems. In *2020 International Russian Automation Conference (RusAutoCon)* (pp. 1031-1036). IEEE. DOI: 10.1109/RusAutoCon49822.2020.9208037

Krishna, M. B. (2016). Security and Trust Management for the Internet of Things: An Rfid and Sensor Network Perspective. In Brooks, T. T. (Ed.), *Cyber-Assurance for the Internet of Things* (1st ed., pp. 137–162). Wiley., DOI: 10.1002/9781119193784.ch4

Krizhevsky, A., Sutskever, I., & Hinton, G. E. (2017). ImageNet classification with deep convolutional neural networks. *Communications of the ACM*, *60*(6), 84–90. DOI: 10.1145/3065386

Ktari, J., Frikha, T., Chaabane, F., Hamdi, M., & Hamam, H. (2022). Agricultural lightweight embedded blockchain system: A case study in olive oil. *Electronics (Basel)*, *11*(20), 3394. DOI: 10.3390/electronics11203394

Kumar, H., Kaushal, R. K., Kumar, N. & Malik, P. K. (2024). Comprehensive Analysis of Blockchain Frameworks and Their Usability in Various Applications. *Convergence of Blockchain and Internet of Things in Healthcare*, 243–262. DOI: 10.1201/9781003466949-14

Kumar, N. (2023). Leveraging artificial intelligence in agriculture: transforming the future of farming.

Kumar, H., Kaushal, R. K., Kumar, N., & Verma, A. (2024). An Analytical Study on the Efficacy of Blockchain Frameworks for Student Grievance Management. *SN Computer Science*, *5*(8), 1071. Advance online publication. DOI: 10.1007/s42979-024-03378-z

Kumar, S., Kumar, D., Dangi, R., Choudhary, G., Dragoni, N., & You, I. (2024). A review of lightweight security and privacy for resource-constrained IoT devices. *Computers, Materials & Continua*, *78*(1), 31–63. DOI: 10.32604/cmc.2023.047084

Kunz, A., Baskaran, S. B. M., & Alexandropoulos, G. C. (2025). Lightweight Security for Ambient-Powered Programmable Reflections with Reconfigurable Intelligent Surfaces. *IEEE Communications Standards Magazine*, *9*(4), 168–174. Advance online publication. DOI: 10.1109/MCOMSTD.2025.3573490

Kuraku, D. S. (2023). Adaptive security framework for IoT: Utilizing AI and ML to counteract evolving cyber threats. *Educational Administration: Theory and Practice*, *29*, 1573–1580.

Laghari, A. A., Khan, A. A., Ksibi, A., Hajjej, F., Kryvinska, N., Almadhor, A., Mohamed, M. A., & Alsubai, S. (2025). A novel and secure artificial intelligence enabled zero trust intrusion detection in industrial internet of things architecture. *Scientific Reports*, *15*(1), 26843. DOI: 10.1038/s41598-025-11738-9 PMID: 40702039

Laghari, A. A., Li, H., Khan, A. A., Shoulin, Y., Karim, S., & Khani, M. A. K. (2024). Internet of Things (IoT) applications security trends and challenges. *Discover Internet of Things*, *4*(1), 36. DOI: 10.1007/s43926-024-00090-5

Lai, Y.-H., Wu, T.-C., Lai, C.-F., Yang, L. T., & Zhou, X. (2021). Cognitive optimal-setting control of AIoT industrial applications with deep reinforcement learning. *IEEE Transactions on Industrial Informatics*, *17*(3), 2116–2123. DOI: 10.1109/TII.2020.2986501

Lama, R., & Karmakar, S. (2025). Secure three-tier authentication approach for agricultural internet of things. *Cyber-Physical Systems*, *11*(3), 241–264. DOI: 10.1080/23335777.2024.2372583

Latour, B. (2005). *Reassembling the social: An introduction to actor-network-theory*. Oxford University Press. DOI: 10.1093/oso/9780199256044.001.0001

Lee, C. C., Lou, R., & Wang, F. (2023). Digital financial inclusion and poverty alleviation: Evidence from the sustainable development of China. *Economic Analysis and Policy*, *77*, 418–434. DOI: 10.1016/j.eap.2022.12.004

Li, M., Mouha, N., Sun, L., & Wang, M. (2022). Revisiting the extension of Matsui's algorithm 1 to linear hulls: application to TinyJAMBU. *IACR transactions on symmetric cryptology*, 161-200.

Liao, R., Yu, S., Huang, Y., Zhu, Z., & Van Gool, L. (2020). PoseGait: Learning pose-based representation for gait recognition. *IEEE Transactions on Circuits and Systems for Video Technology*.

Li, K., Li, C., Yuan, X., Li, S., Zou, S., Ahmed, S. S., & Akan, Ö. B. (2025). Zero-trust foundation models: A new paradigm for secure and collaborative artificial intelligence for internet of things. *IEEE Internet of Things Journal*, *12*(22), 46269–46293. DOI: 10.1109/JIOT.2025.3603957

Lin, Y.-J., Chuang, C.-W., Yen, C.-Y., Huang, S.-H., Chen, J.-Y., & Lee, S.-Y. (2019). Live demonstration: An AIoT wearable ECG patch with decision tree for arrhythmia analysis. In *Proceedings of the IEEE Biomedical Circuits and Systems Conference (BioCAS)*. DOI: 10.1109/BIOCAS.2019.8919138

Litoussi, M., Kannouf, N., El Makkaoui, K., Ezzati, A., & Fartitchou, M. (2020). IoT security: Challenges and countermeasures. *Procedia Computer Science*, *177*, 503–508. DOI: 10.1016/j.procs.2020.10.069

Liu, H., Han, D., & Li, D. (2020). Fabric-iot: A Blockchain-Based Access Control System in IoT. *IEEE Access : Practical Innovations, Open Solutions*, *8*(1), 18207–18218. DOI: 10.1109/ACCESS.2020.2968492

Liu, H., Zhang, J., & Guo, J. (2023). LightGait: Lightweight gait recognition for mobile and edge devices. *Sensors (Basel)*.

Liu, Y., Guo, B., Li, N., Ding, Y., Zhang, Z., & Yu, Z. (2025). CrowdTransfer: Enabling Crowd Knowledge Transfer in AIoT Community. *IEEE Communications Surveys and Tutorials*, *27*(2), 1191–1237. DOI: 10.1109/COMST.2024.3423319

Liu, Y., Huang, P., Yang, F., Huang, K., & Shu, L. (2024). QuAsyncFL: Asynchronous federated learning with quantization for cloud–edge–terminal collaboration enabled AIoT. *IEEE Internet of Things Journal*, *11*(1), 59–69. DOI: 10.1109/JIOT.2023.3290818

Liu, Y., Ma, X., Shu, L., Hancke, G. P., & Abu-Mahfouz, A. M. (2020). From industry 4.0 to agriculture 4.0: Current status, enabling technologies, and research challenges. *IEEE Transactions on Industrial Informatics*, *17*(6), 4322–4334. DOI: 10.1109/TII.2020.3003910

Lu, Z., Zhang, H., Sun, L., Xia, J., Ye, J., & Song, M. (2025). From One to Many: Portable Model Construction With Independent Network Units. *IEEE Internet of Things Journal*, *12*(14), 28092–28101. DOI: 10.1109/JIOT.2025.3566284

Lyu, X., Rani, S., Manimurugan, S., & Feng, Y. (2025). Smart Medical Rescue via Efficient Vehicle Road Cooperation: AIoT Framework. *IEEE Internet of Things Journal*, *12*(3), 3373–3384. DOI: 10.1109/JIOT.2024.3479244

Majumdar, S., & Awasthi, A. (2025). From Vulnerability to Resilience: Securing Public Safety GPS and Location Services with Smart Radio, Blockchain, and AI-Driven Adaptability. *Electronics (Basel)*, *14*(6), 1207. Advance online publication. DOI: 10.3390/electronics14061207

Makihara, Y., Sagawa, R., & Yagi, Y. (2022). Gait recognition for surveillance: A survey. *Computer Vision and Image Understanding*.

Mansoor, S., Iqbal, S., Popescu, S. M., Kim, S. L., Chung, Y. S., & Baek, J. H. (2025). Integration of smart sensors and IOT in precision agriculture: Trends, challenges and future prospectives. *Frontiers in Plant Science*, *16*, 1587869. DOI: 10.3389/fpls.2025.1587869

Maodza, B., & Du Toit, J. (2024). Agricultural Internet of Things (AIoTs) Threat Modeling Using STRIDE-LM. In *International Congress on Information and Communication Technology* (pp. 295-312). Singapore: Springer Nature Singapore. https://doi.org/DOI: 10.1007/978-981-97-3302-6_24

Marwan, M., Ait Temghart, A., Sifou, F., & AlShahwan, F. (2020). A decentralized blockchain-based architecture for a secure cloud-enabled IoT. *Journal of Mobile Multimedia*, *16*(3), 389–412. DOI: 10.13052/jmm1550-4646.1636

Masalila, S., & Sheikh, S. 5353106, A. F.-A. at S. (n.d.). Toward Resilient and Intelligent Infrastructure: A Survey of Smart Monitoring Systems and Emerging Technologies. *Papers.*Ssrn.*Com*, 1–26. https://papers.ssrn.com/sol3/papers.cfm?abstract_id=5353106

Mayer, R. C., Davis, J. H., & Schoorman, F. D. (1995). An integrative model of organizational trust. *Academy of Management Review*, *20*(3), 709–734. DOI: 10.2307/258792

Mazhar, T., Talpur, D. B., Shloul, T. A., Ghadi, Y. Y., Haq, I., Ullah, I., Ouahada, K., & Hamam, H. (2023). Analysis of IoT security challenges and its solutions using artificial intelligence. *Brain Sciences*, *13*(4), 683. DOI: 10.3390/brainsci13040683 PMID: 37190648

McCaig, M., Dara, R., & Rezania, D. (2023). Farmer-centric design thinking principles for smart farming technologies. *Internet of Things : Engineering Cyber Physical Human Systems*, *23*, 100898. DOI: 10.1016/j.iot.2023.100898

McEliece, R. J. (1978). A public-key cryptosystem based on algebraic. *Coding Thv*, *4244*, 114–116.

McGhin, T., Choo, K.-K. R., Liu, C. Z., & He, D. (2019). Blockchain in healthcare applications: Research challenges and opportunities. *Journal of Network and Computer Applications*, *135*, 62–75. DOI: 10.1016/j.jnca.2019.02.027

McKnight, D. H., Cummings, L. L., & Chervany, N. L. (1998). Initial trust formation in new organizational relationships. *Academy of Management Review*, *23*(3), 473–490. DOI: 10.2307/259290

Meckling, J. (2019). Governing renewables: Policy feedback in a global energy transition. *Environment and Planning C. Politics and Space*, *37*(2), 317–338. DOI: 10.1177/2399654418777765

Mehta, R., Sharma, R., Sharma, N., & Sharma, B. B. (2025). Smart Technology in Focus: Legal Frameworks for IoT and AI Integration. *2025 12th International Conference on Computing for Sustainable Global Development (INDIACom)*, 1–5. DOI: 10.23919/INDIACom66777.2025.11115751

Menon, U. V., Kumaravelu, V. B., Kumar, C. V., Rammohan, A., Chinnadurai, S., Venkatesan, R., & Selvaprabhu, P. (2025). AI-powered IoT: A survey on integrating artificial intelligence with IoT for enhanced security, efficiency, and smart applications. *IEEE Access : Practical Innovations, Open Solutions*, *13*, 50296–50339. Advance online publication. DOI: 10.1109/ACCESS.2025.3551750

Mesopotamian Journal of Cyber Security. (n.d.). Cybersecurity challenges in smart cities: An overview and future prospects. Retrieved March 17, 2025, from https://mesopotamian.press/journals/index.php/CyberSecurity/article/view/14

Miao, Y., Zhou, E., Fan, W., Yang, X., Alzahrani, B. A., & Xiong, H. (2025). PassGAT: A Graph Attention Network Framework for Device Authentication in AIoT-Enabled Supply Chain Risk Mitigation. *IEEE Internet of Things Journal, 12*(21), 45160–45174. DOI: 10.1109/JIOT.2025.3601839

Miguel, P., Celdrán, A. H., Xie, N., Bovet, G., Pérez, G. M., & Stiller, B. (2023). FederatedTrust: A solution for trustworthy federated learning. *Future Generation Computer Systems, 152*, 83–98.

Mihailescu, M. I., & Nita, S. L. (2024). Securing Web Data and Privacy in AIoT Systems. In Ortiz-Rodriguez, F., Leyva-Mederos, A., Tiwari, S., Hernandez-Quintana, A. R., & Martinez-Rodriguez, J. L. (Eds.), (pp. 128–172). Advances in Web Technologies and Engineering. IGI Global., DOI: 10.4018/979-8-3693-1487-6.ch007

Mihai, S., Yaqoob, M., Hung, D. V., Davis, W., Towakel, P., Raza, M., Karamanoglu, M., Barn, B., Shetve, D., Prasad, R. V., Venkataraman, H., Trestian, R., & Nguyen, H. X. (2022). Digital twins: A survey on enabling technologies, challenges, trends and future prospects. *IEEE Communications Surveys and Tutorials, 24*(4), 2255–2291. DOI: 10.1109/COMST.2022.3208773

Miller, T., Durlik, I., Kostecka, E., Kozlovska, P., Łobodzińska, A., Sokołowska, S., & Nowy, A. (2025). Integrating Artificial Intelligence Agents with the Internet of Things for Enhanced Environmental Monitoring: Applications in Water Quality and Climate Data. *Electronics (Basel), 14*(4), 696. Advance online publication. DOI: 10.3390/electronics14040696

Ming, W., Guo, X., Lin, B., Yang, T., Zhu, Z., Li, L., Zhang, S., & Yu, X. (2023). DyGait: Exploiting dynamic representations for high-performance gait recognition. *arXiv preprint.*

Mirza, N., Yunis, M., Khalil, A., & Mirza, N. (2024). Towards a conceptual framework for AI-driven anomaly detection in smart city IoT networks for enhanced cybersecurity. *Journal of Innovation & Knowledge, 9*(4), 100601. DOI: 10.1016/j.jik.2024.100601

Mittal, S., Singhal, M., Dublish, M., & Noor, S. (2025). Application of AIoT in Smart Retailing and Consumer Insights. In Tariq, M. U. (Ed.), (pp. 397–430). Advances in Computational Intelligence and Robotics. IGI Global Scientific Publishing., DOI: 10.4018/979-8-3693-8547-0.ch013

Mohamed Shaffril, H. A., Samsuddin, S. F., & Abu Samah, A. (2021). The ABC of systematic literature review: The basic methodological guidance for beginners. *Quality & Quantity*, *55*(4), 1319–1346. DOI: 10.1007/s11135-020-01059-6

Mole, J. S. S., & Shaji, R. S. (2024). Ethereum blockchain for electronic health records: Securing and streamlining patient management. *Frontiers in Medicine*, *11*(September), 1–17. DOI: 10.3389/fmed.2024.1434474 PMID: 39386743

Monrat, A. A., Schelén, O., & Andersson, K. (2022). Applicability Analysis of Blockchain Technology. *2022 IEEE Asia-Pacific Conference on Computer Science and Data Engineering (CSDE)*, 1–8. DOI: 10.1109/CSDE56538.2022.10089307

Monrat, A. A., Schelén, O., & Andersson, K. (2024). A Taxonomy Guideline for Blockchain Platforms. *Journal of Wireless Mobile Networks, Ubiquitous Computing and Dependable Applications*, *15*(2), 286–308. DOI: 10.58346/JOWUA.2024.I2.019

Moore, E., Imteaj, A., Hossain, M. Z., Rezapour, S., & Amini, M. H. (2024). Blockchain-empowered cyber-secure federated learning for trustworthy edge computing. *IEEE Transactions on Artificial Intelligence*, *6*(8), 2110–2118. DOI: 10.1109/TAI.2025.3539258

Moreno, R. T., Garcia-Rodriguez, J., Bernabe, J. B., & Skarmeta, A. (2021). A Trusted Approach for Decentralised and Privacy-Preserving Identity Management. *IEEE Access : Practical Innovations, Open Solutions*, *9*, 105788–105804. DOI: 10.1109/ACCESS.2021.3099837

Morepje, M. T., Sithole, M. Z., Msweli, N. S., & Agholor, A. I. (2024). The influence of E-commerce platforms on sustainable agriculture practices among smallholder farmers in Sub-Saharan Africa. *Sustainability (Basel)*, *16*(15), 6496. DOI: 10.3390/su16156496

Morozov, E., & Bria, F. (2018). *Rethinking the smart city: Democratizing urban technology*. Rosa Luxemburg Stiftung.

Mukherjee, S., Ray, I., Ray, I., Shirazi, H., Ong, T., & Kahn, M. G. (2017). Attribute Based Access Control for Healthcare Resources. *Proceedings of the 2nd ACM Workshop on Attribute-Based Access Control*, 29–40. DOI: 10.1145/3041048.3041055

Mulani, A. O., Sardey, M. P., Kinage, K., Salunkhe, S. S., Fegade, T., & Fegade, P. G. (2024). ML-powered Internet of Medical Things (MLIoMT) structure for heart disease prediction. *Journal of Pharmacology & Pharmacotherapeutics*, *16*(1), 38–45. DOI: 10.1177/0976500X241281490

Namana, M. S. K., & Udaya Kumar, B. (2025). Enhancing Surveillance Systems leveraging AIoT for Advanced Object Detection in Real-Time Security Applications. *Engineering. Technology and Applied Science Research, 15*(3), 22507–22517. DOI: 10.48084/etasr.9926

National Institute of Standards and Technology. (n.d.). *Cybersecurity for the Internet of Things (IoT) Program.* U.S. Department of Commerce. Retrieved April 10, 2025, from https://www.nist.gov/itl/applied-cybersecurity/nist-cybersecurity-iot-program

NextLabs. (2024). NIST 800-207: Zero Trust Architecture. White paper. [Available] https://www.nextlabs.com/wp-content/uploads/2024/11/NextLabs-White-Paper -NIST-800-207-Zero-Trust-Architecture.pdf

Nguyen, T.-P. (2025). AIoT-based indoor air quality prediction for building using enhanced metaheuristic algorithm and hybrid deep learning. *Journal of Building Engineering, 105*, 112448. Advance online publication. DOI: 10.1016/j.jobe.2025.112448

NIST. (2023). *Status Report on the Final Round of the NIST Lightweight Cryptography Standardization Process.* National Institute of Standards and Technology., DOI: 10.6028/NIST.IR.8454

NIST. (2024). *Cybersecurity Framework 2.0.* U.S. National Institute of Standards and Technology. https://www.nist.gov/cyberframework

NIST. (2025). *Status Report on the Fourth Round of the NIST Post-Quantum Cryptography Standardization Process.* National Institute of Standards and Technology., DOI: 10.6028/NIST.IR.8545

Nourildean, S. W. (2024). Artificial Internet of Things (AIoT): A Review. *2024 International Conference on Electrical, Computer and Energy Technologies (ICECET*, 1–7. DOI: 10.1109/ICECET61485.2024.10698612

Nwakpadolu, G. M., Ede, M. O., Okoro, J. O., Nwadi, C. L., Akudo, F. U., Anigbogu, G. N., Ezeanwu, A. B., Edikpa, E. C., Nwadinobi, V. N., & Oneli, J. O. (2024). Effect of psychological intervention in cushioning work-induced stress among secondary school home economics teachers: Implications for policy and administration. *Medicine, 103*(9), e37174. DOI: 10.1097/MD.0000000000037174 PMID: 38428875

Obaidat, M. A., Rawashdeh, M., Alja'afreh, M., Abouali, M., Thakur, K., & Karime, A. (2024). Exploring IoT and Blockchain: A Comprehensive Survey on Security, Integration Strategies, Applications and Future Research Directions. *Big Data and Cognitive Computing, 8*(12), 174. Advance online publication. DOI: 10.3390/ bdcc8120174

Oguejiofor, B. B., Uzougbo, N. S., Kolade, A. O., Raji, A., & Daraojimba, C. (2023). Review of Successful Global Public-Private Partnerships: Extracting key Strategies for Effective US Financial Collaborations. *International Journal of Innovation and Scientific Research, 10*(8), 312–331. DOI: 10.51244/IJRSI.2023.10826

Onike, N. J. (2025). The Internet of Things (IoT) in Farming: Smart Solutions for a Sustainable Future. International Journal of Poverty. *Investment and Development, 5*(1), 31–44. DOI: 10.47941/ijpid.2650

Ouaissa, M., Ouaissa, M., Hidar, T., Sachan, R. C., Mittal, A., & Poddar, S. (2025a). *Information Security Governance using Artificial Intelligence of Things in Smart Environments* (1st ed.). CRC Press., DOI: 10.1201/9781003606307

Palo Alto Networks. (2025). What is the role of AI in threat detection? Retrieved March 17, 2025, from https://origin-www.paloaltonetworks.com/cyberpedia/ai-in-threat-detection

Pancari, S., Rashid, A., Zheng, J., Patel, S., Wang, Y., & Fu, J. (2023). A Systematic Comparison between the Ethereum and Hyperledger Fabric Blockchain Platforms for Attribute-Based Access Control in Smart Home IoT Environments. *Sensors (Basel), 23*(16), 1–28. DOI: 10.3390/s23167046 PMID: 37631581

Pan, T. (2025). An AIoT-Based Home Monitoring System for Arteriovenous Fistula Surveillance in Hemodialysis Patients: Development, Evaluation, and Clinical Potential. *Journal of Multidisciplinary Healthcare, 18*, 5313–5326. DOI: 10.2147/JMDH.S531248 PMID: 40904383

Papernot, N., McDaniel, P., Sinha, A., & Wellman, M. P. (2018). Sok: Security and privacy in machine learning. In *2018 IEEE European symposium on security and privacy (EuroS&P)* (pp. 399-414). IEEE. DOI: 10.1109/EuroSP.2018.00035

Park, H., & Lee, J. (2025). LMSA: A Lightweight Multi-Key Secure Aggregation Framework for Privacy-Preserving Healthcare AIoT. *CMES -. Computer Modeling in Engineering & Sciences, 143*(1), 827–847. DOI: 10.32604/cmes.2025.061178

Perboli, G., Capocasale, V., & Gotta, D. (2020). Blockchain-based transaction management in smart logistics: A saw-tooth framework. In *Proceedings of the IEEE 44th Annual Computers, Software, and Applications Conference (COMPSAC).* https://doi.org/DOI: 10.1109/COMPSAC48688.2020.000-8

Piancharoenwong, A., & Badir, Y. F. (2024). IoT smart farming adoption intention under climate change: the gain and loss perspective. Technological Forecasting and Social Change, 200, 123192. Huo, D., Malik, A. W., Ravana, S. D., Rahman, A. U., & Ahmedy, I. (2024). Mapping smart farming: Addressing agricultural challenges in the data-driven era. *Renewable & Sustainable Energy Reviews, 189*, 113858.

Pinch, T., & Bijker, W. E. (1984). The social construction of facts and artifacts: Or how the sociology of science and the sociology of technology might benefit each other. *Social Studies of Science, 14*(3), 399–441. DOI: 10.1177/030631284014003004

Polymeni, S., Plastras, S., Skoutas, D. N., Kormentzas, G., & Skianis, C. (2023). The impact of 6G-IoT technologies on the development of agriculture 5.0: A review. *Electronics (Basel), 12*(12), 2651. DOI: 10.3390/electronics12122651

Poon, J., & Buterin, V. (2022). *Plasma: Scalable autonomous smart contracts.* https://www.plasma.io/plasma.pdf

Poon, J., & Dryja, T. (2022). *The Bitcoin Lightning Network: Scalable off-chain instant payments.* https://lightning.network/lightning-network-paper.pdf

Porter, Z., Ryan, P., Morgan, P., Al-Qaddoumi, J., Twomey, B., McDermid, J., & Habli, I. (2023). Unravelling responsibility for AI. *arXiv preprint arXiv:2308.02608.*

Powell, J., McCafferty-Leroux, A., Hilal, W., & Gadsden, S. A. (2024). Smart grids: A comprehensive survey of challenges, industry applications, and future trends. *Energy Reports, 11*, 5760–5785. https://doi.org/https://doi.org/10.1016/j.egyr.2024.05.051. DOI: 10.1016/j.egyr.2024.05.051

Pradhan, N. R., & Singh, A. P. (2021). Performance Analysis of a Blockchain Based Peer-to-Peer Energy Trading Framework. *2021 IEEE 4th International Conference on Computing, Power and Communication Technologies, GUCON 2021*, 1–7. DOI: 10.1109/GUCON50781.2021.9573668

Priyadarshini, I. (2024). Anomaly detection of IoT cyberattacks in smart cities using federated learning and split learning. *Big Data and Cognitive Computing, 8*(3), 21. DOI: 10.3390/bdcc8030021

Psarra, E., Apostolou, D., Verginadis, Y., Patiniotakis, I., & Mentzas, G. (2024). Permissioned blockchain network for proactive access control to electronic health records. *BMC Medical Informatics and Decision Making, 24*(1), 303. Advance online publication. DOI: 10.1186/s12911-024-02708-8 PMID: 39407229

Qiao, Y., Munir, M. S., Adhikary, A., Le, H. Q., Raha, A. D., Zhang, C., & Hong, C. S. (2023). Mp-fedcl: Multiprototype federated contrastive learning for edge intelligence. *IEEE Internet of Things Journal*, *11*(5), 8604–8623. DOI: 10.1109/JIOT.2023.3320250

Qiu, X., Yu, J., Zhuang, W., Li, G., & Sun, X. (2023). Channel Prediction-Based Security Authentication for Artificial Intelligence of Things. *Sensors (Basel)*, *23*(15), 6711. Advance online publication. DOI: 10.3390/s23156711 PMID: 37571494

Qureshi, K. N., Jeon, G., & Piccialli, F. (2021). Anomaly detection and trust authority in artificial intelligence and cloud computing. *Computer Networks*, *184*, 107647. DOI: 10.1016/j.comnet.2020.107647

Qureshi, K. N., & Newe, T. (2024a). *Artificial Intelligence of Things (AIoT): New Standards, Technologies and Communication Systems* (1st ed.). CRC Press., DOI: 10.1201/9781003430018

Quy, V. K., Hau, N. V., Anh, D. V., Quy, N. M., Ban, N. T., Lanza, S., Randazzo, G., & Muzirafuti, A. (2022). IoT-enabled smart agriculture: Architecture, applications, and challenges. *Applied Sciences (Basel, Switzerland)*, *12*(7), 3396. DOI: 10.3390/app12073396

Radhakrishnan, I., Jadon, S., & Honnavalli, P. B. (2024). Efficiency and security evaluation of lightweight cryptographic algorithms for resource-constrained IoT devices. *Sensors (Basel)*, *24*(12), 4008. DOI: 10.3390/s24124008

Rahmayanti, D. (2024). Artificial Intelligence of Things (AIoT) To Improve Efficiency and Automation in Industrial 4.0. *Sci-Tech Journal*, *3*(3), 255–270. DOI: 10.56709/stj.v3i3.656

Raj, A., & Prakash, S. (2022). A Privacy-Preserving Authentic Healthcare Monitoring System using Blockchain. *International Journal of Software Science and Computational Intelligence*, *14*(1), 1–23. DOI: 10.4018/IJSSCI.310942

Raj, A., & Prakash, S. (2024). An Efficient Blockchain-Based Access Control Framework for IoT-Healthcare System. *Wireless Personal Communications*, *136*(2), 1017–1045. DOI: 10.1007/s11277-024-11312-y

Rajak, P., Ganguly, A., Adhikary, S., & Bhattacharya, S. (2023). Internet of Things and smart sensors in agriculture: Scopes and challenges. *Journal of Agriculture and Food Research*, *14*, 100776. DOI: 10.1016/j.jafr.2023.100776

Rajesh, G., Raajini, X. M., & Vinayagasundaram, B. (2016). Fuzzy trust-based aggregator sensor node election in Internet of Things. *International Journal of Internet Protocol Technology*, *9*(3), 151. DOI: 10.1504/IJIPT.2016.079550

Rajesh, M., Vengatesan, K., Sitharthan, R., Dhanabalan, S. S., & Gawali, M. B. (2023). Enhancing mobile multimedia trustworthiness through federated AI-based content authentication. *Journal of Mobile Multimedia, 19*(6), 1415–1438. DOI: 10.13052/jmm1550-4646.1963

Raman, A., & Sinha, A. (2020). Privacy, surveillance and public trust: The Aarogya Setu app. *Economic and Political Weekly, 55*(23), 12–15.

Ramyasri, G., & Hussain, S. J. (2021). Access Control of Healthcare Data using Blockchain Technology. *2nd International Conference on Smart Electronics and Communication (ICOSEC)*, 353–357. DOI: 10.1109/ICOSEC51865.2021.9591931

Rane, N. L., Rane, J., Mallick, S. K., & Kaya, Ö. (2024). Federated learning for edge artificial intelligence: Enhancing security, robustness, privacy, personalization, and blockchain integration in IoT. In *Future research opportunities for artificial intelligence in Industry 4.0 and 5.0* (pp. 93–135). Deep Science Publishing. DOI: 10.70593/978-81-981271-0-5_3

Rasooli, M. W., Bhushan, B., & Kumar, N. (2020). Applicability of wireless sensor networks & IoT in saffron & wheat crops: A smart agriculture perspective. *International Journal of Scientific and Technology Research, 9*(2), 2456–2461.

Rathee, G., Garg, S., Kaddoum, G., Choi, B. J., Hassan, M. M., & AlQahtani, S. A. (2023). TrustSys: Trusted Decision Making Scheme for Collaborative Artificial Intelligence of Things. *IEEE Transactions on Industrial Informatics, 19*(1), 1059–1068. DOI: 10.1109/TII.2022.3173006

Rathee, G., Kerrache, C. A., & Calafate, C. T. (2024). A sustainable and trusted solution for IoT-based federated learning using feedback behavior. *Internet of Things : Engineering Cyber Physical Human Systems, 26*, 101177. DOI: 10.1016/j.iot.2024.101177

Ravidas, S., Nguyen, K., & Oualha, N. (2022). Decentralized identity: A survey on emerging trends and challenges. *IEEE Access : Practical Innovations, Open Solutions, 10*, 14038–14060.

Ray, P. P., Dash, D., Salah, K., & Kumar, N. (2021). Blockchain for IoT-Based Healthcare: Background, Consensus, Platforms, and Use Cases. *IEEE Systems Journal, 15*(1), 85–94. DOI: 10.1109/JSYST.2020.2963840

Rinf.tech. (2023). Artificial Intelligence of Things (AIoT): Current State and Future Path. (Online article). https://www.rinf.tech/artificial-intelligence-of-things-aiot-current-state-and-future-path/.

RiskRecon. (2023). Understanding NIST 800-207. [Available] https://blog.riskrecon.com/understanding-nist-800-207

Rose, S., Borchert, O., Mitchell, S., & Connelly, S. *Zero trust architecture. NIST SP 800-207, 2020.*

Rose, S., Borchert, O., Mitchell, S., & Connelly, S. (2020). *Zero Trust Architecture (NIST SP 800-207).* National Institute of Standards and Technology., DOI: 10.6028/NIST.SP.800-207

Ruan, J., Wang, Y., Chan, F. T. S., Hu, X., Zhao, M., Zhu, F., Shi, B., Shi, Y., & Lin, F. (2019). A life cycle framework of green IoT-based agriculture and its finance, operation, and management issues. *IEEE Communications Magazine*, *57*(3), 90–96. DOI: 10.1109/MCOM.2019.1800332

Saeed, F., Shaheen, M., Umer, T., & Farooq, M. S. (2024). Employing federated learning for the implication of digital twin. In *Digital Twins for Wireless Networks: Overview, Architecture, and Challenges* (pp. 93–122). Springer Nature Switzerland.

Safeer, E., Tahir, S., Nawaz, A., Humayun, M., Shaheen, M., & Khan, M. (2025). Advanced hybrid malware identification framework for the Internet of Medical Things, driven by deep learning. *Security and Privacy*, *8*(1), e454. https://doi.org/https://doi.org/10.1002/spy2.454. DOI: 10.1002/spy2.454

Sahu, M. L., Atulkar, M., Ahirwal, M. K., & Ahamad, A. (2022). Cloud-Based Remote Patient Monitoring System with Abnormality Detection and Alert Notification. *Mobile Networks and Applications*, *27*(5), 1894–1909. DOI: 10.1007/s11036-022-01960-4

Salam, A. E., Yousef, S., Duha, A., Eman, A., & Alyaa, A. (2024). Employing mutual information feature selection and LightGBM for intrusion detection in IoT. *ICIC*, *18*(06), 597.

Salayma, M. (2024). Threat modelling in Internet of Things (IoT) environments using dynamic attack graphs. *Frontiers in the Internet of Things*, *3*, 1306465. Advance online publication. DOI: 10.3389/friot.2024.1306465

Salcedo, E., Jalal, S., & Ghosh, R. (2024). Computer vision-based gait recognition on the edge: A survey. *IEEE Transactions on Emerging Topics in Computing*. PMID: 39728223

Salgotra, S., Sharma, B. B., & Rasheed, M. U. (2024, December). IoT_LWC Secure Data Communication for Devices: A Review. In *International Conference on Artificial Intelligence of Things* (pp. 160-171). Cham: Springer Nature Switzerland.

Samadi, V. (2025). Empowering Precision Agriculture with Advanced Technology.

Samanta, S., Sarkar, A., & Kumari, S. (2024). An IoMT data security framework with Hyperledger Fabric for smart cities. *International Journal of Information Technology : an Official Journal of Bharati Vidyapeeth's Institute of Computer Applications and Management*, *16*(8), 4875–4886. Advance online publication. DOI: 10.1007/s41870-024-02181-6

Sánchez, P. M. S., Celdrán, A. H., Xie, N., Bovet, G., Pérez, G. M., & Stiller, B. (2024). Federatedtrust: A solution for trustworthy federated learning. *Future Generation Computer Systems*, *152*, 83–98. DOI: 10.1016/j.future.2023.10.013

Sanjalawe, Y., Al-E'mari, S., Allehyani, B., & Makhadmeh, S. N. (2025). Reinforcement Learning-Guided Hybrid Metaheuristic for Energy-Aware Load Balancing in Cloud Environments. *Algorithms*, *18*(11), 715. DOI: 10.3390/a18110715

Sanjalawe, Y., Al-E'mari, S., Alqurashi, T., Alharbi, Z. H., Makhadmeh, S. N., & Alsharaiah, M. (2025). Adaptive graph attention-based federated learning for IoT intrusion detection: Mitigating poisoning attacks. *PeerJ. Computer Science*, *11*, e3281. DOI: 10.7717/peerj-cs.3281

Saraswat, A., Negi, A., Mittal, K., Sharma, B. B., & Kappal, N. (2022, July). Real-time eyesight power prediction using deep learning methods. In *Proceedings ofThird International Conference on Computing, Communications, and Cyber-Security: IC4S 2021* (pp. 325-339). Singapore: Springer Nature Singapore.

Schiller, E., Aidoo, A., Fuhrer, J., Stahl, J., Ziörjen, M., & Stiller, B. (2022). Landscape of IoT security. *Computer Science Review*, *44*, 1–18. DOI: 10.1016/j.cosrev.2022.100467

Sebestyen, H., Popescu, D. E., & Zmaranda, R. D. (2025). A literature review on security in the Internet of Things: Identifying and analysing critical categories. *Computers*, *14*(2), 61. DOI: 10.3390/computers14020061

Sehgal, N. K., Saxena, M., & Shah, D. N. (2024). Future of Edge AI. In *AI on the Edge with Security: Foundations and Practices* (pp. 239–267). Springer Nature Switzerland.

Sekti, B. A. (2025a). Information Security Awareness. In *User-Centric Cybersecurity Implications for Sustainable Digital Transformation* (pp. 111–145). DOI: 10.4018/979-8-3373-3171-3.ch004

Sekti, B. A. (2025b). IT Service Information Security Management. In *Cases on Information Systems Service Management* (pp. 61–93). DOI: 10.4018/979-8-3373-2352-7.ch003

Sendros, A., Drosatos, G., Efraimidis, P. S., & Tsirliganis, N. C. (2022). Blockchain applications in agriculture: A scoping review. *Applied Sciences (Basel, Switzerland)*, *12*(16), 8061. DOI: 10.3390/app12168061

Seng, K. P., Ang, L. M., & Ngharamike, E. (2022). Artificial intelligence Internet of Things: A new paradigm of distributed sensor networks. *International Journal of Distributed Sensor Networks*, *18*(3). Advance online publication. DOI: 10.1177/15501477211062835

Sfar, A. R., Natalizio, E., Challal, Y., & Chtourou, Z. (2018). A roadmap for security challenges in the Internet of Things. *Digital Communications and Networks*, *4*(2), 118–137. DOI: 10.1016/j.dcan.2017.04.003

Shafique, K., Khawaja, B. A., Sabir, F., Qazi, S., & Mustaqim, M. (2020). Internet of Things (IoT) for next-generation smart systems: A review of current challenges, future trends, and prospects for emerging 5G-IoT scenarios. *IEEE Access : Practical Innovations, Open Solutions*, *8*, 23022–23040. DOI: 10.1109/ACCESS.2020.2970118

Shaghaghi, A., Kaafar, M. A., Scott-Hayward, S., Kanhere, S. S., & Jha, S. (2016, November). Towards policy enforcement point as a service (peps). In *2016 IEEE Conference on Network Function Virtualization and Software Defined Networks (NFV-SDN)* (pp. 50-55). IEEE. DOI: 10.1109/NFV-SDN.2016.7919475

Shah Alam, S., & Latif, M. M. (2025). Influence of Artificial Intelligence of Things (AIoT) on Performance of Hotels: Mediating Effect of Added Value of Controllers and Moderating Effect of Market Turbulence. *Journal of Quality Assurance in Hospitality & Tourism*, •••, 1–24. DOI: 10.1080/1528008X.2025.2540981

Shahzad, A., Chen, W., Shaheen, M., Zhang, Y., & Ahmad, F. (2024). A Robust Algorithm for Authenticated Health Data Access via Blockchain and Cloud Computing. *PLoS One*, *19*(9), 1–25. DOI: 10.1371/journal.pone.0307039 PMID: 39312513

Shahzadi, S., Iqbal, M., Qayyum, Z. U., & Dagiuklas, T. (2017). Infrastructure as a service (IaaS): A comparative performance analysis of open-source cloud platforms. *2017 IEEE 22nd International Workshop on Computer Aided Modeling and Design of Communication Links and Networks (CAMAD)*, 1–6. DOI: 10.1109/CAMAD.2017.8031522

Shaik, T., Tao, X., Higgins, N., Li, L., Gururajan, R., Zhou, X., & Acharya, U. R. (2023). Remote patient monitoring using artificial intelligence: Current state, applications, and challenges. *Wiley Interdisciplinary Reviews. Data Mining and Knowledge Discovery*, *13*(2), 1–31. DOI: 10.1002/widm.1485

Sharma, G., Sharma, G., & Sharma, B. B. (2025a). Comparative Analysis of Deep Learning Models for Tomato Leaf Disease Classification. *2025 12th International Conference on Computing for Sustainable Global Development (INDIACom)*, 1–6. DOI: 10.23919/INDIACom66777.2025.11115590

Sharma, G., Sharma, G., & Sharma, B. B. (2025b). Tomato Plant Disease Detection Using YOLO11. *2025 12th International Conference on Computing for Sustainable Global Development (INDIACom)*, 1–5. DOI: 10.23919/INDIACom66777.2025.11115873

Sharma, K., Kumar, N., & Kaushal, R. K. (2024). Blockchain in Healthcare: Pioneering Transformative Approaches. *2024 IEEE 11th Uttar Pradesh Section International Conference on Electrical, Electronics and Computer Engineering (UPCON)*, 1–6. DOI: 10.1109/UPCON62832.2024.10983842

Sharma, K., Kumar, N., & Kaushal, R. K. (2025). A Study to Investigate Effective Tools and Framework for Blockchain-Based Healthcare Environment. *2025 3rd International Conference on Communication, Security, and Artificial Intelligence, ICCSAI 2025*, 604–609. DOI: 10.1109/ICCSAI64074.2025.11063819

Sharma, R., Sharma, D., Vaidya, P., & Sharma, B. B. (2025). Importance of Artificial Intelligence and the Internet of Things in Smart Agriculture. In V. K. Mathew, A. Chandak, M. Mohan, & Bhumeshwar K. Patle (Eds.), *Metaheuristics in Engineering Applications* (1st ed., Vol. 1). Taylor & Francis Group. DOI: 10.1201/9781003561484-8

Sharma, R., Vaidya, P., & Sharma, B. (2024). A Review on Plant Growth Monitoring using Artificial Intelligence and the Internet of Things. *2024 11th International Conference on Computing for Sustainable Global Development (INDIACom)*, 140–145. DOI: 10.23919/INDIACom61295.2024.10498942

Sharma, B. B., Gupta, G., Vaidya, P., Basheer, S., Memon, F. H., & Thakur, R. N. (2022). Internet of Things-Based Crop Classification Model Using Deep Learning for Indirect Solar Drying. *Wireless Communications and Mobile Computing, 2022*(1), 1455216. Advance online publication. DOI: 10.1155/2022/1455216

Sharma, B. B., & Kumar, N. (2020). Internet of things-based hardware and software for smart agriculture: A review. *Lecture Notes in Electrical Engineering, 597*, 151–157. DOI: 10.1007/978-3-030-29407-6_13

Sharma, B. B., Kumar, R., & Sharma, R. (2025). Enhancing Smart Grid Efficiency: The Role of IoT Blockchain and Fuzzy Set Theory. In Mzili, T., Arya, A. K., Pamucar, D., & Shaheen, M. (Eds.), *Optimization, Machine Learning, and Fuzzy Logic: Theory, Algorithms, and Applications* (1st ed., Vol. 1). IGI Global Scientifc Publishing. DOI: 10.4018/979-8-3693-7352-1.ch011

Sharma, B. B., Vaidya, P., Kumar, N., Tiwari, A., Bansal, S., Faruque, M. R. I., & Al-mugren, K. S. (2025). Enhancing post-harvest sustainability in temperate crops through smart IoT-integrated indirect solar dryer. *Scientific Reports*, *15*(1), 28608. DOI: 10.1038/s41598-025-13499-x PMID: 40764716

Sharma, K., Kumar, N., Kaushal, R. K., & Verma, A. (2025). Privacy and Trustworthiness in Healthcare: A Blockchain and Attribute Based Access Control Integrated Approach. *SN Computer Science*, *6*(7), 1–15. DOI: 10.1007/s42979-025-04421-3

Sharma, P., Jindal, R., & Borah, M. (2020). Blockchain technology for cloud storage: A systematic literature review. *ACM Computing Surveys*, *53*(4), 32. Advance online publication. DOI: 10.1145/3403954

Sharma, R., Kumar, N., & Sharma, B. B. (2022). Applications of Artificial Intelligence in Smart Agriculture: A Review. In Singh, P. K., Singh, Y., Kolekar, M. H., Kar, A. K., & Gonçalves, P. J. S. (Eds.), *Recent Innovations in Computing* (pp. 135–142). Springer Singapore. DOI: 10.1007/978-981-16-8248-3_11

Sharma, R., Sharma, B. B., Vaidya, P., & Naaz, S. (2025). Design and Implementation of Real-Time Tomato Plant Growth Monitoring System using Deep Learning based YOLO and Raspberry Pi. *Applied Artificial Intelligence*, *39*(1), 2590829. DOI: 10.1080/08839514.2025.2590829

Sharma, V., Balusamy, B., Ferrari, G., & Ajmani, P. (2024). *Wireless Communication Technologies: Roles, Responsibilities, and Impact of IoT, 6G, and Blockchain Practices* (1st ed.). CRC Press., DOI: 10.1201/9781003389231

Sharmila, A. H., & Jaisankar, N. (2021). Edge Intelligent Agent Assisted Hybrid Hierarchical Blockchain for Continuous Healthcare Monitoring & Recommendation System in 5G WBAN-IoT. *Computer Networks*, *200*(1), 1–12. DOI: 10.1016/j.comnet.2021.108508

Sharon, T. (2021). When digital health meets digital capitalism, how many common goods are at stake? *Big Data & Society*, *8*(1), 1–12. DOI: 10.1177/2053951721996034

Shen, M., Gu, A., Kang, J., Tang, X., Lin, X., Zhu, L., & Niyato, D. (2023). Blockchains for Artificial Intelligence of Things: A Comprehensive Survey. *IEEE Internet of Things Journal*, *10*(16), 14483–14506. DOI: 10.1109/JIOT.2023.3268705

Shepherd, P., Dagiuklas, T., Alkan, B., & Rodriguez, J. (2025). Dynamic trust management for secure federated learning in critical industrial and IoT networks. In Proceedings of the IEEE International Conference on Communications Workshops (ICC Workshops) (pp. 371–376). DOI: 10.1109/ICCWorkshops67674.2025.11162455

Shilpi, G., Rajesh Kumar, K., Naveen, K., Anshul, V., Kumar, K., Naveen, K., & Verma, A. (2023). Effective Tools and Technologies for IoT and Blockchain-based Remote Patient Monitoring: A Comparative Analysis. *SN Computer Science*, *4*(6), 844–860. DOI: 10.1007/s42979-023-02288-w

Shinde, R., Patil, S., Kotecha, K., Potdar, V., Selvachandran, G., & Abraham, A. (2024). Securing AI-based Healthcare Systems using Blockchain Technology: A State-of-the-Art Systematic Literature Review and Future Research Directions. *Transactions on Emerging Telecommunications Technologies*, *35*(1), 1–48. DOI: 10.1002/ett.4884

Shonubi, J. A. (2025). Multi-Layered Zero Trust Architectures for Cross-Domain Data Protection in Federated Enterprise Networks and High-Risk Operational Environments. *International Journal of Research Publication and Reviews*, *6*(7), 146–169. DOI: 10.55248/gengpi.6.0725.2438

Shor, P. W. (1999). Polynomial-time algorithms for prime factorization and discrete logarithms on a quantum computer. *SIAM Review*, *41*(2), 303–332. DOI: 10.1137/S0036144598347011

Shuaib, K., Abdella, J., Sallabi, F., & Serhani, M. A. (2022). Secure decentralized electronic health records sharing system based on blockchains. *Journal of King Saud University. Computer and Information Sciences*, *34*(8), 5045–5058. DOI: 10.1016/j.jksuci.2021.05.002

Siam, S. I., Ahn, H., Liu, L., Alam, S., Shen, H., Cao, Z., & Zhang, M. (2025). Artificial intelligence of things: A survey. *ACM Transactions on Sensor Networks, 21*(1), 1-75. *arXiv*. https://arxiv.org/abs/2410.19998

Sim, S. H., & Jeong, Y. S. (2021). Multi-blockchain-based iot data processing techniques to ensure the integrity of iot data in aiot edge computing environments. *Sensors (Basel)*, *21*(10), 3515. Advance online publication. DOI: 10.3390/s21103515 PMID: 34070069

Singh, A., Kanaujia, A., Singh, V. K., & Vinuesa, R. (2024). Artificial intelligence for Sustainable Development Goals: Bibliometric patterns and concept evolution trajectories. *Sustainable Development (Bradford)*, *32*(1), 724–754. DOI: 10.1002/sd.2706

Singh, C. S., Naaz, S., & Saranya, G. (2024). IOT-CENTRIC DATA PROTECTION USING DEEP LEARNING TECHNIQUE FOR PRESERVING SECURITY AND PRIVACY IN CLOUD. [IJDSAI]. *International Journal of Data Science and Artificial Intelligence, 02*(03), 81. DOI: 10.66135/ijdsai0203p003

Singh, P., Acharya, B., & Chaurasiya, R. K. (2021). Lightweight cryptographic algorithms for resource-constrained IoT devices and sensor networks. In *Security and Privacy Issues in IoT Devices and Sensor Networks* (pp. 153–185). Academic Press. DOI: 10.1016/B978-0-12-821255-4.00008-0

Singh, S., Sharma, P. K., Moon, S. Y., & Park, J. H. (2024). Advanced lightweight encryption algorithms for IoT devices: Survey, challenges and solutions. *Journal of Ambient Intelligence and Humanized Computing, 15*(2), 1625–1642. DOI: 10.1007/s12652-017-0494-4

Sladojevic, S., Arsenovic, M., Anderla, A., Culibrk, D., & Stefanovic, D. (2016). Deep Neural Networks Based Recognition of Plant Diseases by Leaf Image Classification. *Computational Intelligence and Neuroscience, 2016*, 1–11. Advance online publication. DOI: 10.1155/2016/3289801 PMID: 27418923

Slovic, P. (1987). Perception of risk. *Science, 236*(4799), 280–285. DOI: 10.1126/science.3563507

Solove, D. J., & Citron, D. K. (2018). Risk and anxiety in data breaches. *Texas Law Review, 96*(4), 737–786.

Stahl, B. C. (2021). *Artificial intelligence for a better future: an ecosystem perspective on the ethics of AI and emerging digital technologies.* Springer Nature. DOI: 10.1007/978-3-030-69978-9

Stanko, A., Duda, O., Mykytyshyn, A., Totosko, O., & Koroliuk, R. (2024). Artificial intelligence of things (AIoT): Integration challenges, and security issues. *Proceedings of the BAIT*.

Subahi, A. F. (2024). Advancing Sustainable Cyber-Physical System Development with a Digital Twins and Language Engineering Approach: Smart Greenhouse Applications. *Technologies, 12*(9), 147. DOI: 10.3390/technologies12090147

Suleiman, R., Maradapu Vera Venkata Sai, A., Yu, W., & Wang, C. (2025). Blockchain for Security in Digital Twins. *Future Internet, 17*(9), 385. DOI: 10.3390/fi17090385

Sung, G.-M., Kohale, S. D., Chiang, T.-H., & Chong, Y.-J. (2025). An Artificial Intelligence Home Monitoring System That Uses CNN and LSTM and Is Based on the Android Studio Development Platform. *Applied Sciences (Basel, Switzerland), 15*(3), 1207. Advance online publication. DOI: 10.3390/app15031207

Su, R., Sfar, A. R., Natalizio, E., Moyal, P., & Song, Y.-Q. (2022). Ensuring Trustworthiness in IoIT/AIoT: A Phase-Based Approach. *IEEE Internet of Things Magazine*, *5*(2), 84–88. DOI: 10.1109/IOTM.001.2100190

Tagde, P., Tagde, S., Bhattacharya, T., Tagde, P., Chopra, H., Akter, R., Kaushik, D., & Rahman, M. H. (2021). Blockchain and artificial intelligence technology in e-Health. *Environmental Science and Pollution Research International*, *28*(38), 52810–52831. DOI: 10.1007/s11356-021-16223-0 PMID: 34476701

Taha, M. B., Sanjalawe, Y., Al-Daraiseh, A., Fraihat, S., & Al-E'mari, S. R. (2024). Proactive auto-scaling for service function chains in cloud computing based on deep learning. *IEEE Access : Practical Innovations, Open Solutions*, *12*, 38575–38593. DOI: 10.1109/ACCESS.2024.3375772

Takemura, N., Makihara, Y., Muramatsu, D., Echigo, T., & Yagi, Y. (2018). *Multi-view large population gait dataset and its performance evaluation for cross-view gait recognition*. IPSJ Transactions on Computer Vision and Applications. DOI: 10.1186/s41074-018-0039-6

Talakola, S. (2025). Security Challenges in Autonomous Systems: A Zero-Trust Approach. *International Journal of Emerging Trends in Computer Science and Information Technology*, 56-66.

Talukder, M. B., & Mia, Md. N., Masum, Md. Y., Kabir, F., & Kumar, S. (2025). Encouraging Innovative and Responsible Tourism Through Digital Advancement. In P. Thaichon, P. K. Dutta, A. K. Haghi, & S. Dutta (Eds.), *Digital Disruption in Hospitality, Sustainable Hospitality* (pp. 145–165). Emerald Publishing Limited. DOI: 10.1108/978-1-83662-360-120251007

Talukder, M. B., Das, I. R., & Kumar, S. (2025). From Digital Production to Digital Society in Hospitality: Industry 5.0 Perspectives. In Grima, S., Kaleli, S. S., Baygin, M., & Boztepe, E. (Eds.), *Business Challenges and Opportunities in the Era of Industry 5.0* (pp. 173–193). Emerald Publishing Limited., DOI: 10.1108/978-1-83549-676-320251010

Talukder, M. B., Khan, M. R., & Kumar, S. (2025). The Impact of Gig Economy Trends on Traditional Employment Models: Evidence From Hotel Industry. In Nozari, H. (Ed.), *Dynamic and Safe Economy in the Age of Smart Technologies* (pp. 253–276). IGI Global., DOI: 10.4018/979-8-3693-4369-2.ch016

Tariq, F., Afzaal, A., Anjum, M. J., Kanwal, F., Bashir, K., & Shaheen, M. (2025). Security and Privacy Preservation in Smart Cities During Security Surveillance: A Mapping Study. *Applied Computational Intelligence and Soft Computing*, *2025*(1), 6727022. https://doi.org/https://doi.org/10.1155/acis/6727022. DOI: 10.1155/acis/6727022

Thakor, V. A., Razzaque, M. A., & Khandaker, M. R. (2021). Lightweight cryptography algorithms for resource-constrained IoT devices: A review, comparison and research opportunities. *IEEE Access : Practical Innovations, Open Solutions*, *9*, 28177–28193. DOI: 10.1109/ACCESS.2021.3052867

Thakur, S., Verma, R., Vaidya, P., & Sharma, B. B. (2024). A Review of Current Technologies for Vehicle Tracking and Toll Enforcement. *2024 3rd Edition of IEEE Delhi Section Flagship Conference (DELCON)*, 1–5. DOI: 10.1109/DELCON64804.2024.10866452

Thapliyal, S., Wazid, M., Singh, D. P., Chauhan, R., Mishra, A. K., & Das, A. K. (2024). Secure Artificial Intelligence of Things (AIoT)-enabled authenticated key agreement technique for smart living environment. *Computers & Electrical Engineering*, *118*, 109353. Advance online publication. DOI: 10.1016/j.compeleceng.2024.109353

Tiwari, S., Bhardwaj, B., Arora, D., & Khatri, S. (2024). Challenges and Barriers to Smart Farming Adaptation: A Technical, Economic, and Social Perspective. Smart Agritech: Robotics, AI, and Internet of Things (IoT) in Agriculture, 75-111.

Tiwari, S., Sarma, W., & Srivastava, A. (2022). Integrating artificial intelligence with zero trust architecture: Enhancing adaptive security in modern cyber threat landscape. *International Journal of Research and Analytical Reviews*, *9*, 712–728.

Torabi, H., Mirtaheri, S. L., & Greco, S. (2023). Practical autoencoder based anomaly detection by using vector reconstruction error. *Cybersecurity*, *6*(1), 1. DOI: 10.1186/s42400-022-00134-9

Tripathi, G., Ahad, M. A., & Casalino, G. (2023). A comprehensive review of blockchain technology: Underlying principles and historical background with future challenges. *Decision Analytics Journal, 9*, 100344. https://doi.org/https://doi.org/10.1016/j.dajour.2023.100344

Trivedi, J., Isoaho, J., & Mohammad, T. (2024). A Cloud-based Secure Architecture for Remote Patient Monitoring Integrating OPC UA and Human Digital Twin. *Procedia Computer Science*, *251*(1), 248–255. DOI: 10.1016/j.procs.2024.11.107

Tuler De Oliveira, M., Reis, L. H. A., Verginadis, Y., Mattos, D. M. F., & Olabarriaga, S. D. (2022). SmartAccess: Attribute-Based Access Control System for Medical Records Based on Smart Contracts. *IEEE Access : Practical Innovations, Open Solutions*, *10*(October), 117836–117854. DOI: 10.1109/ACCESS.2022.3217201

Tuli, S., Basumatary, N., Gill, S. S., Kahani, M., Arya, R. C., Wander, G. S., & Buyya, R. (2020). HealthFog: An Ensemble Deep Learning based Smart Healthcare System for Automatic Diagnosis of Heart Diseases in Integrated IoT and Fog Computing Environments. *Future Generation Computer Systems*, *104*(3), 187–200. DOI: 10.1016/j.future.2019.10.043

Tuncel, Y. K., & Öztoprak, K. (2025). SAFE-CAST: Secure AI-federated enumeration for clustering-based automated surveillance and trust in machine-to-machine communication. *PeerJ*, *11*, e2551. PMID: 39896029

U.S. Food and Drug Administration. (2019). *Medtronic recalls insulin pumps due to potential cybersecurity risks*. FDA Safety Communication. Retrieved from https://www.fda.gov/medical-devices/safety-communications

Uddin, M. A., Stranieri, A., Gondal, I., & Balasubramanian, V. (2018). Continuous Patient Monitoring with A Patient Centric Agent: A Block Architecture. *IEEE Access : Practical Innovations, Open Solutions*, *6*(1), 32700–32726. DOI: 10.1109/ACCESS.2018.2846779

Uddin, M. A., Stranieri, A., Gondal, I., & Balasubramanian, V. (2021). A survey on the adoption of blockchain in IoT: Challenges and solutions. *Blockchain: Research and Applications*, *2*(2), 100006.

Ullah, F., Salam, A., Amin, F., Khan, I. A., Ahmed, J., Zaib, S. A., & Choi, G. S. (2024). Deep Trust: A Novel Framework for Dynamic Trust and Reputation Management in the Internet of Things (IoT)-Based Networks. *IEEE Access : Practical Innovations, Open Solutions*, *12*, 87407–87419. DOI: 10.1109/ACCESS.2024.3409273

Upadrista, V., Nazir, S., & Tianfield, H. (2023). Secure data sharing with blockchain for remote health monitoring applications: A review. *Journal of Reliable Intelligent Environments*, *9*(3), 349–368. DOI: 10.1007/s40860-023-00204-w PMID: 37359293

Uprety, A., & Rawat, D. B. (2020). Reinforcement learning for iot security: A comprehensive survey. *IEEE Internet of Things Journal*, *8*(11), 8693–8706. DOI: 10.1109/JIOT.2020.3040957

V, M. & Singh, K. (2025). Enhancing Security and Privacy of IoMT Data for Unconscious Patient With Blockchain. *IEEE Transactions on Network and Service Management, PP*, 1–15. DOI: 10.1109/TNSM.2025.3602117

Vaidya, P., & Sharma, B. B. (2021). Wearable devices: Pros and cons. *Mobile Health: Advances in Research and Applications*, 17–29.

Verma, R., Thakur, S., Vaidya, P., & Sharma, B. B. (2024). Blockchain-Enabled IoT: Revolutionizing Security and Data Integrity in Connected Devices. *2024 3rd Edition of IEEE Delhi Section Flagship Conference (DELCON)*, 1–5. DOI: 10.1109/DELCON64804.2024.10866803

von der Assen, J., Sharif, J., Feng, C., Bovet, G., & Stiller, B. (2024). Asset-driven threat modelling for AI-based systems. *arXiv Preprint arXiv:2403.06512*.

Walia, G. K., Kumar, M., Kumar, S., & Gill, S. S. (2025). Amalgamation of Computational Intelligence and 6G-Enabled AIoT Networks for Industry 4.0. In Kumar, M., Gill, S. S., Kumar, V., & Verma, P. (Eds.), *Computational Intelligence Techniques for 5G Enabled IoT Networks* (pp. 255–265). Springer Nature Switzerland., DOI: 10.1007/978-3-031-82733-4_16

Wallace, A. A. (2022). When AI Meets IoT: AIoT. In Lipschultz, J. H., Freberg, K., & Luttrell, R. (Eds.), *The Emerald Handbook of Computer-Mediated Communication and Social Media* (pp. 481–492). Emerald Publishing Limited., DOI: 10.1108/978-1-80071-597-420221028

Wang, H., Wang, J., & Huang, M. (2013). Building a smart home system with WSN and service robot. *Proceedings - 2013 5th Conference on Measuring Technology and Mechatronics Automation, ICMTMA 2013*, 353–356. DOI: 10.1109/ICMTMA.2013.90

Wang, K., Lu, P., & Xin, Z. (2025). Research on Blockchain Privacy Preservation in Healthcare Systems. *2025 11th International Symposium on System Security, Safety, and Reliability (ISSSR)*, 286–290. DOI: 10.1109/ISSSR65654.2025.00048

Wang, H., Anurag, K. A., Benamer, A. R., Arora, P., Wander, G., Johnson, M. R., Anjana, R. M., Mohan, V., Gill, S. S., Uhlig, S., & Buyya, R. (2025). HealthAIoT: AIoT-driven smart healthcare system for sustainable cloud computing environments. *Internet of Things : Engineering Cyber Physical Human Systems*, *31*, 101555. Advance online publication. DOI: 10.1016/j.iot.2025.101555

Wardana, A. A., Kołaczek, G., & Sukarno, P. (2024). Lightweight, trust-managing, and privacy-preserving collaborative intrusion detection for Internet of Things. *Applied Sciences (Basel, Switzerland)*, *14*(10), 4109. DOI: 10.3390/app14104109

Wazid, M., Das, A. K., & Park, Y. (2021). Blockchain-Envisioned Secure Authentication Approach in AIoT: Applications, Challenges, and Future Research. *Wireless Communications and Mobile Computing, 2021*(1), 3866006. DOI: 10.1155/2021/3866006

WCED. (1987). Development and international economic cooperation: Environment (Report of the World Commission on Environment and Development). United Nations. https://sswm.info/sites/default/files/reference_attachments/UN%20WCED201987%20Brundtland%20Report.pdf

Wei, H., Miao, J., Lv, J., Chen, C.-M., Kumari, S., & Amoon, M. (2025). Secure and Trustworthy Data Management Mechanism for Dance-Consumer Electronics in AIoT. *IEEE Transactions on Consumer Electronics, 71*(1), 1970–1979. DOI: 10.1109/TCE.2024.3471573

Wei, L., Yang, Y., Wu, J., Long, C., & Li, B. (2022). Trust Management for Internet of Things: A Comprehensive Study. *IEEE Internet of Things Journal, 9*(10), 7664–7679. DOI: 10.1109/JIOT.2021.3139989

Wijesundara, W. M. A. B., Lee, J.-S., Aloupogianni, E., Tith, D., Suzuki, H., & Obi, T. (2025). DIDAuth-IoTFW: Decentralized firmware authentication for smart home IoT devices using verifiable credentials. *Internet of Things : Engineering Cyber Physical Human Systems, 34*, 101788. Advance online publication. DOI: 10.1016/j.iot.2025.101788

Wiseman, L., Sanderson, J., Zhang, A., & Jakku, E. (2019). Farmers and their data: An examination of farmers' reluctance to share their data through the lens of the laws impacting smart farming. *NJAS Wageningen Journal of Life Sciences, 90*(1), 100301. DOI: 10.1016/j.njas.2019.04.007

Wu, X., & Liang, J. (2021). A blockchain-based trust management method for Internet of Things. *Pervasive and Mobile Computing, 72*, 101330. DOI: 10.1016/j.pmcj.2021.101330

Xia, G., Chen, J., Yu, C., & Ma, J. (2023). Poisoning attacks in federated learning: A survey. *IEEE Access : Practical Innovations, Open Solutions, 11*, 10708–10722. DOI: 10.1109/ACCESS.2023.3238823

Xiao, X., Tang, Z., Li, C., Jiang, B., & Li, K. (2022). SBPA: Sybil-based backdoor poisoning attacks for distributed big data in AIoT-based federated learning system. *IEEE Transactions on Big Data, 10*(6), 827–838. DOI: 10.1109/TBDATA.2022.3224392

Xia, P., & Hu, F. (2025). Artificial Intelligence of Things Induced Predictive Maintenance of Computer Numerical Control Machine. *Internet Technology Letters*, *8*(5), e70082. Advance online publication. DOI: 10.1002/itl2.70082

Xiong, Z., Cai, Z., Takabi, D., & Li, W. (2021). Privacy threat and defense for federated learning with non-IID data in AIoT. *IEEE Transactions on Industrial Informatics*, •••, 1.

Xiong, Z., Cai, Z., Takabi, D., & Li, W. (2021). Privacy threat and defense for federated learning with non-iid data in AIoT. *IEEE Transactions on Industrial Informatics*, *18*(2), 1310–1321. DOI: 10.1109/TII.2021.3073925

Xu, L. D., Lu, Y., & Li, L. (2021). Embedding blockchain technology into IoT for security: A survey. *IEEE Internet of Things Journal*, *8*(13), 10452–10473. DOI: 10.1109/JIOT.2021.3060508

Yamoah, L. E., Mensah, R. O., & Frimpong, A. (2025). The benefits, challenges and implications for integrating emerging technologies in risk evaluation procedures for supply chains in transportation logistics. *Discover Sustainability*, *6*(1), 476. Advance online publication. DOI: 10.1007/s43621-025-01295-6

Yang, G., Lee, K., Lee, K., Yoo, Y., Lee, H., & Yoo, C. (2022). Resource Analysis of Blockchain Consensus Algorithms in Hyperledger Fabric. *IEEE Access : Practical Innovations, Open Solutions*, *10*(June), 74902–74920. DOI: 10.1109/ACCESS.2022.3190979

Yang, Z., Chen, X., He, Y., Liu, L., Che, Y., Wang, X., Xiao, K., & Xu, G. (2024). An Attribute-based Access Control Scheme using Blockchain Technology for IoT Data Protection. *High-Confidence Computing*, *4*(3), 1–10. DOI: 10.1016/j.hcc.2024.100199

Yaqoob, I., Salah, K., Jayaraman, R., & Al-Hammadi, Y. (2022). Blockchain for Healthcare Data Management: Opportunities, Challenges, and Future Recommendations. *Neural Computing & Applications*, *34*(14), 11475–11490. DOI: 10.1007/s00521-020-05519-w

Yazdinejad, A., Zolfaghari, B., Azmoodeh, A., Dehghantanha, A., Karimipour, H., & Fraser, E.,

Yıldırım, F., Develi, E. I., Meidute-Kavaliauskiene, I., Rostamzadeh, R., & Ghorbani, S. (2025). Symmetric encryption and cryptography algorithms in internet of things. *Pesquisa Operacional*, *45*, e295986. DOI: 10.1590/0101-7438.2025.045.00295986

Yousefnezhad, N., Malhi, A., Keyriläinen, T., & Främling, K. (2023). A Comprehensive Security Architecture for Information Management throughout the Lifecycle of IoT Products. *Sensors (Basel), 23*(6), 3236. Advance online publication. DOI: 10.3390/s23063236 PMID: 36991946

Zaabar, B., Cheikhrouhou, O., Ammi, M., Awad, A. I., & Abid, M. (2021). Secure and Privacy-aware Blockchain-based Remote Patient Monitoring System for Internet of Healthcare Things. *International Conference on Wireless and Mobile Computing, Networking and Communications, 2021-Octob*, 200–205. DOI: 10.1109/WiMob52687.2021.9606362

Zanasi, C., Russo, S., & Colajanni, M. (2024). Flexible zero trust architecture for the cybersecurity of industrial IoT infrastructures. *Ad Hoc Networks, 156*, 103414. DOI: 10.1016/j.adhoc.2024.103414

Zeng, F., Xu, C., Man, D., Jiang, J., & Yang, W. (2025). FLoV2T: A fine-grained malicious traffic classification method based on federated learning for AIoT. *Computer Communications, 242*, 108288. Advance online publication. DOI: 10.1016/j.comcom.2025.108288

Zhang, H., Zheng, W., Zheng, Z., & Nevatia, R. (2023). GaitRef: Gait recognition with refined sequential skeletons. *arXiv preprint.*

Zhang, Y., Luo, Y., Yang, T., Wu, X., & Hu, B. (2025). Eecs-fl: energy-efficient client selection for federated learning in AIoT. *Eurasip Journal on Wireless Communications and Networking, 2025*(1). DOI: 10.1186/s13638-025-02435-2

Zhang, Q., Xue, X., & Yang, J. (2025). Blockchain-Enabled Trustworthy Healthcare Data Sharing Mechanism for Reliable 6G-IoT Networks. *IEEE Internet of Things Journal, PP, 1.* Advance online publication. DOI: 10.1109/JIOT.2025.3564782

Zhang, S., Wang, W., Liu, Z., & Yu, X. (2023). MetaGait: Learning to learn for gait recognition. In *Proceedings of the IEEE/CVF Conference on Computer Vision and Pattern Recognition (CVPR).*

Zhang, W., Bao, Z., Lin, D., Rijmen, V., Yang, B., & Verbauwhede, I. (2015). RECTANGLE: A bit-slice lightweight block cipher suitable for multiple platforms. *Science China. Information Sciences, 58*(12), 1–15. DOI: 10.1007/s11432-015-5459-7

Zhang, W., Du, M., Guo, X., & Xiong, N. N. (2025). SRFL: A swarm-reputation-based autonomic federated learning framework for AIoT. *IEEE Internet of Things Journal, 12*(8), 9687–9700. DOI: 10.1109/JIOT.2024.3509264

Zhang, X., Hu, M., Xia, J., Wei, T., Chen, M., & Hu, S. (2020). Efficient federated learning for cloud-based AIoT applications. *IEEE Transactions on Computer-Aided Design of Integrated Circuits and Systems*.

Zhang, Y., Yutaka, M., Sasabe, M., & Kasahara, S. (2021). Attribute-Based Access Control for Smart Cities: A Smart-Contract-Driven Framework. *IEEE Internet of Things Journal*, *8*(8), 6372–6384. DOI: 10.1109/JIOT.2020.3033434

Zhang, Z., Zhang, H., Wang, J., Hu, X., Li, J., Yu, W., Yu, P., Li, W., Cui, B., Zhu, G., Sood, K., Will, B., & Guan, H. (2023). QKPT: Securing Your Private Keys in Cloud With Performance, Scalability and Transparency. *IEEE Transactions on Dependable and Secure Computing*, *20*(1), 478–491. DOI: 10.1109/TDSC.2021.3137403

Zheng, Q., Wang, X., Khan, M. K., Zhang, W., Gupta, B. B., & Guo, W. (2017). A lightweight authenticated encryption scheme based on chaotic scml for railway cloud service. *IEEE Access : Practical Innovations, Open Solutions*, *6*, 711–722. DOI: 10.1109/ACCESS.2017.2775038

Zhu, Z., Guo, X., Yang, T., Huang, J., Deng, J., Huang, G., & Zhou, J. (2021). Gait recognition in the wild: A benchmark. In *Proceedings of the IEEE/CVF international conference on computer vision* (pp. 14789-14799).

Zichichi, M., Ferretti, S., & D'Angelo, G. (2020). A framework based on distributed ledger technologies for data management and services in intelligent transportation systems. *IEEE Access : Practical Innovations, Open Solutions*, *8*, 100384–100402. DOI: 10.1109/ACCESS.2020.2998012

Ziemba, E. W., & Grabara, D. (2024). Sustainability affected by ICT adoption in enterprises. *Journal of Computer Information Systems*. Advance online publication. DOI: 10.1080/08874417.2024.2321529

About the Contributors

Momina Shaheen is an academic and researcher in computer science with over 8 years of experience in teaching and research. She currently serves as a Lecturer in Computing and Programme Leader at the University of Roehampton London. Her work focuses on edge computing, the Internet of Things, federated learning, and cybersecurity, with applications across smart cities, healthcare, finance, and education. Shaheen holds a B.Sc. in Information Technology, an M.Eng. in Software Engineering, and defended her Ph.D. in Computer Science, focusing on improving deep learning performance in federated machine learning. Her academic contributions include over 46 peer-reviewed publications in Q1 journals, multiple book chapters, and editorial work, earning her an h-index of 9 and over 400 citations. She has taught a wide range of undergraduate and postgraduate modules, including algorithms, software development, artificial intelligence, and data visualization. In addition to her teaching, she leads international collaborations and actively contributes to curriculum design, grant writing, and supervision of research projects. She also served as a reviewer for prominent journals such as Nature (under Early Career Reviewer Program), MDPI Electronics, IEEE Access, IET Information Security, Springer Scientific Reports, PLOS ONE, and ACM Transactions, and has chaired international conferences. Shaheen is committed to fostering innovation in computing education, and intelligent systems.

Jawad Rasheed received a B.S. degree in telecommunication engineering from the National University of Computer and Emerging Sciences, Pakistan. He then moved to Turkey, earning an M.S. degree in electrical and electronics engineering and a Ph.D. in computer engineering. He was a gold medalist and was awarded the Academic Excellence Award for securing straight A's in O' Level exams held by Cambridge University. Later, he also received a prestigious Doctorate and Research Scholarship for his Ph.D. studies (for three years). Dr. Rasheed is currently working as an Associate Professor at the Department of Computer Engineering at Istanbul

Sabahattin Zaim University, Turkey. He is the author/co-author of over 60 articles published in well-reputed journals and highly-ranked conferences. He serves as editor of several reputed journals including PLoS ONE, International Journal of Computational Intelligence Systems, PLoS Digital Health, and Current Medical Imaging. He was guest/lead guest/topic editor for special issues at the Symmetry, Mathematics, Healthcare, Applied Sciences, Electronics, and Journal of Sensor and Actuator Networks. Recently, he served as a book editor for Springer Lecture Notes on Data Engineering and Communications Technologies (Forthcoming Networks and Sustainability in the IoT Era) and Lecture Notes on Network Systems (Forthcoming Networks and Sustainability in the IoT Era). In addition, he is the general chair of IEEE ICAIoT and IEEE/Springer FoNeS-AIoT and chairs the technical program committee of Springer FoNeS-IoT 2021. His research interests include artificial intelligence and image processing. pattern recognition, IoT, LLM, and data analytics.

JAWAD RASHEED received a B.S. degree in telecommunication engineering from the National University of Computer and Emerging Sciences, Pakistan. He then moved to Turkey, earning an M.S. degree in electrical and electronics engineering and a Ph.D. in computer engineering. He was a gold medalist and was awarded the Academic Excellence Award for securing straight A's in O' Level exams held by Cambridge University. Later, he also received a prestigious Doctorate and Research Scholarship for his Ph.D. studies (for three years). Dr. Rasheed is currently working as an Associate Professor at the Department of Computer Engineering at Istanbul Sabahattin Zaim University, Turkey. He is the author/co-author of over 60 articles published in well-reputed journals and highly-ranked conferences. He serves as editor of several reputed journals including PLoS ONE, International Journal of Computational Intelligence Systems, PLoS Digital Health, and Current Medical Imaging. He was guest/lead guest/topic editor for special issues at the Symmetry, Mathematics, Healthcare, Applied Sciences, Electronics, and Journal of Sensor and Actuator Networks. Recently, he served as a book editor for Springer Lecture Notes on Data Engineering and Communications Technologies (Forthcoming Networks and Sustainability in the IoT Era) and Lecture Notes on Network Systems (Forthcoming Networks and Sustainability in the IoT Era). In addition, he is the general chair of IEEE ICAIoT and IEEE/Springer FoNeS-AIoT and chairs the technical program committee of Springer FoNeS-IoT 2021. His research interests include artificial intelligence and image processing. pattern recognition, IoT, LLM, and data analytics.

JAWAD RASHEED received a B.S. degree in telecommunication engineering from the National University of Computer and Emerging Sciences, Pakistan. He then moved to Turkey, earning an M.S. degree in electrical and electronics engineering and a Ph.D. in computer engineering. He was a gold medalist and was awarded the Academic Excellence Award for securing straight A's in O' Level exams held by Cambridge University. Later, he also received a prestigious Doctorate and Research

Scholarship for his Ph.D. studies (for three years). Dr. Rasheed is currently working as an Associate Professor at the Department of Computer Engineering at Istanbul Sabahattin Zaim University, Turkey. He is the author/co-author of over 60 articles published in well-reputed journals and highly-ranked conferences. He serves as editor of several reputed journals including PLoS ONE, International Journal of Computational Intelligence Systems, PLoS Digital Health, and Current Medical Imaging. He was guest/lead guest/topic editor for special issues at the Symmetry, Mathematics, Healthcare, Applied Sciences, Electronics, and Journal of Sensor and Actuator Networks. Recently, he served as a book editor for Springer Lecture Notes on Data Engineering and Communications Technologies (Forthcoming Networks and Sustainability in the IoT Era) and Lecture Notes on Network Systems (Forthcoming Networks and Sustainability in the IoT Era). In addition, he is the general chair of IEEE ICAIoT and IEEE/Springer FoNeS-AIoT and chairs the technical program committee of Springer FoNeS-IoT 2021. His research interests include artificial intelligence and image processing. pattern recognition, IoT, LLM, and data analytics.

Maqbool Khan is a Post-Doctoral Researcher at Software Competence Center Hagenberg (SCCH), Austria and he is also working as an Assistant Professor at Pak-Austria Fachhochschule: Institute of Applied Sciences and Technology (PAF-IAST), Pakistan. Dr. M. Khan obtained a fully funded scholarship for his MS study at HUST and PhD study at Nanjing University in 2011 and 2013 respectively, which was funded by China Scholarship Council (CSC) of China. He has multi-disciplinary expertise and working experience on very diverse topics of Big Data Analytics, Cloud Computing, Predictive Maintenance, Data Science and machine learning. He has more than 10-years of professional experience while working both in industry and academia. He worked in multinational companies like Siemens and Atos. He is a certified Google Cloud Professional Architect. He is an active researcher working on various funded projects with different collaborators and currently he is working on an European Union project titled "Human-AI teaming".

***

Salam Al-E'mari earned her Ph.D. in Cybersecurity from Universiti Sains Malaysia (USM) in 2022. She is the Chair of the Information Security Department and an Assistant Professor at the University of Petra (UoP). With expertise in Blockchain, Deep Learning, and Network Security, she has contributed significantly to cybersecurity research. She previously earned her Bachelor's and Master's in Computer Science from Yarmouk University, Jordan, shaping her strong foundation in security and technology.

Astri Dwi Andriani is an Associate Professor and the Rector of Universitas Putra Indonesia, Indonesia. Her academic expertise is rooted in the social sciences and communication studies, where she explores issues of trust, legitimacy, and governance. Alongside her disciplinary focus, she has developed an active research agenda on Artificial Intelligence (AI), particularly its societal and communicative implications. As both a scholar and university leader, she is dedicated to advancing interdisciplinary inquiry that bridges the humanities, communication, and emerging technologies, with a commitment to building socially responsible and human-centered innovation.

Deswita Anggraini is a researcher in the field of the Internet of Things (IoT) at Esa Unggul University, Jakarta, Indonesia. Her research interests focus on the design and implementation of IoT-based systems, sensor networks, real-time data processing, and smart applications for monitoring and automation. She has been actively involved in academic research projects and practical implementations related to intelligent sensing, embedded systems, and data-driven solutions. Her work reflects strong analytical thinking, technical competence, and a commitment to continuous learning. Through her research activities, Deswita Anggraini aims to contribute to the development of innovative IoT solutions that support efficiency, sustainability, and digital transformation in academic and professional environments.

Ravikumar Ch is an accomplished professional in the field of Computer Science & Engineering, recognized for his contributions to both academia and research. He earned his B.Tech. Degree from Jawaharlal Nehru Technological University in 2004, followed by an M.Tech in Computer Science & Engineering in 2011. Recently, he successfully defended his Ph.D. in Computer Science & Engineering from Lovely Professional University in 2024, focusing on innovative approaches in Cloud Cryptography and blockchain security. With over 14 years of teaching experience and 5 years dedicated to research, Dr. Ravikumar's academic journey includes notable achievements such as receiving the Best Teacher Award from Anurag Engineering College in 2011 for his exceptional delivery of the Operating System subject. His research prowess is evidenced by his authorship of 20 Scopus indexed papers and 5 Web of Science indexed papers, alongside securing 2 patents in areas spanning cloud computing and blockchain technology. Dr. Ravikumar's expertise extends to the forefront of technological advancements, particularly in cloud computing and blockchain.

Fadi Fataftah is a cybersecurity researcher with over 15 years of international academic and industry experience. He holds a PhD in Information Technology and specializes in cloud security, AI-driven cyber defense, and digital-health security.

Fadi Fataftah is a cybersecurity researcher with over 15 years of international academic and industry experience. He holds a PhD in Information Technology and specializes in cloud security, AI-driven cyber defense, and digital-health security.

Yahya Fikri is a Phd researcher in Economic and Management Sciences, specializing in econometrics and statistics, with a strong focus on applying advanced quantitative and qualitative methods to complex economic challenges. His expertise spans time series modeling, data analysis, and statistical inference, areas in which he has consistently advanced both theory and application. Over the course of his academic career, Dr. Fikri has published extensively in peer-reviewed journals, where his contributions have significantly shaped the development and refinement of modern econometric techniques. His scholarly influence is complemented by active participation in international conferences and seminars, where he fosters interdisciplinary collaboration and knowledge exchange across economics, environmental science, and policy domains. And, Dr. Fikri is an associate editor and reviewer in some journals. Dr. Fikri has emerged as a leading voice in examining the nexus of education, poverty, economic growth and sustainable development. By leveraging applied statistics and econometric modeling, his research provides critical insights into the socio-economic impacts of education on poverty, economic growth, and long-term sustainability. Beyond academic contributions, his work carries profound societal relevance. By generating evidence-based models and policy recommendations, Dr. Fikri supports strategies aimed at enhancing economic growth, Ai in education, and environmental sustainability. His research exemplifies how rigorous data-driven analysis can bridge the gap between economic theory and practical solutions to some of the most urgent global challenges. With his blend of methodological precision, interdisciplinary engagement, and commitment to sustainability, Dr. Fikri continues to shape the future of econometric-driven policy and sustainable development research.

Bright Keswani is a Research Professor in the Faculty of Computer Science and Engineering at Poornima University, Jaipur, where he has been serving since June 2023 and is actively associated with the University's Research & Development Cell. He is an accomplished academic and researcher with a strong interdisciplinary orientation, having published numerous book chapters and research papers in reputed Scopus and Web of Science indexed journals. Dr. Keswani completed Post-Doctoral Research from the Department of Creative Technologies and Product Design, National Taipei University of Business (NTUB), Taiwan, where he conducted advanced research in Mobile Ad-Hoc Networks. His research portfolio is further strengthened by the grant of multiple patents, including utility and design patents, reflecting his commitment to innovation and applied research. Known for his academic rigor, professional integrity, and global outlook, Dr. Keswani actively contributes to curriculum design, research mentorship, and the advancement of emerging technologies in higher education.

Shikha Khullar is an accomplished academic and researcher with a Ph.D. in Data Mining and Artificial Intelligence. She currently serves as an Associate Professor at Poornima University, where she is recognized for her dedication to academic excellence and her dynamic involvement in radical research. With a deep-rooted passion for innovation and discovery, Dr. Khullar actively engages in interdisciplinary research that bridges technology and real-world applications, particularly in areas such as intelligent systems, smart data analytics, and sustainable digital solutions. Her work is characterized by a forward-thinking approach, where she not only explores theoretical models but also contributes to practical implementations that address pressing societal and industrial challenges. At Poornima University, she has been instrumental in mentoring young minds, guiding Ph.D. scholars, and contributing to curriculum development in emerging areas such as Artificial Intelligence, Blockchain, and Smart Agriculture Technologies. She is the member of IAENG and ERDA.

S. N Kumar is currently an Associate. Professor, Dept. of Electrical and Electronics Engineering., Amal Jyothi College of Engineering, Kanjirappally, Kerala. He was awarded PhD in Electronics and Communication Engineering from Sathyabama Institute of Science and Technology, Chennai. He has 15 years of teaching experience, and his areas of interest include Medical Image Processing and Embedded System Applications in Telemedicine. He was the Co- Principal Investigator of the DST IDP-funded project and research fellow of the RCA scheme, NTU Singapore. He has edited 3 books, authored 32 book chapters and 30 publications in peer reviewed journals. He had authored 12 text books in engineering discipline.

Sanjeev Kumar Is a Professor in Lovely Professional University Punjab India. He received Undergraduate in Hotel Management from Osmania University, Postgraduate in Tourism Management from Madurai Kamaraj University. He completed Doctor of Philosophy in Hospitality Management in 2019 from Amity University Jaipur India. His research areas lies in food Service Industry, his research focuses on Alcoholic beverages, Event management and Sustainable Management Practices, Metaverse, AI Machine Learning and Artificial Intelligence. He published more than 80 research papers, articles and chapters in Scopus Indexed, UGC Approved and peer reviewed Journals and books. Dr. Sanjeev Kumar participated and acted as resource person in various National and International conferences, seminars, session chair, research workshops and industry talks and his work has been widely cited. Dr. Sanjeev also edited more than 20 books with various International Publishers such as IGI Global, Cambridge Scholars, Emerald, CABI, Bentham Science, Taylor & Francis. Dr Sanjeev is an active researcher and has published numerous research articles in prestigious National and International journals and books.

Yousef K. Sanjalawe is an Assistant Professor specializing in Cybersecurity and Cloud Computing at the University of Jordan (JU), Jordan. He earned his PhD in Cloud Computing from Universiti Sains Malaysia (USM) in 2020, where his research focused on enhancing cloud service broker selection using optimization algorithms. Dr. Sanjalawe has extensive experience in academia, research, and professional training. He has supervised Ph.D. students in Cybersecurity, Cloud Computing, IoT, Fog Computing, Optimization, and Artificial Intelligence (AI). From 2023 to 2024, he served as the Chair of the Cybersecurity Department at the American University of Madaba (AUM), Jordan, and from 2022 to 2024, he was an Assistant Professor in Cybersecurity at AUM.

Dwi Sartika Simatupang is a senior lecturer in Computer Network Systems at Esa Unggul University, Jakarta, Indonesia. She has extensive experience in teaching and research in the fields of computer networks, network security, and information technology infrastructure. Her academic interests focus on network architecture, cybersecurity, and the development of reliable and scalable network systems to support modern digital environments. She has been actively involved in academic teaching, curriculum development, and research initiatives aimed at enhancing the quality of education and technological innovation. Her work reflects strong technical expertise, analytical thinking, and a commitment to advancing knowledge in computer networking and information technology.

Rakesh Kumar Saxena received the M. Tech from Dayalbagh University, Agra, India in 1998 and Ph.D. from MITS Gwalior, Rajeev Gandhi Technical University, Bhopal MP, India. His research area is soft computing, AI, ML, DL and Logic Design. Presently he is working as Professor, CSE in Poornima University Jaipur (Raj.) India. He is Fellow member of Institution of Engineers India, member of International Association of Computer Science and Information Technology (IACSIT), Indian Society for Technical Education (ISTE), Delhi, India and Institution of Electronics and Telecommunication Engineering (IETE), Delhi, India. He is awarded Chartered Engineer in 2017 by IE (I). He had worked on various research projects funded by AICTE, MSME and World bank. He has published 37 Research papers in various Journals of Repute which includes IEEE Xplore, AIP USA etc.

Binastya Anggara Sekti has been a lecturer at the Faculty of Computer Science, Esa Unggul University, Jakarta, since 2016. He is actively involved in the Artificial Intelligence and Information Security Study Group. He holds a Bachelor's degree in Informatics Engineering from the Bandung Institute of Technology and a Master's degree in Information Systems Management from Trisakti University, Jakarta. Prior to entering academia, he accumulated over 25 years of professional experience as an IT practitioner in various companies across Jakarta. His work focused on developing data centers for internet service providers and delivering IT solutions for the manufacturing and oil & gas sectors. His research interests include artificial intelligence, cybersecurity, and the development of IT infrastructure.

Brij Bhushan Sharma received a Bachelor of Technology in Electronics and Communication Engineering in 2012 from Punjab Technical University, Punjab, India. Then he earned a Master of Technology in Electronics and Communication Engineering in 2015 and a PhD in Computer Science Engineering. Dr. Sharma is currently working as an Assistant Professor at Yogananda School of AI Computers and Data Science, Shoolini University of Biotechnology and Management Sciences, Solan, Himachal Pradesh, India. He is the author/co-author of over 27 articles published in well-reputed journals and national/international conferences. He has also over 39 patents to his name. His research interests include the Internet of Things, wireless sensor networks, and power electronics.

Andrew Novan Then is a researcher in the Internet of Things (IoT) and Early Warning System Research Group at Esa Unggul University, Jakarta, Indonesia. His research interests focus on smart sensor networks, real-time monitoring systems, embedded technologies, and the development of IoT-based solutions for early detection and risk mitigation. He has been actively involved in academic research and applied technology projects aimed at improving system reliability, data accuracy, and rapid response mechanisms in intelligent monitoring environments. His work reflects strong analytical thinking, technical competence, and a commitment to innovation in digital sensing technologies. Andrew actively contributes to collaborative research initiatives and scientific publications that support the advancement of IoT applications and early warning technologies for environmental and infrastructure monitoring.

Defia Ulandari is an information technology researcher at Esa Unggul University, Jakarta, Indonesia. Her research interests include information systems development, digital transformation, data management, and applied computing. She has been actively involved in academic research projects and collaborative activities related to system analysis, software development, and the implementation of innovative IT solutions to enhance organizational efficiency and decision-making processes. Her work reflects strong analytical thinking, technical competence, and a commitment to continuous learning. Defia is known for her adaptability and collaborative mindset, and she continues to develop her expertise in emerging technologies to contribute to impactful digital solutions in academic and professional environments.

David Yehezkiel is a programmer and artificial intelligence researcher at Esa Unggul University, Jakarta, Indonesia. His research interests include machine learning, intelligent systems development, software engineering, and data-driven applications. He has been actively involved in programming projects and academic research focusing on the development of AI-based solutions, system automation, and intelligent software applications. His work demonstrates strong technical expertise, analytical thinking, and a commitment to innovation in emerging technologies. David actively contributes to collaborative research initiatives and technology development projects aimed at advancing artificial intelligence applications in academic and professional environments.

Index

A

B

C

D

E

F

G

H

I

L

M

O

P

R

S

T

V

Z

www.ingramcontent.com/pod-product-compliance
Lightning Source LLC
LaVergne TN
LVHW061527290926
849162LV00004B/695